Praise for
Voices in Our Blood

"Meacham, an editor at *Newsweek,* is to be commended for launching and editing such an absorbing and stellar tribute to our struggle." —*Black Issues Book Review*

"A highly satisfying compendium that shines a welcome light onto the troubles of the present day." —*Kirkus Reviews*

"Thoughtful, sensitive, rewarding, and groundbreaking, it belongs on the shelf of every Civil Rights movement scholar and in classrooms and libraries as well." —*Library Journal*

"The articles . . . describe the movement with rare immediacy and enviable insight . . . and make this hefty volume an indispensable work on one of the formative events of the century." —*The Dallas Morning News*

"You're a cold soul if you are not moved by what you read here." —*Arizona Republic*

"While the battle for racial equality has been well covered in documentary films and oral histories, much of its writing has been forgotten. This collection corrects that with powerful fiction and nonfiction." —*American Way*

"Want to read good writing? Want to be reminded of where America has been, and why it is still necessary to keep moving forward? *Voices in Our Blood* should be required reading for our hearts as well as our minds."

—Fort Worth *Star-Telegram*

About the Editor

JON MEACHAM is managing editor of *Newsweek*. Born in Chattanooga in 1969, he is a graduate of The University of the South in Sewanee, Tennessee. Meacham has been a reporter for *The Chattanooga Times* and an editor of *The Washington Monthly*. He and his wife, Keith, live in New York City with their son.

Voices in Our Blood

Voices in Our Blood

◆◆◆

America's Best

on the Civil Rights

Movement

Edited by

Jon Meacham

Random House Trade Paperbacks
New York

Library of Congress Cataloging-in-Publication Data

Voices in our blood: America's best on the civil rights movement /
edited by Jon Meacham.
p.   cm.
Includes index.
ISBN 0-375-75881-X
1. Afro-Americans—Civil rights—History—20th century—Sources.
2. Civil rights movements—United States—History—20th century—Sources.
3. United States—Race relations—Sources. I. Meacham, Jon.
E185.61 .V744   2001
973'.0496073—dc21
00-041474

Random House website address: www.atrandom.com
Printed in the United States of America

2 4 6 8 9 7 5 3 1

Text design by Meryl Sussman Levavi/Digitext

One writes out of one thing only—one's own experience. Everything depends on how relentlessly one forces from this experience the last drop, sweet or bitter, it can possibly give. This is the only real concern of the artist, to re-create out of the disorder of life that order which is art.

—JAMES BALDWIN,
"AUTOBIOGRAPHICAL NOTES"

Contents

Introduction • JON MEACHAM   3

I. BEFORE THE STORM 9

Inheritors of Slavery • RICHARD WRIGHT
*Twelve Million Black Voices: A Folk History of the Negro
in the United States, 1941*   13

North Toward Home • WILLIE MORRIS
1967   32

Notes of a Native Son • JAMES BALDWIN
1955   41

A Pageant of Birds • EUDORA WELTY
The New Republic, October 25, 1943   57

I Know Why the Caged Bird Sings • MAYA ANGELOU
Harper's Magazine, February 1970   61

Opera in Greenville • REBECCA WEST
The New Yorker, June 14, 1947   75

II. INTO THE STREETS 105

America Comes of Middle Age • MURRAY KEMPTON
   He Went All the Way, September 22, 1955   111
   Upon Such a Day, September 10, 1957   113
   Next Day, September 12, 1957   115
   The Soul's Cry, September 13, 1957   117
American Segregation and the World Crisis • WILLIAM FAULKNER
The Segregation Decisions, November 10, 1955   120
The Moral Aspects of Segregation • BENJAMIN E. MAYS
The Segregation Decisions, November 10, 1955   123
The Cradle (of the Confederacy) Rocks • CARL T. ROWAN
Go South to Sorrow, 1957   129
Parting the Waters: America in the King Years • TAYLOR BRANCH
1988   150

Prime Time • HENRY LOUIS GATES, JR.
  Colored People, 1994   154

Letter from the South • E. B. WHITE
  The New Yorker, April 7, 1956   161

Segregation: The Inner Conflict in the South • ROBERT PENN WARREN
  1956   167

Travels with Charley • JOHN STEINBECK
  1962   203

Liar by Legislation • HODDING CARTER
  Look, June 28, 1955   209

Harlem Is Nowhere • RALPH ELLISON
  Harper's Magazine, August 1964   214

An Interview with Malcolm X • ALEX HALEY
  A Candid Conversation with the Militant
  Major-domo of the Black Muslims,
  Playboy, May 1963   218

Wallace • MARSHALL FRADY
  1968   235

Mystery and Manners • FLANNERY O'CONNOR
  1963   267

The Negro Revolt Against "The Negro Leaders" • LOUIS E. LOMAX
  Harper's Magazine, June 1960   268

                    III. THE MOUNTAINTOP   281

"I Have a Dream . . ." • JAMES RESTON
  The New York Times, August 29, 1963   285

Capital Is Occupied by a Gentle Army • RUSSELL BAKER
  The New York Times, August 29, 1963   288

Bloody Sunday • JOHN LEWIS
  Walking with the Wind: A Memoir of the Movement, 1998   292

Mississippi: The Fallen Paradise • WALKER PERCY
  Harper's Magazine, April 1965   318

This Quiet Dust • WILLIAM STYRON
  Harper's Magazine, April 1965   328

When Watts Burned • STANLEY CROUCH
  Rolling Stone's The Sixties, 1977   346

After Watts • ELIZABETH HARDWICK
    Violence in the City—An End or a Beginning?
    The New York Review of Books, March 31, 1966   348

The Brilliancy of Black • BERNARD WEINRAUB
    Esquire, January 1967   352

Representative • CHARLAYNE HUNTER-GAULT
    The New Yorker, April 1, 1967   367

The Second Coming of Martin Luther King • DAVID HALBERSTAM
    Harper's Magazine, August 1967   370

Martin Luther King Is *Still* on the Case • GARRY WILLS
    Esquire, August 1968   389

IV. TWILIGHT   409

"Keep On A-Walking, Children" • PAT WATTERS
    New American Review, January 1969   413

"We in a War—Or Haven't Anybody Told You That?"
    • PETER GOLDMAN
    Report from Black America, 1969   450

Radical Chic: That Party at Lenny's • TOM WOLFE
    New York, June 8, 1970   463

Choosing to Stay at Home: Ten Years After the March on Washington
    • ALICE WALKER
    The New York Times Magazine, August 26, 1973   478

A Hostile and Welcoming Workplace • ELLIS COSE
    The Rage of a Privileged Class, 1993   486

State Secrets • CALVIN TRILLIN
    The New Yorker, May 29, 1995   499

Grady's Gift • HOWELL RAINES
    The New York Times Magazine, December 1, 1991   517

Acknowledgments   529

Permissions Acknowledgments   531

Index   533

Voices in
Our Blood

Introduction

◆

JON MEACHAM

One day in 1957, in Paris, Willie Morris, then a 22-year-old Rhodes scholar, got hold of Richard Wright's Left Bank telephone number. They had both grown up in Mississippi; on the phone, Morris, a descendant of the first territorial governor of the state, told Wright, the son of an illiterate sharecropper, that he was a white Yazoo City boy. "You're from Yazoo?" said Wright, who had expatriated himself to Europe ten years before. "Well, come on over." They went out to an Arab bar and, in Morris's recollection, "got a little drunk together, and talked about the place we had both known. I asked him, 'Will you ever come back to America?' " "No," the novelist said. "I want my children to grow up as human beings." After a time, Morris remembered, "a silence fell between us, like an immense pain—or maybe it was my imagining."

And so there they sat on that awkward, liquid evening, two gifted writers, connected by a common heritage yet hopelessly divided by skin color. Fortunately for the rest of us, what could not be said could be written. "What had I got out of living in America?" Wright mused in his 1945 memoir *Black Boy*, recalling the beginning of his instinct to write his life. "Yes, the whites were as miserable as their black victims. If this country can't find its way to a human path, if it can't inform conduct with a deep sense of life, then all of us, black as well as white, are going down the same drain. . . . I picked up a pencil and held it over a sheet of white paper. . . . I would hurl words into this darkness and wait for an echo, and if an echo sounded, no matter how faintly, I would send other words to tell, to march, to fight, to create a sense of hunger for life that gnaws in us all, to keep alive in our hearts a sense of the inexpressibly human."

A march of words. The work of America's finest authors on race echoes down the decades, illuminating the conflicting, often subtle forces that would meet in the streets in the 1950s and 1960s. We already have many good sources on the great domestic story of the twentieth century, the civil rights movement: documentaries, memoirs, biographies, oral histories, and works of scholarship. What we have not had until now is a collection of the country's best writing on the midcentury crisis, a single volume of the strongest story-telling about the world in which the movement took shape and played itself out. In his *Autobiographical Notes*, James Baldwin says that "it is part of the business of the writer—as I see it—to examine attitudes, to go beneath the surface, to tap the source." The voices in this anthology do just that, capturing the complications behind the public spectacles and charting the competing impulses of grace and rage—the proper province of reporting, reflection, and writing. There are luminous names here: Baldwin, Robert Penn Warren, Alice Walker, William Faulkner, E. B. White, Ralph Ellison, Rebecca West, Murray Kempton, Maya Angelou. There are writers you've never heard of, but whose stories resonate still. The contributors are reporters and artists, novelists and historians, even a poet or two. There are pieces of journalism drafted in the moment, and memoirs composed long after the action. Kempton, the New York columnist, summed up the spirit in which they were all written, and the over-arching stakes of the age, when he wrote, from Nashville in the early autumn of 1957, "In my job we travel, wayfarers . . . and our moments of reward are our moments of engagement. They are moments when tragedy and comedy are all mixed up, and God and the devil contend like scorpions in a bottle inside the soul of a man before us." This book is a record of some of the finest reports from that front. Read together, they tell not just what happened, but why.

As the years wear on, the civil rights movement is turning into a civic fairy tale. Datelines evoke images of combat: Little Rock, Birmingham, Selma, Jackson, Nashville, Tuscaloosa, Clinton, Oxford, Watts. On one side stood the segregationists, holding fast to an old order and unleashing police dogs. On the other were African Americans, marching peaceably or taking seats at segregated lunch counters. In retrospect, everything came together in August 1963, when Martin Luther King, Jr., stood on the steps of the Lincoln Memorial and conjured his Promised Land: a place where his "four little children are judged not by the color of their skin but by the content of their character." (Watching King's speech on television in the White House, President Kennedy remarked, "He's damn good.") A moment later, it seems now, the "White Only" signs came down, the polling booths opened up, and the Dream was more or less fulfilled.

But the truth about the movement is much more complicated. Ambivalence was thick; the death of legalized segregation did not end racial discrimination; the South was not the only region with sins to atone for. Without understanding what a close call the movement really was, we cannot appreciate the courage of those who tried to change a nation's habits of heart and mind, nor can we grasp the fact that even the most remarkable revolutions are never complete. The engines behind the prevailing myth are television and the powerful photographs of days when white people did unthinkable things to black people. However heartbreaking, though, the images do not tell the whole story. John Steinbeck learned this firsthand, in New Orleans in late 1960. The schools were integrating, and whites demonstrated each day. "I had seen photographs in the papers every day and motion pictures on the television screen," Steinbeck wrote in *Travels with Charley*. He made his way to the city and watched as the protestors screamed first at a black girl coming to class. Then came what Steinbeck called "the real show": The mob's most venomous taunts were hurled at a white father and child who were complying with the law. A telling detail: The whites feared blacks but reserved their greatest fury for those of their own kind who broke ranks.

Steinbeck's nuanced reporting and powerful narrative are typical of the writing in this book. Journalism—and many of the pieces here are journalistic—isn't often thought of as art. Dispatches on deadline are usually, as Philip Graham, publisher of *The Washington Post*, once put it, "the first rough draft of history." But the most memorable pieces can be both: They make order out of disorder and capture the passions of a given time and place. Reading the writers collected here, small details and chance thoughts stay in the mind, casting light on big things. There's E. B. White's Florida vacation trip to watch spring training: "A few [blacks] turn up at the ballpark, where they occupy a separate but equal section of the left-field bleachers and watch Negro players on the visiting Braves team using the same bases as white players, instead of separate (but equal) bases." And there's George Wallace's strange surge into the life of the nation, so cinematically captured by Marshall Frady. All these years distant, you can almost smell the stale smoke of the Alabama governor's White Owl cigars and see his sweat as he drawls, "Nigguhs hate whites, and whites hate nigguhs. Everybody knows that deep down." In 1955, Faulkner jotted a quick line to a Memphis newspaper, warning that "We speak now against the day when our Southern people who will resist to the last these inevitable changes in social relations, will, when they have been forced to accept what they at one time might have accepted with dignity and goodwill, will say, 'Why didn't someone tell us this before? Tell us this in time?' "

But people were telling them plenty; too many just didn't want to listen—and never had. The movement's roots lie deep in the American experience. The question of slavery bedeviled the Founding and gave us the Civil War. The stage for the civil rights movement of the twentieth century was set in the nineteenth: in *Plessy v. Ferguson*, the 1896 Supreme Court decision that gave legal authority to the Jim Crow system of "separate but equal." This book begins with the United States of the thirties and forties, the milieu in which whites assumed superiority and blacks had not yet found the legal or political means to fundamentally alter the landscape. Daily life was a curious stew of racism and intimacy. "My boyhood experience," William Styron writes of growing up in the Virginia of the pre–World War II years, "was the typically ambivalent one of most native Southerners, for whom the Negro is taken simultaneously for

granted and as an object of unending concern." Morris recalls both violence
and common interests: He once knocked over a black boy just for sport, but
then walked to school with a black quarterback, talking football. "I don't know
why they treat these niggers so bad," Morris's father would say. "They pay
taxes just like everybody else. If they pay taxes they oughta get to vote. It's as
simple as that." The language shocks today; the condescension rightly enraged
even then. Maya Angelou remembers a white lawman coming to her grandmother's country store to warn her uncle against night riders. For the sheriff it
seemed an act of generosity; to Angelou, it was infuriating. "If on Judgment
Day I were summoned by St. Peter to give testimony to the used-to-be sheriff's
act of kindness, I would be unable to say anything on his behalf," Angelou
writes. "His confidence that my uncle and every other Black man who heard of
the Klan's coming ride would scurry under their houses to hide in chicken
droppings was too humiliating to hear."

What made the nation, in the early fifties, begin to listen to voices like Angelou's? In retrospect, there's a neat theory: that the broadening experience of
World War II, and the growing conviction that America could not very well
fight communism abroad if so much of its population at home was chattel, created a climate in which Jim Crow could not long survive. There is much truth
in this. Carl Rowan, reporting in the mid-fifties, saw it: "I know that this is not
the South I left in 1942. In the greasy apron behind the counter at that fly-
specked honky-tonk there's a guy who talks about Salerno and Anzio and the
gay madames of Paree; in the pool hall, shooting craps with two white guys,
are three Negroes who have been to Guadalcanal, Okinawa, and Heartbreak
Ridge. . . ." Still, the movement snuck up on most blacks and whites. As a
youth in rural West Virginia, Henry Louis Gates, Jr. remembers, "Civil rights
took us all by surprise."

Little things added up. For one, the national press was finally paying attention. That had started around 1947, when Turner Catledge, the Mississippi-
born managing editor of *The New York Times*, dispatched John Popham, an
elegant reporter with a thick Virginia Tidewater accent, to cover the South full-
time—the first journalist to make a permanent beat of the old Confederacy.
Garrulous and charming (a colleague once likened his delivery to "dollops of
sorghum sugar fired from a Gatling gun"), Popham became the godfather of
the Southern story, interpreting the locals to the press corps, and vice versa. At
the Emmett Till murder trial in Sumner, Mississippi, in 1955, Popham
arranged the journalists' seating, once staring down Sheriff H. C. Strider, who
had declared he wouldn't have any "nigger reporters" in his courtroom. In a
column written from Sumner headlined "He Went All the Way," Kempton recounted how Till's uncle dared to testify against the white men who had murdered his nephew. For that time and place, it was a remarkable act of courage,
a defiant and dignified blow against the cruel, white-run prevailing order. In

December of that year, Rosa Parks took her stand when she chose not to get up. Small moments, but they loom large. Parks's decision not to surrender her seat on the bus was, she said, "spontaneous." Once it was made, though, E. D. Nixon, the longtime president of the Alabama branch of A. Philip Randolph's Brotherhood of Sleeping Car Porters, was determined to take advantage of the moment. He called Martin Luther King, Jr.—not quite 27, with a new baby— and asked if a meeting to discuss the Parks case could be held at the young minister's church, not because Nixon sensed greatness in King but because Dexter Avenue Baptist Church was closest to downtown. When the session ran long, a frustrated minister got up to leave, whispering to King, "This is going to fizzle out. I'm going." King replied, "I would like to go, too, but it's in my church."

He didn't go, and the movement began. Nothing was foreordained. John Lewis recalls how the Selma-to-Montgomery march was almost cancelled on March 7, 1965. It happened anyway, and the public push for the Voting Rights Act gathered force that night, when ABC interrupted its broadcast of *Judgment at Nuremberg* to play the footage of Sheriff Jim Clark's troops' attack on Lewis and Hosea Williams as the marchers crossed the Pettus Bridge. In Lewis's voice you can hear the fear and the anger of those who prayed they would win, but didn't know. There were moments, in fact, when they couldn't be sure they would live, much less carry the day. As the tear gas spread and the troopers advanced on Lewis, he thought, "This is it. People are going to die here. *I'm* going to die here." The movement was anything but monolithic. In *Harper's*, Louis E. Lomax details the fissures between the old and the young within the black community; Lewis recalls how quickly the nonviolent movement found itself threatened by the rise of Black Power. King seemed antiquated: to many young eyes he was out of touch. Stokeley Carmichael, by contrast, was the future, offering a radical solution in 1967: "Black people have not only been told they are inferior, but the system maintains it. We are faced in this country with whether or not we want to be equal and let white people define equality for us on their terms as they've always done and thus lose our blackness or whether we should maintain our identity and still be equal. This is Black Power." By the time King went to Memphis in the spring of 1968, the minister was on the cool side of the mountain. He was becoming increasingly interested in Vietnam and economic justice—real issues, to be sure, but they lacked the focus of a campaign to integrate restaurants and buses and the ballot box. For King, the shadows were lengthening at the time of the assassination.

The story of the movement, however, is much more than the story of King—and it isn't over. We must learn from the writers who went before. In *Notes of a Native Son*, Baldwin recounts the Jim Crow world of New Jersey, the Harlem riot of 1943, and perhaps most important, the beginning of wisdom. "It began to seem that one would have to hold in the mind forever two ideas which seemed to be in opposition. The first idea was acceptance, the acceptance, totally without rancor, of life as it is, and men as they are: in the light of this idea, it goes without saying that injustice is a commonplace. But this did not mean that one could be complacent, for the second idea was of equal power: that one must never, in one's own life, accept these injustices as commonplace but must fight them with all one's strength. The fight begins, however, in the heart and it now had been laid to my charge to keep my own heart free of hatred and despair."

Battles of the heart are the fiercest, and most significant, of all. Robert Penn Warren sensed this when he left Connecticut to return South to report and write a little book, *Segregation: The Inner Conflict in the South,* which was published in 1956. Warren's opening lines give this collection its title: "I was going back to look at the landscapes and streets I had known—Kentucky, Tennessee, Arkansas, Mississippi, Louisiana—to look at the faces, to hear the voices, to hear, in fact, the voices in my own blood. A girl from Mississippi had said to me: 'I feel it's all happening inside of me, every bit of it. It's all there.' I know what she meant." The hope is that, after reading this book, the rest of us will, too.

Before the Storm

◆◆◆

In 1940, Richard Wright (1908–1960) published a novel, *Native Son,* to great acclaim. The next year, Viking Press asked him to draft a running text to accompany a series of photographs of black Americans from the archives of the Farm Credit Administration. The editors asked for 20 pages; after research trips to Chicago and the South, where Wright was forced to ride in a segregated railcar, he gave them more than 50. Wright, who would later tend to rush through his work, took pains with the manuscript, once withdrawing it from the publishers for yet more polishing. The result is an impressionistic survey of the prewar landscape, and Wright's essay ends on a note signalling the beginning of the Great Migration, a historic shift that would take millions of African Americans to the North.

They were leaving places like Mississippi. A child of Yazoo City, on the edges of the Delta, Willie Morris (1934–1999) offers a recollection of growing up white in the pre-movement South. Morris's obsession with his homeland would serve the country well in the 1960s, when he became the youngest editor in the history of *Harper's Magazine*. He used its pages to publish pieces on race and civil rights by writers ranging from Ralph Ellison to William Styron. The tone of the *Harper's* coverage in those years—cold-eyed but passionate—gave readers a sophisticated place to come to for dispatches from the front.

As James Baldwin (1924–1987) makes clear, life in the North—specifically in Harlem and New Jersey—was not entirely unlike that in the South. Baldwin (like Wright) had left the United States for Paris. He came home again at a critical hour in the movement: 1954, the year of the Brown school desegregation decision. A friend had suggested Baldwin collect his essays, and he agreed, writing *Notes of a Native Son* before returning to Europe.

Eudora Welty (1909–   ) is best known for her fiction, but in "A Pageant of Birds," a snapshot of a black church in her hometown of Jackson, Mississippi (and one of her very few pieces of reporting), she fulfills the mission she once set for all of her work: "What I do in writing of any character is to try to enter the mind, heart and skin of a human being who is not myself. Whether this happens to be a man or a woman, old or young, with skin black or white, the primary challenge lies in making the jump itself." A church pageant also serves as a jumping-off point for Maya Angelou (1928–   ), who, in a piece that later gave her the title for her autobiography, describes the other side of the childhood Morris lived and Welty saw.

Meanwhile, to many Americans, the old Confederacy was like another country, and in 1947 the English novelist Rebecca West (1892–1983) persuaded *The New Yorker's* Harold Ross to let her cover a lynching case in Greenville, South Carolina. Fresh from writing about the Nuremberg trials, West saw the South's troubles in a larger context and did not pass judgment. "Lately Europe had not been really what any of us could call a peaceable community," she wrote. Ross was fastidious about facts. When West arrived back in New York, a Greenville journalist was brought in "to see if my facts and my account of the locality could be questioned; and a northern lawyer and a southern lawyer were hired to debate together as to whether my view of the case was sound; and then I had to sit up with Harold Ross until four in the morning while he cross-examined me on the proofs." The final piece is an excellent portrait of a town in which, as one Greenville woman told West, race and violence were "just like a fever." As the fifties began, the infection was spreading.

Inheritors of Slavery

*Twelve Million Black Voices: A Folk History of the Negro
in the United States, 1941*

◆

RICHARD WRIGHT

The word "Negro," the term by which, orally or in print, we black folk in the United States are usually designated, is not really a name at all nor a description, but a psychological island whose objective form is the most unanimous fiat in all American history; a fiat buttressed by popular and national tradition, and written down in many state and city statutes; a fiat which artificially and arbitrarily defines, regulates, and limits in scope of meaning the vital contours of our lives, and the lives of our children and our children's children.

This island, within whose confines we live, is anchored in the feelings of millions of people, and is situated in the midst of the sea of white faces we meet each day; and, by and large, as three hundred years of time has borne our nation into the twentieth century, its rocky boundaries have remained unyielding to the waves of our hope that dash against it.

The steep cliffs of this island are manifest, on the whole, in the conduct of whites toward us hour by hour, a conduct which tells us that we possess no rights commanding respect, that we have no claim to pursue happiness in our own fashion, that our progress toward civilization constitutes an insult, that our behavior must be kept firmly within an orbit branded as inferior, that we must be compelled to labor at the behest of others, that as a group we are owned by the whites, and that manliness on our part warrants instant reprisal.

Three hundred years are a long time for millions of folk like us to be held in such subjection, so long a time that perhaps scores of years will have to pass before we shall be able to express what this slavery has done to us, for our personalities are still numb from its long shocks; and, as the numbness leaves our souls, we shall yet have to feel and give utterance to the full pain we shall inherit.

More than one-half of us black folk in the United States are tillers of the soil, and three-fourths of those of us who till the soil are sharecroppers and day laborers.

The land we till is beautiful, with red and black and brown clay, with fresh and hungry smells, with pine trees and palm trees, with rolling hills and swampy delta—an unbelievably fertile land, bounded on the north by the states of Pennsylvania, Ohio, Illinois, and Indiana, on the south by the Gulf of Mexico, on the west by the Mississippi River, and on the east by the Atlantic Ocean.

Our southern springs are filled with quiet noises and scenes of growth. Apple buds laugh into blossom. Honeysuckles creep up the sides of houses. Sunflowers nod in the hot fields. From mossy tree to mossy tree—oak, elm, willow, aspen, sycamore, dogwood, cedar, walnut, ash, and hickory—bright green leaves jut from a million branches to form an awning that tries to shield and shade the earth. Blue and pink kites of small boys sail in the windy air.

In summer the magnolia trees fill the countryside with sweet scent for long miles. Days are slumberous, and the skies are high and thronged with clouds that ride fast. At midday the sun blazes and bleaches the soil. Butterflies flit through the heat; wasps sing their sharp, straight lines; birds fluff and flounce, piping in querulous joy. Nights are covered with canopies sometimes blue and sometimes black, canopies that sag low with ripe and nervous stars. The throaty boast of frogs momentarily drowns out the call and counter-call of crickets.

In autumn the land is afire with color. Red and brown leaves lift and flutter dryly, becoming entangled in the stiff grass and cornstalks. Cotton is picked and ginned; cane is crushed and its juice is simmered down into molasses; yams are grubbed out of the clay; hogs are slaughtered and cured in lingering smoke; corn is husked and ground into meal. At twilight the sky is full of wild geese winging ever southward, and bats jerk through the air. At night the winds blow free.

In winter the forests resound with the bite of steel axes eating into tall trees as men gather wood for the leaden days of cold. The guns of hunters snap and crack. Long days of rain come, and our swollen creeks rush to join a hundred rivers that wash across the land and make great harbors where they feed the gulf or the sea. Occasionally the rivers leap their banks and leave new thick layers of silt to enrich the earth, and then the look of the land is garish, bleak, suffused with a first-day stillness, strangeness, and awe.

But whether in spring or summer or autumn or winter, time slips past us remorselessly, and it is hard to tell of the iron that lies beneath the surface of our quiet, dull days.

To paint the picture of how we live on the tobacco, cane, rice, and cotton plantations is to compete with mighty artists: the movies, the radio, the newspapers, the magazines, and even the Church. They have painted one picture: charming, idyllic, romantic; but we live another: full of the fear of the Lords of the Land, bowing and grinning when we meet white faces, toiling from sun to sun, living in unpainted wooden shacks that sit casually and insecurely upon the red clay.

In the main we are different from other folk in that, when an impulse moves us, when we are caught in the throes of inspiration, when we are moved to better our lot, we do not ask ourselves: "Can we do it?" but: "Will they let us do it?" Before we black folk can move, we must first look into the white man's mind to see what is there, to see what he is thinking, and the white man's mind is a mind that is always changing.

In general there are three classes of men above us: the Lords of the Land—operators of the plantations; the Bosses of the Buildings—the owners of industry; and the vast numbers of poor white workers—our immediate competitors in the daily struggle for bread. The Lords of the Land hold sway over the plantations and over us; the Bosses of the Buildings lend money and issue orders to the Lords of the Land. The Bosses of the Buildings feed upon the Lords of the Land, and the Lords of the Land feed upon the 5,000,000 landless poor whites and upon us, throwing to the poor whites the scant solace of filching from us 4,000,000 landless blacks what the poor whites themselves are cheated of in this elaborate game.

Back of this tangled process is a long history. When the Emancipation Proclamation was signed, there were some 4,000,000 of us black folk stranded and bewildered upon the land which we had tilled under compulsion for two and a half centuries. Sundered suddenly from the only relationship with Western civilization we had been allowed to form since our captivity, our personalities blighted by two hundred and fifty years of servitude, and eager to hold our wives and husbands and children together in family units, some of us turned back to the same Lords of the Land who had held us as slaves and begged for work, resorted to their advice; and there began for us a new kind of bondage: sharecropping.

Glad to be free, some of us drifted and gave way to every vagary of impulse that swept through us, being held in the line of life only by the necessity to work and eat. Confined for centuries to the life of the cotton field, many of us possessed no feelings of family, home, community, race, church, or progress. We could scarcely believe that we were free, and our restlessness and incessant mobility were our naïve way of testing that freedom. Just as a kitten stretches and yawns after a long sleep, so thousands of us tramped from place to place for the sheer sake of moving, looking, wondering, landless upon the land. Arkansas, Missouri, Tennessee, Kentucky, North Carolina, South Carolina, Louisiana, Alabama, Mississippi, Georgia, Virginia, and West Virginia became the home states of us freed blacks.

In 1890 many white people predicted that we black folk would perish in a competitive world; but in spite of this we left the land and kept afloat, wandering from Natchez to New Orleans, from Mobile to Montgomery, from Macon to Jacksonville, from Birmingham to Chattanooga, from Nashville to Louisville, from Memphis to Little Rock—laboring in the sawmills, in the turpentine camps, on the road jobs; working for men who did not care if we lived or died, but who did not want their business enterprises to suffer for lack of labor. During the first decade of the twentieth century, more than one and three-quarter millions of us abandoned the plantations upon which we had been born; more than a million of us roamed the states of the South and the remainder of us drifted north.

Our women fared easier than we men during the early days of freedom; on the whole their relationship to the world was more stable than ours. Their authority was supreme in most of our families inasmuch as many of them had worked in the "Big Houses" of the Lords of the Land and had learned manners, had been taught to cook, sew, and nurse. During slave days they did not always belong to us, for the Lords of the Land often took them for their pleasure. When a gang of us was sold from one plantation to another, our wives would sometimes be kept by the Lords of the Land and we men would have to mate with whatever slave girl we chanced upon. Because of their enforced intimacy with the Lords of the Land, many of our women, after they were too old to work, were allowed to remain in the slave cabins to tend generations of black children. They enjoyed a status denied us men, being called "Mammy"; and through the years they became symbols of motherhood, retaining in their withered bodies the burden of our folk wisdom, reigning as arbiters in our domestic affairs until we men were freed and had moved to cities where cash-paying jobs enabled us to become the heads of our own families.

The economic and political power of the South is not held in our hands; we do not own banks, iron and steel mills, railroads, office buildings, ships, wharves, or power plants. There are some few of us who operate small grocery stores, barber shops, rooming houses, burial societies, and undertaking establishments. But none of us owns any of the basic industries that shape the course of the South, such as mining, lumber, textiles, oil, transportation, or electric power. So, in the early spring, when the rains have ceased and the ground is ready for plowing, we present ourselves to the Lords of the Land and ask to make a crop. We sign a contract—usually our contracts are oral—which allows us to keep one-half of the harvest after all debts are paid. If we have worked upon these plantations before, we are legally bound to plant, tend, and harvest another crop. If we should escape to the city to avoid paying our mounting debts, white policemen track us down and ship us back to the plantation.

The Lords of the Land assign us ten or fifteen acres of soil already bled of its fertility through generations of abuse. They advance us one mule, one plow, seed, tools, fertilizer, clothing, and food, the main staples of which are fat hog meat, coarsely ground corn meal, and sorghum molasses. If we have been lucky the year before, maybe we have saved a few dollars to tide us through the fall months, but spring finds us begging an "advance"—credit—from the Lords of the Land.

From now on the laws of Queen Cotton rule our lives. (Contrary to popular assumption, cotton is a *queen*, not a king. Kings are dictatorial; cotton is not only dictatorial but self-destructive, an imperious woman in the throes of constant childbirth, a woman who is driven by her greedy passion to bear endless bales of cotton, though she well knows that she will die if she continues to give birth to her fleecy children!) If we black folk had only to work to feed the Lords of the Land, to supply delicacies for their tables—as did the slaves of old for their masters—our degradation upon the plantations would not have been the harshest form of human servitude the world has ever known. But we had to raise cotton to clothe the world; cotton meant money, and money meant power and authority and prestige. To plant vegetables for our tables was often forbidden, for raising a garden narrowed the area to be planted in cotton. The world demanded cotton, and the Lords of the Land ordered more acres to be planted—planted right up to our doorsteps!—and the ritual of Queen Cotton became brutal and bloody.

Because they feel that they cannot trust us, the Lords of the Land assign a "riding boss" to go from cotton patch to cotton patch and supervise our work. We pay for the cost of this supervision out of our share of the harvest; we pay interest on the cost of the supplies which the Lords of the Land advance to us; and, because illness and death, rain and sun, boll weevil and storms, are hazards which might work to the detriment of the cotton crop, we agree to pay at harvest a "time price," a sum payable in cotton, corn, or cane, which the Lords of the Land charge us to cover a probable loss on their investment in us.

We who have followed the plow in this fashion have developed a secret life and language of our own. When we were first brought here from our innumerable African tribes, each of us spoke the language of his tribe. But the Lords of the Land decreed that we must be distributed upon the plantations so that no two of us who spoke a common tongue would be thrown together, lest we plot rebellion. So they shackled one slave to another slave of an alien tribe. Our eyes would look wistfully into the face of a fellow-victim of slavery, but we could say no word to him. Though we could hear, we were deaf; though we could speak, we were dumb!

We stole words from the grudging lips of the Lords of the Land, who did not want us to know too many of them or their meaning. And we charged this meager horde of stolen sounds with all the emotions and longings we had; we proceeded to build our language in inflections of voice, through tonal variety, by hurried speech, in honeyed drawls, by rolling our eyes, by flourishing our hands, by assigning to common, simple words new meanings, meanings which enabled us to speak of revolt in the actual presence of the Lords of the Land without their being aware! Our secret language extended our understanding of what slavery meant and gave us the freedom to speak to our brothers in captivity; we polished our new words, caressed them, gave them new shape and color, a new order and tempo, until, though they were the words of the Lords of the Land, they became *our* words, *our* language.

The steady impact of the plantation system upon our lives created new types of behavior and new patterns of psychological reaction, welding us together into a separate unity with common characteristics of our own. We strove each day to maintain that kind of external behavior that would best allay the fear and hate of the Lords of the Land, and over a period of years this dual conduct became second nature to us and we found in it a degree of immunity from daily oppression. Even when a white man asked us an innocent question, some unconscious part of us would listen closely, not only to the obvious words, but also to the intonations of voice that indicated what kind of answer he wanted; and, automatically, we would determine whether an affirmative or negative reply was expected, and we would answer, not in terms of objective truth, but in terms of what the white man wished to hear.

If a white man stopped a black on a southern road and asked: "Say, there, boy! It's one o'clock, isn't it?" the black man would answer: "Yessuh."

If the white man asked: "Say, it's not one o'clock, is it, boy?" the black man would answer: "Nawsuh."

And if the white man asked: "It's ten miles to Memphis, isn't it, boy?" the black man would answer: "Yessuh."

And if the white man asked: "It isn't ten miles to Memphis, is it, boy?" the black man would answer: "Nawsuh."

Always we said what we thought the whites wanted us to say.

So our years pass within the web of a system we cannot beat. Years of fat meat and corn meal and sorghum molasses, years of plowing and hoeing and picking, years of sun and wind and rain—these are the years that do with us what they will, that form our past, shape our present, and loom ahead as the outline of our future.

Most of the flogging and lynchings occur at harvest time, when fruit hangs heavy and ripe, when the leaves are red and gold, when nuts fall from the trees, when the earth offers its best. The thought of harvest steals upon us with a sense of an inescapable judgment. It is time now to settle accounts with the Lords of the Land, to divide the crops and pay old debts, and we are afraid. We have never grown used to confronting the Lords of the Land when the last of the cotton is ginned and baled, for we know beforehand that we have lost yet another race with time, that we are deeper in debt. When word reaches us that the Lords of the Land are bent over the big books down at the plantation commissary, we lower our eyes, shake our heads, and mutter:

> *A naught's a naught,*
> *Five's a figger;*
> *All for the white man,*
> *None for the nigger. . . .*

If the Lord of the Land for whom we are working happens to be a foreigner who came to the United States to escape oppression in Europe, and who has taken to the native way of cheating us, we spit and mutter:

> Red, white, and blue,
>   Your daddy was a Jew,
> Your ma's a dirty dago,
>   Now what the hell is you? . . .

And after we have divided the crops we are still entangled as deeply as ever in this hateful web of cotton culture. We are older; our bodies are weaker; our families are larger; our clothes are in rags; we are still in debt; and, worst of all, we face another year that holds even less hope than the one we have just endured. We know that this is not right, and dark thoughts take possession of our minds. We know that to tread this mill is to walk in days of slow death. When alone, we stand and look out over the green, rolling fields and wonder why it is that living here is so hard. Everything seems to whisper of the possibility of happiness, of satisfying experiences; but somehow happiness and satisfaction never come into our lives. The land upon which we live holds a promise, but the promise fades with the passing seasons.

And we know that if we protest we will be called "bad niggers." The Lords of the Land will preach the doctrine of "white supremacy" to the poor whites who are eager to form mobs. In the midst of general hysteria they will seize one of us—it does not matter who, the innocent or guilty—and, as a token, a naked and bleeding body will be dragged through the dusty streets. The mobs will make certain that our token-death is known throughout the quarters where we black folk live. Our bodies will be swung by ropes from the limbs of trees, will be shot at and mutilated.

And we cannot fight back; we have no arms; we cannot vote; and the law is white. There are no black policemen, black justices of the peace, black judges, black juries, black jailers, black mayors, or black men anywhere in the government of the South. The Ku Klux Klan attacks us in a thousand ways, driving our boys and girls off the jobs in the cities and keeping us who live on the land from protesting or asking too many questions.

This is the way the Lords of the Land keep their power. For them life is a continuous victory; for us it is simply trouble in the land. Fear is with us always, and in those areas where we black men equal or outnumber the whites fear is at its highest. Two streams of life flow through the South, a black stream and a white stream, and from day to day we live in the atmosphere of a war that never ends. Even when the sprawling fields are drenched in peaceful sunshine, it is war. When we grub at the clay with our hoes, it is war. When we sleep, it is war. When we are awake, it is war. When one of us is born, he enters one of the warring regiments of the South. When there are days of peace, it is a peace born of a victory over us; and when there is open violence, it is when we are trying to push back the encroachments of the Lords of the Land.

Sometimes, fleetingly, like a rainbow that comes and vanishes in its coming, the wan faces of the poor whites make us think that perhaps we can join our hands with them and lift the weight of the Lords of the Land off our backs. But, before new meanings can bridge the chasm that has been long created between us, the poor whites are warned by the Lords of the Land that they must cast their destiny with their own color, that to make common cause with us is to threaten the foundations of civilization. Fear breeds in our hearts until each poor white face begins to look like the face of an enemy soldier. We learn that almost all white men feel it is their duty to see that we do not go beyond the prescribed boundaries. And so both of us, the poor black and the poor white, are kept poor, and only the Lords of the Land grow rich. When we black folk are alone together, we point to the poor whites and croon with vindictiveness:

> *I don't like liver*
> *I don't like hash*
> *I'd rather be a nigger*
> *Than poor white trash. . . .*

And then, conversely, when we compare our hopelessness with the vast vistas of progress about us, when we feel self-disgust at our bare lot, when we contemplate our lack of courage in the face of daily force, we are seized with a desire to escape our shameful identification; and, overwhelmed emotionally, we seek to become protectively merged with the least-known and farthest removed race of men we know; yes, when we weigh ourselves and find ourselves wanting, we say with a snicker of self-depreciation:

> *White folks is evil*
> *And niggers is too*
> *So glad I'm a Chinaman*
> *I don't know what to do. . . .*

There is something "funny" about the hate of the poor whites for us and our hate for them. Our minds fight against it, but external reality freezes us into stances of mutual resistance. And the irony of it is that both of us, the poor white and the poor black, are spoken of by the Lords of the Land as "our men." When they stride along and see us working their fields, they point to us and speak of us as though they owned us, saying: "There are our men." Jobs are few and the Lords of the Land know it, and when they refer to us, black or white, we are always "somebody's men."

So we stay fixed in attitudes of opposition, as though the Lords of the Land had waved a magic wand and cast a spell upon us, a spell from which we cannot awaken. And we blacks and whites ride down the years as the plantation system gnaws at the foundations of our characters. The plantation warps us so that some say we black and white upon the land cannot learn to live as other men do. But we know otherwise; we can learn. The Lords of the Land stand in our way; they do not permit the poor whites to make common union with us, for that would mean the end of the Lords' power. To ask questions, to protest, to insist, to contend for a secure institutional and political base upon which to stand and fulfill ourselves is equivalent to a new and intensified declaration of war.

Sometimes a few of us escape the sharecropping system and become home-owners. But gray and blue eyes watch us and if we do not help them in their game of "keeping the niggers down," if we do not ally ourselves with them and partake of their attitudes toward our own black folk, they find fault with us and drive us from our homes. An independent and prosperous black family flourishing amid a vast area of poverty is in itself a powerful enough symbol of aspiration to be a source of trouble, for that black family's mere well-being prods the black thousands, who, if they moved, would disrupt the delicately balanced forces of racial and economic power in the South.

But in spite of this, how eagerly have we taken to the culture of this new land when opportunity was open to us! Knowing no culture but this, what can we do but live in terms of what we see before our eyes each day? From the simple physiological reactions of slave days, from casual relations and sporadic hope, we learn to live the way of life of the Western world. Behind our pushing is the force of life itself, as strong in black men as in white, as emergent in us as in those who contrive to keep us down.

We hear men talk vaguely of a government in far-away Washington, a government that stands above the people and desires the welfare of all. We do not know this government; but the men it hires to execute its laws are the Lords of the Land whom we have known all our lives. We hear that the government wants to help us, but we are too far down at the bottom of the ditch for the fingers of the government to reach us, and there are too many men—the Lords of the Land and the poor whites—with their shoulders pressing tightly together in racial solidarity, forming a wall between us and the government. More to keep faith alive in our hearts than from any conviction that our lot will be bettered, we cling to our hope that the government would help us if it could. But for three hundred years we have been forced to accept the word of men instead of written contracts, for three hundred years we have been forced to rely upon the whimsical kindness of others rather than upon legal agreements; and all this has grown into hallowed tradition, congealed into reflex habit, hardened into a daily ritual, backed by rope and fagot.

When you, your father, and your father's father have lived under a system that permits others to organize your life, how can you get a check the government sends you? The Lords of the Land receive your mail and when you go to the Big House to ask for your check, they look at you and say: "Boy, get back in the field and keep working. We'll take care of your check. Here, you'd better make your mark on it so's we can cash it. We'll feed you until it is used up." Ordinarily you are so deep in debt when you receive a check from the government that you sign it entirely over to the Lords of the Land and forget about it.

Our days are walled with cotton; we move casually among the whites and they move casually among us; our speech is drawled out with slow smiles; there are no loud arguments; no voices are raised in contention; no shouts of passion betray the desire of one to convince the other. It is impossible to debate or maneuver for advantage without colliding; then blood is spilt. Trapped by the plantation system, we beg bread of the Lords of the Land and they give it to us; they need us to work for them. Although our association partakes of an odd sort of father-child relationship, it is devoid of that affinity of blood that restrains the impulse to cruelty, empty of that sense of intimate understanding born of a long proximity of human lives.

We plow, plant, chop, and pick the cotton, working always toward a dark, mercurial goal. We hear that silk is becoming popular, that jute is taking the place of cotton in many lands, that factories are making clothing out of rayon, that scientists have invented a substance called nylon. All these are blows to the reign of Queen Cotton, and when she dies we do not know how many of us will die with her. Adding to our confusion is the gradual appearance of machines that can pick more cotton in one day than any ten of us. How can we win this race with death when our thin blood is set against the potency of gasoline, when our weak flesh is pitted against the strength of steel, when our loose muscles must vie with the power of tractors?

Through the years rumor filters down to us of cotton being grown in Egypt, Russia, Japan, India, in lands whose names we cannot pronounce. We black folk are needed no longer to grow cotton to clothe the world. Moreover, we cannot imagine that there will be so many factories erected in the South— since there are thousands already manufacturing more goods than can be bought—that those of us who cannot earn our bread by growing cotton will get jobs in them. Our future on the plantation is a worry.

Of a summer night, sitting on our front porches, we discuss how "funny" it is that we who raise cotton to clothe the nation do not have handkerchiefs to wipe the sweat from our brows, do not have mattresses to sleep on; we need shirts, dresses, sheets, drawers, tablecloths. When our cotton returns to us— after having been spun and woven and dyed and wrapped in cellophane—its cost is beyond our reach. The Bosses of the Buildings, owners of the factories that turn out the mass of commodities we yearn to buy, have decided that no cheap foreign articles can come freely into the country to undersell the products made by "their own workers."

The years glide on and strange things come. The Lords of the Land, as the cotton market shrinks and prices fall, grow poor and become riding bosses, and the riding bosses grow poor and become tenant farmers, and the tenant farmers grow poor and become sharecroppers, and the sharecroppers grow poor and become day laborers, migrants upon the land whose home is where the next crop is. We ask how such things can happen and we are told that the South is "broke," that it has to borrow money from the Bosses of the Buildings, that it must pay dearly for this hired gold, and that the soil is yielding less because of erosion. As plantation after plantation fails, the Bosses of the Buildings acquire control and send tractors upon the land, and still more of us are compelled to search for "another place." The Bosses of the Buildings now own almost one-third of the plantations of the South, and they are rapidly converting them into "farm factories."

When we grumble about our hard life, the Lords of the Land cry: "Listen, I've borrowed money on my plantation and I'm risking my *land* with you folks!" And we, hungry and barefoot, cry: "And we're risking our *lives* with you!" And that is all that can be said; there is no room for idle words. Everything fits flush, each corner fitting tight into another corner. If you act at all, it is either to flee or to kill; you are either a victim or a rebel.

Days come and days go, but our lives upon the land remain without hope. We do not care if the barns rot down; they do not belong to us, anyway. No matter what improvement we may make upon the plantation, it would give us no claim upon the crop. In cold weather we burn everything in sight to keep us warm; we strip boards from our shacks and palings from the straggling fences. During long winter days we sit in cabins that have no windowpanes; the floors and roofs are made of thin planks of pine. Out in the backyard, over a hole dug in the clay, stands a horizontal slab of oak with an oval opening in it; when it rains, a slow stink drifts over the wet fields.

To supplement our scanty rations, we take our buckets and roam the hillsides for berries, nuts, or wild greens; sometimes we fish in the creeks; at other times our black women tramp the fields looking for bits of firewood, piling their aprons high, coming back to our cabins slowly, like laden donkeys.

If our shacks catch fire, there is nothing much we can do but to snatch our children and run to a safe place and watch the flames eat the dry timbers. There is no fire wagon and there is but little water. Fire, like other things, has its way with us.

Lord, we *know* that this is a hard system! Even while we are hating the Lords of the Land, we know that if they paid us a just wage for all the work we do in raising a bale of cotton, the fleecy strands would be worth more than their weight in gold! Cotton is a drug, and for three hundred years we have taken it to kill the pain of hunger; but it does not ease our suffering. Most people take morphine out of choice; we take cotton because we must. For years longer than we remember, cotton has been our companion; we travel down the plantation road with debt holding our left hand, with credit holding our right, and ahead of us looms the grave, the final and simple end.

We move slowly through sun and rain, and our eyes grow dull and our skin sags. For hours we sit on our porches and stare out over the dusty land, wondering why we are so tired. In the fall the medicine men come and set up their tents, light gas flares, and amuse us with crude jokes. We take the pennies out of the tin can under a plank in the barn and buy patent medicine for Grandpa's malaria-like feeling, for Grandma's sudden chills, for Susie's spasms of hotness, for the strange and nasty rash that eats at Rosa's skin, for Bob's hacking cough that will not leave, for the pain that gnaws the baby's stomach day and night.

Yet we live on and our families grow large. Some people wag their heads in amusement when they see our long lines of ragged children, but we love them. If our families are large, we have a chance to make a bigger crop, for there are more hands to tend the land. But large families eat more, and, although our children lighten the burden of toil, we finish the year as we were before, hungry and in debt. Like black buttercups, our children spring up on the red soil of the plantations. When a new one arrives, neighbors from miles around come and look at it, speculating upon which parent it resembles. A child is a glad thing in the bleak stretches of the cotton country, and our gold is in the hearts of the people we love, in the veins that carry our blood, upon those faces where we catch furtive glimpses of the shape of our humble souls.

Our way of life is simple and our unit of living is formed by the willingness of two or more of us to organize ourselves voluntarily to make a crop, to pool our labor power to wrest subsistence from the stubborn soil. We live just as man lived when he first struggled against this earth. After having been pulverized by slavery and purged of our cultural heritage, we have been kept so far from the sentiments and ideals of the Lords of the Land that we do not feel their way of life deeply enough to act upon their assumptions and motives. So, living by folk tradition, possessing but a few rights which others respect, we are unable to establish our family groups upon a basis of property ownership. For the most part our delicate families are held together by love, sympathy, pity, and the goading knowledge that we must work together to make a crop.

That is why we black folk laugh and sing when we are alone together. There is nothing—no ownership or lust for power—that stands between us and our kin. And we reckon kin not as others do, but down to the ninth and tenth cousin. And for a reason we cannot explain we are mighty proud when we meet a man, woman, or child who, in talking to us, reveals that the blood of our brood has somehow entered his veins. Because our eyes are not blinded by the hunger for possessions, we are a tolerant folk. A black mother who stands in the sagging door of her gingerbread shack may weep as she sees her children straying off into the unknown world, but no matter what they may do, no matter what happens to them, no matter what crimes they may commit, no matter what the world may think of them, that mother always welcomes them back with an irreducibly human feeling that stands above the claims of law or property. Our scale of values differs from that of the world from which we have been excluded; our shame is not its shame, and our love is not its love.

Our black children are born to us in our one-room shacks, before crackling log fires, with rusty scissors boiling in tin pans, with black plantation midwives hovering near, with pine-knot flames casting shadows upon the wooden walls, with the sound of kettles of water singing over the fires in the hearths. . . .

As our children grow up they help us day by day, fetching pails of water from the springs, gathering wood for cooking, sweeping the floors, minding the younger children, stirring the clothes boiling in black pots over the fires in the backyards, and making butter in the churns. . . .

Sometimes there is a weather-worn, pine-built schoolhouse for our children, but even if the school were open for the full term our children would not have the time to go. We cannot let them leave the fields when cotton is waiting to be picked. When the time comes to break the sod, the sod must be broken; when the time comes to plant the seeds, the seeds must be planted; and when the time comes to loosen the red clay from about the bright green stalks of the cotton plants, that, too, must be done even if it is September and school is open. Hunger is the punishment if we violate the laws of Queen Cotton. The seasons of the year form the mold that shapes our lives, and who can change the seasons?

Deep down we distrust the schools that the Lords of the Land build for us and we do not really feel that they are ours. In many states they edit the textbooks that our children study, for the most part deleting all references to government, voting, citizenship, and civil rights. Many of them say that French, Latin, and Spanish are languages not for us, and they become angry when they think that we desire to learn more than they want us to. They say that "all the geography a nigger needs to know is how to get from his shack to the plow." They restrict our education easily, inasmuch as their laws decree that there must be schools for our black children and schools for the white, churches for our black folk and churches for the white, and in public places their signs read: For Colored and For White. They have arranged the order of life in the South so that a different set of ideals is inculcated in the opposing black and white groups.

Yet, in a vague, sentimental sort of way we love books inordinately, even though we do not know how to read them, for we know that books are the gateway to a forbidden world. Any black man who can read a book is a hero to us. And we are joyful when we hear a black man speak like a book. The people who say how the world is to be run, who have fires in winter, who wear warm clothes, who get enough to eat, are the people who make books speak to them. Sometimes of a night we tell our children to get out the old big family Bible and read to us, and we listen wonderingly until, tired from a long day in the fields, we fall asleep.

The Lords of the Land have shown us how preciously they regard books by the manner in which they cheat us in erecting schools for our children. They tax black and white equally throughout the state, and then they divide the money for education unequally, keeping most of it for their own schools, generally taking five dollars for themselves for every dollar they give us. For example, in the state of Mississippi, for every $25 a year that is spent to educate a white child, only $5 a year is spent to educate a black child. In many counties there is no school at all, and where there is one, it is old, with a leaky roof; our children sit on wooden planks made into crude benches without backs. Sometimes seventy children, ranging in age from six to twenty, crowd into the one room which comprises the entire school structure; they are taught by one teacher whose wage is lower and whose conditions of work are immeasurably poorer than those of white teachers.

Many of our schools are open for only six months a year, and allow our children to progress only to the sixth grade. Some of those who are lucky enough to graduate go back as teachers to instruct their brothers and sisters. Many of our children grow to feel that they would rather remain upon the plantations to work than attend school, for they can observe so few tangible results in the lives of those who do attend.

The schoolhouse is usually far away; at times our children must travel distances varying from one to six miles. Busses are furnished for many white children, but rarely for ours. The distances we walk are so legendary that often the measure of a black man's desire to obtain an education is gauged by the number of miles he declares he walked to school when a child.

Sunday is always a glad day. We call all our children to us and comb the hair of the boys and plait the hair of the girls; then we rub their heads with hog fat to make their hair shine. We wrap the girls' hair in white strings and put a red ribbon upon their heads; we make the boys wear stocking caps, that is, we make them pull upon their heads the tops of our stockings, cut and stretched taut upon their skulls to keep their hair in place. Then we rub the hog fat upon their faces to take that dull, ashy look away from skins made dry and rough from the weather of the fields. In clean clothes ironed stiff with starch made from flour, we hitch up the mule to the wagon, pile in our Bibles and baskets of food—hog meat and greens—and we are off to church.

The preacher tells of days long ago and of a people whose sufferings were like ours. He preaches of the Hebrew children and the fiery furnace, of Daniel, of Moses, of Solomon, and of Christ. What we have not dared feel in the presence of the Lords of the Land, we now feel in church. Our hearts and bodies, reciprocally acting upon each other, swing out into the meaning of the story the preacher is unfolding. Our eyes become absorbed in a vision. . . .

. . . a place eternal filled with happiness where dwell God and His many hosts of angels singing His praises and glorifying His name and in the midst of this oneness of being there arises one whose soul is athirst to feel things for himself and break away from the holy band of joy and he organizes revolt in Heaven and preaches rebellion and aspires to take the place of God to rule Eternity and God condemns him from Heaven and decrees that he shall be banished and this Rebel this Satan this Lucifer persuades one-third of all the many hosts of angels in Heaven to follow him and build a new Heaven and down he comes with his angels whose hearts are black with pride and whose souls are hot with vengeance against God who decides to make Man and He makes Man in His own image and He forms him of clay and He breathes the breath of life into him but He warns him against the Rebel the Satan the Lucifer who had been banished from Heaven for his pride and envy and Man lives in a garden of peace where there is no Time no Sorrow and no Death and while Man lives in this happiness there comes to him the Rebel the Satan the Lucifer and he tempts Man and drags him down the same black path of rebellion and sin and God seeing this decrees that Man shall live in the Law and not Love and must endure Toil and Pain and Death and must dig for his bread in the stony earth but while Man suffers God's compassion is moved and God Himself assumes the form of Man's corrupt and weak flesh and comes down and lives and suffers and dies upon a cross to show Man the way back up the broad highway to peace and thus Man begins to live for a time under a new dispensation of Love and not Law and the Rebel the Satan the Lucifer still works rebellion seducing persuading falsifying and God through His prophets says that He will come for a second time bringing not peace but a sword to rout the powers of darkness and build a new Jerusalem and God through His prophets says that the final fight the last battle the Armageddon will be resumed and will endure until the end of Time and of Death. . . .

. . . and the preacher's voice is sweet to us, caressing and lashing, conveying to us a heightening of consciousness that the Lords of the Land would rather keep from us, filling us with a sense of hope that is treasonable to the rule of Queen Cotton. As the sermon progresses, the preacher's voice increases in emotional intensity, and we, in tune and sympathy with his sweeping story, sway in our seats until we have lost all notion of time and have begun to float on a tide of passion. The preacher begins to punctuate his words with sharp rhythms, and we are lifted far beyond the boundaries of our daily lives, upward and outward, until, drunk with our enchanted vision, our senses lifted to the burning skies, we do not know who we are, what we are, or where we are. . . .

We go home pleasantly tired and sleep easily, for we know that we hold somewhere within our hearts a possibility of inexhaustible happiness; we know that if we could but get our feet planted firmly upon this earth, we could laugh and live and build. We take this feeling with us each day and it drains the gall out of our years, sucks the sting from the rush of time, purges the pain from our memory of the past, and banishes the fear of loneliness and death. When the soil grows poorer, we cling to this feeling; when clanking tractors uproot and hurl us from the land, we cling to it; when our eyes behold a black body swinging from a tree in the wind, we cling to it. . . .

Some say that, because we possess this faculty of keeping alive this spark of happiness under adversity, we are children. No, it is the courage and faith in simple living that enable us to maintain this reservoir of human feeling, for we know that there will come a day when we shall pour out our hearts over this land.

Neither are we ashamed to go of a Saturday night to the crossroad dance-hall and slow drag, ball the jack, and Charleston to an old guitar and piano. Dressed in starched jeans, an old silk shirt, a big straw hat, we swing the girls over the plank floor, clapping our hands, stomping our feet, and singing:

> *Shake it to the east*
> *Shake it to the west*
> *Shake it to the one*
> *You love the best. . . .*

It is what makes our boys and girls, when they are ten or twelve years of age, roam the woods, bareheaded and barefoot, singing and whistling and shouting in wild, hilarious chorus a string of ditties that make the leaves of the trees shiver in naked and raucous laughter.

> *I love you once*
> *I love you twice*
> *I love you next to*
> *Jesus Christ. . . .*

And it is this same capacity for joy that makes us hymn:

> *I'm a stranger*
> *Don't drive me away*
> *I'm a stranger*
> *Don't drive me away*
> *If you drive me away*
> *You may need me some day*
> *I'm a stranger*
> *Don't drive me away. . . .*

But there are times when we doubt our songs; they are not enough to unify our fragile folk lives in this competitive world. As our children grow older, they leave us to fulfill the sense of happiness that sleeps in their hearts. Unlike us, they have been influenced by the movies, magazines, and glimpses of town life, and they lack the patience to wait for the consummation of God's promise as we do. We despair to see them go, but we tell them that we want them to escape the deadening life of the plantation. Our hearts are divided: we want them to have a new life, yet we are afraid if they challenge the Lords of the Land, for we know that terror will assail them. As our children learn what is happening on other plantations and up north, the casual ties of our folk families begin to dissolve.

Vast changes engulf our lives. We sit on our front porches, fanning the flies away, and watch the men with axes come through the Southland, as they have already gone through the Northland and the Westland, and whack down the pine, oak, ash, elm, and hickory trees, leaving the land denuded as far as the eye can see. And then rain comes in leaden sheets to slant and scour at the earth until it washes away rich layers of top soil, until it leaves the land defenseless, until all vegetation is gone and nothing remains to absorb the moisture and hinder the violent spreading floods of early spring.

Cotton crops have sapped the soil of its fertility; twenty or thirty years of good cotton farming are enough to drain the land and leave it a hard, yellow mat, a mockery to the sky and a curse to us.

On top of this there come, with a tread as of doom, more and more of the thundering tractors and cotton-picking machines that more and more render our labor useless. Year by year these machines grow from one odd and curious object to be gaped at to thousands that become so deadly in their impersonal labor that we grow to hate them. They do our work better and faster than we can, driving us from plantation to plantation. Black and white alike now go to the pea, celery, orange, grapefruit, cabbage, and lemon crops. Sometimes we walk and sometimes the bosses of the farm factories send their trucks for us. We go from the red land to the brown land, from the brown land to the black land, working our way eastward until we reach the blue Atlantic. In spring we chop cotton in Mississippi and pick beans in Florida; in summer we labor in the peach orchards of Georgia and tramp on to the tobacco crop in North Carolina; then we trek to New Jersey to dig potatoes. We sleep in woods, in barns, in wooden barracks, on sidewalks, and sometimes in jail. Our dog-trot, dog-run, shotgun, and gingerbread shacks fill with ghosts and tumble down from rot.

News comes that there are better places to go, but we know that the next place will be as bad as the last one. Yet we go. Our drifting is the expression of our hope to improve our lives. Season after season the farm factories pass before our eyes, and at the end of the long journey we are filled with nostalgic melancholy, a blurred picture of many places seen and suffered in, a restlessness which we cannot appease.

In 1914, out of the unknown, comes the news that a war is in progress to hold back the Germans, who are determined to wrest markets and lands away from other countries. We hear that the government has decided to keep alien labor out of the country, and a call is made to us to come north and help turn the wheels of industry. At the thought of leaving our homes again, we cry: "What a life it is we live! Our roots are nowhere! We have no home even upon this soil which formed our blood and bones!" But hundreds of thousands of us get on the move once more.

The Lords of the Land pause now and speak kind words to us; they want us to remain upon the plantations. They tell us that they are our best friends; we smile and say nothing. As we abandon the land, odd things happen to us. If one of us should run afoul of the law at harvest time, the Lords of the Land will speak a good word to the sheriff for "his niggers." The law listens and turns us over to the Lords of the Land who pay our fines. Then we labor upon the plantation to pay the debt! But as long as we merely drift from plantation to plantation, the Lords of the Land do not really care. They say: "Niggers don't know what they want. Niggers come and niggers go, but we'll always have the niggers. Only it's hard to keep the books with them moving all the time."

Soon, however, they take a more serious attitude toward us, for the Bosses of the Buildings send men with fair words down from the North, telling us how much money we can make digging in the mines, smelting ore, laying rails, and killing hogs. They tell us that we will live in brick buildings, that we will vote, that we will be able to send our children to school for nine months of the year, that if we get into trouble we will not be lynched, and that we will not have to grin, doff our hats, bend our knees, slap our thighs, dance, and laugh when we see a white face. We listen, and it sounds like religion. Is it really true? Is there not a trick somewhere? We have grown to distrust all white men. Yet they say: "Listen, we need you to work. We'll hire trains to take you away." Then the weekly Negro newspapers supplement their pleas; the Chicago *Defender*, the Pittsburgh *Courier*, the Baltimore *Afro-American*, and many other newspapers paint the North as a land of promise. We cannot help but believe now. We cannot work the cotton fields for thinking of it; our minds are paralyzed with the hope and dread of it. Not to go means lingering here to live out this slow death; to go means facing the unknown. But, strangely, life has already prepared us for moving and drifting. Have we not already roamed the South? Yes, we will go and see. But we do not move. We are scared. Who will go first? Then, suddenly, a friend leaves and we whisper to him to write and tell us if the dream is true. We wait. Word comes. It *is* true! "Come on!" the letters tell us. We go.

It is like this: suddenly, while we are chopping at the clods of clay with a heavy hoe, the riding boss gallops up and says: "Hurry up there, nigger!"

Perhaps for the first time in our lives we straighten our backs, drop the hoe, give a fleeting glance at the white man's face, and walk off.

"Hey, where the hell you going, nigger?"

"I'm shaking the dust of the South off my feet, white man."

"You'll starve up north, nigger."

"I don't care. I'm going to die some day anyhow."

But so many of us are leaving that the Lords of the Land begin to worry.

"Don't go," they say.

"We're already going," we say, and keep leaving.

If we have no money, we borrow it; if we cannot borrow it, we beg it. If the Bosses of the Buildings do not furnish us with a train, we walk until we reach a railroad and then we swing onto a freight. There develops such a shortage of labor in the South that the Lords of the Land order us rounded up and threatened with jail sentences unless we consent to go to the fields and gather the waiting crops. Finally they persuade men of our own race to talk to us.

"Let down your buckets where you are," our black leaders say.

"We're leaving," we answer.

"The white man of the South is your friend," they say.

"How much are they paying you to say that?" we ask.

"You'll freeze up north."

"We don't care."

The Lords of the Land say: "You niggers are going north because you think you'll mix with whites."

"Look at all the half-white boys and girls on the plantations," we answer. "We black men did not do that."

"Don't talk fresh, nigger!"

"We ain't talking; we're leaving!"

"Come on; we'll build you a big school!"

"We'd rather be a lamppost in Chicago than the president of Dixie!"

While we are leaving, our black boys come back from Flanders, telling us of how their white officers of the United States Army had treated them, how they had kept them in labor battalions, how they had jim-crowed them in the trenches even when they were fighting and dying, how the white officers had instructed the French people to segregate them. Our boys come back to Dixie in uniform and walk the streets with quick steps and proud shoulders. They cannot help it; they have been in battle, have seen men of all nations and races die. They have seen what men are made of, and now they act differently. But the Lords of the Land cannot understand them. They take them and lynch them while they are still wearing the uniform of the United States Army.

Our black boys do not die for liberty in Flanders. They die in Texas and Georgia. Atlanta is our Marne. Brownsville, Texas, is our Château-Thierry.

It is a lesson we will never forget; it is written into the pages of our blood, into the ledgers of our bleeding bodies, into columns of judgment figures and balance statements in the lobes of our brains.

"Don't do this!" we cry.

"Nigger, shut your damn mouth!" they say.

"Don't lynch us!" we plead.

"You're not white!" they say.

"Why don't somebody say something?" we ask.

"We told you to shut your damn mouth!"

We listen for somebody to say something, and we still travel, leaving the South. Our eyes are open, our ears listening for words to point the way.

From 1890 to 1920, more than 2,000,000 of us left the land.

North Toward Home

1967

◆

WILLIE MORRIS

One summer morning when I was twelve, I sighted a little Negro boy walking with a girl who must have been his older sister on the sidewalk a block from my house. The little boy could not have been more than three; he straggled along behind the older girl, walking aimlessly on his short black legs from one edge of the sidewalk to the other.

I hid in the shrubbery near the sidewalk in my yard, peering out two or three times to watch their progress and to make sure the street was deserted. The older girl walked by first, and the child came along a few yards behind. Just as he got in front of me, lurking there in the bushes, I jumped out and pounced upon him. I slapped him across the face, kicked him with my knee, and with a shove sent him sprawling on the concrete.

The little boy started crying, and his sister ran back to him and shouted, "What'd he *do* to you?" My heart was beating furiously, in terror and a curious pleasure; I ran into the back of my house and hid in the weeds for a long time, until the crying drifted far away into niggertown. Then I went into the deserted house and sat there alone, listening to every noise and rustle I heard outside, as if I expected some retribution. For a while I was happy with this act, and my head was strangely light and giddy. Then later, the more I thought about it coldly, I could hardly bear my secret shame.

Once before, when I had been a much smaller boy, I had caught a little sparrow trapped on my screen porch, and almost without thinking, acting as if I were another person and not myself, I had fetched a straight pin, stuck it through the bird's head, and opened the door to let him fly away. My hurting the Negro child, like my torturing the bird, was a gratuitous act of childhood cruelty—but I knew later that it was something else, infinitely more subtle and contorted.

For my whole conduct with Negroes as I was growing up in the 1940s was a relationship of great contrasts. On the one hand there was a kind of unconscious affection, touched with a sense of excitement and sometimes pity. On the other hand there were sudden emotional eruptions—of disdain and utter cruelty. My own alternating affections and cruelties were inexplicable to me, but the main thing is that they were largely *assumed* and only rarely questioned. The broader reality was that the Negroes in the town were *there:* they were ours, to do with as we wished. I grew up with this consciousness of some tangible possession, it was rooted so deeply in me by the whole moral atmosphere of the place that my own ambivalence—which would take mysterious shapes as I grew older—was secondary and of little account.

One fact I took for granted was that Negro adults, even Negro adults I encountered alone and had never seen before, would treat me with generosity and affection. Another was some vague feeling for a mutual sharing of the town's past. (I remember going with one of my friends and her parents to take some food to an old Negro woman who lived alone in a cabin in the woods. The old woman told us about growing up in Yazoo, and of the day she saw the Yankee soldiers coming down the road in a cloud of dust. "I looked out the window," she said, "and there was the War, comin' at me from down the road.") Another assumption was that you would never call a Negro woman a "lady" or address her as "ma'am," or say "sir" to a Negro man. You learned as a matter of course that there were certain negative practices and conditions inherently associated with being a nigger. "Keeping a house like a nigger" was to keep it dirty and unswept. A "nigger car" was an old wreck without brakes and with squirrel tails on the radio aerial. "Behaving like a nigger" was to stay out at all hours and to have several wives or husbands. A "nigger street" was unpaved and littered with garbage. "Nigger talk" was filled with lies and superstitions. A "nigger funeral" meant wailing and shouting and keeping the corpse out of the ground for two weeks. A "white nigger store" was owned by a white man who went after the "nigger trade." There were "good niggers" and "bad niggers," and their categories were so formalized and elaborate that you wondered how they could live together in the same town.

Yet in the midst of all this there was the ineluctable attraction of niggertown, which enclosed the white town on all sides like some other world, and the strange heart-pounding excitement that Negroes in a group generated for me. I knew all about the sexual act, but not until I was twelve years old did I know that it was performed with white women for pleasure; I had thought that only Negro women engaged in the act of love with white men just for fun, because they were the only ones with the animal desire to submit that way. So that Negro girls and women were a source of constant excitement and sexual feeling for me, and filled my day-dreams with delights and wonders.

Whenever I go back there and drive through niggertown, it is as if I had never left home. Few of the old shabby vistas seem changed, and time has not moved all these years for me: the strong greasy smells are the same, and the dust in the yards swirling around the abandoned cars, and the countless children with their glazed open eyes on the porches and in the trees and in the road. The Negro grocery stores, the ones my dog and I drove past in the summers, are still patched and covered with advertisements, and the little boys still wait in front for a white man with his golf clubs to drive up and shout, "Caddy!" The farther one goes into niggertown, up Brickyard or down nearer the town dump, the more dank and lean-to the structures: at first there will be the scattering of big, almost graceful houses, wholly painted or partially so, suggesting a slightly forbidding affluence as they always had for me—but back along the fringes of the town there remains that dreadful forlorn impoverishment, those dusty and ruined wooden façades which as a child would send me back toward Grand Avenue as fast as I could get there.

In a small town like this one in the lower South, where the population ran close to half and half, one of the simplest facts of awareness was that Negroes were everywhere: they ambled along the sidewalks in the white neighborhoods, they mowed the grass and clipped the hedges in the broad green lawns, they rode down the streets in their horse-drawn wagons, they were the janitors and cleaning-women in the churches and schools and the laundry-women coming to the back doors for the week's wash. On the main street especially, on Saturdays, the town was filled with them, talking in great animated clusters on the corners, or spilling out of the drugstores and cafés at the far end of the narrow street. Their shouts and gestures, and the loud blare of their music, were so much a part of those Saturdays that if all of them had suddenly disappeared the town would have seemed unbearably ghostly and bereft. The different shades of color were extraordinary, for they ranged from the whitest white to the darkest black, with shades in between as various and distinct as yellows and browns could be. One woman in particular, whom we saw walking through the crowds on Main Street on Saturday nights, could have passed for a member of the women's choir in the white Baptist church. "There's that white nigger again," someone would say. "I wonder what the *others* think of her?" Not until I was fourteen or fifteen did it begin to occur to me to ask myself, "Are we *related?*" And it was about then that I began hearing the story of the two white men who had Thanksgiving and Christmas dinner every year with three Negroes, who were the white men's half-brothers.

There was a stage, when we were about thirteen, in which we "went Negro." We tried to broaden our accents to sound like Negroes, as if there were not

enough similarity already. We consciously walked like young Negroes, mocking their swinging gait, moving our arms the way they did, cracking our
knuckles and whistling between our teeth. We tried to use some of the same expressions, as closely as possible to the way they said them, like: "Hey, *ma-a-a-n,*
whut you *doin'* theah!," the sounds rolled out and clipped sharply at the end for
the hell of it.

My father and I, on Sundays now and then, would go to their baseball
games, sitting way out along the right field line; usually we were the only white
people there. There was no condescension on our part, though the condescension might come later, if someone asked us where we had been. I would say,
"Oh, we been to see the nigger game over at Number Two."

"Number Two" was the Negro school, officially called "Yazoo High Number Two" as opposed to the white high school, which was "Yazoo High Number
One." We would walk up to a Negro our age and ask, "Say, buddy, where you go
to school?" so we could hear the way he said, "Number *Two!*" Number Two was
behind my house a block or so, a strange eclectic collection of old ramshackle
wooden buildings and bright new concrete ones, sprawled out across four or
five acres. When the new buildings went up, some of the white people would
say, "Well, they won't be pretty very *long.*"

Sometimes we would run across a group of Negro boys our age, walking in
a pack through the white section, and there would be bantering, half-
affectionate exchanges: "Hey, Robert, what you *doin'* theah!" and we would
give them the first names of the boys they didn't know, and they would do the
same. We would mill around in a hopping, jumping mass, talking baseball or
football, showing off for each other, and sounding for all the world, with our
accentuated expressions and our way of saying them, like much the same race.
Some days we organized football games in Lintonia Park, first black against
white, then intermingled, strutting out of huddles with our limbs swinging,
shaking our heads rhythmically, until one afternoon the cops came cruising by
in their patrol car and ordered us to break it up.

On Friday afternoons in the fall, we would go to see "the Black Panthers" of
Number Two play football. They played in the discarded uniforms of our high
school, so that our school colors—red, black, and white—were the same, and
they even played the same towns from up in the delta that our high school
played. We sat on the sidelines next to their cheering section, and sometimes a
couple of us would be asked to carry the first-down chains. The spectators
would shout and jump up and down, and even run onto the field to slap one of
the players on the back when he did something outstanding. When one of the
home team got hurt, ten or twelve people would dash out from the sidelines to
carry him to the bench; I suspected some injuries might not have been as
painful as they looked.

The Panthers had a left-handed quarterback named Kinsey, who could
throw a pass farther than any other high school passer I had ever seen. He

walked by my house every morning on the way to school, and I would get in step with him, emulating his walk as we strolled down to Number Two, and talk about last Friday's game or the next one coming up. We would discuss plays or passing patterns, and we pondered how they could improve on their "flea-flicker" which had backfired so disastrously against Belzoni, leading to a tackle's making an easy interception and all but walking thirty yards for a touchdown. "Man, he coulda *crawled* for that touchdown," Kinsey bemoaned. Once I said, "You got to get another kicker," and Kinsey replied, "Lord don't *I* know it," because in the previous game the Yazoo punter had kicked from his own twenty-yard-line, a high cantankerous spiral that curved up, down, and landed right in the middle of his own end zone. But this was a freak, because Kinsey and many of his teammates were not only superb athletes, they played with a casual flair and an exuberance that seemed missing in the white games. A long time after this, sitting in the bleachers in Candlestick Park in San Francisco, I saw a batter for the New York Mets hit a home run over the centerfield fence; the ball hit a rung on the bleachers, near a group of little boys, and then bounced back over the fence onto the outfield grass. Willie Mays trotted over and gingerly tossed the ball underhanded across the wire fence to the boys, who had been deprived of a free baseball, and that casual gesture was performed with such a fine aristocracy that it suddenly brought back to me all the flamboyant sights and sounds of those Friday afternoons watching Number Two.

On Friday nights, when the Yazoo Indians of Number One played, you could see the Number Two boys, watching with their girl friends from the end-zone seats, talking plays and pointing out strategy. One night my father and I went to the hot-dog stand at halftime and saw Dr. Harrison, the Negro dentist who refereed the Number Two games, standing on the fringes of the crowd eating a hot-dog. My father drifted over his way and said, "How're you, Doc?" though not shaking hands, and they stood there until the second half started, talking about the virtues and shortcomings of the Yazoo Indians and the Yazoo Black Panthers.

Co-existing with all this, in no conflict, were the hoaxes we would play on the Negroes, who were a great untapped resource. We would hide in the hedges in my back yard and shoot Negro men who were walking down the sidewalk, aiming BB's at their tails. We would throw dead snakes from the trees into their path, or dead rats and crawfish, or attach a long thread to a dollar bill on the sidewalk and, when the man stooped to pick it up, pull it slowly back into the bushes.

I took to phoning the Negro undertakers, talking in my flawless Negro accent, and exchanges like this would take place:

"Hello, this the undertaker?"

"Yes'm."

"This here's Miss Mobley, from out at Bentonia. I got me a problem."

"What's that?"

"Well, my cousin just died, and I wonder if I can bury him under the house."

"Bury him under the *house?*"

"That right. He never amounted to much to us, and we just want him out of the way quick."

"You can't do it. It's against the *law.*"

"But what if we don't tell nobody? Ain't nobody gonna miss him noway."

"Naw, you can't do it. You got to get a death certificate and things like that."

"Well, we still gonna put him under the house. Is Johnson's Baby Powder a good thing to sprinkle him with?"

"Johnson's *Baby Powder?* Lord no!"

"But it says on the can it's good for the body."

"Lady, you got to have your cousin buried *right.*" So I would give the undertaker the address, and then we would dash to the corner and watch the big black hearse come by on the way to Bentonia.

Or I would pick a Negro number at random from the telephone book, and phone it and say I was Bert Parks, calling from New York City on the Break-the-Bank program. Their number had been chosen out of all the telephones in the United States, and if they could answer three questions they would win $1000. "But I must warn you, Mrs. McGee, you are now *on the air,* and your voice is going into every home in America. Mrs. J. D. McGee, of Yazoo, Mississippi, are you ready for *question number one?*"

"Yessir, an' I hope I can answer it."

"Question number one! Who was the first President of the United States?"

"Why, George Washington was."

"That's absolutely correct, Mrs. McGee," as my fellow conspirators applauded in the background. "Now for question number two, and if you answer it correctly you get a chance to answer our big break-the-bank question. What is the capital of the United States?"

"Washington, D.C. is."

"Very good!" (applause) "Now, Mrs. McGee, are you ready down there in Yazoo for the big jackpot question?"

"Yessir!"

"Here it is. . . . *How many miles in the world?*"

"How many miles in the *world?*"

"That's right."

"The whole thing?"

"All of it."

"Oh Lord, I'll just have to guess. . . . One million!"

"One million? Mrs. McGee, I'm afraid you just missed! The correct answer should have been one million and three."

Several times I recall my father saying, when I was a small boy, "I don't know why they treat these niggers so bad. They pay taxes just like everybody else. If they pay taxes they oughta get to vote. It's as simple as that. If they don't get to vote they ought not to have to pay any taxes."

But one day the police finally caught Willie Johnson, a Negro who had broken into a number of white houses on our street and stolen everything he could carry away with him. He stole my mother's engagement ring from our house, and several pieces of family silver that the Harpers had buried in the dirt floor of their smokehouse before the federal troops had arrived in Raymond. The police brought Willie Johnson to the city hall for questioning, and telephoned all the men whose houses had been broken into to come down and question him. My father took me with him.

It was a stifling hot summer day, so hot that all you had to do was walk into the sun and your armpits and the hair on your head would soon be soaking wet. The room at the city hall was a small one; it was crowded with white men, and several others peered through the open door from the hallway. The police chief was sitting behind a desk, and when he saw my father he shouted, "Come on in and let's talk to this boy." I found a place on the floor next to my father's chair, and then I saw the Negro, sitting in a straight chair, trussed up and sweating as much as I was. The other white men were looking at him, glowering hard and not saying a word. The police chief asked the Negro a few questions, and as I sat there taking it all in I heard a man I knew turn to Willie Johnson and say, in a strangely subdued voice, sounding not at all like himself: "Nigger, I just want to tell you one thing, and you better get it straight, because I ain't gonna repeat it. . . . If I so much as see you walkin' down the sidewalk in front of our house, I'll blow your head off."

A young boy grew up with other things: with the myths, the stories handed down. One of them concerned one of the town's policemen, a gnarled and skinny old man by the time I was growing up, who had shot a Negro on the sidewalk on the lower end of Main Street and stood over him with his pistol to prevent anyone from taking him away while he bled to death. Whether it was apocryphal or not was almost irrelevant, for the terror of that story was quite enough; we saw the policeman almost everyday, making his rounds of the parking meters. "Don't fool with ol' ——," someone would say. "He'd just as soon shoot you as *look* at you," and then recount the legend in gory detail. There was the tale of the white planter, who owned one of the big plantations in the delta. When one of his Negro hands looked too closely at his wife one day, the man got his gun and killed him, and there was no trial.

There were a boy's recurring sense impressions of a hovering violence, isolated acts that remained in my memory long afterward, as senseless and unpatterned later as they had been for me when they happened:

. . . Some white men came to see my father, when I was six or seven years old. I heard them talking at the front door. "We hear the niggers might cause trouble tonight," one of them said. My father went to town to buy some extra shotgun shells, and we locked all our doors and windows when the sun went down.

. . . A Negro shot and killed a white man at the honky-tonk near the town dump. When the time came for him to be executed, they brought the state's portable electric chair in a big truck from Jackson. We drove by and saw it parked in the back yard of the jail. The next day some older boys told me they had stayed up until midnight, with the lights on in their house, to watch all the lights dim when the nigger got killed.

. . . I was playing with some older boys behind the Church of Christ chapel. Three barefooted Negro children appeared in the alley and began rifling through the garbage can. One of them found a rotten apple core and started eating it. The other two stuck their heads inside the can looking for things. We stopped our game to look at them. One of the older boys I was playing with whispered, "Damn little bastards," then said in a loud voice, "What you boys *doin'?*" Before they could answer he ran at them and shouted, "Get outa here, you little coons!" and we all chased them away down the alley.

. . . One rainy night in September one of the Negro shacks in the river bottom near Mound Street toppled over. The shack belonged to a garrulous old Negro named Henry who worked on odd jobs for several white families. When my friends and I found out what had happened, we walked across town to take a look. One of the four stilts had broken, and the whole house had simply flopped down at an angle. Henry and his family had been listening to the radio in the front room, and had slid right into the kitchen. The family had moved out, but there was the house, tilted over at an impossible angle, its backside splintered and broken. A light drizzle was falling, and the more we looked through the rain at that crippled old house the less we could help laughing. The image of Henry, the radio, and the whole family sliding into the kitchen was too much. We laughed all the way home, and more the next day when we saw Henry and asked after his condition, and he said: "I picked up fifty splinters in my ass."

. . . I was walking up Grand Avenue to school. Just as I crossed the railroad track I heard a loud crash several hundred yards to the north. Looking in that direction I saw the early morning freight out of Memphis pushing the remnants of a car along the track on its cowguard. I ran up the track. The train had crashed into a Negro taxicab with a full load of passengers. Blood was everywhere; two people lay mangled and still inside the wrecked car. A third, a

woman, straddled the car and the train. A carload of high school boys on their
way to school screeched around the corner and the boys got out to look at the
wreckage. The woman slowly regained consciousness, looked around her, and
asked, "Where's the train?" One of the high school boys, the star tailback,
replied: "Nigger, you sittin' right on it."

   . . . One morning I awoke to hear that a neighbor had shot a Negro bur-
glar. I ran down to his house, and a large crowd milled around on the porch and
in the front room. Inside, the man was telling what had happened. He pointed
to a bullet hole in the wall, and another in the leg of a table. He had awakened
in the night and saw the nigger in the hallway. He pulled out his automatic and
shot twice, and he heard a moan and saw the nigger running away. When he
telephoned the police, all they had to do was follow the trail of blood to a house
in niggertown. That morning we followed the blood ourselves, little drops and
big ones in the dust of the alley and onto the concrete pavement. Then we came
back and congratulated our neighbor on his aim. More people came in to hear
the story, and he told them: "If that second shot had been two inches to the left,
that woulda been one *good* nigger."

As we grew older, beyond puberty into an involvement with girls, it seemed as
if our own acts took on a more specific edge of cruelty. On Canal Street, across
from the old Greyhound station at the Bayou, there was a concrete bannister
where the Negroes would sit waiting for the busses. On Saturday nights we
would cruise down the street in a car, and the driver would open his door and
drive close to the curb. We would watch while the Negroes, to avoid the car
door, toppled backward off the bannister like dominoes. And the taunts and
threats to the isolated Negroes we saw, on country roads and deserted white
streets, were harder and more cruel than anything we had done as children.

   Deeply involved with the unthinking sadism, and with the sudden curious
affection, were the moments of pity and sorrow. One Fourth of July afternoon
when we were in high school, we went in a large group to one of the lakes in
the delta for swimming and a picnic. A Negro shack on the bank of the lake had
burned to the ground the night before. The father had taken his wife and his
several small children into a bare, floorless cabin nearby, alive with crawling
things that came out of the rotten wood in the walls. All they had saved was the
clothes on their backs. They sat around all day in front of their shack, watching us eat and swim; for hours, it seemed, they hardly moved. Finally my girlfriend and I walked over to them. We discovered that the children had eaten
practically nothing in two days. The children sat there listlessly, not saying a
word; the father said even the fish wouldn't bite for him. My girl started crying.
We went back and told the others, and took up a collection that must have
come to fifteen dollars, and gave them our hotdogs and cokes. The Negro family ate the food and continued to look at us down by the lake. Under their stolid

gaze I felt uncomfortable; I wanted to head back to Grand Avenue again. We packed our things and went to the car, drove through the flat cotton country to town, and resumed our picnic on the back lawn of one of the big houses in our neighborhood.

Notes of a Native Son

1955

♦

JAMES BALDWIN

On the 29th of July, in 1943, my father died. On the same day, a few hours later, his last child was born. Over a month before this, while all our energies were concentrated in waiting for these events, there had been, in Detroit, one of the bloodiest race riots of the century. A few hours after my father's funeral, while he lay in state in the undertaker's chapel, a race riot broke out in Harlem. On the morning of the 3rd of August, we drove my father to the graveyard through a wilderness of smashed plate glass.

The day of my father's funeral had also been my nineteenth birthday. As we drove him to the graveyard, the spoils of injustice, anarchy, discontent, and hatred were all around us. It seemed to me that God himself had devised, to mark my father's end, the most sustained and brutally dissonant of codas. And it seemed to me, too, that the violence which rose all about us as my father left the world had been devised as a corrective for the pride of his eldest son. I had declined to believe in that apocalypse which had been central to my father's vision; very well, life seemed to be saying, here is something that will certainly pass for an apocalypse until the real thing comes along. I had inclined to be contemptuous of my father for the conditions of his life, for the conditions of our lives. When his life had ended I began to wonder about that life and also, in a new way, to be apprehensive about my own.

I had not known my father very well. We had got on badly, partly because we shared, in our different fashions, the vice of stubborn pride. When he was dead I realized that I had hardly ever spoken to him. When he had been dead a long time I began to wish I had. It seems to be typical of life in America, where opportunities, real and fancied, are thicker than anywhere else on the globe, that the second generation has no time to talk to the first. No one, including my father, seems to have known exactly how old he was, but his mother had been born during slavery. He was of the first generation of free men. He, along with thousands of other Negroes, came North after 1919 and I was part of that generation which had never seen the landscape of what Negroes sometimes call the Old Country.

He had been born in New Orleans and had been a quite young man there during the time that Louis Armstrong, a boy, was running errands for the dives and honky-tonks of what was always presented to me as one of the most wicked of cities—to this day, whenever I think of New Orleans, I also helplessly think of Sodom and Gomorrah. My father never mentioned Louis Armstrong, except to forbid us to play his records; but there was a picture of him on our wall for a long time. One of my father's strong-willed female relatives had placed it there and forbade my father to take it down. He never did, but he eventually maneuvered her out of the house and when, some years later, she was in trouble and near death, he refused to do anything to help her.

He was, I think, very handsome. I gather this from photographs and from my own memories of him, dressed in his Sunday best and on his way to preach a sermon somewhere, when I was little. Handsome, proud, and ingrown, "like a toe-nail," somebody said. But he looked to me, as I grew older, like pictures I had seen of African tribal chieftains: he really should have been naked, with war-paint on and barbaric mementos, standing among spears. He could be chilling in the pulpit and indescribably cruel in his personal life and he was certainly the most bitter man I have ever met; yet it must be said that there was something else in him, buried in him, which lent him his tremendous power and, even, a rather crushing charm. It had something to do with his blackness, I think—he was very black—with his blackness and his beauty, and with the fact that he knew that he was black but did not know that he was beautiful. He claimed to be proud of his blackness but it had also been the cause of much humiliation and it had fixed bleak boundaries to his life. He was not a young man when we were growing up and he had already suffered many kinds of ruin; in his outrageously demanding and protective way he loved his children, who were black like him and menaced, like him; and all these things sometimes showed in his face when he tried, never to my knowledge with any success, to establish contact with any of us. When he took one of his children on his knee to play, the child always became fretful and began to cry; when he tried to help one of us with our homework the absolutely unabating tension which emanated from him caused our minds and our tongues to become paralyzed, so that he, scarcely knowing why, flew into a rage and the child, not knowing why, was punished. If it ever entered his head to bring a surprise home for his children, it was, almost unfailingly, the wrong surprise and even the big watermelons he often brought home on his back in the summertime led to the most appalling scenes. I do not remember, in all those years, that one of his children was ever glad to see him come home. From what I was able to gather of his early life, it seemed that this inability to establish contact with other people had always marked him and had been one of the things which had driven him out of New Orleans. There was something in him, therefore, groping and tentative, which was never expressed and which was buried with him. One saw it most clearly when he was facing new people and hoping to impress them. But he never did, not for long. We went from church to smaller and more improbable church, he found himself in less and less demand as a minister, and by the time he died none of his friends had come to see him for a long time. He had lived and died in an intolerable bitterness of spirit and it frightened me, as we drove him to the graveyard through those unquiet, ruined streets, to see how powerful and overflowing this bitterness could be and to realize that this bitterness now was mine.

When he died I had been away from home for a little over a year. In that year I had had time to become aware of the meaning of all my father's bitter warnings, had discovered the secret of his proudly pursed lips and rigid carriage: I had discovered the weight of white people in the world. I saw that this had been for my ancestors and now would be for me an awful thing to live with and that the bitterness which had helped to kill my father could also kill me.

He had been ill a long time—in the mind, as we now realized, reliving instances of his fantastic intransigence in the new light of his affliction and endeavoring to feel a sorrow for him which never, quite, came true. We had not known that he was being eaten up by paranoia, and the discovery that his cruelty, to our bodies and our minds, had been one of the symptoms of his illness was not, then, enough to enable us to forgive him. The younger children felt, quite simply, relief that he would not be coming home anymore. My mother's observation that it was he, after all, who had kept them alive all these years meant nothing because the problems of keeping children alive are not real for children. The older children felt, with my father gone, that they could invite their friends to the house without fear that their friends would be insulted or, as had sometimes happened with me, being told that their friends were in league with the devil and intended to rob our family of everything we owned. (I didn't fail to wonder, and it made me hate him, what on earth we owned that anybody else would want.)

His illness was beyond all hope of healing before anyone realized that he was ill. He had always been so strange and had lived, like a prophet, in such unimaginably close communion with the Lord that his long silences which were punctuated by moans and hallelujahs and snatches of old songs while he sat at the living-room window never seemed odd to us. It was not until he refused to eat because, he said, his family was trying to poison him that my mother was forced to accept as a fact what had, until then, been only an unwilling suspicion. When he was committed, it was discovered that he had tuberculosis and, as it turned out, the disease of his mind allowed the disease of his body to destroy him. For the doctors could not force him to eat, either, and, though he was fed intravenously, it was clear from the beginning that there was no hope for him.

In my mind's eye I could see him, sitting at the window, locked up in his terrors; hating and fearing every living soul including his children who had betrayed him, too, by reaching towards the world which had despised him. There were nine of us. I began to wonder what it could have felt like for such a man to have had nine children whom he could barely feed. He used to make little jokes about our poverty, which never, of course, seemed very funny to us; they could not have seemed very funny to him, either, or else our all too feeble response to them would never have caused such rages. He spent great energy and achieved, to our chagrin, no small amount of success in keeping us away from the people who surrounded us, people who had all-night rent parties to which we listened when we should have been sleeping, people who cursed and drank and flashed razor blades on Lenox Avenue. He could not understand why, if they had so much energy to spare, they could not use it to make their lives better. He treated almost everybody on our block with a most uncharitable asperity and neither they, nor, of course, their children were slow to reciprocate.

The only white people who came to our house were welfare workers and bill collectors. It was almost always my mother who dealt with them, for my father's temper, which was at the mercy of his pride, was never to be trusted. It was clear that he felt their very presence in his home to be a violation: this was conveyed by his carriage, almost ludicrously stiff, and by his voice, harsh and vindictively polite. When I was around nine or ten I wrote a play which was directed by a young, white schoolteacher, a woman, who then took an interest in me, and gave me books to read and, in order to corroborate my theatrical bent, decided to take me to see what she somewhat tactlessly referred to as "real" plays. Theatergoing was forbidden in our house, but, with the really cruel intuitiveness of a child, I suspected that the color of this woman's skin would carry the day for me. When, at school, she suggested taking me to the theater, I did not, as I might have done if she had been a Negro, find a way of discouraging her, but agreed that she should pick me up at my house one evening. I then, very cleverly, left all the rest to my mother, who suggested to my father, as I knew she would, that it would not be very nice to let such a kind woman make the trip for nothing. Also, since it was a schoolteacher, I imagine that my mother countered the idea of sin with the idea of "education," which word, even with my father, carried a kind of bitter weight.

Before the teacher came my father took me aside to ask *why* she was coming, what *interest* she could possibly have in our house, in a boy like me. I said I didn't know but I, too, suggested that it had something to do with education.

And I understood that my father was waiting for me to say something—I didn't quite know what; perhaps that I wanted his protection against this teacher and her "education." I said none of these things and the teacher came and we went out. It was clear, during the brief interview in our living room, that my father was agreeing very much against his will and that he would have refused permission if he had dared. The fact that he did not dare caused me to despise him: I had no way of knowing that he was facing in that living room a wholly unprecedented and frightening situation.

Later, when my father had been laid off from his job, this woman became very important to us. She was really a very sweet and generous woman and went to a great deal of trouble to be of help to us, particularly during one awful winter. My mother called her by the highest name she knew: she said she was a "christian." My father could scarcely disagree but during the four or five years of our relatively close association he never trusted her and was always trying to surprise in her open, Midwestern face the genuine, cunningly hidden, and hideous motivation. In later years, particularly when it began to be clear that this "education" of mine was going to lead me to perdition, he became more explicit and warned me that my white friends in high school were not really my friends and that I would see, when I was older, how white people would do anything to keep a Negro down. Some of them could be nice, he admitted, but none of them were to be trusted and most of them were not even nice. The best thing was to have as little to do with them as possible. I did not feel this way and I was certain, in my innocence, that I never would.

But the year which preceded my father's death had made a great change in my life. I had been living in New Jersey, working in defense plants, working and living among southerners, white and black. I knew about the south, of course, and about how southerners treated Negroes and how they expected them to behave, but it had never entered my mind that anyone would look at me and expect *me* to behave that way. I learned in New Jersey that to be a Negro meant, precisely, that one was never looked at but was simply at the mercy of the reflexes the color of one's skin caused in other people. I acted in New Jersey as I had always acted, that is as though I thought a great deal of myself—I had to *act* that way—with results that were, simply, unbelievable. I had scarcely arrived before I had earned the enmity, which was extraordinarily ingenious, of all my superiors and nearly all my co-workers. In the beginning, to make matters worse, I simply did not know what was happening. I did not know what I had done, and I shortly began to wonder what *anyone* could possibly do, to bring about such unanimous, active, and unbearably vocal hostility. I knew about jim-crow but I had never experienced it. I went to the same self-service restaurant three times and stood with all the Princeton boys before the counter, waiting for a hamburger and coffee; it was always an extraordinarily long time before anything was set before me; but it was not until the fourth visit that I learned that, in fact, nothing had ever been set before me: I had simply picked something up. Negroes were not served there, I was told, and they had been waiting for me to realize that I was always the only Negro present. Once I was told this, I determined to go there all the time. But now they were ready for me and, though some dreadful scenes were subsequently enacted in that restaurant, I never ate there again.

It was the same story all over New Jersey, in bars, bowling alleys, diners, places to live. I was always being forced to leave, silently, or with mutual imprecations. I very shortly became notorious and children giggled behind me when I passed and their elders whispered or shouted—they really believed that I was mad. And it did begin to work on my mind, of course; I began to be afraid to go anywhere and to compensate for this I went places to which I really should not have gone and where, God knows, I had no desire to be. My reputation in town naturally enhanced my reputation at work and my working day became one long series of acrobatics designed to keep me out of trouble. I cannot say that these acrobatics succeeded. It began to seem that the machinery of the organization I worked for was turning over, day and night, with but one aim: to eject me. I was fired once, and contrived, with the aid of a friend from New York, to get back on the payroll; was fired again, and bounced back again. It took a while to fire me for the third time, but the third time took. There were no loopholes anywhere. There was not even any way of getting back inside the gates.

That year in New Jersey lives in my mind as though it were the year during which, having an unsuspected predilection for it, I first contracted some dread, chronic disease, the unfailing symptom of which is a kind of blind fever, a pounding in the skull and fire in the bowels. Once this disease is contracted, one can never be really carefree again, for the fever, without an instant's warning, can recur at any moment. It can wreck more important things than race relations. There is not a Negro alive who does not have this rage in his blood—one has the choice, merely, of living with it consciously or surrendering to it. As for me, this fever has recurred in me, and does, and will until the day I die.

My last night in New Jersey, a white friend from New York took me to the nearest big town, Trenton, to go to the movies and have a few drinks. As it turned out, he also saved me from, at the very least, a violent whipping. Almost every detail of that night stands out very clearly in my memory. I even remember the name of the movie we saw because its title impressed me as being so patly ironical. It was a movie about the German occupation of France, starring Maureen O'Hara and Charles Laughton and called *This Land Is Mine*. I remember the name of the diner we walked into when the movie ended: it was the "American Diner." When we walked in the counterman asked what we wanted and I remember answering with the casual sharpness which had become my habit: "We want a hamburger and a cup of coffee, what do you think we want?" I do not know why, after a year of such rebuffs, I so completely failed to anticipate his answer, which was, of course, "We don't serve Negroes here." This reply failed to discompose me, at least for the moment. I made some sardonic comment about the name of the diner and we walked out into the streets.

This was the time of what was called the "brown-out," when the lights in all American cities were very dim. When we re-entered the streets something happened to me which had the force of an optical illusion, or a nightmare. The streets were very crowded and I was facing north. People were moving in every direction but it seemed to me, in that instant, that all of the people I could see, and many more than that, were moving toward me, against me, and that everyone was white. I remember how their faces gleamed. And I felt, like a physical sensation, a *click* at the nape of my neck as though some interior string connecting my head to my body had been cut. I began to walk. I heard my friend call after me, but I ignored him. Heaven only knows what was going on in his mind, but he had the good sense not to touch me—I don't know what would have happened if he had—and to keep me in sight. I don't know what was going on in my mind, either; I certainly had no conscious plan. I wanted to do something to crush these white faces, which were crushing me. I walked for perhaps a block or two until I came to an enormous, glittering, and fashionable restaurant in which I knew not even the intercession of the Virgin would cause me to be served. I pushed through the doors and took the first vacant seat I saw, at a table for two, and waited.

I do not know how long I waited and I rather wonder, until today, what I could possibly have looked like. Whatever I looked like, I frightened the waitress who shortly appeared, and the moment she appeared all of my fury flowed towards her. I hated her for her white face, and for her great, astounded, frightened eyes. I felt that if she found a black man so frightening I would make her fright worth-while.

She did not ask me what I wanted, but repeated, as though she had learned it somewhere, "We don't serve Negroes here." She did not say it with the blunt, derisive hostility to which I had grown so accustomed, but, rather, with a note of apology in her voice, and fear. This made me colder and more murderous than ever. I felt I had to do something with my hands. I wanted her to come close enough for me to get her neck between my hands.

So I pretended not to have understood her, hoping to draw her closer. And she did step a very short step closer, with her pencil poised incongruously over her pad, and repeated the formula: ". . . don't serve Negroes here."

Somehow, with the repetition of that phrase, which was already ringing in my head like a thousand bells of a nightmare, I realized that she would never come any closer and that I would have to strike from a distance. There was nothing on the table but an ordinary water-mug half full of water, and I picked this up and hurled it with all my strength at her. She ducked and it missed her and shattered against the mirror behind the bar. And, with that sound, my frozen blood abruptly thawed, I returned from wherever I had been, I *saw*, for the first time, the restaurant, the people with their mouths open, already, as it seemed to me, rising as one man, and I realized what I had done, and where I was, and I was frightened. I rose and began running for the door. A round, pot-bellied man grabbed me by the nape of the neck just as I reached the doors and began to beat me about the face. I kicked him and got loose and ran into the streets. My friend whispered, "*Run!*" and I ran.

My friend stayed outside the restaurant long enough to misdirect my pur-suers and the police, who arrived, he told me, at once. I do not know what I said to him when he came to my room that night. I could not have said much. I felt, in the oddest, most awful way, that I had somehow betrayed him. I lived it over and over and over again, the way one relives an automobile accident after it has happened and one finds oneself alone and safe. I could not get over two facts, both equally difficult for the imagination to grasp, and one was that I could have been murdered. But the other was that I had been ready to commit mur-der. I saw nothing very clearly but I did see this: that my life, my *real* life, was in danger, and not from anything other people might do but from the hatred I car-ried in my own heart.

II

I had returned home around the second week in June—in great haste because it seemed that my father's death and my mother's confinement were both but a matter of hours. In the case of my mother, it soon became clear that she had simply made a miscalculation. This had always been her tendency and I don't believe that a single one of us arrived in the world, or has since arrived any-where else, on time. But none of us dawdled so intolerably about the business of being born as did my baby sister. We sometimes amused ourselves, during those endless, stifling weeks, by picturing the baby sitting within in the safe, warm dark, bitterly regretting the necessity of becoming a part of our chaos and stubbornly putting it off as long as possible. I understood her perfectly and congratulated her on showing such good sense so soon. Death, however, sat as purposefully at my father's bedside as life stirred within my mother's womb and it was harder to understand why he so lingered in that long shadow. It seemed that he had bent, and for a long time, too, all of his energies towards dying. Now death was ready for him but my father held back.

All of Harlem, indeed, seemed to be infected by waiting. I had never before known it to be so violently still. Racial tensions throughout this country were exacerbated during the early years of the war, partly because the labor market brought together hundreds of thousands of ill-prepared people and partly be-cause Negro soldiers, regardless of where they were born, received their mili-tary training in the south. What happened in defense plants and army camps had repercussions, naturally, in every Negro ghetto. The situation in Harlem had grown bad enough for clergymen, policemen, educators, politicians, and social workers to assert in one breath that there was no "crime wave" and to offer, in the very next breath, suggestions as to how to combat it. These suggestions always seemed to involve playgrounds, despite the fact that racial skirmishes were occurring in the playgrounds, too. Playground or not, crime wave or not, the Harlem police force had been augmented in March, and the unrest grew—perhaps, in fact, partly as a result of the ghetto's instinctive hatred of policemen. Perhaps the most revealing news item, out of the steady parade of reports of muggings, stabbings, shootings, assaults, gang wars, and accusations of police brutality, is the item concerning six Negro girls who set upon a white girl in the subway because, as they all too accurately put it, she was stepping on their toes. Indeed she was, all over the nation.

I had never before been so aware of policemen, on foot, on horseback, on corners, everywhere, always two by two. Nor had I ever been so aware of small knots of people. They were on stoops and on corners and in doorways, and what was striking about them, I think, was that they did not seem to be talking. Never, when I passed these groups, did the usual sound of a curse or a laugh ring out and neither did there seem to be any hum of gossip. There was certainly, on the other hand, occurring between them communication extraordinarily intense. Another thing that was striking was the unexpected diversity of the people who made up these groups. Usually, for example, one would see a group of sharpies standing on the street corner, jiving the passing chicks; or a group of older men, usually, for some reason, in the vicinity of a barber shop, discussing baseball scores, or the numbers, or making rather chilling observations about women they had known. Women, in a general way, tended to be seen less often together—unless they were church women, or very young girls, or prostitutes met together for an unprofessional instant. But that summer I saw the strangest combinations: large, respectable, churchly matrons standing on the stoops or the corners with their hair tied up, together with a girl in sleazy satin whose face bore the marks of gin and the razor, or heavy-set, abrupt, no-nonsense older men, in company with the most disreputable and fanatical "race" men, or these same "race" men with the sharpies, or these sharpies with the churchly women. Seventh Day Adventists and Methodists and Spiritualists seemed to be hobnobbing with Holyrollers and they were all, alike, entangled with the most flagrant disbelievers; something heavy in their stance seemed to indicate that they had all, incredibly, seen a common vision, and on each face there seemed to be the same strange, bitter shadow.

The churchly women and the matter-of-fact, no-nonsense men had children in the Army. The sleazy girls they talked to had lovers there, the sharpies and the "race" men had friends and brothers there. It would have demanded an unquestioning patriotism, happily as uncommon in this country as it is unde-

sirable, for these people not to have been disturbed by the bitter letters they received, by the newspaper stories they read, not to have been enraged by the
posters, then to be found all over New York, which described the Japanese as
"yellow-bellied Japs." It was only the "race" men, to be sure, who spoke cease-
lessly of being revenged—how this vengeance was to be exacted was not
clear—for the indignities and dangers suffered by Negro boys in uniform; but
everybody felt a directionless, hopeless bitterness, as well as that panic which
can scarcely be suppressed when one knows that a human being one loves is
beyond one's reach, and in danger. This helplessness and this gnawing uneasiness does something, at length, to even the toughest mind. Perhaps the best
way to sum all this up is to say that the people I knew felt, mainly, a peculiar
kind of relief when they knew that their boys were being shipped out of the
south, to do battle overseas. It was, perhaps, like feeling that the most dangerous part of a dangerous journey had been passed and that now, even if death
should come, it would come with honor and without the complicity of their
countrymen. Such a death would be, in short, a fact with which one could
hope to live.

It was on the 28th of July, which I believe was a Wednesday, that I visited
my father for the first time during his illness and for the last time in his life. The
moment I saw him I knew why I had put off this visit so long. I had told my
mother that I did not want to see him because I hated him. But this was not
true. It was only that I *had* hated him and I wanted to hold on to this hatred. I
did not want to look on him as a ruin: it was not a ruin I had hated. I imagine
that one of the reasons people cling to their hates so stubbornly is because they
sense, once hate is gone, that they will be forced to deal with pain.

We traveled out to him, his older sister and myself, to what seemed to be
the very end of a very Long Island. It was hot and dusty and we wrangled, my
aunt and I, all the way out, over the fact that I had recently begun to smoke
and, as she said, to give myself airs. But I knew that she wrangled with me because she could not bear to face the fact of her brother's dying. Neither could I
endure the reality of her despair, her unstated bafflement as to what had happened to her brother's life, and her own. So we wrangled and I smoked and
from time to time she fell into a heavy reverie. Covertly, I watched her face,
which was the face of an old woman; it had fallen in, the eyes were sunken and
lightless; soon she would be dying, too.

In my childhood—it had not been so long ago—I had thought her beautiful. She had been quick-witted and quick-moving and very generous with all
the children and each of her visits had been an event. At one time one of my
brothers and myself had thought of running away to live with her. Now she
could no longer produce out of her handbag some unexpected and yet familiar
delight. She made me feel pity and revulsion and fear. It was awful to realize
that she no longer caused me to feel affection. The closer we came to the hospi-

tal the more querulous she became and at the same time, naturally, grew more dependent on me. Between pity and guilt and fear I began to feel that there was another me trapped in my skull like a jack-in-the-box who might escape my control at any moment and fill the air with screaming.

She began to cry the moment we entered the room and she saw him lying there, all shriveled and still, like a little black monkey. The great, gleaming apparatus which fed him and would have compelled him to be still even if he had been able to move brought to mind, not beneficence, but torture; the tubes entering his arm made me think of pictures I had seen when a child, of Gulliver, tied down by the pygmies on that island. My aunt wept and wept, there was a whistling sound in my father's throat; nothing was said; he could not speak. I wanted to take his hand, to say something. But I do not know what I could have said, even if he could have heard me. He was not really in that room with us, he had at last really embarked on his journey; and though my aunt told me that he said he was going to meet Jesus, I did not hear anything except that whistling in his throat. The doctor came back and we left, into that unbearable train again, and home. In the morning came the telegram saying that he was dead. Then the house was suddenly full of relatives, friends, hysteria, and confusion and I quickly left my mother and the children to the care of those impressive women, who, in Negro communities at least, automatically appear at times of bereavement armed with lotions, proverbs, and patience, and an ability to cook. I went downtown. By the time I returned, later the same day, my mother had been carried to the hospital and the baby had been born.

III

For my father's funeral I had nothing black to wear and this posed a nagging problem all day long. It was one of those problems, simple, or impossible of solution, to which the mind insanely clings in order to avoid the mind's real trouble. I spent most of that day at the downtown apartment of a girl I knew, celebrating my birthday with whiskey and wondering what to wear that night. When planning a birthday celebration one naturally does not expect that it will be up against competition from a funeral and this girl had anticipated taking me out that night, for a big dinner and a night club afterwards. Sometime during the course of that long day we decided that we would go out anyway, when my father's funeral service was over. I imagine I decided it, since, as the funeral hour approached, it became clearer and clearer to me that I would not know what to do with myself when it was over. The girl, stifling her very lively concern as to the possible effects of the whiskey on one of my father's chief mourners, concentrated on being conciliatory and practically helpful. She found a black shirt for me somewhere and ironed it and, dressed in the darkest pants and jacket I owned, and slightly drunk, I made my way to my father's funeral.

The chapel was full, but not packed, and very quiet. There were, mainly, my father's relatives, and his children, and here and there I saw faces I had not seen since childhood, the faces of my father's one-time friends. They were very dark and solemn now, seeming somehow to suggest that they had known all along that something like this would happen. Chief among the mourners was my aunt, who had quarreled with my father all his life; by which I do not mean to suggest that her mourning was insincere or that she had not loved him. I suppose that she was one of the few people in the world who had, and their incessant quarreling proved precisely the strength of the tie that bound them. The only other person in the world, as far as I knew, whose relationship to my father rivaled my aunt's in depth was my mother, who was not there.

It seemed to me, of course, that it was a very long funeral. But it was, if anything, a rather shorter funeral than most, nor, since there were no overwhelming, uncontrollable expressions of grief, could it be called—if I dare to use the word—successful. The minister who preached my father's funeral sermon was one of the few my father had still been seeing as he neared his end. He presented to us in his sermon a man whom none of us had ever seen—a man thoughtful, patient, and forbearing, a Christian inspiration to all who knew him, and a model for his children. And no doubt the children, in their disturbed and guilty state, were almost ready to believe this; he had been remote enough to be anything and, anyway, the shock of the incontrovertible, that it was really our father lying up there in that casket, prepared the mind for anything. His sister moaned and this grief-stricken moaning was taken as corroboration. The other faces held a dark, non-committal thoughtfulness. This was not the man they had known, but they had scarcely expected to be confronted with *him*; this was, in a sense deeper than questions of fact, the man they had not known, and the man they had not known may have been the real one. The real man, whoever he had been, had suffered and now he was dead: this was all that was sure and all that mattered now. Every man in the chapel hoped that when his hour came he, too, would be eulogized, which is to say forgiven, and that all of his lapses, greeds, errors, and strayings from the truth would be invested with coherence and looked upon with charity. This was perhaps the last thing human beings could give each other and it was what they demanded, after all, of the Lord. Only the Lord saw the midnight tears, only He was present when one of His children, moaning and wringing hands, paced up and down the room. When one slapped one's child in anger the recoil in the heart reverberated through heaven and became part of the pain of the universe. And when the children were hungry and sullen and distrustful and one watched them, daily, growing wilder, and further away, and running headlong into danger, it was the Lord who knew what the charged heart endured as the strap was laid to the backside; the Lord alone who knew what one *would* have said if one had had, like the Lord, the gift of the living word. It was the Lord who knew of the impossibility every parent in that room faced: how to prepare the child for the day when the child would be despised and how to *create* in the child—by what means?—a stronger antidote to this poison than one had found for oneself. The avenues, side streets, bars, billiard halls, hospitals, police stations, and even the playgrounds of Harlem—not to mention the houses of correction, the jails, and the morgue—testified to the potency of the poison while remaining silent as to the efficacy of whatever antidote, irresistibly raising the question of whether or not such an antidote existed; raising, which was worse, the question of whether or not an antidote was desirable; perhaps poison should be fought with poison. With these several schisms in the mind and with more terrors in the heart than could be named, it was better not to judge the man who had gone down under an impossible burden. It was better to remember: *Thou knowest this man's fall; but thou knowest not his wrassling.*

While the preacher talked and I watched the children—years of changing their diapers, scrubbing them, slapping them, taking them to school, and scolding them had had the perhaps inevitable result of making me love them, though I am not sure I knew this then—my mind was busily breaking out with a rash of disconnected impressions. Snatches of popular songs, indecent jokes, bits of books I had read, movie sequences, faces, voices, political issues—I thought I was going mad; all these impressions suspended, as it were, in the solution of the faint nausea produced in me by the heat and liquor. For a moment I had the impression that my alcoholic breath, inefficiently disguised with chewing gum, filled the entire chapel. Then someone began singing one of my father's favorite songs and, abruptly, I was with him, sitting on his knee, in the hot, enormous, crowded church which was the first church we attended. It was the Abyssinia Baptist Church on 138th Street. We had not gone there long. With this image, a host of others came. I had forgotten, in the rage of my growing up, how proud my father had been of me when I was little. Apparently, I had had a voice and my father had liked to show me off before the members of the church. I had forgotten what he had looked like when he was pleased but now I remembered that he had always been grinning with pleasure when my solos ended. I even remembered certain expressions on his face when he teased my mother—had he loved her? I would never know. And when had it all begun to change? For now it seemed that he had not always been cruel. I remembered being taken for a haircut and scraping my knee on the footrest of the barber's chair and I remembered my father's face as he soothed my crying and applied the stinging iodine. Then I remembered our fights, fights which had been of the worst possible kind because my technique had been silence.

I remembered the one time in all our life together when we had really spoken to each other.

It was on a Sunday and it must have been shortly before I left home. We were walking, just the two of us, in our usual silence, to or from church. I was in high school and had been doing a lot of writing and I was, at about this time, the editor of the high school magazine. But I had also been a Young Minister and had been preaching from the pulpit. Lately, I had been taking fewer engagements and preached as rarely as possible. It was said in the church, quite truthfully, that I was "cooling off."

My father asked me abruptly, "You'd rather write than preach, wouldn't you?"

I was astonished at his question—because it was a real question. I answered, "Yes."

That was all we said. It was awful to remember that that was all we had *ever* said.

The casket now was opened and the mourners were being led up the aisle to look for the last time on the deceased. The assumption was that the family was too overcome with grief to be allowed to make this journey alone and I watched while my aunt was led to the casket and, muffled in black, and shaking, led back to her seat. I disapproved of forcing the children to look on their dead father, considering that the shock of his death, or, more truthfully, the shock of death as a reality, was already a little more than a child could bear, but my judgment in this matter had been overruled and there they were, bewildered and frightened and very small, being led, one by one, to the casket. But there is also something very gallant about children at such moments. It has something to do with their silence and gravity and with the fact that one cannot help them. Their legs, somehow, seem *exposed,* so that it is at once incredible and terribly clear that their legs are all they have to hold them up.

I had not wanted to go to the casket myself and I certainly had not wished to be led there, but there was no way of avoiding either of these forms. One of the deacons led me up and I looked on my father's face. I cannot say that it looked like him at all. His blackness had been equivocated by powder and there was no suggestion in that casket of what his power had or could have been. He was simply an old man dead, and it was hard to believe that he had ever given anyone either joy or pain. Yet, his life filled that room. Further up the avenue his wife was holding his newborn child. Life and death so close together, and love and hatred, and right and wrong, said something to me which I did not want to hear concerning man, concerning the life of man.

After the funeral, while I was downtown desperately celebrating my birthday, a Negro soldier, in the lobby of the Hotel Braddock, got into a fight with a white policeman over a Negro girl. Negro girls, white policemen, in or out of uniform, and Negro males—in or out of uniform—were part of the furniture of the lobby of the Hotel Braddock and this was certainly not the first time such an incident had occurred. It was destined, however, to receive an unprecedented publicity, for the fight between the policeman and the soldier ended with the shooting of the soldier. Rumor, flowing immediately to the streets outside, stated that the soldier had been shot in the back, an instantaneous and re-vealing invention, and that the soldier had died protecting a Negro woman. The facts were somewhat different—for example, the soldier had not been shot in the back, and was not dead, and the girl seems to have been as dubious a symbol of womanhood as her white counterpart in Georgia usually is, but no one was interested in the facts. They preferred the invention because this in-vention expressed and corroborated their hates and fears so perfectly. It is just as well to remember that people are always doing this. Perhaps many of those legends, including Christianity, to which the world clings began their conquest of the world with just some such concerted surrender to distortion. The effect, in Harlem, of this particular legend was like the effect of a lit match in a tin of gasoline. The mob gathered before the doors of the Hotel Braddock simply began to swell and to spread in every direction, and Harlem exploded.

The mob did not cross the ghetto lines. It would have been easy, for exam-ple, to have gone over Morningside Park on the west side or to have crossed the Grand Central railroad tracks at 125th Street on the east side, to wreak havoc in white neighborhoods. The mob seems to have been mainly interested in some-thing more potent and real than the white face, that is, in white power, and the principal damage done during the riot of the summer of 1943 was to white business establishments in Harlem. It might have been a far bloodier story, of course, if, at the hour the riot began, these establishments had still been open. From the Hotel Braddock the mob fanned out, east and west along 125th Street, and for the entire length of Lenox, Seventh, and Eighth avenues. Along each of these avenues, and along each major side street—116th, 125th, 135th, and so on—bars, stores, pawnshops, restaurants, even little luncheonettes had been smashed open and entered and looted—looted, it might be added, with more haste than efficiency. The shelves really looked as though a bomb had struck them. Cans of beans and soup and dog food, along with toilet paper, corn flakes, sardines and milk tumbled every which way, and abandoned cash registers and cases of beer leaned crazily out of the splintered windows and were strewn along the avenues. Sheets, blankets, and clothing of every description formed a kind of path, as though people had dropped them while running. I truly had not realized that Harlem *had* so many stores until I saw them all smashed open; the first time the word *wealth* ever entered my mind in relation to Harlem was when I saw it scattered in the streets. But one's first, incongruous impression of plenty was countered immediately by an impression of waste. None of this was doing anybody any good. It would have been better to have left the plate glass as it had been and the goods lying in the stores.

It would have been better, but it would also have been intolerable, for Harlem had needed something to smash. To smash something is the ghetto's chronic need. Most of the time it is the members of the ghetto who smash each other, and themselves. But as long as the ghetto walls are standing there will always come a moment when these outlets do not work. That summer, for example, it was not enough to get into a fight on Lenox Avenue, or curse out one's cronies in the barber shops. If ever, indeed, the violence which fills Harlem's churches, pool halls, and bars erupts outward in a more direct fashion, Harlem and its citizens are likely to vanish in an apocalyptic flood. That this is not likely to happen is due to a great many reasons, most hidden and powerful among them the Negro's real relation to the white American. This relation prohibits, simply, anything as uncomplicated and satisfactory as pure hatred. In order really to hate white people, one has to blot so much out of the mind—and the heart—that this hatred itself becomes an exhausting and self-destructive pose. But this does not mean, on the other hand, that love comes easily: the white world is too powerful, too complacent, too ready with gratuitous humiliation, and, above all, too ignorant and too innocent for that. One is absolutely forced to make perpetual qualifications and one's own reactions are always canceling each other out. It is this, really, which has driven so many people mad, both white and black. One is always in the position of having to decide between amputation and gangrene. Amputation is swift but time may prove that the amputation was not necessary—or one may delay the amputation too long. Gangrene is slow, but it is impossible to be sure that one is reading one's symptoms right. The idea of going through life as a cripple is more than one can bear, and equally unbearable is the risk of swelling up slowly, in agony, with poison. And the trouble, finally, is that the risks are real even if the choices do not exist.

"But as for me and my house," my father had said, "we will serve the Lord." I wondered, as we drove him to his resting place, what this line had meant for him. I had heard him preach it many times. I had preached it once myself, proudly giving it an interpretation different from my father's. Now the whole thing came back to me, as though my father and I were on our way to Sunday school and I were memorizing the golden text: *And if it seem evil unto you to serve the Lord, choose you this day whom you will serve; whether the gods which your fathers served that were on the other side of the flood, or the gods of the Amorites, in whose land ye dwell: but as for me and my house, we will serve the Lord.* I suspected in these familiar lines a meaning which had never been there for me before. All of my father's texts and songs, which I had decided were meaningless, were arranged before me at his death like empty bottles, waiting to hold the meaning which life would give them for me. This was his legacy: nothing is ever escaped. That bleakly memorable morning I hated the unbelievable streets and the Negroes and whites who had, equally, made them that way. But I knew that it was folly, as my father would have said, this bitterness was folly. It was necessary to hold on to the things that mattered. The dead man mattered, the new life mattered; blackness and whiteness did not matter; to believe that they did was to acquiesce in one's own destruction. Hatred, which could destroy so much, never failed to destroy the man who hated and this was an immutable law.

It began to seem that one would have to hold in the mind forever two ideas which seemed to be in opposition. The first idea was acceptance, the acceptance, totally without rancor, of life as it is, and men as they are: in the light of this idea, it goes without saying that injustice is a commonplace. But this did not mean that one could be complacent, for the second idea was of equal power: that one must never, in one's own life, accept these injustices as commonplace but must fight them with all one's strength. This fight begins, however, in the heart and it now had been laid to my charge to keep my own heart free of hatred and despair. This intimation made my heart heavy and, now that my father was irrecoverable, I wished that he had been beside me so that I could have searched his face for the answers which only the future would give me now.

A Pageant of Birds

The New Republic, October 25, 1943

◆

E U D O R A   W E L T Y

One summer evening on a street in my town I saw two Negro women walking along carrying big colored paper wings in their hands and talking and laughing. They proceeded unquestioned, the way angels did in their day, possibly, although anywhere else but on such a street the angels might have been looked back at if they had taken their wings off and carried them along over their arms. I followed them to see where they were going, and, sure enough, it was to church.

They walked in at the Farish Street Baptist Church. It stands on a corner in the Negro business section, across the street from the Methodist Church, in a block with the clothing stores, the pool hall, the Booker-T movie house, the doctor's office, the pawnshop with gold in the windows, the café with the fish-sign that says "If They Don't Bite We Catch 'em Anyhow," and the barbershop with the Cuban hair styles hand-drawn on the window. It is a solid, brick-veneered church, and has no hollering or chanting in the unknown tongue. I looked in at the door to see what might be going on.

The big frame room was empty of people but ready for something. The lights were shining. The ceiling was painted the color of heaven, bright blue, and with this to start on, decorators had gone ahead to make the place into a scene that could only be prepared to receive birds. Pinned all around the walls were drawings of birds—bluebirds, redbirds, quail, flamingos, wrens, love-birds—some copied from pictures, and the redbird a familiar cover taken from a school tablet. There was greenery everywhere. Sprigs of snow-on-the-mountain—a bush which grows to the point of complete domination in gar-dens of the neighborhood this time of year—were tied in neat bunches, with single zinnias stuck in, at regular intervals around the room, on the pews and along the altar rail. Over in the corner the piano appeared to be a large mound of vines, with the keyboard bared rather startlingly, like a row of teeth from ambush. On the platform where the pulpit had been was a big easy chair, draped with a red and blue robe embroidered in fleur-de-lys. Above it, two American flags were crossed over a drawing of an eagle copied straight off the back of a dollar bill.

As soon as people began coming into the church, out walked Maude Thompson from the rear, bustling and starched in the obvious role of church leader. She came straight to welcome me. Yes indeed, she said, there was to be a Pageant of Birds at seven o'clock sharp. I was welcome and all my friends. As she talked on, I was pleased to learn that she had written the Pageant herself and had not got it from some Northern YWCA or missionary society, as might be feared. "I said to myself, 'There have been pageants about everything else—why not about birds?' " she said. She told me proudly that each costume had been made by the bird who would wear it.

I brought a friend, and presently we were seated—unavoidably, because we were white—in the front row, with our feet turned sidewise by a large can of zinnias, but in the first of the excitement we were forgotten, and all proceeded as if we weren't there.

Maude Thompson made an announcement to the audience that every-body had better be patient. "Friends, the reason we are late starting is that sev-eral of the birds have to work late and haven't arrived yet. If there are any birds in the audience now, will they *kindly get on back here?*" Necks craned and eyes popped in delight when one girl in a dark-blue tissue-paper dress jumped up from a back pew and skittered out. Maude Thompson clapped her hands for order and told how a collection to be taken up would be used to pay for a piano—"not a new one, but a better one." Her hand was raised solemnly: we were promised, if we were quiet and nice, the sight of even more birds than we saw represented on the walls. The audience fanned, patted feet dreamily, and waited.

The Pageant, decidedly worth waiting for, began with a sudden complete silence in the audience, as if by mass intuition. Every head turned at the same time and all eyes fastened upon the front door of the church.

Then came the entrance of the Eagle Bird. Her wings and tail were of gold and silver tin foil, and her dress was a black and purple kimono. She began a slow pace down the aisle with that truly majestic dignity which only a vast, firmly matured physique, wholly unselfconscious, can achieve. Her hypnotic majesty was almost prostrating to the audience as she moved, as slowly as possible, down the aisle and finally turned and stood beneath the eagle's picture on the wall, in the exact center of the platform. A little Eaglet boy, with propriety her son, about two and a half feet tall, very black, entered from the Sunday School room and trotted around her with a sprightly tail over his knickers, flipping his hands dutifully from the wrist out. He wore bows on each shoulder. No smiles were exchanged—there was not a smile in the house. The Eagle then seated herself with a stifled groan in her chair, there was a strangled chord from the piano, where a Bird now sat, and with the little Eaglet to keep time by waving a flag jutting out from each wing, the congregation rose and sang "The Star-Spangled Banner."

Then the procession of lesser Birds began, and the music—as the pianist watched in a broken piece of mirror hidden in the vines—went gradually into syncopation.

The Birds would enter from the front door of the church, portentously, like members of a bridal party, proceed in absolute and easily distinguishable character down the aisle, cross over, and take their places in a growing circle around the audience. All came in with an assurance that sprang from complete absorption in their roles—erect in their bright wings and tails and crests, flapping their elbows, dipping their knees, hopping and turning and preening to the music. It was like a dance only inasmuch as birds might dance under the circumstances. They would, on reaching the platform, bow low, first to the Eagle Bird, who gave them back a stern look, and then to the audience, and take their positions—never ceasing to fly in place and twitter now and then, never showing recognition or saying one human word to anyone, even each other. There were many more Birds of some varieties than of others; I understood that "you could be what you want to." Maude Thompson, standing in a white uniform beside the piano, made a little evocation of each variety, checking down a list.

"The next group of Birds to fly will be the Bluebirds," she said, and in they flew, three big ones and one little one, in clashing shades of blue crepe paper. They were all very pleased and serious with their movements. The oldest wore shell-rimmed glasses. There were Redbirds, four of them; two Robin Redbreasts with diamond-shaped gold speckles on their breasts; five "Pink-birds"; two Peacocks who simultaneously spread their tails at a point halfway down the aisle; Goldfinches with black tips on their tails, who waltzed slowly and somehow appropriately; Canary birds, announced as "the beautiful Canaries, for pleasure as well as profit," who whistled vivaciously as they twirled, and a small Canary who had a yellow ostrich plume for a crest. There was only one "beautiful Blackbird, alone but not lonesome," with red caps on her wings; there was a head-wagging Purple Finch, who wore gold earrings. There was the Parrot-bird, who was a man and caused shouts—everyone's instant favorite; he had a yellow breast, one green trouser-leg, one red; he was in his shirt sleeves because it was hot, and he had red, green, blue and yellow wings. The lady Parrot (his wife) followed after in immutable seriousness—she had noticed parrots well, and she never got out of character: she ruffled her shoulder feathers, she was cross, she pecked at her wings, she moved her head rapidly from side to side and made obscure sounds, not quite words; she was so good she almost called up a parrot. There was loud appreciation of the Parrots—I thought they would have to go back and come in again. The "Red-headed Peckerwood" was a little boy alone. The "poor little Mourning Dove" was called but proved absent. "And last but not least, the white Dove of Peace!" cried Maude Thompson. There came two Doves, very sanctimonious indeed, with long sleeves, nurse's shoes and white cotton gloves. They flew with restraint, almost sadly.

When they had all come inside out of the night, the Birds filled a complete circle around the congregation. They performed a finale. They sang, lifting up their wings and swaying from side to side to the mounting music, bending and rolling their hips, all singing. And yet in their own and in everybody's eyes they were still birds. They were certainly birds to me.

> *"And I want TWO wings*
> *To veil my face*
> *And I want TWO wings*
> *To fly away,*
> *And I want TWO wings*
> *To veil my face,*
> *And the world can't do me no harm."*

That was their song, and they circled the church with it, singing and clapping with their wings, and flew away by the back door, where the ragamuffins of the alley cried "Oooh!" and jumped aside to let them pass.

I wanted them to have a picture of the group to keep and offered to take it. Maude Thompson said, "Several of the Birds could meet you in front of the church door tomorrow afternoon at four."

There turned out to be a number of rendezvous; but not all the Birds showed up, and I almost failed to get the Eagle, who has some very confining job. The Birds who could make it were finally photographed, however, Maude Thompson supervising the poses. I did not dare interfere. She instructed them to hold up their necks, and reproached the Dove of Peace for smiling. "You ever see a bird smile?"

Since our first meeting I have chanced on Maude Thompson several times. Every time I would be getting on a train, I would see her in the station; she would be putting on a coffin, usually, or receiving one, in a church capacity. She would always tell me how the Pageant was doing. They were on the point of taking it to Forrest or Mount Olive or some other town. Also, the Birds have now made themselves faces and beaks.

"This is going to be one of those things going to grow," said Maude Thompson.

I Know Why the Caged Bird Sings

Harper's Magazine, February 1970

MAYA ANGELOU

"*What you looking at me for?*
I didn't come to stay . . ."

I hadn't so much forgot as I couldn't bring myself to remember. Other things were more important.

"*What you looking at me for?*
I didn't come to stay . . ."

Whether I could remember the rest of the poem or not was immaterial. The truth of the statement was like a wadded-up handkerchief, sopping wet in my fists, and the sooner they accepted it the quicker I could let my hands open and the air would cool my palms.

"*What you looking at me for . . . ?*"

The children's section of the Colored Methodist Episcopal Church of Stamps, Arkansas, was wiggling and giggling over my well-known forgetfulness.

The dress I wore was lavender taffeta, and each time I breathed it rustled, and now that I was sucking in air to breathe out shame it sounded like crepe paper on the back of hearses.

As I'd watched Momma put ruffles on the hem and cute little tucks around the waist, I knew that once I put it on I'd look like a movie star. (It was silk and that made up for the awful color.) I was going to look like one of the sweet little white girls who were everybody's dream of what was right with the world. Hanging softly over the black Singer sewing machine, it looked like magic, and when people saw me wearing it they were going to run up to me and say, "Marguerite [sometimes it was "dear Marguerite"], forgive us, please, we didn't know who you were," and I would answer generously, "No, you couldn't have known. Of course I forgive you."

Just thinking about it made me go around with angel's dust sprinkled over my face for days. But Easter's early morning sun had shown the dress to be a plain ugly cut-down from a white woman's once-was-purple throwaway. It was old-lady-long too, but it didn't hide my skinny legs, which had been greased with Blue Seal Vaseline and powdered with the Arkansas red clay. The age-faded color made my skin look dirty like mud, and everyone in church was looking at my skinny legs.

Wouldn't they be surprised when one day I woke out of my black ugly dream, and my real hair, which was long and blond, would take the place of the kinky mass that Momma wouldn't let me straighten? My light-blue eyes were going to hypnotize them, after all the things they said about "my daddy must of been a Chinaman" (I thought they meant made out of china, like a cup) because my eyes were so small and squinty. Then they would understand why I had never picked up a Southern accent, or spoken the common slang, and why I had to be forced to eat pigs' tails and snouts. Because I was really white and because a cruel fairy stepmother, who was understandably jealous of my beauty, had turned me into a too-big Negro girl, with nappy black hair, broad feet, and a space between her teeth that would hold a number-two pencil.

"What you looking . . ." The minister's wife leaned toward me, her long yellow face full of sorry. She whispered, "I just come to tell you, it's Easter Day." I repeated, jamming the words together, "Ijustcometotellyouit'sEasterDay," as low as possible. The giggles hung in the air like melting clouds that were waiting to rain on me. I held up two fingers, close to my chest, which meant that I had to go to the toilet, and tiptoed toward the rear of the church. Dimly, somewhere over my head, I heard ladies saying, "Lord bless the child" and, "Praise God." My head was up and my eyes were open, but I didn't see anything. Halfway down the aisle, the church exploded with, "Were you there when they crucified my Lord?" and I tripped over a foot stuck out from the children's pew. I stumbled and started to say something, or maybe to scream, but a green persimmon, or it could have been a lemon, caught me between the legs and squeezed. I tasted the sour on my tongue and felt it in the back of my mouth. Then before I reached the door, the sting was burning down my legs and into my Sunday socks. I tried to hold, to squeeze it back, to keep it from speeding, but when I reached the church porch I knew I'd have to let it go, or it would probably run right back up to my head and my poor head would burst like a dropped watermelon, and all the brains and spit and tongue and eyes would roll all over the place. So I ran down into the yard and let it go. I ran, peeing and crying, not toward the toilet out back but to our house. I'd get a whipping for it, to be sure, and the nasty children would have something new to tease me about. I laughed anyway, partially for the sweet release; still, the greater joy came not from being liberated from the silly church but from the knowledge that I wouldn't die from a busted head.

If growing up is painful for the Southern Black girl, being aware of her displacement is the rust on the razor that threatens the throat. It is an unnecessary insult.

|

My brother Bailey and I had come to the musty little town of Stamps when I was three and he four. We had arrived wearing tags on our wrists which instructed—"To Whom It May Concern"—that we were Marguerite and Bailey Johnson, Jr., from Long Beach, California, en route to Stamps, Arkansas, c/o Mrs. Annie Henderson.

Our parents had decided to put an end to their calamitous marriage, and Father shipped us home to his mother. A porter had been charged with our welfare—he got off the train the next day in Arizona—and our tickets were pinned to my brother's inside coat pocket.

I don't remember much of the trip, but after we reached the segregated Southern part of the journey, things must have looked up. Negro passengers, who always traveled with loaded lunch boxes, felt sorry for "the poor little motherless darlings" and plied us with cold fried chicken and potato salad. Years later I discovered that the United States had been crossed thousands of times by frightened Black children traveling alone to their newly affluent parents in Northern cities, or back to grandmothers in Southern towns when the urban North reneged on its economic promises.

The town reacted to us as its inhabitants had reacted to all things new before our coming. It regarded us awhile without curiosity but with caution, and after we were seen to be harmless (and children) it closed in around us, as a real mother embraces a stranger's child. Warmly, but not too familiarly.

We lived with our grandmother and uncle in the rear of the Store (it was always spoken of with a capital s), which she had owned some twenty-five years. Early in the century, Momma (we soon stopped calling her Grandmother) sold lunches to the sawmen in the lumberyard (east Stamps) and the seedmen at the cotton gin (west Stamps). Her crisp meat pies and cool lemonade, when joined to her miraculous ability to be in two places at the same time, assured her business success. From having a mobile lunch counter, she set up a stand between the two points of fiscal interest and supplied the workers' needs for a few years. Then she had the Store built in the heart of the Negro area. Over the years it became the lay center of activities in town. On Saturdays, barbers sat their customers in the shade on the porch of the Store, and troubadours on their ceaseless crawlings through the South leaned across its benches and sang their sad songs of The Brazos while they played juice harps and cigar-box guitars.

The formal name of the Store was the Wm. Johnson General Merchandise Store. Customers could find food staples, a good variety of colored thread, mash for hogs, corn for chickens, coal oil for lamps, light bulbs for the wealthy, shoestrings, hair dressing, balloons, and flower seeds. Anything not visible had only to be ordered. Until we became familiar enough to belong to the Store and it to us, we were locked up in a Fun House of Things where the attendant had gone home for life.

Each year I watched the field across from the Store turn caterpillar green, then gradually frosty white. I knew exactly how long it would be before the big wagons would pull into the front yard and load on the cotton pickers at daybreak to carry them to the remains of slavery's plantations.

During the picking season my grandmother would get out of bed at four o'clock (she never used an alarm clock) and creak down to her knees and chant in a sleep-filled voice, "Our Father, thank you for letting me see this New Day. Thank you that you didn't allow the bed I lay on last to be my cooling board, nor my blanket my winding sheet. Guide my feet this day along the straight and narrow, and help me to put a bridle on my tongue. Bless this house, and everybody in it. Thank you, in the name of your Son, Jesus Christ, Amen." Before she had quite arisen, she called our names and issued orders, and pushed her large feet into home slippers and across the bare lye-washed wooden floor to light the coal-oil lamp.

The lamplight in the Store gave a soft make-believe feeling to our world which made me want to whisper and walk about on tiptoe. The odors of onions and oranges and kerosene had been mixing all night and wouldn't be disturbed until the wooded slat was removed from the door and the early morning air forced its way in with the bodies of people who had walked miles to reach the pickup place.

"Sister, I'll have two cans of sardines."

"I'm gonna work so fast today I'm gonna make you look like you standing still."

"Lemme have a hunk uh cheese and some sody crackers."

"Just gimme a coupla them fat peanut paddies." That would be from a picker who was taking his lunch. The greasy brown-paper sack was stuck behind the bib of his overalls. He'd use the candy as a snack before the noon sun called the workers to rest.

In those tender mornings the Store was full of laughing, joking, boasting, and bragging. One man was going to pick two hundred pounds of cotton, and another three hundred. Even the children were promising to bring home fo' bits and six bits. The champion picker of the day before was the hero of the dawn. If he prophesied that the cotton in today's field was going to be sparse and stick to the bolls like glue, every listener would grunt a hearty agreement. The sound of the empty cotton sacks dragging over the floor and the murmurs of waking people were sliced by the cash register as we rang up the five-cent sales.

If the morning sounds and smells were touched with the supernatural, the late afternoon had all the features of the normal Arkansas life. In the dying sunlight the people dragged, rather than their empty cotton sacks. Brought back to the Store, the pickers would step out of the backs of trucks and fold down, dirt-disappointed, to the ground. No matter how much they had picked, it wasn't enough. Their wages wouldn't even get them out of debt to my grandmother, not to mention the staggering bill that waited on them at the white commissary downtown.

The sounds of the new morning had been replaced with grumbles about cheating houses, weighted scales, snakes, skimpy cotton, and dusty rows. In later years I was to confront the stereotyped picture of gay song-singing cotton pickers with such inordinate rage that I was told even by fellow Blacks that my paranoia was embarrassing. But I had seen the fingers cut by the mean little cotton bolls, and I had witnessed the backs and shoulders and arms and legs resisting any further demands.

Some of the workers would leave their sacks at the Store to be picked up the following morning, but a few had to take them home for repairs. I winced to picture them sewing the coarse material under a coal-oil lamp with fingers stiffening from the day's work. In too few hours they would have to walk back to Sister Henderson's Store, get vittles, and load, again, onto the trucks. Then they would face another day of trying to earn enough for the whole year with the heavy knowledge that they were going to end the season as they started it. Without the money or credit necessary to sustain a family for three months. In cotton-picking time the late afternoons revealed the harshness of Black Southern life, which in the early morning had been softened by nature's blessing of grogginess, forgetfulness, and the soft lamplight.

II

When Bailey was six and I a year younger, we used to rattle off the times tables with the speed I was later to see Chinese children in San Francisco employ on their abacuses. Our summer-gray potbellied stove bloomed rosy red during winter, and became a severe disciplinarian threat if we were so foolish as to indulge in making mistakes.

Uncle Willie used to sit, like a giant black Z (he had been crippled as a child), and hear us testify to the Lafayette County Training School's abilities. His face pulled down on the left side, as if a pulley had been attached to his lower teeth, and his left hand was only a mite bigger than Bailey's, but on the second mistake or on the third hesitation his big overgrown right hand would catch one of us behind the collar, and in the same moment would thrust the culprit toward the dull red heater, which throbbed like a devil's toothache. We were never burned, although once I might have been when I was so terrified I tried to jump onto the stove to remove the possibility of its remaining a threat. Like most children, I thought if I could face the worst danger voluntarily, and *triumph*, I would forever have power over it. But in my case of sacrificial effort I was thwarted. Uncle Willie held tight to my dress and I only got close enough to smell the clean dry scent of hot iron. We learned the times tables without understanding their grand principle, simply because we had the capacity and no alternative.

The tragedy of lameness seems so unfair to children that they are embarrassed in its presence. And they, most recently off nature's mold, sense that they have only narrowly missed being another of her jokes. In relief at the narrow escape, they vent their emotions in impatience and criticism of the unlucky cripple.

Momma related times without end, and without any show of emotion, how Uncle Willie had been dropped when he was three years old by a woman who was minding him. She seemed to hold no rancor against the baby-sitter, nor for her just God who allowed the accident. She felt it necessary to explain over and over again to those who knew the story by heart that he wasn't "born that way."

In our society, where two-legged, two-armed strong Black men were able at best to eke out only the necessities of life, Uncle Willie, with his starched shirts, shined shoes, and shelves full of food, was the whipping boy and butt of jokes of the underemployed and underpaid. Fate not only disabled him but laid a double-tiered barrier in his path. He was also proud and sensitive. Therefore he couldn't pretend that he wasn't crippled, nor could he deceive himself that people were not repelled by his defect.

Only once in all the years of trying not to watch him, I saw him pretend to himself and others that he wasn't lame. Coming home from school one day, I saw a dark car in our front yard. I rushed in to find a strange man and woman (Uncle Willie said later they were schoolteachers from Little Rock) drinking Dr. Peppers in the cool of the Store. I sensed a wrongness around me, like an alarm clock that had gone off without being set.

I knew it couldn't be the strangers. Not frequently, but often enough, travelers pulled off the main road to buy tobacco or soft drinks in the only Negro store in Stamps. When I looked at Uncle Willie, I knew what was pulling my mind's coattails. He was standing erect behind the counter, not leaning forward or resting on the small shelf that had been built for him. Erect. His eyes seemed to hold me with a mixture of threat and appeal.

I dutifully greeted the strangers and roamed my eyes around for his walking stick. It was nowhere to be seen. He said, "Uh . . . this this . . . this . . . uh, my niece. She's . . . uh . . . just come from school." Then to the couple—"You know . . . how, uh, children are . . . th-th-these days . . . they play all d-d-day at school and c-c-can't wait to get home and pl-play some more."

The people smiled, very friendly.

He added, "Go on out and pl-play, Sister."

The lady laughed in a soft Arkansas voice and said, "Well, you know, Mr. Johnson, they say, You're only a child once. Have you children of your own?"

Uncle Willie looked at me with an impatience I hadn't seen in his face even when he took thirty minutes to loop the laces over his high-topped shoes. "I . . . I thought I told you to go . . . go outside and play."

Before I left I saw him lean back on the shelves of Garret Snuff, Prince Albert, and Spark Plug chewing tobacco.

"No ma'am . . . no ch-children and no wife." He tried a laugh. "I have an old m-m-mother and my brother's t-two children to l-look after."

The couple left after a few minutes, and from the back of the house I watched the red car scare chickens, raise dust, and disappear toward Magnolia.

Uncle Willie was making his way down the long shadowed aisle between the shelves and the counter—hand over hand, like a man climbing out of a dream. I stayed quiet and watched him lurch from one side, bumping to the other, until he reached the coal-oil tank. He put his hand behind that dark recess and took his cane in the strong fist and shifted his weight on the wooden support. He thought he had pulled it off.

I'll never know why it was important to him that the couple (he said later that he'd never seen them before) would take a picture of a whole Mr. Johnson back to Little Rock. He must have tired of being crippled, as prisoners tire of penitentiary bars and the guilty tire of blame. The high-topped shoes and the cane, his uncontrollable muscles and thick tongue, and the looks he suffered of either contempt or pity had simply worn him out, and for one afternoon, one part of an afternoon, he wanted no part of them.

I understood and felt closer to him at the moment than ever before or since.

During these years in Stamps, I met and fell in love with William Shakespeare. He was my first white love. Although I enjoyed and respected Kipling, Poe, Butler, Thackeray, and Henley, I saved my young and loyal passion for Paul Lawrence Dunbar, Langston Hughes, James Weldon Johnson, and W.E.B. Du Bois's "Litany at Atlanta." But it was Shakespeare who said, "When in disgrace with fortune and men's eyes." It was a state with which I felt myself most fa-

miliar. I pacified myself about his whiteness by saying that after all he had been
dead so long it couldn't matter to anyone anymore.

Bailey and I decided to memorize a scene from *The Merchant of Venice*, but
we realized that Momma would question us about the author and that we'd
have to tell her that Shakespeare was white, and it wouldn't matter to her
whether he was dead or not. So we chose "The Creation" by James Weldon
Johnson instead.

III

Until I was thirteen and left Arkansas for good, the Store was my favorite place
to be. Alone and empty in the mornings, it looked like an unopened present
from a stranger. Opening the front doors was pulling the ribbon off the unexpected gift. The light would come in softly (we faced north), easing itself over
the shelves of mackerel, salmon, tobacco, thread. It fell flat on the big vat of
lard and by noontime during the summer the grease had softened to a thick
soup. Whenever I walked into the Store in the afternoon, I sensed that it was
tired. I alone could hear the slow pulse of its job half done. But just before bed-
time, after numerous people had walked in and out, had argued over their bills,
or joked about their neighbors, or just dropped in "to give Sister Henderson a
'Hi y'all,' " the promise of magic mornings returned to the Store and spread itself over the family in washed life waves.

Momma opened boxes of crispy crackers and we sat around the meat block
at the rear of the Store. I sliced onions, and Bailey opened two or even three
cans of sardines and allowed their juice of oil and fishing boats to ooze down
and around the sides. That was supper. In the evening, when we were alone like
that, Uncle Willie didn't stutter or shake or give any indication that he had an
"affliction." It seemed that the peace of a day's ending was an assurance that
the covenant God made with children, Negroes, and the crippled was still in effect.

Throwing scoops of corn to the chickens and mixing sour dry mash with
leftover food and oily dishwater for the hogs were among our evening chores.
Bailey and I sloshed down twilight trails to the pigpens, and standing on the
first fence rungs we poured down the unappealing concoctions to our grateful
hogs. They mashed their tender pink snouts down into the slop, and rooted and
grunted their satisfaction. We always grunted a reply only half in jest. We were
also grateful that we had concluded the dirtiest of chores and had only gotten
the evil-smelling swill on our shoes, stockings, feet, and hands.

Late one day, as we were attending to the pigs, I heard a horse in the front
yard (it really should have been called a driveway, except that there was
nothing to drive into it), and ran to find out who had come riding up on a
Thursday evening. The used-to-be sheriff sat rakishly astraddle his horse. His

nonchalance was meant to convey his authority and power over even dumb animals. How much more capable he would be with Negroes, it went without saying.

His twang jogged in the brittle air. From the side of the Store, Bailey and I heard him say to Momma, "Annie, tell Willie he better lay low tonight. A crazy nigger messed with a white lady today. Some of the boys'll be coming over here later." Even after the slow drag of years, I remember the sense of fear which filled my mouth with hot, dry air, and made my body light.

The "boys"? Those cement faces and eyes of hate that burned the clothes off you if they happened to see you lounging on the main street downtown on Saturday. Boys? It seemed that youth had never happened to them. Boys? No, rather men who were covered with graves' dust and age without beauty or learning. The ugliness and rottenness of old abominations.

If on Judgment Day I were summoned by St. Peter to give testimony to the used-to-be sheriff's act of kindness, I would be unable to say anything in his behalf. His confidence that my uncle and every other Black man who heard of the Klan's coming ride would scurry under their houses to hide in chicken droppings was too humiliating to hear. Without waiting for Momma's thanks, he rode out of the yard, sure that things were as they should be and that he was a gentle squire, saving those deserving serfs from the laws of the land, which he condoned.

Immediately, while his horse's hoofs were still loudly thudding the ground, Momma blew out the coal-oil lamps. She had a quiet, hard talk with Uncle Willie and called Bailey and me into the Store.

We were told to take the potatoes and onions out of their bins and knock out the dividing walls that kept them apart. Then with a tedious and fearful slowness Uncle Willie gave me his rubber-tipped cane and bent down to get into the now-enlarged empty bin. It took forever before he lay down flat, and then we covered him with potatoes and onions, layer upon layer, like a casserole. Grandmother knelt praying in the darkened Store.

It was fortunate that the "boys" didn't ride into our yard that evening and insist that Momma open the Store. They would have surely found Uncle Willie and just as surely lynched him. He moaned the whole night through as if he had, in fact, been guilty of some heinous crime. The heavy sounds pushed their way up out of the blanket of vegetables and I pictured his mouth pulling down on the right side and his saliva flowing into the eyes of new potatoes and waiting there like dewdrops for the warmth of morning.

IV

Bailey was the greatest person in my world. And the fact that he was my brother, my only brother, and I had no sisters to share him with, was such good fortune that it made me want to live a Christian life just to show God that I was grateful. Where I was big, elbowy, and grating, he was small, graceful, and smooth. When I was described by our playmates as being shit color, he was lauded for his velvet-black skin. His hair fell down in black curls, and my head was covered with black steel wool. And yet he loved me.

When our elders said unkind things about my features (my family was handsome to a point of pain for me), Bailey would wink at me from across the room, and I knew that it was a matter of time before he would take revenge. He would allow the old ladies to finish wondering how on earth I came about, then he would ask, in a voice like cooling bacon grease, "Oh Mizeriz Coleman, how is your son? I saw him the other day, and he looked sick enough to die."

Aghast, the ladies would ask, "Die? From what? He ain't sick."

And in a voice oilier than the one before, he'd answer with a straight face, "From the Uglies."

I would hold my laugh, bite my tongue, grit my teeth, and very seriously erase even the touch of a smile from my face. Later, behind the house by the black-walnut tree, we'd laugh and laugh and howl. Bailey could count on very few punishments for his consistently outrageous behavior, for he was the pride of the Henderson/Johnson family.

His movements, as he was later to describe those of an acquaintance, were activated with oiled precision. He was also able to find more hours in the day than I thought existed. He finished chores, homework, read more books than I, and played the group games on the side of the hill with the best of them. He could even pray out loud in church, and was apt at stealing pickles from the barrel that sat under the fruit counter and Uncle Willie's nose.

After our early chores were done, while Uncle Willie or Momma minded the Store, we were free to play the children's games, as long as we stayed within yelling distance. Playing hide-and-seek, his voice was easily identified, singing, "Last night, night before, twenty-four robbers at my door. Who all is hid? Ask me to let them in, hit 'em in the head with a rolling pin. Who all is hid?" In follow-the-leader, naturally he was the one who created the most daring and interesting things to do. And when he was on the tail of the pop-the-whip, he would twirl off the end like a top, spinning, falling, laughing, finally stopping just before my heart beat its last, and then he was back in the game, still laughing.

Of all the needs (there are none imaginary) a lonely child has, the one that must be satisfied, if there is going to be hope and a hope of wholeness, is the unshaking need for an unshakable God. My pretty Black brother was my Kingdom Come.

In Stamps the segregation was so complete that most Black children didn't really, absolutely know what whites looked like. Other than that they were different, to be dreaded, and in that dread was included the hostility of the power-less against the powerful, the poor against the rich, the worker against the worked-for, and the ragged against the well-dressed. I remember never believ-ing that whites were really real.

Many women who worked in their kitchens traded at our Store, and when they carried their finished laundry back to town they often set the big baskets down on our front porch to pull a singular piece from the starched collection and show either how graceful was their ironing hand or how rich and opulent was the property of their employers.

I looked at the items that weren't on display. I knew, for instance, that white men wore shorts, as Uncle Willie did, and that they had an opening for taking out their "things" and peeing, and that white women's breasts weren't built into their dresses, as people said, because I saw their brassieres in the bas-kets. But I couldn't force myself to think of them as people. People were Mrs. LaGrone, Mrs. Hendricks, Momma, Reverend Sneed, Lillie B, and Louise and Rex. Whitefolks couldn't be people because their feet were too small, their skin too white and see-throughy, and they didn't walk on the balls of their feet the way people did—they walked on their heels like horses.

People were those who lived on my side of town. I didn't like them all, or, in fact, any of them very much, but they were people. These others, the strange pale creatures that lived in their alien unlife, weren't considered folks. They were whitefolks.

V

Some families of powhitetrash lived on Momma's farmland behind the school. Sometimes a gaggle of them came to the Store, filling the whole room, chasing out the air, and even changing the well-known scents. The children crawled over the shelves and into the potato and onion bins, twanging all the time in their sharp voices like cigar-box guitars. They took liberties in my Store that I would never dare. Since Momma told us that the less you say to whitefolks (or even powhitetrash) the better, Bailey and I would stand, solemn, quiet, in the displaced air. But if one of the playful apparitions got close to us, I pinched it. Partly out of angry frustration and partly because I didn't believe in its flesh re-ality.

They called my uncle by his first name and ordered him around the Store. He, to my crying shame, obeyed them in his limping dip-straight-dip fashion. My grandmother, too, followed their orders, except that she didn't seem to be servile because she anticipated their needs.

"Here's sugar, Miz Potter, and here's baking powder. You didn't buy soda last month, you'll probably be needing some."

Momma always directed her statements to the adults, but sometimes, oh painful sometimes, the grimy, snotty-nosed girls would answer her. "Naw, Annie . . ."—to Momma? Who owned the land they lived on? Who forgot more than they would ever learn? If there was any justice in the world, God should strike them dumb at once!—"Just give us some extry sody crackers, and some more mackerel."

At least they never looked in her face, or I never caught them doing so. Nobody with a smidgen of training, not even the worst roustabout, would look right in a grown person's face. It meant the person was trying to take the words out before they were formed. The dirty little children didn't do that, but they threw their orders around the Store like lashes from a cat-o'-nine-tails.

When I was around ten years old, those scruffy children caused me the most painful and confusing experience I had ever had with my grandmother. One summer morning, after I had swept the dirt yard of leaves, spearmint-gum wrappers, and Vienna-sausage labels, I raked the yellow-red dirt, and made half-moons carefully, so that the design stood out clearly and masklike. I put the rake behind the Store and came through the back of the house to find Grandmother on the front porch in her big, wide white apron. The apron was so stiff by virtue of the starch that it could have stood alone. Momma was admiring the yard, so I joined her. It truly looked like a flat redhead that had been raked with a big-toothed comb. Momma didn't say anything but I knew she liked it. She looked around, hoping one of the community pillars would see the design before the day's business wiped it out. Then she looked upward toward the school. My head had swung with hers, so at just about the same time we saw a troop of the powhitetrash kids marching over the hill and down by the side of the school.

I looked to Momma for direction. She did an excellent job of sagging from her waist down, but from the waist up she seemed to be pulling for the top of the oak tree across the road. Then she began to moan a hymn. Maybe not to moan, but the tune was so slow and the meter so strange that she could have been moaning. She didn't look at me again. When the children reached halfway down the hill, halfway to the Store, she said without turning, "Sister, go on inside."

I wanted to beg her, "Momma, don't wait for them. Come on inside with me. If they come in the Store, you go to the bedroom and let me wait on them. They only frighten me if you're around. Alone I know how to handle them," but of course I couldn't say anything, so I went in and stood behind the screen door.

Before the girls got to the porch I heard their laughter crackling and popping like pine logs in a cooking stove. I suppose my lifelong paranoia was born in those cold, molasses-slow minutes. They came finally to stand on the ground in front of Momma. At first they pretended seriousness. Then one of them wrapped her right arm in the crook of her left, pushed out her mouth, and started to hum. I realized that she was aping my grandmother. Another said, "Naw, Helen, you ain't standing like her. This here's it." Then she lifted her chest, folded her arms, and mocked that strange carriage that was Annie Henderson. Another laughed, "Naw, you can't do it. Your mouth ain't pooched out enough. It's like this."

I thought about the rifle behind the door, but I knew I'd never be able to hold it straight, and the .410, our sawed-off shotgun, which stayed loaded and was fired every New Year's night, was locked in the trunk and Uncle Willie had the key on his chain. Through the fly-specked screen door, I could see that the arms of Momma's apron jiggled from the vibrations of her humming. But her knees seemed to have locked as if they would never bend again.

She sang on. No louder than before, but no softer either. No slower or faster.

The dirt of the girls' cotton dresses continued on their legs, feet, arms, and faces to make them all of a piece. Their greasy uncolored hair hung down, uncombed, with a grim finality. I knelt to see them better, to remember them for all time. The tears that had slipped down my dress left unsurprising dark spots, and made the front yard blurry and even more unreal. The world had taken a deep breath and was having doubts about continuing to revolve.

The girls had tired of mocking Momma and turned to other means of agitation. One crossed her eyes, stuck her thumbs in both sides of her mouth, and said, "Look here, Annie." Grandmother hummed on and the apron strings trembled. I wanted to throw a handful of black pepper in their faces, to throw lye on them, to scream that they were dirty, scummy peckerwoods, but I knew I was as clearly imprisoned behind the scene as the actors outside were confined to their roles.

One of the smaller girls did a kind of puppet dance while her fellow clowns laughed at her. But the tall one, who was almost a woman, said something very quietly, which I couldn't hear. They all moved backward from the porch, still watching Momma. For an awful second I thought they were going to throw a rock at Momma, who seemed (except for the apron strings) to have turned into stone herself. But the big girl turned her back, bent down, and put her hands flat on the ground—she didn't pick up anything. She simply shifted her weight and did a hand stand.

Her dirty bare feet and long legs went straight for the sky. Her dress fell down around her shoulders, and she had on no drawers. The slick pubic hair made a brown triangle where her legs came together. She hung in the vacuum of that lifeless morning for only a few seconds, then wavered and tumbled. The other girls clapped her on the back and slapped their hands.

Momma changed her song to "Bread of Heaven, bread of Heaven, feed me till I want no more."

I found that I was praying too. How long could Momma hold out? What new indignity would they think of to subject her to? Would I be able to stay out of it? What would Momma really like me to do?

Then they were moving out of the yard, on their way to town. They bobbed their heads and shook their slack behinds and turned, one at a time:

"'Bye, Annie."

"'Bye, Annie."

"'Bye, Annie."

Momma never turned her head or unfolded her arms, but she stopped singing and said, "'Bye, Miz Helen, 'bye, Miz Ruth, 'bye, Miz Eloise."

I burst. A firecracker July-the-Fourth burst. How could Momma call them Miz? The mean nasty things. Why couldn't she have come inside the sweet, cold Store when we saw them breasting the hill? What did she prove? And then if they were dirty, mean, and impudent, why did Momma have to call them Miz?

She stood another whole song through and then opened the screen door to look down on me crying in rage. She looked until I looked up. Her face was a brown moon that shone on me. She was beautiful. Something had happened out there, which I couldn't completely understand, but I could see that she was happy. Then she bent down and touched me as mothers of the church "lay hands on the sick and afflicted" and I quieted.

"Go wash your face, Sister." And she went behind the candy counter and hummed, "Glory, glory, hallelujah, when I lay my burden down." I threw the well water on my face and used the weekday handkerchief to blow my nose. Whatever the contest had been out front, I knew Momma had won.

I took the rake back to the front yard. The smudged footprints were easy to erase. I worked for a long time on my new design and laid the rake behind the wash pot. When I came back in the Store, I took Momma's hand and we both walked outside to look at the pattern.

It was a large heart with lots of hearts growing smaller inside, and piercing from the outside rim to the smallest heart was an arrow. Momma said, "Sister, that's right pretty." Then she turned back to the Store and resumed, "Glory, glory hallelujah, when I lay my burden down."

Opera in Greenville

The New Yorker, June 14, 1947

◆

REBECCA WEST

The note of Greenville, South Carolina, is rhetorical. Among the stores and offices on Main Street there is a vacant lot that suddenly pretends to be a mountain glade, with a stream purling over a neatly assembled rockfall; and in the foreground there is staked a plaque bearing the words "Greenville City Water Works. 1939. The water supply of Greenville, South Carolina, pure, sparkling, life's most vital element, flows by gravity from an uncontaminated mountain watershed of nine thousand acres, delivered through duplicated pipe lines, fourteen million gallons capacity, a perfect water for domestic and industrial uses." Not in such exuberant terms would the existence of a town water supply be celebrated in the North or in my native England, and no deduction can be drawn from this that is damaging to the South. The exuberance of the inscription is actually a sober allusion to reality. Here one remembers that water is a vital element, as it is not in the North or in England. One is always thinking about water, for one is always wanting to have a drink or take a shower or get some clothes washed. The heat of the South is an astonishment to the stranger. When the lynching trial in Greenville came to its end, late in May, it was full summer there, and the huge, pale bush roses that grow around the porches were a little dusty. Greenville was as hot as the cities that lie on the Spanish plains, as Seville and Cordoba. But in those cities the people do not live a modern life, they do not work too grimly, and they sleep in the afternoons; here they keep the same commercial hours as in New York, and practice the hard efficiency that is the price this age asks for money. On this point they fool the stranger. It is the habit of the mills and other factories to build themselves outside the city limits to dodge taxation. So Greenville has a naïve-looking Main Street, with cross streets that run, after a block or two, into residential sections, where the white houses stand among gardens that look as if they were presently going to pass into woods and fields and the clear countryside; and it has a population of 35,000. But outside Greenville city, in Greenville County, there are 137,000 people, 123,000 of whom live within ten miles of the city. In fact, the lynching for which thirty-one men were being tried in the Court House was committed not, as might be imagined by an interested person who was trying to size the matter up by looking at a map and gazetteer, in a backward small town, but in a large, modern city.

To sustain the life of a large, modern city in this cloying, clinging heat is an amazing achievement. It is no wonder that the white men and women in Greenville walk with a slow, dragging pride, as if they had taken up a challenge and intended to defy it without end. These people would deny that it is the climate that has challenged them. They speak of the coolness of the nights almost before the stranger has mentioned the heat of the day. When they name the antagonist against whom they have to pit themselves, they simply and passionately and frequently name the North, with the same hatred, the profounder because it is insolently unrequited, that the Irish feel for the English. But the stranger will obstinately continue to admire them for living and working in this land over which the sun seems to be bending low, and for doing more than live and work: for luxuriating in rhetoric, and topping rhetoric with opera. Near the center of Greenville there stands an old white church, with a delicate spire and handsome steps leading down from a colonnade—the kind of building that makes an illusion of space around itself. This is the First Baptist Church. In there, on Sunday evenings, there is opera. The lovely girls with their rich hair curling around their shoulders and their flowered dresses showing their finely molded throats and arms sit beside the tall young men, whose pale shirts show the squareness of their shoulders and the slimness of their waists, and they join in coloratura hymns with their parents and their grandparents, who sing, like their children, with hope and vehemence, having learned to take things calmly no more than the older characters in opera. As they sing, the women's dresses become crumpled wraps, the men's shirts cling to them, although the service does not begin till eight o'clock at night. But, undistracted by the heat, they listen, still and yet soaring, to the anthems sung by an ecstatic choir and to a sermon that is like a bass recitative, ending in an aria of faith, mounting to cadenzas of adoration. In no other place are Baptists likely to remind a stranger of Verdi.

In the Court House, also, there was opera. This is a singularly hideous building, faced with yellow washroom tiles, standing in Main Street, next to the principal hotel, which, it should be noted for those who want to understand the character of Greenville, is cleaner and more comfortable and kinder to the appetite than most of the great New York hotels at this moment. The courtroom is about the size of the famous court at the Old Bailey in London. In the body of the courtroom there were chairs for about three hundred white persons. The front rows were occupied by the thirty-one defendants who were being tried for lynching a Negro early on the morning of February 17th of this year. With the exception of three young men, one a member of a wealthy mill-owning family, one a salesman, and one a restaurant proprietor, these defendants were all

Greenville taxi-drivers. Many people, including a number of Greenville residents, some of whom desired them to be acquitted of all charges on the ground that lynching is a social prophylactic, talked of them as if they were patently and intensely degraded. As a matter of fact, they covered a wide range of types, most of them very far from repulsive. Some were quite good-looking and alert young men; most were carefully and cleanly dressed; some were manifest eccentrics. The most curious in aspect was a young man of twenty-five who must have weighed about three hundred pounds. The contours of his buttocks and stomach suggested that they were molded in some ductile substance like butter, and his face, which was smiling and playful, was pressed upward, till it turned toward the ceiling, by an enormous accumulation of fat under the chin and jaws. His name was Joy, and he was known as Fat Joy. The most conspicuous by reason of character was Roosevelt Carlos Hurd, Sr., who was a taxi-driver also working as a taxi dispatcher, a man of forty-five with hair that stood up like a badger's coat, eyes set close together and staring out under glum brows through strong glasses, and a mouth that was unremitting in its compression. He looked like an itinerant preacher devoted to the worship of a tetchy and uncooperative God. In his statement, he had declared that his education had stopped in the second grade. This did not necessarily imply that he was of weak intelligence. When he was a boy, there were no laws against child labor in the State of South Carolina, and it is probable that he went to work. Several of the statements made by other defendants alleged that Mr. Hurd was the actual trigger man of the lynching, the man who fired the shot that killed the Negro.

Nearly all these defendants were exercising a right their state permits to all persons accused of a capital offense. They had brought their families to sit with them in court. Many had their wives beside them, young women, for the most part very young women, in bright cotton and rayon dresses, their curled hair wild about them. A number of these women had brought their children with them; one had five scrambling over her. All the children were plump and comely, and though some were grimy, all of them were silent and miraculously court-broken. Mr. Hurd, though married and a father, was accompanied only by his own father, a thin and sharp-nosed man, his eyes censorious behind gold-rimmed spectacles, the whole of him blanched and shrivelled by austerity as by immersion in a caustic fluid. It was altogether plain that at any moment he and his son might become possessed by the idea that they were appointed God's arm and instrument, and that their conception of God would render the consequence of this conviction far from reasonably bland.

It was said by the anti-lynching element in the town that the families had been brought into court to sit with the defendants in order to soften the hearts of the jurors. But certainly they liked to be there, and the defendants liked to have them there. It is quite untrue to imagine, as was often said, that the defendants were sure of being acquitted. They were extremely afraid of what might be coming to them, and so were their families. Several of the wives sat in close embrace with their husbands, shaken from time to time by the inimitable convulsions of distress. One pregnant girl in a green dress sat throughout the trial with an arm thrown about her young husband's shoulder, rubbing her pudgy and honest and tear-stained face against his arm. Many of the men, including some who seemed to take no particular interest in their wives, obviously enjoyed playing with their children. One tall and dark young man with an intelligent face sat with his wife, who was dressed with noticeable good taste, and two pretty little daughters. During the recesses, he spread his legs wide apart, picked up one or the other of the little girls under her armpits, and swung her back and forth between his knees. He would look down on her with adoration as she gurgled with joy, but if she became too noisy, he would stop and set her down with a slight frown and a finger to his lips. It was the oddest gesture to see in this trial, in this place. Mr. Hurd's father was also there out of profound concern for the person whom he loved, though he made no physical manifestation except for occasionally biting his lips and lowering his head. His part was to confirm his son's title to rectitude, his inheritance of grace. It was so hot in the court that the women at the press table all wore fresh dresses every day and almost every man except the attorneys and officers of the court sat in their shirts. But Mr. Hurd's father, from the beginning to the end of the case, wore a neat blue coat and a conservative tie. Most of the defendants and their relatives, but never Mr. Hurd or his father, chewed gum throughout the proceedings, and some chewed bubble gum. So, until the press made unfriendly comment, did two of the attorneys.

Behind the defendants and their families sat something under two hundred of such white citizens of Greenville as could find the time to attend the trial, which was held during working hours. Some were drawn from the men of the town who are too old or too sick to work, or who do not enjoy work and use the Court House as a club, sitting on the steps, chewing and smoking and looking down on Main Street through the hot, dancing air, when the weather is right for that, and going inside when it is better there. They were joined by a certain number of men and women who did not like the idea of people being taken out of jail and murdered, and by others who liked the idea quite well. None of these expressed their opinions very loudly. There were also a number of the defendants' friends. Upstairs, in the deep gallery, sat about a hundred and fifty Negroes, under the care of two white bailiffs. Many of them, too, were court spectators by habit. It is said that very few members of the advanced group of colored people in the town were present. There were reasons, reticently guarded but strongly felt, that they did not want to make an issue of the case. They thought it best to sit back and let the white man settle whether or not he liked mob rule. But every day there went into court a number of colored men and women who were conspicuously handsome and fashionably dressed, and had resentment and the proud intention not to express it written all over them. They might be put down as Negroes who feel the humiliation of their race so deeply that they will not even join in the orthodox movements for its emancipation, because these are, to their raw sensitiveness, tainted with the assumption that Negroes have to behave like good children to win a favorable report from the white people. In the shadows of the balcony the dark faces of these people could not be seen. Their clothes sat there, worn by sullen space. The shoulders of a white coat drooped; a hat made of red roses tilted sidewise, far sidewise. The only Negroes who were clearly visible and bore a label were two young men who sat in the front row of the balcony every day, cheerful and dignified, with something more than spontaneous cheerfulness and dignity, manifestly on parade. They were newspapermen from two Northern Negro journals. They had started at the press table down in the front of the court, for the newspaper people there, Northern and Southern, national and local, had made no objection, and neither had the judge. But one of the defense attorneys said that it was as good as giving the case to him to have a nigger sitting at the press table along with white men and women, and this remark was repeated. Also, the local Negroes intimated that they would take it as a favor if the Northern Negroes went up into the gallery. So they took their seats up there, where, it may be remarked, it was quite impossible to get anything like a complete record of the proceedings. Then there was a very strong agitation to get them to come back to the press table. But that turned out to be inspired by the defense. Such was the complication of this case.

It was complicated even to the extent of not being a true lynching case, although the man taken from prison was a Negro and the men charged with killing him were white. Or, rather, it was not a pure lynching case. The taxi-drivers of Greenville are drawn from the type of men who drive taxis anywhere. They are people who dislike steady work in a store or a factory or an office, or have not the aptitude for it, have a certain degree of mechanic intelligence, have no desire to rise very far in the world, enjoy driving for its own sake, and are not afraid of the dangers that threaten those who are on the road at night. They are, in fact, tough guys, untainted by intellectualism, and their detachment from the stable life of the community around them gives them a clan spirit that degenerates at times into the gang spirit. The local conditions in Greenville encourage this clan spirit. In every big town, the dangers that threaten taxi-drivers as they go about their work are formidable and shameful to society, and they increase year by year. In Greenville, they are very formidable indeed. A great many people are likely to hire taxis, for there are relatively few automobiles in the region; two-thirds of the people who are likely to hire a Greenville taxi live in small communities or isolated homes; it is so hot for the greater part of the year that people prefer to drive by night. Hence the taxi-drivers spend a great part of their time making journeys out of town after dark.

In consequence, a large number of taxi-drivers have during the last few years been robbed and assaulted, sometimes seriously, by their fares. The number of these crimes that has not been followed by any arrest is, apparently, great enough to make the taxi-drivers feel aggrieved. The failure to make an arrest has been especially marked in cases in which the assailants were supposedly Negroes, for the reason, it is said, that Negroes are hard to identify. The taxi-drivers therefore had a resentment against fares who assaulted them, Negroes in general, and the police. In defense of the police, it is alleged that investigation of these crimes is made difficult because a certain number of them never happen at all. Taxi-drivers who have got into money troubles have been known to solve them by pretending that they have been robbed of their money by fares, whom they describe as Negroes in order to cash in on racial prejudice.

On February 15, 1947, an incident occurred that drew the taxi-drivers of Greenville very close together. A driver named Brown picked up a Negro fare, a boy of twenty-four called Willie Earle, who asked him to drive to his mother's home in Pickens County, about eighteen miles from Greenville. Mrs. Earle, by the way, had given birth to Willie when she was fourteen. Both Willie Earle and Brown had been the victims of tragedy. Willie Earle had been a truck driver and had greatly enjoyed his occupation. But he was an epileptic, and though his mates conspired with him to conceal this fact from his employer, there came a day when he fell from the truck in a fit and injured himself. His employer, therefore, quite properly decided that he could not employ him on a job in which he was so likely to come to harm, and dismissed him. He could not get any other employment as a truck driver and was forced to work as a construction laborer, an occupation that he did not like so well and that brought him less money. He became extremely depressed, and began to drink heavily. His fits became more frequent, and he developed a great hostility to white men. He got into trouble, for the first time in his life, for a sudden and unprovoked assault on a contractor who employed him, and was sent to the penitentiary, from which he had not been long released when he made his journey with Brown. Brown's tragedy was also physical. He had been wounded in the first World War and had become a taxi-driver, although he was not of the usual type, because his state of health obliged him to take up work that he could leave when he needed rest. He was a man of thoughtful and kindly character. A Greenville resident who could be trusted told me that in the course of some social-service work he had come across a taxi-driver and his wife who had suffered exceptional misfortune, and that he had been most impressed by the part that Brown had played in helping them to get on their feet again. "You could quite fairly say," this resident told me, "that Brown was an outstanding man, who was a good influence on these taxi boys, and always tried to keep them out of trouble. Lynching is just the sort of thing he wouldn't have let them get into."

Willie Earle reached his home that night on foot. Brown was found bleeding from deep knife wounds beside his taxi a mile or two away and was taken to a hospital, where he sank rapidly. Willie was arrested, and put in Pickens County Jail. Late on the night of February 16th, the melancholy and passionate Mr. Roosevelt Carlos Hurd was, it was said, about certain business. Later, the jailer of the Pickens County Jail telephoned to the sheriff's office in Greenville to say that a mob of about fifty men had come to the jail in taxicabs and forced him to give Willie Earle over to them. A little later still, somebody telephoned to the Negro undertaker in the town of Pickens to tell him that there was a dead nigger in need of his offices by the slaughter-pen in a byroad off the main road from Greenville to Pickens. He then telephoned the coroner of Greenville County, whose men found Willie Earle's mutilated body lying at that place. He had been beaten and stabbed and shot in the body and the head. The bushes around him were splashed with his brain tissue. His own people sorrowed over his death with a grief that was the converse of the grief Brown's friends felt for him. They mourned Brown because he had looked after them; Willie Earle's friends mourned him because they had looked after him. He had made a number of respectable friends before he became morose and intractable.

Thirty-six hours after Willie Earle's body had been found, no arrest had been made. This was remarkable, because the lynching expedition—if there was a lynching expedition—had been planned in a café and a taxicab office that face each other across the parking lot at the back of the Court House. On the ground floor of the Court House is the sheriff's office, which has large windows looking on the parking lot. A staff sits in that office all night long. But either nobody noticed a number of taxi-drivers passing to and fro at hours when they would normally be going off duty or nobody remembered whom he had seen when he heard of a jail break by taxi-drivers the next day. When the thirty-six hours had elapsed, Attorney General Tom C. Clark sent in a number of F.B.I. men to look hard for the murderers of Willie Earle. This step evoked, of course, the automatic resentment against federal action which is characteristic of the South; but it should have been remembered that the murderers were believed to number about fifty, and Greenville had nothing like a big enough police staff to cope with such an extensive search. The sensitivity based on a concern for States' rights was inflamed by a rumor that Attorney General Clark had sent in the F.B.I. men without consulting, or even informing, the Governor of South Carolina. Whether this rumor was true or false, it was believed, and it accounted for much hostility to the trial which had nothing to do with approval of lynching. Very soon the F.B.I. had taken statements from twenty-six men, who, along with five others whom they had mentioned in their statements, were arrested and charged with committing murder, being accessories before or after the fact of murder, and conspiring to murder. It is hard to say, now that all these defen-

dants have been acquitted of all these charges, how the statements are to be regarded. They consist largely of confessions that the defendants were concerned
in the murder of Willie Earle. But the law has pronounced that they had no
more to do with the murder than you or I or President Truman. The statements
must, therefore, be works of fiction, romances that these inhabitants of
Greenville were oddly inspired to weave around the tragic happenings in their
midst. Here is what one romancer invented about the beginnings of that evil:

> Between ten and eleven P.M. on February 16, 1947, I was at the Blue Bird Cab Of-
> fice and heard some fellows, whose identities I do not know, say that the nigger
> ought to be taken out and lynched. I continued to work until about two A.M. Febru-
> ary 17, 1947, at which time I returned to the Blue Bird Taxi Office where R. C.
> Hurd was working on the switchboard. After I had been at the office for a few min-
> utes, Hurd made several telephone calls to other taxicab companies in Greenville,
> including the Yellow Cab Company, the Commercial Cab Company, and the
> Checker Cab Company. He asked each company to see how many men it wanted to
> go to Pickens. Each time he called he told them who he was. When he finished mak-
> ing the calls, he asked me to drive my cab, a '39 Ford coach which is number
> twenty-nine (29), and carry a load of men to Pickens. I told him that he was "the
> boss." He then got a telephone call from one of the taxicab companies and he told
> them he would not be able to go until Earl Humphries, night dispatcher, got back
> from supper. After Earl Humphries returned from supper, Hurd, myself, Ernest
> Stokes, and Henry Culberson and Shephard, all Blue Bird drivers, got in Culber-
> son's cab, which was a '41 Ford colored blue. We rode to the Yellow Cab Company
> on West Court Street followed by Albert Sims in his cab. At the Yellow Cab Com-
> pany, we met all the other cab drivers from the cab companies. After all got orga-
> nized, the orders given me by R. C. Hurd were to go back and pick up my cab at the
> Blue Bird Office. I would like to say here that Hurd had already made arrangements
> for everybody to meet at the Yellow Cab Company.

These sentences touch on the feature that disquiets many citizens of Greenville: A great deal was going on, at an hour when the city is dead, right under
the sheriff's windows, where a staff was passing the night hours without, presumably, many distractions. They also touch on the chief peril of humanity.
Man, born simple, bravely faces complication and essays it. He makes his mind
into a fine wire that can pry into the interstices between appearances and ex-
tract the secret of the structural intricacy of the universe; he uses the faculty
of imitation he inherits from the ape to create on terms approximating this
intricacy of creation; so there arrive such miracles as the telephone and the
internal-combustion engine, which become the servants of the terrible simplicity of Mr. Hurd, and there we are back at the beginning again.
    A string of about fifteen automobiles lined up for the expedition. All but
one of these were taxicabs. In their statements, the taxi-drivers spoke of the

one that was not a taxi as a "civilian" automobile and of the people who were not taxi-drivers as "civilians." When they got to Pickens County Jail, which lies on the corner of a highway and a side road, about twenty miles from Greenville, some of them parked on the highway and some on the side road. A taxi shone its spotlight on the front door, and they called the jailer down. When they told him they had come for the Negro, he said, "I guess you boys know what you're doing," and got the jail keys for them. The only protest that he seems to have uttered was a request that the men should not use profanity, in case his wife should hear it. He also, with a thoughtfulness of which nobody can complain, pointed out that there were two Negroes in the jail, and indicated which of the two had been guilty of nothing worse than passing a bad check. This surrender of Willie Earle by the jailer has been held by many people to be one of the worst features of the case. It is thought that the jailer showed cowardice in handing the Negro over to the mob, and that his protest about profanity meant that he had strained at a gnat but swallowed a camel. When I visited Pickens County Jail, however, I found that the situation was not as it appeared at a safe distance.

The jail is a mellow red-brick building, planned with much fantasy by somebody who had seen pictures of castles in books and had read the novels of Sir Walter Scott and Mrs. Radcliffe, or had been brought up by people who had read them. It is a building that the Sitwells would enjoy. The front part is in essence like any home in the district, with two stories and a porch running around it. But at the corner looking on the highway and the side road there rises a rounded and crenellated tower, and over both the front door and the side door are arches and crenellations which suggest that the words "dungeon" and "oubliette" were running through the architect's mind, but that it was a kind mind, interested in the picturesque rather than in the retributive. This part of the jail, which seems to be the jailer's residence and office, is joined to a small, oblong building, severe except for a continuance of feudal fantasy along the parapet, with six barred windows on the first story and six on the second. The cells must be extremely small, and it is probable that the jail falls far below modern standards, but there is a pleasantly liberal notice hanging on the side door which announces that visitors' hours are from nine to eleven in the morning and from two to four in the afternoon. The floor of the porch is crumbling. On a wooden table there is a scarlet amaryllis. Beside it stands the jailer's wife, and it can be well understood that her husband would not wish her to hear profanity. She wears spectacles, a pink cotton sunbonnet, a blue-flowered cotton frock, a brown apron streaked with absent-minded cooking. She speaks sweetly but out of abstraction; her bones are as fragile as a bird's, her eyes look right through her spectacles, right through this hot and miserable world, at a wonder. She is a Methodist. God is about her as an enveloping haunt. Such of her as is on earth cooks for the prisoners, who usually number five or six, and for fifteen or sixteen people in the poorhouse up the road. She has a daughter to help her, but the daughter too is gentle and delicate, and has a child to care for. They are tired, gracious, manifestly not cherished by destiny.

As I stood on the porch with them, I reflected that if I were in charge of that jail and a mob came to ask me for a prisoner, I would hand him over without the smallest show of resistance. The jail is far beyond shouting distance of the center of Pickens Town. On one side of it is a large vacant lot. On the other side, beyond a tumble-down fence, a long cabin that seems to be occupied by two or three families stands in a paddock where a couple of lean cows graze. Three women were standing about on the porch with their children, all pale and dispirited. (A startling hint as to the economics of the district was given by some particulars I collected regarding the terms on which most people become inmates of this jail. In Pickens County, a man who is run in for drunkenness is usually fined twelve dollars, with the alternative of going to jail for thirty days; if he has been drunk and disorderly, he gets sixty days or twenty-four dollars; if he has driven an automobile while drunk, he gets ninety days or fifty-two dollars.) Opposite the jail there are larger houses, which may be inhabited by more vigorous people, but the highway is wide and anybody answering the jailer's call for help would have to come a considerable distance without cover. My misgivings about the possibility of showing ideal courage in Pickens County Jail were confirmed when the jailer, Mr. Ed Gilstrap, arrived. He was a stout man in his sixties, with that passive and pliant air of geniality that is characteristic of men who hold small political appointments. He wore khaki overalls with green suspenders, and a derby. When he removed this to greet me, it was disclosed that there ran down his bald scalp a new scar, appallingly deep and about three to four inches long. He did not spontaneously mention the incident that had led to this injury, but, asked about it, he explained that on April 23rd, nine weeks after the lynching, three prisoners had tried to break out of the jail, and while he was preventing them, one had hit him over the head with an iron pipe. What had he done? He had shot at them and killed one and wounded another. The wounded one was still in the hospital. "I wish I had killed him," said Mr. Gilstrap, not unamiably, just with simple realism, "for he was the one who hit me with the pipe." And the third man? "He is still right here in jail," said Mr. Gilstrap. "We try to be fair to him. We're feeding him just the same as before."

The men who took Willie Earle away were in a state of mind not accurately to be defined as blood lust. They were moved by an emotion that is held high in repute everywhere and especially high in this community. All over the world friendship is regarded a sacred bond, and in South Carolina it is held that it should override nearly all other considerations. Greenville had at first felt some surprise that one of the defense attorneys, Mr. Thomas Wofford, had accepted the case. It was not easy for a stranger to understand this surprise, for the case might have been tailored to fit Mr. Wofford; but all the same, surprise was generally felt. When, however, it was realized that the group of defendants he represented included the half-brother of a dead friend of Mr. Wofford, his action was judged comprehensible and laudable. It is not to be wondered at, therefore, if in Greenville a group of very simple people, grieving over the cruel slaughter of a beloved friend, felt that they had the right to take vengeance into their own hands. They would feel it more strongly if there was one among them who believed that all is known, that final judgment is possible, that if Brown was a good man and Willie Earle was a bad man, the will of God regarding these two men was quite plain. It would, of course, be sheer nonsense to pretend that the men, whoever they were, who killed Willie Earle were not affected in their actions by the color of Willie Earle's skin. They certainly did not believe that the law would pursue them—at least, not very far or very fast—for killing a Negro. But it is more than possible that they would have killed Willie Earle even if he had been white, provided they had been sure he had murdered Brown. The romances in statement form throw a light on the state of mind of those who later told of getting Willie Earle into a taxi and driving him to a quiet place where he was to be killed. One says that a taxi-driver sat beside him and "talked nice to him." He does not mean that he talked in a way that Willie Earle enjoyed but that the taxi-drivers thought that what he was saying was elevating. Mr. Hurd described how Willie Earle sat in the back seat of a Yellow Cab and a taxi-driver knelt on the front seat and exhorted him, "Now you have confessed to cutting Mr. Brown, now we want to know who was the other Negro with you." Willie Earle answered that he did not know; and it appears to be doubtful that there was another Negro with him. The taxi-driver continued, in the accents of complacent pietism, "You know we brought you out here to kill you. You don't want to die with a lie in your heart and on your tongue."

Brown's friends were in the state of bereavement that is the worst to bear. Brown was not dead. He was dying, and they could do nothing to save him. They were in that state of frustration that makes atheists at the deathbed of their loved ones curse God. "They then drug the Negro out of the car," said Mr. Hurd in his statement. ("Drug" is certainly a better word than "dragged.") Nobody speaks of doing anything there beside the slaughter-pen; they all speak of hearing things. One heard "the tearing of cloth and flesh," another heard "some licks like they were pounding him with the butt end of a gun." Some heard the Negro say, "Lord, you done killed me." Some saw as well as heard. "I saw," stated one, "Hurd aim the single shotgun towards the ground in the direction of where I judged the Negro was laying and pulled the trigger; I then heard the shot fired. I then heard Hurd ask someone to give him another shell." But Mr. Hurd also is among those who heard but did not do. He did not even see. "When I seen they were going to kill the Negro," he stated, "I just turned around, because I did not want to see it."

People can become accustomed to committing acts of cruelty; recent Europe proves that. But the first act of cruelty disgusts and shames far past the unimaginative man's power of prevision. The men who had joined the lynching party in the mood of righteous men fulfilling a duty did not, according to their statements, enjoy the actual lynching. "I only heard one report from a gun because I immediately drove away," stated one. "I have worked only one night since then," stated another. Fat Joy, another says, was overcome by terror on the way home, and drove up to one of the taxis and said, "Let's drive side by side; I think the law is coming." But it was only the civilian car that had been with them all night. Of their return to the town another states, "I got out at the Southern depot and went into the Southern Café. I got a cup of coffee. The man George, a Greek, behind the counter said, 'Did you get him?' I said, 'Who do you mean?' He said, 'You know.' I said, 'I don't know what you're talking about.' " It was so little like what they had expected that even Mr. Hurd informed the F.B.I. that he thought it had all been a mistake, and recalled that he had never been in trouble for anything before. That the deed sickened them was proved beyond a shadow of doubt in the Court House. When Sam Watt, the assistant but more conspicuous prosecuting attorney, read from the statements the details of what had been done to Willie Earle and described them as the detestable horrors that they were, the defendants were ashamed. They did not like their wives to hear them; and indeed their wives were also sickened. Mr. Hurd's father himself, whose loyalty to Mr. Hurd will be unshakable in eternity, looked down his long nose, so might an Inquisitor look, suddenly smitten with doubt of the purging flame. That hour passed. There were those at the trial who saw to that. But in that hour the defendants surely hated evil and loved good.

Years ago a poet in New York, babbling the indecencies of early parenthood, told a gathering that his child of two already enjoyed having poetry read to him. Someone asked what poetry he read to it. "Shelley and some of my own work," he answered. "That," said the false friend, "gives the kid the whole range." This trial gave the kid the whole range. The judge, J. Robert Martin, Jr., is very local. He knows all about rhetoric and opera. His speech arouses wonder as to how the best sort of stenographer, who takes down by sounds and not by sense, is not wholly baffled in the South, where "You gentlemen must apportion your time" is converted into "Yo' ge'men, must appo'tion yo' taiaime," with a magnificent vibrato on the diphthongs and a strong melodic line to the whole. He is so good that though he is local he expands the local meaning, and recalls that the great Southerners are great men to the whole world. He has humor but hates a clown. He would have given much to have had the court fully decorous; when an important personage of the region took his seat on the dais and threw his raincoat over the law books on the Judge's table, it irked him. His love of handsomeness, and fine manners extends to the intellectual world.

His charge to the jury was both powerful and beautifully shaped. Throughout the trial he stood on the skyline, proclaiming his hostility to lawlessness and his determination to keep his court uncontaminated, with a solid and unremitting positiveness that must have made him a personal enemy of every reactionary in the state.

The leader for the prosecution was nominally Robert T. Ashmore, the Greenville County solicitor, a gentle and courteous person. But the leading prosecuting attorney was Sam Watt, who comes from the neighboring town of Spartanburg, a lawyer of high reputation throughout the South, a much more dynamic person. He was assigned to the case by the Attorney General of the State of South Carolina at the suggestion of the Governor, about ten days after the F.B.I. men had gone in. When he arrived, the preliminaries of the case were over; and they had been conducted in a disastrous fashion. The taking of statements from accused persons is one of the most delicate processes of police work. All over the world, police forces are likely to become corrupt and tyrannous, and are then apt to coerce accused persons into making confessions. This is generally recognized. It is very hard to examine accused persons in places that are not more or less private, and therefore it is very hard to know when they have or have not been coerced. While there is no reason to believe that the F.B.I. men used any illegitimate methods, it is true that they took these statements in circumstances that did not protect them from the charge that the defendants gave them under duress. It is also true that the statements amounted to frank confessions of participation in a capital crime. It is actually not at all uncommon for criminals who have committed acts which touch them deeply to make such confessions. But this is not so generally recognized. So this was very dubious material to bring before a jury, and indeed at least one of the defense attorneys flatly declared that they would be fools to believe that twenty-six men would incriminate themselves unless under compulsion. But the mishandling went a great deal farther than that. The statements, which were not sworn, might have been supplemented when the defendants applied to be released under bond, for it was perfectly possible to demand that the applicants should again recite their connection with the crime in the form of sworn affidavits prepared by their own attorneys. This had not been done. The defendants had been turned loose unconditionally, and most of them, by the time Sam Watt came into the case, had returned to their duties as taxi-drivers. Any stranger visiting the town of Greenville during late February, March, April, or early May of this year was as likely as not to be driven from the station by a person awaiting trial for murder and conspiracy to murder. But it is not necessary to bring the stranger into it. The citizens of Greenville also used these taxis, and it would be interesting to know how they liked the idea.

A prosecutor who introduced these statements in court would be a very lucky man if he could support them by strong corroborative evidence, and a

very unlucky one if he could not. Mr. Watt and Mr. Ashmore had at their dis-
posal nothing like the evidence that might convince a jury that these statements had not been obtained by duress, or, rather, prevent the jury from using
a suspicion of duress as an excuse for an acquittal. It was true that one of the
defendants had handed over to the police a gun that was damaged, and that the
gun was of the same make as a gun that several men had described in their
statements as being used by one of their number to beat the dying Negro until
it broke under the force of his blows. This, however, was not such satisfactory
evidence as it appears, because the man who was supposed to have broken the
gun on the Negro's body did not himself admit in his statement that he had
used it to beat the Negro, and each of the statements was evidence only against
the man who made it and not against the men mentioned in it. This is not mere
legal fussiness but a sensible provision, as the statements were not sworn and
could not have been subjected to cross-examination by the attorneys of the
mentioned persons unless the makers of the statements went into the witness
box, which they did not do. There was also the testimony of one Roy Stansell,
proprietor of a tourist camp on the Pickens Highway, at which some of the
taxis had stopped. This merely proved that the expedition had been on the road;
it did not connect the men with the jail break or the murder. There was also the
unfortunate U. G. Fowler, a taxi-driver who gave evidence that he had been
asked to join the party and had refused. But even he had heard the purpose of
the expedition announced only by a voice to which he could not pin a name.
There must have been a great many taxi-drivers who could have given much
more pointed evidence along these lines. Why they did not do so was revealed
before the end of the trial. U. G. Fowler was set upon as he was driving along a
country road, beaten, and threatened with death. He appeared before a local
judge and made complaint, but the judge refused to swear out a warrant for the
arrest of the men who had beaten him. So Mr. Fowler left town.

   It cannot be said, therefore, that the prosecution had put together a valid
argument for a conviction. Timid muddling by someone or by some people who
were not only muddlers but had an eye on the political weather had drawn
most of its claws. As the case was handled, the jury cannot be blamed for returning an acquittal. If it had convicted on any of the indictments, even on the
least, which related to conspiracy, either the verdict would have been reversed
by a superior court or a very dangerous precedent would have been established. The trial had not the pleasing pattern, the agreeable harmony and
counterpoint, of good legal process, however much the Judge tried to redeem it.
But whether the jury returned their verdict of not guilty because they recognized the weakness of the State's case, it was hard to guess. It was the habit of
certain people connected with the case to refer to the jury with deep contempt,
as a parcel of boobs who could be seduced into swallowing anything by anybody who knew how to tickle them up by the right mixture of brutish prejudice

and corny sentimentality; and it was odd to notice that the people who most despised the jury were those who most despised the Negroes. To me, the jurymen
looked well built and well groomed; and they stayed awake, which is the first
and most difficult task of a juror, although they, like the attorneys, kept their
coats on when the heat was a damp, embracing fever. I marvelled at nothing
about this jury except its constitution. As Greenville is a town with, it is said,
twenty-five millionaires and a large number of prosperous and well-educated
people, it may have seemed peculiar that the jury should consist of two salesmen, a farmer, a mechanic, a truck driver, and seven textile workers. Some of
the prosperous citizens had indeed appeared on the list of the veniremen from
which the jurors were selected, but they had been singularly fortunate in being
challenged by the attorneys. The unpopular task of deciding a lynching case
therefore fell to an unfavored group who had not the money to hire a bodyguard or to leave the town. They would, let us remember, have been in a most
difficult position if they had returned a verdict of guilty. They might not have
been murdered, like Willie Earle, or beaten up, like U. G. Fowler, but they would
never have been able to take a taxi again with an easy mind, and that would be
a considerable inconvenience in Greenville. It is one of the mysteries of this
case that the trial was not shifted to another town.

Of the prosecuting attorneys, Mr. Ashmore made a speech that was not very
spirited but was conscientious and accepted the moral values common to civilized people without making any compromise. Sam Watt, who has a deep and
passionate loathing of violence and disorder, and who is such a good attorney
that the imperfections of the case must have vexed him to his soul, handled the
situation in his own way by using the statements to build up a picture of the
lynching in all its vileness. It was while the defendants were listening to this
speech that they hated evil and that they desired to renounce it. It was a great,
if highly local, speech, and it is possible that some of its effect will survive,
though the close of the case cancelled it for the moment. That cancellation was
due to the remarkable freedom of two of the defense attorneys from the moral
values accepted by Mr. Ashmore and Mr. Watt. The two other defense attorneys
accepted them, one wholly, the other partly. Mr. Bradley Morrah, Jr., accepted
them wholly, Mr. Ben Bolt partly.
    Mr. Bradley Morrah, Jr., is a young man who is a member of the State Leg-
islature. He was representing a strange defendant, his cousin, Mr. John B.
Marchant, who is twenty-eight and the son of a widow of good family who is
greatly loved in the town. Mr. Marchant was the driver of the "civilian car" that
accompanied the string of taxicabs to the lynching. According to his story, he
was leading the contemplative life in a café opposite the Yellow Cab office in the
early hours of February 17th when he saw the expedition forming and joined
it out of sheer curiosity. He was extremely disconcerted when he discovered its

object, and though he did not dare leave the party, he did not approach the scene of action but waited some distance away. Mr. Marchant apparently spends much of his time accompanying the sheriff's men on their night work just as a hobby, and he certainly visited the sheriff's office next day and volunteered a statement before there was any need. There is no reason to disbelieve his account.

Both Mr. Marchant and Mr. Morrah gave the impression that they were stranded in the wrong century, like people locked in a train that has been shunted onto a siding. Mr. Morrah was as old-fashioned in appearance as Governor Dewey; he looked like a dandy of 1890. He was very likable, being small and delicately made yet obviously courageous; and there was nothing unlikable in his oratory. He told the court that he had known his cousin for twenty-five years and knew that he had never had a vicious thought, and he wished that it was possible for him to take John Marchant's heart out of his breast and turn it over in his hand so that the jury could see that there was not an evil impulse in it. He was going on to say that he could picture John Marchant "with his mother, my aunt," when Sam Watt rose and said, "I object. There is no evidence about the Marchant family." The Judge allowed the objection. Mr. Morrah altered the phrase to "I can picture him surrounded by his loved ones," and said that he "stood firmly bottomed, like a ship," and warned the jury that if they convicted him, the facts "would rankle in the hearts of men throughout the state, from the rock-ribbed brow of Caesar's Head to the marshes of Fort Sumter" and someplace else on the sea, and that "the ghosts of Hampton's men would rise to haunt you." But there was nothing barbarous in his speech. He was a transparently honest and kindly and dutiful person, and he depreciated no civilized standard, though it was startling when he ended his speech with the statement that the prosecution of Marchant reminded him of words spoken two thousand years ago, "Forgive them, Father, for they know not what they do." Mr. Marchant was really not that good.

But great play was made with the Scripture; it might almost be called ball play. The Bible belonging to Greenville County Court House is in terrible shape. Like many Bibles, it has a flounce, or valance, of leather protecting its edges, and this is torn and crumbling, while its boards are cracked, and small wonder. Its quietest hours are when it is being sworn upon; at any other time, it is likely to be snatched up from the small stand on which it rests, which is like that used for potted plants in some homes, and waved in the air, held to an attorney's breast, thrust out over the jury box, and hurled back to its resting place in a convulsion of religious ecstasy. Some of the Bible-tossing in this case was inspired by sincere conviction. But it looked as if a great deal was done in cold sacrilege to impress the jury, who were assumed to be naïvely pious. This was only one of the cynical efforts to exploit the presumed naïveté of the twelve men in the box. The subjects of these efforts were, as well as religion, alcohol, the hatred of the state for the nation, the hatred of the South for the North, and the hatred of the white man for the Negro. This last the Judge had expressly ruled should not be mentioned in court. Of the four defense attorneys, Mr. Morrah obeyed this ruling, Mr. John Bolt Culbertson and Mr. Thomas Wofford openly defied it, and Mr. Ben Bolt, who stood somewhere in the scale between Mr. Morrah and the other two, skated round it.

Mr. Ben Bolt is a slow-moving, soft-voiced, gray-haired person of noble appearance, who is said to make many speeches about the common man. The industrial development of the South is evidently producing the same crop of liberal attorneys that were produced in England and the Northern states in the similar stage of their development. Mr. Bolt began his speech by a plea for racial tolerance, celebrating the life of dear old Aunt Hester, who aided his dear mother to guide his footsteps and who now lies in a grave that he often visits, always with the feeling that he ought to take his shoes off, since it is hallowed ground. Laying hold of the exhausted Bible, he changed the subject and recalled that the Supreme Court has ruled the Bible to be part of the common law of the State of South Carolina, and he pointed out that the Bible condemns conviction without several witnesses. It was not necessary to bring in the Bible to explain that, but Mr. Bolt was certainly going about his proper business when he proceeded to demonstrate the insufficiency of the evidence against the defendants. He passed on, however, to make an attack on the credibility of the witness U. G. Fowler that was embarrassing in its fatuity and seeming insincerity. This witness had been asked what his initials stood for, and had amazed the court by saying that he did not know, that they did not stand for anything but themselves. To people who questioned him outside court, he said that his mother had called him after a brother of hers and had never explained to him what his full name was. I am told by local experts that the uncle was probably called Huger, like many people in parts of South Carolina nearer the sea; it is the name of a Southern family of Huguenot origin, and it is pronounced "U.G." by the simple folk who have borrowed it. Mr. Bolt tried to disseminate another explanation. "That don't sound exactly Southern to me," he said. "Those initials certainly don't stand for Robert E. Lee or Stonewall Jackson." He was attempting to engender prejudice against this person by suggesting that his parents had christened him Ulysses Grant. This eminently sensible person was talking what he obviously knew to be humbug, out of his fathomless contempt for the jury. How little that school of thought realizes the dangers of contempt was demonstrated by a remark he made when he was representing the lynching as an episode that nobody but the meddlesome federal authorities would ever have thought of making a fuss over. When he was speaking of the F.B.I. agents, he said, "Why, you would have thought someone had found a new atomic bomb," but "all it was was a dead nigger boy." This is not a specifically Southern attitude. All over the world there are people who may use the atomic bomb because they have forgotten that it is our duty to regard all lives, however alien and even repellent, as equally sacred.

Mr. John Bolt Culbertson's speeches were untainted by any regard for the values of civilization. He went all the way over to the dead-nigger-boy school of thought. Mr. Culbertson is a slender, narrow-chested man with a narrow head. His sparse hair is prematurely white, his nose is sharp, and his face is colorless except for his very pink lips. He wears rimless spectacles and his lashes are white. The backs of his hands are thickly covered with fine white hairs. In certain lights, he gives the impression of being covered with frost. He has a great reputation in the South as a liberal. He is the local attorney for the C.I.O. and has worked actively for it. He has also been a friend to the emancipation of the Negroes and has supported their demands for better education and the extension of civil rights. He recently made an address to Negro veterans, which took courage on his part and gave them great happiness. He is one of the very few white men in these parts who shake hands with Negroes and give them the prefix of Mr. or Mrs. or Miss. Not long ago, an article in the *New Republic* hailed him as one of the true liberal leaders of the South. Many young people in Greenville who wish to play a part in the development of the New South look to him as an inspiring teacher, and many Negroes feel a peculiar devotion to him. Mr. Culbertson belongs to the school of oratory that walks up and down in front of the jury box. At the climactic points of his speeches, he adopts a crouching stance, puts his hands out in front of him, parallel to one another, and moves them in a rapid spin, as if he were a juggler and they were plates. Finally he shoots one hand forward and propels his argument with it. His choreography was especially vigorous when he was putting in a little work on the jury's possible prejudice against alcohol. He was attempting to discredit the evidence of the tourist-camp proprietor who had identified the alleged lynchers. His knees went down. "Doesn't this man"—his hands went forward—"own a honky-tonk . . . a camp"—his knees went lower; his hands came further forward—"where they sell"—his right hand shot out; his voice caught in his throat with horror and then cracked across space like a whip—"BEER?" It is not illegal to sell beer in South Carolina. I do not think that Mr. Culbertson, though a man of most sober habits, is a teetotaller. Had the outburst been simply an unlovely piece of hypocrisy, based on a profound contempt for his fellow-men, it would have sounded much the same; and it would have sounded equally irreconcilable with liberalism as that word is generally understood.

Mr. Culbertson pandered to every folly that the jurors might be nursing in their bosoms. He spoke of the defendants as "these So'th'n boys." Only two or three could be considered boys. The ages of the others ranged from the late twenties to the fifties. It was interesting, by the way, to note how all the attorneys spoke with a much thicker Southern accent when they addressed the jury than when they were talking with their friends. Mr. Culbertson attacked the

F.B.I. agents in terms that either meant nothing or meant that it was far less important to punish a murder than to keep out the federal authorities. He made the remark, strange to hear in a court of law, "If a Democratic administration could do that to us, what would a Republican administration do to us down here?" He appeared later to be declaring that the F.B.I. had been sent in by the administration to provide an anti-lynching case to win the Northern vote, in a Democratic seat that was not likely to go Republican even after a lynching prosecution. He himself, it may be noted, is a former F.B.I. agent, and was, it is said, famous for his zeal. He used his hope that the jury were xenophobes to make an attack on the freedom of the press. He pointed to the press table and declared that because of this fussy insistence on the investigation of a murder there was now a trial to which Northern papers had sent representatives; and the implication was that they had come for the purpose of mocking and insulting the South. "*Lai-ai-aife* and *Tai-ai-aime*," he chanted with the accent that was so much stronger in the courtroom than it sounded in the hotel lobby or the drugstore, "have sent representatives." The Judge pointed out that Mr. Culbertson had no evidence of the existence of these people and that they therefore could not be discussed.

The thread on which these pearls were strung appeared to be the argument that the murder of Willie Earle was of very slight importance except for its remote political consequences. Mr. Culbertson was to prove that he did not give this impression inadvertently. He went into his crouching stance, his hands were spinning, he shone with frosty glee, exultantly he cried, "Willie Earle is dead, and I wish more like him was dead." There was a delighted, giggling, almost coquettish response from the defendants and some of the spectators. Mr. Hurd and his father looked fortified. There was a gasp from others of different mind. Thunderously, the Judge called him to order: "You confine yourself to my ruling or I'll stop you from arguing to the jury." Culbertson, smiling at the defendants, almost winking at them, said, "I didn't refer to Willie Earle as a Negro." When the Judge bade him be careful, he continued, still flirting with his audience, "There's a law against shooting a dog, but if a mad dog were loose in my community, I would shoot the dog and let them prosecute me." A more disgusting incident cannot have happened in any court of law in any time.

The attitude of Greenville toward this speech was disconcerting. Prosperous Greenville did not like it, but it likes very little that Mr. Culbertson does, and it explained that one could expect nothing better from him, because he is a liberal. If it was objected that this was precisely not the kind of speech that could be expected from a liberal, this Greenville answered that it was a horrid speech, and that liberals are horrid, an argument that cannot be pursued very far. The response of the liberal section of Greenville was not any easier to take. The liberals made no attempt to conceal the important fact that two of the defendants were close connections of a C.I.O. official. But they insisted that Mr. Culbertson is sincerely liberal, and apparently, if they rejected him, there is no local liberal of anything like his energy to take his place. To rationalize their continued acceptance of him, they had to adopt a theory that will do them no moral good at all. They admitted that it would have been awkward for his relations with the local C.I.O. if he had refused to appear for the defendants, and they claimed that he was right not to refuse, because nothing is of equal importance to the necessity of introducing the C.I.O. into the South. When they were asked why he used such squalid arguments in court, they replied that it is a lawyer's duty to do everything he can to win his case for his clients, and that as he believed these arguments would appeal to the jury, he was obliged to use them. That is, of course, pure moonshine. In no system of jurisprudence is there a moral obligation on a lawyer who accepts the task of defending an accused murderer to go so near justifying murder as John Bolt Culbertson did in his passage about Willie Earle and the mad dog. This recalls many like accommodations that were made by lawyers in Italy and Germany during the early days of the Fascist and Nazi Parties. They relaxed their traditional principles and practice because the establishment of the Party seemed a necessity that had precedence over all others. But it is not generally understood that the C.I.O. is the kind of party that demands such sacrifices.

If Mr. Culbertson's conduct of the case has confused and depraved the standards of young liberal Greenville, it has done something just as unpleasant to the Negroes. The connection that links the defendants and the C.I.O. is known to every Negro in town. The uneducated Negroes have invented their own legend on the subject. Mr. Culbertson's home, they believe, done belong to C.I.O., and C.I.O. done say it put Mr. Culbertson's furniture right out on the sidewalk if Mr. Culbertson don't save their folks' good name. Then they laugh, with a roaring, jeering cynicism that is a humiliation to every white man and woman in the land.

It was for the speech made by the fourth defense attorney, Mr. Thomas Wofford, that Greenville apologized most unhappily, though most laconically. Mr. Wofford is a person whom the town likes, or, to put it more accurately, for whom it feels an uneasy emotional concern. He is a man in his late thirties, red-haired, lightly built, and quick on his feet, intelligent, nerve-ridden, well mannered, with a look in his eyes like a kicking horse. He must have been a very attractive and hopeful boy. He has always been fortunate. His uncle and his father-in-law are famous lawyers, and he has had the brains to make the best of the opportunities these relationships have given him. He is said to have political ambitions. In the preliminary stages of the case, when the Judge was compiling a list of questions to be put to the veniremen to determine their suitability as jurors in this case, Sam Watt desired that they should be asked if they were members of any "secret organization, lodge, or association." Mr. Wofford objected, on the grounds that such a question might be "embarrassing."

All the defense attorneys exaggerated their Southern accents and assumed a false ingenuousness when they addressed the jury, but none more so than Mr. Wofford. This elegantly attired and accomplished person talked as if he had but the moment before taken his hands off the plow; and he was careful to mop the sweat from his brow, because it is well known that the simple admire an orator who gives out even from the pores. He excelled his colleagues not only in this play acting but in his contempt for the jury. He assumed that they hated strangers, as the stupid do. He assumed that they would be stingy about money, as the poor often are. So he referred to the F.B.I. investigation as a "case of what I call 'meddler's itch,'" pointed out the F.B.I. agents who were sitting in court, and cried out in indignation because the State had closed its case four days before, "and here they are, staying at government expense." He must have known quite well that the F.B.I. would only be performing its duty if it ordered its agents to stay till the end of the case, so that they could hear the attorneys' comments on their activities. He was against the F.B.I.; he was also against the local representatives of the law. "If you're going to enforce all the laws, why don't you prosecute the jailer?" he asked. "It took," he cried scornfully, "a nigger undertaker to find out there had been a lynching." Everybody and everything was wrong, it seemed, except murderers and the idea of murder. Like Mr. Culbertson, he disregarded the Judge's ruling that no alleged action of Willie Earle was to be mentioned as affording "justification, mitigation, or excuse" for the lynching. It was rumored in the recess preceding Mr. Wofford's speech that he meant to flout this ruling, and he did so with evident deliberation. He said, "Mr. Watt argues, 'Thou shalt not kill.' I wonder if Willie Earle had ever read that statement." This was as flagrant a defense of the lynching as Mr. Culbertson's remark "Willie Earle is dead, and I wish more like him was dead" and the allusion to the mad dog. But it was much more dangerous, because it was not obviously disgusting. Mr. Culbertson was plainly seeking to please and enroll as allies people in court and outside who could not for one moment be thought of as representing the highest traditions of Greenville or the South. Mr. Wofford was careful to look and speak in such a manner that people who did not fully understand the implications of his defense might think he was upholding those traditions. When the Judge checked him and ordered the remark stricken off the records, he showed a remarkable lack of deference to the Court, but again in such a way that many people might have thought that he was defending the cause of justice and democracy. And it would be interesting to know what he was really defending. "We people get along pretty well," he said, "until they start interfering with us in Washington and points North," and he spoke of the Northern armies that had laid waste the South in the Civil War. He abused the "Northern agitators, radio commentators, and certain publications" for interfering in this case. He said that "they refer to us as 'a sleepy little town.' They say we are a backward state and poor—and we are. But this state is ours. To the historian, the South is the Old South. To the poet, it is the Sunny South. To the prophet, it is the New South. But to us, it is *our* South. I wish to God they'd leave us alone." This would be an attitude that one would respect in the case of the ordinary citizen of Greenville. But in view of Mr. Wofford's desire not to embarrass secret organizations, his hostility to all law-enforcement agencies, and his attitude toward murder, it would be interesting to know what he wanted to be left alone to do.

It would not be fair to chronicle the speeches of the last two defense attorneys, without emphasizing that they were in no way representative of Greenville. Some hours after Mr. Wofford had spoken, a man that Greenville looks up to paused in the lobby of the principal hotel to say to me, "I would like you to know that we were very disappointed in Tom's speech. We hoped he would do better." A nice man was putting something nicely. Greenville was more at ease the next day, the tenth day of the trial, when Judge Martin made his charge to the jury. The courtroom was fuller than ever before. There were now heavy showers, but the heat had not broken, so the women were still in summer dresses and the men in their shirts, while the rain fell in rods past the windows. In the front row of the seats, within the bar of the court, were the Judge's wife and three daughters, all spectacular beauties, with magnificent black eyes and silky black curls. The youngest child, who is not yet in her teens, was dressed in a pink-checked muslin frock and had a special charm. The Judge's charge to the jury struck oddly on the ears of strangers, for by the law of South Carolina the Judge cannot comment on the evidence; he must do no more than analyze the law applying to the evidence and define the verdicts that it is possible to return against the accused persons. It is not easy to see the purpose of the law. If the intention is to prevent the common man from being hoodwinked by his superiors, there is equal reason for forbidding the prosecuting and defending attorneys from making closing speeches. For what it was, Judge Martin's charge was masterly, but it represented a legal position very favorable to the defendants. They were charged with murder and conspiracy, and there was very little evidence except their own statements. No man had in his statement confessed to murder. Nearly all had confessed to conspiracy. But, as the Judge put it, "the State cannot establish a conspiracy by the alleged statements of the individual defendants alone." However, the Judge also seemed at some pains to make the jury understand that if they acquitted the defendants on the charges relating to murder and found them guilty of conspiracy, the sentences passed on them could not exceed ten years.

Shortly after three o'clock, the jury went out to consider their verdict and the Judge left the bench. He had directed that the defendants need not be taken out, and might sit in court and visit with their families and friends. So now the court turned into a not enjoyable party, at which one was able to observe more closely certain personalities of the trial. There was Mrs. Brown, the widow of the murdered taxi-driver, a spare, spectacled woman of the same austere type as the Hurds. She was dressed in heavy but smart mourning, with a veiled hat tipped sharply on one side, and she was chewing gum. So, too, was the professional bondsman who was the animating spirit of the committee that had raised funds for the defense of the defendants, a vast, blond, baldish man with the face of a brooding giant baby; but he was not genteel, as she was—he opened his mouth so wide at every chew that his gum became a matter of public interest. It had been noticeable during the trial that whenever the Judge showed hostility to the introduction of race hatred into the proceedings, this man's chewing became particularly wide and vulpine. A judge from another local court, and various other Greenville citizens, drifted up to the press table and engaged the strangers in defensive conversation. The Southern inferiority complex took charge. They supposed that an English visitor would be shocked by the lynching, but it was impossible for anybody to understand who had always lived in a peaceable community where there was no race problem. Would I please remember that when colored people were killed in race riots in the North nobody said anything about it, and that it was only when these things happened in the South that people made a fuss about them, because all Northern congressmen were voted for by black men? They added that anyway they were sure that my Northern friends had told me very unkind things about the South. I said what I had been saying constantly since my arrival: that lately Europe had not been really what one could call a peaceable community, and that my standards of violence were quite high and that the lynching party did not seem very important to me as an outbreak of violence but that it was important as an indication of misery; that we English had a very complex and massive race problem in South Africa, where one of the indubitably great men of the British Empire, General Smuts, professed views on the color bar which would strike Greenville as fairly reactionary; and that my Northern friends, on hearing that I was going to the lynching party, had remarked that while Southern lawlessness has a pardonable origin in a tragic past, Northern lawlessness has none and is therefore far more disgraceful. What I said brought no response. We might have been sitting each in a glass case built by history. I laid hold of arguments that had once been clothed in flesh, that still to me were of the heart as well as of the brain; I said that my father had settled in the South, that his first wife had been a Southern lady, that he spoke of her dead goodness and grace as partly her own and partly her local heritage, and that he had brought me up to think of the South as a paradise and of the reconstruction period as hell. Still nothing registered. Here was a curtain cut of the same stuff as hangs between England and Ireland.

I was glad when the common attention was distracted by Mr. Hurd. Everybody was now circulating freely in the court. Fat Joy seemed to be everywhere.

Two of the attorneys and a friend had sat in the jury box for some time, but they had gone and two of the defendants had taken their place and were sitting with their feet up on the ledge. David Fredenthal, the *Life* artist, had been passing about the court making sketches from various points of view, and now he had come to ask Mr. Hurd, who was in his usual place, not far from the press table, if he would sit for him. Mr. Hurd became quite wooden with shyness, but his attorney and his father urged him to have his picture drawn. He came forward and sat stiffly in a chair within the bar of the court. It could be seen that he was really delighted. Mr. Hurd's father hovered about him, watching the artist with the greatest curiosity but too well mannered to come and look over his shoulder, as the hardier Mr. Culbertson and I were doing. Gradually, people noticed that Mr. Hurd was being drawn, and several of the defendants came and stood beside us. They became quite silent. Mr. Fredenthal is a draftsman of the modern school, with the vagrant, caricaturing line of Feliks Topolski, and they were plain folks who like their art strictly representational. After the drawing was finished, Mr. Hurd's father very politely asked if he might see it. When he was given it, he stood still and looked down on it for a minute. His son asked for it and he handed it to him without saying a word. This was probably one of the most acutely disappointing moments in their lives. He returned it to his father, who handed it back to the artist with a bow, forcing his features into a courteous smile. Then they rose and went away and sat down in their usual seats, staring in front of them. The defendants who had been watching the artist then took up the drawing, seemingly to make sure that it really was as crazy as they had thought it from a distance, set it down with a murmur of thanks, and drifted away.

Edward Clark, the *Life* photographer, should have been a novelist; he detects the significant characters and episodes in the welter of experience as an Indian guide sees game in the forest. He said to me, "I want you to come and talk to one of the defendants and look at his hands." He took me over to a fair man in his early thirties, a plump and smiling person in his shirtsleeves, who looked rather like Leon Errol. It was his wife who came daily to the court with five children. Clark introduced us and said, "Now show us what you have got on your hands." The man held them out proudly. On the four fingers of his left hand he had tattooed, just above the knuckles, the letters "L-O-V-E." And on the four fingers of his right hand he had the letters "H-A-T-E." Then he flipped up the thumbs. "T" was on the left thumb, "O" was on the right. "Love to hate," he read. He had done it himself, he said; he had a tattooing outfit. The more you washed the letters, the brighter they got. He had done it when he was seventeen, he said, and when I asked him why, he broke into laughter and said, "Lack of sense, I reckon, lack of sense. Leastways, that's what a lot of folks round here would tell you." This man had married a girl of thirteen ten years before. She had had a child every year, of which six were living. They lived in a street on the outskirts of Greenville which is counted one of its worst sections, though to the stranger's eye it looks pleasant enough, since the houses are set far apart in a pretty countryside. But the houses are old and poorly built and unsanitary, and the psychological climate is at once depressed and ferocious. The poor white population lived there, but as prosperity waxed in the twenties they moved out to better quarters and the Negroes moved in. Then came the depression, and the whites lost their jobs or their pay was cut, and they were glad to get back to their old quarters whenever they could, even though it meant living beside the Negroes, whom they hated more than ever, because they now were anxious to do the menial jobs that till then had been left to the Negroes. This man had grown up during this horrible period when blacks and whites snarled at each other like starved dogs fighting over a garbage can. There was no necessity to darken his world. But people who talked like Mr. Culbertson and Mr. Wofford had given him fears he need never have felt. "Don't take my picture," he said to Clark. "These days I drive a truck up North and I know what they would do to me if they knew I'd been in this."

A red-headed defendant was telling us that his old schoolteacher had sent him twenty dollars to help pay for his defense, when it was announced that the Judge was going out to dinner and would not be back until half past nine. The defendants were taken to the jail to have their dinner; it was there discovered that during the courtroom party they had acquired several quarts of rye. The press went out after them, because it was obvious that the jury, even if they came to a decision, could not announce their verdict till the Judge returned. At a little after half past eight, it was known that the jury had sounded its buzzer, which meant that they had made up their minds. This certainly meant that the accused persons had been acquitted of all charges. The jurymen had been out only five hours and a quarter, and they would have had to stay out much longer than that before all of them would have consented to a conviction; and they would have had to stay out much longer before they could have announced that they had failed to agree. This last, which would have led to the declaration of a mistrial, was what many people hoped for, since it would have meant that the defendants were not flattered by a proclamation of innocence, while at the same time there was no conviction, no risk of race riots, and no breach of tradition. But it was hardly any use hoping for this, since no juror who stood against an acquittal could be certain that some other juror would not betray him; and, as the fate of Mr. U. G. Fowler had shown, a juror would not be unduly pusillanimous if he let that consideration weigh with him. The press knew what the verdict was and knew there was still an hour till the Judge would return. Yet we knew too that it is not what happens that matters so much as how it happens. Every event of any magnitude changes life unpredictably. There would by now be something happening in the Court House that we could not have guessed would happen. So we got up from the table in the hotel dining room, where they were serving a beautiful meal that never was eaten, and ran into the street and through a heavy rain and up the Court House steps and along the corridor and up the staircase into the courtroom, and there it was, the thing we could not have guessed.

The place was given up to gloom. All the spectators who were not connected with the case had long since gone home to supper, and so had most of the defendants' friends, and those members of the defendants' families who had duties at their homes. The defendants had not yet been brought back from jail. So their wives and fathers and mothers had been sitting in the hall, now empty and full of shadows, looking at the press table, where there were no journalists; at the bench, where there was no judge; at the jury box, where there was no jury; and a fear of nothingness had come upon them. The wives were huddled in twos and threes, and most of these child-bearing children were weeping bitterly. The girl in green was sitting in the universal attitude of anguish, her head bent, the fingers of one hand spread along the hairline on her brow, the wrist brought down on the bridge of her nose. Mr. Hurd's father sat slowly turning his straw hat around and around on his knee, looking down his long nose at the floor. The windows showed us the sluices of the rain pouring between us and a night palpitating and dyed scarlet by an electric sign on the hotel. Up in the gallery, thirteen Negroes were sitting in attitudes of fatigue and despair. Behind them, three windows looked on a night whitened by the lights of Main Street.

This had been a miserable case for these Negroes. They had not even been able to have the same emotional release that would have been granted them if Willie Earle had been an innocent victim, a sainted martyr. It happened that the night Willie Earle had hired Brown to take him into Pickens County, he went into a store in the Negro quarter, carrying a cheap cardboard suitcase. He accidentally dropped it on the floor at the feet of an older man, a university graduate who is one of the most influential figures in the Negro community of Greenville. The suitcase burst open and the contents were scattered all over the floor. The older man was surprised when Willie made no move to bend down and repack his suitcase, looked at him, saw that he was very drunk, so himself knelt down and did it for him. Hence the higher grades of colored people, though referring to Earle with admirable charity and understanding as a maimed soul who acted without knowledge, made no issue of the case, as they would have done if the victim had been normal and blameless. It happened that the only constructive proposal concerning this morass of misery stretching out to infinity round this case that I heard during my stay at Greenville came from a Negro. That, oddly enough, was a plea for the extension of the Jim Crow system. "There is nothing I wish for more," he said, "than a law that would prohibit Negroes from riding in taxicabs driven by white men. They love to do it. We all love to do it. Can't you guess why? Because it is the only time we can pay a white man to act as a servant to us. And that does something to me, even though I can check up on myself and see what's happening. I say to myself, 'This is fine! I'm hiring this white man! He's doing a chore for me!' " He threw his head back and breathed deeply and patted his chest, to show how he felt. "If riding in a white taxicab does that to me, what do you think it does to Negroes who haven't been raised right or are full of liquor? Then queer things happen, mighty queer things. Killing is only one of them." It is apparently the practice in many other Southern towns, such as Savannah, that whites use only taxis with white drivers and Negroes use only taxis with Negro drivers.

No more Negroes went into the gallery. There were still only thirteen when the verdict was given. But the courtroom slowly filled up during the hour and a half that elapsed before the Judge's return. The bondsman who had organized the defense fund came in and sat with a friend, who also resembled a giant baby; they whispered secrets in each other's ears, each screening his mouth with a huge hand while the other hand held, at arm's length, a tiny cigarette, as if a wreath of smoke could trouble their massiveness. The widow Brown ranged the aisles hungrily, evidently believing that an acquittal would ease her much more than it possibly could. The attorneys came in one by one and sat at their tables. Mr. Wofford was, as they say down there, happy as a skunk, flushed and gay and anecdotal. He and his group made a cheerful foreground to the benches where the wives of the defendants, fortified by their returning friends, wept less than before but still were weeping. As one of the Southern newspapermen looked about him at the scene, his face began to throb with a nervous twitch. At length, the Judge was seen standing at the open door of his chambers, and the defendants were brought into court. They were all very frightened. They bore themselves creditably, but their faces were pinched with fear. Mr. Hurd, though he was still confused, seemed to be asking himself if he had not been greatly deceived. Fat Joy was shifting along, wearing sadness as incongruously as fat men do. As they sat down, their wives clasped them in their arms, and they clung together, melting in the weakness of their common fear. The Judge came onto the bench and took some measures for the preservation of order in the court. He directed that all people should be cleared from the seats within the bar of the court unless they had a direct interest in the case or were of the press. The bondsman who had organized the defense committee was in such a seat and did not at first rise to go, but the court officials made him go. The people thus ejected stood around the walls of the room. Those by the windows turned to look at the downpour of the rain, which was now torrential. The Judge ordered all the officers of the court to take up positions in the aisles and to be ready for anyone who started a demonstration. They stood there stiffly, and the defendants' wives, as if this were the first sign of a triumph for severity, trembled and hid their faces. The jury entered. One juror was smil-

ing; one was looking desperately ashamed; the others looked stolid and secre-
tive, as they had done all through the trial. They handed the slips on which
they had recorded their verdicts to the clerk of the court, who handed them to
the Judge. He read them through to himself, and a flush spread over his face.

As soon as the clerk had read the verdicts aloud and the Judge had left the
bench and the courtroom, which he did without thanking the jury, the courtroom became, in a flash, something else. It might have been a honky-tonk, a
tourist camp where they sold beer, to use Mr. Culbertson's comminatory
phrase. The Greenville citizens who had come as spectators were filing out quietly and thoughtfully. Whatever their opinions were, they were not to recover
their usual spirits for some days. As they went, they looked over their shoulders
at the knot of orgiastic joy that had instantly been formed by the defendants
and their supporters. Mr. Hurd and his father did not give such spectacular
signs of relief as the others. They gripped each other tightly for a moment, then
shook hands stiffly, but in wide, benedictory movements, with the friends who
gathered around them with the ardent feeling that among the defendants Mr.
Hurd especially was to be congratulated. The father and son were grinning
shyly, but in their eyes was a terrible light. They knew again that they were the
chosen vessels of the Lord. Later, Mr. Hurd, asked for a statement, was to say,
"Justice has been done . . . both ways." Meanwhile, the other defendants were
kissing and clasping their wives, their wives were laying their heads on their
husbands' chests and nuzzling in an ecstasy of animal affection, while the
laughing men stretched out their hands to their friends, who sawed them up
and down. They shouted, they whistled, they laughed, they cried; above all,
they shone with self-satisfaction. In fact, make no mistake, these people interpreted the verdict as a vote of confidence passed by the community. They interpreted it as a kind of election to authority.

They must have been enormously strengthened in this persuasion by the
approval of Mr. Culbertson, who, as soon as the Judge had left court, had leapt
like a goat from chair to table and from table to chair, the sooner to wring the
hands of his clients. Oddly, Mr. Ashmore, the prosecuting attorney, was also
busy telling the defendants how glad he was that they had been acquitted, with
the rallying smile of a schoolmaster who is telling his pupils that he had to keep
them in for a little because they really were too boisterous, but that he knew all
the time what fine, manly fellows they were. Clark had now produced his camera and flashlight and was standing on a chair, taking photographs of the cel-
ebrations. The defendants were delighted and jumped up on chairs to pose for
him, their friends standing below them and waving and smiling toward the
camera, so that they could share in the glory. In these pictorial revels, Mr. Culbertson was well to the fore. First he posed with the Hurds. Then he formed part
of a group that neither Greenville nor the C.I.O. could greatly enjoy if they
should see it in *Life.* On a chair stood Fat Joy, bulging and swelling with plea-

sure, and on his right stood the bondsman and on his left Mr. Culbertson, bar-
ing their teeth in ice-cold geniality, and each laying one hard hand on the boy's
soft bulk and raising the other as if to lead a cheer. It is unlikely that Mr. Culbertson was unaware of the cynical expression on Clark's face, and he knew
perfectly well what other members of the press were thinking of him. But he
did not care. *Life* is a national weekly. Mr. Culbertson does not want to be a national figure. He means to be a highly successful local figure. My future, he was
plainly saying to himself, is in Greenville and this is good enough for Greenville,
so let's go. It will be astonishing if he is right. At that, he was a more admirable
figure than Mr. Wofford, however, because at least his credo had brought him
out into the open standing alongside the people whose fees he had taken and
whose cause he had defended. But on hearing the verdict, Mr. Wofford, who
possibly has an intention of becoming a national figure, had vanished with the
speed of light and was doubtless by this time at some convenient distance, wip-
ing his mouth and saying, "Lord, I did not eat."

There could be no more pathetic scene than these taxi-drivers and their
wives, the deprived children of difficult history, who were rejoicing at a salvation that was actually a deliverance to danger. For an hour or two, the trial had
built up in them that sense of law which is as necessary to man as bread and
water and a roof. They had known killing for what it is: a hideousness that
begets hideousness. They had seen that the most generous impulse, not subjected to the law, may engender a shameful deed. For indeed they were sick at
heart when what had happened at the slaughter-pen was described in open
court. But they had been saved from the electric chair and from prison by men
who had conducted their defense without taking a minute off to state or imply
that even if a man is a murderer one must not murder him and that murder is
foul. These people had been plunged back into chaos. They had been given by
men whom they naïvely trusted the most wildly false ideas of what conduct the
community will tolerate. It is to be remembered that in their statements these
men fully inculpated each other. At present they are unified by the trial, but
when the tension is over, there will come into their minds that they were not so
well treated as they might have been by their friends. Then the propaganda for
murder which was so freely dished out to them during their trial may bear its
fruit. Not only have they, along with everyone else, been encouraged to use the
knife and the gun in ways that may get them into trouble—for it is absurd to
think of Greenville as a place whose tolerance of disorder is unlimited—but
they have been exposed to a greater danger of having the knife and the gun
used on them. The kind of assault by which Mr. Brown died is likely to be encouraged by the atmosphere that now hangs over Greenville. These wretched
people have been utterly betrayed.

It was impossible to watch this scene of delirium, which had been conjured
up by a mixture of clownishness, ambition, and sullen malice, without feeling

a desire for action. Supposing that one lived in a town, decent but tragic, which had been trodden into the dust and had risen again, and that there were men in that town who threatened every force in that town which raised it up and encouraged every force which dragged it back into the dust; then lynching would be a joy. It would be, indeed, a very great delight to go through the night to the home of such a man, with a few loyal friends, and walk in so softly that he was surprised and say to him, "You meant to have your secret bands to steal in on your friends and take them out into the darkness, but it is not right that you should murder what we love without paying the price, and the law is not punishing you as it should." And when we had driven him to some place where we would not be disturbed, we would make him confess his treacheries and the ruses by which he had turned the people's misfortunes to his profit. It would be only right that he should purge himself of his sins. Then we would kill him, but not quickly, for there would be no reason that a man who had caused such pain should himself be allowed to flee quickly to the shelter of death. The program would have seemed superb had it not been for two decent Greenville people, a man and a woman, who stopped as they went out of the courtroom and spoke to me, because they were so miserable that they had to speak to someone. "This is only the beginning," the man said. He was right. It was the beginning of a number of odd things. Irrational events breed irrational events. The next day I was to see a Negro porter at the parking place of a resort hotel near Greenville insult white guests as I have never seen a white hotel employee insult guests; there were to be minor assaults all over the state; there was to be the lynching party in North Carolina. "It is like a fever," said the woman, tears standing in her eyes behind her glasses. "It spreads, it's an infection, it's just like a fever." I was prepared to admit that she, too, was right.

II

Into the Streets

◆◆◆

On May 17, 1954, just before 1 P.M. in Washington, Chief Justice Earl Warren announced the opinion of the Court in *Brown v. Board of Education.* "Separate but equal" was now unconstitutional; so, therefore, were segregated schools. A year later, the court would rule that its decision be enforced "with all deliberate speed" — for the segs, there was no real hope of returning to the old order. At an integrated dinner during a meeting of the Southern Historical Association at the Peabody Hotel in Memphis the next year, William Faulkner (1897– 1962) and Morehouse College president Benjamin E. Mays (1895–1984) talked about the decision and the new world struggling to be born. Faulkner was the descendant of a Confederate colonel; Mays, born the son of a South Carolina sharecropper, had risen within the ranks of the African-American church and academy. Their remarks were published in a pamphlet, though Faulkner's best line—"We speak now against the day when our Southern people who will resist to the last these inevitable changes in social relations will, when they have been forced to accept what they at one time might have accepted with dignity and goodwill, will say, 'Why didn't someone tell us this before? Tell us this in time?' "—was in fact part of a letter to the editor of a Memphis paper a few days later.

Even beyond the school question, 1955 was a pivotal year. In Money, Mississippi, the bludgeoned corpse of 14-year-old Emmett Till was fished out of the Tallahatchie River. Till had been down from Chicago, visiting cousins; he boasted he had a white girlfriend back home. His cousins challenged him to go talk to the white female cashier at a crossroads store, and Till did, allegedly saying, "Bye, baby," as he walked out. A few nights later the woman's husband and brother-in-law rode out to Till's uncle's place, rounded up the youth, and murdered him, tying his body to a cotton gin and dumping it in the river. Back in Chicago, Till's mother insisted on an open casket, and the pictures of the boy's disfigured head put a human face on Southern lynchings. The trial unfolded in Sumner. Murray Kempton (1918–1997) sent a column back to New York describing Till's uncle's courage in identifying the men who took the teenager from home—and who were predictably acquitted. In the 1950s and '60s, Kempton, one of the great newspaper columnists of the century, wrote largely for the *New York Post;* an elegant man who could quote Aeschylus while chronicling the vicissitudes of life in the Mafia, he once showed up for dinner during the Till trial in British walking shorts. The race story fascinated him, and he also covered the integration crisis in Nashville, a standoff orchestrated by John Kasper, a roaming white supremacist.

By December 1955, the action moved from Mississippi to Montgomery, where Carl T. Rowan (1925–2000) chronicled the bus boycott and the emergence of Martin Luther King, Jr. Rowan's life experience and natural gifts—a native Tennessean who had moved North, served overseas, and could write gracefully—equipped him well to sense nuances that might elude journalists from outside the region. Decades later, in this excerpt from his groundbreaking 1988 biography of King, *Parting the Waters: America in the King Years,* Taylor Branch (1947–) re-creates the young minister's debut as the spokesman for the boycott at a mass meeting at Montgomery's Holt Street Baptist Church in the days after Rosa Parks's arrest.

In the fifties, television was a new force in American life, and it fueled the movement, as Henry Louis Gates, Jr. (1950–) recalls in the 1993 memoir of his childhood in rural West Virginia—a book he wrote, he says, so that his young daughters could grasp the milieu in which he had grown up. "As artlessly and honestly as I can," Gates said, "I have tried to evoke the colored world of the fifties, a Negro world of the early sixties, and the advent of a black world of the later sixties, from the point of view of the boy I was." In a "Letter from the South" to *The New Yorker* in 1956, E. B. White (1899–1985) suggested that embarrassment about the "silliness" of Jim Crow might one day help bring it down.

But that was still a long way off. Born in Guthrie, Kentucky, educated at Vanderbilt University in Nashville, Robert Penn Warren (1905–1989) had moved to Connecticut, and to Yale, by 1954. In the aftermath of the *Brown* decision, the novelist-poet-critic agreed to do a piece for *Life* on desegregation in the South. He took two trips home and, back in the North, battled the flu as he wrote a 20,000-word chronicle of his journeys; for *Life,* he cut it down to an 8,000-word article entitled "Divided South Searches for Its Soul." In September 1956, Random House published the complete text as *Segregation: The Inner Conflict in the South,* which is reprinted here. One of Warren's conclusions: "History, like nature, knows no jumps. Except the jump backward, maybe."

In New Orleans, John Steinbeck (1902–1968) absorbed the local crisis and talked it all over with whites and blacks in the trailer he drove around the country with his poodle, Charley. Back in Mississippi, there were a few white voices of tolerance: Hodding Carter (1907–1972), of the *Delta Democrat-Times* in Greenville, Mississippi, was one of a collection of moderate Southern editors and publishers (Atlanta's Ralph McGill was another) who tried to nudge their readers toward the middle. In the piece reprinted here, Carter recounts how the state legislature officially branded him a liar after he denounced the White Citizens Councils.

The author of the classic novel *Invisible Man,* Ralph Ellison (1914–1994) grew up in Oklahoma City. More Southwestern than Southern, the city was not as racially riven as those in the Deep South, though Ellison did go to Alabama to attend the Tuskegee Institute in 1933. In 1936 he moved to New York, where he studied sculpture and met Langston Hughes, who introduced him to Richard Wright. In his 1964 essay collected here, Ellison points out that the crisis of race extended beyond the Southern borders, to Harlem.

There was another, increasingly important, story taking shape: the rise of the Nation of Islam. In 1959, a documentary about the sect entitled *The Hate That Hate Produced* brought Elijah Muhammad and his disciple Malcolm X to the country's attention. Researched by Louis E. Lomax (whose *Harper's* piece, "The Negro Revolt Against 'The Negro Leaders,' " is found later in the section) for *The Mike Wallace Show,* the program was broadcast about the same time Alex Haley (1921–1992), an aspiring writer nearing retirement after 20 years in the Coast Guard, heard about the Muslims from a friend. Haley then embarked on a piece for *Reader's Digest;* the story, "Mr. Muhammad Speaks," appeared in early 1960. He co-authored a second article on the Muslims for the *Saturday Evening Post,* then convinced Malcolm to sit for a *Playboy* interview, which is included here. As he laid out his aggressive manifesto, Malcolm X doubted Haley's promise that the magazine would publish the interview verbatim: "You know that devil's not going to print that!" he would say after an especially vehement anti-Christian or anti-white remark. "He was very much taken aback," Haley recalled, "when *Playboy* kept its word." The interview then led to *The Autobiography of Malcolm X,* which Haley wrote from long sessions with Malcolm, who was assassinated in 1965.

Down South, Alabama Governor George Wallace became a force to be reckoned with, first in the 1963 standoff over the integration of the University of Alabama and, as the decade wore on, in presidential politics. Marshall Frady (1942–) paints a portrait of the segregationist pol who had started out as a moderate, lost, and sworn that race would never beat him again. "It was sometime back in the spring of 1966, when I was covering the Alabama governor's campaign for *Newsweek,*" Frady recalls, "that it occurred to me George Wallace was worth a book as the palpable, breathing articulation into flesh of Willie Stark in Robert Penn Warren's *All the*

King's Men." That was the year Wallace was running his wife, Lurleen, for governor since he couldn't constitutionally succeed himself. Frady's epiphany: At a rally in Birmingham, Wallace was pumping up the crowd, and "the sense I got from his oration to that multitude was, 'I am you and you are me,' and that's when I realized: This is Willie Stark."

In a little-known 1963 interview, Flannery O'Connor (1925–1964) offered a vision of the role manners might play in bringing peace to the war between the races. She knew, however, that "good manners seldom make the papers." Sit-ins *were* making news. As Louis E. Lomax (1922–1970) points out, young black activists did what their parents' and grandparents' generations had not: genuinely and effectively challenge the status quo. Lomax understood the emerging intricacies within black America—between violent and nonviolent and between young and old. A freelance journalist and expatriate Georgian, Lomax wrote a book called *The Negro Revolt* in 1962 and was a critic of the established black leadership and an integrationist. He occasionally debated Malcolm X; in fact, when Malcolm delivered his most famous speech in Cleveland in April 1964, Lomax had been the first speaker on the program. Malcolm's title: "The Ballot or the Bullet."

America Comes of Middle Age

◆

MURRAY KEMPTON

He Went All the Way

Sumner, Mississippi, September 22, 1955

Mose Wright, making a formation no white man in his county really believed he would dare to make, stood on his tiptoes to the full limit of his sixty-four years and his five feet three inches yesterday, pointed his black, workworn finger straight at the huge and stormy head of J. W. Milam and swore that this was the man who dragged fourteen-year-old Emmett Louis Till out of his cottonfield cabin the night the boy was murdered.

"There he is," said Mose Wright. He was a black pigmy standing up to a white ox. J. W. Milam leaned forward, crooking a cigaret in a hand that seemed as large as Mose Wright's whole chest, and his eyes were coals of hatred.

Mose Wright took all their blast straight in his face, and then, for good measure, turned and pointed that still unshaking finger at Roy Bryant, the man he says joined Milam on the night-ride to seize young Till for the crime of whistling suggestively at Bryant's wife in a store three miles away and three nights before.

"And there's Mr. Bryant," said Mose Wright and sat down hard against the chair-back with a lurch which told better than anything else the cost in strength to him of the thing he had done. He was a field Negro who had dared try to send two white men to the gas chamber for murdering a Negro.

He sat in a court where District Attorney Gerald Chatham, who is on his side, steadily addressed him as Uncle Mose and conversed with him in a kind of pidgin cotton-picker's dialect, saying "axed" for "asked" as Mose Wright did and talking about the "undertaker man."

Once Chatham called him "Old Man Mose," but this was the kindly, contemptuous tolerance of the genteel; after twenty-one minutes of this, Mose Wright was turned over to Defense Counsel Sidney Carlton and now the manner was that of an overseer with a field hand.

Sidney Carlton roared at Mose Wright as though he were the defendant, and every time Carlton raised his voice like the lash of a whip, J. W. Milam would permit himself a cold smile.

And then Mose Wright did the bravest thing a Delta Negro can do; he stopped saying "sir." Every time Carlton came back to the attack, Mose Wright pushed himself back against his chair and said "That's right" and the absence of the "sir" was almost like a spit in the eye.

When he had come to the end of the hardest half hour in the hardest life possible for a human being in these United States, Mose Wright's story was shaken; yet he still clutched its foundations. Against Carlton's voice and Milam's eyes and the incredulity of an all-white jury, he sat alone and refused to bow.

If it had not been for him, we would not have had this trial. It will be a miracle if he wins his case; yet it is a kind of miracle that, all on account of Mose Wright, the State of Mississippi is earnestly striving here in this courtroom to convict two white men for murdering a Negro boy so obscure that they do not appear to have even known his name.

He testified yesterday that, as Milam left his house with Emmett Till on the night of August 28, he asked Mose Wright whether he knew anyone in the raiding party. "No, sir, I said I don't know nobody."

Then Milam asked him how old he was, and Mose Wright said sixty-four and Milam said, "If you knew any of us, you won't live to be sixty-five."

And, after the darkened car drove off, with his great-nephew, Mose Wright drove his hysterical wife over to Sumner and put her on the train to Chicago, from which she has written him every day since to cut and run and get out of town. The next day, all by himself, Mose Wright drove into nearby Greenwood and told his story in the sheriff's office.

It was a pathetic errand; it seems a sort of marvel that anything was done at all. Sheriff George Smith drove out to Money around 2 P.M. that afternoon and found Roy Bryant sleeping behind his store. They were good friends and they talked as friends about this little boy whose name Smith himself had not bothered to find out.

Smith reported that Roy had said that he had gone down the road and taken the little boy out of "Preacher's" cabin, and brought him back to the store and, when his wife said it wasn't the right boy, told him to go home.

Sheriff Smith didn't even take Bryant's statement down. When he testified to it yesterday, the defense interposed the straight-faced objection that this was after all the conversation of two friends and that the state shouldn't embarrass the sheriff by making him repeat it in court. Yet, just the same, Sheriff Smith arrested Roy Bryant for kidnaping that night.

When the body supposed to be Emmett Till's was found in the river, a deputy sheriff drove Mose Wright up to identify it. There was no inquest. Night before last, the prosecution fished up a picture of the body which had been in the Greenwood police files since the night it was brought in, but there was no sign the sheriff knew anything about it, and its discovery was announced as a coup for the state. But, with that apathy and incompetence, Mose Wright almost alone has brought the kidnapers of his nephew to trial.

The country in which he toiled and which he is now resigned to leaving will never be the same for what he has done. Today the state will put on the stand three other field Negroes to tell how they saw Milam and Bryant near the murder scene. They came in scared; one disappeared while the sheriff's deputies were looking for him. They, like Mose Wright, are reluctant heroes; unlike him, they have to be dragged to the test.

They will be belted and flayed as he was yesterday, but they will walk out with the memory of having been human beings for just a little while. Whatever the result, there is a kind of majesty in the spectacle of the State of Mississippi honestly trying to convict two white men on the word of four Negroes.

And we owe that sight to Mose Wright, who was condemned to bow all his life, and had enough left to raise his head and look the enemy in those terrible eyes when he was sixty-four.

Upon Such a Day

Nashville, September 10, 1957

7:55 A.M., September 9—The ladies of North Nashville were on parade, in sweat socks one, in formless cotton sacking others, with signs saying, "Keep Our White Schools White"; "Keep Your Kids Home"; and "KKKK," which stands for Knights of the Ku Klux Klan. Their husbands, the knights, stood protected behind them, on the grass around Glenn School. One knight held up a sign saying: "What God Has Put Asunder [sic], Let No Man Put Together." A little girl pointed to him and said, "Gee, there's Carol Sue's daddy," and, with her mother and her little brother, joined the little clump of indecisive who milled not in or out but on the rim.

8:15 A.M., same day—A convertible came by; the ladies of North Nashville set up their tribal cries. The police told its driver to park down the road. He came out, at last, a large man, holding by the hand his daughter, a small Negro child named Lajuanda Street, and followed by a woman with her child, Sinclair Lee, Jr., and a man with glasses and his daughter Jacqueline Faye Griffith. The children were all first-graders. "If that don't make my blood boil," said a woman. The children passed through the crowd; they were out of sight; nothing of this historic parade could be seen except Harold Street, who was bulkier than anyone there. One of the knights looked at Harold Street and thought better of pushing him, and pushed M. J. Griffith, who is smaller, instead.

"You'll come out of there feet up," one of the Valkyries shrieked. City Detective C. E. Burris, a fat man in a Panama hat, shoved the knight halfway across the walkway. The menace collapsed. The cry came up safely from the back: "You see what they do to the white people. Who's gonna take up for the white people?"

9 A.M.—Some thirty-odd mothers, dragging their children, had come out, each one to be greeted by wild cries. Three or four of the children were crying. Their mother comforted two of them by giving them signs saying "Keep Our White Schools White." They were not quite large enough to carry this burden; the sign kept bowing and falling away. But a white woman walked the gantlet escorting her two children late to school. One of the Valkyries called her a tedious obscenity. She answered: "You tend to your business and I'll tend to mine."

10 A.M.—John Kasper, taller than all his flock, with his felt hat sweated through, was telling the crowd that the jails weren't big enough for all of them. "The niggers are in there now; we're gonna continue the boycott." A cop said everyone should get up on the sidewalk, "because we don't want nobody to get run over." "We're gonna stand and stand and stand," said John Kasper.

10:15 A.M.—Edna Jean Moore, arrested at Fehr School for throwing a stick of wood at a Negro mother, was bailed out for $10 and brought back to the scene of the resistance in a KKK car. A mother whispered in a little girl's ear, and having learned that lesson, her child, a blond, marched the sidewalk, chanting, "Go home, niggers, go home, niggers."

11 A.M.—The intervening minutes had been occupied with Kasper on the need to keep on, keep on. Jones School was very peaceful. Inside, a visitor looked into room 105, and saw first-grader Charlie Battles, with the smile all children have at peace, playing blind man's buff with the white kids. It seemed a pleasant place to watch and wait; Charlie Battles sat down and began working earnestly with another child on his drawings, and before long the first day of school was over.

Mrs. Pauline Brommer, Charlie Battles's new teacher, said that the children had been bothered a little by the clatter outside, and that they had asked what it was. "I told them," she said: "Those were mommies and daddies; they're just waiting for us to finish school.

"It was," she said, "a delightful day. I wasn't sure at the beginning just how it would be, but we began to play the game of sharing, and right away Charlie said he had a song to share with us, and he gave the most wonderful imitation of Elvis Presley singing 'Hound Dog' and the children just loved it." Her visitor left walking past a sign which said: "God is the author of segregation."

There were very few of them really, these criers against the daylight, and, once school was out, Nashville was as it always had been. They met at seven fifteen, 400 or so of them, on the steps of its War Memorial, and, with the city going about its shopping hours unheeding, listened to John Kasper. It was a date-night audience.

"We've started from nothin'," cried John Kasper. "They said it couldn't be done but we did it. Let's start hating the nigger until we get him out of our schools. Let's say we want him either to be a dead nigger or back to Africa." The audience laughed. "We say no peace," said John Kasper. "We say attack, attack, attack. There ain't any jails big enough." A high school boy, who preferred not to give his name, bawled he would die before he'd let yer little brother grow up to marry one of them black et ceteras, et ceteras. The crowd went trooping up the steps of Nashville's State Capitol to better affront Governor Frank Clement.

John Kasper held up a rope, and everybody laughed and cheered. This is Dixie, he said, the best and most bloodthirsty people under God's skies. "Let's for one time show what a white man can do." He announced that ten men would pass through the crowd soliciting funds. The crowd began to flee, while the high school boy, still anonymous in his red sweater, said: "It's like a football game; we're not out for love; we're out for blood and victory."

It was horribly ugly, and it was about nothing. Upon such a day, Charles Battles played blind man's buff with the white children on his first day in school.

Next Day

Nashville, September 12, 1957

The gathering place of the Klans of Nashville had been moved yesterday from the streets to the City Court where Judge Andrew Doyle adjusts the passions of the disorderly poor.

In Judge Doyle's court, by tradition, Negro and white, although united in trouble, sit segregated as spectators. As defendants, they are intermixed in the bullpen where they await trial. A man was saying yesterday that the quickest way to get integrated in Nashville is to resist a cop in the cause of segregation.

The judge was gentle enough with most of the rioters who were before him for loitering. Glowering and disturbing, they are a thin-blooded crowd, most of them; the passion which had flared in them Monday was down to soggy mush. G. H. Akins, who had been calling the cops to come and fight him in front of Caldwell School Tuesday, broke down and blubbered, with his two little girls clutching his knees before the judge. To such as these Andrew Doyle gave $5 fines; he knew they would not trouble him again.

He saved his moral indignation for people worthy of it. Marvin Sullins, a farmer in his fifties, was before him for hitting a thirteen-year-old Negro boy in front of Caldwell School Tuesday. William Jackson had been running from an assaulting corps of white children when Marvin Sullins got him. The police had found a pair of brass knuckles on Marvin Sullins when they brought him in.

William Jackson told his story and looked up at Marvin Sullins's eyes. Marvin Sullins had not the moral force to brag about his moment of struggle for the purity of the white South; he mumbled that he couldn't have hit this boy: "He's too little." Judge Doyle said "Yer a coward," and fined him $200 and told him he could never again be a free patient at the county hospital, and Marvin Sullins shuffled off to the county workhouse to render his payment to the God which watches over little children.

Then John Kasper came in on the counts of vagrancy, loitering and disorderly conduct. Andrew Doyle looked at him and saw only William Jackson who was chased on the street by white boys and was caught and hit by a fifty-five-year-old man. The point to him was not about fascism or racism or other abstract things; it was that John Kasper makes his war on little boys.

Floyd Peek, a county constable, told of Kasper's standing on the steps of the State Capitol and waving a rope and telling the poor that blood should run in the streets. John Kasper, dream-walking, stumbling in his speech, kept asking if he had said that, like the man who had blacked out on whisky the night before and was asking around town what had he done. He is an apprentice demagogue in a section whose politicians can summon up passion as Horowitz plays the piano. It is extraordinary the passion this essentially passionless man can arouse. Assistant City Attorney Robert Jennings cried out for a punishment that would degrade John Kasper and bring him to his knees in atonement:

"I hope your Honor fines him so much that he will be unable to pay and have to go to our workhouse where they'll put him behind a clean broom and send him back to those schools to clean up the debris he's left behind in our streets."

I would swear that John Kasper winced. And then Andrew Doyle raised his eyes from the docket and stared straight at John Kasper, and the back of John Kasper's neck went red with the blush that small boys cannot hold back and his eyes had no sight in them. Andrew Doyle spoke without a note and he drew the line where it belonged:

"I only wish," he said, "we had enough policemen to take you by the seat of yer britches and the nape of yer neck and throw you outside the city limits of Nashville as far as possible.

"Yer purpose was to cause trouble and fatten yer pocketbook with the dimes and dollars of irresponsible and uneducated people. You go into homes and take food from their mouths when they can hardly feed their own children. You pass the hat to nobody but people who can't afford to give the money you take from them. I wish I could do more on the vagrancy charge, but the only thing that I can do is to fine you $50 and that is what I will do, because you are the worst vagrant ever to hit the city of Nashville and the state of Tennessee, and I hope we never see another like you."

And then Andrew Doyle fairly cried out from the scar that the sight of little Willie Jackson had left upon what should by now be a calloused memory:

"We tried this white man just now for something that happened as a direct result of what you have agitated. He had no more sense than to attack an itty bitty kid. Only a coward would take after an innocent child rather than pick on somebody his own size."

And having said this, Andrew Doyle fined John Kasper $200 on four counts. There was an indecisive floundering about for a bondsman; none was found, and John Kasper went back to the workhouse. At midnight last night, he remained unbailed; it seemed impossible that this shaker of the earth could not raise $200. It may be that he has been left, as so much of his battleground is, morally exhausted, and will go stumbling tomorrow as a city prisoner cleaning the streets in the company of some defaulting Saturday night drunk who might be white or might be colored, because only accident and pauperism brought him here.

The point of it, I think, was moral exhaustion. The schools were emptier than they had been the day before; some of the Negro children even stayed home. The father of one of them said yesterday that he was tired and that he just didn't think he would mess with it today. So long had it been since Monday. The sidewalks in front of the schools were barren of disturbers of the peace; the cops lounged in the sun before Jones School, and Cecil Ray, a little Negro boy who has come here every day, was by now quite the pet of the policemen. Nashville will pick itself up and begin again today. Yesterday it was used up. The moment of purgation was, for John Kasper and everyone else, the moment of exhaustion.

The Soul's Cry

Nashville, September 13, 1957

John Kasper was cleaning the bars of the city jail yesterday. It was just the latest of the waiting rooms in which he tarries, this permanent vagrant, between his wanderings across the face of the South between the gutter and the sewer.

John Kasper lives nowhere except in the backs of old cars with a pile of leaflets as his pillow.

But, if John Kasper is of the air, the Reverend Fred Stroud is of the earth. Fred Stroud—"Call me Brother Stroud; that's what my people call me"—is pastor of the Bible Presbyterian Church. He is twenty-four years out of Georgia's Columbia Theological Seminary; he is twenty years out of the Southern Presbyterian Church, which he declared "officially apostate" in 1938, and seceded, carrying some 400 members of his congregation with him.

Fred Stroud is chaplain of the ragged, temporarily routed army which went into the streets here Monday to fight integration of Nashville's schools. He roamed from school to school that day, a short, lantern-jawed man carrying a sign proclaiming: "God is the author of segregation: Sixth Corinthians."

Fred Stroud is immobilized now. Mayor Ben West has moved to enjoin him from preaching in the streets. He sat yesterday in his study looking out over the shabby streets of "this receding neighborhood" he holds as a fortress of the fundamental creed. He looks at an indifferent city, a city of people who are unlike him because they do not really care. His verse in the Bible is the verse of the truly committed, the verse in Revelations which says—be thou hot or cold; if thou art lukewarm I will spew you out of my mouth. It is, I confess, my verse too.

"I wouldn't say John Kasper is a failure," he told one caller yesterday. "Not everybody who gets in jail is a failure. Just keep looking up, boy. That's all I know to do, just keep looking up. The Lord will take care of us; he always has."

He hung up, and told his two visitors of "my soul's cry for Nashville.

"John Kasper found me here and I will be here if he has to leave. I have been standing alone here since 1938 against all the modernist preachers." He riffled the Bible: "There's not one word of compromise in this. Christ set his face steadfastly to go to Jerusalem."

He waved his hand in the direction of the comfortable churches across the river. "They preach the false philosophy that it is un-Christian to fight. They're teaching the fatherhood of God and the brotherhood of all mankind. But, unless a man has been born again, he cannot claim to be a child of God.

"Christ hated mixing. God has always been a segrationist."

One of his visitors asked Brother Stroud what he had thought of his flock boiling in the streets last Monday.

"It just shows a sincerity," he said. "They have convictions. They don't want to be pushed around."

Is John Kasper saved, the visitor wondered?

"Of course, John knows no more about theology than you do. He went to Columbia. But he tells me now that he is a believer in the Lord Jesus Christ."

Fred Stroud is a wandering holy man, an eater of locusts. He preaches in the market and in the streets.

It is odd what forms of witness God chooses for his ministers. While Fred Stroud stalked the streets on Tuesday, Robert Kelly, rector of a Negro Methodist Church, visited the homes of the parents who had enrolled their children and were, most of them, afraid to go back.

"I told them," Robert Kelly said yesterday, "that, if they were afraid to go and take them in, that I would take them in." Fred Stroud is not alone among the committed.

But, if this is Armageddon, one of Fred Stroud's visitors asked, are you not lonely and weary among the few who battle for the Lord in this city of neutrals?

The light of the message came to Fred Stroud's eyes under their jutting, tangled brows:

"What do you know about Armageddon?" he said. "Are you saved?"

The visitor said that he was not. "Boy," said Mr. Stroud, "can you face the lake of fire?"

It was time for the sinner to flee the tender of grace. "Before you go," said Fred Stroud, "could we stop for a moment for prayer?"

He put one hand on his New York visitor's hand, and another on the shoulder of William Emerson, of *Newsweek*, a Georgian of charming mien and traditional outlook.

"Oh, Lord," cried Fred Stroud on his knees, "watch over this good boy from Georgia and save this poor boy from New York. He is alone and suffering; come to him, save him, and perhaps he will grow up to preach Thy gospel."

Then, "Oh, Lord," he cried, alone with his vision, "You know that I don't hate anyone. I just feel sorry for ole Ben West, I just feel sorry for these niggers."

In my job we travel, wayfarers as rootless as—if less vandalic than—John Kasper, and our moments of reward are our moments of engagement. They are moments when tragedy and comedy are all mixed up, and God and the devil contend like scorpions in a bottle inside the soul of a man before us. Oh, Lord, Fred Stroud cries, You know I don't hate anybody. Fred Stroud has sacrificed life and comfort, and he does yet not know inside himself whether God or the devil sends him into the streets, and makes him happy when a mob chases a Negro away from a school.

What I have said about him probably makes very little sense. He is my brother. We are bound together, he and Emerson and I, through all eternity by that horrible, desperate prayer.

American Segregation
and the World Crisis

The Segregation Decisions, November 10, 1955

◆

WILLIAM FAULKNER

For the moment and for the sake of the argument, let's say that, a white Southerner and maybe even any white American, I too curse the day when the first
Negro was brought against his will to this country and sold into slavery. Because that doesn't matter now. To live anywhere in the world of A.D. 1955 and
be against equality because of race or color, is like living in Alaska and being
against snow.

Inside the last two years I have seen (a little of some, a good deal of others)
Japan, the Philippines, Siam, India, Egypt, Italy, West Germany, England and
Iceland. Of these countries, the only one I would say definitely will not be communist ten years from now, is England. And if these other countries do not remain free, then England will no longer endure as a free nation. And if all the
rest of the world becomes communist, it will be the end of America too as we
know it; we will be strangled into extinction by simple economic blockade since
there will be no one anywhere anymore to sell our products to; we are already
seeing that now in the problem of our cotton.

And the only reason all these countries are not communist already, is
America, not just because of our material power, but because of the idea of individual human freedom and liberty and equality on which our nation was
founded, and which our founding fathers postulated the name of America to
mean. These countries are still free of communism simply because of that—
that belief in individual liberty and equality and freedom—that one belief powerful enough to stalemate the idea of communism. We have no other weapon
to fight communism with but this, since in diplomacy we are children to communist diplomats, and in production we will always lag behind them since
under monolithic government all production can go to the aggrandizement of
the State. But then, we don't need anything else, since that idea—that simple
belief of man that he can be free—is the strongest force on earth; all we need to
do is, use it.

Because it is glib and simple, we like to think of the world situation today as
a precarious and explosive balance of two irreconcilable ideologies confronting

each other; which precarious balance, once it totters, will drag the whole world into the abyss along with it. That's not so. Only one of the forces is an ideology, an idea. Because the second force is the simple fact of Man: the simple belief of individual man that he can and should and will be free. And if we who so far are still free, want to continue to be free, all of us who are still free had better confederate, and confederate fast, with all others who still have a choice to be free—confederate not as black people nor white people nor pink nor blue nor green people, but as people who still are free with all other people who still are free; confederate together and stick together too, if we want a world or even a part of a world in which individual man can be free, to continue to endure.

And we had better take in with us as many as we can get of the nonwhite peoples of the earth who are not completely free yet but who want to be and intend to be, before that other force which is opposed to individual freedom, befools and gets them. Time was when the nonwhite was content to—anyway, did—accept his instinct for freedom as an unrealizable dream. But not any more; the white man himself taught him different with that phase of his—the white man's—own culture which took the form of colonial expansion and exploitation based and morally condoned on the premise of inequality not because of individual incompetence, but of mass race or color. As a result of which, in only ten years, we have watched the nonwhite peoples expel, by bloody violence when necessary, the white man from all of the middle east and Asia which he once dominated. And into that vacuum has already begun to move that other and inimical power which people who believe in freedom are at war with—that power which says to the nonwhite man: "We don't offer you freedom because there is no such thing as freedom; your white overlords whom you just threw out have already proved that to you. But we offer you equality: at least equality in slavedom; if you are to be slaves, at least you can be slaves to your own color and race and religion."

We, the western white man who does believe that there exists an individual freedom above and beyond this mere equality of slavedom, must teach the nonwhite peoples this while there is yet a little time left. We, America, who are the strongest force opposing communism and monolithicism, must teach all other peoples, white and nonwhite, slave or (for a little while yet) still free. We, America, have the best chance to do this because we can do it here, at home, without needing to send costly freedom expeditions into alien and inimical places already convinced that there is no such thing as freedom and liberty and equality and peace for all people, or we would practice it at home.

The best chance and the easiest job, because our nonwhite minority is already on our side; we don't need to sell them on America and freedom because they are already sold; even when ignorant from inferior or no education, even despite the record and history of inequality, they still believe in our concepts of freedom and democracy.

That is what America has done for them in only three hundred years. Not *to* them: *for* them, because to our shame we have made little effort so far to teach them to be Americans, let alone to use their capacities to make of ourselves a stronger and more unified America:—the people who only three hundred years ago were eating rotten elephant and hippo meat in African rain-forests, who lived beside one of the biggest bodies of inland water on earth and never thought of a sail, who yearly had to move by whole villages and tribes from famine and pestilence and human enemies without once thinking of a wheel, yet in only three hundred years in America produced Ralph Bunche and George Washington Carver and Booker T. Washington, who have yet to produce a Fuchs or Rosenberg or Gold or Greenglass or Burgess or McLean or Hiss, and for every prominent communist or fellow-traveler like Robeson, there are a thousand white ones.

I am not convinced that the Negro wants integration in the sense that some of us claim to fear he does. I believe he is American enough to repudiate and deny by simple American instinct any stricture or regulation forbidding us to do something which in our opinion would be harmless if we did it, and which we probably would not want to do anyway. I think that what he wants is equality, and I believe that he too knows there is no such thing as equality *per se*, but only equality *to:* equal right and opportunity to make the best one can of one's life within one's capacity and capability, without fear of injustice or oppression or threat of violence. If we had given him this equal right to opportunity ninety or fifty or even ten years ago, there would have been no Supreme Court decision about how we run our schools.

It is our white man's shame that in our present southern economy, the Negro must not have economic equality; our double shame that we fear that giving him more social equality will jeopardize his present economic status; our triple shame that even then, to justify ourselves, we must becloud the issue with the purity of white blood; what a commentary that the one remaining place on earth where the white man can flee and have his blood protected and defended by law, is Africa—Africa: the source and origin of the people whose presence in America will have driven the white man to flee from defilement.

Soon now all of us—not just Southerners nor even just Americans, but all people who are still free and want to remain so—are going to have to make a choice. We will have to choose not between color nor race nor religion nor between East and West either, but simply between being slaves and being free. And we will have to choose completely and for good; the time is already past now when we can choose a little of each, a little of both. We can choose a state of slavedom, and if we are powerful enough to be among the top two or three or ten, we can have a certain amount of license—until someone more powerful rises and has us machine-gunned against a cellar wall. But we cannot choose freedom established on a hierarchy of degrees of freedom, on a caste system of equality like military rank. We must be free not because we claim freedom, but because we practice it; our freedom must be buttressed by a homogeny equally and unchallengeably free, no matter what color they are, so that all the other inimical forces everywhere—systems political or religious or racial or national—will not just respect us because we practice freedom, they will fear us because we do.

◆◆◆

[*Editor's note*—On December 1, Mr. Faulkner extended views expressed in his Memphis paper with the following statement]:

The question is no longer of white against black. It is no longer whether or not white blood shall remain pure, it is whether or not white people shall remain free.

We accept insult and contumely and the risk of violence because we will not sit quietly by and see our native land, the South, not just Mississippi but all the South, wreck and ruin itself twice in less than a hundred years, over the Negro question.

We speak now against the day when our Southern people who will resist to the last these inevitable changes in social relations will, when they have been forced to accept what they at one time might have accepted with dignity and goodwill, will say, "Why didn't someone tell us this before? Tell us this in time?"

The Moral Aspects of Segregation

The Segregation Decisions, November 10, 1955

◆

BENJAMIN E. MAYS

Whenever a strong dominant group possesses all the power, political, educational, economic, and wields all the power; makes all the laws, municipal, state and federal, and administers all the laws; writes all constitutions, municipal, state and federal, and interprets these constitutions; collects and holds all the money, municipal, state, and federal, and distributes all the money; determines all policies—governmental, business, political and educational; when that group plans and places heavy burdens, grievous to be borne, upon the backs of the weak, that act is immoral. If the strong group is a Christian group or a follower of Judaism both of which contend that God is creator, judge, impartial, just, universal, love and that man was created in God's image, the act is against God and man—thus immoral. If the strong group is atheistic, the act is against humanity—still immoral.

No group is wise enough, good enough, strong enough, to assume an omnipotent and omniscient role; no group is good enough, wise enough to restrict the mind, circumscribe the soul, and to limit the physical movements of another group. To do that is blasphemy. It is a usurpation of the role of God.

If the strong handicaps the weak on the grounds of race or color, it is all the more immoral because we penalize the group for conditions over which it has no control, for being what nature or nature's God made it. And that is tantamount to saying to God, "You made a mistake, God, when you didn't make all races white." If there were a law which said that an illiterate group had to be segregated, the segregated group could go to school and become literate. If there were a law which said that all peoples with incomes below $5,000 a year had to be segregated, the people under $5,000 a year could strive to rise above the $5,000 bracket. If there were a law which said that men and women who did not bathe had to be segregated, they could develop the habit of daily baths and remove the stigma. If there were a law which said that all groups had to be Catholics, the Jews and Protestants could do something about it by joining the Catholic Church. But to segregate a man because his skin is brown or black, red or yellow, is to segregate a man for circumstances over which he has no control. And of all immoral acts, this is the most immoral.

So the May 17, 1954, Decision of the Supreme Court and all the decisions against segregation are attempts on the part of the judges involved to abolish a great wrong which the strong has deliberately placed upon the backs of the weak. It is an attempt on the part of federal and state judges to remove this stigma, this wrong through constitutional means, which is the democratic, American way.

I said a moment ago that if the strong deliberately picks out a weak racial group and places upon it heavy burdens that act is immoral. Let me try to analyze this burden, segregation, which has been imposed upon millions of Americans of color. There are at least three main reasons for legal segregation in the United States.

1. The first objective of segregation is to place a legal badge of inferiority upon the segregated, to brand him as unfit to move freely among other human beings. This badge says the segregated is mentally, morally, and socially unfit to move around as a free man.
2. The second objective of segregation is to set the segregated apart so that he can be treated as an inferior: in the courts, in recreation, in trans-

portation, in politics, in government, in employment, in religion, in education, in hotels, in motels, restaurants and in every other area of American life. And all of this has been done without the consent of the segregated.

3. The third objective of legalized segregation follows from the first two. It is designed to make the segregated believe that he is inferior, that he is nobody and to make him accept willingly his inferior status in society. It is these conditions which the May 17, 1954, Decision of the Supreme Court and other federal decisions against segregation are designed to correct—to remove this immoral stigma that has been placed upon 16 million Negro Americans, and these are the reasons every thinking Negro wants the legal badge of segregation removed so that he might be able to walk the earth with dignity, as a man, and not cringe and kowtow as a slave. He believes that this is his God-given right on the earth.

Segregation is immoral because it has inflicted a wound upon the soul of the segregated and so restricted his mind that millions of Negroes now alive will never be cured of the disease of inferiority. Many of them have come to feel and believe that they are inferior or that the cards are so stacked against them that it is useless for them to strive for the highest and the best. Segregate a race for ninety years, tell that race in books, in law, in courts, in education, in church and school, in employment, in transportation, in hotels and motels, in the government that it is inferior—it is bound to leave its damaging mark upon the souls and minds of the segregated. It is these conditions that the federal courts seek to change.

Any country that restricts the full development of any segment of society retards its own growth and development. The segregated produces less, and even the minds of the strong group are circumscribed because they are often afraid to pursue the whole truth and they spend too much time seeking ways and means of how to keep the segregated group in "its place." Segregation is immoral because it leads to injustice, brutality, and lynching on the part of the group that segregates. The segregated is somebody that can be pushed around as desired by the segregator. As a rule equal justice in the courts is almost impossible for a member of the segregated group if it involves a member of the group imposing segregation. The segregated has no rights that the segregator is bound to respect.

The chief sin of segregation is the distortion of human personality. It damages the soul of both the segregator and the segregated. It gives the segregated a feeling of inherent inferiority which is not based on facts, and it gives the segregator a feeling of superiority which is not based on facts. It is difficult to know who is damaged more—the segregated or the segregator.

It is a false accusation to say that Negroes hail the May 17, 1954, Decision of the Supreme Court because they want to mingle socially with white people. Negroes want segregation abolished because they want the legal stigma of inferiority removed and because they do not believe that equality of educational opportunities can be completely achieved in a society where the law brands a group inferior. When a Negro rides in a Pullman unsegregated he does it not because he wants to ride with white people. He may or may not engage in conversations with a white person. He wants good accommodations. When he eats in an unsegregated diner on the train, he goes in because he is hungry and not because he wants to eat with white people. He goes to the diner not even to mingle with Negroes but to get something to eat. But as he eats and rides he wants no badge of inferiority pinned on his back. He wants to eat and ride with dignity. No Negro clothed in his right mind believes that his social status will be enhanced just because he associates with white people.

It is also a false accusation to say that Negroes are insisting that segregated schools must be abolished today or tomorrow, simultaneously all over the place. As far as I know, no Negro leader has ever advocated that, and they have not even said when desegregation is to be a finished job. They do say that the Supreme Court is the highest law of the land and we should respect that law. Negro leaders do say that each local community should bring together the racial groups in that community, calmly sit down and plan ways and means not how they can circumvent the decision but how they can implement it and plan together when and where they will start. They will be able to start sooner in some places than in others and move faster in some places than in others but begin the process in good faith and with good intent. To deliberately scheme, to deliberately plan through nefarious methods, through violence, boycott and threats to nullify the Decision of the highest law in the land is not only immoral but it encourages a disregard for all laws which we do not like.

We meet the moral issue again. To write into our constitutions things that we do not intend to carry out is an immoral act. I think I am right when I say that most of our states, certainly some of them, say in their constitutions "separate but equal." But you know as well as I do that on the whole the gulf of inequality in education widened with the years. There was no serious attempt nor desire in this country to provide Negroes with educational opportunities equal to those for whites. The great surge to equalize educational opportunities for Negroes did not begin until after 1935 when Murray won his suit to enter the law school of the University of Maryland. It is also clear that the millions poured into Negro education in the last 20 years were appropriated not so much because it was right but in an endeavor to maintain segregation.

We brought this situation upon ourselves. We here in the South have said all along that we believe in segregation but equal segregation. In 1896 in the Louisiana case, *Plessy versus Ferguson,* the United States Supreme Court confirmed the doctrine "separate but equal." But from 1896 to 1935 there was practically nothing done to make the separate equal. When Murray won his case in 1935, we knew we had to move toward equalization. Since 1935 many suits have been won.

It would have been a mighty fine thing if we had obeyed the Supreme Court in 1896 and equalized educational opportunities for Negroes. If we had done that the problem would have been solved because gradually the separate school system would have been abolished and we would have been saved from the agony and fear of this hour. We didn't obey the Supreme Court in 1896 and we do not want to obey it now.

Let me say again that the May 17, 1954, Decision of the Supreme Court is an effort to abolish a great evil through orderly processes. And we are morally obligated to implement the Decision or modify the federal constitution and say plainly that this constitution was meant for white people and not for Negroes and that the Declaration of Independence created mostly by the mind of the great southerner, Thomas Jefferson, was meant for white people and not Negroes. Tell the world honestly that we do not believe that part of the Declaration of Independence which says in essence that all men are created equal, that they are endowed by their creator with certain inalienable rights, that among these are life, liberty and the pursuit of happiness.

We are morally obligated to abolish legalized segregation in America or reinterpret the Christian Gospel, the Old and New Testaments, and make the Gospel say that the noble principles of Judaism and Christianity are not applicable to colored peoples and Negroes. Tell the world honestly and plainly that the Fatherhood of God and the Brotherhood of Man cannot work where the colored races are involved. We are morally obligated to move toward implementing the Decision in the deep South or lose our moral leadership in the world. If we do not do it, we must play the role of hypocrisy, preaching one thing and doing another. This is the dilemma which faces our democracy.

The eyes of the world are upon us. One billion or more colored people in Asia and Africa are judging our democracy solely on the basis of how we treat Negroes. White Europe is watching us too. I shall never forget the day in Lucknow, India, when nine reporters from all over India questioned me for 90 minutes about how Negroes are treated in the United States. I shall remember to my dying day the event in 1937 when the principal of an untouchable school introduced me to his boys as an untouchable from the United States. At first it angered me. But on second thought I knew that he was right. Though great progress has been made, for which I am grateful, I and my kind are still untouchables in many sections of the country. There are places where wealth, decency, culture, education, religion, and position will do no good if a Negro. None of these things can take away the mark of untouchability. And the world knows this.

Recently a group of colored students from Asia, Africa, the Middle East and South America were visiting an outstanding Southern town. All the colored people except those from Africa and Haiti could live in the downtown hotels. The Africans and the Haitians had to seek refuge on the campus of a Negro College. That incident was known to all the other colored students and it will be told many times in Europe, Asia, Africa—and it will not help us in our efforts to democratize the world.

Not long ago a Jew from South Africa and a man from India were guests of a Negro professor. He drove them for several days through the urban and rural sections of his state. The Negro, the host, a citizen of the United States, could not get food from the hotels and restaurants. His guests, one a Jew and the other an Indian, had to go in and buy food for him. The man who introduced me in India as an untouchable was right. The Negro is America's untouchable.

Two or three years ago a friend of mine was traveling in Germany. He met a German who had traveled widely in the United States. He told my friend that he hangs his head in shame every time he thinks of what his country did to the Jews—killing six million of them. But he told my friend that after seeing what segregation has done to the soul of the Negro in the South, he has come to the conclusion that it is worse than what Hitler and his colleagues did to the Jews in Germany. He may be wrong but this is what he is telling the people in Germany.

Make no mistake—as this country could not exist half slave and half free, it cannot exist half segregated and half desegregated. The Supreme Court has given America an opportunity to achieve greatness in the area of moral and spiritual things just as it has already achieved greatness in military and industrial might and in material possessions. It is my belief that the South will accept the challenge of the Supreme Court and thus make America and the South safe for democracy.

If we lose this battle for freedom for 15 million Negroes we will lose it for 145 million whites and eventually we will lose it for the world. This is indeed a time for greatness.

The Cradle (of the Confederacy) Rocks

Go South to Sorrow, 1957

◆

CARL T. ROWAN

When the Citizens Council leader finished outlining his proposals for economic coercion, he told his Mississippi audience boastfully: "I think the Negro will be humble."

Yes, the Negro knows how to be humble. How long did he sing his spirituals under the burdens of animal labor, pray at the sight of new oppressions and say "yassuh" a little louder for the new white boss? Poor, powerless and humble, waiting for God to quicken the white man's sense of decency, waiting for the day when the Constitution would be big enough to serve as a hiding place. How long? So now—when the tension is high, and legislators are legislating, and the crosses burn again, and an eerie new cry of danger comes from the peanut patches and from beneath the weeping willows where the white men meet—who would expect the Negro to be anything but humble?

Yet I know that this is not the South I left in 1942. In the greasy apron behind the counter at that flyspecked honky-tonk there's a guy who talks about Salerno and Anzio and the gay madames of Paree; in the pool hall, shooting craps with two white guys, are three Negroes who have been to Guadalcanal, Okinawa and Heartbreak Ridge; preaching every Sunday at the Baptist church, trying to lure them out of the pool hall and the honky-tonk, is a man who went North to study the white folks' Bible and to bring back some of the religion of Plato, Rousseau and Paine.

So I wonder how humble this 1956 Negro will be . . . can be. I wonder . . . and once again it is 1953, six months before the Supreme Court was to utter those words that told the world that, for better or worse, the South would never be the same. Yes, 1953—and these are days of optimism about race relations in America. Only here and there a hint or a threat of bloodshed or violence over segregation. But I could not take these threats seriously. I was in the heart of South Carolina, and I had heard too many white men and women utter a quiet, "don't quote me" prayer for a court ruling against segregation, to believe that the majority of these people would ever sit timid and confused while those lawless elements of intimidation and coercion grasped the reins of government and the forces of society. I could see that the plain and simple Negroes of Clarendon County, the people behind the starched and polished briefs that lay before the Supreme Court, were not unduly afraid. After all, when I had walked down the street in Summerton, B. E. Hardy, a Negro farmer, stopped to tell me that he was "in the thick of the fight" to end segregation. I mentioned to Hardy that the mayor of Summerton had just been lecturing me about how the humble Negroes in the county preferred segregation. I told Hardy that a farmer at the mayor's office, waiting for a loan, was hasty to agree.

Hardy pushed his face close to mine and barked: "We got too damn many Negroes around here who ain't nothing but a white man's tool. They ought to've been dead before they were born; then they wouldn't be around to raise so many children to grow up ignorant because their parents are cowards enough to say they don't want their children to have their just dues."

I talked with other Negroes in Summerton, and as I walked toward my car, ready to leave town, a hand tapped me on the arm. It was farmer Hardy, back to find out what I thought of the courage of Negroes in his county.

I told him that I had found them far more courageous than I had expected, but that the fighting words on both sides had aroused fear among some people that conflict and bloodshed might ensue.

"That's kinda strange to me," the farmer said. "Here we been sending American boys across the seas to fight and die for principles that wasn't always easy to understand. But here we got a clear-cut American principle of democracy. Don't tell me they gonna let a little talk of riots and bloodshed make 'em weak-kneed and mealy-mouthed.

"You just let 'em know that we Negroes down here are like Gideon's army. A few went down like dogs and lapped the water. The rest were fit to fight."

A few minutes later my colleague Bonham Cross, a Minneapolis *Tribune* photographer, and I were cruising slowly along the highway from Summerton to Columbia. I gazed across cotton fields and into the shacks that hundreds of Negroes called home. I thought of that one big word that hovered over Dixie: *Segregation.* A feeling of inadequacy crept over me. How could I explain the feelings inside farmer Hardy that made him compare militant Negroes with Gideon's army? How do you make a white man understand the stigma that is an inevitable concomitant of racial segregation? How do you make the white majority of Americans understand the Negroes' knowledge, based on experience, that segregation *is* a badge of inferiority pinned upon the segregated by the segregators? How do you explain racial segregation to the three poorly dressed lads we saw playing outside their shack on a chilly morning with drippings from their noses reaching into their mouths? What does segregation mean to the little Negro girl standing over the black washpot in front of the shanty where there is less than a dream of a bathtub or running water?

Photographer Bonham Cross and I got out of the car and walked toward the shanty, under which pigs wandered from the pens close by. I watched what appeared to be a million flies as they crawled along the wooden steps and on the arms and legs of the tots who came to the porch to see what these two strangers—one of them white and with a camera—were doing in their yard.

Yes, I thought, even the pigs and the flies were part of this issue of segregation. For in some measure they were a reflection on the education that South Carolina had given the parents of these youngsters, a measure of the extent to which second-class citizenship saps initiative, robs man of his *raison d'être.*

And the dilapidated house, the backyard privy, the crude equipment in which the little girl washed clothes were reflections of a discriminatory economic system that Negroes insist is linked to segregation. I asked myself what I knew my readers would ask: Why don't they paint the shack, scrub the steps so the flies will go away, move the pigpens farther away and scrub the children and comb their hair? A big question—one that involves the incentive and self-respect that are lacking among the illiterate and the impoverished everywhere. But this apathy is difficult to understand when one has not lived where there is little education, little reason for incentive, little basis for self-respect.

Now, in 1956, I knew that the white man still did not understand, did not want to understand, this burden of the stigma of segregation. He laid his plans for coercion, passed oppressive law on top of oppressive law and even stacked the deck in his local courts, but he never ceased telling himself and the visiting press about how the Negro prefers segregation.

There was J. B. Easterly with his spurious story about the national "all-Negro" group being organized to maintain segregation; there were the editorials and the politicians asserting over and over again that "outside influences" were upsetting "the fine relationship between whites and Negroes in the South"; there were hundreds of whites parroting the same argument James F. Byrnes had given me in 1953 about how "only the Negro agitators and false leaders" desired integration.

It gave me a queasy, frightening feeling deep inside to listen to these arguments and realize that pills of self-deception were being dispensed and swallowed so generally across the South that a semi-literate cement-block builder in Louisiana in 1956 was using, almost verbatim, the rationalizations used almost three years earlier by a man who had held some of the highest positions this democracy can bestow upon an individual.

J. B. Easterly told us that the Negro preferred segregation because he is better off in the South than in the North. "One southern state—South Carolina—employs more Negro teachers than all your goddamn meddling northern states put together."

Like Byrnes, Easterly neglected to mention the fact that teaching is practically the only professional state job a Negro can hold in the Deep South; or the fact that a strictly segregated system demands that South Carolina find 7,000 Negro teachers; or that these factors explain why so many Negroes are in the teaching profession in the Deep South. Easterly and others went on with the words of Byrnes, who told me in 1953 that there are about the same number of Negroes in New York City as in South Carolina and that, considering the relative poorness of South Carolina, Negroes in New York City are worse off.

(This is what the bureau of census reports for 1950:

In the New York metropolitan area, 579,410 Negroes over fourteen reported a median annual income of $1,707. In South Carolina, 506,436 Negroes over fourteen reported median annual incomes of $525.

In New York the median income for whites over fourteen was $2,517 compared with $1,684 for whites in South Carolina, indicating that New York is wealthier, even to the extent that a Negro in New York has a higher median income than a white person in South Carolina.

Allowing for this greater wealth, census figures show that the Negro still is better off in New York City. There his income is more than half that of the whites; in South Carolina it is less than one-third that of whites.)

So I listened to these white men—defiant today, wielding the big stick, predicting that the Negro will be humble; angelic tomorrow, disobeying the court only to do obedience to God, only to help the Negro who wants segregation, only fulfilling the white man's paternal duty to act as the Negro's best friend.

But even as I listened, sometimes disheartened and often confused, I could see that although there might be reasons to fear for my native South and my country, there should be no despair for the Negro. Swirling all about me and the white man was new evidence that the new Negro might not be humble.

In the early evening hours of December 1, 1955, a bright yellow bus passed through the court square in the heart of Montgomery, Alabama, and stopped in front of the Empire Theater. When a bespectacled, soft-voiced Negro seamstress refused to get up and yield her seat to white passengers, the white citizens of "the Cradle of the Confederacy" began to see the nation's most dramatic demonstration of the existence of this new Negro.

But let us tell that story in much of its detail, for in it is all the conflict, the pathos, the individual courage, the sacrifice, the spirit of Gandhi, the hope and the hopelessness that is the Southland of today.

On this Montgomery City Lines bus, with seating capacity of thirty-six, twenty-four Negroes and twelve white people sat in the traditional Jim Crow pattern: the Negroes to the rear, the whites to the front. Several passengers of both races were standing. Not only was this tradition, but the law, for the Montgomery city code required bus drivers to assign seats to passengers so as to separate whites from Negroes. The city code gave bus drivers police powers for the purpose of enforcing racial segregation.

At the Empire Theater stop, several white passengers boarded the bus, whereupon the driver asked four Negroes to stand so the whites might sit.

Three Negroes complied, but Mrs. Rosa Parks, a forty-two-year-old seamstress at a department store and a well-known and highly respected citizen, refused. She said later that her action was spontaneous. Perhaps it was from tiredness, perhaps the resentment that is welling up high inside the new Negro was manifesting itself.

The bus driver called a policeman, who took Mrs. Parks off the bus to the police station, where she was charged with violating the city's segregation law. Trial was set for the following Monday, December 5, and Mrs. Parks was released on bond.

The news spread quickly through a Negro community where deep bitterness already existed over the bus situation. There had been many charges that bus drivers used abusive language toward Negro passengers. During 1955, two other Negro women had been taken off the bus, arrested and fined, although they contended that they were seated according to bus company policy. One Negro mother had stirred anger among the 60,000 Negroes in the metropolitan area when she told about a driver's alleged action when she put her two infants on the front seat while getting change from her purse. She said the driver ordered her to take the children from the seat, and without giving her a chance to place them elsewhere, lunged the bus forward, throwing the children onto the floor.

When word of Mrs. Parks' arrest reached the rougher element in the tavern district, they began to organize. "Goddamn it, we're gonna make it safe for our women," said one tough guy. "These bus drivers either dog 'em or date 'em."

But several Negro ministers were informed that these Negroes were oiling their pistols, sharpening their switch blades, and building up an arsenal of pipes, baseball bats and spiked sticks. The ministers got busy. On December 3, two days before the trial, the Negro community was flooded with mysterious circulars asking Negroes to stage a one-day protest by refusing to ride buses on the day of the trial. As yet, there has been no public admission as to who arranged for and distributed the circulars, but it is my belief that the job was done by the ministers, seeking to prevent the hoodlum element from carrying out its threat to "beat the hell out of a few bus drivers." On Sunday, December 4, many Negro ministers included in their sermons a request that Negroes protest Mrs. Parks' arrest by staying off buses the following day.

On Monday, after the newspapers had given even wider circulation to the protest plans, probably eighty per cent of the Negro bus riders went to their jobs by bicycle, taxi, truck, wagon or on foot, covering distances up to ten miles. City officials were somewhat disturbed, but officials of Montgomery City Lines, a subsidiary of National City Lines of Chicago, were alarmed, for Montgomery's Negroes represented seventy per cent of the company's passengers.

On Monday, Mrs. Parks was found guilty of disobeying the bus driver and fined $10 and $4 cost. This angered Negroes even more. That night, 5,000 Negroes overflowed the Holt Street Baptist Church, where, according to press reports, some forty-seven Negro ministers and one white one, the Reverend Robert S. Graetz of the all-Negro Trinity Lutheran Church, led the crowd through hymn-singing and speech-making and produced a solid corps of citizens determined to produce changes in the transportation system of Montgomery. They extended the boycott—or "protest" as they called it—until such time as the bus company and city officials agreed to (1) more courteous treatment of Negroes; (2) seating on a first-come-first-served basis, agreeing that Negroes would continue to fill the bus from the rear and whites from the front; and (3) that Negro bus drivers be employed on predominantly Negro lines.

Negro citizens founded the Montgomery Improvement Association to direct the protest and to work out new means of transportation for Negroes. Named president of the association was a quiet, pacifist-type, twenty-seven-year-old minister with a doctorate in religion from Boston University, the Reverend Martin Luther King, Jr., pastor of the Dexter Avenue Baptist Church.

At dawn the following morning, Montgomery was a strange sight. People accustomed to seeing as many as two hundred Negro domestics awaiting buses at Montgomery and Lee Streets saw none. Instead, beginning at 5 A.M., they saw a straggling parade of the young and the aged, hiking to their jobs. They saw some three hundred Negro-owned automobiles—old clunks fresh from used-car lots and new family "chariots"—picking up other Negro workers. They saw the wife of a Negro doctor halt her shiny Cadillac to offer a ride to domestic workers.

"I'm sure glad this protest started," a Negro maid whispered to the doctor's wife. "Otherwise, I never would've got to ride in a car like this."

They saw empty and near-empty buses, and wealthy white women, in housecoats and pincurls, driving to get Negro servants. Occasionally they saw a white citizen using his car to give free rides to Negroes.

The bus company reported that a half-dozen or so of its buses were stoned and shot at as they rolled through Negro neighborhoods. The Negro ministers—who had achieved the almost unbelievable by pulling the hoodlums out of the crap games and honky-tonks into the churches where they sang hymns, gave money, shouted amen and wept over the powerful speeches—quickly went to the public with paid advertisements in the daily press:

1. Non-violence—
    At no time have the participants of this movement advocated or anticipated violence. We stand willing and ready to report and give any assistance in exposing persons who resort to violence. This is a movement of passive resistance, depending on moral and spiritual forces. We, the oppressed, have no hate in our hearts for the oppressors, but we are, nevertheless, determined to resist until the cause of justice triumphs.

2. Coercion—

There has not been any coercion on the part of any leader to force anyone to stay off the buses. The rising tide of resentment has come to fruition. This resentment has resulted in a vast majority of the people staying off the buses willingly and voluntarily.

3. Arbitration—

We are willing to arbitrate. We feel that this can be done with men and women of good will. However, we find it rather difficult to arbitrate in good faith with those whose public pronouncements are anti-Negro and whose only desire seems to be that of maintaining the status quo. We call upon men of good will, who will be willing to treat this issue in the spirit of Him whose birth we celebrate at this season, to meet with us. We stand for Christian teachings and the concepts of democracy for which men and women of all races have fought and died.

Now the boycott was practically ninety-five per cent effective, and the bus company was suffering losses estimated at $3,200 per day. The Negroes had organized a car pool, posting unsigned and unidentified schedules on telephone poles or the sides of buildings. These schedules listed some forty pickup points at which workers could get rides from 6 to 8:30 A.M. and from 3 to 6 P.M. City policemen, under orders from a white supremacist police commissioner, became extra zealous in enforcing the city's traffic laws. To avoid violating regulations governing taxis, automobiles operating in the Negro pool charged no fares. Funds were collected for gasoline at the churches and at rallies which became regular events.

Tension rose. National City Lines of Chicago sent a representative to Montgomery to look into the trouble. The mayor of Montgomery, W. A. Gayle, himself an ardent segregationist, called a meeting to which several citizens were invited, including a leader of the Montgomery White Citizens Council. Out of this meeting the mayor appointed a committee to try to reach a solution.

The Negroes observed that among the whites appointed was the White Citizens Council leader, and they contended that the whites were not prepared to bargain in good faith. Whites accused the Negroes of not wanting to reach a solution. On matters of disagreement, the sixteen-member committee split along racial lines—eight Negroes against eight whites.

Now the citizenry began to observe that something revolutionary was taking place in the heart of Alabama. But large numbers of whites still were unwilling to believe that this was the mark of the new Negro. On December 13, the Montgomery *Advertiser,* a newspaper which had been skillful at saying "nice" things about Negroes just often enough to stay in the "liberal" column, while cutting their throats when it really counted, declared editorially:

"A lot of grief can be averted if whites and Negroes in these parts dismiss their emotions long enough to take a cool, practical look at the consequences of boycott and counter-boycott . . . as a matter of enlightened self-interest. . . .

"The bus boycott here is a painful economic injury to the company.

"But as a matter of the facts of life, Negro leaders should reckon with two realities:

"The white man's economic artillery is far superior, better emplaced, and commanded by more experienced gunners.

"Second, the white man holds all the offices of government machinery. There will be white rule as far as the eye can see.

"Are those not facts of life?"

Mayor Gayle and others quickly charged that Negroes were being kept off the buses by fear. Gayle charged that "outside influences" were "stirring this thing up." He promised police protection to anyone who wanted to ride the buses, adding that Montgomery "has good impartial law enforcement, with equal treatment for white and black. We have offered them equal accommodations and everything else. But they want integration—that's the whole thing."

But one of the leading citizens of Montgomery, Miss Juliette Morgan, saw the Negroes' protest as a fine example of the spirit and the discipline of Mahatma Gandhi. In a letter to the editor of the *Advertiser*, she wrote:

"The Negroes of Montgomery seem to have taken a lesson from Gandhi—and our own Thoreau, who influenced Gandhi. Their own task is greater than Gandhi's, however, for they have greater prejudice to overcome.

"One feels that history is being made in Montgomery these days, the most important in her career. It is hard to imagine a soul so dead, a heart so hard, a vision so blinded and provincial as not to be moved with admiration at the quiet dignity, discipline and dedication with which the Negroes have conducted their boycott. . . .

"It is sad indeed that the most reasonable and moderate requests presented to the bus company and City Commission by the Reverend M. L. King were met with such a 'Ye rebels! Disperse!' attitude as voiced by their attorney and others. No, the law must be enforced with all pharisaical zeal and inflexibility. Well, I say the law ought to be changed. . . .

"I am all for law and order, the protection of person and property against violence, but I believe the Constitution and Supreme Court of the United States constitute the supreme law of the land. I find it ironical to hear men in authority who are openly flouting this law speak piously of law enforcement.

"I also find it hard to work up sympathy for the bus company. . . . Three times I've gotten off the bus because I could not countenance the treatment of Negroes. I should have gotten off on several other occasions. Twice I have heard a certain driver with high seniority mutter quite audibly 'black ape.' I could not tell whether the Negro heard or not, but I did and felt insulted.

"It is interesting to read editorials on the legality of this boycott. They make me think of that famous one that turned America from a tea- to a coffee-drinking nation. Come to think of it, one might say that this nation was founded upon a boycott.

"The likening of the bus boycott to those of the White Citizens Councils is misleading. The difference in the causes and in the spirit behind each is vast. Just compare the speeches delivered at Selma and here in the City Hall with those at the Holt Street Baptist Church Monday night. Read them side by side as reported in the *Advertiser*—and blush."

These were extremely interesting words from an Alabama white woman, and they must have been heartening words to those Negroes who wondered whether they walked alone. They certainly were important words, for there were many whites, including the editors of the daily papers, seeking to put the Negro protesters in the same camp as the members of the White Citizens Councils who had resorted to economic coercion in order to defy the decision of the United States Supreme Court.

I asked Dr. King if he saw any difference between what the Negroes were doing and what the Citizens Councils were doing.

"Ours is an open and above-board protest for the birth of justice," said the young minister. "The White Citizens Councils' is a surreptitious movement for the perpetuation of injustice, to preserve what is illegal, to maintain a deadening status quo.

"This," added Dr. King, "is democracy being transformed from thin paper to thick action. Negroes long infected with the crippling paralysis of fear are tired of the long nights of captivity and are now reaching out for the daybreak of freedom."

By now, white Montgomery was shocked—shocked at the determination of Negroes who said: "We will not retreat one inch in our fight to secure and hold our American citizenship. The history books will write of us as a race of people who in Montgomery County, state of Alabama, country of the United States, stood up and fought for their rights as American citizens, as citizens of a democracy."

But always, the leaders of the protest kept their hand atop those Negroes who once were eager to resort to violence. Pastor Graetz, the young white minister who had stood beside the Negroes through the bitterest kind of harassment, wrote the National Lutheran Council that the Negroes of Montgomery were "conducting a real 'love' campaign":

"Week after week [the Negro] ministers proclaimed, 'We must love our enemies. Don't ever let them bring you down so low that you will hate them. We don't want to harm anyone. . . .'

"And the white leaders of Montgomery are at a loss. They do not know how to meet such a campaign. If we were to take up arms, they could defeat us in battle. If we were to engage in full-scale economic warfare, they could starve us into submission. But they know not how to respond to the regular prayers that we send up in their behalf."

As I moved about Montgomery, it became obvious that the Negro people sensed that the white man of Montgomery was at a loss. In all the eighteen years I had lived in the South, in my three extended trips back since World War II, I had never seen such spirit among a group of Negroes. When a Negro minister, working for the car pool, offered a ride to an old woman who obviously had walked a long distance, he said: "Sister, aren't you getting tired?"

"My soul has been tired for a long time," she replied. "Now my feet are tired and my soul is resting."

The Reverend R. D. Abernathy, pastor of First Baptist Church and one of the leaders in the protest, told me of a seventy-year-old Negro woman who limped to his church one morning looking for a car-pool ride to work. All the cars were out.

"You're old and crippled, and it's cold," a young Negro said to the woman. "You take the bus to work. We'll understand."

"Children, I ain't got many days left," the old woman replied. "So I ain't walking for myself. I'm walking for my grandson. I want him to be able to pay his money and take his seat."

The old woman hobbled off.

One Negro woman quit her $12-a-week domestic job and devoted her time to the boycott when the white woman for whom she worked refused to drive her home from work.

"I told her that if I took a taxi, I would have only four dollars left, and I'd rather be rested and proud with no money than tired and humiliated with four dollars—so good-bye," the woman reported.

Still Montgomery's police commissioner, Clyde Sellers (one of the three commissioners who would have to rule on any concessions granted the Negroes), insisted that he was unimpressed by the Negroes' protest. He boldly joined the local White Citizens Council. The Montgomery *Advertiser* reminded the public of its December 13 warning that white people held all the big ammunition, and then pointed out that by joining the pro-segregation group, Sellers had in effect made the city's police force an arm of the White Citizens Council. The editorial was more a passed-along threat than an expression of the *Advertiser*'s desire to help Negroes, though.

The *Advertiser* reported that its poll showed white citizens overwhelmingly in support of the bus company. The Alabama Council on Human Relations, an interracial group, reported that letters from whites to the city's newspapers were running five to one in favor of the Negroes' position.

Negro leaders said one gauge of white opinion—at least, whites in higher educational and economic brackets—was the fact that employers did not try to force Negroes to ride buses.

"One white woman fired her Negro cook for refusing to ride," reported Fred D. Gray, twenty-five-year-old Negro lawyer and a leading figure in the protest, "but the white woman next door hired the Negro as she left the first house!"

He told of another domestic who got tired of walking and took the bus. Her white employer found out and fired her with this lecture: "If you have no race pride—if your own people can't trust you—then I can't trust you in my house."

Whites like Grover C. Hall, Jr., editor of the *Advertiser,* and Commissioner Sellers said it just wasn't so. The boycott couldn't be spontaneous, they argued.

My colleague, Kleeman, and I asked Hall's city editor, Joe Azbell, if Negroes were using intimidation to keep Negroes off buses.

"They haven't been able to convict anybody," he replied. "One man was arrested on a policeman's complaint, but they had to release him."

We asked Hall if Negroes were using coercion.

"It's indisputable on any assumptive basis," he replied. I paused to figure out how something assumptive could be indisputable, but was interrupted by Hall, who was quite sensitive about two northern reporters even coming to Montgomery.

"So many Negroes are leaving here for the East that pretty soon you fellows can stay home and cover the story," he cracked.

"Wherever the story is—New Jersey, Minnesota or Montgomery—we'll be there, for if it affects part of the nation, it affects all the nation," I replied.

When I expressed a desire to cover a meeting of the White Citizens Council scheduled for that evening, Hall advised me not to.

"I know that crowd—it's pretty rough," he said. "Now if you want a good city editor's tip, why don't you ride a bus and tell what they do to a Negro? That's how you find out about the labor-union-type goons."

(I took this tip, going to a busy intersection in the heart of the Negro community. I got bored because no one bothered me while I awaited the bus. While Kleeman stood nearby watching, I strolled across the street in front of a tavern and inquired of three Negroes whether I was waiting in the right place.

"Mister, you know about the buses—about the boycott?" one of them asked me.

"Sure—but that doesn't mean I can't ride if I want to, does it?"

A second Negro rushed to say that "goddamn right he can ride—nobody gonna bother you long as I'm here. Damn right you can ride if you want to."

Suddenly the bus was there. I smiled as I ran to it, for I heard one of the three Negroes say: "Man, there goes a queer one."

Kleeman and I noticed that a Negro nurse boarded the bus as we did. We learned that she rode it every night and had not been molested by any "union-type goons.")

Kleeman and I left the *Advertiser* office agreed that we should find out more about who was behind the boycott, and how it functioned. I telephoned a Negro leader who convinced a group of Negroes holding a "strategy meeting" on the boycott that they should let me sit in.

At the home of Mrs. JoAnn Robinson, an English instructor at Alabama

State College (Negro), I found the "brains" behind the protest. Present were the Reverend A. W. Wilson, fifty-three, pastor of the Holt Street Baptist Church; the Reverend W. J. Powell, forty-seven, pastor of the A.M.E. Zion Church; Reverend Abernathy; Mrs. R. T. Adair, wife of a Negro doctor; Dr. King; Gray; and Mrs. Robinson.

They talked freely of the "protest"—although they insisted that as leaders, they were not proud of what was taking place.

"If only the whites could realize that we are working to help Montgomery," said Mrs. Adair. "As long as they keep Negroes bottlenecked, intimidated and ignorant, they keep themselves ignorant.

"Oh, it pains me deeply when I think of the brain power and the man hours that we have poured into this thing. Think how many constructive things we could do for the city if they did not force us to spend every second struggling for basic decency.

"The white man in this town just does not want to believe that this is a people's movement," added Mrs. Adair. "In that fact lies the real tragedy of our South: because of segregation there is no communication between whites and Negroes."

When asked about alleged "Negro goon squads," attorney Gray insisted that not the slightest intimidation was needed to keep Negroes off buses. Almost every Negro in Montgomery had been humiliated at one time or the other by a bus driver, he said, so the Rosa Parks case was merely the culmination of many grievances.

Gray cited cases of bus drivers' cursing some Negro women, trying to date others, and of their forcing pregnant Negro women to stand so white youths might sit. He reeled off names like Claudette Colvin, Alberta Smith, Mrs. Viola White—these among the five women and two children who were arrested in 1955 (one Negro man was killed by a policeman) when they ignored a driver's order to stand.

This, Gray said, is what united all the Negro ministerial groups in Montgomery and provoked them to speak for 60,000 Negroes: "Our cup of tolerance has run over. Our people . . . prefer to walk rather than endure more."

II

But the white man figured the Negro still would be humble. And still available was that old technique used all over the world to keep the underprivileged underprivileged, that old technique used for decades in the South to keep the Negro "in his place": divide and rule. White Montgomery officials set about trying just that. On Saturday night, January 21, 1956, I sat down to dinner in Minneapolis. In a couple of hours I would drive to the corner drugstore to get the Minneapolis *Sunday Tribune*, in which Kleeman and I were telling the story of Montgomery, in its forty-ninth day of the bus boycott. My telephone rang and the news editor asked if I was sitting or standing. After receiving an assurance that my heart could take any bad news, he told me that Associated Press had just filed a dispatch announcing that the Negro ministers of Montgomery had agreed to end their boycott. I first expressed disgust over the idea of having to leave dinner to try to change our story from what suddenly had become ancient history to something up-to-date. My second reaction was disbelief. I telephoned Dr. King, who told me that he had not seen city officials, that the protest leaders had held a meeting of their own, and that they had not agreed to end the boycott. I telephoned attorney Gray, who advised me that neither he nor any other boycott leader had met with city officials or agreed to end their protest. I checked with Associated Press, which said its Montgomery correspondent had filed the story attributing it to Commissioner Sellers. I telephoned Sellers, who told me that three Negro ministers, "a Presbyterian, a Holiness Bishop and a Baptist," had met with him and other white leaders and had agreed to end the boycott.

"Could you give me the names of these ministers?" I asked.

"You know, we don't really know these Nigras down here," Sellers replied, assuming that I was white. "We just know these Nigras by what they represent, not by name."

I advised the police commissioner that I had just talked with the boycott leaders and that they had denied any settlement. He expressed no surprise. I asked if he felt the ministers with whom he conferred could end the boycott. Sellers said he did not think the three ministers had enough influence, "but they might start other Nigras to thinking." He said that if Montgomery Negroes refused the offer of January 21 (which was a promise for more courtesy, but a denial of the other demands), Negroes could "go on walking because we have met with them for the last time."

The Montgomery reporter had failed even to telephone the Negro leaders of the protest, but had filed his unsubstantiated "agreement" story as part of what the Negroes promptly labeled "a scheme to divide and mislead Negroes." The protest leaders set about identifying the three Negroes who had met with the white officials. These three ministers denied agreeing to any compromise plan for ending the boycott. They said that they had been "duped" into attending the meeting.

When their divisive scheme failed, Montgomery officials were furious. Mayor Gayle, who was one of those who proclaimed loudly that Negroes preferred segregation, expressed disgust over rumors that even his Negro help, who had been saying "Yassuh, Boss" at work, were hurrying to church, where they put large portions of their wages into the collection plate for the NAACP. On January 23, Gayle issued a bristling statement after announcing that he and his fellow members of the city commission had joined the White Citizens Council. He said that the White Citizens of Montgomery had "pussyfooted around on this boycott long enough and it has come time to be frank and honest.

". . . There seems to be a belief on the part of the Negroes that they have the white people hemmed up in a corner and they are not going to give an inch until they can force the white people of our community to submit to their demands—in fact, swallow all of them," he said.

"The Negro leaders have forced the bus boycott into a campaign between whether the social fabric of our community will continue to exist or will be destroyed by a group of Negro radicals who have split asunder the fine relationships which have existed between the Negro and white people for generations. . . .

"The white people are firm in their convictions that they do not care whether the Negroes ever ride a city bus again if it means that the social fabric of our community is to be destroyed so that the Negroes will start riding the buses again.

"It is not that important to whites that the Negroes ride the buses. This is not a matter of a bus boycott. It is a matter of a community relationship.

"The Negro leaders have proved they are not interested in ending the boycott but rather in prolonging it so that they may stir up racial strife. The Negro leaders have proved they will say one thing to a white man and another thing to a Negro. They have proved it again and again. . . .

"When and if the Negro people desire to end the boycott, my door is open to them. But until they are ready to end it, there will be no more discussions."

Mayor Gayle was especially vexed about the white families who gave car rides to their Negro help, or paid their taxi fares. He said that the cooks and maids boycotting the buses "are fighting to destroy our social fabric just as much as the Negro radicals who are leading them. The Negroes are laughing at white people behind their backs. . . . They think it's very funny and amusing that whites who are opposed to the Negro boycott will act as chauffeurs to Negroes who are boycotting the buses. When a white person gives a Negro a single penny for transportation or helps a Negro with his transportation, even if it's a block ride, he is helping the Negro radicals who lead the boycott. The Negroes have made their own bed, and the whites should let them sleep in it."

Meanwhile, the city officials, particularly the policemen under Clyde Sellers, had adopted a few "get-tough" tactics of their own. Dr. King was arrested and fined on a charge of driving thirty-five miles an hour in a thirty-mile zone. City officials set out to press charges against young attorney Fred Gray, who had filed a suit on behalf of several Negro citizens, challenging the constitutionality of the bus segregation laws of Montgomery. The charge against Gray was that he acted unscrupulously and contrary to the principles of a good lawyer because he filed the suit "against the wishes" of some of the people listed as plaintiffs.

But not all the people who felt the whip of the get-tough policy were Negroes. Pastor Graetz, the white minister at Trinity Lutheran Church (he objects to its being referred to as all-Negro. "We have four white members—my wife, myself, and our two children, and pretty soon there will be five") had had his moments of harassment. Two weeks after the boycott began, Pastor Graetz went out on his routine chore of driving Negroes to work. After one trip, he pulled up to a parking meter at the main downtown pickup and dispatch station for Negroes seeking rides. The minister loaded five Negro women into his car and drove off, unaware that a sheriff's car was following him. A block or so from the drugstore, the sheriff's car pulled alongside and its driver motioned Pastor Graetz to the curb.

"What are you doing? Running a taxi?" asked the officer, who, the minister discovered, was Sheriff Mac Sim Butler. The sheriff accused the minister of picking up passengers in the taxi zone, demanded his license and then asked who his five passengers were.

"Just friends," Pastor Graetz replied.

"Friends!" Butler exploded back at him, as if to ask what white man in Alabama would have Negro friends. The sheriff told the women to remain in the car while the minister went with him to the county jail.

"When we got to the jail, he took me inside and left me alone in the office for a few moments. I was grateful for that, because it gave me a chance to pray a bit," Pastor Graetz remembers.

A deputy sheriff was sent out to ask the five women how much they were paying for the ride (the pastor, aware of the law, had charged nothing but urged his riders to contribute the equivalent of bus fare to the boycott expense fund).

The deputy searched the pastor's car and brought in copies of his newsletter to other ministers, a list of jitney pickup stations—"and," said Pastor Graetz with a grin, "a copy of our church budget, which didn't interest him much."

There followed lectures to the minister by the deputy sheriff along the line of "we like things the way things are around here and we don't intend to have anybody change them." The Bible, the deputy said, supports segregation.

Meanwhile, Sheriff Butler had disappeared. Soon he returned and told Pastor Graetz he had been to see a judge, who would not allow him to charge the pastor either with running a taxicab or with hauling whites and Negroes together.

There followed some more discussion with the deputy, "who just couldn't understand how I could be a Christian and a minister and believe the things I believe."

Then—after being detained about half an hour—the young minister was released (as his five passengers had been earlier).

After Pastor Graetz was the subject of an extensive—and largely fair and factual—article on the editorial page of the Montgomery *Advertiser,* he began receiving abusive calls.

One man, who reached the minister by telephone, exploded: "If I was you I wouldn't call myself a pastor. You're a no-good son of a bitch."

Later the pastor discovered that someone had slashed two tires on his new Chevrolet and poured sugar in his gasoline tank.

The Lutheran minister took all this in stride, just as Negro minister King had taken it in stride when someone planted dynamite under his home; just as NAACP leader E. D. Nixon took it in stride when dynamite was exploded in his front yard.

Pastor Graetz merely kept church people informed of what it meant to be a white man trying to live up to what he believed to be Christian principles amid this kind of tension. The twenty-seven-year-old, lean-faced Lutheran said he and his family felt like the circus lion tamer: "Our heads are in the lion's mouth."

But Pastor Graetz insisted that he did not feel overly courageous. "There are others who have made, and are still making, much bolder confessions while in 'enemy territory.' Some of them, especially ministers, have been driven out. A few have paid the supreme price of their lives."

Pastor Graetz could still laugh—laugh at the way the segregationists labeled him a "northern agitator" or a "Yankee carpetbagger," even though he was born and reared in West Virginia, where segregation also was a way of life until this decade, when the nation's courts and its new conscience began to produce change.

Pastor Graetz could ignore these labels, he said, because "a Negro minister who has lived in Montgomery for several years spent the first part of his life just across the county line, about thirty miles away. He says that every time trouble breaks out, he is branded as an outside agitator.

"People scratch their heads and wonder what this 'nigger-lovin' ' white preacher is up to. They suspect and have said so privately that the church sent me to Montgomery to stir up racial tension."

But in the early days of the boycott Pastor Graetz had explained quite simply why he felt obligated to join Negroes in their protest.

"Pie in the sky by and by may be a fine thing to look forward to," he told an official of the Lutheran church. "But my people [his congregation] deserve the opportunity to live a decent life in this world, too."

He also gave his answer to a reporter from the Montgomery *Advertiser:*

"The reactionary element in the South will stop at nothing to maintain their strangle hold on the Negro population, whom they still hold in virtual economic slavery.

"I have been told that I am a kind of symbol to my people. Many of them had long ago concluded that it was scarcely possible for a white person to be a Christian. But now they know that, with some of us, Christianity is more than pious profession of the lips. . . .

"I know that I shall be criticized for my stand. I may even suffer violence. But I cannot minister to souls alone. My people also have bodies."

Some weeks later Pastor Graetz's home was dynamited while he and the family were away. But he turned the other cheek—and went back to Montgomery.

III

Now what hope was there for a solution to the racial strife in Montgomery? On one side stood city officials who had announced boldly that they stood for segregation, that they were members of "the uptown Ku Klux Klan." On the other side were some 60,000 Negroes, united, as Negro people never before had been united, by harassment, bombings, intimidation—and most of all, united by the wise, dignified leadership that caused a sense of pride and achievement to well up inside the lowliest Negro. In the middle, of course, was a bus company, losing money, the first victim in "the battle of Montgomery."

Surely, now, Mayor Gayle must feel that Negroes were laughing out loud at the white people of Alabama—white people who, as the Montgomery *Advertiser* had warned so many weeks earlier, enjoyed superior economic artillery, white men who held all the offices of government machinery. Even editor Hall must have wondered by now whether or not there would be white rule as far as the eye could see.

Well, the showdown had to come. Sooner or later someone would have to find out whether the white man's control of the machinery of government would be enough to beat down these Negroes and put them "in their place." Those who visited the transportation centers, Negro drugstores, pool halls and barber shops would have seen much reason to doubt the possibility of this, because this Negro movement not only embodied courage but had cloaked itself with an armor of humor and a willingness to suffer that was becoming almost legendary.

But the city officials made their move. In March, 1956, they indicted ninety-odd Negroes, including twenty-four ministers, under an almost forgotten anti-labor law enacted in 1921 making it a misdemeanor to conspire "without a just cause or legal excuse" to hinder any company in its conduct of business.

The Negroes, men, women and church leaders, were arrested, fingerprinted and released on bond. A wave of anger and indignation rolled over the Negro community like the giant mushroom from a hydrogen bomb. But Dr. King cautioned Negroes against anger and violence: "Even if we are arrested every day, let no man drag you so low as to hate."

So in the late days of March the white men set up their machinery at the Montgomery County Courthouse—where, for a century, Negroes had gone in meekness—to test it against the black man's weapon of "passiveness and love."

But this time, Negroes walked straight and even haughtily down a gloomy corridor with its sign asserting that "Gentlemen will not and others must not spit on the floor." All who could not crowd inside the shabby old building, to huddle in anger beneath the American flag, stood outside to murmur and roar support and determination for the man on trial inside.

The first defendant (the Negroes had demanded separate trials) was Dr. King, who was accused, in effect, of organizing the Montgomery Improvement Association for the purpose of unjustly boycotting the bus company and forcing upon it the illegal demands of the Negro community. Dr. King's attorneys—from the NAACP, which now had stepped into the Montgomery boycott for the first time—were prepared to prove that the "protest" was spontaneous and that it arose from a just cause.

Dr. King, his eight lawyers and the Negro spectators, many wearing crosses urging "Father forgive them," listened intently as the prosecutor produced evidence that the Montgomery Improvement Association had spent some $30,000 in support of the boycott. He produced witnesses who testified that force had been used to maintain the boycott, and the Negro courthouse janitor bragged that he knocked down a Negro who threatened to whip him if he didn't stop riding the bus. The prosecutor gave no evidence that the defendant was linked to any violence; the record showed that, in fact, Dr. King had urged Negroes against violence.

When time came for the defense to show the "just cause" that provoked a spontaneous protest, Della Perkins took the stand and testified that a driver once called her "an ugly black ape." Georgia Gilmore said that when she boarded a bus the driver hollered, "Come out, nigger, and go in the back door," and that when she stepped off he drove away. Sadie Brooks said she saw a Negro man forced from a bus at pistol-point because he did not have the correct change. Martha Walker said her blind husband's leg was injured when a bus driver shut a door on him and drove on. Stella Brooks testified that her husband was shot to death when he refused to obey a bus driver, but the judge ordered this testimony stricken from the record because Stella Brooks did not see the shooting.

After four dramatic days of testimony, Circuit Judge Eugene Carter reached a quick verdict; he found Dr. King guilty, fined him $500 and assessed him $400 for court costs. Dr. King appealed and was released on bond.

Outside that old courthouse, the throng of Negroes raised their voices in rebellious tones such as the Deep South had never heard before. A minister shouted out plans for a mass prayer meeting that night.

"Y'all gonna be there?" demanded a bass-voiced man.

"Yes, Jesus, yes," replied a roly-poly woman just after the crowd had shouted a loud "Yes."

"Y'all gonna ride them buses?" bellowed the bass-voiced man.

"No," roared the crowd.

"You're damn right we ain't," added the roly-poly woman.

Now the cold winter rains had stopped. Flowers were blooming in Alabama. A deeper green came over the weeping-willow trees. Negro Montgomery began to forget about the worn-out brakes and the slipping clutches in the family cars that were volunteered for the transportation pool. Now a fleet of sleek station wagons rolled down the streets, bearing the names of the Negro churches. City officials had denied a request by the Negroes for permission to operate their own bus company.

A new element of conflict arose when, on April 23, 1956, the United States Supreme Court dismissed as frivolous an appeal from a Court of Appeals decision in Richmond, Virginia, holding that racial segregation on intrastate buses violated the Federal Constitution. This case arose from a lawsuit filed in South Carolina by a Negro who had been ordered by a bus driver to sit in the "Negro section" of a bus.

Newspapermen hastily interpreted this as a decision by the Supreme Court outlawing intrastate transit segregation. Several transit firms in the South quickly announced that they would cease enforcing segregation, among them Montgomery City Lines. It developed, however, that by a technicality, the Supreme Court actually had made no clear ruling on segregation.

Montgomery city officials demanded that the bus company resume its old policy of having drivers enforce segregation. The bus company, still in a financial pinch despite a fifty-per-cent fare increase, refused to do so. The city turned to Circuit Judge Walter B. Jones, who ruled on May 9 that the bus company would have to continue a policy of segregation.

But Montgomery knew, as all the South must know, that the last word had not been spoken, for the legality of bus segregation in the state was being challenged (by the NAACP at the request of Montgomery Negroes) before a three-judge federal court panel. On June 5, these judges, all southerners, voted two to one that bus segregation in Montgomery violated the Constitution. Judge Richard T. Rives of the Fifth U.S. Circuit Court of Appeals and Judge Frank M. Johnson, Jr., of the United States Middle District Court, signed the majority opinion. Judge Seybourn Lynne of the Northern Alabama United States District Court in Birmingham dissented.

The decision was hailed by Dr. King as "a great victory for democracy and justice." There was hope, the happy Negroes cried, so long as the Citizens Councils could not buy or intimidate the federal courts.

On June 28, attorneys for the state appealed the federal panel's decision to the United States Supreme Court. Pending this decision, segregation continued in the once-quiet capital, the old Cradle of the Confederacy; so did the Negroes' boycott. In the besieged and bewildered Southland, the battle lines were shaping up for a new kind of conflict: a new Negro with an old Constitution against the old South with a new-style Ku Klux Klan.

Once again it was time for the nation's highest tribunal to speak. Meanwhile, black Montgomery would continue to walk and ride those church-sponsored station wagons. But each day brought new troubles for their operators. Most any speed seemed too fast for the city's traffic laws; suddenly, no Negro could make a proper left turn. Finally, the segregationists found a way (and with very little trouble in the Alabama courts) to ban the use of the station wagons altogether.

On November 13, 1956, even as the Negroes turned to the federal courts in an effort to regain use of the station wagons, the Supreme Court spoke: the lower federal court was correct when it said on June 5 that an Alabama law and a Montgomery ordinance requiring racial separation violated the Negroes' constitutional rights.

The next night 2,000 cheering Negroes held another mass meeting and voted to end their eleven-month-old protest as soon as the Supreme Court order was delivered to the local court.

Alabama State Senator Sam Engelhardt called the Supreme Court ruling "another attempt by a group of misguided zealots in Washington to torpedo constitutional government." To him it meant nothing that all these Washington "zealots" had done was say "amen" to what two white Alabama judges had said five months earlier.

Montgomery's white leaders, beaten but defiant, announced that they would fight the Supreme Court ruling "with every lawful means." But the Negro citizens had no doubt but that they had scored a great victory, that a "new age" had dawned in which American Negroes would use this technique of "non-violent protest" to end segregation in other areas of life.

A year after the beginning of the boycott, Montgomery Negroes conducted a week-long institute on "non-violence and social change," at which their leader, Dr. King, said:

"If we are to speed up the coming of the new age we must have the moral courage to stand up and protest against injustice wherever we find it. Wherever we find segregation we must have the fortitude to passively resist it. . . . This will mean suffering and sacrifices. It might even mean going to jail. . . . we must be willing to fill up the jailhouses of the South. It might even mean physical death. But if physical death is the price that some must pay to free their children from a permanent life of psychological death, then nothing could be more honorable."

On December 21, 1956, the Supreme Court's decree was delivered to Montgomery. Dr. King and other Negro ministers led a return to the buses after workshop demonstrations of courtesy, including advice that Negroes should sit beside whites only if no other seats were available. "We are not returning to the buses to abuse anyone, or to gloat over any so-called victory over the white people of Montgomery," Dr. King said. "We shall go back in a spirit of love and humility."

On December 22 newspapers all over the country headlined stories that Negroes had ridden unsegregated without any unpleasant incidents. But there were ominous reports of carloads of white men, members of the Citizens Council, observing buses, sometimes following them.

Then there came a report that three white men had beaten a teen-age Negro girl as she got off a bus. A few days later Dr. King announced in a sermon that during the night someone had fired a shotgun blast into his front door. Then snipers began to shoot at buses, hitting one Negro woman passenger in the leg.

Meanwhile, the movement to secure compliance with the court ruling had spread to other cities. The Reverend F. L. Shuttlesworth, a thirty-four-year-old Negro minister in Birmingham, led a group of Negroes in an unsegregated bus ride. Birmingham police, who have given the city a reputation as one of the most racially brutal in the world, arrested three Negroes. During the night, Reverend Shuttlesworth's home was ripped by a dynamite explosion. Miraculously, no one was killed.

The young minister went before his congregation (and the nation's television cameras) the next day and took note of the fact that millions of Americans were in anguish over Communist Russia's rape of Hungary. Reverend Shuttlesworth said that he shared this concern; that he approved President Eisenhower's humane decision to raise the quota for Hungarian refugees; but that he wanted to say this to Americans:

"You cannot go on throwing bread to Hungarians and bombs at us."

Birmingham Negroes returned to segregated riding, pending a court test of the city's right to enforce its segregation ordinance—a court decision that now was a foregone conclusion. But the pattern of violence was spreading. The situation became so bad in Tallahassee that Florida's Governor LeRoy Collins ordered all bus service halted. Negro ministers in Atlanta began a desegregation movement, provoking Governor Marvin Griffin to alert the National Guard, a body Talmadge had once threatened to use to keep segregation.

In the early darkness of January 10, 1957, four Negro churches and the homes of two ministers were dynamited in Montgomery. One of the homes was that of Reverend Graetz, the white Lutheran. No one was killed, but only because eleven sticks of dynamite placed at the Graetz home failed to explode.

Montgomery buses were ordered halted and Governor James E. Folsom offered a $2,000 reward for the arrest and conviction of the bomb-throwers.

"The issue now is no longer segregation on city buses. . . . The issue is whether it is safe to live in Montgomery, Alabama," declared the *Advertiser.*

Amid this angry furor, the Southern Regional Council in Atlanta announced that many cities—Little Rock, Pine Bluff, Fort Smith and Hot Springs, Arkansas; Charlotte, Greensboro, Durham and Winston-Salem, North Carolina; Richmond, Norfolk, Portsmouth, Newport News, Petersburg, Charlottesville, Fredericksburg, Lynchburg and Roanoke, Virginia; San Antonio, Corpus Christi and Dallas, Texas; and Knoxville, Tennessee—had quietly ended bus segregation.

As the violence continued in the Deep South, some fifty Negro leaders assembled in Atlanta. They appealed jointly to President Eisenhower, whom Negroes had favored with more of their votes than any Republican presidential candidate in decades, for a trip South and a speech asking southerners to respect law and order.

All along, there had been a growing cry that the President had taken the comfortable refuge of pretending that the South's struggles over desegregation were not the business of his administration. Many felt that his aloofness—timidity, even—had added to the boldness of hoodlums and lawless groups and forced southerners of good will to run to shelter. But there was little room for evasion of this challenge from Atlanta, this request that the man most able to articulate the moral conscience of the nation walk into the midst of southerners and say that the girl-beaters and dynamite-throwers were betraying and dishonoring America. Nevertheless, early in February, Presidential Assistant Sherman Adams advised Dr. King that President Eisenhower had decided against making any such speech in the South.

Parting the Waters:
America in the King Years

1988

◆

TAYLOR BRANCH

King stood silently for a moment. When he greeted the enormous crowd of strangers, who were packed in the balconies and aisles, peering in through the windows and upward from seats on the floor, he spoke in a deep voice, stressing his diction in a slow introductory cadence. "We are here this evening—for serious business," he said, in even pulses, rising and then falling in pitch. When he paused, only one or two "yes" responses came up from the crowd, and they were quiet ones. It was a throng of shouters, he could see, but they were waiting to see where he would take them. "We are here in a general sense, because first and foremost—we are American citizens—and we are determined to apply our citizenship—to the fullness of its means," he said. "But we are here in a specific sense—because of the bus situation in Montgomery." A general murmur of assent came back to him, and the pitch of King's voice rose gradually through short, quickened sentences. "The situation is not at all new. The problem has existed over endless years. Just the other day—just last Thursday to be exact—one of the finest citizens in Montgomery—not one of the finest Negro citizens—but one of the finest citizens in Montgomery—was taken from a bus—and carried to jail and arrested—because she refused to give up—to give her seat to a white person."

The crowd punctuated each pause with scattered "Yeses" and "Amens." They were with him in rhythm, but lagged slightly behind in enthusiasm. Then King spoke of the law, saying that the arrest was doubtful even under the segregation ordinances, because reserved Negro and white bus sections were not specified in them. "The law has never been clarified at that point," he said, drawing an emphatic "Hell, no" from one man in his audience. "And I think I speak with—with legal authority—not that I have any legal authority—but I think I speak with legal authority behind me—that the law—the ordinance—the city ordinance has never been totally clarified." This sentence marked King as a speaker who took care with distinctions, but it took the crowd nowhere. King returned to the special nature of Rosa Parks. "And since it had to happen, I'm happy it happened to a person like Mrs. Parks," he said, "for nobody can doubt the boundless outreach of her integrity. Nobody can doubt the height of her character, nobody can doubt the depth of her Christian commitment." That's right, a soft chorus answered. "And just because she refused to get up, she was arrested," King repeated. The crowd was stirring now, following King at the speed of a medium walk.

He paused slightly longer. "And you know, my friends, there comes a time," he cried, "when people get tired of being trampled over by the iron feet of oppression." A flock of "Yeses" was coming back at him when suddenly the individual responses dissolved into a rising cheer and applause exploded beneath the cheer—all within the space of a second. The startling noise rolled on and on, like a wave that refused to break, and just when it seemed that the roar must finally weaken, a wall of sound came in from the enormous crowd outdoors to push the volume still higher. Thunder seemed to be added to the lower register—the sound of feet stomping on the wooden floor—until the loudness became something that was not so much heard as it was sensed by vibrations in the lungs. The giant cloud of noise shook the building and refused to go away. One sentence had set it loose somehow, pushing the call-and-response of the Negro church service past the din of a political rally and on to something else that King had never known before. There was a rabbit of awesome proportions in those bushes. As the noise finally fell back, King's voice rose above it to fire again. "There comes a time, my friends, when people get tired of being thrown across the abyss of humiliation, where they experience the bleakness of nagging despair," he declared. "There comes a time when people get tired of being pushed out of the glittering sunlight of life's July, and left standing

amidst the piercing chill of an Alpine November. There . . ." King was making
a new run, but the crowd drowned him out. No one could tell whether the roar
came in response to the nerve he had touched, or simply out of pride in a
speaker from whose tongue such rhetoric rolled so easily. "We are here—we are
here because we are tired now," King repeated.

Perhaps daunted by the power that was bursting forth from the crowd,
King moved quickly to address the pitfalls of a boycott. "Now let us say that we
are not here advocating violence," he said. "We have overcome that." A man in
the crowd shouted, "Repeat that! Repeat that!" "I want it to be known throughout Montgomery and throughout this nation that we are Christian people,"
said King, putting three distinct syllables in "Christian." "The only weapon
that we have in our hands this evening is the weapon of protest." There was a
crisp shout of approval right on the beat of King's pause. He and the audience
moved into a slow trot. "If we were incarcerated behind the iron curtains of a
communistic nation—we couldn't do this. If we were trapped in the dungeon
of a totalitarian regime—we couldn't do this. But the great glory of American
democracy is the right to protest for right." When the shouts of approval died
down, King rose up with his final reason to avoid violence, which was to distin-
guish themselves from their opponents in the Klan and the White Citizens
Council. "There will be no crosses burned at any bus stops in Montgomery," he
said. "There will be no white persons pulled out of their homes and taken out
on some distant road and murdered. There will be nobody among us who will
stand up and defy the Constitution of this nation."

King paused. The church was quiet but it was humming. "My friends," he
said slowly, "I want it to be known—that we're going to work with grim and
bold determination—to gain justice on the buses in this city. And we are not
wrong. We are not wrong in what we are doing." There was a muffled shout of
anticipation, as the crowd sensed that King was moving closer to the heart of
his cause. "If we are wrong—the Supreme Court of this nation is wrong," King
sang out. He was rocking now, his voice seeming to be at once deep and high-
pitched. "If we are wrong—God Almighty is wrong!" he shouted, and the
crowd seemed to explode a second time, as it had done when he said they were
tired. Wave after wave of noise broke over them, cresting into the farthest
reaches of the ceiling. They were far beyond Rosa Parks or the bus laws. King's
last cry had fused blasphemy to the edge of his faith and the heart of theirs. The
noise swelled until King cut through it to move past a point of unbearable tension. "If we are wrong—Jesus of Nazareth was merely a utopian dreamer and
never came down to earth! If we are wrong—justice is a lie." This was too
much. He had to wait some time before delivering his soaring conclusion, in a
flight of anger mixed with rapture: "And we are determined here in Montgomery—to work and fight until justice runs down like water, and righteousness like a mighty stream!" The audience all but smothered this passage from

Amos, the lowly herdsman prophet of Israel who, along with the priestly Isaiah, was King's favorite biblical authority on justice.

He backed off the emotion to speak of the need for unity, the dignity of protest, the historical precedent of the labor movement. Comparatively speaking, his subject matter was mundane, but the crowd stayed with him even through paraphrases of abstruse points from Niebuhr. "And I want to tell you this evening that it is not enough for us to talk about love," he said. "Love is one of the pinnacle parts of the Christian faith. There is another side called justice. And justice is really love in calculation. Justice is love correcting that which would work against love." He said that God was not just the God of love: "He's also the God that standeth before the nations and says, 'Be still and know that I am God—and if you don't obey Me I'm gonna break the backbone of your power—and cast you out of the arms of your international and national relationships.' " Shouts and claps continued at a steady rhythm as King's audacity overflowed. "Standing beside love is always justice," he said. "Not only are we using the tools of persuasion—but we've got to use the tools of coercion." He called again for unity. For working together. He appealed to history, summoning his listeners to behave so that sages of the future would look back at the Negroes of Montgomery and say they were "a people who had the moral courage to stand up for their rights." He said they could do that. "God grant that we will do it before it's too late." Someone said, "Oh, yes." And King said, "As we proceed with our program—let us think on these things."

The crowd retreated into stunned silence as he stepped away from the pulpit. The ending was so abrupt, so anticlimactic. The crowd had been waiting for him to reach for the heights a third time at his conclusion, following the rules of oratory. A few seconds passed before memory and spirit overtook disappointment. The applause continued as King made his way out of the church, with people reaching to touch him. Dexter members marveled, having never seen King let loose like that. Abernathy remained behind, reading negotiating demands from the pulpit. The boycott was on. King would work on his timing, but his oratory had just made him forever a public person. In the few short minutes of his first political address, a power of communion emerged from him that would speak inexorably to strangers who would both love and revile him, like all prophets. He was twenty-six, and had not quite twelve years and four months to live.

Prime Time

Colored People, 1994

◆

HENRY LOUIS GATES, JR.

I guess some chafed more than others against the mundane impediments of the color line. "It's no disgrace to be colored," the black entertainer Bert Williams famously observed early in this century, "but it is awfully inconvenient." For most of my childhood, we couldn't eat in restaurants or sleep in hotels, we couldn't use certain bathrooms or try on clothes in stores. Mama insisted that we dress up when we went to shop. She was a fashion plate when she went to clothing stores, and wore white pads called shields under her arms so her dress or blouse would show no sweat. We'd like to try this on, she'd say carefully, articulating her words precisely and properly. We don't buy clothes we can't try on, she'd say when they declined, as we'd walk, in Mama's dignified manner, out of the store. She preferred to shop where we had an account and where everyone knew who she was.

As for me, I hated the fact that we couldn't sit down in the Cut-Rate. No one colored was allowed to, with one exception: my father. It was as if there were a permanent TAKE-AWAY ONLY sign for colored people. You were supposed to stand at the counter, get your food to go, and leave. I don't know for certain why Carl Dadisman, the proprietor, wouldn't stop Daddy from sitting down. But I believe it was in part because Daddy was so light-complected, and in part because, during his shift at the phone company, he picked up orders for food and coffee for the operators, and Dadisman relied on that business. At the time, I never wondered if it occurred to Daddy not to sit down at the Cut-Rate when neither his wife nor his two children were allowed to, although now that I am a parent myself, the strangeness of it crosses my mind on occasion.

Even when we were with Daddy, you see, we had to stand at the counter and order takeout, then eat on white paper plates using plastic spoons, sipping our vanilla rickeys from green-and-white paper cups through plastic flexible-end straws. Even after basketball games, when Young Doc Bess would set up the team with free Cokes after one of the team's many victories, the colored players had to stand around and drink out of paper cups while the white players and cheerleaders sat down in the red Naugahyde booths and drank out of glasses. Integrate? I'll shut it down first, Carl Dadisman had vowed. He was an odd-looking man, with a Humpty-Dumpty sort of head and bottom, and weighing four or five hundred pounds. He ran the taxi service, too, and was just as nice as he could be, even to colored people. But he did not want us sitting in his booths, eating off his plates and silverware, putting our thick greasy lips all over his glasses. He'd retire first, or die.

He had a heart attack one day while sitting in the tiny toilet at his place of business. Daddy and some other men tried to lift him up, while he was screaming and gasping and clutching his chest, but he was stuck in that cramped space. They called the rescue squad at the Fire Department. Lowell Taylor and Pat Amoroso came. Lowell was black and was the star of the soccer team at the high school across the river in Westernport. He looked like Pele, down to the shape of his head.

They sawed and sawed and sawed, while the ambulance and the rescue squad sat outside on Third Street, blocking the driveway to the town's parking lot. After a while, Carl Dadisman's cries and moans became quieter and quieter. Finally, they wedged in a couple of two-by-fours and dragged out his lifeless body. By then it made little difference to Carl that Lowell was black.

Maybe Carl never understood that the racial dispensation he took for granted was coming to an end. As a child, I must once have assumed that this dispensation could no more be contested than the laws of gravity, or traffic lights. And I'm not sure when I realized otherwise.

I know that I had rich acquaintance early on with the inconveniences to which Bert Williams alluded. But segregation had some advantages, like the picnic lunch Mama would make for the five-hour train ride on the National Limited to Parkersburg, where you had to catch the bus down to the state capital, Charleston, to visit her sister Loretta. So what if we didn't feel comfortable eating in the dining car? Our food was better. Fried chicken, baked beans, and potato salad . . . a book and two decks of cards . . . and I didn't care if the train ever got there. We'd sing or read in our own section, munching that food and feeling sorry for the people who couldn't get any, and play 500 or Tonk or Fish with Mama and Daddy, until we fell asleep.

The simple truth is that the civil rights era came late to Piedmont, even though it came early to our television set. We could watch what was going on Elsewhere on television, but the marches and sit-ins were as remote to us as, in other ways, was the all-colored world of *Amos 'n' Andy*—a world full of black lawyers, black judges, black nurses, black doctors.

Politics aside, though, we were starved for images of ourselves and searched TV to find them. Everybody, of course, watched sports, because Piedmont was a big sports town. Making the big leagues was like getting to Heaven, and everybody had hopes that they could, or a relative could. We'd watch the games day and night, and listen on radio to what we couldn't see. Everybody knew the latest scores, batting averages, rbi's, and stolen bases. Everybody knew the standings in the leagues, who could still win the pennant and how. Everybody liked the Dodgers because of Jackie Robinson, the same way everybody still voted Republican because of Abraham Lincoln. Sports on the mind, sports in the mind. The only thing to rival the Valley in fascination was the big-league baseball diamond.

I once heard Mr. James Helms say, "You got to give the white man his due when it comes to technology. One on one, though, and it's even-steven. Joe Louis showed 'em that." We were obsessed with sports in part because it was the only time we could compete with white people even-steven. And the white people, it often seemed, were just as obsessed with this primal confrontation between the races as we were. I think they integrated professional sports, after all those years of segregation, just to capitalize on this voyeuristic thrill of the forbidden contact. What interracial sex was to the seventies, interracial sports were to the fifties. Except for sports, we rarely saw a colored person on TV.

Actually, I first got to know white people as "people" through their flickering images on television shows. It was the television set that brought us together at night, and the television set that brought in the world outside the Valley. We were close enough to Washington to receive its twelve channels on cable. Piedmont was transformed from a radio culture to one with the fullest range of television, literally overnight. During my first-grade year, we'd watch *Superman, Lassie,* Jack Benny, Danny Thomas, *Robin Hood, I Love Lucy, December Bride,* Nat King Cole (of course), *Wyatt Earp, Broken Arrow,* Phil Silvers, Red Skelton, *The $64,000 Question, Ozzie and Harriet, The Millionaire, Father Knows Best, The Lone Ranger,* Bob Cummings, *Dragnet, The People's Choice, Rin Tin Tin, Jim Bowie, Gunsmoke, My Friend Flicka, The Life of Riley, Topper,* Dick Powell's *Zane Grey Theater, Circus Boy,* and Loretta Young—all in prime time. My favorites were *The Life of Riley,* in part because he worked in a factory like Daddy did, and *Ozzie and Harriet,* in part because Ozzie never seemed to work at all. A year later, however, *Leave It to Beaver* swept most of the others away.

With a show like *Topper,* I felt as if I was getting a glimpse, at last, of the life that Mrs. Hudson, and Mrs. Thomas, and Mrs. Campbell, must be leading in their big mansions on East Hampshire Street. Smoking jackets and cravats, spats and canes, elegant garden parties and martinis. People who wore suits to eat dinner! This was a world so elegantly distant from ours, it was like a voyage to another galaxy, light-years away.

Leave It to Beaver, on the other hand, was a world much closer, but just out of reach nonetheless. Beaver's street was where we wanted to live, Beaver's house where we wanted to eat and sleep, Beaver's father's firm where we'd have liked Daddy to work. These shows for us were about property, the property that white people could own and that we couldn't. About a level of comfort and ease at which we could only wonder. It was the world that the integrated school was going to prepare us to enter and that, for Mama, would be the prize.

If prime time consisted of images of middle-class white people who looked nothing at all like us, late night was about the radio, listening to *Randy's Record Shop* from Gallatin, Tennessee. My brother, Rocky, kept a transistor radio by his bed, and he'd listen to it all night, for all I knew, long after I'd fallen asleep. In 1956, black music hadn't yet broken down into its many subgenres, except for large divisions such as jazz, blues, gospel, rhythm and blues. On *Randy's*, you were as likely to hear The Platters doing "The Great Pretender" and Clyde McPhatter doing "Treasure of Love" as you were to hear Howlin' Wolf do "Smokestack Lightning" or Joe Turner do "Corrine, Corrine." My own favorite that year was the slow, deliberate sound of Jesse Belvin's "Goodnight, My Love." I used to fall asleep singing it in my mind to my Uncle Earkie's girlfriend, Ula, who was a sweet caffè latté brown, with the blackest, shiniest straight hair and the fullest, most rounded red lips. Not even in your dreams, he had said to me one day, as I watched her red dress slink down our front stairs. It was my first brush with the sublime.

We used to laugh at the way the disc jockey sang "Black Strap Lax-a-teeves" during the commercials. I sometimes would wonder if the kids we'd seen on TV in Little Rock or Birmingham earlier in the evening were singing themselves to sleep with *their* Ulas.

Lord knows, we weren't going to learn how to be colored by watching television. Seeing somebody colored on TV was an event.

"Colored, colored, on Channel Two," you'd hear someone shout. Somebody else would run to the phone, while yet another hit the front porch, telling all the neighbors where to see it. And *everybody* loved *Amos 'n' Andy*—I don't care what people say today. For the colored people, the day they took *Amos 'n' Andy* off the air was one of the saddest days in Piedmont, about as sad as the day of the last mill pic-a-nic.

What was special to us about *Amos 'n' Andy* was that their world was *all* colored, just like ours. Of course, *they* had their colored judges and lawyers and doctors and nurses, which we could only dream about having, or becoming— and we *did* dream about those things. Kingfish ate his soft-boiled eggs delicately, out of an egg cup. He even owned an acre of land in Westchester County, which he sold to Andy, using the facade of a movie set to fake a mansion. As far as we were concerned, the foibles of Kingfish or Calhoun the lawyer were the foibles of individuals who happened to be funny. Nobody was likely to confuse them with the colored people we knew, no more than we'd confuse ourselves with the entertainers and athletes we saw on TV or in *Ebony* or *Jet*, the magazines we devoured to keep up with what was happening with the race. And people took special relish in Kingfish's malapropisms. "I denies the allegation, Your Honor, and I resents the alligator."

In one of my favorite episodes of *Amos 'n' Andy*, "The Punjab of Java-Pour," Andy Brown is hired to advertise a brand of coffee and is required to dress up as a turbaned Oriental potentate. Kingfish gets the bright idea that if he dresses up as a potentate's servant, the two of them can enjoy a vacation at a luxury hotel for free. So attired, the two promenade around the lobby, running up an enormous tab and generously dispensing "rubies" and "diamonds" as tips. The plan goes awry when people try to redeem the gems and discover them to be colored glass. It was widely suspected that this episode was what prompted two Negroes in Baltimore to dress like African princes and demand service in a segregated four-star restaurant. Once it was clear to the management that these were not American Negroes, the two were treated royally. When the two left the restaurant, they took off their African headdresses and robes and enjoyed a hearty laugh at the restaurant's expense. "They weren't like our Negroes," the maître d' told the press in explaining why he had agreed to seat the two "African princes."

Whenever the movies *Imitation of Life* and *The Green Pastures* would be shown on TV, we watched with similar hunger—especially *Imitation of Life.* It was never on early; only the late *late* show, like the performances of Cab Calloway and Duke Ellington at the Crystal Palace. And we'd stay up. Everybody colored. The men coming home on second shift from the paper mill would stay up. Those who had to go out on the day shift and who normally would have been in bed hours earlier (because they had to be at work at 6:30) would stay up. As would we, the kids, wired for the ritual at hand. And we'd all sit in silence, fighting back the tears, watching as Delilah invents the world's greatest pancakes and a down-and-out Ned Sparks takes one taste and says, flatly, "We'll box it." Cut to a big white house, plenty of money, and Delilah saying that she doesn't want her share of the money (which should have been *all* the money); she just wants to continue to cook, clean, wash, iron, and serve her good white lady and her daughter. (Nobody in our living room was going for *that.*) And then Delilah shows up at her light-complected daughter's school one day, unexpectedly, to pick her up, and there's the daughter, Peola, ducking down behind her books, and the white teacher saying, I'm sorry, ma'am, there must be some mistake. We have no little colored children here. And then Delilah, spying her baby, says, Oh, yes you do. Peola! Peola! Come here to your mammy, honey chile. And then Peola runs out of the room, breaking her poor, sweet mother's heart. And Peola continues to break her mother's heart, by passing, leaving the race, and marrying white. Yet her mama understands, always understands, and, dying, makes detailed plans for her own big, beautiful funeral, complete with six white horses and a carriage and a jazz band, New Orleans style. And she dies and is about to be buried, when, out of nowhere, comes grown-up Peola, saying, "Don't die, Mama, don't die, Mama, I'm sorry, Mama, I'm sorry," and throws her light-and-bright-and-damn-near-white self onto her mama's casket. By this time, we have stopped trying to fight back the tears and are boo-hooing all over the place. Then we turn to our *own* mama and tell her how much we love her and swear that we will *never, ever* pass for white. I promise, Mama. I promise.

Peola had sold her soul to the Devil. This was the first popular Faust in the black tradition, the bargain with the Devil over the cultural soul. Talk about a cautionary tale.

The Green Pastures was an altogether more uplifting view of things, our Afro Paradiso. Make way for the Lawd! Make way for the Lawd! And Rex Ingram, dressed in a long black frock coat and a long white beard, comes walking down the Streets Paved with Gold, past the Pearly Gates, while Negroes with the whitest wings of fluffy cotton fly around Heaven, playing harps, singing spirituals, having fish fries, and eating watermelon. Hard as I try, I can't stop seeing God as that black man who played Him in *The Green Pastures* and seeing Noah as Rochester from the Jack Benny show, trying to bargain with God to let him take along an extra keg of wine or two.

Civil rights took us all by surprise. Every night we'd wait until the news to see what "Dr. King and dem" were doing. It was like watching the Olympics or the World Series when somebody colored was on. The murder of Emmett Till was one of my first memories. He whistled at some white girl, they said; that's all he did. He was beat so bad they didn't even want to open the casket, but his mama made them. She wanted the world to see what they had done to her baby.

In 1957, when I was in second grade, black children integrated Central High School in Little Rock, Arkansas. We watched it on TV. All of us watched it. I don't mean Mama and Daddy and Rocky. I mean *all* the colored people in America watched it, together, with one set of eyes. We'd watch it in the morning, on the *Today* show on NBC, before we'd go to school; we'd watch it in the evening, on the news, with Edward R. Murrow on CBS. We'd watch the Special Bulletins at night, interrupting our TV shows.

The children were all well scrubbed and greased down, as we'd say. Hair short and closely cropped, parted, and oiled (the boys); "done" in a "permanent" and straightened, with turned-up bangs and curls (the girls). Starched shirts, white, and creased pants, shoes shining like a buck private's spit shine. Those Negroes were *clean*. The fact was, those children trying to get the right to enter that school in Little Rock looked like black versions of models out of *Jack & Jill* magazine, to which my mama had subscribed for me so that I could see what children outside the Valley were up to. "They handpicked those children," Daddy would say. "No dummies, no nappy hair, heads not too kinky, lips not too thick, no disses and no dats." At seven, I was dismayed by his cynicism. It bothered me somehow that those children would have been chosen, rather than just having shown up or volunteered or been nearby in the neighborhood.

Daddy was jaundiced about the civil rights movement, and especially about the Reverend Dr. Martin Luther King, Jr. He'd say all of his names, to drag out his scorn. By the mid-sixties, we'd argue about King from sunup to sundown. Sometimes he'd just mention King to get a rise from me, to make a sagging evening more interesting, to see if I had *learned* anything real yet, to see how long I could think up counter arguments before getting so mad that my face would turn purple. I think he just liked the color purple on my face, liked producing it there. But he was not of two minds about those children in Little Rock.

The children would get off their school bus surrounded by soldiers from the National Guard and by a field of state police. They would stop at the steps of the bus and seem to take a very deep breath. Then the phalanx would start to move slowly along this gulley of sidewalk and rednecks that connected the steps of the school bus with the white wooden double doors of the school. All kinds of crackers would be lining that gulley, separated from the phalanx of children by rows of state police, who formed a barrier arm in arm. Cheerleaders from the all-white high school that was desperately trying to stay that way were dressed in those funny little pleated skirts, with a big red *C* for "Central" on their chests, and they'd wave their pom-poms and start to cheer: "Two, four, six, eight—We don't want to integrate!" And all those crackers and all those rednecks would join in that chant as if their lives depended on it. Deafening, it was: even on our twelve-inch TV, a three-inch speaker buried along the back of its left side.

The TV was the ritual arena for the drama of race. In our family, it was located in the living room, where it functioned like a fireplace in the proverbial New England winter. I'd sit in the water in the galvanized tub in the middle of our kitchen, watching the TV in the next room while Mama did the laundry or some other chore as she waited for Daddy to come home from his second job. We watched people getting hosed and cracked over their heads, people being spat upon and arrested, rednecks siccing fierce dogs on women and children, our people responding by singing and marching and staying strong. Eyes on the prize. Eyes on the prize. George Wallace at the gate of the University of Alabama, blocking Autherine Lucy's way. Charlayne Hunter at the University of Georgia. President Kennedy interrupting our scheduled program with a special address, saying that James Meredith will *definitely* enter the University of Mississippi; and saying it like he believed it (unlike Ike), saying it like the big kids said "It's our turn to play" on the basketball court and walking all through us as if we weren't there.

Whatever tumult our small screen revealed, though, the dawn of the civil rights era could be no more than a spectator sport in Piedmont. It was almost like a war being fought overseas. And all things considered, white and colored Piedmont got along pretty well in those years, the fifties and early sixties. At least as long as colored people didn't try to sit down in the Cut-Rate or at the Rendezvous Bar, or eat pizza at Eddie's, or buy property, or move into the white neighborhoods, or dance with, date, or dilate upon white people. Not to mention try to get a job in the craft unions at the paper mill. Or have a drink at the white VFW, or join the white American Legion, or get loans at the bank, or just generally get out of line. Other than that, colored and white got on pretty well.

Letter from the South

The New Yorker, April 7, 1956

◆

E. B. WHITE

After the lions had returned to their cages, creeping angrily through the chutes, a little bunch of us drifted away and into an open doorway nearby, where we stood for a while in semi-darkness, watching a big brown circus horse go harumphing around the practice ring. His trainer was a woman of about forty, and the two of them, horse and woman, seemed caught up in one of those desultory treadmills of afternoon from which there was no apparent escape. The day was hot, and we kibitzers were grateful to be briefly out of the sun's glare. The long rein, or tape, by which the woman guided her charge counterclockwise in this dull career formed the radius of their private circle, of which she was the revolving center; and she, too, stepped a tiny circumference of her own, in order to accommodate the horse and allow him his maximum scope. She had on a short-skirted costume and a conical straw hat. Her legs were bare and she wore high heels, which probed deep into the loose tanbark and kept her ankles in a state of constant turmoil. The great size and meekness of the horse, the repetitious exercise, the heat of the afternoon, all exerted a hypnotic charm that invited boredom; we spectators were experiencing a languor—we neither expected relief nor felt entitled to any. We had paid a dollar to get into the grounds, to be sure, but we had got our dollar's worth a few minutes before, when the lion trainer's whiplash had got caught around a toe of one of the lions. What more did we want for a dollar?

Behind me I heard someone say, "Excuse me, please," in a low voice. She was halfway into the building when I turned and saw her—a girl of sixteen or seventeen, politely threading her way through us onlookers who blocked the entrance. As she emerged in front of us, I saw that she was barefoot, her dirty little feet fighting the uneven ground. In most respects she was like any of two or three dozen showgirls you encounter if you wander about the winter quarters of Mr. John Ringling North's circus, in Sarasota—cleverly proportioned, deeply browned by the sun, dusty, eager, and almost naked. But her grave face and the naturalness of her manner gave her a sort of quick distinction and brought a new note into the gloomy octagonal building where we had all cast our lot for a few moments. As soon as she had squeezed through the crowd, she spoke a word or two to the older woman, whom I took to be her mother, stepped to the ring, and waited while the horse coasted to a stop in front of her. She gave the animal a couple of affectionate swipes on his enormous neck and then swung herself aboard. The horse immediately resumed his rocking canter, the woman goading him on, chanting something that sounded like "Hop! Hop!"

In attempting to recapture this mild spectacle, I am merely acting as recording secretary for one of the oldest of societies—the society of those who, at one time or another, have surrendered, without even a show of resistance, to the bedazzlement of a circus rider. As a writing man, or secretary, I have always felt charged with the safekeeping of all unexpected items of worldly or unworldly enchantment, as though I might be held personally responsible if even a small one were to be lost. But it is not easy to communicate anything of this nature. The circus comes as close to being the world in microcosm as anything I know; in a way, it puts all the rest of show business in the shade. Its magic is universal and complex. Out of its wild disorder comes order; from its rank smell rises the good aroma of courage and daring; out of its preliminary shabbiness comes the final splendor. And buried in the familiar boasts of its advance agents lies the modesty of most of its people. For me the circus is at its best before it has been put together. It is at its best at certain moments when it comes to a point, as through a burning glass, in the activity and destiny of a single performer out of so many. One ring is always bigger than three. One rider, one aerialist, is always greater than six. In short, a man has to catch the circus unawares to experience its full impact and share its gaudy dream.

The ten-minute ride the girl took achieved—as far as I was concerned, who wasn't looking for it, and quite unbeknownst to her, who wasn't even striving for it—the thing that is sought by performers everywhere, on whatever stage, whether struggling in the tidal currents of Shakespeare or bucking the difficult motion of a horse. I somehow got the idea she was just cadging a ride, improving a shining ten minutes in the diligent way all serious artists seize free moments to hone the blade of their talent and keep themselves in trim. Her brief tour included only elementary postures and tricks, perhaps because they were all she was capable of, perhaps because her warmup at this hour was unscheduled and the ring was not rigged for a real practice session. She swung herself off and on the horse several times, gripping his mane. She did a few knee-stands—or whatever they are called—dropping to her knees and quickly bouncing back up on her feet again. Most of the time she simply rode in a standing position, well aft on the beast, her hands hanging easily at her sides, her head erect, her straw-colored ponytail lightly brushing her shoulders, the blood of exertion showing faintly through the tan of her skin. Twice she managed a one-foot stance—a sort of ballet pose, with arms outstretched. At one point the neck strap of her bathing suit broke and she went twice around the ring in the classic attitude of a woman making minor repairs to a garment. The fact that she was standing on the back of a moving horse while doing this invested the matter with a clownish significance that perfectly fitted the spirit of the circus—jocund, yet charming. She just rolled the strap into a neat ball and stowed it inside her bodice while the horse rocked and rolled beneath her in dutiful innocence. The bathing suit proved as self-reliant as its owner and stood up well enough without benefit of strap.

The richness of the scene was in its plainness, its natural condition—of horse, of ring, of girl, even to the girl's bare feet that gripped the bare back of her proud and ridiculous mount. The enchantment grew not out of anything that happened or was performed but out of something that seemed to go round and around and around with the girl, attending her, a steady gleam in the shape of a circle—a ring of ambition, of happiness, of youth. (And the positive pleasures of equilibrium under difficulties.) In a week or two, all would be changed, all (or almost all) lost: the girl would wear makeup, the horse would wear gold, the ring would be painted, the bark would be clean for the feet of the horse, the girl's feet would be clean for the shoes that she'd wear. All, all would be lost.

As I watched with the others, our jaws adroop, our eyes alight, I became painfully conscious of the element of time. Everything in the hideous old building seemed to take the shape of a circle, conforming to the course of the horse. The rider's gaze, as she peered straight ahead, seemed to be circular, as though bent by force of circumstance; then time itself began running in circles, and so the beginning was where the end was, and the two were the same, and one thing ran into the next and time went round and around and got nowhere. The girl wasn't so young that she did not know the delicious satisfaction of having a perfectly behaved body and the fun of using it to do a trick most people can't do, but she was too young to know that time does not really move in a circle at all. I thought: "She will never be as beautiful as this again"—a thought that made me acutely unhappy—and in a flash my mind (which is too much of a busybody to suit me) had projected her twenty-five years ahead, and she was now in the center of the ring, on foot, wearing a conical hat and high-heeled shoes, the image of the older woman, holding the long rein, caught in the treadmill of an afternoon long in the future. "She is at that enviable moment in life [I thought] when she believes she can go once around the ring, make one complete circuit, and at the end be exactly the same age as at the start." Everything in her movements, her expression, told you that for her the ring of time was perfectly formed, changeless, predictable, without beginning or end, like the ring in which she was travelling at this moment with the horse that wallowed under her. And then I slipped back into my trance, and time was circular again—time, pausing quietly with the rest of us, so as not to disturb the balance of a performer.

Her ride ended as casually as it had begun. The older woman stopped the horse, and the girl slid to the ground. As she walked toward us to leave, there was a quick, small burst of applause. She smiled broadly, in surprise and pleasure; then her face suddenly regained its gravity and she disappeared through the door.

It has been ambitious and plucky of me to attempt to describe what is indescribable, and I have failed, as I knew I would. But I have discharged my duty to my society; and besides, a writer, like an acrobat, must occasionally try a stunt that is too much for him. At any rate, it is worth reporting that long before the circus comes to town, its most notable performances have already been given. Under the bright lights of the finished show, a performer need only reflect the electric candle power that is directed upon him; but in the dark and dirty old training rings and in the makeshift cages, whatever light is generated, must come from original sources—from internal fires of professional hunger and delight, from the exuberance and gravity of youth. It is the difference between planetary light and the combustion of stars.

The South is the land of the sustained sibilant. Everywhere, for the appreciative visitor, the letter S insinuates itself into the scene: in the sound of sea and sand, in the singing shell, in the heat of sun and sky, in the sultriness of the gentle hours, in the siesta, in the stir of birds and insects. In contrast to the softness of its music, the South is also cruel and hard and prickly. A little striped lizard, flattened along the sharp green bayonet of a yucca, wears in its tiny face and watchful eye the pure look of death and violence. And all over the place, hidden at the bottom of their small sandy craters, the ant lions lie in wait for the ant that will stumble into their trap. (There are three kinds of lions in this region: the lions of the circus, the ant lions, and the Lions of the Tampa Lions Club, who roared their approval of segregation at a meeting the other day—all except one, a Lion named Monty Gurwit, who declined to roar and thereby got his picture in the paper.)

The day starts on a note of despair: the sorrowing dove, alone on its telephone wire, mourns the loss of night, weeps at the bright perils of the unfolding day. But soon the mockingbird wakes and begins an early rehearsal, setting the dove down by force of character, running through a few slick imitations, and trying a couple of original numbers into the bargain. The redbird takes it from there. Despair gives way to good humor. The southern dawn is a pale affair, usually, quite different from our northern daybreak. It is a triumph of gradualism; night turns to day imperceptibly, softly, with no theatrics. It is subtle and undisturbing. As the first light seeps in through the blinds I lie in bed half awake, despairing with the dove, sounding the A for the brothers Alsop. All seems lost, all seems sorrowful. Then a mullet jumps in the bayou outside the bedroom window. It falls back into the water with a smart smack. I have asked several people why the mullet incessantly jump and I have received a variety of answers. Some say the mullet jump to shake off a parasite that annoys them. Some say they jump for the love of jumping—as the girl on the horse seemed to ride for the love of riding (although she, too, like all artists, may have been shaking off some parasite that fastens itself to the creative spirit and can be got rid of only by fifty turns around a ring while standing on a horse).

In Florida at this time of year, the sun does not take command of the day until a couple of hours after it has appeared in the east. It seems to carry no authority at first. The sun and the lizard keep the same schedule; they bide their time until the morning has advanced a good long way before they come fully forth and strike. The cold lizard waits astride his warming leaf for the perfect moment; the cold sun waits in his nest of clouds for the crucial time.

On many days, the dampness of the air pervades all life, all living. Matches refuse to strike. The towel, hung to dry, grows wetter by the hour. The newspaper, with its headlines about integration, wilts in your hand and falls limply into the coffee and the egg. Envelopes seal themselves. Postage stamps mate with one another as shamelessly as grasshoppers. But most of the time the days are models of beauty and wonder and comfort, with the kind sea stroking the back of the warm sand. At evening there are great flights of birds over the sea, where the light lingers; the gulls, the pelicans, the terns, the herons stay aloft for half an hour after land birds have gone to roost. They hold their ancient formations, wheel and fish over the Pass, enjoying the last of day like children playing outdoors after suppertime.

To a beachcomber from the North, which is my present status, the race problem has no pertinence, no immediacy. Here in Florida I am a guest in two houses—the house of the sun, the house of the State of Florida. As a guest, I mind my manners and do not criticize the customs of my hosts. It gives me a queer feeling, though, to be at the center of the greatest social crisis of my time and see hardly a sign of it. Yet the very absence of signs seems to increase one's awareness. Colored people do not come to the public beach to bathe, because they would not be made welcome there; and they don't fritter away their time visiting the circus, because they have other things to do. A few of them turn up at the ballpark, where they occupy a separate but equal section of the left-field bleachers and watch Negro players on the visiting Braves team using the same bases as the white players, instead of separate (but equal) bases. I have had only two small encounters with "color." A colored woman named Viola, who had been a friend of my wife's sister years ago, showed up one day with some laundry of ours that she had consented to do for us, and with the bundle she brought a bunch of nasturtiums, as a sort of natural accompaniment to the delivery of clean clothes. The flowers seemed a very acceptable thing and I was touched by them. We asked Viola about her daughter, and she said she was at Kentucky State College, studying voice.

The other encounter was when I was explaining to our cook, who is from Finland, the mysteries of bus travel in the American Southland. I showed her the bus stop, armed her with a timetable, and then, as a matter of duty, mentioned the customs of the Romans. "When you get on the bus," I said, "I think you'd better sit in one of the front seats—the seats in back are for colored people." A look of great weariness came into her face, as it does when we use too many dishes, and she replied, "Oh, I know—isn't it silly!"

Her remark, coming as it did all the way from Finland and landing on this sandbar with a plunk, impressed me. The Supreme Court said nothing about silliness, but I suspect it may play more of a role than one might suppose. People are, if anything, more touchy about being thought silly than they are about being thought unjust. I note that one of the arguments in the recent manifesto of Southern congressmen in support of the doctrine of "separate but equal" was that it had been founded on "common sense." The sense that is common to one generation is uncommon to the next. Probably the first slave ship, with Negroes lying in chains on its decks, seemed commonsensical to the owners who operated it and to the planters who patronized it. But such a vessel would not be in the realm of common sense today. The only sense that is common, in the long run, is the sense of change—and we all instinctively avoid it, and object to the passage of time, and would rather have none of it.

The Supreme Court decision is like the Southern sun, laggard in its early stages, biding its time. It has been the law in Florida for two years now, and the years have been like the hours of the morning before the sun has gathered its strength. I think the decision is as incontrovertible and warming as the sun, and, like the sun, will eventually take charge.

But there is certainly a great temptation in Florida to duck the passage of time. Lying in warm comfort by the sea, you receive gratefully the gift of the sun, the gift of the South. This is true seduction. The day is a circle—morning, afternoon, and night. After a few days I was clearly enjoying the same delusion as the girl on the horse—that I could ride clear around the ring of day, guarded by wind and sun and sea and sand, and be not a moment older.

Segregation: The Inner Conflict in the South

1956

◆

ROBERT PENN WARREN

"I'm glad it's you going," my friend, a Southerner, long resident in New York, said, "and not me." But I went back, for going back this time, like all the other times, was a necessary part of my life. I was going back to look at the land-scapes and streets I had known—Kentucky, Tennessee, Arkansas, Mississippi, Louisiana—to look at the faces, to hear the voices, to hear, in fact, the voices in my own blood. A girl from Mississippi had said to me: "I feel it's all happening inside of me, every bit of it. It's all there."

I know what she meant.

To the right, the sun, cold and pale, is westering. Far off, a little yellow plane scuttles down a runway, steps awkwardly into the air, then climbs busily, learn-ing grace. Our big plane trundles ponderously forward, feeling its weight like a fat man, hesitates, shudders with an access of sudden, building power, and with a new roar in my ears, I see the ground slide past, then drop away, like a dream. I had not been aware of the instant we had lost that natural contact.

Memphis is behind me, and I cannot see it, but yonder is the river, glitter-ing coldly, and beyond, the tree-sprigged flats of Arkansas. Still climbing, we tilt eastward now, the land pivoting away below us, the tidy toy farms, white houses, silos the size of a spool of white thread, or smaller, the stock ponds bright like little pieces of gum wrapper dropped in brown grass, but that brown grass is really trees, the toy groves with shadows precise and long in the level-ing light.

Arkansas has pivoted away. It is Mississippi I now see down there, the land slipping away in the long light, and in my mind I see, idly, the ruined, gaunt, classic clay hills, with the creek bottoms throttled long since in pink sand, or the white houses of Holly Springs, some of them severe and beautiful, or High-way 61 striking south from Memphis, straight as a knife edge through the sad and baleful beauty of the Delta country, south toward Vicksburg and the Fed-eral cemeteries, toward the fantasia of Natchez.

It seems like a thousand years since I first drove that road, more than twenty-five years ago, a new concrete slab then, dizzily glittering in the August sun-blaze, driving past the rows of tenant shacks, Negro shacks set in the infinite cotton fields, and it seems like a hundred years since I last drove it, last week, in the rain, then toward sunset the sky clearing a little, but clouds solid and low on the west like a black range of mountains frilled upward with an edge of bloody gold light, quickly extinguished. Last week I noticed that more of the shacks were ruinous, apparently abandoned. More, but not many, had an electric wire running back from the road. But when I caught a glimpse, in the dusk, of the interior of a lighted shack, I usually saw the coal-oil lamp. Most shacks were not lighted. I wondered if it was too early in the evening. Then it was early no longer. Were that many of the shacks abandoned?

Then we would pass in the dark some old truck grudging and clanking down the concrete, and catch, in the split-second flick of our headlamps, a glimpse of the black faces and the staring eyes. Or the figure, sudden in our headlight, would rise from the roadside, dark and shapeless against the soaked blackness of the cotton land: the man humping along with the croker sack on his shoulders (containing what?), the woman with a piece of sacking or paper over her head against the drizzle now, at her bosom a bundle that must be a small child, the big children following with the same slow, mud-lifting stride in the darkness. The light of the car snatches past, and I think of them behind us in the darkness, moving up the track beside the concrete, seeing another car light far yonder toward Memphis, staring at it perhaps, watching it grow, plunge at them, strike them, flick past. They will move on, at their pace. Yes, they are still here.

I see a river below us. It must be the Tennessee. I wonder on which side of us Shiloh is, and guess the right, for we must have swung far enough north for that. I had two grandfathers at Shiloh, that morning of April 6, 1862, young men with the other young men in gray uniforms stepping toward the lethal spring thickets of dogwood and redbud, to the sound of bird song. "One hundred and sixty men we took in the first morning, son. Muster the next night, and it was sixteen answered." They had fallen back on Corinth, into Mississippi.

The man in the seat beside me on the plane is offering me a newspaper. I see the thumb of the hand clutching the paper. The nail is nearly as big as a quarter, split at the edges, grooved and horny, yellowish, with irrevocable coal-black grime deep under the nail and into the cuticle. I look at the man. He is a big man, very big, bulging over the seat, bulging inside his blue serge. He is fiftyish, hair graying. His face is large and raw-looking, heavy-jowled, thick gray eyebrows over small, deep-set, appraising eyes. His name, which he tells me, sounds Russian or Polish, something ending in *-ski*.

I begin to read the paper, an article about the riots at the University of Alabama. He notices what I am reading. "Bet you thought I was from down here," he said. "From the way I talk. But I ain't. I was born and raised in New York City, but I been in the scrap business down here ten years. Didn't you think I was from down here?"

"Yes," I say, for that seems the sociable thing to say.

He twists his bulk in the blue serge and reaches and stabs a finger at the headline about Alabama. "Folks could be more gen'rous and fair-thinking," he says. "Like affable, you might say, and things would work out. If folks get affable and contig'ous, you might say, things sort of get worked out in time, but you get folks not being affable-like and stirring things up and it won't work out. Folks on both sides the question."

He asks me if I don't agree, and I say, sure, I agree. Sure, if folks were just affable-like.

I am thinking of what a taxi driver had said to me in Memphis: "Looks like the Lucy girl wouldn't want to go no place where people throw eggs at her and sich. But if they'd jist let her alone, them Goodrich plant fellers and all, it would blow over. What few niggers come would not have stayed no duration. Not when they found she couldn't git the social stuff, and all."

And what the school superintendent, in middle Tennessee, had said: "You take a good many people around here that I know, segregationists all right, but when they read about a thousand to one, it sort of makes them sick. It is the unfairness in that way that gets them."

And an organizer of one of the important segregation groups, a lawyer, when I asked him if Autherine Lucy wasn't acting under law, he creaked his swivel chair, moved his shoulders under his coat, and touched a pencil on his desk, before saying: "Yes—yes—but it was just the Federal Court ruled it."

And a taxi driver in Nashville, a back-country man come to the city, a hard, lean, spare face, his lean, strong shoulders humped forward over the wheel so that the clavicles show through the coat: "A black-type person and a white-type person, they ain't alike. Now, the black-type person, all they think about is fighting and having a good time and you know what. Now, the white-type person is more American-type, he don't mind fighting but he don't fight to kill for fun. It's that cannibal blood you caint git out."

Now, on the plane, my companion observes me scribbling something in a notebook.

"You a writer or something?" he asks. "A newspaper fellow, maybe?"

I say yes.

"You interested in that stuff?" he asks, and points to the article. "Somebody ought to tell 'em not to blame no state, not even Alabam' or Mississippi, for what the bad folks do. Like stuff in New York or Chicago. Folks in Mississippi got good hearts as any place. They always been nice and good-hearted to me, for I go up to a man affable. The folks down here is just in trouble and can't claw out. Don't blame 'em, got good hearts but can't claw out of their trouble. It is hard to claw out from under the past and the past way."

He asks me if I have been talking to a lot of people.

I had been talking to a lot of people.

I had come to the shack at dusk, by the brimming bayou, in the sea of mud where cotton had been. The cold drizzle was still falling. In the shack, on the hickory chair, the yellow girl, thin but well made, wearing a salmon sweater and salmon denim slacks, holds the baby on her knee and leans toward the iron stove. On the table beyond her is an ivory-colored portable radio and a half-full bottle of Castoria. On the other side of the stove are her three other children, the oldest seven. Behind me, in the shadowy background, I know there are faces peering in from the other room of the shack, black faces, the half-grown boys, another girl I had seen on entering. The girl in the salmon sweater is telling me how she heard her husband had been killed. "Livin in town then, and my sister, she come that night and tole me he was shot. They had done shot him dead. So I up and taken out fer heah, back to the plantation. Later, my sister got my chillen and brought 'em. I ain't gonna lie, mister. I tell you, I was scairt. No tellin if that man what done it was in jail or no. Even if they had arrest him, they might bon' him out and he come and do it to me. Be mad because they 'rest him. You caint never tell. And they try him and 'quit him, doan know as I kin stay heah. Even they convick him, maybe I leave. Some good folks round heah and they helpin me, and I try to appreciate and be a prayin chile, but you git so bore down on and nigh ruint and sort of brainwashed, you don't know what. Things git to goin round in yore head. I could run out or somethin, but you caint leave yore chillen. But look like I might up and leave. He git 'quitted, that man, and maybe I die, but I die goin."

This is the cliché. It is the thing the uninitiate would expect. It is the cliché of fear. It is the cliché come fresh, and alive.

There is another image. It is morning in Nashville. I walk down Union Street, past the Negro barbershops, past the ruinous buildings plastered over with placards of old circuses and rodeos, buildings being wrecked now to make way for progress, going into the square where the big white stone boxlike, ugly and expensive Davidson County Court House now stands on the spot where the old brawling market once was. Otherwise, the square hasn't changed much, the same buildings, wholesale houses, liquor stores, pawnshops, quick lunches, and the same kind of people stand on the corners, countrymen, in khaki pants and mackinaw coats, weathered faces and hard, withdrawn eyes, usually pale eyes, lean-hipped men ("narrow-assted" in the country phrase) like the men who rode with Forrest, the farm wives, young with a baby in arms, or middle-aged and work-worn, with colored cloths over the head, glasses, false teeth, always the shopping bag.

I walk down toward the river, past the Darling Display Distribution show window, where a wax figure stands in skirt and silk blouse, the fingers spread on one uplifted hand, the thin face lifted with lips lightly parted as though in eternal, tubercular expectation of a kiss. I see the power pylons rising above the river mist. A tug is hooting upriver in the mist.

I go on down to the right, First Street, to the replica of Fort Nashborough, the original settlement, which stands on the riverbank under the shadow of warehouses. The stockade looks so child-flimsy and jerry-built jammed against the massive, soot-stained warehouses. How could the settlers have ever taken such protection seriously? But it was enough, that and their will and the long rifles and the hunting knives and the bear-dogs they unleashed to help them when they broke the Indians at the Battle of the Bluffs. They took the land, and remain.

I am standing in the middle of the empty stockade when a boy enters and approaches me. He is about fifteen, strongly built, wearing a scruffed and tattered brown leather jacket, blue jeans, a faded blue stocking cap on the back of his head, with a mop of yellow hair hanging over his forehead. He is a fine-looking boy, erect, manly in the face, with a direct, blue-eyed glance. "Mister," he said to me, "is this foh't the way it was, or they done remodeled it?"

I tell him it is a replica, smaller than the original and not on the right spot, exactly.

"I'm glad I seen it, anyway," he says. "I like to go round seeing things that got history, and such. It gives you something to think about. Helps you in a quiz sometimes, too."

I ask him where he goes to school.

"Atlanta," he says. "Just come hitchhiking up this a-way, looking at things for interest. Like this here foh't."

"You all been having a little trouble down your way," I ask, "haven't you?"

He looks sharply at me, hesitates, then says: "Niggers—you mean niggers?"

"Yes."

"I hate them bastards," he says, with a shuddering, automatic violence, and averts his face and spits through his teeth, a quick, viperish, cut-off expectoration.

I say nothing, and he looks at me, stares into my face with a dawning belligerence, sullen and challenging, and suddenly demands: "Don't you?"

"I can't say that I do," I reply. "I like some and I don't like some others."

He utters the sudden obscenity, and removes himself a couple of paces from me. He stops and looks back over his shoulder. "I'm hitching on back to Atlanta," he declares in a flat voice, "this afternoon," and goes on out of the fort.

This, too, is a cliché. The boy, standing on the ground of history and heroism, his intellect and imagination stirred by the fact, shudders with that other, automatic emotion which my question had evoked. The cliché had come true: the cliché of hate. And somehow the hallowedness of the ground he stood on had vindicated, as it were, that hate.

The boy in the fort was the only person to turn from me, but occasionally there would be a stiffening, a flicker of suspicion, an evasion or momentary refusal of the subject, even in the casual acquaintance of lobby or barroom. At one of the new luxurious motels near Clarksdale (the slick motels and the great power stations and booster stations, silver-glittering by day and jewel-glittering by night, are the most obvious marks of the new boom), a well-dressed young man is talking about a movie being made down near Greenville. The movie is something about cotton, he says, by a fellow named Williams. Anyway, they had burned down a gin in the middle of the night, just for the movie. The woman at the desk (a very good blue dress that had cost money, a precise, respectable middle-aged mouth, pince-nez) speaks up: "Yes, and they say it's the only movie ever made here didn't criticize Mississippi."

"Criticize?" I ask. "Criticize how?"

She turns her head a little, looks at the man with her behind the desk, then back at me. "You know," she says, "just criticize."

I see the eyes of the man behind the desk stray to the license of our car parked just beyond the glass front. It has a Tennessee license, a U-Drive-It from Memphis.

"Criticize?" I try again.

The man had been busy arranging something in the drawer behind the desk. Suddenly, very sharply, not quite slamming, he shoves the drawer shut. "Heck, you know," he says.

"Didn't they make another movie over at Oxford?" I ask.

The man nods, the woman says yes. I ask what that one had been about. Nobody has seen it, not the woman, neither of the men. "It was by that fellow Faulkner," the woman says. "But I never read anything he ever wrote."

"I never did either," the man behind the desk says, "but I know what it's like. It's like that fellow Hemingway. I read some of his writings. Gory and on the seedy side of life. I didn't like it."

"That's exactly right," the woman says, and nods. "On the seedy side of life. That fellow Faulkner, he's lost a lot of friends in Mississippi. Looking at the seedy side."

"Does he criticize?" I ask.

She turns away. The man goes into a door behind the desk. The well-dressed young man has long since become engrossed in a magazine.

My Tennessee license, and Tennessee accent, hadn't been good enough credentials in Clarksdale, Mississippi. But on one occasion, the accent wasn't good enough even in Tennessee, and I remember sitting one evening in the tight, tiny living room (linoleum floor, gas heater, couch, one chair, small table with TV) of an organizer of a new important segregation group (one-time official of the Klan, this by court record) while he harangues me. He is a fat but powerful man, face fat but not flabby, the gray eyes squinty, set deep in the flesh, hard and sly by turns, never genial, though the grin tries to be when he has scored a point and leans forward at me, creaking the big overstuffed chair, his big hands crossed on his belly. He is a hill-man, come to town from one of the counties where there aren't too many Negroes, but he's now out to preserve, he says, "what you might name the old Southern way, what we was raised up to."

He is not out for money. ("I just git one dollar ever fellow I sign, the other two goes to Mr. Perkins at headquarters, for expense. Hell, I lose money on hit, on my gasoline.") No, he's not out for money, but something else. He is clearly a man of force, force that somehow has never found its way, and a man of language and leadership among his kind, the angry and ambitious and disoriented and dispossessed. It is language that intoxicates him now. He had been cautious at first, had thought I was from the FBI (yes, he had had a brush with them once, a perjury indictment), but now it seems some grand vista is opening before him and his eyes gleam and the words come.

He is talking too much, tangling himself. All the while his wife (very handsome, almost beautiful, in fact, bobbed, disordered black hair around a compact, smooth-chiseled, tanned face, her body under a flimsy dress tight and compact but gracefully made) has been standing in the deep shadow of the doorway to a room beyond, standing patiently, hands folded but tense, with the fingers secretly moving, standing like the proper hill-wife while the menfolks talk.

"Excuse me," she suddenly says, but addressing me, not the husband, "excuse me, but didn't you say you were born down here, used to live right near here?"

I say yes.

She takes a step forward, coming out of the shadow. "Yes," she says, "yes," leaning at me in vindictive triumph, "but you never said where you're living now!"

And I remember sitting with a group of college students, and one of them, a law student it develops, short but strong-looking, dark-haired and slick-headed, dark bulging eyes in a slick, rather handsome, arrogant—no, bumptious—face, breaks in: "I just want to ask one question before anything starts. I just want to ask where you're from."

Suspicion of the outlander, or of the corrupted native, gets tangled up sometimes with suspicion of the New York press, but this latter suspicion may exist quite separately, on an informed and reasoned basis. For instance, I have seen a Southern newspaperman of high integrity and ability (an integrationist, by the way) suddenly strike down his fist and exclaim: "Well, by God, it's just a fact, it's not in them not to load the dice in a news story!" And another, a

man publicly committed to maintaining law and order, publicly on record
against the Citizens Councils and all such organizations: "*Life* magazine's editorial on the Till case, that sure fixed it. If Till's father had died a hero's death
fighting for liberty, as *Life* said, that would have been as irrelevant as the actual
fact that he was executed by the American army for rape-murder. It sure makes
it hard."

There is the Baptist minister, an educated and intelligent man, who, when
I show him an article in the *Reader's Digest,* an article mentioning that the
Southern Baptist Convention had voted overwhelmingly for support of the
Supreme Court decision, stiffens and says to me: "Look—look at that title!"

I didn't need to look. I knew what it was: "The Churches Repent."

But there is another suspicion story. A Negro told me this. A man from
New Haven called on him, and upon being asked politely to take a chair, said:
"Now, please, won't you tell me about the race problem."

To which the Negro replied: "Mister, I can't tell you a thing about that.
There's nothing I could tell to you. If you want to find out, you better just move
down here and live for a while."

That is the something else—the instinctive fear, on the part of black or
white, that the massiveness of experience, the concreteness of life, will be violated; the fear of abstraction. I suppose it is this fear that made one man, a subtle and learned man, say to me: "There's something you can't explain, what
being a Southerner is." And when he said that, I remembered a Yankee friend
saying to me: "Southerners and Jews, you're exactly alike, you're so damned
special."

I had said it for a joke.

But had I?

In the end people talked, even showed an anxiety to talk, to explain something.
Even the black Southerners, a persecuted minority, too, would talk, for over
and over, the moment of some sudden decision would come: "All right—all
right—I'll tell it to you straight. All right, there's no use beating around the
bush."

But how fully can I read the words offered in the fullest efforts of candor?

It is a town in Louisiana, and I am riding in an automobile driven by a
Negro, a teacher, a slow, careful man, who puts his words out in that fashion,
almost musingly, and drives his car that way, too. He has been showing me the
Negro business section, how prosperous some of it is, and earlier he had said he
would show me a section where the white men's cars almost line up at night.
Now he seems to have forgotten that sardonic notion in the pleasanter, more
prideful task. He has fallen silent, seemingly occupied with his important business of driving, and the car moves deliberately down the street. Then, putting
his words out that slow way, detachedly as though I weren't there, he says:
"You hear some white men say they know Negroes. Understand Negroes. But

it's not true. No white man ever born ever understood what a Negro is think-ing. What he's feeling."

The car moves on down the empty street, negotiates a left turn with ma-jestic deliberation.

"And half the time that Negro," he continues, "he don't understand, ei-ther."

I know that the man beside me had once, long back, had a bright-skinned, pretty wife. She had left him to be set up by a well-off white man (placée is the old word for it). The Negro man beside me does not know that I know this, but I have known it a long time, and now I wonder what this man is thinking as we ride along, silent again.

Just listening to talk as it comes is best, but sometimes it doesn't come, or the man says, "You ask me some questions," and so, bit by bit, a certain pattern of questions emerges, the old obvious questions, I suppose—the questions people respond to or flinch from.

What are the white man's reasons for segregation?

The man I am talking to is a yellow man, about forty years old, shortish, rather fat, with a very smooth, faintly Mongolian face, eyes very shrewd but ready to smile. When the smile really comes, there is a gold tooth showing, to become, in that gold face, part of the sincerity of the smile. His arms seem somewhat short, and as he sits very erect in a straight chair, he folds his hands over his stomach. He gives the impression of a man very much at home in him-self, at peace in himself, in his dignity, in his own pleasant, smooth-skinned plumpness, in some sustaining humorousness of things. He owns a small busi-ness, a shoe-shop with a few employees.

"What does the white man do it for?" he rephrases the question. He pauses, and you can see he is thinking, studying on it, his smooth yellow face com-pressing a little. All at once the face relaxes, a sort of humorous ripple, humor-ous but serious too, in a sort of wry way, before the face settles to its blandness. "You know," he says, "you know, years and years I look at some white feller, and I caint never figure him out. You go long with him, years and years, and all of a sudden he does something. I caint figure out what makes him do the way he does. It is like a mystery, you might say. I have studied on it."

Another Negro, a very black man, small-built and intense, leans forward in his chair. He says it is money, so the white man can have cheap labor, can make the money. He is a bookish man, has been to a Negro college, and though he has never been out of the South, his speech surprises me the way my native ear used to be surprised by the speech of a Negro born and raised, say, in Akron, Ohio. I make some fleeting, tentative association of his speech, his edu-cation, his economic interpretation of things; then let the notion slide.

"Yeah, yeah," the yellow man is saying, agreeing, "but—" He stops, shakes his head.

"But what?" I ask.

He hesitates, and I see the thumbs of the hands lightly clasped across his belly begin to move, ever so slowly, round and round each other. "All right," he says, "I might as well say it to you."

"Say what?"

"Mongrelization," he says, "that's what a white man will say. You ask him and he'll say that. He wants to head it off, he says. But—" He grins, the skin crinkles around his eyes, the grin shows the gold tooth. "But," he says, "look at my face. It wasn't any black man hung it on me."

The other man doesn't seem to think this is funny. "Yes," he says, "yes, they claim they don't want mongrelization. But who has done it? They claim Negroes are dirty, diseased, that that's why they want segregation. But they have Negro nurses for their children, they have Negro cooks. They claim Negroes are ignorant. But they won't associate with the smartest and best-educated Negro. They claim . . ." And his voice goes on, winding up the bitter catalogue of paradoxes. I know them all. They are not new.

The smooth-faced yellow man is listening. But he is thinking, too, the yellow blandness of his face creaming ever so little with his slow, humorous intentness. I ask him what he is thinking.

He grins, with philosophic ruefulness. "I was just studying on it," he says. "It's all true, what Mr. Elmo here says. But there must be something behind it all. Something he don't ever say, that white feller. Maybe . . ." He pauses, hunting for the formulation. "Maybe it's just pridefulness," he says, "him being white."

Later, I am talking with the hill-man organizer, the one with the handsome wife who asks me where I live now, and he is telling me why he wants segregation. "The Court," he says, "hit caint take no stick and mix folks up like you swivel and swull eggs broke in a bowl. Naw," he says, "you got to raise 'em up, the niggers, not bring the white folks down to nigger level." He illustrates with his pudgy, strong hands in the air before him, one up, one down, changing levels. He watches the hands, with fascination, as though he has just learned to do a complicated trick.

How would you raise the level? I ask.

"Give 'em good schools and things, yeah. But"—and he warms to the topic, leaning at me—"I'd 'bolish common-law marriage. I'd put 'em in jail fer hit, and make 'em learn morals. Now, a nigger don't know how to treat no wife, not even a nigger wife. He whup her and beat her and maybe carve on her jaw with a pocketknife. When he ought to trick and pet her, and set her on his knee like a white man does his wife."

Then I talk with a Negro grade-school teacher, in the country, in Tennessee. She is a mulatto woman, middle-aged, with a handsome aquiline face, rather Indian-looking. She is sitting in her tiny, pridefully clean house, with a prideful bookcase of books beyond her, talking with slow and detached tones. I know what her story has been, years of domestic service, a painfully acquired education, marriage to a professional man, no children ("It was a cross to bear, but maybe that's why I love 'em so and like to teach 'em not my own").

I ask her why white people want to keep segregation.

"You ought to see the schoolhouse I teach in," she says, and pauses, and her lips curl sardonically, "set in the mud and hogs can come under it, and the privies set back in the mud. And see some of the children that come there, out of homes with nothing, worse than the schoolhouse, no sanitation or cleanness, with disease and dirt and no manners. You wouldn't blame a white person for not wanting the white child set down beside them." Then with a slow movement of the shoulders, again the curl of the lips: "Why didn't the Federal government give us money ten years ago for our school? To get ready, to raise us up a little to integrate. It would have made it easier. But now—"

But now? I ask.

"You got to try to be fair," she says.

I am talking with an official of one of the segregation outfits, late at night, in his house, in a fringe subdivision, in a small living room, with red velvet drapes at the one window, a TV set, new, on a table, a plastic or plaster bas-relief of a fox hunter hung on the wall, in color, the hunting coat very red and arrogant. My host is seventy-five years old, bald except for a fringe of gray hair, sallow-skinned, very clean and scrubbed-looking, white shirt but no tie, a knife-edge crease to his hard-finish gray trousers. He smokes cigarettes, one after another, with nervous, stained fingers.

He was born in North Kentucky, romantically remembers the tobacco nightriders ("Yeah, it was tight, nobody talked tobacco much, you might get shot"), remembers the Civil War veterans ("even the GAR's") sitting round, talking to the kids ("Yeah, they talked their war, they had something to remember and be proud of, not like these veterans we got nowadays, nothing to be proud of"), started out to be a lawyer ("But Blackstone got too dry, but history now, that's different, you always get something out of it to think about"), but wound up doing lots of things, finally, for years, a fraternal organizer.

Yes, he is definitely a pro, and when he talks of Gerald L. K. Smith he bursts out, eyes a-gleam: "Lord, that man's mailing list would be worth a million dollars!" He is not the rabble-rouser, the crusader, but the persuader, the debater, the man who gives the reasons. He is, in fact, a very American type, the oldfashioned, self-made, back-country intellectual—the type that finds apotheosis in Mark Twain and Abraham Lincoln. If he is neither of them, if he says "gondorea" and "enviromental" and "ethnolology," if something went wrong, if nothing ever came out quite right for him along the long way, you can still sense the old, unappeased hungers, the old drives of a nameless ambition. And he is sadly contemptuous of his organizers, who "aren't up to it," who "just aren't posted on history and ethnolology," who just haven't got "the old gray matter."

I ask him why the white man wants segregation.

"He'll say one thing and another," he says, "he knows in his bones it ain't right to have mixing. But you got to give him the reasons, explain it to him. It is the ethnolology of it you got to give. You got to explain how no *Negroes*"—he pronounces it with the elaborate polemical correctness, but not for polemics, just to set himself off intellectually, I suppose, from the people who might say *nigger*—"explain how no Negroes ever created a civilization. They are parasites. They haven't got the stuff up here." And he taps his forehead. "And explain how there is just two races, white and black, and—"

"What about the Bible," I ask, "doesn't the Bible say three?"

"Yes, but you know, between you and me, I don't reckon you have to take much stock in the Bible in this business. I don't take much stock in Darwin in some ways, either. He is too enviromental, he don't think enough about the blood. Yes, sir, I'll tell you, it's hard to come by good books on ethnolology these days. Got a good one from California the other day, though. But just one copy. Been out of print a long time. But like I was saying, the point is there's just two races, black and white, and the rest of them is a kind of mixing. You always get a mess when the mixing starts. Take India. They are a pure white people like you and me, and they had a pretty good civilization, too. Till they got to shipping on a little Negro blood. It don't take much to do the damage. Look at 'em now."

That is his argument. It is much the same argument given me by another official of another segregation group, whom I sit with a week later in another state, a lawyer, forty-five or -six, of strong middle height, sandy blond, hands strong, with pale hairs and square-cut, scrubbed-looking nails. He is cagey at first, then suddenly warm, in an expanding, sincere, appealing way. He really wants to explain himself, wants to be regarded as an honest man, wants to be liked. I do like him, as he tells about himself, how he had gone to college, the hard way I gather, had prepared to be a teacher of history in high school, had given that up, had tried business in one way or another, had given that up, had studied law. "You ought to know my politics, too," he says. He was New Deal till the Court-packing plan. "That disgusted me," he says, and you believe him. Then he was for Willkie, then for Dewey, then Dixiecrat, then for Eisenhower. (I remember another lawyer, hired by another group: "Hell, all Southerners are Republicans at heart, conservative, and just don't know they're Republican.")

But Eisenhower doesn't satisfy my friend now. "We'll elect our own President. Our organization isn't just Southern. We're going national. Plenty of people in Chicago and other places feel like we do. And afraid of a big central government, too. We'll elect our own President and see how Chief Justice Warren's decision comes out."

I ask if the main point is the matter of States' rights, of local integrity.

"Yes, in a way," he says, "but you got to fight on something you can rouse people up about, on segregation. There's the constitutional argument, but your basic feeling, that's what you've got to trust—what you feel, not your reasons for it. But we've got argument, reasons."

He hesitates, thumps the desk top in a quick tattoo of his strong, scrubbed-looking fingers (he isn't a nervous man in the ordinary sense, but there are these sudden bursts), twists himself in his chair, then abruptly leans forward, jerks a drawer open (literally jerks it), and thrusts an envelope at me. "Heck, you might as well see it," he says.

I look at it. The stuff is not new. I have seen it before, elsewhere. It was used in the last gubernatorial campaign in Tennessee, it was used in the march on the Capitol at Nashville a few weeks ago. There are the handbills showing "Harlem Negro and White Wife," lying abed, showing "Crooner Roy Hamilton & Teenage Fans," who are white girls, showing a schoolyard in Baltimore with Negro and white children, "the new look in education." On the back of one of the handbills is a crudely drawn valentine-like heart, in it the head of a white woman who (with feelings not indicated by the artist) is about to be kissed by a black man of the most primitive physiognomy. On the heart two vultures perch. Beneath it is the caption: "The Kiss of Death."

Below are the "reasons": "While Russia makes laws to protect her own race she continues to prod us to accept 14,000,000 Negroes as social equals and we are doing everything possible to please her. . . . Segregation is the law of God, not man. . . . Continue to rob the white race in order to bribe the Asiatic and Negro and these people will overwhelm the white race and destroy all progress, religion, invention, art, and return us to the jungle. . . . Negro blood destroyed the civilization of Egypt, India, Phoenicia, Carthage, Greece, and it will destroy America!"

I put the literature into my pocket, to join the other samples. "If there's trouble," I ask, "where will it begin?"

"We don't condone violence," he says.

"But if—just suppose," I say.

He doesn't hesitate. "The redneck," he says, "that's what you call 'em around here. Those fellows—and I'm one of them myself, just a redneck that got educated—are the ones who will feel the rub. He is the one on the underside of the plank with nothing between him and the bare black ground. He's got to have something to give him pride. Just to be better than something."

To be better than something: so we are back to the pridefulness the yellow man had talked about. But no, there is more, something else.

There is the minister, a Baptist, an intellectual-looking man, a man whose face indicates conscience and thoughtfulness, pastor of a good church in a good district in a thriving city. "It is simple," he says. "It is a matter of God's will and revelation. I refer you to Acts 17—I don't remember the verse. This is the passage the integrationists are always quoting to prove that integration is Christian. But they won't quote it all. It's the end that counts."

I looked it up: *And hath made of one blood all nations of men for to dwell on all the face of the earth, and hath determined the times before appointed, and the bounds of their habitation.*

There is the very handsome lady of forty-five, charming and witty and gay, full of dramatic mimicry, a wonderful range of phrase, a quick sympathy, a totally captivating talker of the kind you still occasionally find among women of the Deep South, but never now in a woman under forty. She is sitting before the fire in the fine room, her brother, big and handsome but barefoot and rigid drunk, opposite her. But she gaily overrides that small difficulty ("Oh, don't mind him, he's just had a whole bottle of brandy. Been on a high-lonesome all by himself. But poor Jack, he feels better now"). She has been talking about the Negroes on her plantation, and at last, about integration, but that only in one phrase, tossed off as gaily and casually as any other of the evening, so casual as to permit no discussion: "But of course we have to keep the white race intact."

But the husband, much her senior, who has said almost nothing all evening, lifts his strong, grizzled old face, and in a kind of *sotto voce* growl, not to her, not to me, not to anybody, utters: "In power—in power—you mean the white race in power."

And I think of another Southerner, an integrationist, saying to me: "You simply have to recognize a fact. In no county where the Negroes are two to one is the white man going to surrender political power, not with the Negroes in those counties in their present condition. It's not a question of being Southern. You put the same number of Yankee liberals in the same county and in a week they'd be behaving the same way. Living with something and talking about it are two very different things, and living with something is always the slow way."

And another, not an integrationist, from a black county, saying: "Yeah, let 'em take over and in six months you'd be paying the taxes but a black sheriff would be collecting 'em. You couldn't walk down the sidewalk. You'd be communized, all right."

But is it power. Merely power? Or any of the other things suggested thus far?

I think of a college professor in a section where about half the population is Negro. The college has no Negro students, but—"The heat is on," he says. "But listen, brother," he says, "lots of our boys don't like it a bit. Not a bit."

I ask would it be like the University of Alabama.

"It would be something, brother. I'll tell you that, brother. One of our boys—been fooling around with an organization uptown—he came to me and asked me to be sure to let him know when a nigger was coming, he and some friends would stop that clock. But I didn't want to hear student talk. I said, son, just don't tell me."

I asked what the faculty would do.

"Hide out, brother, hide out. And, brother, I would, too."

Yes, he was a segregationist. I didn't have to ask him. Or ask his reasons, for he was talking on, in his rather nasal voice—leaning happily back in his chair in the handsome office, a spare, fiftyish man, dark-suited, rather dressy, sharp-nosed, with some fringe-remnants of sandy hair on an elongated, slightly freckled skull, rimless glasses on pale eyes: "Yeah, brother, back in my county there was a long ridge running through the county, and one side the ridge was good land, river bottom, and folks put on airs there and held niggers, but on the other side of the ridge the ground so pore you couldn't grow peas and nothing but pore white trash. So when the Civil War came, the pore white trash, as the folks who put on airs called them, just picked down the old rifle off the deer horns over the fireplace and joined the Federals coming down, just because they hated those fellows across the ridge. But don't get me wrong, brother. They didn't want any truck with niggers, either. To this day they vote Republican and hate niggers. It is just they hate niggers."

Yes, they hate niggers, but I am in another room, the library of a plantation house, in Mississippi, and the planter is talking to me, leaning his length back at ease, speaking deliberately from his high-nosed, commanding face, the very figure of a Wade Hampton or Kirby Smith, only the gray uniform and cavalry boots not there, saying: "No, I don't hate Negroes. I never had a minute's trouble with one in my life, and never intend to. I don't believe in getting lathered up, and I don't intend to get lathered up. I simply don't discuss the question with anybody. But I'll tell you what I feel. I came out of the university with a lot of ideals and humanitarianism, and I stayed by it as long as I could. But I tell you now what has come out of thirty years of experience and careful consideration. I have a deep contempt for the Negro race as it exists here. It is not so much a matter of ability as of character. Character."

He repeats the word. He is a man of character, it could never be denied. Of character and force. He is also a man of fine intelligence and good education. He reads Roman history. He collects books on the American West. He is widely traveled. He is unusually successful as a planter and businessman. He is a man of human warmth and generosity, and eminent justice. I overhear his wife, at this moment, talking to a Negro from the place, asking him if she can save some more money for him, to add to the hundred dollars she holds, trying to persuade him.

The husband goes on: "It's not so much the hands on my place, as the lawyers and doctors and teachers and insurance men and undertakers—oh, yes, I've had dealings all around, or my hands have. The character just breaks down. It is not dependable. They pay lip service to the white man's ideals of conduct. They say, yes, I believe in honesty and truth and morality. But it is just lip service. Most of the time. I don't intend to get lathered up. This is just my private opinion. I believe in segregation, but I can always protect myself and my family. I dine at my club and my land is my own, and when I travel, the places I frequent have few if any Negroes. Not that I'd ever walk out of a restaurant, for I'm no professional Southerner. And I'd never give a nickel to the Citizens Council or anything like that. Nor have any of my friends, that I know of. That's townspeople stuff, anyway."

Later on, he says: "For years, I thought I loved Negroes. And I loved their humor and other qualities. My father—he was a firster around here, first man to put glass windows in for them, first to give them a written monthly statement, first to do a lot to help them toward financial independence—well, my father, he used to look at me and say how it would be. He said, son, they will knock it out of you. Well, they did. I learned the grimness and the sadness."

And later, as we ride down the long row of the houses of the hands, he points to shreds of screening at windows, or here and there a broken screen door. "One of my last experiments," he says, dourly. "Three months, and they poked it out of the kitchen window so they could throw slops on the bare ground. They broke down the front door so they could spit tobacco juice out on the porch floor."

We ride on. We pass a nicely painted house, with a fenced dooryard, with flower beds, and flower boxes on the porch, and good bright-painted porch furniture. I ask who lives there. "One of the hands," he says, "but he's got some energy and character. Look at his house. And he loves flowers. Has only three children, but when there's work he gets it done fast, and then finds some more to do. Makes $4,500 to $5,000 a year." Some old pride, or something from the lost days of idealism, comes back into his tone.

I ask what the other people on the place think of the tenant with the nice house.

"They think he's just lucky." And he mimics, a little bitterly, without any humor: "Boss, looks lak Jefferson's chillen, they jes picks faster'n mine. Caint he'p it, Boss."

I ask what Jefferson's color is.

"A real black man, a real Negro, all right. But he's got character."

I look down the interminable row of dingy houses, over the interminable flat of black earth toward the river.

Now and then, I encounter a man whose argument for segregation, in the present context, has nothing to do with the Negro at all. At its simplest level its spokesman says: "I don't give a durn about the niggers, they never bother me one way or another. But I don't like being forced. Ain't no man ever forced me."

But the law always carries force, you say.

"Not this law. It's different. It ain't our law."

At another level, the spokesman will say it is a matter of constitutionality, pure and simple. He may even be an integrationist. But this decision, he will say, carries us one more step toward the power state, a cunningly calculated step, for this decision carries a moral issue and the objector to the decision is automatically put in the role of the enemy of righteousness. "But wait till the next decision," he will say. "This will be the precedent for it, and the next one won't have the moral façade."

Precedent for what? you ask.

"For government by sociology, not law," he will say.

"Is it government by law," one man asks me, "when certain members of the Supreme Court want to write a minority decision, and the great conciliator conciliates them out of it, saying that the thing is going to be controversial enough without the Court splitting? Damn it, the Court should split, if that's the honest reading of the law. We want the reading of the law, not the concili- ation by sociology. Even if we don't happen to like the kind of law it turns out to be in a particular case."

And another man: "Yes, government by sociology not law is a two-edged business. The next guy who gets in the saddle just picks another brand of soci- ology. And nothing to stop him, for the very notion of law is gone."

Pridefulness, money, level of intelligence, race, God's will, filth and disease, power, hate, contempt, legality—perhaps these are not all the words that get mentioned. There is another thing, whatever the word for it. An eminent Negro scholar, is, I suppose, saying something about that other thing. "One thing," he says, "is that a lot of people down here just don't like change. It's not merely desegregation they're against so much, it's just the fact of any change. They feel some emotional tie to the way things are. A change is disorienting, es- pecially if you're pretty disoriented already."

Yes, a lot of them are disoriented enough already, uprooted, driven from the land, drawn from the land, befuddled by new opportunities, new ambitions, new obligations. They have entered the great anonymity of the new world.

And I hear a college student in the Deep South: "You know, it's just that people don't like to feel like they're spitting on their grandfather's grave. They feel some connection they don't want to break. Something would bother them if they broke it."

The young man is, I gather, an integrationist. He adds: "And sometimes something bothers them if they don't break it."

Let us give a name now to whatever it is that the eminent Negro scholar and the young white college boy were talking about. Let us, without meaning to be ironical, call it piety.

What does the Negro want?

The plump yellow man, with his hands folded calmly over his belly, the man who said it is the white man's "pridefulness," thinks, and answers the new question. "Opportunity," he says. "It's opportunity a man wants."

For what? I ask.

"Just to get along and make out. You know, like anybody."

"About education, now. If you got good schools, as good as anybody's, would that satisfy you?"

"Well—" the yellow man begins, but the black, intense-faced man breaks in. "We never had them, we'd never have them!"

"You might get them now," I say, "under this pressure."

"Maybe," the yellow man agrees, "maybe. And it might have satisfied once. But"—and he shakes his head—"not now. That doctrine won't grip now."

"Not now," the intense-faced man says. "Not after the Supreme Court decision. We want the law."

"But when?" I ask. "Right now? Tomorrow morning?"

"The Supreme Court decision says—" And he stops.

"It says deliberate speed," I say, "or something like that."

"If a Negro wants to study medicine, he can't study it. If he wants to study law, he can't study it. There isn't any way in this state for him to study it."

"Suppose," I say, "suppose professional and graduate schools got opened. To really qualified applicants, no funny business either way. Then they began some sort of staggered system, a grade or two at a time, from either top or bottom. Would something like that satisfy you? Perhaps not all over the state at the same time, some place serving as a sort of pilot for others where the going would be rougher."

The yellow man nods. The intense-faced man looks down at his new and newly polished good black shoes. He looks across at the wall. Not looking at me, he says: "Yes, if it was in good faith. If you could depend on it. Yes."

He hates to say it. At least, I think he hates to say it. It is a wrench, grudging.

I sit in another room, in another city, in the Deep South, with several men, two of them Negroes. One Negro is the local NAACP secretary, a man in build, color and quality strangely like the black, intense-faced man. I am asking again what will satisfy the Negroes. Only this time the intense-faced man does not as readily say, yes, a staggered system would be satisfactory. In fact, he doesn't say it at all. I ask him what his philosophy of social change is, in a democracy. He begins to refer to the law, to the Court, but one of the white men breaks in.

This white man is of the Deep South, born, bred and educated there. He is a middle-aged man, tall, rather spare but not angular, the impression of the lack of angularity coming, I suppose, from a great deliberation in voice and movement, a great calmness in voice and face. The face is an intellectual's face, a calm, dedicated face, but not a zealot's. His career, I know, has been identified with various causes of social reform. He has sat on many committees, has signed many things, some of them things I personally take to be nonsense. What he says now, in his serene voice, the words and voice being really all that

I know of him, is this: "I know that Mr. Cranford here"—and he nods toward this black, intense-faced man—"doesn't want any change by violence. He knows—we know—that change will take time. He wants a change in a Christian way that won't aggravate to violence. We have all got to live together. It will take time."

Nobody says anything. After a moment I go back to my question about the philosophy of social change. Wearily the intense-faced man says something, something not very relevant, not evasive, just not relevant. I let the matter drop. He sits with his head propped on his right hand, brow furrowed. He is not interested in abstractions. Why should he be?

Again, it is the Deep South, another town, another room, the bright, new-sparkling living room of the house of a Negro businessman, new furniture, new TV, new everything. There are several white men present, two journalists, myself (I've just come along to watch, I'm not involved), some technicians, and about ten Negroes, all in Sunday best, at ease but slightly formal, as though just before going in to a church service. Some of the Negroes, I have heard, are in the NAACP.

The technicians are rigging up their stuff, lights and cameras, etc., moving arrogantly in their own world superior to human concerns. In the background, in the dining room, the wife of our host, a plump fortyish mulatto, an agreeable-looking woman wearing a new black dress with a discreet white design on it, stands watching a big new electric percolator on a silver tray. Another silver tray holds a bottle of Canadian whiskey, a good whiskey, and glasses. When someone comes out of the kitchen, I catch a glimpse of a gray-haired Negro woman wearing a maid's uniform.

It is a bright, sunny, crisp day outside. The coffee is bubbling cheerfully. Out the window I see a little Negro girl, about ten years old, with a pink bow in her hair, an enormous bow, come out of a small pink house with aquamarine trim and shutters, and a dull blue roof. She stands a moment with the pink bow against the aquamarine door, then moves through the opening in the clipped privet hedge, a very tidy, persnickety hedge, and picks her way down the muddy street, where there is no sidewalk.

One of the journalists is instructing a Negro who is to be interviewed, a tall, well-set-up, jut-nosed, good-looking dark-brown man in a blue suit. He has a good way of holding his head. "Now, you're supposed to tell them," the journalist is saying, "what a lot of hogwash this separate but equal stuff is. What you said to me last night."

Pedagogical and irritable, one of the technicians says: "Quiet, quiet!"

They take a voice level. The dark-brown man is very much at ease, saying: "Now is the time for all good men to come to the aid of their country."

The interview begins. The dark-brown man, still very much at ease, is saying: ". . . and we're not disturbed. The only people disturbed are those who have not taken an unbiased look. We who have taken our decision, we aren't disturbed." He goes on to say the Negroes want an interracial discussion on the "how" of desegregation—but with the background understanding that the Court decision is law.

The journalist cuts in: "Make it simple and direct. Lay it on the line."

The tall brown man is unruffled. There is sweat on his face now, but from the lamps. He wipes his face, and patiently, condescendingly, smiles at the journalist. "Listen," he says, "you all are going back to New York City. But we stay here. We aren't afraid, but we live here. They know what we think, but it's a way of putting it we got to think about."

He says it is going to take some time to work things out, he knows that, but there is a chorus from the Negroes crowded back out of range of the camera: "Don't put no time limit—don't put any time on it—no ten or fifteen years!"

The dark-brown man doesn't put any time on it. He says all they want is to recognize the law and to sit down in a law-abiding way to work out the "how" and the "when."

"That's good, that's all right!" the chorus decides.

Leave the "how" in detail up to the specialists in education. As for the "when"—the dark-brown, jut-nosed man hesitates a second: "Well, Negroes are patient. We can wait a little while longer."

The dark-brown man gets up to his considerable height, wipes the sweat off his face, asks the journalist: "You got your playback?"

The chorus laughs. It is indulgent laughter of human vanity and such. Sure, any man would like to hear his voice played back, hear himself talking.

There is no playback. Not now, anyway.

The dark-brown man is receiving the handshakes, the shoulder-slaps, of his friends. They think he did well. He did do well. He looks back over his shoulder at the white men, grins. "When I got to leave," he says, "who's going to give me that job as chauffeur? I see that nice Cadillac sitting out front there."

There are the quick, deep-throated giggles.

I turn to a Negro beside me. "Ten years ago," I ask, "would this have been possible?"

"No," he says.

Then there is another house, the tangle of wires, the jumble of rig and lights, and another Negro being arranged for an interview. There is no air of decorous festivity here, just a businesslike bustle, with the Negro waiting. This one will be knocked off quick. It's getting on to lunch.

This one, one of the journalists told me, is supposed to be the Uncle Tom. He is a middle-aged man, fair-sized, tallish, medium brown, with a balding, rather high forehead. He is wearing a good dark suit. His manner is dignified, slow, a little sad. I have known him before, know something about him. He had begun life as waterboy on a plantation, back in the times when "some folks didn't think a thing of bloodying a Negro's head, just for nothing, and I have seen their heads bloodied." But a white man on the plantation had helped him ("Noticed I was sort of quick and took an interest in things, trying to learn"), and now he is a preacher. For a voice level, he does not say: "Now is the time for all good men to come to the aid of their country." He says: "Jesus wept, Jesus wept, Jesus wept."

The journalist tells him he is supposed to say some good things for segregation.

The Negro doesn't answer directly to that. "If you have some opinions of your own," he says, "your own people sometimes call you a son-of-a-gun, and sometimes the white people call you a son-of-a-gun."

Your own people. And I remember that the men at the last house had said: "Don't tell him you've seen us, don't tell him that or you won't get him to talk."

Is integration a good thing? the journalist asks him, and he says: "Till Negro people get as intelligent and self-sustaining they can't mix." But he flares up about discrimination along with segregation: "That's what makes Negroes bitter, wage differentials, no good jobs, that and the ballot." As for the Court decision, he says: "It's something for people to strive for, to ascertain their best."

I break in—I don't think the machinery is going yet—and ask about humiliation as a bar to Negro fulfillment.

"Segregation did one thing," he says. "No other race but the Negroes could build up as much will to go on and do things. To get their goals."

What goals? I ask.

"Just what anybody wants, just everything people can want to be a citizen," he says.

This isn't what the journalist has come for.

Things aren't promising too well. Uncle Tom is doing a disappearing act, Old Black Joe is evaporating, the handkerchief-head, most inconveniently, isn't there. The genie has got out of the bottle clearly labeled: *Negro* segregationist.

But maybe the genie can be coaxed back into the bottle. The sad-mannered man is, the journalist suggests, a pro-segregationist in that he thinks segregation built a will to achieve something.

The machinery gets going, the mike is lifted on its rod, the slow, sad voice speaks: "For segregation has test steel into the Negro race and this is one valuable point of segregation—segregation has proven that Negroes in the South, where it's practiced most, have done a fine job in building an economic strength beyond that of many other sections in the United States of America. Negroes own more farmland in Mississippi than any other state in the United States that is engaged in agriculture."

He goes along, he says, "with the idea you should have a moderate approach. You will never be able to integrate children on the school campus, the mothers holding a lot of bitterness in their hearts against each other white and colored."

It will take time, he says. "It is absurd otherwise, it's just foolish thinking for people to believe you can get the South to do in four or five years what they have been doing in the North for one hundred years. These people are emotional about their tradition, and you've got to have an educational program to change their way of thinking and this will be a slow process."

Yes, the genie is safely back in the labeled bottle. Or is he?

For the slow, sad voice is saying: ". . . has got to outthink the white man, has got to outlive the white man . . ."

Is saying: ". . . no need of saying that the South won't ever integrate . . ."

Is saying: ". . . not ultimate goal just to go to white schools and travel with white people on conveyances over the country. No, the Negro, he is a growing people and he will strive for all the equalities belonging to any American citizen. He is a growing people."

Yes, Uncle Tom is gone again, and gone for good. Too bad for the program. I wondered if they got this last part on tape.

The Negro turns to the journalist and asks if he has interviewed other people around.

"Yes, saw Mr. So-and-so of the Citizens Council."

Had we interviewed any other Negroes?

"Oh, some," after a shade of hesitation.

Had we seen So-and-so and So-and-so?

"No—why, no. Well, we want to thank you . . ."

We leave the sad-mannered, slow man and we know that he knows. He isn't a big enough fool not to know. White men have lied to him before. What is one more time after all the years?

Besides, what if you do tell him a lie?

There are, as a matter of fact, in Arkansas, Negroes who go from door to door collecting money to fight integration. There *are* Uncle Toms.

So it all evens out.

I ask my question of the eminent Negro scholar. His reply is immediate: "It's not so much what the Negro wants as what he doesn't want. The main point is not that he has poor facilities. It is that he must endure a constant assault on his ego. He is denied human dignity."

And I think of the yellow girl wearing the salmon sweater and slacks, in the shack in the sea of mud, at dusk, the girl whose husband has been shot, and she says: "It's how yore feelings git tore up all the time. The way folks talk, sometimes. It ain't what they say sometimes, if they'd jes say it kind."

She had gone to a store, in another town, for some dress goods, and had requested a receipt for the minister who manages the fund raised in her behalf. By the receipt the saleswoman identifies her and asks if "that man up yonder is still in jail for killing a nigger."

"Well," the girl had said, "if you want to put it that a-way."

"They can't do anything to a man for something he does drunk," the sales-woman has said.

The girl has laid the package down on the counter. "If you want it that a-way," she has said, "you kin take back yore dress goods. They's other places to buy."

She tells me the story.

And I think of another woman, up in Tennessee, middle-aged, precise, the kind of woman who knows her own competent mind, a school inspector for county schools, a Negro. "We don't want to socialize. That's not what we want. We do everything the white folks do already, even if we don't spend as much money doing it. And we have more fun. But I don't want to be insulted. If some-body has to tell you something, about some regulation or other, they could say it in a low, kind voice, not yell it out at you. And when I go to a place to buy something, and have that dollar bill in my hand, I want to be treated right. And I won't ride on a bus. I won't go to a restaurant in a town where there's just one. I'll go hungry. I won't be insulted at the front door and then crawl around to the back. You've got to try to keep some respect."

And in Tennessee again, the Negro at the biracial committee meeting says: "My boy is happy in the Negro school where he goes. I don't want him to go to the white school and sit by your boy's side. But I'd die fighting for his right to go." "We don't want to socialize," the woman in Tennessee says.

The college student, a Negro, in Tennessee, says: "The Negro doesn't want social equality. My wife is my color. I'm above wanting to mix things up. That's low class. Low class of both races."

The Negro man in Mississippi says: "Take a Negro man wanting a white woman. A man tends to want his own kind, now. But the white folks make such an awful fuss about it. They make it seem so awful special-like. Maybe that's what makes it sort of prey on some folks' mind."

And I remember the gang rape by four Negroes of a white woman near Memphis last fall, shortly after the Till killing. "One of our boys was killed down in Mississippi the other day and we're liable to kill you," one of the Negroes said as they bludgeoned the man who was with the woman and told him to get going.

This is a question for Negroes only. *Is there any difference between what the Negro feels at the exclusions of segregation, and what a white man feels at the exclusions which he, any man, must always face at some point?*

"Yes, it's different," the Negro college administrator says, "when your fate is on your face. Just that. It's the unchangeableness. But a white man, even if he knows he can't be President, even if he knows the chances for his son are one in many millions—long odds—still there's an idea there."

And the Negro lawyer: "Yes, it's different. But it's not easy to name it. Take how some unions come in and make some plant build nice rest rooms, one for white, one for Negroes, but same tile, same fixtures and all. But off the white ones, there's a little lounge for smoking. To make 'em feel superior to somebody. You see what I mean, how it's different?"

He thinks some more. "Yes," he says, "I got my dreams and hopes and aspirations, but me, I have to think what is sort of possible in the possibilities and probabilities. Some things I know I can't think on because of the circumstances of my birth."

And he thinks again, looking out of the window, over Beale Street. "Yes, there's a difference," he says. "A Negro, he doesn't really know some things, but he just goes walking pregnant with worries, not knowing their name. It's he's lost his purpose, somewhere. He goes wandering and wondering, and no purpose."

I look out the window, too, over Beale Street. It is late afternoon. I hear the pullulation of life, the stir and new tempo toward evening, the babble of voices, a snatch of laughter. I hear the remorseless juke boxes. They shake the air.

What's coming?

"Whatever it is," the college student in the Deep South says, "I'd like to put all the Citizens Council and all the NAACP in one room and give every man a baseball bat and lock 'em in till it was over. Then maybe some sensible people could work out something."

What's coming? I say it to the country grade-school superintendent. He is a part-time farmer, too, and now he is really in his role as farmer, not teacher, as we stand, at night, under the naked light of a flyspecked 200-watt bulb hanging from the shed roof, and he oversees two Negroes loading sacks of fertilizer on a truck. "I know folks round here," he says, and seeing his hard, aquiline, weathered face, with the flat, pale, hard eyes, I believe him.

"They aren't raised up to it," he says. "Back in the summer now, I went by a lady's house to ask about her children starting to school. Well, she was a real old-timey gal, a gant-headed, barefoot, snuff-dipping, bonnet-wearing, hard-ankled old gal standing out in the tobacco patch, leaning on her hoe, and she leaned at me and said, 'Done hear'd tell 'bout niggers gonna come in,' and before I could say anything, she said, 'Not with none of my young 'uns,' and let out a stream of ambeer."

"Would you hire a Negro teacher?" I asked.

"I personally would, but folks wouldn't stand for it, not now, mostly those who never went much to school themselves. Unless I could prove I couldn't get white." He paused. "And it's getting damned hard to get white, I tell you," he says.

I ask if integration will come.

"Sure," he says, "in fifty years. Every time the tobacco crop is reduced, we lose just that many white sharecroppers and Negroes. That eases the pain."

What's coming? And the Methodist minister, riding with me in the dusk, in the drizzle, by the flooded bayou, says: "It'll come, desegregation and the vote and all that. But it will be twenty-five, thirty years, a generation. You can preach love and justice, but it's a slow pull till you get the education." He waves a hand toward the drowned black cotton fields, stretching on forever, toward the rows of shacks marshaled off into the darkening distance, toward the far cypresses where dusk is tangled. "You can see," he says. "Just look, you can see."

What's coming? I ask the young lawyer in a mid-South city, a lawyer retained by one of the segregation outfits. "It's coming that we got to fight this bogus law," he says, "or we'll have a lot of social dis-tensions. The bogus law is based on social stuff and progress and just creates dis-tension. But we're gaining ground. Some upper-class people, I mean a real rich man, is coming out for us. And we get rolling, a Southern President could repack the Court. But it's got so a man can't respect the Supreme Court. All this share-the-wealth and Communist stuff and progress. You can't depend on law any more."

What can you depend on? I ask.

"Nothing but the people. Like the Civil War."

I suggest that whatever the constitutional rights and wrongs of the Civil War were, we had got a new Constitution out of it.

"No," he said, "just a different type of dog saying what it is."

I ask if, in the end, the appeal would be to violence.

"No, I don't believe in violence. I told Mr. Perkins, when we had our mass meeting, to keep the in-ci-dents down. But you get a lot of folks and there's always going to be in-ci-dents."

I ask if at Tuscaloosa the mob hadn't dictated public policy.

"Not dictate exactly." And he smiles his handsome smile. "But it was a lot of people."

He has used the word *progress,* over and over, to damn what he does not like. It is peculiar how he uses this laudatory word—I can imagine how he would say it in other contexts, on public occasions, rolling it on his tongue—as the word now for what he hates most. I wonder how deep a cleavage the use of that word indicates.

What's coming? I ask the handsome, aristocratic, big gray-haired man, sitting in his rich office, high over the city, an ornament of the vestry, of boards of directors, of club committees, a man of exquisite simplicity and charm, and a member of a segregation group.

"We shall exhaust all the legal possibilities," he says.

I ask if he thinks his side will win. The legal fight, that is.

He rolls a cigarette fastidiously between the strong, white, waxy forefinger and thumb. "No," he says. "But it is just something you have to do." He rolls the cigarette, looking out the window over the city, a city getting rich now, "filthy rich," as somebody has said to me. There is the undertone and unceasing susurrus of traffic in the silence of his thoughts.

"Well," he says at last, "to speak truth, I think the whole jig is up. We'll have desegregation right down the line. And you know why?"

I shake my head.

"Well, I'll tell you. You see those girls in my office outside, those young men. Come from good lower-middle-class homes, went to college a lot of them. Well, a girl comes in here and says to me a gentleman is waiting. She shows him in. He is as black as the ace of spades. It just never crossed that girl's mind, what she was saying, when she said a gentleman was waiting." He pauses. "Yes, sir," he says, "I just don't know why I'm doing it."

I am thinking of walking down Canal Street, in New Orleans, and a man is saying to me: "Do you know how many millions a year the Negroes spend up and down this street?"

No, I had said, I didn't know.

He tells me the figure, then says: "You get the logic of that, don't you?"

What's coming? And the college student says: "I'll tell you one thing that's coming, there's not going to be any academic freedom or any other kind around here if we don't watch out. Now, I'm a segregationist, that is, the way things are here right now, but I don't want anybody saying I can't listen to somebody talk about something. I can make up my own mind."

What's coming? And a state official says: "Integration sure and slow. A creeping process. If the NAACP has got bat sense, not deliberately provoking things as in the University of Alabama deal. They could have got that girl in quiet and easy, but that wouldn't satisfy them. No, they wanted the bang. As for things in general, grade schools and high schools, it'll be the creeping process. The soft places first, and then one county will play football or basketball with Negroes on the team. You know how it'll be. A creeping process. There'll be lots of court actions, but don't let court actions fool you. I bet you half the superintendents over in Tennessee will secretly welcome a court action in their county. Half of 'em are worried morally and half financially, and a court action just gets 'em off the hook. They didn't initiate it, they can always claim, but it gets them off the hook. That's the way I would feel, I know."

What's coming? I ask the taxi driver in Memphis. And he says: "Lots of dead niggers round here, that's what's coming. Look at Detroit, lots of dead niggers been in the Detroit River, but it won't be a patch on the Ole Mississippi. But hell, it won't stop nothing. Fifty years from now everybody will be gray anyway, Jews and Germans and French and Chinese and niggers, and who'll give a durn?"

The cab has drawn to my destination. I step out into the rain and darkness. "Don't get yourself drownded now," he says. "You have a good time now. I hope you do."

What's coming? And a man in Arkansas says: "We'll ride it out. But it looked like bad trouble one time. Too many outsiders. Mississippians and all. They come back here again, somebody's butt will be busted."

And another man: "Sure, they aim for violence, coming in here. When a man gets up before a crowd and plays what purports to be a recording of an NAACP official, an inflammatory sex thing, and then boasts of having been in on a lynching himself, what do you call it? Well, they got him on the witness stand, under oath, and he had to admit he got the record from Patterson, of the Citizens Council, and admitted under oath the lynching statement. He also admitted under oath some other interesting facts—that he had once been indicted for criminal libel but pleaded guilty to simple libel, that he has done sixty days for contempt of court on charges of violating an injunction having to do with liquor. Yeah, he used to run a paper called *The Rub Down*—that's what got him into the libel business. What's going to happen if a guy like that runs things? I ask you."

What's coming? And the planter leans back with the glass in his hand. "I'm not going to get lathered up," he says, "because it's no use. Why is the country so lathered up to force the issue one way or the other? Democracy—democracy has just come to be a name for what you like. It has lost responsibility, no local integrity left, it has been bought off. We've got the power state coming on, and communism or socialism, whatever you choose to call it. Race amalgamation is inevitable. I can't say I like any of it. I am out of step with the times."

What's coming? I ask the Episcopal rector, in the Deep South, a large handsome man, almost the twin of my friend sitting in the fine office overlooking the rich city. He has just told me that when he first came down from the North, a generation back, his bishop had explained it all to him, how the Negroes' skull capacity was limited. But, as he has said, brain power isn't everything, there's justice, and not a member of his congregation wasn't for conviction in the Till case.

"But the Negro has to be improved before integration," he says. "Take their morals, we are gradually improving the standard of morality and decency."

The conversation veers, we take a longer view. "Well, anthropologically speaking," he says, "the solution will be absorption, the Negro will disappear."

I ask how this is happening.

"Low-class people, immoral people, libertines, wastrels, prostitutes and such," he says.

I ask if, in that case, the raising of the moral level of the Negro does not prevent, or delay, what he says is the solution.

The conversation goes into a blur.

What's coming? And the young man from Mississippi says: "Even without integration, even with separate but pretty good facilities for the Negro, the Negro would be improving himself. He would be making himself more intellectually and socially acceptable. Therefore, as segregationists, if we're logical, we ought to deny any good facilities to them. Now, I'm a segregationist, but I can't be that logical."

What's coming? And the officer of the Citizens Council chapter says: "Desegregation, integration, amalgamation—none of it will come here. To say it will come is defeatism. It won't come if we stand firm."

And the old man in north Tennessee, a burly, full-blooded, red-faced, raucous old man, says: "Hell, son, it's easy to solve. Just blend 'em. Fifteen years and they'll all be blended in. And by God, I'm doing my part!"

Out of Memphis, I lean back in my seat on the plane, and watch the darkness slide by. I know what the Southerner feels going out of the South, the relief, the expanding vistas. Now, to the sound of the powerful, magnanimous engines bearing me through the night, I think of that, thinking of the new libel laws in Mississippi, of the academic pressures, of academic resignations, of the Negro facing the shotgun blast, of the white man with a nice little hard-built business being boycotted, of the college boy who said: "I'll just tell you, everybody is *scairt.*"

I feel the surge of relief. But I know what the relief really is. It is the relief from responsibility.

Now you may eat the bread of the Pharisee and read in the morning paper, with only a trace of irony, how out of an ultimate misery of rejection some Puerto Rican schoolboys—or is it Jews or Negroes or Italians?—who call themselves something grand, the Red Eagles or the Silver Avengers, have stabbed another boy to death, or raped a girl, or trampled an old man into a bloody mire. If you can afford it, you will, according to the local mores, send your child to a private school, where there will be, of course, a couple of Negro children on exhibit. And that delightful little Chinese girl who is so good at dramatics. Or is it finger painting?

Yes, you know what the relief is. It is the flight from the reality you were born to.

But what is that reality you have fled from?

It is the fact of self-division. I do not mean division between man and man in society. That division is, of course, there, and it is important. Take, for example, the killing of Clinton Melton, in Glendora, Mississippi, in the Delta, by a man named Elmer Kimbell, a close friend of Milam (who had been acquitted of the murder of Till, whose car was being used by Kimbell at the time of the killing of Melton, and to whose house Kimbell returned after the deed).

Two days after the event, twenty-one men—storekeepers, planters, railroad men, schoolteachers, preachers, bookkeepers—sent money to the widow for funeral expenses, with the note: "Knowing that he was outstanding in his race, we the people of this town are deeply hurt and donate as follows." When the Lions Club met three days after the event, a resolution was drawn and signed by all members present: "We consider the taking of the life of Clinton Melton an outrage against him, against all the people of Glendora, against the people of Mississippi as well as against the entire human family. . . . We humbly confess in repentance for having so lived as a community that such an evil occurrence could happen here, and we offer ourselves to be used in bringing to pass a better realization of the justice, righteousness and peace which is the will of God for human society."

And the town began to raise a fund to realize the ambition of the dead man, to send his children to college; the doctor of Glendora offered employment in his clinic to the widow; and the owner of the plantation where she had been raised offered to build for her and her children a three-room house.

But, in that division between man and man, the jury that tried Elmer Kimbell acquitted him.

But, in that same division between man and man, when the newspaper of Clarksdale, Mississippi, in the heart of the Delta, ran a front-page story of the acquittal, that story was bracketed with a front-page editorial saying that there had been some extenuation for acquittal in the Till case, with confusion of evidence and outside pressures, but that in the Melton case, there had been no pressure and "we were alone with ourselves and we flunked it."

Such division between man and man is important. As one editor in Tennessee said to me: "There's a fifth column of decency here, and it will, in the end, betray the extremists, when the politicians get through." But such a division between man and man is not as important in the long run as the division within the individual man.

Within the individual there are, or may be, many lines of fracture. It may be between his own social idealism and his anger at Yankee Phariseeism. (Oh, yes, he remembers that in the days when Federal bayonets supported the black Reconstruction state governments in the South, not a single Negro held elective office in any Northern state.) It may be between his social views and his fear of the power state. It may be between his social views and his clan sense. It may be between his allegiance to organized labor and his racism—for status or blood purity. It may be between his Christianity and his social prejudice. It may be between his sense of democracy and his ingrained attitudes toward the Negro. It may be between his own local views and his concern for the figure America cuts in the international picture. It may be between his practical concern at the money loss to society caused by the Negro's depressed condition and his own personal gain or personal prejudice. It may be, and disastrously, between his sense of the inevitable and his emotional need to act against the inevitable.

There are almost an infinite number of permutations and combinations, but they all amount to the same thing: a deep intellectual rub, a moral rub, anger at the irremediable self-division, a deep exacerbation at some failure to find identity. That is the reality.

It expresses itself in many ways. I sit for an afternoon with an old friend, a big, weather-faced, squarish man, a farmer, an intelligent man, a man of good education, of travel and experience, and I ask him questions. I ask if he thinks we can afford, in the present world picture, to alienate Asia by segregation here at home. He hates the question. "I hate to think about it," he says. "It's too deep for me," he says, and moves heavily in his chair. We talk about Christianity— he is a churchgoing man—and he says: "Oh, I know what the Bible says, and Christianity, but I just can't think about it. My mind just shuts up."

My old friend is an honest man. He will face his own discomfort. He will not try to ease it by passing libel laws to stop discussion or by firing professors.

There are other people whose eyes brighten at the thought of the new unity in the South, the new solidarity of resistance. These men are idealists, and they dream of preserving the traditional American values of individual-ism and localism against the anonymity, irresponsibility, and materialism of the power state, against the philosophy of the ad-man, the morality of the Kin-sey report, and the gospel of the bitch-goddess. *To be Southern again:* to re-create a habitation for the values they would preserve, to achieve in unity some clar-ity of spirit, to envisage some healed image of their own identity.

Some of these men are segregationists. Some are desegregationists, but these, in opposing what they take to be the power-state implications of the Court decision, find themselves caught, too, in the defense of segregation. And defending segregation, both groups are caught in a paradox: in seeking to pre-serve individualism by taking refuge in the vision of a South redeemed in unity and antique virtue, they are fleeing from the burden of their own individual-ity—the intellectual rub, the moral rub. To state the matter in another way, by using the argument of *mere* social continuity and the justification by mere *mores*, they think of a world in which circumstances and values are frozen; but the essence of individuality is the willingness to accept the rub which the flux of things provokes, to accept one's fate in time. What heroes would these ideal-ists enshrine to take the place of Jefferson and Lee, those heroes who took the risk of their fate?

Even among these people some are in discomfort, discomfort because the new unity, the new solidarity, once it descends from the bright new world of Idea, means unity with some quite concrete persons and specific actions. They say: "Yes—yes, we've got to unify." And then: "But we've got to purge certain elements."

But who will purge whom? And what part of yourself will purge another part?

"Yes, it's our own fault," the rich businessman, active in segregation, says. "If we'd ever managed to bring ourselves to do what we ought to have done for the Negro, it would be different now, if we'd managed to educate them, get them decent housing, decent jobs."

So I tell him what a Southern Negro professor had said to me. He had said that the future now would be different, would be hopeful, if there could just be "one gesture of graciousness" from the white man—even if the white man didn't like the Supreme Court decision, he might try to understand the Negro's view, not heap insult on him.

And the segregationist, who is a gracious man, seizes on the word. "Graciousness," he says, "that's it, if we could just have managed some graciousness to the race. Sure, some of us, a lot of us, could manage some graciousness to individual Negroes, some of us were grateful to individuals for being gracious to us. But you know, we couldn't manage it for the race." He thinks a moment, then says: "There's a Negro woman buried in the family burial place. We loved her."

I believe him when he says it. And he sinks into silence, feeling the rub, for the moment anyway, between the man who can talk in terms of graciousness, in whatever terms that notion may present itself to him, and the man who is a power for segregation.

This is the same man who has said to me, earlier, that he knows integration to be inevitable, doesn't know why he is fighting it. But such a man is happier, perhaps, than those men, destined by birth and personal qualities to action and leadership, who in the face of what they take to be inevitable feel cut off from all action. "I am out of step with the times," one such man says to me, and his wife says, "You know, if we feel the way we do, we ought to do something about it," and he, in some deep, inward, unproclaimed bitterness, says, "No, I'm not going to get lathered up about anything."

Yes, there are many kinds of rub, but I suppose that the commonest one is the moral one—the Christian one, in fact, for the South is still a land of faith. There is, of course, the old joke that after the Saturday night lynching, the congregation generally turns up a little late for church, and the sardonic remark a man made to me about the pro-integration resolution of the Southern Baptist Convention: "They were just a little bit exalted. When they got back with the home folks a lot of 'em wondered how they did it."

But meanwhile, there are the pastors at Glendora and Hoxie and Oxford and other nameless places. And I remember a pastor, in Tennessee, a Southerner born and bred, saying to me: "Yes, I think the Court decision may have set back race equality—it was coming fast, faster than anybody could guess, because so quiet. But now some people get so put out with the idea of Negroes in church, they stop me on the street and say if I ever let one in, they won't come to church. So I ask about Heaven, what will they do in Heaven?

" 'Well,' one woman said, 'I'll just let God segregate us.'

" 'You'll *let* God segregate you?' I said, and she flounced off. But I ask, where is Christianity if people can't worship together? There's only one thing to try to preach, and that is Christ. And there's only one question to ask, and that is what would Christ do?"

Will they go with him? I ask.

"They are good Christian people, most of them," he says. "It may be slow, but they are Christians."

And in a town in south Kentucky, in a "black county," a Confederate county, where desegregation is now imminent in the high schools, the super-intendent says to me: "The people here are good Christian people, trying to do right. When this thing first came up, the whole board said they'd walk out. But the ministers got to preaching, and the lawyers to talking on it, and they came around."

I asked how many were influenced by moral, how many by legal, consider-ations.

About half and half, he reckons, then adds: "I'm a Rebel myself, and I don't deny it, but I'm an American and a law-abiding citizen. A man can hate an idea but know it's right, and it takes a lot of thinking and praying to bring your-self around. You just have to uncover the unrecognized sympathy in the white man for the Negro humiliation."

Fifty miles away I shall sit in a living room and hear some tale of a Negro coming to somebody's front door—another house—and being admitted by a Negro servant and being found by the master of the house, who says: "I don't care if Susie did let you in. I don't care if Jesus Christ let you in. No black son-of-a-bitch is coming to my front door."

After the tale, there is silence. All present are segregationist, or I think they are.

Then one woman says: "Maybe he did take a lot on himself, coming to the front door. But I can't stand it. He's human."

And another woman: "I think it's a moral question, and I suffer, but I can't feel the same way about a Negro as a white person. It's born in me. But I pray I'll change."

The successful businessman in Louisiana says to me: "I have felt the moral question. It will be more moral when we get rid of segregation. But I'm human enough—I guess it's human to be split up—to want things just postponed till my children are out of school. But I can't lift my finger to delay things."

But this man, privately admitting his division of feeling, having no inten-tion of public action on either side, is the sort of man who can be trapped, ac-cidentally, into action.

There is the man who got the letter in the morning mail, asking him to serve as chairman of a citizens committee to study plans for desegregation in his county. "I was sick," he says, "and I mean literally sick. I felt sick all day. I didn't see how I could get into something like that. But next morning, you know, I did it."

That county now has its schedule for desegregation.

There is another man, a lawyer, who has been deeply involved in a desegregation action. "I never had much feeling of prejudice, but hell, I didn't have any theories either, and I now and then paid some lip service to segregation. I didn't want to get mixed up in the business. But one night a telephone call came. I told the man I'd let him know next day. You know, I was sick. I walked on back in the living room, and my wife looked at me. She must have guessed what it was. 'You going to do it?' she asked me. I said, hell, I didn't know, and went out. I was plain sick. But next day I did it. Well," he says, and grins, and leans back under the shelves of lawbooks, "and I'm stuck with it. But you know, I'm getting damned tired of the paranoiacs and illiterates I'm up against."

Another man, with a small business in a poor county, "back in the shelf country," he calls it, a short, strong-looking, ovoidal kind of man, with his belt cutting into his belly when he leans back in his office chair. He is telling me what he has been through. "I wouldn't tell you a lie," he says. "I'm Southern through and through, and I guess I got every prejudice a man can have, and I certainly never would have got mixed up in this business if it hadn't been for the Court decision. I wouldn't be out in front. I was just trying to do my duty. Trying to save some money for the county. I never expected any trouble. And we might not have had any if it hadn't been for outsiders, one kind and another.

"But what nobody understands is how a man can get cut up inside. You try to live like a Christian with your fellowman, and suddenly you find out it is all mixed up. You put in twenty-five years trying to build up a nice little business and raise up a family, and it looks like it will all be ruined. You get word somebody will dynamite your house and you in it. You go to lawyers and they say they sympathize, but nobody'll take your case. But the worst is, things just go round and round in your head. Then they won't come a-tall, and you lay there in the night. You might say, it's the psychology of it you can't stand. Getting all split up. Then, all of a sudden, somebody stops you on the street and calls you something, a so-and-so nigger-lover. And you know, I got so mad, not a thing mattered any more. I just felt like I was all put back together again."

He said he wished he could write it down, how awful it is for a man to be split up.

Negroes, they must be split up, too, I think. They are human, too. There must be many ways for them to be split up. I remember asking a Negro schoolteacher if she thought Negro resentment would be a bar to integration. "Some of us try to teach love," she says, "as well as we can. But some of us teach hate. I guess we can't help it."

Love and hate, but more than that, the necessity of confronting your own motives: *Do we really want to try to work out a way to live with the white people or*

*do we just want to show them, pay off something, show them up, rub their noses in
it?*

And I can imagine the grinding anger, the sense of outrage of a Negro crying out within himself: *After all the patience, after all the humility, after learning
and living those virtues, do I have to learn magnanimity, too?*

Yes, I can imagine the outrage, the outrage as some deep, inner self tells
him, yes, he must.

I am glad that white people have no problem as hard as that.

The taxi drew up in front of the apartment house, and I got out, but the driver
and I talked on for a moment. I stood there in the rain, then paid him, and ran
for the door. It wasn't that I wanted to get out of the rain. I had an umbrella. I
wanted to get in and write down what he had said.

He was a local man, born near Nashville, up near Goodlettsville, "raised up
with niggers." He had been in the army, with lots of fighting, Africa, Sicily, Italy,
but a lot of time bossing work gangs. In Africa, at first, it had been Arabs, but
Arabs weren't "worth a durn." Then they got Negro work battalions.

But here are the notes:

*Niggers a lot better than Arabs, but they didn't hurt themselves—didn't any of
'em git a hernia for Uncle Sam—race prejudice—but it ain't our hate, it's the hate
hung on us by the old folks dead and gone. Not I mean to criticize the old folks, they
done the best they knew, but that hate, we don't know how to shuck it. We got that
God-damn hate stuck in our craw and can't puke it up. If white folks quit shoving the
nigger down and calling him a nigger, he could maybe get to be a asset to the South
and the country. But how stop shoving?*

We are the prisoners of our history.

Or are we?

There is one more interview I wish to put on record. I shall enter it by question
and answer.

Q. You're a Southerner, aren't you?
A. Yes.
Q. Are you afraid of the power state?
A. Yes.
Q. Do you think the Northern press sometimes distorts Southern news?
A. Yes.
Q. Assuming that they do, why do they do it?
A. They like to feel good.
Q. What do you think the South ought to do about that distortion?
A. Nothing.
Q. Nothing? What do you mean, nothing?

A. The distortion—that's the Yankees' problem, not ours.

Q. You mean they ought to let the South work out a way to live with the Negro?

A. I don't think the problem is to learn to live with the Negro.

Q. What is it, then?

A. It is to learn to live with ourselves.

Q. What do you mean?

A. I don't think you can live with yourself when you are humiliating the man next to you.

Q. Don't you think the races have made out pretty well, considering?

A. Yes. By some sort of human decency and charity, God knows how. But there was always an image of something else.

Q. An image?

A. Well, I knew an old lady who grew up in a black county, but a county where relations had been, as they say, good. She had a fine farm and a good brick house, and when she got old she sort of retired from the world. The hottest summer weather and she would lock all the doors and windows at night, and lie there in the airless dark. But sometimes she'd telephone to town in the middle of the night. She would telephone that somebody was burning the Negroes out there on her place. She could hear their screams. Something was going on in her old head which in another place and time would not have been going on in her old head. She had never, I should think, seen an act of violence in her life. But something was going on in her head.

Q. Do you think it is chiefly the redneck who causes violence?

A. No. He is only the cutting edge. He, too, is a victim. Responsibility is a seamless garment. And the northern boundary of that garment is not the Ohio River.

Q. Are you for desegregation?

A. *Yes.*

Q. When will it come?

A. Not soon.

Q. When?

A. When enough people, in a particular place, a particular county or state, cannot live with themselves any more. Or realize they don't have to.

Q. What do you mean, don't have to?

A. When they realize that desegregation is just one small episode in the long effort for justice. It seems to me that that perspective, suddenly seeing the business as little, is a liberating one. It liberates you from yourself.

Q. Then you think it is a moral problem?

A. Yes, but no moral problem gets solved abstractly. It has to be solved in a context for possible solution.

Q. Can contexts be changed?

A. Sure. We might even try to change them the right way.

Q. Aren't you concerned about possible racial amalgamation?

A. I don't even think about it. We have to deal with the problem our historical moment proposes, the burden of our time. We all live with a thousand unsolved problems of justice all the time. We don't even recognize a lot of them. We have to deal only with those which the moment proposes to us. Anyway, we can't legislate for posterity. All we can do for posterity is to try to plug along in a way to make them think we—the old folks—did the best we could for justice, as we could understand it.

Q. Are you a gradualist on the matter of segregation?

A. If by gradualist you mean a person who would create delay for the sake of delay, then no. If by gradualist you mean a person who thinks it will take time, not time as such, but time for an educational process, preferably a calculated one, then yes. I mean a process of mutual education for whites and blacks. And part of this education should be in the actual beginning of the process of desegregation. It's a silly question, anyway, to ask if somebody is a gradualist. Gradualism is all you'll get. History, like nature, knows no jumps. Except the jump backward, maybe.

Q. Has the South any contribution to make to the national life?

A. It has made its share. It may again.

Q. How?

A. If the South is really able to face up to itself and its situation, it may achieve identity, moral identity. Then in a country where moral identity is hard to come by, the South, because it has had to deal concretely with a moral problem, may offer some leadership. And we need any we can get. If we are to break out of the national rhythm, the rhythm between complacency and panic.

This is, of course, an interview with myself.

Travels with Charley

1962

◆

J O H N   S T E I N B E C K

While I was still in Texas, late in 1960, the incident most reported and pictured in the newspapers was the matriculation of a couple of tiny Negro children in a New Orleans school. Behind these small dark mites were the law's majesty and the law's power to enforce—both the scales and the sword were allied with the infants—while against them were three hundred years of fear and anger and terror of change in a changing world. I had seen photographs in the papers every day and motion pictures on the television screen. What made the newsmen love the story was a group of stout middle-aged women who, by some curious definition of the word "mother," gathered every day to scream invectives at children. Further, a small group of them had become so expert that they were known as the Cheerleaders, and a crowd gathered every day to enjoy and to applaud their performance.

This strange drama seemed so improbable that I felt I had to see it. It had the same draw as a five-legged calf or a two-headed foetus at a sideshow, a distortion of normal life we have always found so interesting that we will pay to see it, perhaps to prove to ourselves that we have the proper number of legs or heads. In the New Orleans show, I felt all the amusement of the improbable abnormal, but also a kind of horror that it could be so.

At this time the winter which had been following my track ever since I left home suddenly struck with a black norther. It brought ice and freezing sleet and sheeted the highways with dark ice. I gathered Charley from the good doctor. He looked half his age and felt wonderful, and to prove it he ran and jumped and rolled and laughed and gave little yips of pure joy. It felt very good to have him with me again, sitting up right in the seat beside me, peering ahead at the unrolling road, or curling up to sleep with his head in my lap and his silly ears available for fondling. That dog can sleep through any amount of judicious caresses.

Now we stopped dawdling and laid our wheels to the road and went. We could not go fast because of the ice, but we drove relentlessly, hardly glancing at the passing of Texas beside us. And Texas was achingly endless—Sweetwater and Balinger and Austin. We bypassed Houston. We stopped for gasoline and coffee and slabs of pie. Charley had his meals and his walks in gas stations.

Night did not stop us, and when my eyes ached and burned from peering too long and my shoulders were side hills of pain, I pulled into a turnout and crawled like a mole into my bed, only to see the highway writhe along behind my closed lids. No more than two hours could I sleep, and then out into the bitter cold night and on and on. Water beside the road was frozen solid, and people moved about with shawls and sweaters wrapped around their ears.

Other times I have come to Beaumont dripping with sweat and lusting for ice and air-conditioning. Now Beaumont with all its glare of neon signs was what they called froze up. I went through Beaumont at night, or rather in the dark well after midnight. The blue-fingered man who filled my gas tank looked in at Charley and said, "Hey, it's a dog! I thought you had a nigger in there." And he laughed delightedly. It was the first of many repetitions. At least twenty times I heard it—"Thought you had a nigger in there." It was an unusual joke—always fresh—and never Negro or even Nigra, always Nigger or rather Niggah. That word seemed terribly important, a kind of safety word to cling to lest some structure collapse.

And then I was in Louisiana, with Lake Charles away to the side in the dark, but my lights glittered on ice and glinted on diamond frost, and those people who forever trudge the roads at night were mounded over with cloth against the cold. I dogged it on through La Fayette and Morgan City and came in the early dawn to Houma, which is pronounced Homer and is in my memory one of the pleasantest places in the world. There lives my old friend Doctor St. Martin, a gentle, learned man, a Cajun who has lifted babies and cured colic among the shell-heap Cajuns for miles around. I guess he knows more about Cajuns than anyone living, but I remembered with longing other gifts of Doctor St. Martin. He makes the best and most subtle martini in the world by a process approximating magic. The only part of his formula I know is that he uses distilled water for his ice and distills it himself to be sure. I have eaten black duck at his table—two St. Martin martinis and a brace of black duck with a burgundy delivered from the bottle as a baby might be delivered, and this in a darkened house where the shades have been closed at dawn and the cool night air preserved. At that table with its silver soft and dull, shining as pewter, I remember the raised glass of the grape's holy blood, the stem caressed by the doctor's strong artist fingers, and even now I can hear the sweet little health and welcome in the singing language of Acadia which once was French and now is itself. This picture filled my frosty windshield, and if there had been traffic would have made me a dangerous driver. But it was pale yellow frozen dawn in Houma and I knew that if I stopped to pay my respects, my will and my determination would drift away on the particular lotus St. Martin purveys and we would be speaking of timeless matters when the evening came, and another evening. And so I only bowed in the direction of my friend and scudded on toward New Orleans, for I wanted to catch a show of the Cheerleaders.

Even I know better than to drive a car near trouble, particularly Rocinante, with New York license plates. Only yesterday a reporter had been beaten and his camera smashed, for even convinced voters are reluctant to have their moment of history recorded and preserved.

So, well on the edge of town I drove into a parking lot. The attendant came to my window. "Man, oh man, I thought you had a nigger in there. Man, oh man, it's a dog. I see that big old black face and I think it's a big old nigger."

"His face is blue-gray when he's clean," I said coldly.

"Well I see some blue-gray niggers and they wasn't clean. New York, eh?"

It seemed to me a chill like the morning air came into his voice. "Just driving through," I said. "I want to park for a couple of hours. Think you can get me a taxi?"

"Tell you what I bet. I bet you're going to see the Cheerleaders."

"That's right."

"Well, I hope you're not one of those troublemakers or reporters."

"I just want to see it."

"Man, oh man, you going to see something. Ain't those Cheerleaders something? Man, oh man, you never heard nothing like it when they get going."

I locked Charley in Rocinante's house after giving the attendant a tour of the premises, a drink of whisky, and a dollar. "Be kind of careful about opening the door when I'm away," I said. "Charley takes his job pretty seriously. You might lose a hand." This was an outrageous lie, of course, but the man said, "Yes, sir. You don't catch me fooling around with no strange dog."

The taxi driver, a sallow, yellowish man, shriveled like a chickpea with the cold, said, "I wouldn't take you more than a couple of blocks near. I don't go to have my cab wrecked."

"Is it that bad?"

"It ain't is it. It's can it get. And it can get that bad."

"When do they get going?"

He looked at his watch. "Except it's cold, they been coming in since dawn. It's quarter to. You get along and you won't miss nothing except it's cold."

I had camouflaged myself in an old blue jacket and my British navy cap on the supposition that in a seaport no one ever looks at a sailor any more than a waiter is inspected in a restaurant. In his natural haunts a sailor has no face and certainly no plans beyond getting drunk and maybe in jail for fighting. At least that's the general feeling about sailors. I've tested it. The most that happens is a kindly voice of authority saying, "Why don't you go back to your ship, sailor? You wouldn't want to sit in the tank and miss your tide, now would you, sailor?" And the speaker wouldn't recognize you five minutes later. And the Lion and Unicorn on my cap made me even more anonymous. But I must warn anyone testing my theory, never try it away from a shipping port.

"Where you from?" the driver asked with a complete lack of interest.

"Liverpool."

"Limey, huh? Well, you'll be all right. It's the goddamn New York Jews cause all the trouble."

I found myself with a British inflection and by no means one of Liverpool. "Jews—what? How do they cause trouble?"

"Why, hell, mister. We know how to take care of this. Everybody's happy and getting along fine. Why, I *like* niggers. And them goddamn New York Jews come in and stir the niggers up. They just stay in New York there wouldn't be no trouble. Ought to take them out."

"You mean lynch them?"

"I don't mean nothing else, mister."

He let me out and I started to walk away. "Don't try to get too close, mister," he called after me. "Just you enjoy it but don't mix in."

"Thanks," I said, and killed the "awfully" that came to my tongue.

As I walked toward the school I was in a stream of people all white and all going in my direction. They walked intently like people going to a fire after it has been burning for some time. They beat their hands against their hips or hugged them under coats, and many men had scarves under their hats and covering their ears.

Across the street from the school the police had set up wooden barriers to keep the crowd back, and they paraded back and forth, ignoring the jokes called to them. The front of the school was deserted but along the curb United States marshals were spaced, not in uniform but wearing armbands to identify them. Their guns bulged decently under their coats but their eyes darted about nervously, inspecting faces. It seemed to me that they inspected me to see if I was a regular, and then abandoned me as unimportant.

It was apparent where the Cheerleaders were, because people shoved forward to try to get near them. They had a favored place at the barricade directly across from the school entrance, and in that area a concentration of police stamped their feet and slapped their hands together in unaccustomed gloves.

Suddenly I was pushed violently and a cry went up: "Here she comes. Let her through. . . . Come on, move back. Let her through. Where you been? You're late for school. Where you been, Nellie?"

The name was not Nellie. I forget what it was. But she shoved through the dense crowd quite near enough to me so that I could see her coat of imitation fleece and her gold earrings. She was not tall, but her body was ample and full-busted. I judge she was about fifty. She was heavily powdered, which made the line of her double chin look very dark.

She wore a ferocious smile and pushed her way through the milling people, holding a fistful of clippings high in her hand to keep them from being crushed. Since it was her left hand I looked particularly for a wedding ring, and saw that there was none. I slipped in behind her to get carried along by her wave, but the crush was dense and I was given a warning too. "Watch it, sailor. Everybody wants to hear."

Nellie was received with shouts of greeting. I don't know how many Cheerleaders there were. There was no fixed line between the Cheerleaders and the crowd behind them. What I could see was that a group was passing newspaper clippings back and forth and reading them aloud with little squeals of delight.

Now the crowd grew restless, as an audience does when the clock goes past curtain time. Men all around me looked at their watches. I looked at mine. It was three minutes to nine.

The show opened on time. Sound of sirens. Motorcycle cops. Then two big black cars filled with big men in blond felt hats pulled up in front of the school. The crowd seemed to hold its breath. Four big marshals got out of each car and from somewhere in the automobiles they extracted the littlest Negro girl you ever saw, dressed in shining starchy white, with new white shoes on feet so little they were almost round. Her face and little legs were very black against the white.

The big marshals stood her on the curb and a jangle of jeering shrieks went up from behind the barricades. The little girl did not look at the howling crowd but from the side the whites of her eyes showed like those of a frightened fawn. The men turned her around like a doll, and then the strange procession moved up the broad walk toward the school, and the child was even more a mite because the men were so big. Then the girl made a curious hop, and I think I know what it was. I think in her whole life she had not gone ten steps without skipping, but now in the middle of her first skip the weight bore her down and her little round feet took measured, reluctant steps between the tall guards. Slowly they climbed the steps and entered the school.

The papers had printed that the jibes and jeers were cruel and sometimes obscene, and so they were, but this was not the big show. The crowd was waiting for the white man who dared to bring his white child to school. And here he came along the guarded walk, a tall man dressed in light gray, leading his frightened child by the hand. His body was tensed as a strong leaf spring drawn to the breaking strain; his face was grave and gray, and his eyes were on the ground immediately ahead of him. The muscles of his cheeks stood out from clenched jaws, a man afraid who by his will held his fears in check as a great rider directs a panicked horse.

A shrill, grating voice rang out. The yelling was not in chorus. Each took a turn and at the end of each the crowd broke into howls and roars and whistles of applause. This is what they had come to see and hear.

No newspaper had printed the words these women shouted. It was indicated that they were indelicate, some even said obscene. On television the sound track was made to blur or had crowd noises cut in to cover. But now I heard the words, bestial and filthy and degenerate. In a long and unprotected life I have seen and heard the vomitings of demoniac humans before. Why then did these screams fill me with a shocked and sickened sorrow?

The words written down are dirty, carefully and selectedly filthy. But there was something far worse here than dirt, a kind of frightening witches' Sabbath. Here was no spontaneous cry of anger, of insane rage.

Perhaps that is what made me sick with weary nausea. Here was no principle good or bad, no direction. These blowzy women with their little hats and their clippings hungered for attention. They wanted to be admired. They simpered in happy, almost innocent triumph when they were applauded. Theirs was the demented cruelty of egocentric children, and somehow this made their insensate beastliness much more heartbreaking. These were not mothers, not even women. They were crazy actors playing to a crazy audience.

The crowd behind the barrier roared and cheered and pounded one another with joy. The nervous strolling police watched for any break over the barrier. Their lips were tight but a few of them smiled and quickly unsmiled. Across the street the U.S. marshals stood unmoving. The gray-clothed man's legs had speeded for a second, but he reined them down with his will and walked up the school pavement:

The crowd quieted and the next cheer lady had her turn. Her voice was the bellow of a bull, a deep and powerful shout with flat edges like a circus barker's voice. There is no need to set down her words. The pattern was the same; only the rhythm and tonal quality were different. Anyone who has been near the theater would know that these speeches were not spontaneous. They were tried and memorized and carefully rehearsed. This was theater. I watched the intent faces of the listening crowd and they were the faces of an audience. When there was applause, it was for a performer.

My body churned with weary nausea, but I could not let an illness blind me after I had come so far to look and to hear. And suddenly I knew something was wrong and distorted and out of drawing. I knew New Orleans, I have over the years had many friends there, thoughtful, gentle people, with a tradition of kindness and courtesy. I remembered Lyle Saxon, a huge man of soft laughter. How many days I have spent with Roark Bradford, who took Louisiana sounds and sights and created God and the Green Pastures to which He leadeth us. I looked in the crowd for such faces of such people and they were not there. I've seen this kind bellow for blood at a prize fight, have orgasms when a man is gored in the bull ring, stare with vicarious lust at a highway accident, stand patiently in line for the privilege of watching any pain or any agony. But where were the others— the ones who would be proud they were of a species with the gray man—the ones whose arms would ache to gather up the small, scared black mite?

I don't know where they were. Perhaps they felt as helpless as I did, but they left New Orleans misrepresented to the world. The crowd, no doubt, rushed home to see themselves on television, and what they saw went out all over the world, unchallenged by the other things I know are there.

Liar by Legislation

Look, June 28, 1955

◆

HODDING CARTER

It happened on April Fools' Day. But it wasn't a joke to me or to the majority of the Mississippi House of Representatives who, by formal resolution, voted on April 1, 1955, that I had lied, slandered my state, and betrayed the South in a *Look* magazine article (March 22 issue) about the Citizens' Councils—the militant Southern white groups which have been organized to discourage school integration and Negro suffrage.

Perhaps in the history of state legislatures, often citizens have been made liars by legislation. But I doubt that any of them received the accolade under the same conditions as I did.

April 1 was the final day of a special legislative session at which our Mississippi lawmakers had been seeking feverishly, and finally with success, to find new money to equalize the dual school systems, as a means of avoiding racial integration. April 1 was as usual the opening day of the turkey hunting season. With four friends, a cook, and a guide, I was turkey hunting forty miles from my home town, Greenville, Mississippi. Our headquarters was the *Mistuh Charley*, my newspaper's cabin cruiser, and we were playing cards aboard her that afternoon after an unsuccessful opening day.

The game was interrupted by a low-flying plane that dropped a bundle near the wooded shoreline. I kept on playing cards, but John Gibson, the *Delta Democrat-Times* business manager and my publishing associate, went out and found the bundle. He returned and handed me some sheets of paper. "You'd better read this," he said.

I did, and for the time being I lost interest in cards and turkeys. Joe Call, a cotton-duster pilot and friend, had dropped a press association report of what the House of Representatives had done, together with a note from my wife. I read the note first:

"We've played the story on page one as second lead. Everybody's calling for your answer. When can we get it and what else shall we do? Love, Betty."

Then I read the wire service report. It was like being kicked in the stomach by eighty-nine angry jackasses. That number of state legislators, with nineteen opposed and thirty-two others not voting, had officially branded me a liar.

During two hours of angry debate preceding the vote, I had been described in terms not often used by lawmakers. I was a Negro lover and a scalawag, a lying newspaperman, a person who "as far as the white people of Mississippi are concerned, should have no rights." I had sold out the South for 50,000 pieces of silver. (Note to *Look:* You owe me money.)

The elderly Speaker of the House, a perpetual seceder and a backer of the Citizens' Councils, cast a vote for the resolution, gratuitously, although ordinarily he would not vote on any measure except to break a tie. I was defended by a few, notably the two young lawyer-legislators from Greenville and another young representative, Joel Blass of Stone County. Blass told how he also had felt the Councils' lash because he had opposed a Council-backed constitutional amendment making it possible to abandon the state's public school system. The fact that these men are young is important to this story and to the future of Mississippi.

My hunting companions thought the whole thing was funny. I didn't, even though they assured me—and I agreed—that a Mississippi legislative majority was mentally and morally incapable of insulting anybody. I ducked below and started writing. I'm glad, I guess, that my fellow turkey stalkers talked me into watering down the original editorial. [The watered-down version is reproduced here. *Ed.*]

Liar by Legislation

By a vote of 89 to 19, the Mississippi House of Representatives has resoluted the editor of this newspaper into a liar because of an article I wrote about the Citizens' Councils for *Look* magazine. If this charge were true it would make me well qualified to serve with that body. It is not true. So, to even things up, I herewith resolve by a vote of 1 to 0 that there are 89 liars in the state legislature beginning with Speaker Sillers and working way on down to Rep. Eck Windham of Prentiss, a political loon whose name is fittingly made up of the words "wind" and "ham."

As for the article, I stand by it. This action by a majority of the House of Representatives only serves to add new proof to what I wrote. There is one editor of this newspaper. I vote only in Washington County. The Citizens' Councils claim 30,000 members who vote all over the state. That is explanation enough for the resolution.

I am grateful to the 19 legislators, and especially to Greenville's two representatives, who voted against the resolution. I am also appreciative of the sane comments of Rep. Joel Blass of Stone County who likewise has been a target of the dishonest and contemptible tactics used by the Citizens' Councils against anyone who differs with them or their methods.

I am hopeful that this fever, like the Ku Kluxism which rose from the same kind of infection will run its course before too long a time. Meanwhile, those 89 character mobbers can go to hell, collectively or singly, and wait there until I back down. They needn't plan on returning.

Hodding Carter

I decided to wait until the next morning to telephone in the reply I had written. We turned on the radio and heard how I had been done in, and then went on playing cards.

But in the woods on the rest of the hunt I couldn't forget what had happened. I did a lot of thinking about my twenty-three years as editor and publisher of small newspapers, four years in Louisiana and the last nineteen in Mississippi. I had never looked on myself as a starry-eyed crusader or an unfriendly critic of my homeland. No book or editorial or article I had ever written, including the *Look* article, would so identify me. I do like to believe that we've tried on our paper to take seriously the idea of man's equality. But we've been generally orthodox newspaper people, my wife and I.

I have noted, however, that an editor is remembered longest for his unpleasant comments—and for comments made about him. Long ago in Louisiana that odious anti-Semite, Gerald L. K. Smith, said that I had been run out of Mississippi as a young newspaperman and would be run out of Louisiana. Every now and then, some politician will repeat that preposterous fantasy as gospel. When I won a Pulitzer Prize for editorial writing in 1946, the late Theodore G. Bilbo, then running for re-election to the United States Senate, told his listeners that "no self-respecting Southern white man would accept a prize given by a bunch of nigger-loving, Yankeefied Communists for editorials advocating the mongrelization of the race."

When, ten years earlier, in 1936, ours had been the first Mississippi paper to print a picture showing a Negro in a favorable light—it was of Jesse Owens, the Olympic triple winner—some of the readers who canceled their subscriptions said that our action was part of a Communist plot to end segregation.

When (and this again was unique in Mississippi) we began using the courtesy title "Mrs." before the names of Negro women in news stories, the tale spread that we would soon demand "social equality" for Negroes. And every time we have come out for anything that some of our special pleaders or Stone Agers haven't liked—from the Blue Cross nearly twenty years ago to a good word for the United Nations—we have known we could expect the same emotional cacophony, and that the cumulative roaring would echo loudest during political campaigns. But never had we been ganged up on by a state legislature. Most of all, I wanted to know what this thing portended.

I've been trying to figure it out ever since. I think I've come up with some answers, and I'd like to say first that I'm not as worried as I was about Mississippi or our newspaper or anything except our politicians. Perhaps the reaction of so many of my home town and Southern fellow citizens, and my fellow newspapermen, particularly in Mississippi, is what keeps me from being worried.

When I got home, I asked our two Greenville legislators what they thought about the resolution. Both had strongly defended me on the floor. Young Joe

Wroten, a lawyer and a minister's son, didn't mince words. "Some of our people who pay lip service to constitutional government pay homage in practice to a government of men," he said. "The resolution was abortive thought control by legislation against facts, and I don't like it. But maybe those venomous attacks on freedom of the press may wake people to the danger of a clandestine government of men." And Joe punned: "—a Klandestine klavern of men. . . ."

Jimmy Robertshaw, likewise a lawyer, was more amused than disturbed. "It's partly because they were scared, partly because they're sore at the Supreme Court, and partly because they were on edge after twelve weeks of looking for money," he said. "And some of them, don't forget, are Council members. But I would like to think that they're ashamed, too, and don't want people outside to know that the Councils really exist."

Joe and Jimmy are two of the legislative minority that wouldn't go along. Numerically, they aren't important. But numerically and otherwise, the letters that continue to pile up as an aftermath of the *Look* article and its legislative sequel do seem to me to be important. I have received more than 2,000 letters about the Council piece. They've run about three to two in my favor in the South, and better than that elsewhere. Heartening is the preponderance of letters from young people, especially servicemen; clergymen of all faiths; educators and fellow newspapermen, and the accent of so many of them has been upon the Christian challenge. The several hundred that quickly followed the resolution favored our side at least nineteen to one. I think this shows that Americans dislike seeing people ganged up on.

It is significant, too, that the critical letters were overwhelmingly emotional, often anti-Semitic, and, when unsigned as many were, contained filthy personal attacks and threats. Some, of course, came from people honestly disturbed over the Supreme Court ruling and wondering whether the Councils' program of economic terrorism is not the South's only anti-integration weapon.

A man in Alaska sent $100 to be used as I saw fit to oppose the Councils. Three priests, each from different communities and one of them 300 miles away, came to Greenville within a few days of each other to offer aid and comfort to this battered Episcopalian. But an unidentified telephone caller told me to get out of town before I was carried out.

Less trivial than threats or insults have been the efforts at boycott, only spasmodic before the *Look* article appeared, but now accelerated. We've lost circulation in some areas, but we've managed to hold to our 12,500 average. We've been hurt a little in our commercial printing and office-supply sidelines. So far, none of our advertisers has knuckled under to the arrogant demands of Council spokesmen that they join the Councils, or taken away their advertising from us on penalty of losing the trade of Council members. This economic weapon was announced last summer as being planned for use only against Negroes who tried to vote or enter their children in white schools, but it has been turned against anyone who doesn't go along with the Councils.

It seems to me that the general reaction to the legislature's blast, and the failure so far of any boycott, points up something that our non-Southern friends possibly don't know. The thinking people of Mississippi and the South are a long way ahead of their politicians; and those of us who seem to be in a completely rebuffed minority aren't as alone or as out of step as legislators and Councils might lead the outsider to believe.

I don't mean that many white Southerners are willing to have public schools integrated now, especially in the Deep South where numerical pressures are greatest. But they know that inflammatory political behavior and the formation of vigilante groups aren't the answer any more than would be a Supreme Court edict ordering complete integration next fall. There must be a middle ground.

That brings up something personal. I've been pretty much a middle-of-the-roader all my life. Some of my fellow Southerners think otherwise. They've been conditioned largely by political demagogues to believe that anybody who challenges extremism in the South is in league with the Supreme Court, the N.A.A.C.P., the Communist party, the mass-circulation magazines, and everybody north of the Mason-Dixon Line to destroy the Southern way of life. There's a lot of it I do want destroyed. There's a lot I want to keep.

And some of my non-Southern correspondents have been wrong also, though in a kindlier way. They envision a dangerous life for the Southern dissenter, or, at the best, a social and economic martyrdom. That, I am glad to say, just isn't so, though it could have been twenty years ago.

We live normal small-town lives in Greenville. That means we're busy with all kinds of matters besides racial problems. According to my calendar for the general period between the *Look* article and the legislature's resolution, I was chairman, so help me, of the Rotary Club's Ladies' Night; planned a spring boating weekend with the skipper of the Sea Scouts whose unofficial flagship is the *Mistuh Charley*, and gave a wiener roast for the Cub Scouts, including my youngest, whose den father I am; met three times with my fellow directors of the Chamber of Commerce; awarded the annual *Democrat-Times* plaques to the outstanding man and woman citizen; served as ringmaster for our neighborhood teen-agers' Cypress Saddle Club show; met with our monthly discussion group, a dozen business and professional men, in my home; judged a college and high school newspaper contest; went to two square dances; attended the Tulane University annual Board of Visitors meeting; began work on a talk for the convention of the Mississippi Bankers Association; helped my wife entertain for two engaged daughters of friends, and for each of our two older sons home from college and school for Easter holidays; planned a board meeting of the Mississippi Historical Society, of which I'm president; and worked with my wife on the 150-year history of the Episcopal Diocese of Louisiana. This accounting is only partial, but it doesn't leave much time for scalawagging.

A great many of my friends, and uncounted thousands of other Southerners, are too busy to spend time on boycotts and threats even were they so inclined. A good many other thousands, however, do seem to have the time and inclination, too. The Southern struggle, it seems to me, is not so much between two races as between these groups. In four or five Deep Southern states, the Supreme Court and the Negro stand on the sidelines. In these states, integration is distant. In their public schools, it will be no more than token for as far ahead as I can see. The gradual adjustment will be aided by accompanying improvement in the Negro's economic status; by Negro migration which will reduce the pressure of numbers; by the tolerance of those who today are our young; and by the persistent growth of the idea that democracy and Christianity and man's responsibility for his brother are all facets of the same bright dream.

I know that, against these forces, the South's braying demagogues, its Klans and Councils and Southern Gentlemen, Inc., cannot forever stand. As our eldest son, who is twenty, disdainfully told our ten-year-old, who has been delighted with all the excitement:

"If you think this is something, you should have been around when I was in the fifth grade. . . ."

Or when I was.

Harlem Is Nowhere

Harper's Magazine, August 1964

RALPH ELLISON

To live in Harlem is to dwell in the very bowels of the city; it is to pass a labyrinthine existence among streets that explode monotonously skyward with the spires and crosses of churches and clutter under foot with garbage and decay. Harlem is a ruin—many of its ordinary aspects (its crimes, its casual violence, its crumbling buildings with littered areaways, ill-smelling halls, and vermin-invaded rooms) are indistinguishable from the distorted images that appear in dreams, and which, like muggers haunting a lonely hall, quiver in the waking mind with hidden and threatening significance. Yet this is no dream but the reality of well over four hundred thousand Americans; a reality which for many defines and colors the world. Overcrowded and exploited politically and economically, Harlem is the scene and symbol of the Negro's perpetual alienation in the land of his birth.

But much has been written about the social and economic aspects of Harlem; I am here interested in its psychological character—a character that arises from the impact between urban slum conditions and folk sensibilities. Historically, American Negroes are caught in a vast process of change that has swept them from slavery to the condition of industrial man in a space of time so telescoped (a bare eighty-five years) that it is possible literally for them to step from feudalism into the vortex of industrialism simply by moving across the Mason-Dixon Line.

This abruptness of change and the resulting clash of cultural factors within the Negro personality account for some of the extreme contrasts found in Harlem, for both its negative and its positive characteristics. For if Harlem is the scene of the folk-Negro's death agony, it is also the setting of his transcendence. Here it is possible for talented youths to leap through the development of decades in a brief twenty years, while beside them white-haired adults crawl in the feudal darkness of their childhood. Here a former cotton picker develops the sensitive hands of a surgeon, and men whose grandparents still believe in magic prepare optimistically to become atomic scientists. Here the grandchildren of those who possessed no written literature examine their lives through the eyes of Freud and Marx, Kierkegaard and Kafka, Malraux and Sartre. It explains the nature of a world so fluid and shifting that often within the mind the real and the unreal merge, and the marvelous beckons from behind the same sordid reality that denies its existence.

Hence the most surreal fantasies are acted out upon the streets of Harlem; a man ducks in and out of traffic shouting and throwing imaginary grenades that actually exploded during World War I; a boy participates in the rape-robbery of his mother; a man beating his wife in a park uses boxing "science" and observes Marquess of Queensberry rules (no rabbit punching, no blows beneath the belt); two men hold a third while a lesbian slashes him to death with a razor blade; boy gangsters wielding homemade pistols (which in the South of their origin are but toy symbols of adolescent yearning for manhood) shoot down their young rivals. Life becomes a masquerade, exotic costumes are worn every day. Those who cannot afford to hire a horse wear riding habits; others who could not afford a hunting trip or who seldom attend sporting events carry shooting sticks.

For this is a world in which the major energy of the imagination goes not into creating works of art, but to overcome the frustrations of social discrimination. Not quite citizens and yet Americans, full of the tensions of modern man, but regarded as primitives, Negro Americans are in desperate search for an identity. Rejecting the second-class status assigned them, they feel alienated and their whole lives have become a search for answers to the questions: Who am I, What am I, Why am I, and Where? Significantly, in Harlem the reply to the greeting, "How are you?" is very often, "Oh, man, I'm *nowhere*"—a phrase revealing an attitude so common that it has been reduced to a gesture, a seemingly trivial word. Indeed, Negroes are not unaware that the conditions of their lives demand new definitions of terms like *primitive* and *modern, ethical* and *unethical, moral* and *immoral, patriotism* and *treason, tragedy* and *comedy, sanity* and *insanity.*

But for a long time now—despite songs like the "Blow Top Blues" and the eruption of expressions like *frantic, buggy,* and *mad* into Harlem's popular speech, doubtless a word-magic against the states they name—calm in face of the unreality of Negro life becomes increasingly difficult. And while some seek relief in strange hysterical forms of religion, in alcohol and drugs, others learn to analyze the causes for their predicament and join with others to correct them.

In relation to their Southern background, the cultural history of Negroes in the North reads like the legend of some tragic people out of mythology, a people which aspired to escape from its own unhappy homeland to the apparent peace of a distant mountain; but which, in migrating, made some fatal error of judgment and fell into a great chasm of mazelike passages that promise ever to lead to the mountain but end ever against a wall. Not that a Negro is worse off in the North than in the South, but that in the North he surrenders and does not replace certain important supports to his personality. He leaves a relatively static social order in which, having experienced its brutality for hundreds of years—indeed, having been formed within it and by it—he has developed those techniques of survival to which Faulkner refers as "endurance," and an ease of movement within explosive situations which makes Hemingway's definition of courage, "grace under pressure," appear mere swagger. He surrenders the protection of his peasant cynicism—his refusal to hope for the fulfillment of hopeless hopes—and his sense of being "at home in the world" gained from confronting and accepting (for day-to-day living, at least) the obscene absurdity of his predicament. Further, he leaves a still authoritative religion which gives his life a semblance of metaphysical wholeness; a family structure which is relatively stable; and a body of folklore—tested in life-and-death terms against his daily experience with nature and the Southern white man—that serves him as a guide to action.

These are the supports of Southern Negro rationality (and, to an extent, of the internal peace of the United States); humble, but of inestimable psychological value,* they allow Southern Negroes to maintain their almost mystical hope for a future of full democracy—a hope accompanied by an irrepressible

---

*Their political and economic value is the measure of both the positive and negative characteristics of American democracy.

belief in some Mecca of equality, located in the North and identified by the magic place names New York, Chicago, Detroit. A belief sustained (as all myth is sustained by ritual) by identifying themselves ritually with the successes of Negro celebrities, by reciting their exploits and enumerating their dollars, and by recounting the swiftness with which they spiral from humble birth to head-line fame. And doubtless the blasting of this dream is as damaging to Negro personality as the slum scenes of filth, disorder, and crumbling masonry in which it flies apart.

When Negroes are barred from participating in the main institutional life of society, they lose far more than economic privileges or the satisfaction of salut-ing the flag with unmixed emotions. They lose one of the bulwarks which men place between themselves and the constant threat of chaos. For whatever the assigned function of social institutions, their psychological function is to pro-tect the citizen against the irrational, incalculable forces that hover about the edges of human life like cosmic destruction lurking within an atomic stockpile.

And it is precisely the denial of this support through segregation and dis-crimination that leaves the most balanced Negro open to anxiety.

Though caught not only in the tensions arising from his own swift history, but in those conflicts created in modern man by a revolutionary world, he cannot participate fully in the therapy which the white American achieves through patriotic ceremonies and by identifying himself with American wealth and power. Instead, he is thrown back upon his own "slum-shocked" institutions.

But these, like his folk personality, are caught in a process of chaotic change. His family disintegrates, his church splinters; his folk wisdom is dis-carded in the mistaken notion that it in no way applies to urban living; and his formal education (never really his own) provides him with neither scientific de-scription nor rounded philosophical interpretation of the profound forces that are transforming his total being. Yet even his art is transformed; the lyrical rit-ual elements of folk jazz—that artistic projection of the only real individuality possible for him in the South, that embodiment of a superior democracy in which each individual cultivated his uniqueness and yet did not clash with his neighbors—have given way to the near-themeless technical virtuosity of bebop, a further triumph of technology over humanism. His speech hardens; his movements are geared to the time clock; his diet changes; his sensibilities quicken; and his intelligence expands. But without institutions to give him di-rection, and lacking a clear explanation of his predicament—the religious ones being inadequate, and those offered by political and labor leaders obviously in-complete and opportunistic—the individual feels that his world and his per-sonality are out of key. The phrase "I'm nowhere" expresses the feeling borne in upon many Negroes that they have no stable, recognized place in society. One's identity drifts in a capricious reality in which even the most commonly held assumptions are questionable. One "is" literally, but one is nowhere; one wanders dazed in a ghetto maze, a "displaced person" of American democracy.

And as though all this were not enough of a strain on a people's sense of the rational, the conditions under which it lives are seized upon as proof of its inferiority. Thus the frustrations of Negro life (many of them the frustrations of *all* life during this historical moment) permeate the atmosphere of Harlem with a hostility that bombards the individual from so many directions that he is often unable to identify it with any specific object. Some feel it the punishment of some racial or personal guilt and pray to God; others (called "evil Negroes" in Harlem) become enraged with the world. Sometimes it provokes dramatic mass responses.

And why have these explosive matters—which are now a problem of our foreign policy—been ignored? Because there is an argument in progress between black men and white men as to the true nature of American reality. Following their own interests, whites impose interpretations upon Negro experience that are not only false but, in effect, a denial of Negro humanity. Too weak to shout down these interpretations, Negroes live nevertheless as they have to live, and the concrete conditions of their lives are more real than white men's arguments.

An Interview with Malcolm X

A Candid Conversation with the Militant Major-domo of the Black Muslims

Playboy, May 1963

ALEX HALEY

Within the past five years, the militant American Negro has become an increasingly active combatant in the struggle for civil rights. Espousing the goals of unqualified equality and integration, many of these outspoken insurgents have participated in freedom rides and protest marches against their segregationist foes. Today, they face opposition from not one, but two inimical exponents of racism and segregation: the white supremacists and the Black Muslims. A relatively unknown and insignificant radical religious Negro cult until a few years ago, the Muslims have grown into a ded-

icated, disciplined nationwide movement which runs its own school, publishes its own newspaper, owns stores and restaurants in four major cities, buys broadcast time on 50 radio stations throughout the country, stages mass rallies attended by partisan crowds of 10,000 and more, and maintains its own police force of judo-trained athletes called the Fruit of Islam.

Predicated on the proposition that the black man is morally, spiritually and intellectually superior to the white man, who is called a "devil," Muslim doctrine dooms him to extermination in an imminent Armageddon—along with Christianity itself, which is denounced as an opiate designed to lull Negroes—with the promise of heaven—into passive acceptance of inferior social status. Amalgamating elements of Christianity and Mohammedanism (both of which officially and unequivocally disown it) and spiked with a black-supremacy version of Hitler's Aryan racial theories, Muslimism was founded in 1931 by Elijah Poole, a Georgia-born ex–factory worker who today commands unquestioning obedience from thousands of followers as the Honorable Elijah Muhammad, Messenger of Allah. At the right hand of God's Messenger stands 36-year-old Malcolm Little, a lanky onetime dining-car steward, bootlegger, pimp and dope pusher who left prison in 1952 to heed Muhammad's message, abandoned his "slave name," Little, for the symbolic "X" (meaning identity unknown), and took an oath to abstain thereafter from smoking, drinking, gambling, cursing, dancing and sexual promiscuity—as required of every Muslim. The ambitious young man rose swiftly to become the Messenger's most ardent and erudite disciple, and today wields all but absolute authority over the movement and its membership as Muhammad's business manager, trouble shooter, prime minister and heir apparent.

In the belief that knowledge and awareness are necessary and effective antitoxins against the venom of hate, Playboy asked Malcolm X to submit to a cross-examination on the means and ends of his organization. The ensuing interview was conducted at a secluded table in a Harlem restaurant owned by the Muslims. Interrupting his replies occasionally with a sip of black African coffee and whispered asides to deferential aides, the dark-suited minister of Harlem's Muslim Temple Number Seven spoke with candor and—except for moments of impassioned execration of all whites—the impersonal tone of a self-assured corporation executive.

Many will be shocked by what he has to say; others will be outraged. Our own view is that this interview is both an eloquent statement and a damning self-indictment of one noxious facet of rampant racism. As such, we believe it merits publication—and reading.

PLAYBOY: What is the ambition of the Black Muslims?

MALCOLM X: Freedom, justice and equality are our principal ambitions. And to faithfully serve and follow the Honorable Elijah Muhammad is the guiding goal of every Muslim. Mr. Muhammad teaches us the knowledge of our own selves, and of our own people. He cleans us up—morally, mentally and spiritually— and he reforms us of the vices that have blinded us here in the Western society.

He stops black men from getting drunk, stops their dope addiction if they had it, stops nicotine, gambling, stealing, lying, cheating, fornication, adultery, prostitution, juvenile delinquency. I think of this whenever somebody talks about someone investigating us. Why investigate the Honorable Elijah Muhammad? They should subsidize him. He's cleaning up the mess that white men have made. He's saving the Government millions of dollars, taking black men off of welfare, showing them how to do something for themselves. And Mr. Muhammad teaches us love for our own kind. The white man has taught the black people in this country to hate themselves as inferior, to hate each other, to be divided against each other. Messenger Muhammad restores our love for our own kind, which enables us to work together in unity and harmony. He shows us how to pool our financial resources and our talents, then to work together toward a common objective. Among other things, we have small businesses in most major cities in this country, and we want to create many more. We are taught by Mr. Muhammad that it is very important to improve the black man's economy, and his thrift. But to do this, we must have land of our own. The brainwashed black man can never learn to stand on his own two feet until he is on his own. We must learn to become our own producers, manufacturers and traders; we must have industry of our own, to employ our own. The white man resists this because he wants to keep the black man under his thumb and jurisdiction in white society. He wants to keep the black man always dependent and begging—for jobs, food, clothes, shelter, education. The white man doesn't want to lose somebody to be supreme over. He wants to keep the black man where he can be watched and retarded. Mr. Muhammad teaches that as soon as we separate from the white man, we will learn that we can do without the white man just as he can do without us. The white man knows that once black men get off to themselves and learn they can do for themselves, the black man's full potential will explode and he will *surpass* the white man.

PLAYBOY: Do you feel that the Black Muslims' goal of obtaining "several states" is a practical vision?

MALCOLM X: Well, *you* might consider some things practical that are really impractical. Wasn't it impractical that the Supreme Court could issue a desegregation order nine years ago and there's still only eight percent compliance? Is it practical that a hundred years after the Civil War there's not freedom for black men yet? On the record for integration you've got the President, the Congress, the Supreme Court—but show me your integration, where is it? That's practical? Mr. Muhammad teaches us to be for what's *really* practical—that's separation. It's more natural than integration.

PLAYBOY: In the view of many, that is highly debatable. However: In a recent interview, Negro author-lecturer Louis Lomax said, "Eighty percent, if not more, of America's 20,000,000 Negroes vibrate sympathetically with the Muslims' indictment of the white power structure. But this does not mean we agree with them in their doctrines of estrangement or with their proposed resolutions of the race problem." Does this view represent a consensus of opinion among Negroes? And if so, is it possible that your separationist and anti-Christian doctrine have the effect of alienating many of your race?

MALCOLM X: Sir, you make a mistake listening to people who tell you how much our stand alienates black men in this country. I'd guess actually we have the sympathy of 90 percent of the black people. There are 20,000,000 dormant Muslims in America. A Muslim to us is somebody who is for the black man; I don't care if he goes to the Baptist Church seven days a week. The Honorable Elijah Muhammad says that a black man is born a Muslim by nature. There are millions of Muslims not aware of it now. All of them will be Muslims when they wake up; that's what's meant by the Resurrection.

Sir, I'm going to tell you a secret: the black man is a whole lot smarter than white people think he is. The black man has survived in this country by fooling the white man. He's been dancing and grinning and white men never guessed what he was thinking. Now you'll hear the bourgeois Negroes pretending to be alienated, but they're just making the white man *think* they don't go for what Mr. Muhammad is saying. This Negro that will tell you he's so against us, he's just protecting the crumbs he gets from the white man's table. This kind of Negro is so busy trying to be *like* the white man that he doesn't know what the real masses of his own people are thinking. A fine car and house and clothes and liquor have made a lot think themselves different from their poor black brothers. But Mr. Muhammad says that Allah is going to wake up all black men to see the white man as he really is, and see what Christianity has done to them. The black masses that are waking up don't believe in Christianity anymore. All it's done for black men is help to keep them slaves. Mr. Muhammad is teaching that Christianity, as white people see it, means that whites can have their heaven here on earth, but the black man is supposed to catch his hell here. The black man is supposed to keep believing that when he dies, he'll float up to some city with golden streets and milk and honey on a cloud somewhere. Every black man in North America has heard black Christian preachers shouting about "tomorrow in good old Beulah's Land." But the thinking black masses today are interested in *Muhammad's* Land. The Promised Land that the Honorable Elijah Muhammad talks about is right here on this earth. Intelligent black men today are interested in a religious doctrine that offers a solution to their problems right now, right here on this earth, while they are alive.

You must understand that the Honorable Elijah Muhammad represents the fulfillment of Biblical prophecy to us. In the Old Testament, Moses lived to see his enemy, Pharaoh, drowned in the Red Sea—which in essence means that Mr. Muhammad will see the completion of his work in his lifetime, that he will live to see victory gained over his enemy.

PLAYBOY: The Old Testament connection seems tenuous. Are you referring to the Muslim judgment day which your organization's newspaper, *Muhammad Speaks*, calls "Armageddon" and prophesies as imminent?

MALCOLM X: Armageddon deals with the final battle between God and the Devil. The Third World War is referred to as Armageddon by many white statesmen. There won't be any more war after then because there won't be any more warmongers. I don't know when Armageddon, whatever form it takes, is supposed to be. But I know the time is near when the white man will be finished. The signs are all around us. Ten years ago you couldn't have *paid* a Southern Negro to defy local customs. The British Lion's tail has been snatched off in black Africa. The Indonesians have booted out such would-be imperialists as the Dutch. The French, who felt for a century that Algeria was theirs, have had to run for their lives back to France. Sir, the point I make is that all over the world, the old day of standing in fear and trembling before the almighty white man is *gone*!

PLAYBOY: You refer to whites as the guilty and the enemy; you predict divine retribution against them; and you preach absolute separation from the white community. Do not these views substantiate that your movement is predicated on race hatred?

MALCOLM X: Sir, it's from Mr. Muhammad that the black masses are learning for the first time in 400 years the real truth of how the white man brainwashed the black man, kept him ignorant of his true history, robbed him of his self-confidence. The black masses for the first time are understanding that it's not a case of being anti-white or anti-Christian, but it's a case of seeing the true nature of the white man. We're anti-evil, anti-oppression, anti-lynching. You can't be anti- those things unless you're also anti- the oppressor and the lyncher. You can't be anti-slavery and pro-slavemaster; you can't be anti-crime and pro-criminal. In fact, Mr. Muhammad teaches that if the present generation of *whites* would study their own race in the light of their true history, they would be anti-white themselves.

PLAYBOY: Are you?

MALCOLM X: As soon as the white man hears a black man say that he's through loving white people, then the white man accuses the black man of hating him. The Honorable Elijah Muhammad doesn't teach hate. The white man isn't *important* enough for the Honorable Elijah Muhammad and his followers to spend any time hating him. The white man has brainwashed himself into believing that all the black people in the world want to be cuddled up next to him. When he meets what we're talking about, he can't believe it, it takes all the wind out of him. When we tell him we don't want to be around him, we don't want to be like he is, he's staggered. It makes him re-evaluate his 300-year myth about the black man. What I want to know is how the white man, with the blood of black people dripping off his fingers, can have the audacity to be asking black people do they hate him. That takes a lot of nerve.

PLAYBOY: How do you reconcile your disavowal of hatred with the announcement you made last year that Allah had brought you "the good news" that 120 white Atlantans had just been killed in an air crash en route to America from Paris?

MALCOLM X: Sir, as I see the law of justice, it says as you sow, so shall you reap. The white man has reveled as the rope snapped black men's necks. He has reveled around the lynching fire. It's only right for the black man's true God, Allah, to defend us—and for us to be joyous because our God manifests his ability to inflict pain on our enemy. We Muslims believe that the white race, which is guilty of having oppressed and exploited and enslaved our people here in America, should and will be the victims of God's divine wrath. All civilized societies in their courts of justice set a sentence of execution against those deemed to be enemies of society, such as murderers and kidnapers. The presence of 20,000,000 black people here in America is proof that Uncle Sam is guilty of kidnaping—because we didn't come here voluntarily on the *Mayflower.* And 400 years of lynchings condemn Uncle Sam as a murderer.

PLAYBOY: We question that all-inclusive generalization. To return to your statement about the plane crash, when Dr. Ralph Bunche heard about it, he called you "mentally depraved." What is your reaction?

MALCOLM X: I know all about what Dr. Bunche said. He's always got his international mouth open. He apologized in the UN when black people protested there. You'll notice that whenever the white man lets a black man get prominent, he has a job for him. Dr. Bunche serves the white man well—he represents, speaks for and defends the white man. He does none of this for the black man. Dr. Bunche has functioned as a white man's tool, designed to influence international opinion on the Negro. The white man has Negro local tools, national tools, and Dr. Bunche is an international tool.

PLAYBOY: Dr. Bunche was only one of many prominent Negroes who deplored your statement in similar terms. What reply have you to make to these spokesmen for your own people?

MALCOLM X: Go ask their opinions and you'll be able to fill your notebook with what white people want to hear Negroes say. Let's take these so-called spokesmen for the black men by types. Start with the politicians. They never attack Mr. Muhammad personally. They realize he has the sympathy of the black masses. They know they would alienate the masses whose votes they need. But the black civic leaders, they do attack Mr. Muhammad. The reason is usually that they are appointed to their positions by the white man. The white man pays them to attack us. The ones who attack Mr. Muhammad the most are the ones who earn the most. Then take the black religious leaders, they also attack Mr. Muhammad. These preachers do it out of self-defense, because they know he's waking up Negroes. No one believes what the Negro preacher preaches except those who are mentally asleep, or in the darkness of ignorance about the true situation of the black man here today in this wilderness of North America. If you will take note, sir, many so-called Negro leaders who once attacked the Honorable Elijah Muhammad don't do so anymore. And he never speaks against them in the personal sense except as a reaction if they speak against him. Islam is a religion that teaches us never to attack, never to be the aggressor—but you can waste somebody if he attacks you. These Negro leaders have become aware that whenever the Honorable Elijah Muhammad is caused by their attack to level his guns against them, they always come out on the losing end. Many have experienced this.

PLAYBOY: Do you admire and respect any other American Negro leaders—Martin Luther King, for example?

MALCOLM X: I am a Muslim, sir. Muslims can see only one leader who has the qualifications necessary to unite all elements of black people in America. This is the Honorable Elijah Muhammad.

PLAYBOY: Many white religious leaders have also gone on record against the Black Muslims. Writing in the official NAACP magazine, a Catholic priest described you as "a fascist-minded hate group," and B'nai B'rith has accused you of being not only anti-Christian but anti-Semitic. Do you consider this true?

MALCOLM X: Insofar as the Christian world is concerned, dictatorships have existed only in areas or countries where you have Roman Catholicism. Catholicism conditions your mind for dictators. Can you think of a single Protestant country that has ever produced a dictator?

PLAYBOY: Germany was predominantly Protestant when Hitler—

MALCOLM X: Another thing to think of—in the 20th Century, the Christian Church has given us two heresies: fascism and communism.

PLAYBOY: On what grounds do you attribute these "isms" to the Christian Church?

MALCOLM X: Where did fascism start? Where's the second-largest Communist party outside of Russia? The answer to both is Italy. Where is the Vatican? But let's not forget the Jew. Anybody that gives even a just criticism of the Jew is instantly labeled anti-Semite. The Jew cries louder than anybody else if anybody criticizes him. You can tell the truth about any minority in America, but make a true observation about the Jew, and if it doesn't pat him on the back, then he uses his grip on the news media to label you anti-Semite. Let me say just a word about the Jew and the black man. The Jew is always anxious to *advise* the black man. But they never advise him how to solve his problem the way the Jews solved their problem. The Jew never went sitting-in and crawling-in and sliding-in and freedom-riding, like he teaches and helps Negroes to do. The Jews stood up, and stood together, and they used their ultimate power, the economic weapon. That's exactly what the Honorable Elijah Muhammad is trying to teach black men to do. The Jews pooled their money and *bought* the hotels that barred them. They bought Atlantic City and Miami Beach and anything else they wanted. Who owns Hollywood? Who runs the garment industry, the largest industry in New York City? But the Jew that's advising the Negro joins the NAACP, CORE, the Urban League, and others. With money donations, the Jew gains control, then he sends the black man doing all this wading-in, boring-in, even burying-in—everything but buying-in. Never shows him how to set up factories and hotels. Never advises him how to own what he wants. No, when there's something worth owning, the Jew's got it.

PLAYBOY: Isn't it true that many Gentiles have also labored with dedication to advance integration and economic improvement for the Negro, as volunteer workers for the NAACP, CORE and many other interracial agencies?

MALCOLM X: A man who tosses worms in the river isn't necessarily a friend of the fish. All the fish who take him for a friend, who think the worm's got no hook in it, usually end up in the frying pan. All these things dangled before us by the white liberal posing as a friend and benefactor have turned out to be nothing but bait to make us think we're making progress. The Supreme Court decision has never been enforced. Desegregation has never taken place. The promises have never been fulfilled. We have received only tokens, substitutes, trickery and deceit.

PLAYBOY: What motives do you impute to *Playboy* for providing you with this opportunity for the free discussion of your views?

MALCOLM X: I think you want to sell magazines. I've never seen a sincere white man, not when it comes to helping black people. Usually things like this are done by white people to benefit themselves. The white man's primary interest is not to elevate the thinking of black people, or to waken black people, or white people either. The white man is interested in the black man only to the extent that the black man is of use to him. The white man's interest is to make money, to exploit.

PLAYBOY: Is there any white man on earth whom you would concede to have the Negro's welfare genuinely at heart?

MALCOLM X: I say, sir, that you can never make an intelligent judgment without evidence. If any man will study the entire history of the relationship between the white man and the black man, no evidence will be found that justifies any confidence or faith that the black man might have in the white man today.

PLAYBOY: Then you consider it impossible for the white man to be anything but an exploiter and a hypocrite in his relations with the Negro?

MALCOLM X: Is it wrong to attribute a predisposition to wheat before it comes up out of the ground? Wheat's characteristics and nature make it wheat. It differs from barley because of its nature. Wheat perpetuates its own characteristics just as the white race does. White people are born devils by nature. They don't become so by deeds. If you never put popcorn in a skillet, it would still be popcorn. Put the heat to it, it will pop.

PLAYBOY: You say that white men are devils by nature. Was Christ a devil?

MALCOLM X: Christ wasn't white. Christ was a black man.

PLAYBOY: On what Scripture do you base this assertion?

MALCOLM X: Sir, Billy Graham has made the same statement in public. Why not ask *him* what Scripture he found it in? When Pope Pius XII died, *Life* magazine carried a picture of him in his private study kneeling before a black Christ.

PLAYBOY: Those are hardly quotations from Scripture. Was He not reviled as "King of the Jews"—a people the Black Muslims attack?

MALCOLM X: Only the poor, brainwashed American Negro has been made to believe that Christ was white, to maneuver him into worshiping the white man. After becoming a Muslim in prison, I read almost everything I could put my hands on in the prison library. I began to think back on everything I had read and especially with the histories, I realized that nearly all of them read by the general public have been made into white histories. I found out that the history-whitening process either had left out great things that black men had done, or some of the great black men had gotten whitened.

PLAYBOY: Would you list a few of these men?

MALCOLM X: Well, Hannibal, the most successful general that ever lived, was a black man. So was Beethoven; Beethoven's father was one of the blackamoors that hired themselves out in Europe as professional soldiers. Haydn, Beethoven's teacher, was of African descent. Columbus, the discoverer of America, was a half-black man.

PLAYBOY: According to biographies considered definitive, Beethoven's father, Johann, was a court tenor in Cologne; Haydn's parents were Croatian; Columbus' parents were Italian—

MALCOLM X: Whole black empires, like the Moorish, have been whitened to hide the fact that a great black empire had conquered a white empire even before America was discovered. The Moorish civilization—black Africans—conquered and ruled Spain; they kept the light burning in Southern Europe. The word "Moor" means "black," by the way. Egyptian civilization is a classic example of how the white man stole great African cultures and makes them appear today as white European. The black nation of Egypt is the only country that has a science named after its culture: Egyptology. The ancient Sumerians, a black-skinned people, occupied the Middle Eastern areas and were contemporary with the Egyptian civilization. The Incas, the Aztecs, the Mayans, all dark-skinned Indian people, had a highly developed culture here in America, in what is now Mexico and northern South America. These people had mas-

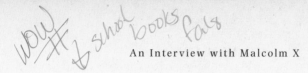

tered agriculture at the time when European white people were still living in mud huts and eating weeds. But white children, or black children, or grownups here today in America don't get to read this in the average books they are exposed to.

PLAYBOY: Can you cite any authoritative historical documents for these observations?

MALCOLM X: I can cite a great many, sir. You could start with Herodotus, the Greek historian. He outright described the Egyptians as "black, with woolly hair." And the American archaeologist and Egyptologist James Henry Breasted did the same thing.

PLAYBOY: You seem to have based your thesis on the premise that all nonwhite races are necessarily black.

MALCOLM X: Mr. Muhammad says that the red, the brown and the yellow are indeed all part of the black nation. Which means that black, brown, red, yellow, all are brothers, all are one family. The white one is a stranger. He's the odd fellow.

PLAYBOY: Since your classification of black peoples apparently includes the light-skinned Oriental, Middle Eastern and possibly even Latin races as well as the darker Indian and Negroid strains, just how do you decide how light-skinned it's permissible to be before being condemned as white? And if Caucasian whites are devils by nature, do you classify people by degrees of devilishness according to the lightness of their skin?

MALCOLM X: I don't worry about these little technicalities. But I know that white society has always considered that one drop of black blood makes you black. To me, if one drop can do this, it only shows the power of one drop of black blood. And I know another thing—that Negroes who used to be light enough to pass for white have seen the handwriting on the wall and are beginning to come back and identify with their own kind. And white people who also are seeing the pendulum of time catching up with them are now trying to join with blacks, or even find traces of black blood in their own veins, hoping that it will save them from the catastrophe they see ahead. But no devil can fool God. Muslims have a little poem about them. It goes, "One drop will make you black, and will also in days to come save your soul."

PLAYBOY: As one of this vast elite, do you hold the familiar majority attitude toward minority groups—regarding the white race, in this case, as inferior in quality as well as quantity to what you call the "black nation"?

MALCOLM X: Thoughtful white people *know* they are inferior to black people. Even [Senator James] Eastland knows it. Anyone who has studied the genetic phase of biology knows that white is considered recessive and black is considered dominant. When you want strong coffee, you ask for black coffee. If you want it light, you want it weak, integrate it with white milk. Just like these Negroes who weaken themselves and their race by this integrating and intermixing with whites. If you want bread with no nutritional value, you ask for white bread. All the good that was in it has been bleached out of it, and it will consti-pate you. If you want pure flour, you ask for dark flour, whole-wheat flour. If you want pure sugar, you want dark sugar.

PLAYBOY: If all whites are devilish by nature, as you have alleged, and if black and white are essentially opposite, as you have just stated, do you view all black men—with the exception of their non-Muslim leaders—as fundamentally an-gelic?

MALCOLM X: No, there is plenty wrong with Negroes. They have no society. They're robots, automatons. No minds of their own. I hate to say that about us, but it's the truth. They are a black body with a white brain. Like the monster Frankenstein. The top part is your bourgeois Negro. He's your integrator. He's not interested in his poor black brothers. He's usually so deep in debt from try-ing to copy the white man's social habits that he doesn't have time to worry about nothing else. They buy the most expensive clothes and cars and eat the cheapest food. They act more like the white man than the white man does him-self. These are the ones that hide their sympathy for Mr. Muhammad's teach-ings. It conflicts with the sources from which they get their white-man's crumbs. This class to us are the fence-sitters. They have one eye on the white man and the other eye on the Muslims. They'll jump whichever way they see the wind blowing. Then there's the middle class of the Negro masses, the ones not in the ghetto, who realize that life is a struggle, who are conscious of all the injustices being done and of the constant state of insecurity in which they live. They're ready to take some stand against everything that's against them. Now, when this group hears Mr. Muhammad's teachings, they are the ones who come forth faster and identify themselves, and take immediate steps toward trying to bring into existence what Mr. Muhammad advocates. At the bottom of the social heap is the black man in the big-city ghetto. He lives night and day with the rats and cockroaches and drowns himself with alcohol and anes-thetizes himself with dope, to try and forget where and what he is. That Negro has given up all hope. He's the hardest one for us to reach, because he's the deepest in the mud. But when you get him, you've got the best kind of Muslim. Because he makes the most drastic change. He's the most fearless. He will stand the longest. He has nothing to lose, even his life, because he didn't have that in the first place. I look upon myself, sir, as a prime example of this category—and as graphic an example as you could find of the salvation of the black man.

PLAYBOY: Could you give us a brief review of the early life that led to your own "salvation"?

MALCOLM X: Gladly. I was born in Omaha on May 19, 1925. My light color is the result of my mother's mother having been raped by a white man. I hate every drop of white blood in me. Before I am indicted for hate again, sir—is it wrong to hate the blood of a rapist? But to continue: My father was a militant follower of Marcus Garvey's "Back to Africa" movement. The Lansing, Michigan, equivalent of the Ku Klux Klan warned him to stop preaching Garvey's message, but he kept on and one of my earliest memories is of being snatched awake one night with a lot of screaming going on because our home was afire. But my father got louder about Garvey, and the next time he was found bludgeoned in the head, lying across streetcar tracks. He died soon and our family was in a bad way. We were so hungry we were dizzy and we had nowhere to turn. Finally the authorities came in and we children were scattered about in different places as public wards. I happened to become the ward of a white couple who ran a correctional school for white boys. This family liked me in the way they liked their house pets. They got me enrolled in an all-white school. I was popular, I played sports and everything, and studied hard, and I stayed at the head of my class through the eighth grade. That summer I was 14, but I was big enough and looked old enough to get away with telling a lie that I was 21, so I got a job working in the dining car of a train that ran between Boston and New York City.

On my layovers in New York, I'd go to Harlem. That's where I saw in the bars all these men and women with what looked like the easiest life in the world. Plenty of money, big cars, all of it. I could tell they were in the rackets and vice. I hung around those bars whenever I came in town, and I kept my ears and eyes open and my mouth shut. And they kept their eyes on me, too. Finally, one day a numbers man told me that he needed a runner, and I never caught the night train back to Boston. Right there was when I started my life in crime. I was in all of it that the white police and the gangsters left open to the black criminal, sir. I was in numbers, bootleg liquor, "hot" goods, women. I sold the bodies of black women to white men, and white women to black men. I was in dope, I was in everything evil you could name. The only thing I could say good for myself, sir, was that I did not indulge in hitting anybody over the head.

PLAYBOY: By the time you were 16, according to the record, you had several men working for you in these various enterprises. Right?

MALCOLM X: Yes, sir. I turned the things I mentioned to you over to them. And I had a good working system of paying off policemen. It was here that I learned that vice and crime can only exist, at least the kind and level that I was in, to the degree that the police cooperate with it. I had several men working and I was a steerer myself. I steered white people with money from downtown to whatever kind of sin they wanted in Harlem. I didn't care what they wanted, I knew where to take them to it. And I tell you what I noticed here—that my best customers always were the officials, the top police people, businessmen, politicians and clergymen. I never forgot that. I met all levels of these white people, supplied them with everything they wanted, and I saw that they were just a filthy race of devils. But despite the fact that my own father was murdered by whites, and I had seen my people all my life brutalized by whites, I was still blind enough to mix with them and socialize with them. I thought they were gods and goddesses—until Mr. Muhammad's powerful spiritual message opened my eyes and enabled me to see them as a race of devils. Nothing had made me see the white man as he is until one word from the Honorable Elijah Muhammad opened my eyes overnight.

PLAYBOY: When did this happen?

MALCOLM X: In prison. I was finally caught and spent 77 months in three different prisons. But it was the greatest thing that ever happened to me, because it was in prison that I first heard the teachings of the Honorable Elijah Muhammad. His teachings were what turned me around. The first time I heard the Honorable Elijah Muhammad's statement, "The white man is the devil," it just clicked. I am a good example of why Islam is spreading so rapidly across the land. I was nothing but another convict, a semi-illiterate criminal. Mr. Muhammad's teachings were able to reach into prison, which is the level where people are considered to have fallen as low as they can go. His teachings brought me from behind prison walls and placed me on the podiums of some of the leading colleges and universities in the country. I often think, sir, that in 1946, I was sentenced to 8 to 10 years in Cambridge, Massachusetts, as a common thief who had never passed the eighth grade. And the next time I went back to Cambridge was in March 1961, as a guest speaker at the Harvard Law School Forum. This is the best example of Mr. Muhammad's ability to take nothing and make something, to take nobody and make somebody.

PLAYBOY: Your rise to prominence in the Muslim organization has been so swift that a number of your own membership have hailed you as their articulate exemplar, and many anti-Muslims regard you as the real brains and power of the movement. What is your reaction to this sudden eminence?

MALCOLM X: Sir, it's heresy to imply that I am in any way whatever even equal to Mr. Muhammad. No man on earth today is his equal. Whatever I am that is good, it is through what I have been taught by Mr. Muhammad.

PLAYBOY: Be that as it may, the time is near when your leader, who is 65, will have to retire from leadership of the Muslim movement. Many observers predict that when this day comes, the new Messenger of Allah in America—a role which you have called the most powerful of any black man in the world—will be Malcolm X. How do you feel about this prospect?

MALCOLM X: Sir, I can only say that God chose Mr. Muhammad as his Messenger, and Mr. Muhammad chose me and many others to help him. Only God has the say-so. But I will tell you one thing. I frankly don't believe that I or anyone else am worthy to succeed Mr. Muhammad. No one preceded him. I don't think I could make the sacrifice he has made, or set his good example. He has done more than lay down his life. But his work is already done with the seed he has planted among black people. If Mr. Muhammad and every identifiable follower he has, certainly including myself, were tomorrow removed from the scene by more of the white man's brutality, there is one thing to be sure of: Mr. Muhammad's teachings of the naked truth have fallen upon fertile soil among 20,000,000 black men here in this wilderness of North America.

PLAYBOY: Has the soil, in your opinion, been as fertile for Mr. Muhammad's teachings elsewhere in the world—among the emerging nations of black Africa, for instance?

MALCOLM X: I think not only that his teachings have had considerable impact even in Africa but that the Honorable Elijah Muhammad has had a greater impact on the world than the rise of the African nations. I say this as objectively as I can, being a Muslim. Even the Christian missionaries are conceding that in black Africa, for every Christian conversion, there are two Muslim conversions.

PLAYBOY: Might conversions be even more numerous if it weren't for the somewhat strained relations which are said by several Negro writers to exist between the black people of Africa and America?

MALCOLM X: Perhaps. You see, the American black man sees the African come here and live where the American black man can't. The Negro sees the African come here with a sheet on and go places where the Negro—dressed like a white man, talking like a white man, sometimes as wealthy as the white man—can't go. When I'm traveling around the country, I use my real Muslim name, Malik Shabazz. I make my hotel reservations under that name, and I always see the same thing I've just been telling you. I come to the desk and always see that "here-comes-a-Negro" look. It's kind of a reserved, coldly tolerant cordiality. But when I say "Malik Shabazz," their whole attitude changes: they snap to respect. They think I'm an African. People say what's in a name? There's a whole lot in a name. The American black man is seeing the African respected as a human being. The African gets respect because he has an identity and cultural roots. But most of all because the African owns some land. For these reasons he has his human rights recognized, and that makes his civil rights automatic.

PLAYBOY: Do you feel this is true of Negro civil and human rights in South Africa, where the doctrine of apartheid is enforced by the government of Prime Minister Verwoerd?

MALCOLM X: They don't stand for anything different in South Africa than America stands for. The only difference is over there they *preach* as well as practice apartheid. America preaches freedom and practices slavery. America preaches integration and practices segregation. Verwoerd is an honest white man. So are the [Mississippi Governor Russ] Barnetts, [Arkansas Governor Orval] Faubuses, Eastlands and Rockwells. They want to keep all white people white. And we want to keep all black people black. As between the racists and the integrationists, I highly prefer the racists. I'd rather walk among rattlesnakes, whose constant rattle warns me where they are, than among those

Northern snakes who grin and make you forget you're still in a snake pit. Any white man is against blacks. The entire American economy is based on white supremacy. Even the religious philosophy is, in essence, white supremacy. A white Jesus. A white Virgin. White angels. White everything. But a black Devil, of course. The "Uncle Sam" political foundation is based on white supremacy, relegating nonwhites to second-class citizenship. It goes without saying that the social philosophy is strictly white supremacist. And the educational system perpetuates white supremacy.

PLAYBOY: Are you contradicting yourself by denouncing white supremacy while praising its practitioners, since you admit that you share their goal of separation?

MALCOLM X: The fact that I prefer the candor of the Southern segregationist to the hypocrisy of the Northern integrationist doesn't alter the basic immorality of white supremacy. A devil is still a devil whether he wears a bed sheet or a Brooks Brothers suit. The Honorable Elijah Muhammad teaches separation simply because any forcible attempt to integrate America completely would result in another Civil War, a catastrophic explosion among whites which would destroy America—and still not solve the problem. But Mr. Muhammad's solution of separate black and white would solve the problem neatly for both the white and black man, and America would be saved. Then the whole world would give Uncle Sam credit for being something other than a hypocrite.

PLAYBOY: Do you feel that the Administration's successful stand on the integration of James Meredith into the University of Mississippi has demonstrated that the Government—far from being hypocritical—is sympathetic with the Negro's aspirations for equality?

MALCOLM X: What was accomplished? It took 15,000 troops to put Meredith in the University of Mississippi. Those troops and $3,000,000—that's what was spent—to get one Negro in. That $3,000,000 could have been used much more wisely by the Federal Government to elevate the living standards of all the Negroes in Mississippi.

PLAYBOY: Then in your view, the principle involved was not worth the expense. Yet it is a matter of record that President Kennedy, in the face of Southern opposition, championed the appointment of Dr. Robert Weaver as the first Negro Cabinet member. Doesn't this indicate to you, as it does to many Negro leaders, that the Administration is determined to combat white supremacy?

MALCOLM X: Kennedy doesn't *have* to fight; he's the President. He didn't have any fight replacing [successive Secretary(s) of Health, Education, and Welfare] Ribicoff with Celebrezze. He didn't have any trouble putting Goldberg on the Supreme Court. He hasn't had any trouble getting anybody in but Weaver and Thurgood Marshall. He wasn't worried about Congressional objection when he challenged U.S. Steel. He wasn't worried about either Congressional reaction or Russian reaction or even world reaction when he blockaded Cuba. But when it comes to the rights of the Negro, who helped to put him in office, then he's afraid of little pockets of white resistance.

PLAYBOY: Has *any* American President, in your opinion—Lincoln, FDR, Truman, Eisenhower, Kennedy—accomplished anything for the Negro?

MALCOLM X: None of them have ever done anything for Negroes. All of them have tricked the Negro, and made false promises to him at election times which they never fulfilled. Lincoln's concern wasn't freedom for the blacks but to save the Union.

PLAYBOY: Wasn't the Civil War fought to decide whether this nation could, in the words of Lincoln, "endure permanently half slave and half free"?

MALCOLM X: Sir, many, many people are completely misinformed about Lincoln and the Negro. That war involved two thieves, the North and the South, fighting over the spoils. The further we get away from the actual incident, the more they are trying to make it sound as though the battle was over the black man. Lincoln said that if he could save the Union without freeing the slaves, he would. But after two years of killing and carnage he found out he would *have* to free the slaves. He wasn't interested in the slaves but in the Union. As for the Emancipation Proclamation, sir, it was an empty document. If it freed the slaves, why, a century later, are we still battling for civil rights?

PLAYBOY: Despite the fact that the goal of racial equality is not yet realized, many sociologists—and many Negro commentators—agree that no minority group on earth has made as much social, civil and economic progress as the American Negro in the past 100 years. What is your reaction to this view?

MALCOLM X: Sir, I hear that everywhere almost exactly as you state it. This is one of the biggest myths that the American black man himself believes in. Every immigrant ethnic group that has come to this country is now a genuinely first-class citizen group—every one of them but the black man, who was here when they came. While everybody else is sharing the fruit, the black man is just now starting to be thrown some seeds. It is our hope that through the Honorable Elijah Muhammad, we will at last get the soil to plant the seeds in. You talk about the progress of the Negro—I'll tell you, mister, it's just because the Negro has been in America while *America* has gone forward that the Negro appears to have gone forward. The Negro is like a man on a luxury commuter train doing 90 miles an hour. He looks out of the window, along with all the white passengers in their Pullman chairs, and he thinks *he's* doing 90, too. Then he gets to the men's room and looks in the mirror—and he sees he's not really getting anywhere at all. His reflection shows a black man standing there in the white uniform of a dining-car steward. He may get on the 5:10, all right, but he sure won't be getting off at Westport.

PLAYBOY: Is there anything then, in your opinion, that could be done—by either whites or blacks—to expedite the social and economic progress of the Negro in America?

MALCOLM X: First of all, the white man must finally realize that *he's* the one who has committed the crimes that have produced the miserable condition that our people are in. He can't hide this guilt by reviling us today because we answer his criminal acts—past and present—with extreme and uncompromising resentment. He cannot hide his guilt by accusing us, his victims, of being racists, extremists and black supremacists. The white man must realize that the sins of the fathers are about to be visited upon the heads of the children who have continued those sins, only in more sophisticated ways. Mr. Elijah Muhammad is warning this generation of white people that they, too, are also facing a time of harvest in which they will have to pay for the crime committed when their grandfathers made slaves out of us.

But there *is* something the white man can do to avert this fate. He must atone—and this can only be done by allowing black men, those who choose, to leave this land of bondage and go to a land of our own. But if he doesn't want a mass movement of our people away from this house of bondage, then he should separate this country. He should give us several states here on American soil, where those of us who wish to can go and set up our own government, our own economic system, our own civilization. Since we have given over 300 years of our slave labor to the white man's America, helped to build it up for him, it's only right that white America should give us everything *we* need in finance and materials for the next 25 years, until our own nation is able to stand on its feet. Then, if the Western Hemisphere is attacked by outside enemies, we would have both the capability and the motivation to join in defending the hemisphere, in which we would then have a sovereign stake.

The Honorable Elijah Muhammad says that the black man has served under the rule of all the other peoples of the earth at one time or another in the past. He teaches that it is now God's intention to put the black man back at the top of civilization, where he was in the beginning—before Adam, the white man, was created. The world since Adam has been white—and corrupt. The world of tomorrow will be black—and righteous. In the white world there has been nothing but slavery, suffering, death and colonialism. In the black world of tomorrow, there will be *true* freedom, justice and equality for all. And that day is coming—sooner than you think.

PLAYBOY: If Muslims ultimately gain control as you predict, do you plan to bestow "*true* freedom" on white people?

MALCOLM X: It's not a case of what would we do, it's a case of what would God do with whites. What does a judge do with the guilty? Either the guilty atone, or God executes judgment.

Wallace

1968

◆

MARSHALL FRADY

On a cold, rain-flicked night in 1967 a rickety twin-engine Convair 240 began a blind and uncertain descent through low clouds, abruptly breaking out over the scattered watery lights of Concord, New Hampshire. It came in headlong, less by instruments and calculation than with a precipitous lurching optimism.

A damp huddle of greeters was waiting in the dark, and they waggled dime-store Confederate flags when he emerged from the plane—a stumpy little man with heavy black eyebrows and bright black darting eyes and a puglike bulb of a nose who looked as if he might have stepped out of an eighteenth-century London street scene by Hogarth. Wrapped in a black raincoat, he bobbed spryly down the steps as flashbulbs stammered in the rain. Someone held an umbrella over his head while he said a few words to the newsmen. Asked if he were offended because no local officials were there to welcome him, he answered jauntily, "Naw"—his voice rising just a bit—"Naw, 'cause it's the workin' folks all over this country who're gettin' fed up and are gonna turn this country around, and a whole heap of politicians are gonna get run over when they do." With that, he was bundled into a car at the head of the waiting cavalcade, and, with a swift surge, everyone—he, his entourage, the reporters, his local supporters—vanished into the night. One had the peculiar fleeting impression that a squad of commandos or guerrillas, irregulars at any rate, had just landed in the dark and was now loose in the New England countryside.

At a press conference that evening in a crammed smoke-hazed motel room on the outskirts of Concord, he seemed—peering over a thicket of microphones that came up almost to his chin, perspiring and a little haggard in the harsh glare of television lights—an improbable apparition. His baggy dark suit was buttoned tightly over his paunch, with a tab-collar shirt hugging the bulky knot of an inexpensive tie. His breast pocket was bulging with plastic-tip White Owl cigars and scraps of paper on which were scribbled random notes, addresses, telephone numbers. He looked somewhat like a traveling novelty salesman. But what this chunky little man was occupied with, what had brought him out of the night from distant Alabama all the way to this New Hampshire motel room, was the election of the next President of the United States—an

event now only a year away. He carefully affected, out of deference to this un-
familiar assembly, a subdued and amiable manner, with much congenial winking, and his grammar and enunciation were studiously precise, faintly stilted.
(On the flight up, he had mused, "Them New Hampshire folks, you know, they
a little more restrained and genteel than Alabama folks. They gotten kind of
overbred up there.") At one point, he announced, "Well, I'm mighty happy to
be among all you very intelligent-lookin' folks." But later, when he interrupted
a woman reporter, "What's that, honey? Could you say that again? I don't hear
too good," turning his head with his hand cupped behind his ear so that he had
to look at her out of the corner of his eye, he seemed solemnly impervious to
the ripple of titters in the room.

Morning revealed a landscape that had the tidy miniature quality of a
model train set, with a trivial city skyline under washed drab skies. It was alien
country. Though the month was April, the weather was wintry—not his kind
of weather—as if the South and North described not so much regions as perpetual weathers, summerland and winterland. Syracuse, into which he had
ventured the week before, had had a profoundly remote look about it, cold and
wan under bare bleak trees, with junkyards, power lines, and oil tanks set out
in wide weedy fields and cement trucks moving through a rubble of construction. All the towns in the North where he was appearing seemed generations
older than those in Alabama, and over Concord's streets there was a kind of
static quiescence, a worn and antique quality. When he spoke that afternoon in
the square downtown, he was regarded from the capitol lawn by an incredu-
lously scowling statue of Daniel Webster, and his grits-and-gravy voice blared
down a main street that was a turn-of-the-century tintype of stark brick buildings crested with Yankee brass eagles.

But it could have been a rally on a musky spring afternoon in Suggsville,
Alabama. His finger stabbing downward, his eyes crackling, the microphone
ringing under the impetuous barrage of his voice, he barked, "If one of these
two national parties don't wake up and get *straight*, well, I can promise that you
and me, we gonna stir something up all over this country. . . ." Afterward he
greeted people along the sidewalks with an instant, easy intimacy: "Honey, I
'preciate yawl comin' on out here today in this cold, heunh? Tell yo folks hello
for me, heunh?" When a small girl suddenly kissed him square on the mouth,
he looked around him for a moment—at all the pleasant faces, at the moil of reporters, at the candy-green capitol lawn, the thin exquisite sunshine, the vast
benign blue sky—and grinned almost blissfully.

Driving on to Dartmouth later for an evening speech, through Devil-and-
Daniel Webster country—weathervanes atop white wooden farmhouses, stone
fences and apple orchards, birches and dark cedars sheltering small secret
ponds the color of graphite—he removed his wetly chewed cigar to remark,
"This sho does look like North Alabama, don't it?" He found the thought cheer-

ing. "Yes, sir," he murmured happily, "you go up there around Gurley, New Hope, Grays Chapel—country up there looks just like this," and he leaned back in his seat and returned his cigar to his mouth, satisfied.

Two hours later, after nightfall, over the still, shadowed campus at Dartmouth, there pulsed a dull, steady roar from the auditorium where he was speaking. Scattered groups of students were hurrying toward the sound under the dark trees, but people were already milling under the windows and around the front steps. Inside, students were standing along the walls and sitting on windowsills and in the aisles, and the noise they were making was like a single continuous howl existing independent and disembodied above their open mouths. On the stage, while a student tried to read questions submitted by the audience, he paced restlessly, exhilarated by the violence heavy in the air. Occasionally he spat into his handkerchief and then plunged it back into his hip pocket. When he pounced to the microphone to answer a question, it was as if he were deliberately lobbing incendiary pronouncements into the crowd. He would crouch, looking up, his left arm gripping the lectern and his right swinging and whipping with pointed finger, as if he were furiously cranking himself up: "I'm not against dissent now, but I believe anybody that stands up like this professor in New Jersey and says they *long* for a victory by the Vietcong over the American imperialist troops, and anybody that goes out raising *bluhd* and *money* for the Vietcong against American servicemen, they oughtta be drug by the hair of their heads before a grand jury and indicted for *treason*, 'cause that's what they guilty of, and I promise you if I—" And then he would step back and spit into his handkerchief again, shooting it back into his hip pocket as the roar rose around him.

At one point there was a charge by students down the center aisle, led by a young professor with fine-spun hair and a freshly scrubbed cherubic complexion—but his mild face was now flushed, his tie askew, his eyes manic and glaring as he tried to flail his way through campus police and plainclothesmen, bellowing with a crack in his voice, "Get out of here! Get out of here! You are an outrage!" That berserk charge—anarchic and hopeless, an abandonment of fairness, proprieties, all civilized approaches, a retreat to simple brute action— testified not only to despair and fury over the fact that this man could be speaking there at all, but to a sinking of the heart over the absurdly serious import of that figure's audacious aspirations, a dread that something sinister and implacable was afoot in the land. As he was hustled offstage during the short melee, he glanced quickly back over his shoulder at the furor with a curious, bemused, almost awed expression.

Outside, after his speech, his car was engulfed. White and Negro students kicked the fenders and hammered on the hood, and one policeman was hauled back into the maw of the crowd and disappeared into it, his crumpled cap reappearing a moment later in the hand of a student, who waved it high in the air in triumph. And it seemed as if he, too, this stubby little man, might be on the point of vanishing, consumed whole by the kind of popular violence he so savors. As the crowd seethed around his car, there were glimpses of him sitting in the back seat, his face not worried, but just empty whenever the reeling TV lights washed over it, huddling behind the rolled-up windows with his cigar, all of him as small and still and inert as a rabbit in a burrow while hounds swirl and bay in the grass around it. The car began to ease forward, slowly nosing through the mob—he still not moving, looking to neither the right nor the left—and then, rapidly, it was gone.

At the least, he is a simple primitive natural phenomenon, like weeds or heat-lightning. He is a mixture of innocence and malevolence, humor and horror. "He's simply more alive than all the others," declared a woman reporter after the Dartmouth fray. "These professors like Galbraith, Schlesinger, the politicians and bureaucrats in Washington—God knows, I've been around all of them, and they don't really know what's going on. You saw those people in that auditorium while he was speaking—you saw their eyes. He made those people feel something *real* for once in their lives. You can't help but respond to him. Me—my heart was pounding, I couldn't take my eyes off him, there were all those people screaming. You almost *love* him, though you know what a little gremlin he actually is."

Many still find it hard to regard George Corley Wallace as anything other than merely the most resourceful, durable, and unabashed of the Southern segregationist governors. But the fact is, he passed that point long ago, and has intruded himself now into the history of the nation. He has become, at the least, a dark poltergeist whose capacity for mischief in the land is formidable. The havoc he seems sure to cause in the procedure of electing the next President of the United States has already raised substantial doubts about the system: he has materialized as the grim joker in the deck. More soberingly, the significance of his candidacy invokes certain questions about the basic health of the American society, both at this time and in the future.

To many he portends the eventual arrival of a final racist psychology into American politics. It seems certain that his candidacy can only increase the racial alienation in the country. A moderate Alabama politician declares, "What he's trying to do in the nation is what he's managed to do in Alabama. When you draw the line the way he does, the whites go with the white, and the blacks with the black, and when that happens, you're in for warfare." A former Alabama senator echoes, "It's conceivable that he could win a state like Illinois or even California when he puts the hay down where the goats can get at it. He can use all the other issues—law and order, running your own schools, protecting property rights—and never mention race. But people will know he's telling them, 'A nigger's trying to get your job, trying to move into your neighborhood.' What Wallace is doing is talking to them in a kind of shorthand, a kind of code."

At the same time, despite his public protestations that he is only an Alabama segregationist, what Wallace has been encountering in the violent demonstrations that have greeted him as he has junketed over the nation has been the same instinct he venerates in cabdrivers and dirt-farmers, "that tells you when you can trust somebody and when you can't." If a Birmingham steelworker or a country barber in Marengo County "knew Castro was a Commie just by instinct," so do Negroes and most liberals know "by instinct, just by looking at him and hearing him talk," that Wallace is a racist. Segregation is necessarily predicated on racism, and it doesn't have to be of the malevolent variety—it can be Wallace's kind of faint amicable contempt. Racism, fundamentally, is the persuasion that there is an innate, generic, permanent difference between the races in all the traits that describe humanity. Actually, Wallace himself once confided to a reporter in the lobby of a Cleveland hotel, removing his cigar for a moment to whisper behind his hand, "Let 'em call me a racist. It don't make any difference. Whole heap of folks in this country feel the same way I do. Race is what's gonna win this thing for me."

The simple prospect that his candidacy could impinge upon the system to the extent of throwing the presidential election into the House of Representatives (with giddy swiftness the outrageous becomes the possible and then the probable) can only make more acute the cornered mentality among America's disenchanted and estranged. "By God," muttered a young liberal after one of Wallace's campus appearances, "this could be the time. Just because all the others have missed before—the Know-Nothings, Joe McCarthy, Goldwater— that doesn't mean they'll keep on missing. This could be it. He might be the one with the right combination." The desperate outbursts of violence that attend his wanderings about the country leave one with the uneasy feeling that alienations, not only racial but also intellectual, have reached the point in our society where the potential for revolution is more palpable than ever before.

Actually, Wallace could be only one reflection of a general shattering of the American society, a disintegration into fragments. The American mystics—such as Norman Mailer—are unintelligible to the sturdy American Boy Scouts like Ronald Reagan and Billy Graham. Lyndon Johnson could never understand Timothy Leary or Allen Ginsberg. Stokely Carmichael could never understand Roger Blough. The efficacy of dialogue seems to be waning, and with it a sense of the American community. It's like a new Tower of Babel. Nothing seems to mean anything anymore except action. For Wallace, talk is finally not for the purpose of communication, explanation, or persuasion, but just another form of action: rhetoric. Action is all. The unsettling thing about his candidacy now is that it will tend to reduce America's disaffected, those who view him as an omen of a wider mentality, to a reliance on the same brute processes.

In this sense, Wallace represents the dark side of the moon of the American democracy—the tradition of direct popular violent action in community crises. He belongs fundamentally to the vigilante ethic, with certain apocalyptic overtones, and the potential in any social crisis for violent confrontation and climax enthralls him. One autumn evening in 1966, driving back to a Birmingham hotel after a shopping-center rally, he sat in the back seat of his car, gesturing in the glare of headlights behind him. "Nigguh comes up to a white woman down here like they do up North, tryin' all that stuff, he's gonna get shot. Yessuh. Or get his head busted. That's why we don't have any of that business down here. They know what's gonna happen to 'em. They start a riot down here, first one of 'em to pick up a brick gets a bullet in the brain, that's all. And then you walk over to the next one and say, 'All right, pick up a brick. We just want to see you pick up one of them bricks, now!' Let 'em see you shoot down a few of 'em, and you got it stopped. Bob McNair, guvnuh over there in South Carolina, he's one of them *nice* fellas, you know, he don't go for that kinda talk—like Carl Sanders over there in Georgia. Now, I like Carl, I don't know whether he likes me particularly or not, but I got nothing against him. But he's one of those nice fellas wantin' to moderate everything. But, of course, he found out you can't do that. Like ole Ivan Allen over there. Knocked him offa that car, you know, those rioters, when he was tryin' to talk to them. They oughtta done more than that. Hell, we got too much dignity in government now, what we need is some *meanness*. You elect one of those steelworkers guvnuh, you talk about a revolution—damn, there'd be shootin' and tearin' down and burnin' up and killin' and bloodlettin' sho *nuff*. Steelworker wouldn't have to think about it—he'd just go ahead and do it. Anyway, I been tellin' folks for years, you ask if I hadn't, that there'd be fightin' in the streets one day between rightists and leftists, between whites and blacks. Hell, all we'd have to do right now is march on the federal courthouse there in Montgomery, take over the post office and lock up a few of those judges, and by sunset there'd be a revolution from one corner of this nation to the other. We could turn this country right around."

It has become Wallace's conviction—more than conviction, visceral sensation—that he exists as the very incarnation of the "folks," the embodiment of the will and sensibilities and discontents of the people in the roadside diners and all-night chili cafés, the cabdrivers and waitresses and plant workers, as well as a certain harried Prufrock population of dingy-collared department-store clerks and insurance salesmen and neighborhood grocers: the great silent American Folk which have never been politically numbered as the Wallace candidacy promises to number them. His candidacy poses questions about what illusions we may have been under about the American public. There's no doubt he has sensed a subterranean political consciousness congenial to him. In *The Earl of Louisiana*, A. J. Liebling suggests that "if Hoover by some disas-

trous miracle had been reelected in 1932, Huey [Long] might within two years
have crystallized around himself all the discontent, rational and irrational, in
the country. . . ." In this time, if there is an ominous conspiracy underway in
the United States, it would be the silent massive *suspicion* of a conspiracy which
threatens home, job, status, the accustomed order of life. And Wallace's varia-
tion of Long's coalition of frustration is a "fusion" of the working man with the
large industrialists and tycoons of Mid-America. "We got part of it already," he
declares; "we got the workin' man, and now we're gonna get the other part of
it—the high hoi-polloi. They gonna come around, you wait." Indeed, when he
has appeared before large groups of industrialists, the receptions have been robust. At a patio party recently in New Orleans' French Quarter, an oil million-
aire from Dallas allowed, "I'd vote for him in a minute, and give him all the
money I could, if I just felt I could trust him—if he wouldn't wind up getting
tamed by Washington like Lester Maddox over there in Georgia. I'm a Republican, but I'd love to support him, and every one of my friends—oilmen, fellows
in wheat—feel the same way."

Nevertheless, the man himself seems hopelessly implausible as a national
political figure. For one thing, he looks on the entire world as merely an extension of Barbour County, Alabama, where he grew up—full of chillun and folks,
some of them liars and cheats and no-counts, most of them decent people
minding their own business, whose interests are simple and who are polite to
each other, but with a certain measure of orneriness and villainy going on, the
best answers to which are Barbour County's kind of commonsense solutions.
In an age of freeways and high-rise apartments, he seems a whimsical
anachronism: his are essentially village sensibilities.

More than anything else, he is a consummate political and cultural articulation of the South, where life is simply more glandular than it is in the rest of
the nation. Southerners tend to belong and believe through blood and weather
and common earth and common enemy and common travail, rather than belonging, believing, cerebrally. The tribal instinct is what they answer to. That is
part of the reason why the most recent incarnations of the Boston Abolition-
ists—those gaunt, tense, electric youths from the snows of the North and the
seasonless hothouse clime of California who, lank hair falling over ethereal
faces, ventured into Negro neighborhoods in Alabama and Mississippi—were
not only incomprehensible but also faintly repulsive to most Southerners. They
were tinged with the perversion of having subjected life to ideas. Any politician
like Eugene McCarthy, with his diaphanous abstractions, would be impossible
in the South. The region is ruled by humid passion, and a fine old-fashioned
sense of sin. There is a lingering romance of violence, a congenital love for
quick and final physical showdowns. Not just the filling-station attendants, the
cabdrivers and deputy sheriffs and beauticians and tabernacle evangelists, but
also Rotarians, bankers, teachers, the urbanites of Atlanta and Charlotte,

stockbrokers and reporters who have moved away to the cities of the North—virtually all those born in the South have about them, to a certain degree, that air of an immediate and casual familiarity with violence, a quality of loosely leashed readiness for mayhem. Even those Southerners who come from large cities—although, say, having martinis in some expensive New York restaurant, surrounded by Continental waiters and chandeliers—seem to have emerged from another dimension where the days are fevered and dreaming with honeysuckle and wisteria, from a different and more passionate play of life, a slow, sensuous, easy, lyrical, savage marriage of man and earth. They carry with them the sense of another landscape—primeval mountains, scruffy pine hills populated with mules and moonshiners, cottonland as level and limitless as the sea, fierce skies—a land where winters are only a dull and sullen hiatus with a pale ghost of the sun passing through vague chill rains.

Wallace is a direct product of this society where things—be they theories or institutions or political machines—do not count for so much as passion and people. Accordingly, he operates outside the conventional political wisdom. There has been an almost childlike naïveté about the way he has undertaken to run for President. One afternoon shortly after his wife's election as governor, he sat in his office and calculated, almost as an afterthought, the financial strategy for his whole national campaign, scribbling on the back of a memo pad with his ball-point pen: "Let's see, we got better'n $380,000 when we went into three states back in '64, three goes into fifty about seventeen times—don't it?—yes, and seventeen times $380,000 that oughtta be—that's $6,460,000. That oughtta be enough." In fact, he seems to regard formal political organization with a vague contempt, as a sign of political effeteness, an absence of vitality—as if he is already naturally blessed with what political organization exists to create. His simple directness is, at once, part of his absurdity and part of his genius.

"Power comes from the people," he declares, "and if my health holds up, I'm gonna change things in this country. Anyway, I don't have a single thing to lose, and everything to gain." Indeed, there is surrounding him an uncanny aura of limitless possibility, of adventure, of incredible prospects—a feeling that anything is possible. The sheer hope, the happy half-reckless presumption of his candidacy for the highest office in the land, gives one the sense that the demonic is still at work in human affairs, even in this age of computers and slide rules and pundits and public-relations task forces: that life and politics, after all, are simply larger than arithmetic. Accordingly, his candidacy is a reminder that anything, including the unthinkable, can happen in a democracy. In the same way that he went into the 1964 Northern presidential primaries in touch with potentials that no one else seemed to be in touch with, he has proceeded this time from absolutely nothing—not precedent, rumor, or normal political equations, polls, press, or the patronage of the American establishment—but merely from his own clear sense and vision of the democratic possibilities for himself. For him to have aspired seriously to the presidency right now, in this age—or even to have expected to figure importantly in the election—has required more originality, audacity, optimism, and dauntlessness than has ever been required of any other significant presidential candidate in this nation's history, including Huey Long.

In the final analysis, whatever becomes of him in the months ahead, it seems probable that George Wallace will be recorded as the greatest of the American demagogues—the classic of his species. That is true not only because of the magnitude of the rapport he has already invoked in the country (television having enlarged the stump to the size of the continent), but because of his own nature as a politician and a human being. He is really more elemental than Huey Long; it is quite beyond him, for instance, to take a case of whiskey up to the top floor of a hotel and come back down six weeks later with *Every Man a King.* He doesn't think about it all enough to write a book about it. He is more essential than that. Abstractions do not really exist for him. "He doesn't ever talk about purposes, causes, destinies, anything like that," says one Alabama politician. "He differs from every other politician I've ever known in that respect." Wallace himself cheerfully allows, "Naw, we don't stop and figger, we don't think about history or theories or none of that. We just go ahead. Hell, history can take care of itself." In this rude sense, he is the most existential politician in the country today. He seems empty of any private philosophy or persuasions reached in solitude and stillness. He is made up, in mind and sensibilities, of the clatter and chatter and gusting impulses of the marketplace, the town square, the barbershop. His morality is the morality of the majority. "The majority of the folks aren't gonna want to do anything that ain't right," he insists. He is the ultimate product of the democratic system.

Not only are abstract ethics alien to him, but he entertains a particular antipathy to people who live and act from them. It's something like the Dionysian principle applied to politics. "Hell, intellectuals, when they've gotten into power, have made some of the bloodiest tyrants man has ever seen," he maintains. "These here liberals and intellectual morons, they don't believe in nothing but themselves and their theories. They don't have any faith in people. Lot of 'em don't really *like* people, when you get right down to it." (His own vision of man is the old vision—man is perpetually embattled on this earth, his state fixed and imperfectible, composed of natural wickedness and natural virtue in a balance that can never really be altered, poverty and grief and injustice and conflict irrevocable parts of his lot. "Life's basically a fight," declares Wallace. "People have to go out and make a livin', have to fight snow and cold and heat and natural disasters. People enjoy fightin'. That's the way folks are. . . ." Accordingly, he operates on the most elemental assumptions about the nature of the human species, such as: "Nigguhs hate whites, and whites hate nigguhs. Everybody knows that deep down.")

His political mystique of "the common folks" reduces everyone to a simple and almost biological common denominator. While standing at the edge of a crowd waiting to speak at a 1966 rally, he declared to reporters, "When the liberals and intellectuals say the people don't have any sense, they talkin' about *us* people—they talkin' about the people here. But hell, you can get good solid information from a man drivin' a truck, you don't need to go to no college professor. The fella on the street has got a better mind and instincts than these here sissy-britches intellectual morons, like the editor of *The Birmingham News,* for instance. He's just one man, that's all he is. You take this fella here—" Without taking his eyes from the reporters, he reached out at random and pulled over an elderly man, dressed in coveralls and an old army field jacket, with a light frosting of beard on his cheeks. "—this fella here, he's one man too, just like the editor of *The Birmingham News.* He weighs just as much as the editor of *The Birmingham News—*" The man listened with a mute, bashful pleasure and an awkward little grin while Wallace held on to his elbow. "—he's got eyes and ears and a mouth just like the editor of *The Birmingham News.* He's got a mind, too—fact, he's got a better mind. And the editor of *The Birmingham News* has got just one vote, like this fella here. So who is the editor of *The Birmingham News?* Folks like this fella here know just by instinct, just by havin' lived with folks, more'n all the newspaper editors and professors up yonder at Harvard will ever know. Any truck driver'd know right off what to do at the scene of an accident, but you take a college professor, he'd just stand around lookin', with his hands in his pockets and gettin' sick."

As a private person, Wallace himself is curiously vague and weightless. He seems only marginally and incidentally aware of home and family, food and friends, the gentle comforts that bless the lives of ordinary men. One of his oldest associates declares, "Whenever he comes over here to eat, he's just not conscious of anything except the people around him. He knows where the ketchup and the milk are, but that's all. Because he's only here to keep on talking to somebody. He never knows what he's eating because he's too busy talking—it could be filet mignon he's eating, it could be hamburger, it could be the end of his tie, he don't know. Just that whatever it is, he wants to put ketchup on it."

Neither does money interest him. His one luxurious indulgence, reports a Montgomery businessman, "is having his fingers manicured downtown at the Exchange Hotel Barber Shop by Edna Taylor." What money arrangements have been necessary in past campaigns have been quietly attended to by aides, out of his sight, out of his knowledge. Finance, high or low, leaves him wretchedly bored anyway; as one observer has noted, it would seem he never got beyond decimals.

He seems to exist in a constant state of energy and ebullience that never vanishes altogether but simply flares and pales. It's as if, at the instant in his childhood when he comprehended what he was going to do, time simply ceased for him, and he began to exist in the same tense charged moment—the absolute fact of his destiny, a condition of will that was quite outside time.

"He don't have no hobbies," declares an old crony from Wallace's hometown. "He don't do any honest work. He don't drink. He ain't got but one serious appetite, and that's votes." It is the recollection of one official in Wallace's home county that since 1947 there has been only one election in which Wallace's name was not on the ballot for something. When he was a small child, remembers his grandmother, "He couldn't bear to see anything thrown away. His grandfather would drop a piece of paper in the wastebasket, and he would fetch it right back out and say, 'Well, Grandpa, this is *some* good. . . .' " And it's as if he is still collecting scraps from his grandfather's wastebasket, as if he were born with a compulsive, indiscriminate acquisitiveness. Shaking hands in a Birmingham shopping center during the 1966 governor's race, he paused in the midst of the crowd before one man, holding onto his hand, and inquired earnestly, "Yes, now, and how is Faye? Now, she was in St. Vincent's, wasn't she? I meant to write her a letter—" He released the man for a moment and plunged both hands into his coat pockets, bringing up two thick fistfuls of business cards and folded envelopes, dog-eared, a bit soiled, covered with scribbles; he shuffled furiously through them, intent and absorbed, oblivious now of the crowd and everything else around him, until he found a vacant space on the back of one relatively fresh envelope on which he promptly scribbled yet another name and address, swiftly returning both handfuls to his coat pockets and seizing the man's hand again. "Now, you tell her we gonna write her, heunh?" A lady from his hometown recalls, "I kept after him to see a friend of mine who was in the hospital, and he'd whine and grumble, 'You know, I just hate to go anywhere nowadays, so many people want to shake my hand.' But he finally agreed, and when we walked into the hospital room, a nurse made the mistake of telling him, 'Some people down the hall would like to say hello to you, Governor.' He looked at her real bright and quick and said, 'Oh, yeah? Say there are?' Before I knew it, he was right back out the door, running up and down that hall shaking hands with patients, some of them people flat on their backs who could hardly talk and probably wouldn't even live until election time." He has a way of showing up, unannounced and solemn and reverential, at funerals in remote places all over the state, slipping discreetly into a back pew of the church, and later at the graveside, after the burial, shaking hands, a commiserating singsong in his voice, with the family and friends of the deceased and the minister and the mortuary officials.

His voraciousness lends to everyone, indiscriminately, a certain dearness—invokes in him an automatic compassion and solicitude. "He don't even like for us to talk about his enemies," says one of his aides. "He'll hear you cussin' out some no-good sonuvabitch that everybody agrees is no good, and he'll say, 'Now, you wrong about that fella, he's a good ole boy, you ought not to

talk about him that way.' " It's something like a miser's fanatic abhorrence of waste, and it extends even to Negro voters. During one of his campaigns he told a group of Negro educators in a secret meeting on a Negro campus, "Now, when I get out here speakin' to folks, don't pay any attention to what I say, 'cause I'm gonna have to fuss at yawl a little. But I don't mean any of it." And during the 1966 campaign, as he was riding to an afternoon rally, a newsman in the car with him mentioned that one Alabama Negro leader had suggested privately that if Wallace would only give some small sign of amicability, make some token gesture, it was still possible that the Negroes in the state could gather behind him. Even though it was already obvious that Wallace would obliterate his Republican opponent, this piece of news caused him to snatch his cigar out of his mouth and peer sharply at the newsman: "Said they could, eh? 'Cose, they realize I couldn't be meetin' with them in public or anything like that. But, uh—what kinda sign you reckon they'd want?"

In turn, it seems impossible for him to believe that anyone could just simply and naturally not like him. "It bothers him no end to think anybody living is against him," declares one of his old associates. "He'll hear about somebody didn't vote for him, he'll worry over that fella, think about him, more'n he will his friends. He finds out you aren't with him on something, he takes that to mean you're against him altogether. He'll sometimes call you around eleven at night and wheedle, wheedle, argue, argue." When finally reduced to accept the mysterious finality of someone's hostility, he and his people attribute it to some psychological defect in the person, to some peculiar and esoteric long-smoldering grudge, or to simple mental affliction—it's a sad sign that the individual concerned has deserted the company of normal and decent folks, has forsaken the human race.

It was about 1964 that his passion began to embrace the entire nation. When he places long-distance calls, he is given to chatting with the operator first: "Honey, this is George Wallace—uh, guv'n'Alabama—yes, well, you know I've gotten a lot of support from you communications workers. I want to thank yawl, you folks been mighty good to me. You know, when I was up there in Wisconsin—" talking on until the operator finally, gently, suggests that perhaps she should put his call on through. "Well, thank you, honey. Now, you tell yo family hello for me, heunh?" Trying once to reach a political contact in Denver, he was connected by mistake with an anonymous bar somewhere in the outer reaches of Colorado, and he immediately engaged the bartender in a long and cozy conversation. An old but now disaffected comrade says, "You sit in his office, and he's sifting through his mail all the time—you know, scooping it up with both hands, letting it spill through his fingers back on the desk, over and over again. He'll pick up one letter, right in the middle of a conversation about something else, and say, 'Look ahere, here's a letter I got all the way from I-dee-ho. . . .' "

In Alabama Wallace has managed to pass the point of being just the most popular politician in the memory of the state. He has become a Folk Hero. Alabama, along with the rest of the South, has been changing into something more like the rest of the nation, and in the process, a particular devastation is being worked among its people. In his transition from the gentle earth to the city—the filling stations, the power lines, the merciless asphalt, the neon Jumboburger drive-ins—the Southern yeoman has acquired a quality of metallic ferocity. At the same time, the central fact about the South continues to be its defeat in the Civil War. There lingers a kind of mortal irreconcilability, an incapacity to forget—embarking on a kind of folk crusade a century ago, throwing everything into it, making a total commitment of honor and valor and hope and pride, it could not afford to lose: but it did. The malaise of spirit that disaster left behind has not been dispelled by the South's transmogrification into an imitation of the North, and has only been deepened by its recent ten years of racial anguish. What Wallace has done in Alabama is assume the legacy of defeat, the burden of his state's embarrassment before the rest of the nation, its lurking sense of guilt and pettiness, dread and futility. "They think he's the greatest thing that's ever come along," snorts one Alabama judge. "He keeps tellin' 'em, 'You the children of Israel, you gonna lead this country out of the wilderness!' Well, goddamn. We at the bottom of everything you can find to be at the bottom of, and yet we gonna save the country. We lead the country in illiteracy and syphilis, and yet we gonna lead the damn country out of the wilderness. . . ."

"I don't have no inferiority complex about runnin' for President," Wallace announced in town squares all over Alabama during his wife's campaign for governor. "I want you to know, when I go to the guvnuhs' conferences, I don't sit on the third row or the fourth row or even the second row. I sit on the front row, because I represent just as good and refined and cultured people as anybody else there. They talk like you and me hadn't got enough sense to turn around. They say you voted ignorantly when you voted for me four years ago. But I want to let yawl in on a little secret. These here national politicians like Humphrey and Johnson and Nixon, they don't hang their britches on the wall and then do a flyin' jump into 'em every mornin', they put 'em on one britches leg at a time, just like the folks here in Chilton County. Earl Warren on the Supreme Court, he's one of them big Republicans, and he's done more against you'n'me than anybody else in this country. He hadn't got enough brains in his whole head to try a chicken thief in Chilton County. I promise you, we gonna stir sump'n up all over this country, from Maine to California. We not powerful personally, it's all you good people here in Chilton County. Why, when you go to Lima-Peru or Berlin-Germany or Geneva-Switzerland or even"—one waits, suspended, to see if it will come, and it does—"Paris-France, they've all heard about Alabama. This is the first time in yo history so many big politicos been worried about us. They say we gonna hurt 'em, and I'll tell you sump'n: I *wanta* hurt 'em, 'cause they've hurt us long enough, and I'm tired of it. The Republicans now, they havin' to meet in banks tryin' to figger out what they gonna do about us down here. I'm not talkin' about the good banks of Chilton County or Alabama, I'm talking about the Chase National and the Wall Street crowd. You know, they used to meet in little biddy banks to talk about us, but this time, we got 'em meetin' in the *biggest bank in the world* talkin' about you'n'me and what they gonna do about Guvnuh Wallace down here in Alabama. . . ."

The fact is, the rest of the nation has probably never been quite so real to Alabamians as it is right now. His forays into the North and the West, answering what most Alabamians had come to consider a sudden inexplicable conspiracy by the nation to torment them after leaving them in peace for nearly one hundred years, have caused them to rediscover America. There is an almost palpable sense of excitement and national involvement abroad in the state, even if it tends to be edged with belligerence. This has been one of Wallace's accidental gifts to his people; he has, in this sense, enlarged their lives. Former governor John Patterson allows, "When Wallace was elected governor, the people in Alabama didn't know the difference between a preferential primary and the real thing. What he's done is educate 'em." One of Wallace's old boxing coaches asked a pair of newsmen: "Now, okay, I wish you'd answer a question for me. He's running for President here. Everybody says he's got to win something. Now, exactly, how can it happen? I mean, I'd really like to know." It's the same kind of wonder and dazed titillation the Hebrews probably felt on the shore of the Red Sea just after they learned it was going to open for them and then engulf their enemies. In cities and towns all over Alabama, people in restaurants during lunch hour are counting electoral votes, neglecting their desserts to make urgent calculations on wet napkins with ballpoint pens. One of Wallace's aides admits, "All these little farmhouses stuck way out in the woods, they all got a TV set now, you know. When those folks see Wallace on there standin' up to these big-city slick-hair boys, that's not just *him* talkin'. That's *them* on there. . . ."

In turn, Wallace's own identification with "the folks" is almost sensuous, almost mystic. They are his only reality. He feels that without them he is nothing, and with them he is everything and cannot be intimidated. In fact, what makes Wallace the ultimate demagogue is that, behind his indefatigable scrambling, his ferocious concentration, his inexhaustible ambition, there seems to lurk a secret, desperate suspicion that facing him, aside from and beyond his political existence, is nothingness—an empty, terrible white blank. It's as if, when the time finally arrives for him to cease to be a politician, he will simply cease to be. His terror of being alienated from "the folks" is like the terror of not being able to breathe. Probably the most traumatic period of his life was the interval between the Alabama Senate's startling refusal to permit him to succeed himself (late fall, 1965) and the spring primary that nominated his wife. The state Senate's blunt defiance was the first serious political repudiation he had suffered since becoming governor, and through the long winter of doubt that followed, there was a vast silence from the people—a silence in which there occurred repeated little ominous intimations that he might be falling, might indeed have already fallen. The worst part of it was, he couldn't really know—there was no final way to find out until the spring primary.

That harrowing winter even affected him physically. Seen lunching one February afternoon in the state capitol's bleak basement cafeteria, he had the look of a small rodent that was slowly starving: the skin over his cheekbones and narrow forehead was taut, glazed, and yellowish, his ink-black hair was combed back long and thin and scraggly to the nape of his neck, there were hollows behind his ears like empty sockets, and in his eyes was a ragged despair. He waited fretfully for the others at the table to finish eating, tearing off shreds of paper napkin with his gnawed rusty fingers and wadding them into tiny moist pills which he arrayed along the rim of his plate. He kept working almost viciously at his teeth with a toothpick, his lips curled back in an unconscious snarl.

But when, in the spring, the decision was finally made to run his wife, he seemed restored, whole, even peaceful again. In a packed café one afternoon shortly after the start of the campaign, after exchanging hugs and kisses and ardent double-fisted handshakes—oddly suggestive of secret fraternity grips— with the sun-scorched ginghamed and khakied folk filing past his table, he turned back to his plate and speculated with some glee, savagely hammering out ketchup onto his hamburger with the heel of his hand, about what "those Anglo-Saxons" in the several counties in which Negroes were running for sheriff would do to any Negro who might be elected. "The Black Panthers talkin' all the time about rev-o-lu-tion if one of their boys wins. A nigguh sheriff—the folks over there just ain't gonna stand for any kind of stuff such as that. When those Anglo-Saxon people get stirred up, boy, they don't mess around. Wouldn't one of them nigguhs last thirty minutes if he was to have the misfortune of gettin' elected." He went on to express the hope that John Doar, frequent Justice Department emissary into Alabama, would be shot between the eyes before too very long. Later, after his hamburger and buttermilk, as he stood outside in his shirtsleeves in the warm May sunshine waiting for his wife to finish her short introductory speech, he seemed possessed of the high vivid exhilaration of someone who had just emerged from a long and dangerous illness.

Lurleen won the spring primary dizzyingly, drawing more votes than her nine opponents combined. The general election campaign began in the late fall, and though Lurleen technically was the candidate, it was more like a long celebration by Wallace of the reaffirmation of his existence. As one veteran

Alabama reporter has noted, "He's never quite so alive as when he's out on the road again running for something. Each time, it's like his own little personal Easter."

The last week of that campaign began in soft October weather. The mornings were fine and bright and watery, just warm enough to produce a light dew of sweat on the upper lip. In the exhausted drab little towns where most of the rallies were held, the crowd would be gathered in a parking lot beside a brick store with a dimming inscription:

LEHMAN FURN. CO.

WARM MORNING HEATER

Drink

Royal Crown

Cola

and the hillbilly band on the flatbed trailer—pale youths, luxuriously coiffured, wearing twinkly, sequined black-and-gold suits with gold valentines running up their pants legs from black boots—would still be conjuring people out of the countryside with the lickety-split, devilish fiddle music, sawing them on out of the stores: farmers, filling-station workers, slippered women with their hair pinched up in curlers. The band would alternate spry gospel music with abject love ballads—forlorn, inconsolable, stricken, yelping, tragic, full of death, loss, violence, insanity, tears, night—which, with the arrival of the Wallace cars, would abruptly switch to rapid wheedling music while a large bell, carried from rally to rally in the back of a truck, would begin clangoring.

Wallace, in his faintly iridescent beetle-black suit, spurted out of his car, coming up on the first handshake with a slight dip, bending his knees, and then swooping upward, a flourish of body jazz, and then moved along the edge of the throng while the band kept playing, he fidgeting with his cuffs and scuffing at the pavement with the toes of his shoes, like a fighter shuffling about in his corner before the opening gong. While Lurleen spoke, he huddled with the local candidates behind the platform, and people passing behind him gave him light pats on the shoulder, which he accepted, not even turning around. (At one stop, a small pack of young razorbacks stood near him and loudly observed, "He's a rough-lookin' little devil, ain't he?" Wallace went over to them and, grinning, shook hands all around. "Glad to see you fellas out here today, heunh? Yawl doin' all right?")

When Lurleen stepped back to a spatter of applause, he would skip snappily up on the platform, take off his three-vent coat, and briskly roll up his shirtsleeves, once, twice, leaving bulky cuffs high on his biceps. Behind the microphone, his hipwork was fancy, vigorous, and vaguely obscene, with one blunt little paw constantly stroking the microphone stand: "These unidentified flyin' objects people are seein' outta airplane windows, they not flyin' saucers, they these intellectual morons and national politicians havin' runnin' humanitarian fits about my wife's candidacy down here. . . ." (Lurleen's principal function in the campaign, besides her brief overture speeches, was to supply Wallace with a clipping or magazine from the pack she kept in her lap whenever he thrust his hand toward her—"See here, they got a picture of yo guvnuh in this magazine that goes all over this nation"—he flourishing the item and then swiftly returning it to her as he went on, she placing it back neatly in the battered packet in her lap and getting the next clipping ready and then sitting primly with her hands folded over it as she waited.) "The national press now, anything's that bad about yo guvnuh, oh yes, they gonna run that. But anything good—why, you know, one national magazine had an article by a lady out in California during one of the guvnuhs' conferences, called us Dogpatch folks down here 'cause of the way we dressed. Well, I want to tell you something, the woman that wrote that article, I wisht you had seen what *she* was wearin'." Jubilant whoops from the crowd. "The *Life* magazine—yeah, I think they out here with us today, and the *Newsweek* and the *Time*, they all here— they wrote an article criticizin' my wife for not goin' to the guvnuhs' meetings when we were out there in California. Well, of course, she wasn't guvnuh then, and they had a program for the guvnuhs' wives and they had conferences for the guvnuhs. But for the benefit of the *Life* magazine—and there's some of 'em with us today—I just want to say that next year, after she's elected guvnuh, she'll go to the guvnuhs' conferences, and I'll go out with the guvnuhs' wives." There was another roar of guffaws, and one old-timer chortled to his friend, "Damn little rascal, he would too. He'd cut up a time with 'em."

His addresses everywhere were extended monologues rather than speeches, a hectic one-man argument without any real beginning, progression, or end. He added to and took from his sack of notions sparingly, line by line. The total effect was like that of an orchestra perpetually tuning up—a cacophony of peeves and exasperations. His points were scattershot, his climaxes came hurly-burly. At one stop, in the middle of his address, he was abruptly silenced by the deafening hoot and clatter of a freight train barging interminably past behind him, and he finally adlibbed in a loud voice, "I'm glad to see our railroad folks go by, 'cause they've endorsed my wife too, and I hope we can always keep them runnin'. Yessuh." He manages to exploit any interruption, assimilate any distraction.

His head tilting to one side, one hand plunged in his pants pocket and the other chopping and stabbing the air, his hips pumping and scooping furiously, he told the crowds, "You get a bayonet in yo back with the national Democrats, and you get a bayonet in yo back with the national Republicans. This Richard Milhouse 'Tricky Dick' Nixon, he hadn't got the sense of a Chilton County mule. He comes down here to talk about Alabama politics like it was some kind of his business. Sure, I went over to Mississippi to make a speech awhile back, but it was just a philosophy speech over there at the state fair. But I'll tell you, if I had said as much and done as much against the state of Mississippi as 'Tricky Dick' Nixon has said and done against the state of Alabama, I wouldn't have the brass to go within a *hunnert* miles of Mississippi, I'd just go around it or over it or something. And this Romney, singin' all those songs about overcomin' evuhthing—and Bobby Kennedy: he's the one that wants to give blood to the Communists all the time. Now, he's gone to South Africa tellin' them what to do in South Africa. Maybe he'll stay there this time. And now they wantin' to transfer yo chillun ten miles over in another county so they can conduct *social experiments* on 'em. And if you get a book sayin' Robert E. Lee was a good man, and the Confederate flag was a symbol of honor, they can put in books sayin' Robert E. Lee was a bad, vulgar man, and the Confederate flag was a symbol of dishonor. But I'll tell you, the mommas and poppas all over this country are mighty mad about them movin' their little chillun around like this. Emanuel Celler, he called yo guvnuh a devil, but then he found out they were gonna transfer his chillun too all the way across New York City, so now he's sayin' he's gonna have to look into all this guideline mess. But I tell you, if they don't all wake up, I'm gonna go all over this country tellin' those folks in Washington, 'You better mind about our chillun. You triflin' with our chillun now, and you better watch out.' . . ."

Afterward, he would lean from the platform to shake the hands of the people filing past below him—when there was a gap in the line, his hand would grope about in the air until someone stepped up to take it. Finally, stepping down from the platform and submerging himself in the crowd, he would keep a tight clasp on someone—sometimes two at once—as he turned to talk to still another over his shoulder, and in pursuit of unshaken hands he would sometimes drag people along with him, through shrubbery and rain puddles, as if reluctant to release them until he had fastened himself to the next hand. There would slowly come over the faces of the people caught in Wallace's grasp the expression of faintly amused embarrassment. At times he would unexpectedly break through the crowd into empty space, and propelled by sheer momentum, walk in aimless circles, trailed by his bodyguards, until he found the edge of the throng again, pulling himself back into their midst with double-handed clutches, his face fixed in a cozy little nose-wrinkling, teeth-gritting grin of gratification: "Yes, yes, I know yo uncle, he works down at H. L. Green's. Tell him hello for us, heunh? He sho is our friend. I saw yawl up the road, I believe, I sho 'preciate yawl bein' with us today, heunh? I 'preciate yawl's suppote, you know Hollis Jackson died. Honey, thank you very much, heunh? Glad to see you—yes, how is yo daughter now? Well, you tell her I been thinkin' about her. Hi, sweetie pie, honey, thank you. Yes, you know, I still miss Mr. Roy. I heard, I understand she was goin' to the junior high. 'Cose, her daddy got killed, you know. I sho will. I be glad to shake hands with her. She in the car? Yeah, all right, I'll be over there in a minute. . . ." He seemed somehow to be caressing, fondling, stroking, kneading the masses between his hands, and he would sometimes draw an out-of-state reporter close to him and inquire, sotto voce, "How you like these Alabama folks, hunh? They all right, ain't they?" and bob off without waiting for an answer. At several places he was approached by local young businessmen who asked him with poignant anxiety if it were possible to bring a factory of some kind into their community—a desperation to be found in every town in Alabama, no matter how small. Wallace would rub his hands together and tell them, "Now, you just keep tryin', and you know it'll all come about," and the young men would nod—"Yes. Well, thank you, Guvnuh. Anything you could do would be appreciated"—and wander away, somewhat dispirited. But Wallace was obviously buoyant when making his way through the crowds. He would pluck fistfuls of black snap-on Wallace ties from the hawkers and distribute them himself. "Here, here you go. Here's you one. And you, too."

Inevitably there would be a flock of elderly ladies sitting in plastic lawn chairs or cane-bottom rockers under a tree or on the courthouse porch, patiently waiting for him, and when he finally approached them, they would all chorus, reaching for him with heavy wattled arms, "Good ole boy. We all pray for you. . . ." "Sleep tight, honey, you gonna make it. . . ." "I love you. I just love you. . . ." "God bless you. You're God's man for us. . . ." As the crowd began thinning away, he would bounce on back to his car—a suggestion in his spry, ebullient haste of a schoolboy skipping and hopping—sometimes stopping to smooth out a drooping Wallace sticker on a car bumper, personally tidying up, sprucing up, putting the finishing touches on a good situation. Before leaving, though, his party would usually have to wait a few minutes while he retreated to a men's room. Finding one for Wallace—or, as his bodyguards put it, "giving him a chance to do what he wants to do"—was an unusually persistent problem all through the campaign, coming up virtually at every stop. At one gathering in a community Democratic headquarters, Wallace, while ecstatically shaking hands all around, began standing briefly on his tiptoes to glance furtively over the tops of partitions in the room, and finally, after an urgent hurried conference outside between the bodyguards and some local party officials, Wallace was conducted to the rear of a closed filling station next door.

Eating seemed to him a tedious distraction, an interruption best gotten out of the way fast in order to return to more interesting matters. When his party stopped at a school cafeteria for lunch, Wallace shook hands all the way to the feed counter. After he had settled himself at a table with his tray, a teacher came over and stood beside him for a full fifteen minutes confiding to him such pieces of news as, "Fifteen boys the other day broke into a farmhouse over yonder and tore things up pretty bad. We caught 'em and got it straightened out now. There was one colored boy with 'em." It was like a local village elder making a report to a touring tribal chief. Wallace listened, grasping a huge glass of tea with his stubby fingers and taking quick little sips, pushing food on his fork with a roll, looking up at the man only when he turned to leave, lunging to give him a fleeting pat on the back. "Well, awfully good to see you again, heunh? Tell yo folks hello for me." He managed to keep his mouth full for the duration of the meal, despite frequent pauses to turn and shake the hands of passing students. "Yes, yes, yawl in the ginnin' business, I know yo folks. You tell Charlie hello for me, heunh?" Once he turned automatically, his hand already in midair, only to discover three young Negro girls passing him with their trays, their faces serenely averted as they floated on past him. He quickly returned his attention to his plate without so much as a blink.

Toward the middle of the week the weather turned abruptly cold, and there was a flavor of woodsmoke in the November afternoons. Finally, one night, it snowed. The next morning the air was lyrically icy. Entering the little town of New Hope, Wallace's cavalcade pulled up behind a cotton gin, with a cold wind shivering puddles of melted snow beneath wagonloads of cotton, and smoke blowing through the bare pecan trees overhead. The band now looked a bit frozen and bleak in their sequins, but they were gamely whunking on for the crowd. At the edges of the gathering stood the inevitable old men, their faces and necks like those of turkeys, standing mute and alone, isolated even from each other, hands shoved deep in their coveralls, khaki shirts buttoned up all the way to their Adam's apples, their old mouse-gray felt hats yanked low over their eyes. Wallace and his bodyguards were now wearing overcoats, and Wallace spoke with his coat collar turned up against the wind. Later, down in the crowd, he would pause among the hands to dab his lips swiftly with Chapstick.

Back in his car, he put on dark glasses and lighted an oversized cigar as the party pulled away. He looked, huddling against the door, as diminutive as a dwarf; he had, indeed, something of a dwarf's quick, nimble, nervous alacrity, as well as that peculiar suggestion of danger: undersized, stumpy, brisk, he inevitably strikes one as vaguely dangerous, or at least as one secretly and suspiciously busy, in a room full of women taller than he. Yet, despite his size, he seemed in this small enclosure pent and cramped. After just coming from the crowd, where his presence dominated all the out-of-doors, his energy and urgency overwhelmed everyone riding with him now. Looking out the window, he mused, "New Hope, Alabama. Yessuh, I carried New Hope in 1962...." And he recited the voting figures from New Hope in the 1958 and 1962 races for governor. There seems to be at work inside him some swift tabulation, as if, in privacy, whenever he stopped talking to remove or to receive his cigar, there might escape from inside him, briefly, a smooth, furious clicking and jingling, like an office full of adding machines all going at once.

As the car plunged on along a country road, Wallace observed, "This is some of the prettiest land you ever saw, ain't it? You know, we just about in Tennessee up here." Wallace asked someone about a local family—"They got a farm over there in the holler, don't they?"—and as the car grew steadily warmer, he began rummaging up other names, families: "Now, Bladon's wife, her name was Lila Mann, you know. There's all those Manns. . . . And Dewey, Dewey's still around, ain't he? He had that heart attack not long ago, you know." It seemed he had converted the entire state into his personal neighborhood, that every community was as familiar and intimate to him as his own flesh. Noticing an accident at an intersection ahead of them, Wallace abruptly broke off his monologue, snapped up straight in the seat, and peered at the scene through his dark glasses, turning his head as the car carried him past it, as if he had homed in on it with radar. "You reckon they all right?" he demanded. "Duhdn't anybody look hurt, do they? Reckon we oughtta stop? Reckon they called an ambulance yet?" He was reassured that things already seemed to be well in hand, and he leaned back in the seat and reinserted his cigar in his mouth. Then, going through a small town, he noticed a Negro in a pickup truck immediately behind. He turned in the crowded seat to wave out the back window, muttering, "Hi. Hi, there, fella." The Negro's face behind the truck's windshield looked down on him with a stolid impassivity. Wallace redoubled the vigor of his waves. "He must not recognize me," he explained. His men, with some uneasiness, began talking about something else. Wallace ignored them, though, even when they tried to fetch him away from the back window with cheerful calls, "Ain't that right, guvnuh?" He kept twisting around for another flurry of waves, in deep and remote concentration now. "He don't see me, see?" he murmured, more to himself than to anyone else, his face meanwhile grimacing in faintly grotesque expressions of amiability. At last, as the car turned a corner and lost the truck, he faced front again and declared in triumph, "You see that? He saluted, just at the last minute."

Now he began reminiscing about his expeditions into the North during 1963 and 1964. "Hell, some of these places, they was breakin' glass and knockin' heads and I don't know what all." He smiled slyly. "The police up there, you know, they hate those pickets—they'd wade into them with those big nightsticks of theirs, and you could hear heads cracking all over the place. Actually, a professor, I'm tellin' you, came out and tried to let the air outta our tires. That's right. The sheriff up there kicked him straight up in the air, said, 'What the *hell* do you think you're doin'?' Yessuh. Kicked him six feet straight up in the air. One place we went to, the professors were all wearin' black armbands. Goddamn, idn't that silly? I went in this room full of professors, and every one of 'em had on a black armband. I just stood there a minute and looked around and said, 'Who died?' Yeah, I looked around. 'Somebody die around here? Hunh? Who dead? Somebody dead?' " The car filled with laughter, but Wallace remained deadpan. "Up there on them Northern campuses, they just don't seem to have any manners. I don't know what's wrong with them up there. Damn uncultured, ignorant intellectuals."

He fell to talking about his opponent, Republican James Martin, a former congressman. "He gets up there, he sounds like a senator, you know. He sounds just like a nigguh preacher or senator. He gets up there and starts out, 'Naaoww, brethrenn. Ah—' " Here, Wallace sat forward in the seat, pulled back his coat, puffed out his chest, and delivered himself of a few deep mimicking phrases, his right hand, still holding the cigar, making scooping motions like an opera singer ladling out notes. His companions were guffawing, but his face remained solemn. He did it again. "Yeah, he sounds like that. Kind of pompous, you know. Well, you can't have that insincere ring, you got to talk to the folks. Martin oughtta run for senator, he sounds so much like one. But that's the way he is. He goes to church every Sunday. I go to church too, but I always slip in the back of the pew so nobody'll notice. But Martin, do you know he'll walk slap down there to the front row every Sunday morning? That's right. He's like Strom Thurmond. They got to heckling him one time when he was speaking to a Yankee audience, and he stood up there and"—his voice sank to a deep stentorian bray—" 'Well, I'm a U-nited States senatuh, Ah don't have to take such as this,' got all huffy and walked off, you know. That just don't get it." He sank back, crossed his legs cozily, and took a few rapid chugs on his cigar as he gazed for a moment out the window at the snow. Abruptly he observed, "Look at that snow. Lots of it, ain't there? You know what ole Jim Folsom said, 'It's all them atom bums.' " Guffaws erupted around him again, but Wallace only smiled, continued gazing out the window, and kept teasing the line, a favorite habit of his. "Yeah, all them atom *bums*. Big Jim said it was all them atom *bums* goin' off everywhere causin' the funny weather. Yeah. Atom *bums*." He leaned back, smiling, comfortable, tasting the end of his cigar, still looking out the window. Then, abruptly, he said, "Yeah, I don't believe in usin' religion in my campaigns like he does." In conversation he is given to making sudden blind swerves which set off hectic mental scrambles in his listeners to reassemble, reinvoke the context to which he has already secretly, by himself, returned. One thinks, "Like *he* does. He. Oh. Oh, yes. Martin. He has picked up after Martin walks slap down to the front of the church every Sunday morning. . . ." It's as if he keeps several themes running simultaneously, because one alone would be inadequate to his energies and concentration. He is like a ringmaster reclining serenely in the middle of the rapt attention of trained animals, watching, with a kind of remote lazy relish, the furious, desperate, scurrying adjustment that breaks out around him each time he blows a different whistle. "They all the time tryin' to get me to preach a lay sermon in pulpits over the state. But I don't believe in usin' no pulpit. I mean, I don't believe in anybody gettin' up there in a pulpit unless they an ordained preacher. I mean, we all got our faults. We all weak, you know."

All the while, he was keeping an ever-vigilant eye out for Wallace stickers, frequently interrupting his monologue to murmur happily, "Lookathere, there's one." Finally he leaned forward, placing his hands together on the back of the front seat, to notify one of his aides, "We oughtta got better glue. The glue wasn't too good on our stickers this year, I seen a lot of 'em kind of hangin' off. Don't know what the matter is. 'Course, these nigguhs been tearin' a lot of 'em off at the car washes, they tell me."

As they approached the town of the next rally, the driver informed Wallace, "About twenty minutes early, Guvnuh." Wallace mumbled through his cigar, "Well, we don't want to be gettin' down there no twenty minutes early, it wouldn't look right. Just drive around town a little bit, let's look at the folks here."

When they finally began heading for the rally, Wallace, as usual, started fretting about what the size of the crowd was likely to be, inventing an exhaustive and ingenious variety of reasons why it wouldn't be large. He worried about the cold—to him, the deadliest enemy of political rallies, North or South. When someone in the car offered, "A lot of people came out here to hear you last spring in the rain," he snapped, "That don't mean anything. It was warm, a warm rain. A little summer rain on their shirtsleeves, that's all right. But folks don't like much to come out in cold like this." When the site came into view— a spot on the edge of town, along the highway—Wallace lunged forward, thrusting his head alongside that of his aide in the front seat, his forehead actually bumping the window. "Yeah, there's some folks," he declared. "I see some folks." And leaving his wetly chewed cigar in the ashtray, he scrambled out into music, excitement, extended hands.

When the last rally of the day was finished, there would emerge among the Wallace party, Lurleen excepted, a private holiday air, a festival or party exuberance, a spirit of happy release, with jubilant calls and the energetic slamming of car doors filling the dusk. Wallace would usually take aside whatever reporter happened still to be on hand and inquire one last time, his voice low and almost conspiratorial, "Well, what you think? We gonna get any votes up here?"

Among the last to leave all of Wallace's rallies were two women—a young girl, dowdily dressed, with pale skin and bad teeth and a cringing twangy voice and moist mournful woebegone eyes, and her mother, a smaller and more sprightly woman who nevertheless had the same air of besieged endurance. The two of them were entertainers of a sort. In summers, they packed their belongings into an ancient black Cadillac and journeyed down to Miami Beach, where they played a succession of dumpy little hotels, the daughter manning an organ and the mother briskly accompanying her on a set of drums. "We play "Dixie" real good and loud and clear for those Yank-kees down there," the daughter likes to declare, with the shy brave pride of a Salvation Army maid reporting on her missionary efforts with a cornet outside a corner saloon. Now free-lance members of Wallace's entourage, they peddled campaign records on the fringe of the crowd at each stop, holding samples high in the air and soundlessly waggling them to catch people's attention—having not a lot of success, since most people were facing the other way. But they showed up at each rally, that shattered expression in their eyes, smiling abjectly, with an air of having gamely and even gaily borne unspeakable suffering, which they could never for a moment be able to describe or forget, but which they would not allow to get them down, either—that embattled but plucky air which women have when left, the last functioning survivors of their family, with nothing in this world to rely on but each other. At the end of each rally, Wallace would call to them before he got into his car, as if it were the first time he had noticed they had joined him, "Mighty glad to see yawl out here with us today, heunh?"

Toward the close of the campaign, a day was spent in the state's largest city, Birmingham. It is, in Alabama, the closest thing to alien turf for Wallace, not only because of its relative sophistication, but because the Republican party is particularly robust there. "You know, I ain't really their type here," Wallace remarked, driving into town. "They got a lot of genteel folks here." But the first rallies that morning were held in a fairly congenial section of the city: the mill villages, with their close streets of little brick and frame houses ranked endlessly under pecan and chinaberry trees, where one passes 1949 Dodge coupes with rubber buzzards dangling from the rear-view mirrors or plastic figurines of Jesus set on the dashboards. At each stop that morning there were unusually large delegations of minor politicians on hand, and they collected around Wallace like a cloud of pilot fish.

Around noon, driving to a Birmingham hotel, Wallace declared as the car passed a bank, "We stopped in there for a minute this morning, and all the girls in there were for us. Real genteel girls. You could tell they was college girls, you know. You have to have a college education to work in a bank. Yeah, they were for us." He then mused, "My grandmother lives here, gonna be celebrating her ninety-ninth birthday tomorrow." Someone in the car suggested he visit her with photographers for the occasion, but he dismissed that: "It'd look like I was using her politically, to campaign with. A fella just can't use his ninety-nine-year-old grandmother. . . ." He paused. "Can he?"

At the hotel he led a charge down winding marble steps to the men's room, his cigar in his hand, and then went back upstairs, pausing only a moment to refire his cigar, to the sunny dining room, where a waitress greeted him cordially with one quick grind of the twist, which Wallace, just barely, just perceptibly under his suit coat, reciprocated. When he was seated, the waitress told him he could quit his newspaper ads, he was already too far ahead for anything to happen to him. Tickled, he grabbed her hand by the fingertips and gave it a fond little shake. "Honey, you say we don't need to run 'em anymore?" He looked at the other people at the table expectantly, in delight. "Say we don't need any more ads, hunh? Say we already got it?" He finally released her hand when she began to take the order. She recommended tapioca pudding for dessert, and Wallace inquired, "Tapioca—now what would that be like?" She told him what was in it, and he said, "Well, honey, I think I'll just have me a little bowl of banana pudding." When she left, Wallace informed the people at his table, "You know, her daughter was in an automobile accident not long ago up on the mountain. It killed her dead." Toward the end of the meal, a crony came over and sat at the table, a heavy pie-faced fellow whose name, caught fleetingly, seemed to be Jimmie Moon. Moon began telling Wallace about the recent misfortunes of a local patriarch. "Yeah, he's got cancer of the rectum, all his garbage is coming out here—" Moon demonstrated, his hands forming a large circle in the vicinity of his watch pocket. "Twelve months is gonna get him, but he don't know it yet." Wallace meditated a moment over his banana pudding. "Well, send a telegram, 'Sorry to hear you're under the weather, but glad to hear you're feeling better.' "

He then fell to chatting about the rally to be held that afternoon in the Birmingham suburb of Vestavia. "This here's gonna be a silk-stocking district. I don't really know why I'm going out there. They got one of the most elegant clubs in the United States up there on the side of that mountain, with the most beautiful view you ever saw. They call it The Club." One arm hitched over the back of his chair, his legs crossed, he dislodged a speck of food with his toothpick and chewed it ruminatively for a moment. "'Cose, I ain't no The Club type myself. These folks where we goin', they got it all, they don't want to give it to nobody. You go put a nigguh in their school, it ain't like it is with a poor workin' man over there on the other side of town—the rich folks can send their chillun to a private school. They ain't the ones gettin' run over and trampled, it's the steelworkers and metalworkers here."

With some relish he recalled the time Birmingham had been dropped from the itinerary of the touring New York Metropolitan Opera because all the local hotels refused to accommodate the integrated company. "There was some soprano couldn't stand not to stay with the nigguhs in the bunch. So I told 'em to take their fa-sal-las and re-ti-does somewhere else. We could do without 'em. Only opera anybody around here cares about anyway is the Grand Ole Opry. The folks down home in Barbour County got real upset with me when they heard the opera wasn't coming to Birmingham—they thought it was gonna be the Grand Ole Opry. There's more real culture in that anyway, than in all this European singin'. Those are real folk songs right from the earth, right from life. Those are real people in the Grand Ole Opry."

But driving to Vestavia, he continued to fret: "This here's gonna be Martin country, now. Got-rocks country—that's what ole Jim Folsom used to say. These the got-rocks folks." He sat forward once and declared, "There's a fella in a big car got a Wallace sticker. We got a few doctors with us, I guess." Sitting back again, he murmured, "I'm gonna give 'em a speech out here, anyway."

But it was listless, distracted, and vaguely pathetic. The shopping center was filled, in the gathering dusk, with women in slacks and knit sweaters holding poodles, small boys with John-John haircuts, and small girls in Winnie-the-Pooh dresses, an expensive and well-preened assembly of suburbanites who were chattering as much to each other as they were listening to Wallace's voice blaring electronically from the amplifiers on the flatbed trailer. A good many of them simply sat in their cars waiting for someone to come back from one of the stores. Wallace's monologue, his repertoire of phrases, was plainly unsuited to them. He seemed aware of it, and peculiarly deferential and eager to be friendly anyway. Referring to a recount of votes during the Maryland primary race he entered, he said, "What they did was recapitulate on us—you folks may know what that means, but I don't," and changed one of his references to "all these folks in their air-conditioned country clubs" to "some people in their air-conditioned offices, they may not understand. . . ."

The party returned to the hotel before going on to the last rally, at Roebuck, a somewhat homier section of Birmingham. Wallace, after Vestavia, was eager to be back on more familiar ground. On the way to Roebuck, Wallace suddenly demanded of a local politician in the car, "I don't spose we gonna carry Vestavia, are we?" The politician made the mistake of agreeing that things indeed did not look sunny in Vestavia, and Wallace quickly barked, "Well, you say that, but you know we didn't do too bad out there in the spring, I recall. . . ." The politician rode the rest of the way in chastened silence.

There was a huge crowd waiting in the shopping-center parking lot where the rally was scheduled. The wind was black and sharp and wicked now, and as Wallace passed through the crowd, platform-bound, there were frequent whiffs of bourbon. He was welcomed lustily. One small snugly bundled lady tugged at the sleeve of a Wallace bodyguard and told him, "Now, you take good care of that boy, you hear?" After his speech, back down in the crowd, he was heartily hugged and bussed. "God bless you, Guvnuh Wallace. . . . I believe we got the most Christian guvnuh in the United States. . . ." As they pressed about him, he chattered jubilantly, "Yawl get cold out here? Hope we didn't keep yawl too long. Watch out there, don't mash the baby. . . ." He was engulfed for a full twenty minutes. A Negro, a young schoolteacher, surfaced briefly and announced, with only the slightest flutter of his eyelashes, "I pledge to you my support," and then promptly sank back out of sight. Finally, before Wallace returned to his car, there was one last picture for a group of college students. "I hope that turns out good, heunh?" Wallace said. "Yawl want to take another one just to make sure?" Back in his car at last, he declared, after lighting up a fresh cigar, "Now, that's the way I like to end the day." Vestavia had been more than neutralized.

With the rallies of the last day, he drifted closer and closer to Barbour County, his home, so that now it seemed as if he had been circling the whole week, drawing nearer and nearer to his origins. When he arrived in Abbeville, a little town some forty miles from the Barbour County seat of Clayton, he was in another clime, warmer, mellower, easier—southeastern Alabama's flat peanut country. A large crowd was already gathered under the pecan trees on the town square. Drugstore and dime-store neons glimmered around them in the blue twilight, and in the air there was the faint smell of fresh soap. When Wallace finished his address and stepped down into the crowd, he seemed to pull the people close around him, like a bird finally folding and preening his wings. There was only one more rally left, in Clayton. By now Lurleen looked weary and strangely frightened, as if it had come to her at last that the next day she was going to be elected the governor of a state. At moments through the campaign, she had seemed almost to crumple. Wallace, after he had finished shaking hands and started back to his car, would see her sitting in the car behind his, and, his door opened and one foot already inside, he would gesture irritably to her, arching his hand as if he were flinging seed over the town at large, and mutter, so that she could not possibly have heard him, "C'mon, honey, you got to go into the stores and things, you got to *see* 'em, you got to *speak* to 'em now. . . ." And there had been brief furtive arguments. Once, at the end of a day's campaigning in central Alabama, the two of them talked for a moment while the rest of the party stood aside waiting, Wallace leaning in the door of her car and she sitting across the seat from him against the other door, listening to him with a faint frown of harried, hopeless exasperation. A light rain began falling, ending the argument, Wallace abruptly shutting her door and getting into his own car, and as the caravan pulled away, she sat with her chin still in her hand, gazing out into the dusk.

The car now carried him the final miles to Clayton. It was only seventeen miles from Clio, the village where he had grown up and to which he had returned after the war to commence his political life. Not long after that, he had moved on up to Clayton, and since then, it has served as what home he could be said to have. He huddled in the back seat against the door, as small and self-absorbed as a twelve-year-old boy, abstractedly fingering the door lever and window latch as he peered out at the night.

At last, he said, his voice low now and a little thick and hoarse, "I like to touch people. It does something good to you, to see how people like you. A lot of places, people have passed little children up to me, saying, 'Let him touch them!' " He demonstrated, raising his short arms. "There even been folks standing out there in the rain lots of places. It really makes you feel humble." For a while he was quiet again, looking out the window. As the car approached a small litter of weakly lit stores, he leaned forward. "This here's Blue Springs, where we used to go swimming all the time. It's got a natural spring comes out of the ground. Old Confederate veterans used to like to have their reunions here back during the teens and the twenties. It used to be a real popular resort community, but you can see it's pretty run down now. But we're fixin' it up with a big picnic area, gonna turn it into a place like all them other resort areas with natural springs." He said to his driver, "Jemison, reckon we could stop and take a look at it? Ain't we got a little time yet?" Jemison wheeled off the highway and charged down into a grassy area, followed by the caravan. "This here's good, you can stop," said Wallace. "Keep your lights on it, now, so I can see it." He scrambled out and walked in the glare of the car's lights toward a black shine of water ahead of him, stepping a little high in the wet grass, his bodyguards and the rest of his party trailing after him. The night was cool, hushed, sweet with dew, filled with the myriad stitch of crickets. Wallace stopped abruptly and gestured with his cigar over the vague dark expanse of water. "We used to take running jumps off the bank here when we were boys. We gonna brick all this in here, see, where there's just mud now. We got picnic and camping areas over yonder. It's gonna be a real nice park." He tromped on around the water, eager, aimless, as if trying to find some spot where he would be able to see it all and enclose its shape once more in his mind, all the while talking and flourishing his cigar, his entourage tumbling after him and the waiting headlights of the other cars flaring in the night. "Yeah," he said, "you can't see it so good now, but all this has been built on during my administration. We fixin' it up real nice." (But in daylight the recreation area has a scraped and denuded look. Ancient trees once shaded the water, but they have vanished, bulled down and replaced with scraggly knee-high seedlings spaced with arithmetic regularity around concrete tables and benches, geometrically abstract picnic shelters painted in pastels, and blacktop driveways with raw new concrete gullies. There is even, beside the swimming hole with its natural spring, a wire-fenced pool with diving boards. The place is usually absolutely deserted. A native of Blue Springs once protested to Wallace, "It just don't seem to look like it used to." Wallace assured him, "Well, now, we still got lots of work to do out there. We gonna get it back lookin' the same. You can tell all the folks out there not to worry, we gonna fix it." But he seemed to sense that something had gone grievously wrong with this project. It made him profoundly uncomfortable.)

Back on the highway to Clayton, Wallace became increasingly chatty. The car whined over a short bridge, and he said, "Sikes Creek. Ole Sikes Creek. We used to go swimming there some—fish, set out hooks, catch catfish—kill snakes. Used to go out in the river hunting moccasins that'd be hanging around in the trees." He leaned forward, close to the ear of Oscar Harper, one of his aides in the front seat. "You ever do that, Oscar? Go out looking for them moccasins hanging up in them trees?" Before Harper could answer, Wallace leaned back again and mused, "You know, I haven't seen a snake on this road this whole year, I don't believe. Used to see them all the time. Back when I was driving this road a lot by myself, I used to run over them all the time—hit 'em, and then back up over 'em, and then get out and whup 'em with a stick. But you just don't see 'em anymore. I don't know what the matter is. . . ."

The nostalgic sites were coming to him thicker and faster out of the night, surfacing for a moment in the fleeting glare of the car lights and then sucked back into the sightless dark. "That's Bonny Smith's, where we used to shell oysters. . . . And there's Ben Bell's house. He's had a Wallace for Governor sign in his yard there since 1958, said he was gonna keep that sign nailed to that tree until I was elected governor. Now, he says he's gonna keep it up there until I'm elected President. And there's that old cotton gin, and the church I used to go to."

Clio was only a brief flicker of feeble street lights outside the windows, and then the car was on the Billy Watson Highway—a skinny graveled road that Wallace had named for the old Barbour County political impresario who had been one of his original patrons. Watson, in fact, had been probably the single most important person in Wallace's life, the relation between them like that between manager and fighter. Now seventy, Watson was spending his declining diabetic years in Clayton watching with a private high amusement the progress of the protégé he had helped loose on the public. Oscar Harper—a thin, quick man with a sharp face and pale eyes and almost white hair, and a mouth always adorned with a cigar just like Wallace's—chuckled from the front seat, "Billy says not enough signs on his highway tellin' folks who it belongs to. He says he wants one at least every fifteen miles." Wallace gave a hint of a snicker. "Yeah? Well, I don't know how many votes this thing's lost for us already. You know, I got a letter the other day sayin' this road was in pretty bad shape, full of chuckholes and things. Why can't we blacktop this someday soon?" Harper replied, "Billy ain't interested in improvin' the pavement particularly. He just wants some more signs up." Wallace snickered again. "That damn Watson. He ain't satisfied I named a highway for him, he wants his name on signs all over the place. I might just take the durn thing back again, he ain't satisfied with it." After a pause Wallace inquired, "You reckon he's gonna be able to make it out tonight for the rally? He's been awful sick here lately and all. . . ." Harper said, "Hell, Billy'd have to be dead before he'd miss bein' where there was a crowd and excitement goin' on." Wallace gazed out the window for a moment and then idly observed, "Well, they got the grass cut down mighty nice along here."

Suddenly the car was slowing into the outskirts of Clayton. "This is a pretty little town," observed Wallace. "All little towns are pretty." The car eased around the square, where that night's rally was to be held, turned a corner, went a short distance down a quiet street in deep shadows, and then pulled into the back yard of an old white frame house sheltered by large and generous trees. Wallace and Lurleen had lived there before he became governor, when it was an apartment house, and they had wound up buying it as Wallace's fortunes rose; but it was still only a token and tentative settling place, occupied now by Wallace's paternal grandmother. Called Momma Mae, she was a frail little lady with soft white luminous hair like spun glass, as thin as a bamboo slat, with a sparrowlike face and small round eyes behind rimless glasses. She greeted Wallace at the screened back door with a dry brief kiss on the cheek, as he murmured, "Hi, Momma Mae, how you feelin'?" and bolted on into the house. Harper and the bodyguards drove off to eat supper somewhere else, leaving Wallace and Lurleen there.

Wallace now was hurrying from room to room, furiously smoking his cigar, looking as if he were being propelled from one quick discharge of smoke to the next, and leaving behind him a thin trail of ash. His coat still buttoned, he paused in each room only long enough for a swift embracing glance—the spacious front parlor with clay-colored rug and green draperies and an old burnt-umber velour couch, a lot of chill air hanging between the furniture and the high ceiling this autumn evening; the back bedroom, with green floral wallpaper and thickets of family photographs on dresser and chest of drawers; the small cold dining room, with an arrangement of white chrysanthemums placed in the precise middle of a table on a white doily. Here Wallace squatted on his heels to rummage through shelves below a wall cabinet. Lurleen presently entered the room and asked, "What are you digging for, George?" He mumbled, "Scrapbook I just wanted to find." She told him, "It's not there, George. I moved it with some other things up yonder to Montgomery." He continued shuffling through the shelves until she repeated, her voice higher, "George, honest, it's not *there.*"

He retreated to the pine-paneled den and watched television while waiting for supper, slouched low and deep on the sofa, his tiny heels crossed on the coffee table. Lurleen looked in, and he asked her, "How you like that Abbeville crowd, honey?" "It was all right," she said. "That was a good crowd," he informed her. Then he said, "What you gonna tell 'em tonight?" and she replied, with a touch of a smile, "I'm gonna say howdy." Wallace merely looked back at the TV—he didn't think her remark very funny.

Supper—served in the large kitchen, with its formica breakfast table and, on one of the damp yellow walls, a display of undersized plastic fruit—consisted of coffee, homemade chicken salad, pimento cheese, and more coffee. The talk around the table was of the town's Republicans, a conversation conducted mostly by the women in the shrill and slightly incredulous tones of outrage and scandal, Wallace listening to them with small sniggers. Presently a neighbor—an elderly effusive woman—walked into the kitchen without knocking and cried, "Oh, George!" Wallace now was like a small boy basking in the adoration of fond womenfolk. When he rose to leave with Lurleen, Momma Mae followed him out to the back porch, telling him, "Now, you can stay here whenever you want. That's your bedroom back there, George, that's your bathroom."

There was a huge throng at the square in front of the courthouse, with the combined country high-school bands bleating lustily. The air was warmish, with an almost springlike flush and promise of rain, but Wallace, when he pitched out of the car, asked the first people who approached him, "Yawl cold? It's not too cold, is it?" A woman came up and squeezed his hand and said softly, "How you, George?" her eyes twinkling with tears. "I sho am glad to be back home," he declared. The music, with a few stray squawks and honks, abruptly dwindled into silence, and the local Methodist minister opened the rally with a prayer: "Tonight, our Father, we thank Thee for Lurleen and George. We pray that Thou will use them. . . ." It did seem a special and beautiful night, limpid and sweet and filled with love and the tender thrill of homecoming. Wallace whispered to an aide, "Watson out here tonight?" and he was told, "No, Guv-nuh, I ain't seen him yet."

Lurleen gave her talk, her voice ringing over the hushed crowd. Waiting for her to finish, Wallace stood by his car in a small, momentarily empty circle, his head ducked, pulling thoughtfully at his jowls, hearing finally the spatter of clapping as Lurleen turned from the mike. Then, with his own hillbilly band breaking into a spry mischievous, hot-diggety-dog "Dixie," he was on.

Afterward he leaned down from the flatbed trailer, his bodyguards having to catch him by the coattails to keep him from tumbling into the surge of faces below him. "Hi, Josephine. Martha, honey, glad to see you. Listen, now, yawl be careful goin' home, heunh? Birdy, honey—Mr. Charlie, how are you? Don't yawl stay up too late, now, honey." An old lady, when he took her hand, fairly wriggled with fondness and wrinkled up her face. "Bless you heart, we need you so much!" A young mother lifted up her little girl for a handshake, a bless-ing. An old man in a corduroy coat strained up to him on his tiptoes to mutter the message he had been waiting all evening to deliver: "We got a little sumpum over yonder now to pick you up if you want—it's what we got it here for, now." When Wallace declined, the old man announced, "Well, I think I'm gonna have me a little. But I'm keepin' it for you, in case you decide later on." Wallace clung to a pretty girl's hand. "Aw, Lucille, honey, I didn't recognize you"—burst of happy laughter under him—"I got sinus trouble, you know, and it's kind of hard to see sometimes."

It was over now. Dismounting from the platform, Wallace found the youths who had traveled through the campaign distributing bumper stickers ahead of his rallies, and he told them, "Boys, we'll wind up in California someplace. . . ." He then wandered over to the Dixie Academy fried-chicken stand, a booth that had been set up on the square for the evening to raise funds for a private school in the county—a hasty assembly of raw planks now dappled with puddles of melted ice in the bleak glare of a string of light bulbs. He told the townsmen who were closing it, "I'll see all yawl in the mornin'. I'll be around with you boys tomorrow for the votin', heunh?" The square now was nearly deserted, with paper blowing in a light, damp, late night wind and a few people still lin-gering under the street lights, quietly talking. From somewhere came a high hoot of mountain laughter. Wallace made for his car, giving an unlit cigar two swift licks and then popping it into his mouth still unlit. Then he noticed, heading toward him like a pair of pale specters, the two women who had been following him all over the state in their aged black Cadillac. The girl, her damp dark eyes still stricken and full of suffering, whined to him with a brave little smile, "We done recorded a victory song." He instantly swerved to avoid them, calling to them over his shoulder, "Well, I 'preciate yawl bein' with us. Goodbye, sweetie. We'll see yawl, heunh?"

He could have spent the night there in Clayton, where he was to vote the next day, but, too energized, he decided to drive back to Montgomery. Lurleen went on ahead of him in another car. Before following her, he dropped by his brother's house, a few blocks from the square. There was a yardful of cars, and as Wallace got out, he exclaimed, not unhappily, "Godamightydamn, look at them people. I'll never get away." The den of his brother's home was paneled in the same bright yellow pine as Momma Mae's, but with the addition of a large brick fireplace. As soon as he entered, he asked, "Don't guess Watson made it out tonight, did he?" and someone answered, "Didn't see him, George."

A few members of the national press were waiting for him; they were a trifle uneasy, laughing a bit too quickly and loudly at the banter going on around them among the assembled townfolk. Cokes were served, the bottoms of the bottles wrapped in paper napkins. Wallace settled himself on a sofa with a jaunty, "Well, what yawl wanna distort tonight?" The newspeople from New York and Washington and Chicago all laughed heartily, but their eyes were quite blank. It was a short session.

After they left, Wallace was informed that Watson had "passed out" at the supper table that evening before the rally. "It was just the excitement, probably," someone said, "and he'd probably had a couple too. You know Billy." A moment later, someone phoned to say Watson had suffered an insulin shock but was coming out of it. "Well," snorted Wallace, "don't let him know we been askin' about him. He might get the idea we worryin' about him or something." But he seemed vaguely troubled.

On the way back to Montgomery, he talked for a while about Martin, the Republican candidate: "He's dead now. He's finished. He might could of been senator, but he ain't gonna be nothing now. He fixed himself, we didn't do it. People say we used to be close, me'n'him, but it wasn't like that—he tried to get close to me, but I was never close to him." He finally subsided into silence. As the car hummed on through the night on the long drive back to Montgomery, he periodically leaned forward to peer out the window at passing cars and trucks, still checking for Wallace stickers.

Mystery and Manners

1963

♦

FLANNERY O'CONNOR

We're all grotesque and I don't think the Southerner is any more grotesque than anyone else; but his social situation demands more of him than that elsewhere in this country. It requires considerable grace for two races to live together, particularly when the population is divided about 50-50 between them and when they have our particular history. It can't be done without a code of manners based on mutual charity. I remember a sentence from an essay of Marshall McLuhan's. I forget the exact words, but the gist of it was, as I recollect it, that after the Civil War, formality became a condition of survival. This doesn't seem to me any less true today. Formality preserves that individual privacy which everyone needs and, in these times, is always in danger of losing. It's particularly necessary to have in order to protect the rights of both races. When you have a code of manners based on charity, then when the charity fails—as it is going to do constantly—you've got those manners there to preserve each race from small intrusions upon the other. The uneducated Southern Negro is not the clown he's made out to be. He's a man of very elaborate manners and great formality, which he uses superbly for his own protection and to insure his own privacy. All this may not be ideal, but the Southerner has enough sense not to ask for the ideal but only for the possible, the workable. The South has survived in the past because its manners, however lopsided or inadequate they may have been, provided enough social discipline to hold us together and give us an identity. Now those old manners are obsolete, but the new manners will have to be based on what was best in the old ones—in their real basis of charity and necessity. In practice, the Southerner seldom underestimates his own capacity for evil. For the rest of the country, the race problem is settled when the Negro has his rights, but for the Southerner, whether he's white or colored, that's only the beginning. The South has to evolve a way of life in which the two races can live together with mutual forbearance. You don't form a committee to do this or pass a resolution: both races have to work it out the hard way. In parts of the South these new manners are evolving in a very satisfactory way, but good manners seldom make the papers.

The Negro Revolt Against "The Negro Leaders"

Harper's Magazine, June 1960

◆

Louis E. Lomax

For nearly a century a small "ruling class" has served as spokesman—and has planned the strategy—for all American Negroes. Now it is being overwhelmed by an upsurge of aggressive young people, who feel that the NAACP is far too conservative and slow-moving.

As Pastor Kelly Miller Smith walked to the lectern to begin his Sunday sermon, he knew his parishioners wanted and needed more than just another spiritual message. The congregation—most of them middle-class Americans, many of them university students and faculty members—sat before him waiting, tense; for Nashville, like some thirty-odd other Southern college towns, on that first Sunday in March of this year, was taut with racial tension in the wake of widespread student demonstrations against lunch-counter discrimination in department stores.

Among the worshipers in Pastor Smith's First Baptist Church were some of the eighty-five students from Fisk and from Tennessee Agricultural and Industrial University who had been arrested and charged with conspiracy to obstruct trade and commerce because they staged protests in several of Nashville's segregated eating places. Just two days before, Nashville police had invaded Mr. Smith's church—which also served as headquarters for the demonstrators—and arrested one of their number, James Lawson, Jr., a Negro senior theological student at predominantly white Vanderbilt University, on the same charge.

The adult members of the congregation were deeply troubled. They knew, as did Negroes all over America, that the spontaneous and uncorrelated student demonstrations were more than an attack on segregation: they were proof that the Negro leadership class, epitomized by the National Association for the Advancement of Colored People, was no longer the prime mover of the Negro's social revolt.

Each protest had a character of its own, tailored to the local goals it sought to achieve. Neither the advice nor the aid of recognized Negro leaders was sought until after the students had set the policy, engaged the enemy, and joined the issue. Despite the probability that the demonstrations would be met with violence, the students took direct action, something Negro leadership organizations consistently counseled against. By forcing these organizations not only to come to their aid but to do their bidding, these militant young people completely reversed the power flow within the Negro community.

"*Father forgive them,*" Mr. Smith began, "*for they know not what they do.*" And for the next half-hour, the Crucifixion of Christ carried this meaning as he spoke:

"*The students sat at the lunch counters alone to eat and, when refused service, to wait and pray. And as they sat there on that southern Mount of Olives, the Roman soldiers, garbed in the uniforms of Nashville policemen and wielding night sticks, came and led the praying children away. As they walked down the streets, through a red light, and toward Golgotha, the segregationist mob shouted jeers, pushed and shoved them, and spat in their faces, but the suffering students never said a mumbling word. Once the martyr mounts the Cross, wears the crown of thorns, and feels the pierce of the sword in his side there is no turning back.*

"*And there is no turning back for those who follow in the martyr's steps,*" the minister continued. "*All we can do is to hold fast to what we believe, suffer what we must suffer if we would win, and as we face our enemy let us say, 'Father, forgive them, for they know not what they do.'*"

The New Gospel

This new gospel of the American Negro is rooted in the theology of desegregation; its major prophets are Christ, Thoreau, Gandhi, and Martin Luther King. But its missionaries are several thousand Negro students who—like Paul, Silas, and Peter of the early Christian era—are braving incalculable dangers and employing new techniques to spread the faith. It is not an easy faith, for it names the conservative Negro leadership class as sinners along with the segregationists. Yet, this new gospel is being preached by clergymen and laymen alike wherever Negroes gather.

Negro businessman John Brooks temporarily deserted his place in a picket line around Thalhimers department store, in Richmond, to make this comment to newsmen:

"The Bible says, 'A little child shall lead them,' but it didn't say these children should have to drag us. We should willingly follow these young people's example. I am suggesting that mothers picket one day, ministers the next, doctors the next, and so on until we bring segregation to its knees."

And all over the South the Negro masses said, "Amen." So ran the litany as the once reluctant elders walked and shouted in cadence behind their off-spring. Without doubt, the students had delivered a telling blow against the centralization of Negro leadership.

The demonstrators have shifted the desegregation battle from the court-room to the market place, and have shifted the main issue to one of individual dignity, rather than civil rights. Not that civil rights are unimportant—but, as these students believe, once the dignity of the Negro individual is admitted, the debate over his right to vote, attend public schools, or hold a job for which he is qualified becomes academic.

Thus, the Negro question, as Tocqueville called it, comes full circle, back to where it started late in the seventeenth century when Christian and puritan America, supported by a good deal of spurious scholarship, downgraded the Negro from villenage (a state he shared with the entire servant class of that era) to slavery, by arguing the inferiority of the Negro as a human being—a soul to be saved, most certainly, but a being somewhat lower than the white Christian with respect to the angels. This concept endured during Reconstruc-tion in the South after the Civil War and formed the foundation upon which the complex and sometimes contradictory structure of segregation was built.

Negro leaders spent seventy-five years remodeling that structure, trying to make it more livable by removing such horrible reminders of the past as lynch-ings, denial of the ballot, restrictive covenants in housing, and inequalities of public facilities. Only after the intractable Deep South emasculated every move toward equalization did the Negro leadership class sue for school integration. Even then it was a segmented, room-by-room assault. But these student demonstrators have—in effect—put dynamite at the cornerstone of segrega-tion and lit the fuse.

This revolt, swelling under ground for the past two decades, means the end of the traditional Negro leadership class. Local organization leaders were caught flat-footed by the demonstrations; the parade had moved off without them. In a series of almost frantic moves this spring, they lunged to the front and shouted loud, but they were scarcely more than a cheering section—lead-ers no more. The students completed their bold maneuver by jabbing the lead-ership class in its most vulnerable spot: the Southern schoolteachers. Many of these, as the Norfolk *Journal and Guide* put it, "were ordered to stop the demon-strations or else!" Most Negro school administrators kept silent on the matter; a few of them, largely heads of private colleges, supported the students; while others—notably Dr. H. C. Trenholm of Alabama State College—were forced by white politicians to take action against the students. As a Negro reporter from New York, I talked with scores of Southern Negro leaders and they admitted without exception that the local leadership class was in dire difficulty.

National leadership organizations fared only slightly better. The NAACP rushed its national youth secretary, Herbert Wright, into the area to conduct "strategy and procedure" conferences for the students.* Lester Granger, the executive director of the Urban League, issued a statement saying the demonstrations were "therapeutic for those engaged in them and a solemn warning to the nation at large"—this despite the fact that, in Mr. Granger's words, "the League does not function in the area of public demonstrations."

The NAACP does not always move with such swiftness when local groups, some of them laced with NAACP members, set off independent attacks on racial abuse. The Montgomery bus boycott is a classic case in point. But the impact of these new student demonstrations was such that the NAACP was forced to support the students or face a revolt by its Southern rank and file. This does not impeach the NAACP's motives for entering the demonstrations—its motives and work have the greatest merit—but it does illustrate the reversal of the power flow within the Negro community.

"The demonstrations are not something we planned," NAACP public-relations director Henry Moon told me. "The students moved on their own. We didn't know what was going on until it happened. However, it should be kept in mind that many of the students involved are NAACP people."

The NAACP on Top

The NAACP's frank admission that it had no part in planning a demonstration against segregation that resulted in upwards of a thousand Negroes being jailed—coupled with its prompt defense of the demonstrators—marks the end of the great era of the Negro leadership class: a half-century of fiercely guarded glory, climaxed by the historic school desegregation decision of 1954, during which the NAACP by dint of sheer militancy, brains, and a strong moral cause became the undisputed commander-in-chief of the Negro's drive for equality. These demonstrations also ended a two-century-long *modus vivendi* based on the myth of the Negro leader.

The phrase "Negro leadership class" pops up, Minerva-like, in most histories and essays about the Negro. White writers generally take its validity for granted, but Negro writers, of late, when they speak analytically of the Negro leader, do so with contempt.

The myth of a Black Moses, the notion that Negroes had or needed a leader, began to take shape in the early years of the nation when a troubled America viewed the Negro as an amorphous mass undulating in the wilderness of igno-

*The NAACP was not the first organization to offer aid to the students. At the invitation of Dr. George Simkins, president of the Greensboro, North Carolina, NAACP branch, the Congress of Racial Equality (CORE) sent field workers to the scene several days before the NAACP moved into action. An unimpeachable source told me that Dr. Simkins has been severely criticized by NAACP officials for this.

rance rather than as individuals, each to be dealt with purely on merit. When the myth took on flesh, the Negro leader had the provincial outlook of the white community that fashioned him: in the pre–Civil War North, Frederick Douglass, leading his people out of slavery; in the South, the plantation preacher.

Had Emancipation meant that the Negro would become just another of the racial strains to be absorbed into the American melting pot, the myth of the Negro leader would have evaporated. But as Abraham Lincoln so clearly stated, this is precisely what Emancipation did not mean. Consequently, the myth not only continued but took on even greater significance.

There were three chief prerequisites for becoming a Negro leader: (1) approbation of the white community, (2) literacy (real or assumed), and (3) some influence over the Negro masses. Each community spawned an array of "professors," "doctors" (not medical men), "preachers," "bishops," "spokesmen" who sat down at the segregated arbitration table and conducted business in the name of the Negro masses.

These leaders received their credentials and power both from the white community and from the Negro masses, who stood humble before their white-appointed leaders. This status was heady stuff for the early-twentieth-century Negro elite, many of whom could remember the snap of the master's whip, and they began to function as a social class. As a result, three generations of educated Negroes dreamed of an equal but separate America in which white power spoke only to black power and black power spoke only to God, if even to Him.

But the Negro leadership class has produced some practical and positive results: the concept provided America with an easy way of doing business with a people it had wronged and did not understand; it provided a platform for talented Negroes—many of whom were dedicated to the interests of the masses. During the last three decades, however, Negro leadership organizations, based in the North and with a national approach to the Negro's problem, eclipsed the local leaders. The heads of these organizations assumed the general title of "Leader of Leaders."

The NAACP rose in power during the decade of the 'forties by winning a series of court victories which broke down restrictive covenants and ordered Southern states to equalize the salaries of Negro and white schoolteachers and the facilities of Negro and white public schools. Its position was further strengthened when the Urban League fell into disfavor, as far as Negroes were concerned, because of its reluctance to give aid to Negro labor unionists. Then, in 1949, two of the Negro members of the League's board of directors resigned, claiming that white real-estate operators controlled the League.

The NAACP, on the other hand, saw the sign in the sky and was more definite in its support of the Negro labor unionists. As a result, the NAACP also eclipsed A. Philip Randolph and his Pullman porters' union—the third of the "Big Three" Negro leadership organizations—and at mid-century it stood atop the heap.

But the NAACP's main ally was the upsurge of freedom that swept the world in the wake of Nazism and in the face of Communism. Far-reaching social change was in the air. It *could* happen here. Who would bring it? How? The NAACP had the center of the stage; its position was based on solid performance; Negroes—smarting under the charge that they forever fight among themselves—closed ranks around "Twenty West Fortieth Street," the New York headquarters of the NAACP.

And so a curtain was lowered between the opponents and the advocates of a broader desegregation. It was a sham curtain, to be sure, for there was no unity on either side. But for the Negro, as has been true so often in the past, the well-reasoned lie worked. Negro writers, clergymen, schoolteachers, lawyers, social workers—all who commanded a public platform—agreed without conspiring that we would not disagree in public with the NAACP. Many of us felt that the NAACP was too committed to legalism; not committed enough to direct action by local people. There was an endless parade in and out of the NAACP's national office of Negroes who felt that the desegregation fight should take on a broader base. But until the spring of 1958, four years after the school desegregation decision, not a single desegregation-minded Negro engaged in serious open debate with the NAACP. Even then, unfortunately, the debate came in terms of personalities rather than policy.

The decade of the 'fifties was an incredible era for the Negro leadership class, particularly for the NAACP. That the NAACP hung together at all is a monument to its vitality as well as to the effectiveness of its muffling curtain.

First off, by suing for school integration the NAACP immobilized the majority of the Negro leadership class. The entire structure of the Negro community was designed to function in a separate but equal America. Negro newspapers, in addition to being protest organs, were the social Bibles of Negro society. They had their "400" and a list of the year's best-dressed women. The Negro church was ofttimes more Negro than church. Negro businesses depended upon the concept of a Negro community for survival (as late as 1958 Negro businessmen in Detroit criticized the NAACP for holding its annual convention at a "white" downtown hotel, which meant that local Negro merchants failed to benefit from the gathering). The dilemma of the Negro teacher was even more agonizing. If Negroes really meant business about integration, then it was obvious that the Negro leadership class could remain leaders only by working to put themselves out of business.

The Bitterness Under the Glamor

To this one must add the internal problems of the NAACP itself. In 1948–49, Walter White, then the executive secretary of the NAACP, divorced his Negro wife and married Poppy Cannon, a white woman. This brought on an organizational crisis that might have resulted in ruin if the board of directors had not given Mr. White a year's leave of absence. Nobody expected Mr. White to return to his post and Roy Wilkins, who had been Mr. White's loyal assistant for almost twenty years, turned in an excellent performance as acting executive secretary. But the following spring Mr. White did return. Another organizational crisis was averted by making him secretary of external affairs and Mr. Wilkins secretary of internal affairs. Things remained that way until 1955, when Mr. White died. Nor was that the only separatist movement going on within the NAACP. Since 1939 the entity known to the public as the NAACP has actually been two organizations: the NAACP, headed by the late Walter White and now by Roy Wilkins, and the NAACP Legal Defense and Education Fund, headed by Thurgood Marshall.

The initial reason for the separation was to provide tax relief for contributors to the Legal Defense and Education Fund, which functions solely as a legal redress organization. The NAACP, on the other hand, maintains a lobby in Washington and so its contributors are not entitled to tax exemptions. For fifteen years, however, the two organizations maintained quarters in the same building and shared an interlocking directorate. In 1952 the Legal Defense and Education Fund moved to separate quarters and in 1955 the interlocking directorate was ended. The tax matter aside, the cleavage came about as a result of deep internal troubling, the details of which are still in the domain of "no comment." In the midst of all this, Mrs. Franklin D. Roosevelt left the NAACP board for reasons that have never been fully disclosed.

The lynching of Emmett Till in Mississippi produced yet another crisis for the Negro leadership class. Mrs. Mamie Bradley, Till's mother, became a *cause célèbre* and Negro leadership organizations became locked in a bitter struggle over just where Mrs. Bradley would speak and under whose auspices. But even before Mrs. Bradley started her speaking tour there was the famous Chicago wash-pot incident. Till's body lay in state in a Chicago funeral home: somehow—nobody, including the funeral director, knows just how—a wash pot covered with fine chicken wire was placed at the head of the bier. Thousands of Negroes filed by to see the grim remains, and as they passed they dropped money in the wash pot. How many times the pot was filled and emptied, nobody knows; nobody knows where the money went. I was among the newsmen who went to check the wash-pot story but when we got there the pot, complete with chicken wire and money, had vanished.

After the funeral, Mrs. Bradley embarked on an NAACP-sponsored speaking tour, traveling by air, with secretary. Bitter disputes about money raised during her appearances came from all sections and her tour finally petered out.

Nevertheless, these were glamorous years for successful Negroes; almost all got the title of Negro leader. Their names and faces appeared on ads endorsing soap, cigarettes, whiskeys, and ladies' personal items. Adam Clayton Powell endured in Congress, always reminding his flock that, some ten years earlier, he was the first Negro to call the late Senator Theodore Bilbo, of Mississippi, a "cesspool"; Paul Robeson called a press conference and announced that Negroes would not fight with America against Russia; Jackie Robinson took a day off from the Brooklyn Dodgers to assure the House Un-American Activities Committee that Mr. Robeson was wrong. Indeed we would fight. Joe Louis, who had dispelled doubts during the dark days of Dunkirk by proclaiming, "America will win 'cause God is on our side," made an all-expense-paid visit to a Washington, D.C., courtroom and embraced the defendant, James Hoffa, in full view of the jury, peppered with Negroes. Father Divine announced that he brought about integration, and he had a white wife to prove it!

Enter the Students

These incidents—some humorous, some tragic, but all of them significant— had a grave impact on the Negro leadership class; a less stout-hearted group would have exploded from so much internal combustion. But it was the tense drama of school integration that provided the bailing wire for a show of unity.

I was there and it was a moving and unforgettable experience to see Negro students at Clinton, Sturgis, Clay, and Little Rock dodge bricks as they raced to and from school under armed guard. It was a magnificent hour for these fortuitously elite youngsters, many of whom became international heroes. But few of us lost sight of the Negro masses in these cities. They were still called "Jim," "Mary," "Aunt Harriet," and "Uncle Job"; they had to buy clothes they were not allowed to try on; their homes were searched by police without warrants; their heads were bloodied, their jobs threatened if they dared protest. They darted in and out of drug and department stores where they dared not sit down. They were denied free access to the polls, and if they received a just day in court it was usually when all parties concerned were Negroes.

Despite the march of well-scrubbed, carefully selected Negro students into previously all-white schools, it was crystal clear that the fundamental question of the Negro's dignity as an individual had not been resolved. The glory was the NAACP's and nobody begrudged it. Yet, there was a widespread doubt that a nationally directed battle of attrition that took so long and cost so much to bring so little to so few would ever get to the heart of the issue.

There were many local heroes during the decade of the 'fifties: they all had a brief hour, were clasped to the breasts of national leadership organizations, but when their public-relations and fund-raising value slipped they fell into disuse.

Mrs. Daisy Bates, president of the Arkansas State NAACP and the undisputed moving spirit behind the integration of Little Rock's Central High School, affords an example of life behind the monolithic curtain.

The Spingarn Medal of 1958, voted annually by the NAACP to the person or persons who have contributed most to racial advancement during the previous year, was awarded to the Little Rock Nine. When the students received notice of the award and realized that it did not include Mrs. Bates—whose home had been bombed, her business destroyed—they rejected the citation. The powers-that-be at Twenty West Fortieth Street reversed themselves and Mrs. Bates was included in the award, which she and the students accepted with full smiles, amid thunderous ovations. The Negro press reported the Bates case in great detail and interpreted the incident as overt evidence of the covert pressure the NAACP had been exerting on local Negro leaders for some time.

Dr. King and Mr. Wilkins

The curtain had begun to lift; it had achieved a great good, for it had produced a façade of unity; yet it had cloaked some terrible wrongs, including the smothering of homegrown, local Negro leaders who, even then, sensed the restlessness of the masses. The Reverend Dr. Martin Luther King, Jr. was the lone successful exception, and even he came into international prominence mainly because the NAACP refused to help the Montgomery bus boycotters when they at first demanded something less than full integration.

Acting on pleas from Negroes in other Southern communities, Dr. King organized the Southern Christian Leadership Council (the organization has undergone several name changes but this is the current one) to instigate non-violent protests in Southern cities. The NAACP has a most active program all through the South and a clash between the two organizations—that is to say, Dr. King and Mr. Wilkins—seemed inevitable. To end rumors of a power struggle between them, Dr. King flew to New York and made a public show of purchasing life memberships in the NAACP for himself and his Montgomery Improvement Association. Dr. King and Mr. Wilkins then embarked on a series of infrequent private talks that may go down in history as the Negro leadership class's great and final hour.

The King-Wilkins talks of 1957–58 undoubtedly covered the issue of just who would do what and where, but central in the discussion was the common knowledge that many NAACP members were disenchanted with Wilkins' leadership. The two men came out from the talks as one, each co-sponsoring the activities of the other's organization.

Dr. King and Mr. Wilkins joined also with A. Philip Randolph to sponsor the highly successful Washington Prayer Pilgrimage of 1957, during which Dr. King emerged, to quote editor James Hicks, of the *Amsterdam News*, "as the number-one Negro leader." But the following year King and Wilkins ignored the sentiments of some five hundred Negro spokesmen, representing three hundred leadership organizations, at the Summit Meeting of Negro Leadership and gave their reluctant endorsement to the Senate's watered-down civil-rights proposal. The Negro press reacted with shock.

The criticism was even worse when, a few months later, King, Wilkins, and Randolph met with President Eisenhower to explain why Negroes were displeased with the first civil-rights bill to be passed in eighty-three years. The *Afro-American*'s Louis Lautier wrote: "Ike charmed the Negro leaders and neither of them uttered a word of criticism."

Little Rock kept the NAACP in the foreground, while a near-fatal stiletto wound at the hands of a crazed Harlem woman—and internal difficulties with his own Montgomery Association—rendered Dr. King almost inactive for some eighteen months. But this year, Dr. King moved to Atlanta and began to give the lion's share of his time to the Southern Christian Leadership Council. Mr. Wilkins was on hand and the NAACP appeared as co-sponsor when the Council launched a South-wide voting drive on behalf of the Negro masses.

In one sense it was 1958 all over again. Congress was locked in a civil-rights debate that we all knew would culminate in some kind of legislation. Both Dr. King and Mr. Wilkins were on hand backstage as liberal Congressmen planned their moves. But in another, perhaps more significant, sense the early months of this year were unlike 1958. Negroes, particularly the youth, were restless; they were tired of compromises, piecemeal legislation, and token integration which, as Martin Luther King phrased it, "is a new form of discrimination covered up with certain niceties and complexities." A small but growing segment of the Negro population had joined a Muslim faith that preaches the superiority of the black man and the imminent destruction of the white man. Then there is the matter of Africa: hardly a week passes that that awakening giant's cries for "Free DOOM" don't ring out over the radio and television into the ears of American Negroes—ashamed, as they most certainly are, that they are still oppressed. The law, particularly in the South, was against them; but for the militant young people this was the time for all good Negroes to be in jail.

Meanwhile the Negro leadership class—itself often guilty of rank, class, and color discrimination—was continuing to operate under a concept that begged the question of the dignity of the Negro individual. The literature of Negro progress is littered with such terms as "the talented tenth," "the exceptional Negro," "the new Negro," "the break-through Negro," and in recent years "the accepted" and "the assimilated Negro." Sharing the outlook of the white liberals who finance them, and sincerely so, Negro leadership organizations have focused their attention, by and large, on matters that are of interest to the talented Negro rather than the Negro masses. By so doing the Negro leadership class ignored the basic problem of human dignity in favor of themselves and their white peers—a distinction which the segregationists refused to accept. Thus an impassable void has separated the leaders of both sides for the past decade; and the ordinary Negro has been in the no man's land between.

The lunch-counter demonstrations moved to the center of the void, and menaced both principals: the recalcitrant South, by striking closer to the heart of segregation than any other widespread local movements have ever struck before; the Negro leadership class, by exposing its impotence.

The Negro leadership class, still torn by jealousy, dissension, and power struggles, rushed to the aid of the students and their mass supporters, and attempted to make complete recovery by "correlating" and "co-ordinating" the movements. But as one Southern NAACP branch president said to me, "How can I correlate something when I don't know where and when it's going to happen?"

I found that established leaders don't have the same fire in their stomachs that the students and the rallying Negro masses have. As the Southern Regional Council interim report on the demonstrations reflects, Southern leaders, Negro and white, are saying, "Before this happened we could have integrated lunch counters. Now it is almost impossible." What the report does not explain is why the lunch counters were not already integrated. This, again, is black power talking to white power about something neither fully understands.

The Genius Behind It

When I talked to the students and their mass supporters I heard them quote the *Wall Street Journal*, of all things, to show that they had hit the segregationists in the pocketbook. I also discovered that in March five Southern cities had already yielded to the demands of the demonstrators and were serving Negroes at lunch counters without incident. Eighteen other cities had interracial committees working to resolve the matter. In each case the students have made it plain that they will not accept segregation in any form.

But neither the students nor their real supporters dwelt unduly on such practical results. For them, individually and as a group, the victory came when they mustered the courage to look the segregationists in the face and say, "I'm no longer afraid!"

The genius of the demonstrations lies in their spirituality; in their ability to enlist every Negro, from the laborer to the leader, and inspire him to seek suffering as a badge of honor. By employing such valid symbols as singing, praying, reading Gandhi, quoting Thoreau, remembering Martin Luther King, preaching Christ, but most of all by suffering themselves—being hit by baseball bats, kicked, and sent to jail—the students set off an old-fashioned revival that has made integration an article of faith with the Negro masses who, like other masses, are apathetic toward voting and education.

Now the cook, the maid, the butler, and the chauffeur are on fire with the new faith. For the first time since slavery the South is facing a mass revolt against segregation. There is no total explanation for what has happened. All I know is that as I talked with the participants I realized that people were weary of the very fact of segregation. They were no longer content "to let the NAACP do it"; they wanted to get into the fight and they chose the market place, the great center of American egalitarianism, not because it had any overwhelming significance for them but because it was there—accessible and segregated. To-morrow—and they all believe there will be a tomorrow—their target will be something else.

Few of the masses who have come to the support of these students realize that in attacking segregation under the banner of idealism they are fighting a battle they refused for five years to enter in the name of legalism. But there is a twinkle in the Southern Negro's eye. One gets the feeling that he is proud, now that he has come to full stature and has struck out with one blow against both segregation and the stifling control of Negro leaders.

In all truth, the Negro masses have never been flattered by the presence of these leaders, many of whom—justifiably or not—they suspected were Judas goats. The Negro masses will name leaders and will give them power and re-sponsibility. But there will never again be another class of white-oriented lead-ers such as the one that has prevailed since 1900.

What's Left?

For the Negro masses this is the laying down of a heavy burden. As the deep South is slowly learning, it faces a race of Negro *individuals*—any of whom, acting out of deep religious faith, may at any moment choose the most avail-able evidence of segregation and stage a protest. And when he does the entire Negro community will close ranks about him.

If Negro leadership organizations accept this verdict of change gracefully they can find a continuing usefulness as a reservoir of trained personnel to aid the local Negro in pressure techniques and legal battles. Indeed, within four weeks after the lunch-counter demonstrations began, just such a pattern was established. I have investigated the mechanics of the demonstrations in twenty-six cities and in each instance I found that the students and their local supporters moved first on their own; CORE came in by invitation and provided classes in techniques of non-violence; and the NAACP provided lawyers and bondsmen for those who were arrested. If Negro leadership organizations don't accept this state of affairs, they will be replaced, as they were in Mont-gomery.

Thurgood Marshall and the NAACP Legal Defense and Education Fund have already set an excellent pattern which other leadership organizations will do well to study. As a symbol, Mr. Marshall inspires local citizens to act; when they do act, and at their request, Marshall brings the skill of his organization to their defense. Thurgood Marshall's role as the inspiring servant of the masses accounts for much of what has been accomplished to date in and for the United States—including his appearance in London as counsel to the Kenya natives.

Negro leadership organizations know what the revolt means and are about reconciled to being servants rather than catalysts—at least I think so. I cannot say the same for the Negro leadership class as a whole. My month-long investigation unearthed a good deal of foot-dragging by moneyed Negroes in high places. They are not too pleased to see young Negro students sit down at the conference table with Southern white city officials. Some Negro college presidents are set to execute strange maneuvers. I would not be surprised, for example, if some of the student demonstrators who are studying under grants from foundations suddenly find their scholarships have been canceled on recommendation from their college presidents . . . for "poor scholarship." But nobody noticed their scholarship until they sat down at a previously all-white lunch counter.

The student demonstrators have no illusions. They know the segregationists are not their only enemies. But the students told me they are not prejudiced—they are willing to stand up to their enemies, Negro and white alike.

It is not premature, then, to write this epitaph to the Negro leader while at the same time announcing the birth of the Negro individual. The christening has already begun; the funeral is yet a few days off. This is as it should be, America being committed, as it most certainly is, to orderly social transition. But there is no reason whatsoever to doubt that both events will come off on schedule.

III

The Mountaintop

◆◆◆

For a moment—a brief one, running roughly from the March on Washington on August 28, 1963, to the signing of the Voting Rights Act on August 6, 1965—the movement hit its peak. In retrospect, King's stirring sermon at the March is one of the high notes of the American Century. As James Reston (1909–1995) and Russell Baker (1925–) pointed out in the next day's *New York Times,* white Washington had been braced for the worst, and there were complications ahead as the politicians tried to figure out where to go from here. Reston was the newspaper's Washington bureau chief, and Baker had just become a columnist but was writing a feature for the front page—and he started the day in a helicopter. "There was great fear there would be rioting," Baker recalls, "so the *Times* chartered a chopper. But it was so quiet that I had the pilot go over my house and I checked out the roof. Finally I had him land at National Airport and went to the Lincoln Memorial."

The Civil Rights Act passed in 1964; the next goal was federal voting rights legislation. The bill would be passed in Washington, but the forces that produced the law met far from the capital, on a bridge in Alabama. In an excerpt from his memoirs, John Lewis (1940–   ), the young activist who had conquered a childhood stutter by preaching to chickens on his Alabama farm and whose Student Nonviolent Coordinating Committee (SNCC) had been at the forefront of the movement, recalls the 1965 Selma-to-Montgomery march, and the televised beatings he endured when white officers assaulted him and his comrades on the Pettus Bridge. The images from that attack galvanized the nation, and the Voting Rights Act was not far behind.

Walker Percy (1916–1990), physician and novelist, explains how the death of the Southern white moderate fueled the anarchy that afflicted Mississippi in the early and mid-1960s, concluding on a note of hope: "Someday a white Mississippian is going to go to New York, make the usual detour through Harlem, and see it for the foul cheerless warren that it is; and instead of making him happy as it does now, it is going to make him unhappy. Then the long paranoia, this damnable sectional insanity, will be one important step closer to being over." William Styron (1925–   ) details his discovery of Nat Turner, the leader of the slave rebellion. Willie Morris of *Harper's* had written Styron around 1964 and asked if he would do something for the magazine. Styron declined the first time, but when Morris contacted him again and asked for a piece to include in a special issue of the magazine marking the centennial of the end of the Civil War, Styron, who had been at work on *The Confessions of Nat Turner,* offered what became *This Quiet Dust.* Two years later, *Harper's* would publish a 45,000-word excerpt of Styron's novel.

As the sixties wore on, temperatures rose. Stanley Crouch (1945–   ) was working as a speechwriter for an antipoverty program in Los Angeles in 1965, the summer Watts burned. "I went up because there had been some static," Crouch says. "I wanted to check it out, and then all hell broke loose. The Malcolm X rhetoric was beginning to affect how people thought—you know, 'You can't love your enemy.' " More than 2,000 National Guardsmen were called in, and by the time it was over, there had been 3,934 arrests and 37 people were dead. Crouch recalled the scene for *Rolling Stone* years later, and the novelist and critic Elizabeth Hardwick (1916–) analyzed "Violence in the City—An End or a Beginning? A Report by the Governor's Commission on the Los Angeles Riots," when it came out the spring after the violence.

As the national riots of the mid-1960s—after Watts came Detroit, Newark, and many others—unfolded, the Black Power movement began to gather force. Arguing that the time had come for confrontation, not compromise, Stokely Carmichael wrested control of the Student Nonviolent Coordinating Committee from John Lewis. Bernard Weinraub (1938–) was a young *New York Times* reporter when *Esquire* called and asked him to do a freelance piece on Carmichael. Weinraub's profile of the Black Panther's frenetic life on the road, "The Brilliancy of Black," was one of the first major looks at this rising figure. "I think he was a bit flattered that someone from *Esquire* would want to follow him around," Weinraub recalls. "He was accustomed to news coverage, but not magazine pieces." Carmichael's rise, and the appeal of Panther-like tactics, were forcing King and his nonviolent lieutenants to the margins of the movement. Charlayne Hunter-Gault (1942–), who had integrated the University of Georgia and then moved to New York to work for *The New Yorker,* caught up with Julian Bond, one of the key strategists of the movement's glory days and by then a Georgia state representative. In a "Talk of the Town" (the editorial "we" was standard style for that section of the magazine for years), Hunter-Gault asked what Bond made of the future. "[F]or the Movement," Bond told Hunter-Gault, "lack of interest is more killing than lack of money."

David Halberstam (1934–), just back from overseas duty with *The New York Times,* sensed the same thing. As a young reporter in Mississippi and Tennessee in the fifties and very early sixties, Halberstam had covered the first civil rights days. After tours for the *Times* in Vietnam, Africa, and Eastern Europe, he came home in the spring of 1967 and soon moved to *Harper's Magazine.* The movement he saw now was different from the one he had known. For his first *Harper's* piece, Halberstam caught up with King as the minister—still improbably young—turned his attention from segregation to the poor and Vietnam. "I spent about two weeks with him," Halberstam recalls, "and it was clear that Martin was about to hit a wall. As he came North, everybody wanted something from him, and you could feel the burden he was carrying on his shoulders."

Halberstam's article was published in August 1967. Eight months later, in Memphis, James Earl Ray killed King on the balcony outside Room 306 of the Lorraine Motel. Garry Wills (1934–   ) was living in Baltimore at the time. "The minute I heard King had been shot," he says, "I got one of the last seats on the plane to Memphis." Once Wills landed, he headed for the funeral home where King had been taken; there were only three journalists—Wills, a *Detroit Free Press* reporter, and a photographer from *Life*—inside the building when the undertakers emerged with King's body. Wills had been writing regularly for *Esquire* and called the magazine's editor, Harold Hayes, the day after he got to Tennessee and asked if Hayes wanted a piece. "Absolutely," the editor replied.

"I Have a Dream . . ."

The New York Times, August 29, 1963

◆

JAMES RESTON

Abraham Lincoln, who presided in his stone temple today above the children of the slaves he emancipated, may have used just the right words to sum up the general reaction to the Negro's massive march on Washington. "I think," he wrote to Gov. Andrew G. Curtin of Pennsylvania in 1861, "the necessity of being ready increases. Look to it." Washington may not have changed a vote today, but it is a little more conscious tonight of the necessity of being ready for freedom. It may not "look to it" at once, since it is looking to so many things, but it will be a long time before it forgets the melodious and melancholy voice of the Rev. Dr. Martin Luther King Jr. crying out his dreams to the multitude.

It was Dr. King who, near the end of the day, touched the vast audience. Until then the pilgrimage was merely a great spectacle. Only those marchers from the embattled towns in the Old Confederacy had anything like the old crusading zeal. For many the day seemed an adventure, a long outing in the late summer sun—part liberation from home, part Sunday School picnic, part political convention, and part fish-fry.

But Dr. King brought them alive in the late afternoon with a peroration that was an anguished echo from all the old American reformers. Roger Williams calling for religious liberty, Sam Adams calling for political liberty, old man Thoreau denouncing coercion, William Lloyd Garrison demanding emancipation, and Eugene V. Debs crying for economic equality—Dr. King echoed them all.

"I have a dream," he cried again and again. And each time the dream was a promise out of our ancient articles of faith: phrases from the Constitution, lines from the great anthem of the nation, guarantees from the Bill of Rights, all ending with a vision that they might one day all come true.

Find Journey Worthwhile

Dr. King touched all the themes of the day, only better than anybody else. He was full of the symbolism of Lincoln and Gandhi, and the cadences of the Bible.

He was both militant and sad, and he sent the crowd away feeling that the long journey had been worthwhile.

This demonstration impressed political Washington because it combined a number of things no politician can ignore. It had the force of numbers. It had the melodies of both the church and the theater. And it was able to invoke the principles of the founding fathers to rebuke the inequalities and hypocrisies of modern American life.

There was a paradox in the day's performance. The Negro leaders demanded equality "now," while insisting that this was only the "beginning" of the struggle. Yet it was clear that the "now," which appeared on almost every placard on Constitution Avenue, was merely an opening demand, while the exhortation to increase the struggle was what was really on the leaders' minds.

The question of the day, of course, was raised by Dr. King's theme: Was this all a dream or will it help the dream come true?

No doubt this vast effort helped the Negro drive against discrimination. It was better covered by television and the press than any event here since President Kennedy's inauguration, and since indifference is almost as great a problem to the Negro as hostility, this was a plus.

None of the dreadful things Washington feared came about. The racial hooligans were scarce. Even the local Nazi, George Lincoln Rockwell, minded his manners, which is an extraordinary innovation for him. And there were fewer arrests than any normal day for Washington, probably because all the saloons and hootch peddlers were closed.

Politicians Are Impressed

The crowd obviously impressed the politicians. The presence of nearly a quarter of a million petitioners anywhere always makes a Senator think. He seldom ignores that many potential votes, and it did not escape the notice of Congressmen that these Negro organizations, some of which had almost as much trouble getting out a crowd as the Washington Senators several years ago, were now capable of organizing the largest demonstrating throng ever gathered at one spot in the District of Columbia.

It is a question whether this rally raised too many hopes among the Negroes or inspired the Negroes here to work harder for equality when they got back home. Most observers here think the latter is true, even though all the talk of "Freedom NOW" and instant integration is bound to lead to some disappointment.

The meetings between the Negro leaders on the one hand and President Kennedy and the Congressional leaders on the other also went well and probably helped the Negro cause. The Negro leaders were careful not to seem to be putting improper pressure on Congress. They made no specific requests or threats, but they argued their case in small groups and kept the crowd off Capitol Hill.

Whether this will win any new votes for the civil rights and economic legislation will probably depend on the over-all effect of the day's events on the television audience.

The Major Imponderable

This is the major imponderable of the day. The speeches were varied and spotty. Like their white political brethren, the Negroes cannot run a political meeting without letting everybody talk. Also, the platform was a bedlam of moving figures who seemed to be interested in everything except listening to the speaker. This distracted the audience.

Nevertheless, Dr. King and Roy Wilkins, head of the National Association for the Advancement of Colored People, and one or two others got the message across. James Baldwin, the author, summed up the day succinctly. The day was important in itself, he said, and "what we do with this day is even more important."

He was convinced that the country was finally grappling with the Negro problem instead of evading it; that the Negro himself was "for the first time" aware of his value as a human being and was "no longer at the mercy of what the white people imagine the Negro to be."

Merely the Beginning

On the whole, the speeches were not calculated to make Republican politicians very happy with the Negro. This may hurt, for without substantial Republican support, the Kennedy program on civil rights and jobs is not going through.

Apparently this point impressed President Kennedy, who listened to some of the speeches on television. When the Negro leaders came out of the White House, Dr. King emphasized that bipartisan support was essential for passage of the Kennedy civil rights program.

Aside from this, the advantages of the day for the Negro cause outran the disadvantages.

Above all, they got over Lincoln's point that "the necessity of being ready increases." For they left no doubt that this was not the climax of their campaign for equality but merely the beginning, that they were going to stay in the streets until they could get equality in the schools, restaurants, houses and employment agencies of the nation, and that, as they demonstrated here today, they had found an effective way to demonstrate for changes in the laws without breaking the law themselves.

Capital Is Occupied by a Gentle Army

The New York Times, August 29, 1963

◆

RUSSELL BAKER

No one could remember an invading army quite as gentle as the 200,000 civil rights marchers who occupied Washington today.

For the most part, they came silently during the night and early morning, occupied the great shaded boulevards along the Mall, and spread through the parklands between the Washington Monument and the Potomac.

But instead of the emotional horde of angry militants that many had feared, what Washington saw was a vast army of quiet, middle-class Americans who had come in the spirit of the church outing.

And instead of the tensions that had been expected, they gave this city a day of sad music, strange silences and good feeling in the streets.

It was apparent from early morning that this would be an extraordinary day. At 8 A.M. when rush-hour traffic is normally creeping bumper-to-bumper across the Virginia bridges and down the main boulevards from Maryland, the streets had the abandoned look of Sunday morning.

From a helicopter over the city, it was possible to see caravans of chartered buses streaming down New York Avenue from Baltimore and points North, but the downtown streets were empty. Nothing moved in front of the White House, nor on Pennsylvania Avenue.

A Day of Siege

For the natives, this was obviously a day of siege and the streets were being left to the marchers.

By 9:30, the number of marchers at the assembly point by the Washington Monument had reached about 40,000, but it was a crowd without fire. Mostly, people who had traveled together sat on the grass or posed for group portraits against the monument, like tourists on a rare visit to the capital.

Here and there, little groups stood in the sunlight and sang. A group of 75 young people from Danville, Va., came dressed in white sweatshirts with crudely cut black mourning bands on their sleeves.

"We're mourning injustice in Danville," explained James Bruce, a 15-year-old who said he has been arrested three times for participating in demonstrations there.

Standing together, the group sang of the freedom fight in a sad melody with words that went, "Move on, move on, move on with the freedom fight; move on, move on, we're fighting for equal rights."

Other hymns came from groups scattered over the grounds, but there was no cohesion in the crowd.

Instead, a fair grounds atmosphere prevailed. Marchers kept straggling off to ride the elevators to the top of the monument. Women sat on the grass and concentrated on feeding babies.

Among the younger members of the crowd, beards were in high vogue, "It's just that we're so busy saving the world that we don't have time to shave," Kyle Valkar, 19-year-old Washingtonian, explained.

Up on the slope near the monument's base, Peter Ottley, president of the Building Services International Union, Local 144, in New York City, was ignoring the loudspeaker and holding a press conference before about 100 of his delegates.

He thought the march would "convince the legislators that something must be done, because it is the will of the people to give equality to all."

In the background, the amplifier was presenting Joan Baez, the folk singer.

One Note of Bitterness

In one section of the ground, a group from Americus and Albany, Ga., was gathered under its own placards singing its own hymn. The placards conveyed an uncharacteristic note of bitterness.

"What is a state without justice but a robber band enlarged?" asked one. Another bore the following inscription: "Milton Wilkerson—20 stitches. Emanuel McClendon—3 stitches (Age 67). James Williams—broken leg."

Charles Macken, 15, of Albany, explained the placard in a deep Georgia accent.

"That's where the police beat these people up," he said.

Over the loudspeaker, Roosevelt Johnson was urged to come claim his lost son, Lawrence.

From the monument grounds the loudspeaker boomed an announcement that the police had estimated that 90,000 marchers were already on the scene.

At 10:56 the loudspeaker announced desperately that "we are trying to locate Miss Lena Horne," and a group from Cambridge, Md., was kneeling while the Rev. Charles M. Bowen of Bethel A.M.E. Church prayed:

"We know truly that we will—we shall—overcome—some day," he was saying.

The Cambridge group rose and began a gospel hymn and clapped and swayed. The loudspeaker was saying, "Lena—wherever you are—."

Many were simply picnicking. They had brought picnic baskets and thermos jugs and camp stools, and lunched leisurely in the soft August sunshine. Some stretched out to doze on the grass.

Singer Introduced

At 11:10 Bobby Darin, the teen-age pop singer, was being introduced over the amplifier. He was, he announced, "Here as a singer, and I'm proud and kind of choked up."

The marchers by this time, however, had had enough of the Monument grounds. Spontaneously, without advice from the platform, they began to flow away, moving toward the Lincoln Memorial, where the official program was to begin at noon.

Thousands simply began to move out into Constitution Avenue, and in a few minutes it was tens of thousands. They trooped leisurely out into the boulevard and moved happily along in a strange mood of quiet contentment.

By 11:55, much of the crowd had regrouped at the Lincoln Memorial, where the speaker's platform was set on the top step under the Lincoln statue.

This made an impressive stage for the star performers, but it was a bad theater for most of the audience, which was dispersed down the sides of the reflecting pool for a third of a mile.

Still the crowd remained in good temper, and many who could not find comfortable space in the open with a clear view up to the Memorial steps filtered back under the trees and sat down on their placards.

On the platform, Roy Wilkins, executive secretary of the National Association for the Advancement of Colored People, surveyed the sea of people and said, "I'm very satisfied. It looks like a Yankee game."

Photographers Busy

Inside, under the Lincoln statue, the photographers were deployed five deep around Burt Lancaster, Harry Belafonte and Charlton Heston. On metal chairs in the guest sections, Marlon Brando and Paul Newman were submitting to microphone interviewers.

As the crowd on the steps thickened and gradually became an impassable mass, the extraordinary politeness that characterized the day was dramatized every time an elbow was crooked.

People excused themselves for momentarily obstructing a view, excused themselves for dropping cigarette ashes on shoeshines.

When the marshals called for a clear path, hundreds hastened to fall aside
with a goodwill rarely seen in the typical urban crowd. The sweetness and patience of the crowd may have set some sort of national high-water mark in
mass decency.

The program at the Memorial began with more music. Peter, Paul and
Mary, a folk-singing trio were there "to express in song what this meeting is all
about," as Ossie Davis, the master of ceremonies, put it.

Then there was Josh White, in a gray short-sleeved sports shirt, singing
"ain't nobody gonna stop me, nobody gonna keep me, from marchin' down
freedom's road."

And the Freedom Singers from Mississippi, a hand-clapping group of hot
gospel shouters whom Mr. Davis introduced as "straight from one of the prisons of the South."

"They've been in so many, I forget which one it is," he added.

At 1:19 P.M. there was the Rev. Fred L. Shuttlesworth, president of the Alabama Christian Movement for Human Rights and a leader of the Birmingham
demonstrations.

A 1:28 P.M. Miss Baez was singing "Little baby don't you cry, you know
your mama won't die, all your trials will soon be over."

As she sang, Mayor Wagner of New York made his appearance, walking
down the Memorial steps.

Bunche Speaks

Miss Baez was followed by Dr. Ralph Bunche.

"Anyone who cannot understand the significance of your presence here
today," he said, "is blind and deaf." The crowd roared approval.

Then came Dick Gregory, the comedian.

"The last time I saw this many of us," he said, "Bull Connor was doing all
the talking." The reference was to Eugene (Bull) Connor, who was police commissioner of Birmingham during the spring demonstrations there.

To many of the marchers, the program must have begun to seem like eternity, and the great crowd slowly began dissolving from the edges. Mr. Lancaster
read a lengthy statement from 1,500 Americans in Europe. They were in favor
of the march. Mr. Belafonte read a statement endorsed by a large group of actors, writers and entertainers. They also favored the march.

Bob Dylan, a young folk singer, rendered a lugubrious mountain song
about "The day Medgar Evers was buried from a bullet that he caught." Mr.
Lancaster, Mr. Belafonte and Mr. Heston found time dragging, stood up to
stretch and chat, and set off pandemonium among the photographers. Mr.
Brando submitted to another microphone interviewer.

Speaking Begins

At 1:59 the official speaking began. For those who listened it was full of noble statement about democracy and religious sincerity, but the crowd was dissolving fast now.

These missed two of the emotional high points of the day. One was Mahalia Jackson's singing, which seemed to bounce off the Capitol far up the mall. The other was the speech of the Rev. Dr. Martin Luther King Jr., president of the Southern Christian Leadership Conference.

Long before that, however, huge portions of the crowd had drifted out of earshot. Thousands had moved back into Constitution Avenue to walk dreamily in the sun. The grass for blocks around was covered with sleepers. Here and there a man sat under a tree and sang to a guitar.

Mostly though, the "marchers" just strolled in the sunshine. Most looked contented and tired and rather pleased with what they had done.

Bloody Sunday

Walking with the Wind: A Memoir of the Movement, 1998

◆

JOHN LEWIS

I've been back to Selma many times since that fateful Sunday afternoon. Normally I'm with a large crowd, gathered for one anniversary or another of that '65 march. The town is alive with noise and excitement on such days, but the rest of the time it remains today what it was back then: a sleepy, dying little Southern community. Many of the storefronts along its downtown Broad Street are boarded up, with handwritten FOR LEASE signs taped on the windows. The businesses that are left—Rexall Drugs, the El Ranchero cafe, Walter Craig Sportsman's Headquarters ("TONS OF GUNS" is its slogan)—point more to the past than they do to the future.

The Dallas County Courthouse is still there, its steps that same pale green, though the building itself has now been painted the color of cream. Brown's Chapel, of course, still stands as well, with the same arched whitewashed ceiling inside, the same rows of folding, theater-style seats up in its U-shaped balcony.

There's a monument in front of the church, a bust of Dr. King, which, on my most recent visit there, was coated with a thin dusting of snow. The unlikely snowfall had brought out children by the dozen in the dirt yards of the Carver projects, across the street from the church. They were hooting and hollering, trying valiantly to make snowmen out of the sprinkling of powder that lay on the ground. A couple of them were having a snowball fight, hiding from one another behind the streetside markers that commemorate the history that was written here in 1965.

None of those children was alive back then, but most of them know better than any historian the details of what happened on March 7 of that year. They've heard the story so many times, from parents and grandparents, from neighbors and friends—from the people who were there.

How could anyone ever forget a day like that?

It was brisk and breezy, a few puffs of purplish clouds scattered across the clear blue sky. By the time I arrived at Brown's Chapel, about half past noon, there were already close to five hundred marchers gathered on the ballfield and basketball courts beside and beyond the church. Some of the SCLC staffers were holding impromptu training sessions, teaching the people how to kneel and protect their bodies if attacked.

Hosea and Bevel were off to the side, huddled with Andy Young, the three of them talking animatedly, as if something was wrong. And there was something wrong. Dr. King, it turned out, had decided late the day before to postpone the march until Monday. He'd missed too many preaching commitments at his church in Atlanta, he explained. He needed to deliver his sermon that weekend. The march from Selma, he decided, would have to wait a day. That was the message Andy Young had been sent to deliver.

Hosea was clearly upset. So was Bevel. The people were here, and they were ready. There was no way to turn them back home now.

This was the first I'd heard of this news. Later I would learn that there were other factors that had affected Dr. King's decision, the most serious being a death threat, of which there had been several during the previous two months. Dr. King was initially leaning toward still coming, but his staff talked him out of it.

Or so the story goes. There is still disagreement and speculation today among many people about King's decision not to march that day. There is still resentment among a lot of people, especially SNCC members, who saw this as nothing but abandonment, a cop-out.

I don't feel that way. First of all, I can't imagine anyone questioning the courage of Martin Luther King Jr. Beyond that, in terms of the specific circumstances of that Sunday, no one in SNCC was in any position to criticize Dr. King.

As far as I was concerned, they had lost the right to pass judgment of any kind on this march the moment they decided not to take part in it.

After seeing that the march could not be stopped, Andy Young went inside the church and called Dr. King in Atlanta. They talked over the situation, and King instructed Andy to choose one among them—Andy, Hosea or Bevel—to join me as co-leader of the march. The other two would remain behind to take care of things in case there was trouble.

Andy returned with that news, and the three of them proceeded to flip coins to see who would join me. The odd man would march; the other two would stay.

The odd man turned out to be Hosea, and so that little slice of history was settled—by the flip of a quarter.

It was mid-afternoon now, and time to assemble. A team of doctors and nurses from a group called the Medical Committee for Human Rights had arrived the day before on a flight from New York and set up a makeshift clinic in the small parsonage beside the church. We expected a confrontation. We knew Sheriff Clark had issued yet another call the evening before for even more deputies. Mass arrests would probably be made. There might be injuries. Most likely, we would be stopped at the edge of the city limits, arrested and maybe roughed up a little bit. We did not expect anything worse than that.

And we did *not* expect to march all the way to Montgomery. No one knew for sure, until the last minute, if the march would even take place. There had been a measure of planning, but nowhere near the preparations and logistics necessary to move that many people in an orderly manner down fifty-four miles of highway, a distance that would take about five days for a group that size to cover.

Many of the men and women gathered on that ballfield had come straight from church. They were still wearing their Sunday outfits. Some of the women had on high heels. I had on a suit and tie, a light tan raincoat, dress shoes and my backpack. I was no more ready to hike half a hundred miles than anyone else. Like everyone around me, I was basically playing it by ear. None of us had thought much further ahead than that afternoon. Anything that happened beyond that—if we were allowed to go on, if this march did indeed go all the way to Montgomery—we figured we would take care of as we went along. The main thing was that we *do* it, that we march.

It was close to 4 P.M. when Andy, Hosea, Bevel and I gathered the marchers around us. A dozen or so reporters were there as well. I read a short statement aloud for the benefit of the press, explaining why we were marching today. Then we all knelt to one knee and bowed our heads as Andy delivered a prayer.

And then we set out, nearly six hundred of us, including a white SCLC staffer named Al Lingo—the same name as the commander of Alabama's state troopers.

We walked two abreast, in a pair of lines that stretched for several blocks. Hosea and I led the way. Albert Turner, an SCLC leader in Perry County, and Bob Mants were right behind us—Bob insisted on marching because I was marching; he told me he wanted to be there to "protect" me in case something happened.

Marie Foster and Amelia Boynton were next in line, and behind them, stretching as far as I could see, walked an army of teenagers, teachers, undertakers, beauticians—many of the same Selma people who had stood for weeks, months, *years,* in front of that courthouse.

At the far end, bringing up the rear, rolled four slow-moving ambulances.

I can't count the number of marches I have participated in in my lifetime, but there was something peculiar about this one. It was more than disciplined. It was somber and subdued, almost like a funeral procession. No one was jostling or pushing to get to the front, as often happened with these things. I don't know if there was a feeling that something was going to happen, or if the people simply sensed that this was a special procession, a "leaderless" march. There were no big names up front, no celebrities. This was just plain folks moving through the streets of Selma.

There was a little bit of a crowd looking on as we set out down the red sand of Sylvan Street, through the black section of town. There was some cheering and singing from those onlookers and from a few of the marchers, but then, as we turned right along Water Street, out of the black neighborhood now, the mood changed. There was no singing, no shouting—just the sound of scuffling feet. There was something holy about it, as if we were walking down a sacred path. It reminded me of Gandhi's march to the sea. Dr. King used to say there is nothing more powerful than the rhythm of marching feet, and that was what this was, the marching feet of a determined people. That was the only sound you could hear.

Down Water Street we went, turning right and walking along the river until we reached the base of the bridge, the Edmund Pettus Bridge.

There was a small posse of armed white men there, gathered in front of the *Selma Times-Journal* building. They had hard hats on their heads and clubs in their hands. Some of them were smirking. Not one said a word. I didn't think too much of them as we walked past. I'd seen men like that so many times.

As we turned onto the bridge, we were careful to stay on the narrow sidewalk. The road had been closed to traffic, but we still stayed on the walkway, which was barely wide enough for two people.

I noticed how steep it was as we climbed toward the steel canopy at the top of the arched bridge. It was too steep to see the other side. I looked down at the river and saw how still it was, still and brown. The surface of the water was stirred just a bit by the late-afternoon breeze. I noticed my trench coat was riffling a little from that same small wind.

When we reached the crest of the bridge, I stopped dead still.

So did Hosea.

There, facing us at the bottom of the other side, stood a sea of blue-helmeted, blue-uniformed Alabama state troopers, line after line of them, dozens of battle-ready lawmen stretched from one side of U.S. Highway 80 to the other.

Behind them were several dozen more armed men—Sheriff Clark's posse—some on horseback, all wearing khaki clothing, many carrying clubs the size of baseball bats.

On one side of the road I could see a crowd of about a hundred whites, laughing and hollering, waving Confederate flags. Beyond them, at a safe distance, stood a small, silent group of black people.

I could see a crowd of newsmen and reporters gathered in the parking lot of a Pontiac dealership. And I could see a line of parked police and state trooper vehicles. I didn't know it at the time, but Clark and Lingo were in one of those cars.

It was a drop of one hundred feet from the top of that bridge to the river below. Hosea glanced down at the muddy water and said, "Can you swim?"

"No," I answered.

"Well," he said, with a tiny half smile, "neither can I.

"But," he added, lifting his head and looking straight ahead, "we might have to."

Then we moved forward. The only sounds were our footsteps on the bridge and the snorting of a horse ahead of us.

I noticed several troopers slipping gas masks over their faces as we approached.

At the bottom of the bridge, while we were still about fifty feet from the troopers, the officer in charge, a Major John Cloud, stepped forward, holding a small bullhorn up to his mouth.

Hosea and I stopped, which brought the others to a standstill.

"*This is an unlawful assembly,*" Cloud pronounced. "*Your march is not conducive to the public safety. You are ordered to disperse and go back to your church or to your homes.*"

"May we have a word with the major?" asked Hosea.

"*There is no word to be had,*" answered Cloud.

Hosea asked the same question again, and got the same response.

Then Cloud issued a warning: "*You have two minutes to turn around and go back to your church.*"

I wasn't about to turn around. We were there. We were not going to run. We couldn't turn and go back even if we wanted to. There were too many people.

We could have gone forward, marching right into the teeth of those troopers. But that would have been too aggressive, I thought, too provocative. God knew what might have happened if we had done that. These people were ready to be arrested, but I didn't want anyone to get hurt.

We couldn't go forward. We couldn't go back. There was only one option left that I could see.

"We should kneel and pray," I said to Hosea.

He nodded.

We turned and passed the word back to begin bowing down in a prayerful manner.

But that word didn't get far. It didn't have time. One minute after he had issued his warning—I know this because I was careful to check my watch—Major Cloud issued an order to his troopers.

"*Troopers*," he barked. "*Advance!*"

And then all hell broke loose.

The troopers and possemen swept forward as one, like a human wave, a blur of blue shirts and billy clubs and bullwhips. We had no chance to turn and retreat. There were six hundred people behind us, bridge railings to either side and the river below.

I remember how vivid the sounds were as the troopers rushed toward us— the clunk of the troopers' heavy boots, the whoops of rebel yells from the white onlookers, the clip-clop of horses' hooves hitting the hard asphalt of the highway, the voice of a woman shouting, "Get 'em! *Get* the niggers!"

And then they were upon us. The first of the troopers came over me, a large, husky man. Without a word, he swung his club against the left side of my head. I didn't feel any pain, just the thud of the blow, and my legs giving way. I raised an arm—a reflex motion—as I curled up in the "prayer for protection" position. And then the same trooper hit me again. And everything started to spin.

I heard something that sounded like gunshots. And then a cloud of smoke rose all around us.

Tear gas.

I'd never experienced tear gas before. This, I would learn later, was a particularly toxic form called C-4, made to induce nausea.

I began choking, coughing. I couldn't get air into my lungs. I felt as if I was taking my last breath. If there was ever a time in my life for me to panic, it should have been then. But I didn't. I remember how strangely calm I felt as I thought, This is it. People are going to die here. *I'm* going to die here.

I really felt that I saw death at that moment, that I looked it right in its face. And it felt strangely soothing. I had a feeling that it would be so easy to just lie down there, just lie down and let it take me away.

That was the way those first few seconds looked from where I stood—and lay. Here is how Roy Reed, a reporter for *The New York Times*, described what he saw:

The troopers rushed forward, their blue uniforms and white helmets blurring into a flying wedge as they moved.

The wedge moved with such force that it seemed almost to pass over the waiting column instead of through it.

The first 10 or 20 Negroes were swept to the ground screaming, arms and legs flying, and packs and bags went skittering across the grassy divider strip and on to the pavement on both sides.

Those still on their feet retreated.

The troopers continued pushing, using both the force of their bodies and the prodding of their nightsticks.

A cheer went up from the white spectators lining the south side of the highway.

The mounted possemen spurred their horses and rode at a run into the retreating mass. The Negroes cried out as they crowded together for protection, and the whites on the sidelines whooped and cheered.

The Negroes paused in their retreat for perhaps a minute, still screaming and huddling together.

Suddenly there was a report like a gunshot and a grey cloud spewed over the troopers and the Negroes.

"Tear gas!" someone yelled.

The cloud began covering the highway. Newsmen, who were confined by four troopers to a corner 100 yards away, began to lose sight of the action.

But before the cloud finally hid it all, there were several seconds of unobstructed view. Fifteen or twenty nightsticks could be seen through the gas, flailing at the heads of the marchers.

The Negroes broke and ran. Scores of them streamed across the parking lot of the Selma Tractor Company. Troopers and possemen, mounted and unmounted, went after them.

I was bleeding badly. My head was now exploding with pain. That brief, sweet sense of just wanting to lie there was gone. I needed to get up. I'd faded out for I don't know how long, but now I was tuned back in.

There was mayhem all around me. I could see a young kid—a teenaged boy—sitting on the ground with a gaping cut in his head, the blood just gushing out. Several women, including Mrs. Boynton, were lying on the pavement and the grass median. People were weeping. Some were vomiting from the tear gas. Men on horses were moving in all directions, purposely riding over the top of fallen people, bringing their animals' hooves down on shoulders, stomachs and legs.

The mob of white onlookers had joined in now, jumping cameramen and reporters. One man filming the action was knocked down and his camera was taken away. The man turned out to be an FBI agent, and the three men who attacked him were later arrested. One of them was Jimmie George Robinson, the man who had attacked Dr. King at the Hotel Albert.

I was up now and moving, back across the bridge, with troopers and posse-men and other retreating marchers all around me. At the other end of the bridge, we had to push through the possemen we'd passed outside the *Selma Times-Journal building.*

"Please, *no,*" I could hear one woman scream.

"God, we're being *killed!*" cried another.

With nightsticks and whips—one posseman had a rubber hose wrapped with barbed wire—Sheriff Clark's "deputies" chased us all the way back into the Carver project and up to the front of Brown's Chapel, where we tried get-ting as many people as we could inside the church to safety. I don't even recall how I made it that far, how I got from the bridge to the church, but I did.

A United Press International reporter gave this account of that segment of the attack:

> The troopers and possemen, under Gov. George C. Wallace's orders to stop the Ne-groes' "Walk for Freedom" from Selma to Montgomery, chased the screaming, bleeding marchers nearly a mile back to their church, clubbing them as they ran.
>
> Ambulances screamed in relays between Good Samaritan Hospital and Brown's Chapel Church, carrying hysterical men, women and children suffering head wounds and tear gas burns.

Even then, the possemen and troopers, 150 of them, including Clark him-self, kept attacking, beating anyone who remained on the street. Some of the marchers fought back now, with men and boys emerging from the Carver homes with bottles and bricks in their hands, heaving them at the troopers, then retreating for more. It was a scene that's been replayed so many times in so many places—in Belfast, in Jerusalem, in Beijing. Angry, desperate people hurling whatever they can at the symbols of authority, their hopeless fury much more powerful than the futile bottles and bricks in their hands.

I was inside the church, which was awash with sounds of groaning and weeping. And singing and crying. Mothers shouting out for their children. Children screaming for their mothers and brothers and sisters. So much confu-sion and fear and anger all erupting at the same time.

Further up Sylvan Street, the troopers chased other marchers who had fled into the First Baptist Church. A teenaged boy, struggling with the posse-men, was thrown through a church window there.

Finally Wilson Baker arrived and persuaded Clark and his men to back off to a block away, where they remained, breathing heavily and awaiting further orders.

A crowd of Selma's black men and women had collected in front of the church by now, with SNCC and SCLC staff members moving through and try-ing to keep them calm. Some men in the crowd spoke of going home to get guns. Our people tried talking them down, getting them calm. Kids and teenagers continued throwing rocks and bricks.

The parsonage next to the church looked like a MASH unit, with doctors and nurses tending to dozens of weeping, wounded people. There were cuts and bumps and bruises, and a lot of tear gas burns, which were treated by rinsing the eyes with a boric acid solution.

Relays of ambulances sent by black funeral homes carried the more seriously wounded to Good Samaritan Hospital, Selma's largest black health-care facility, run by white Catholics and staffed mostly by black doctors and nurses. One of those ambulance drivers made ten trips back and forth from the church to the hospital and to nearby Burwell Infirmary, a smaller clinic. More than ninety men and women were treated at both facilities, for injuries ranging from head gashes and fractured ribs and wrists and arms and legs to broken jaws and teeth. There was one fractured skull—mine, although I didn't know it yet.

I didn't consider leaving for the hospital, though several people tried to persuade me to go. I wanted to do what I could to help with all this chaos. I was so much in the moment, I didn't have much time to think about what had happened, nor about what was yet to come.

By nightfall, things had calmed down a bit. Hosea and I and the others had decided to call a mass meeting there in the church, and more than six hundred people, many bandaged from the wounds of that day, arrived. Clark's possemen had been ordered away, but the state troopers were still outside, keeping a vigil.

Hosea Williams spoke to the crowd first, trying to say something to calm them. Then I got up to say a few words. My head was throbbing. My hair was matted with blood clotting from an open gash. My trench coat was stained with dirt and blood.

I looked out on the room, crammed wall to wall and floor to ceiling with people. There was not a spot for one more body. I had no speech prepared. I had not had the time or opportunity to give much thought to what I would say. The words just came.

"I don't know how President Johnson can send troops to Vietnam," I said. "I don't see how he can send troops to the Congo. I don't see how he can send troops to *Africa*, and he can't send troops to Selma, Alabama."

There was clapping, and some shouts of "Yes!" and "Amen!"

"Next time we march," I continued, "we may have to keep going when we get to Montgomery. We may have to go on to *Washington*."

When those words were printed in *The New York Times* the next morning, the Justice Department announced it was sending FBI agents to Selma to investigate whether "unnecessary force was used by law officers and others." For two months we'd been facing "unnecessary force," but that apparently had not been enough. This, finally, was enough.

Now, after speaking, it was time for me to have my own injuries examined. I went next door to the parsonage, where the doctors took one look at my head and immediately sent me over to Good Samaritan. What I remember most about arriving there was the smell in the waiting room. The chairs were jammed with people from the march—victims and their families—and their clothing reeked of tear gas. The bitter, acrid smell filled the room.

The nurses and nuns were very busy. Priests roamed the room, comforting and calming people. When one of the nurses saw my head, I was immediately taken through and X-rayed. My head wound was cleaned and dressed, then I was admitted. By ten that night, exhausted and groggy from painkillers, I finally fell asleep.

It was not until the next day that I learned what else had happened that evening, that just past 9:30 P.M., ABC Television cut into its Sunday night movie—a premiere broadcast of Stanley Kramer's *Judgment at Nuremberg*, a film about Nazi racism—with a special bulletin. News anchor Frank Reynolds came onscreen to tell viewers of a brutal clash that afternoon between state troopers and black protest marchers in Selma, Alabama. They then showed fifteen minutes of film footage of the attack.

The images were stunning—scene after scene of policemen on foot and on horseback beating defenseless American citizens. Many viewers thought this was somehow part of the movie. It seemed too strange, too ugly to be real. It *couldn't* be real.

But it was. At one point in the film clip, Jim Clark's voice could be heard clearly in the background: "Get those goddamned niggers!" he yelled. "And get those goddamned *white* niggers."

The American public had already seen so much of this sort of thing, countless images of beatings and dogs and cursing and hoses. But something about that day in Selma touched a nerve deeper than anything that had come before. Maybe it was the concentrated focus of the scene, the mass movement of those troopers on foot and riders on horseback rolling into and over two long lines of stoic, silent, unarmed people. This wasn't like Birmingham, where chanting and cheering and singing preceded a wild stampede and scattering. This was a face-off in the most vivid terms between a dignified, composed, completely nonviolent multitude of silent protestors and the truly malevolent force of a heavily armed, hateful battalion of troopers. The sight of them rolling over us like human tanks was something that had never been seen before.

People just couldn't believe this was happening, not in America. Women and children being attacked by armed men on horseback—it was impossible to believe.

But it had happened. And the response from across the nation to what would go down in history as Bloody Sunday was immediate. By midnight that evening, even as I lay asleep in my room over at Good Samaritan, people from as far away as New York and Minnesota were flying into Alabama and driving to Selma, forming a vigil of their own outside Brown's Chapel. President Johnson, who had been contacted by the Justice Department almost immediately after the attack, watched the ABC footage that evening. He knew he would have to respond. Dr. King, too, was informed of what had happened as soon as the President—Andy Young called King in Atlanta, and the two agreed that now there *would* be a march. They made plans to file a request the first thing in the morning, asking for a federal injunction barring state interference in a massive Selma-to-Montgomery march.

That request arrived the next morning, Monday, in Montgomery, on the desk of Federal District Judge Frank Johnson—the same judge who had issued the injunction four years earlier providing us with safe passage out of Montgomery during the Freedom Ride.

Banner headlines, with four-column photographs—many showing the trooper clubbing me as I lay on the ground with my arm upraised—appeared that Monday morning in newspapers around the world. By midday I was receiving telegrams and cards and flowers from total strangers. A wreath arrived from an elderly woman in Southern California: "A FORMER ALABAMIAN," the card read. "WE ARE WITH YOU."

Dr. King and Ralph Abernathy came to see me. They told me what was going on outside, that people all across the country were with us, that they were going to have this march. "It's going to happen, John," Dr. King told me. "Rest assured it is going to happen."

John Doar, from the Justice Department, came to interview me about the attack, to take a deposition of sorts. The federal government was now very involved in this thing.

The hospital staff kept the press away from my room, except for a UPI photographer, who was allowed in to shoot a picture, I saw no reporters at all.

I was in a lot of pain that day. And I felt very strange lying in that bed. With all my arrests and injuries over the years, I had never actually been admitted to a hospital before. I'd been treated, but never admitted. And I did not like it. I felt very restless and a little bit frightened. Maybe it was the drugs, but I had visions of someone slipping into the room and doing something to me. I felt vulnerable, helpless.

Worst of all, though, was the sense of being cut off. I was hearing about everything secondhand, if at all. It was killing me not to know what was going on outside that hospital, because I knew there was plenty going on.

And I was right.

Several carloads, and a truckload as well, of SNCC field workers from Mississippi had rushed in that day, along with a chartered plane of staff people from Atlanta—Forman and others. All told, more than thirty SNCC people had arrived in Selma by that afternoon.

They came with a mixture of hurt and outrage and shame and guilt. They were concerned for the local people of Selma, and also for one of their own. I had been hurt, and they didn't like it. It made them mad. It got them excited, too. This was an emergency, a crisis, something to *respond* to. It was like firemen who hadn't had a fire to put out in a long time. Now everyone wanted to be the first to get to the blaze.

None of them came to see me in the hospital, except for Lafayette Surrney, whose purpose was to collect information for a press release. I really wasn't hurt about that. I guessed that they were probably very busy.

And I was right. Word came from Judge Johnson that Monday afternoon that he would not grant an injunction without a hearing, and he would not be able to hold a hearing any sooner than Thursday. That evening the SCLC and SNCC leadership—Dr. King, Andy Young and others of the SCLC; Forman, Willie Ricks and Fay Bellamy of SNCC, along with Jim Farmer, who'd come on the scene to represent CORE—argued over whether they should risk losing the judge's support by staging a march before getting his approval, or risk losing credibility and momentum by waiting patiently until he issued his injunction.

Unlike two days earlier, when he had been dead set against SNCC's participation, Forman was now pushing hard to march, and to march *now*. Hosea was with him, as was Farmer. Most of the others leaned toward accepting Judge Johnson's terms. If I had been there, I would have said we should march and let the courts do what they would—what they *should*. I wouldn't have gone as far as Forman, who was furious that this judge was telling us to wait—he called Judge Johnson's offer "legal blackmail"—but I would have said this was no time to stop and sit still.

Our SNCC people were even more fed up with the SCLC than they had been two days before. King's staff had prepared a fund-raising ad to be placed in *The New York Times*, showing a photograph of me being beaten on the bridge. That really bothered a lot of our people. The way Julian later put it to one reporter, "It was *our* chairman who was leading the march. . . . SCLC was hogging all the publicity and all the money and doing very little to deserve it. . . . We just resented SCLC's ability to capitalize on things we thought we were doing."

I understood that resentment. But again, I felt that SNCC had lost the upper hand completely, along with any right to complain, by not being part of that march. When Julian said it was "our chairman" leading the march, he was ignoring the fact that our leadership had pointedly decided the night before that I would march *not* as the chairman of SNCC but as myself. There was something wrong with trying to have it both ways now. I had played the role of a go-between up until this point, bridging my roles with both SNCC and the SCLC, but clearly that was going to be harder to do from here on out.

The final decision at that Monday night meeting was left up to Dr. King, and he decided there would be no march on Tuesday. Then he left with the others to attend a rally at Brown's Chapel. The place was packed; the atmosphere was overwhelmingly emotional, and apparently it overwhelmed Dr. King as well, who stunned everyone who had been at that meeting by announcing to the crowd that there *would* be a march the next day.

Late that night and on into the next morning, the SNCC and SCLC leaders met at the home of a local black dentist, Dr. Sullivan Jackson, to hash out the plans for the Tuesday march. State and federal authorities had issued official statements forbidding it. George Wallace actually claimed he had "saved lives" by having Lingo and Clark and their men stop us that Sunday afternoon—the counties ahead, the places we would have to pass through to get to Montgomery, said the governor, were much more dangerous than anything we faced in Selma. Those same dangers, he now claimed, were too great to allow us to march on this day.

Dr. King and the others were up until 4 A.M. trying to work out some sort of compromise with government officials in the face of a restraining order against this march issued by Judge Johnson. King spoke by phone early that morning with Attorney General Katzenbach in Washington. Then, after a few hours' sleep, King met with several federal officials, including John Doar and former Florida governor LeRoy Collins, who was now director of the Justice Department's Community Relations Service and who had been sent by President Johnson to mediate this situation. After Collins met with King that morning, he went to talk to state and local officials, including Lingo and Clark, who were once again stationed with their troops at the east end of the bridge.

No one besides Dr. King and a few of his closest staffers knew exactly what was decided by those early-morning phone calls and meetings. When a column of two thousand marchers led by Dr. King left Brown's Chapel early that afternoon, walking the same route toward the same bridge we'd tried to cross that Sunday, they all assumed they were headed for Montgomery. When they were stopped at the bridge by a U.S. marshal who read aloud Judge Johnson's order against this march, they assumed this was just a formality. And when Dr. King then led the column over the crest of the bridge to the bottom of the other side, where the armed troopers were massed once again, the marchers steeled themselves for another attack.

This time, though, the troopers stood still and simply watched as Dr. King brought the column to a halt and led the marchers in prayer. Then they sang "We Shall Overcome." And then, as the troopers moved aside to open the way east to Montgomery, Dr. King turned around and headed *back* to the church.

The marchers were shocked and confused. They had no idea what was going on. They had come to put their bodies on the line, and now they were backing down, retreating, going home. They followed Dr. King—what else could they do? But they were disappointed. Many were openly angry.

Jim Forman was absolutely livid. When he—and everyone else—learned that Dr. King had made an agreement with federal officials that morning to march only to the bridge, as a symbolic gesture, and then to turn back and await Judge Johnson's hearing later that week, he exploded, denouncing Dr. King's "trickery" and saying that this was the last straw. SNCC had had enough. There would be no more working with the SCLC. There would be no waiting for any judge's injunction. SNCC was finished with waiting, finished with Selma. It was time to do something on our own, said Forman. Within twenty-four hours he shifted our manpower and focus from Selma to the streets of Montgomery, where SNCC-led student forces from Tuskegee Institute and Alabama State University began laying siege to the state capitol with a series of demonstrations more overt and aggressive than anything seen in Selma. Taunting, provoking, clashing with mounted policemen—the SNCC protests that week in Montgomery would prove to be nothing like our nonviolent campaign in Selma.

All this news hit me like a windstorm when I was released from the hospital that Tuesday night. I was still in great pain—my head was pounding. My skull was fractured. I'd had a serious concussion. The doctors told me I needed more treatment and suggested I see some specialists up in Boston. But there was no way I was going to Boston. There was no time. I'd already lain in that hospital long enough. It was driving me crazy.

One good thing about the three days I spent in that hospital bed was that it gave me a lot of time to think, to reflect. I had every reason to be discouraged. My feelings and philosophy about the movement, about our strategies and tactics, my commitment to nonviolence, my loyalty to Dr. King were all increasingly putting me at odds with many of my SNCC colleagues. We even differed about the events of that Tuesday, about Dr. King's "double-dealing," as some of them called it. I had no problem with what Dr. King did. I thought it was in keeping with the philosophy of the movement, that there comes a time when you must retreat, and that there is nothing wrong with retreating. There is nothing wrong with coming back to fight another day. Dr. King knew—we all knew—that Judge Johnson was going to give us what we were asking for if we simply followed procedure, followed the rules.

But I was in the minority. Most of the people in SNCC were sick of procedure, sick of the rules. Some were sick of me. By all rights, I should have been despondent when I came out of that hospital, but I wasn't. Quite the opposite. I guess I've always been a person who looks at the big picture rather than focusing on little details. That's probably a curse as much as it is a blessing. But that's what I saw that Tuesday night as I emerged from that hospital—the big picture. And it looked wonderful. I was convinced now more than ever that we would prevail. The response we had gotten nationally in the wake of that Sunday attack was so much greater than anything I'd seen since I'd become a part of the movement for civil rights. It was greater than the Freedom Rides, greater than the March on Washington, greater than Mississippi Summer. The country seemed truly aroused. People were really moved. During the first forty-eight hours after Bloody Sunday, there were demonstrations in more than eighty cities protesting the brutality and urging the passage of a voting rights act. There were speeches on the floors of both houses of Congress condemning the attack and calling for voting rights legislation. A telegram signed by more than sixty congressmen was sent to President Johnson, asking for "immediate" submission of a voting rights bill.

Yes, we had serious problems with SNCC. They would have to be worked out, and I had no doubt they would be. But meanwhile, the movement had an incredible amount of momentum. When I came out of the hospital that Tuesday night, despite all the buzz among my SNCC colleagues about the "betrayal" that afternoon, I was exhilarated.

There was a rally that night at Brown's Chapel, and I was overjoyed to be there. People in the press were pushing and pushing about the "split" between SNCC and the SCLC. They asked me openly about it. I told them, no, there was no split. How could there be a split, I said, between two groups that have never pretended to be one?

"I am not going to engage in any public discussion of organizational problems," I stated. "SCLC is not the enemy. George Wallace and segregation are the enemy."

Ivanhoe Donaldson put it a different way. "Within the movement," he told one reporter, "we are a family. Arguments take place in any family."

He couldn't have put it any better. And the wisest families, he might have added, keep their arguments to themselves. Yes, we had problems among ourselves and with the SCLC, but I wasn't about to discuss them with the press.

That night, after the rally at Brown's, I went home with one of the families in the Carver project, the Wests, and slept like a baby. It was not until the next morning that I heard what had happened while I was asleep.

More than four hundred out-of-town ministers—most of them white— had taken part in the march that afternoon. After the rally that evening, three of them went and had dinner at Walker's Cafe, the diner that was such a favorite among movement people. After their meal, as they walked back toward the church, they lost their way and wound up passing through a poor white section of town. As they went by a little bar called the Silver Moon, a crowd from inside the bar came out and surrounded them. Before they knew what was happening, one of the three, a thirty-eight-year-old Unitarian minister from Boston named James J. Reeb, was clubbed in the head by a full baseball-style swing of a bat. He was so badly injured that the local emergency room staff put him in an ambulance and sent him on to Birmingham University Hospital, where he was listed Wednesday morning in critical condition with a large blood clot in his brain.

Thursday, with the Reverend Reeb's condition headlined in the newspapers, I went to Montgomery for the beginning of the federal court hearing on the SCLC request for an injunction to block state interference and allow a Selma-to-Montgomery march. Walking back into Frank Johnson's courtroom, where I'd testified four years earlier during the Freedom Ride, felt familiar in some ways, but different in one hugely important one. Four years earlier, the governor of Alabama was John Patterson. He was the figure of state authority who was squared off against the federal figure, Judge Johnson. Now the governor was George Wallace, a man whose clashes with Judge Johnson went back for years and years.

Frank Johnson and George Wallace had been classmates at the University of Alabama in the 1930s, but other than that they had next to nothing in common. While Wallace was from the same southeastern, deeply Confederate part of the state as I, Johnson grew up in north Alabama, near Tennessee, in a county that had actually sided with the Union during the Civil War. Early in his career Johnson established a reputation for fairness and reason in the face of racists. During the Montgomery bus boycott he was a member of a three-judge panel that handed down a decision in favor of desegregation. Later, he sat on another panel that struck down Alabama's poll-tax law. In 1958 he ordered the voter registration records of Barbour County to be turned over to the U.S. Civil Rights Commission. The Barbour County circuit judge who held those records refused to give them up. Only after Johnson threatened him with a contempt charge did the circuit judge relent and give up the records. That judge was George Wallace.

In the wake of that episode, Wallace famously called Johnson an "integrating, carpetbagging, scalawagging, race-mixing, bald-faced liar." Now, seven years later, the two were squaring off again, this time with Wallace sitting in the governor's mansion.

We had spent several days meeting with our lawyers—Fred Gray, Arthur Shores, Orzell Billingsley and J. L. Chestnut—preparing our case, which was to establish that our rights had been repeatedly violated during our two-month campaign in Selma, often through violent means, and that this march, as a method of demonstrating our *right* to those rights, should be allowed.

We expected the hearing to extend over several days, which it did. I testified, describing in detail my experience the Sunday of the attack on the Edmund Pettus Bridge. The FBI agents who witnessed that attack also testified. A film clip of the attack—three minutes of footage shot by Larry Pierce for CBS—was shown, and when the courtroom lights were turned back on, Judge Johnson stood silently, shook his head, straightened his robe and called for a recess. He was visibly disgusted.

On the third day of the hearing Colonel Lingo testified and indicated that the order to use force that day came straight from George Wallace. He didn't come right out and say it then, but years later, when Lingo was running for sheriff of Jefferson County, he was explicit. "I was ordered to cause the scene that the troopers made," he said. "Who ordered me? The governor! Governor George C. Wallace ordered me to stop the marchers even if we had to use force, to bring this thing to a halt. He said that we'd teach other niggers to try to march on a public highway in Alabama. He said that he was damned if he would allow such a thing to take place."

Whether Wallace actually ordered it or not, he certainly condoned the attack that took place that Sunday. And he never criticized it. In fact, even as Judge Johnson's hearing was moving into its third day, Wallace was on his way to Washington to meet with President Johnson and try to convince the President to step in and stop us from marching. That meeting wound up backfiring on Wallace. Not only did Johnson not agree to help Wallace, but he emerged from the meeting and made a stunning announcement to the reporters waiting outside:

> The events of last Sunday cannot and will not be repeated, but the demonstrations in Selma have a much larger meaning. They are a protest against a deep and very unjust flaw in American democracy itself.
>
> Ninety-five years ago our Constitution was amended to require that no American be denied the right to vote because of race or color. Almost a century later, many Americans are kept from voting simply because they are Negroes.
>
> Therefore, this Monday I will send to the Congress a request for legislation to carry out the amendment of the Constitution.

That was Saturday, March 13. The Reverend Reeb had passed away two nights earlier, prompting even more demonstrations across the country in support of our efforts in Selma. That Sunday, Forman and I flew to New York for a march in Harlem protesting the events in Alabama. Several thousand people, most of them black, a great many dressed in white Masonic uniforms, paraded, then listened as I told them what had happened and what was *going* to happen in Selma.

Meanwhile, down in Montgomery, as well as in cities across the country, SNCC-led demonstrations were heating up. There were sit-ins at the Justice Department and protests outside the White House. I heard later that President Johnson actually complained at a meeting that Sunday night that his daughter Luci couldn't study because of all the noise outside.

The next day, Monday, I was back in Montgomery for the fourth day of the hearing. It was clear now that Judge Johnson was going to give us the injunction we wanted. He asked us that day to submit a plan for the march we wanted to make. We went back that afternoon—Andy Young, Hosea Williams, Jack Greenberg, who was head of the NAACP's Legal Defense Fund, several other SCLC people and I—to the Albert Pick Motel in Montgomery and drew up details of the number of people we expected to march, the route we would follow and the number of days it would take.

Then I headed back to Selma, where a rally was held that afternoon in honor of the Reverend Reeb. More than two thousand people marched through downtown Selma to the courthouse steps, where Dr. King led a twenty-minute service, with Jim Clark's deputies looking on but doing nothing to stop it.

I was in Selma that night when I got word that there had been an outburst of violence earlier that afternoon in Montgomery, where several hundred SNCC demonstrators—mainly the Tuskegee Institute and Alabama State students organized by Forman—had clashed with police and mounted deputies who tried to stop them from demonstrating. When the police began pushing in and physically shoving the students aside, some of the students responded by throwing rocks, bricks and bottles. That brought the mounted possemen forward, swinging clubs and whips. When the students ran, the possemen chased them on horseback, actually riding up onto the porches of private homes. At least one glass door was broken by the charge of a deputy on horseback.

I was horrified to hear this. It was almost surreal. The violence seemed to be getting wilder and wilder each day. I talked to Forman early that evening on the phone and agreed that we should stage a march the next day to protest the extremity of the possemen's attack. I had the final day of Judge Johnson's hearing to attend in the morning, but I would be there for the march after that.

After talking with Forman, I settled in that night at the home of Dr. Jackson, the Selma dentist, to watch President Johnson make a live televised address to Congress. Dr. King and several SCLC staffers were also squeezed into Dr. and Mrs. Jackson's small living room. The President had invited Dr. King and me to come up to Washington that night and join the audience for his speech, but we decided the place for us to be was Selma.

And so, along with 70 million other Americans who watched the broadcast that evening, we listened to Lyndon Johnson make what many others and I consider not only the finest speech of his career, but probably the strongest speech any American president has ever made on the subject of civil rights. It began powerfully:

> At times history and fate meet at a single time in a single place to shape a turning point in man's unending search for freedom. So it was at Lexington and Concord. So it was a century ago at Appomattox. So it was last week in Selma, Alabama.

It moved toward a climax with a focus on voting rights:

> Rarely in any time does an issue lay bare the secret heart of America itself. . . . The issue of equal rights for American Negroes is such an issue. And should we defeat every enemy, and should we double our wealth and conquer the stars and still be unequal to this issue, then we will have failed as a people and as a nation.

And it peaked with the President citing our favorite freedom song, the anthem, the very heart and soul, of the civil rights movement:

> Even if we pass this bill, the battle will not be over. What happened in Selma is part of a far larger movement which reaches into every section and state of America. It is the effort of American Negroes to secure for themselves the full blessings of American life.
>
> Their cause must be our cause too. Because it is not just Negroes, but really it is all of us who must overcome the crippling legacy of bigotry and injustice.
>
> And we *shall* overcome.

All told, the speech was forty-five minutes long. It was interrupted forty times by applause, twice by standing ovations. I was deeply moved. Lyndon Johnson was no politician that night. He was a man who spoke from his heart. His were the words of a statesman and more; they were the words of a poet. Dr. King must have agreed. He wiped away a tear at the point where Johnson said the words "We shall overcome."

Predictably, not everyone was so moved. I was not surprised to hear Jim Forman attack the speech. The President's reference to our anthem was a "tinkling empty symbol," Forman told one reporter. "Johnson," he later said to another writer, "spoiled a good song that day."

We never did have time to discuss the speech, Forman and I. Events were tumbling much too swiftly. The next morning I was back in Montgomery, watching our attorneys hand Judge Johnson the plans for our march. The hearing was now over. Johnson would make his decision by the following day.

That afternoon—gray, overcast, with a steady rain drizzling down—I joined Forman, Dr. King and others at the front of a group of six hundred people marching from the state capitol to the Montgomery County Courthouse to protest the violence of the day before. To this day, photos from that day's march, showing us wearing ponchos and raincoats, are mistakenly presented as if they were taken during the march from Selma to Montgomery, which they were not. That march was yet to come.

That evening, at a rally called by SCLC officials, with Dr. King and Abernathy in the audience, along with dozens of middle-class, mainstream black ministers, Forman stunned everyone with one of the angriest, most fiery speeches made by a movement leader up to that point.

> There's only one man in the country that can stop George Wallace and those posses.
>
> These problems will not be solved until the man in that shaggedy old place called the White House begins to shake and gets on the phone and says, "Now listen, George, we're coming down there and throw you in jail if you don't stop that mess." . . .

I said it today, and I will say it again. If we can't sit at the table of democracy, we'll knock the fucking legs *off!*

The fact that he quickly caught himself and muttered the words "Excuse me" was lost on almost everyone there. This was a church. Not only were those pews filled with ministers, but there were women and children in the audience, too. They were shocked. I was not. I'd heard Forman use that kind of language many times at SNCC meetings. But I was dismayed. That was not the language of the nonviolence movement. That was not the *message* of the movement, at least not of the movement I was a part of. And that was what was most significant to me about that speech, not the fact that Forman's words were so bold and profane, but the fact that they pointed the way down a road SNCC was headed that I knew I would not be able to travel.

Even Dr. King, when he stepped to the podium after Forman was finished, had trouble restoring calm. People were visibly upset. Several had already gotten up to leave. Then, as if on some sort of cue, one of Dr. King's staffers arrived, approached the podium and had a word with King, who nodded, smiled and waved everyone quiet.

Judge Johnson, Dr. King announced, had issued his ruling. The march from Selma to Montgomery would be allowed.

The judge's written order, officially released the next morning, beautifully and succinctly summarized what we had been through in Selma, and *why* we had gone through it:

> The evidence in this case reflects that . . . an almost continuous pattern of conduct
> has existed on the part of defendant Sheriff Clark, his deputies, and his auxiliary
> deputies known as "possemen" of harassment, intimidation, coercion, threatening
> conduct, and, sometimes, brutal mistreatment toward these plaintiffs and other
> members of their class. . . .
>
> The attempted march alongside U.S. Highway 80 . . . on March 7, 1965, in
> volved nothing more than a peaceful effort on the part of Negro citizens to exercise
> a classic constitutional right: that is, the right to assemble peaceably and to petition
> one's government for the redress of grievances.
>
> . . . it seems basic to our constitutional principles that the extent of the right
> to assemble, demonstrate and march peaceably along the highways and streets in
> an orderly manner should be commensurate with the enormity of the wrongs that
> are being protested and petitioned against. In this case, the wrongs are enormous.
> The extent of the right to demonstrate against these wrongs should be determined
> accordingly.

We had told the judge the march would begin on Sunday, March 21. This was Wednesday. That gave us five days to prepare. And this time, as compared to our small, spontaneous effort on Bloody Sunday, there would *be* preparation, as

well as the full participation of SNCC, the SCLC, the NAACP, the Urban League
and every other civil and human rights organization in the United States. In
many ways, this event promised to be as big as the March on Washington. The
numbers would be nowhere near that many, of course, but unlike the demonstration in Washington, which was a rally more than an actual march, this
was literally going to be a mass *movement* of people, thousands and thousands
of them, walking down a highway, cutting through the heart of the state of
Alabama.

The next five days were a swirl of activity, much like preparing an army for
an assault. Marchers, not just from Selma but from across the nation, were mo-
bilized and organized, route sections and schedules were mapped out, printed
up and distributed, tents big enough to sleep people by the hundreds were se-
cured. Food. Security. Communications. There were thousands of details to
take care of, and thousands of dollars, most of it raised by the SCLC, to be spent.
Just a quick scan of the records from that week indicates both the enormity and
the tediousness of this undertaking:

- 700 air mattresses at $1.45 each
- 700 blankets donated by local churches and schools
- Four carnival-sized tents rented for $430 apiece
- 17,000 square feet of polyethylene for ground cloth, at a cost of $187
- 700 rain ponchos
- Two 2,500-watt generators for lighting campsites
- 2,000 feet of electrical wiring

Walkie-talkies, flashlights, pots and pans and stoves for cooking . . . the list
went on and on. And so did the manpower. A crew of twelve ministers—we
called them the "fish and loaves committee"—was responsible for transporting
food to each campsite each evening. Ten local women cooked the evening
meals in church kitchens in Selma. Ten others made sandwiches around the
clock. Squads of doctors and nurses from the same Medical Committee for
Human Rights that had provided the physicians who tended the wounded on
Bloody Sunday now geared up for a different kind of casualty, with dozens of
cases of rubbing alcohol and hundreds of boxes of Band-Aids, for the
marchers' sore muscles and blistered feet.

Meanwhile, state and federal authorities were doing their part to prepare.
The two westbound lanes of Highway 80 between Selma and Montgomery
would be closed off for the five days of the march—all traffic in both directions
would be routed onto the eastbound lanes. At the order of President Johnson,
more than 1,800 armed Alabama National Guardsmen would line the fifty-
four-mile route, along with two thousand U.S. Army troops, a hundred FBI
agents and a hundred U.S. marshals. Helicopters and light planes would patrol
the route from the air, watching for snipers or other signs of trouble, and de-

molition teams would clear the way ahead of us, inspecting bridges and bends in the road for planted explosives.

That Saturday night, the evening before the march would begin, more than two hundred people came to spend the night in Brown's Chapel. We all made short speeches—Bevel and Diane, Andy Young and I. Dick Gregory couldn't help working a little routine into his speech. "It would be just our luck," he said, looking ahead to our arrival in Montgomery, "to find out that Wallace is colored."

When we awoke Sunday morning, more than three thousand people had gathered outside the church. Dr. King greeted them with a speech intended to make the local Selmans among them comfortable with the middle-class professionals and out-of-town celebrities who had arrived to join them. We were all very sensitive about this, about keeping the focus as much as possible on the people who had brought this historic day about, the everyday men and women of Selma. We made a point to put them at the front of the march, right behind the row that led the way.

That row included Dr. King and his wife, Coretta, A. Philip Randolph, Ralph Bunche, Ralph and Juanita Abernathy, Andy Young, Hosea, me, Forman, Dick Gregory and Rabbi Abraham Heschel of the Jewish Theological Seminary of America, a biblical-looking man with a long, flowing white beard. When he walked up to join us, one onlooker shouted out, "There goes *God!*"

Someone arrived with an armful of Hawaiian leis, which were placed around each of our necks. Abernathy stepped forward and announced, "Wallace, it's all over now."

And then we stepped off, 3,200 people walking in a column that stretched a mile long.

Ahead of us rolled a television truck, its lights and cameras trained on Dr. King's every step.

Behind us walked an unimaginable cross section of American people.

There was a one-legged man on crutches—Jim Leatherer, from Saginaw, Michigan—who answered each person who thanked him for coming by thanking them in return. "I believe in you," he said over and over again. "I believe in democracy."

There was a couple from California pushing a baby in a stroller.

Assistant Attorneys General John Doar and Ramsey Clark were both there, walking among the crowd like everyone else.

Cager Lee, Jimmie Lee Jackson's elderly grandfather, who had been wounded the night Jimmie Lee was killed, was with us. It was hard for him to do even a few miles a day, but Mr. Lee was bound and determined to do them. "Just got to tramp some more," he said, nodding his head and pushing on.

Ministers, nuns, labor leaders, factory workers, schoolteachers, firemen— people from all walks of life, from all parts of the country, black and white and Asian and Native American, walked with us as we approached the same bridge where we'd been beaten two weeks before. The same troopers were there again, but this time National Guardsmen were there as well, and we passed over the river without incident, trailed by two truckloads of soldiers and a convoy of Army jeeps.

And now we were out of the city, the pebble-and-tar pavement of Highway 80 carrying us on into the countryside, through swampy marshland, past mossy Spanish oaks, rolling red clay farmland, and small, twisting creeks and rivers.

There was some jeering from occasional white onlookers gathered here and there along the shoulder of the road. Profanities from passing traffic were pretty constant. A man in a car with the words "Coonsville, USA" painted on its doors drove beside us for several days. And a private plane passed over the first day, dropping a small snowstorm of hate leaflets. But other than a couple of small incidents—one white marcher was hit in the face when he walked over to a filling station for a Coke, and bricks were thrown into a campsite one night, injuring several sleeping marchers—there was no actual violence.

We covered seven miles the first day, accompanied by the constant clicking of cameras as dozens of photographers and reporters circled us all the way. We stopped that night at a prearranged site, as spelled out in the plans we had given Judge Johnson. A man named David Hall, who worked for the Carver housing project as a maintenance manager and who owned an eighty-acre farm at the east edge of Dallas County, offered his land for us to pitch our tents that first night. The father of eight children, Mr. Hall, who was black, was asked whether he feared retaliation from the white community for doing us such a favor. "The Lord," he answered simply, "will provide."

That was basically the same answer a seventy-five-year-old woman named Rosa Steele gave when asked how she felt about letting us stay our second night on her 240-acre farm in Lowndes County. "I'm not afraid," said Mrs. Steele. "I've lived my three score and ten."

It was cold that first evening, below freezing as a matter of fact. More than two thousand of the marchers bedded down beneath three large tents. In the morning they would have to head back to Selma—Judge Johnson's order included a stipulation that we limit the number of marchers the second day to three hundred, since we'd be passing through a section of Lowndes County where the road narrowed from four to two lanes. The marchers that night made the most of their evening together. They clapped hands, built huge fires, sang and soaked in that Freedom High until they finally fell asleep.

The other thousand or so people who had walked with us that day were driven back to Selma that night in a caravan of cars and trucks. I was among them. Before allowing me to make this march at all, my doctors insisted that I sleep in a bed each evening. They did not want me spending the nights on hard ground, out in the cold. My head was still bothering me badly enough that I agreed with them. I would walk that entire fifty-four-mile route, but I spent each night back in Selma, with a doctor nearby in case something went wrong with my head.

That Monday, the second day, I rejoined the group and put on an orange vest, which we had decided each of the three hundred people chosen to march that day would wear for identification. We moved much more swiftly that day, covering sixteen miles by nightfall. Dr. King left that evening to fulfill a speaking engagement in Cleveland. He would be back two days later for the last leg of the march.

Tuesday the number of marchers swelled back to three thousand as the road widened back to four lanes and we were allowed to lift the limitation. The skies darkened early, and a torrential downpour began that lasted all day. To beat back the rain, we started a song, a little chant written by a guy named Len Chandler:

> *Pick 'em up and lay 'em down,*
> *All the way from Selma town.*

The weather was miserable, but no one complained. No one got tired. No one fell back. To me, there was never a march like this one before, and there hasn't been one since. The incredible sense of community—of *communing*—was overwhelming. We felt bonded with one another, with the people we passed, with the entire nation. The people who came out of their homes to watch as we passed by—rural people, almost all of them black, almost all of them dirt poor—waved and cheered, ran into their kitchens and brought us out food, brought us something to drink. More than a few of them put down what they were doing and joined us.

We covered eleven miles that day as well, and sixteen the next. And now we were just outside Montgomery. We were sunburned, windburned, weary, looking like the "last stragglers of a lost battalion," as one reporter described it. Our final stop was a place called the City of St. Jude, a Catholic complex of a church, a hospital and a school located two miles from Montgomery, operated through charity to serve the black community. Dr. King was there when we arrived, along with a crowd of 1,500 people that swelled by the hundreds every hour, as night fell and the scene turned into a celebration, a festival.

Dozens of celebrities arrived for a massive outdoor concert organized by—whom else?—Harry Belafonte. The entertainers included Tony Bennett, Sammy Davis Jr., Billy Eckstine, Shelley Winters, Ossie Davis, Leonard Bernstein, Nina Simone, Odetta, Johnny Mathis, Nipsey Russell, Peter, Paul and Mary, the Chad Mitchell Trio, Anthony Perkins, Elaine May, George Kirby, Joan Baez and Dick Gregory. They all performed that evening on a makeshift stage fashioned from stacks of coffins loaned by a local black funeral home. Yes, *coffins.*

It was a spectacle, a salute to Selma, with more than 20,000 people gathered under the stars for four hours of songs, speeches and sketches. At one point a reporter asked Elaine May if she thought this show and all these celebrities were turning this serious march into a circus. She snapped back, "The only real circus is the state of Alabama and George Wallace."

The next morning—a spectacularly sunny day—we went to see Governor Wallace, 50,000 of us. It was six miles from St. Jude's to the state capitol building. There had been yet another death threat made on Dr. King, and so, as a precaution, several ministers were dressed in the same blue suit he wore that day and marched beside him, to confuse any would-be snipers.

Into downtown we came, around the fountain on Court Square, where slaves had watered their owners' horses in antebellum times, up Dexter Avenue past the church where Dr. King preached when he was a minister in Montgomery and finally out onto the open square in front of the sun-drenched silver-and-white state capitol building. I could see the Alabama state flag flying high above the rotunda dome, along with the flag of the Confederacy. But the American flag was nowhere in sight. Neither was George Wallace, though we learned later that he watched the entire afternoon, peeking out through the drawn blinds of the governor's office.

A podium had been set up on the trailer of a flatbed truck, along with a microphone and loudspeakers. Peter, Paul and Mary sang. Then came the speakers: Ralph Bunche, Roy Wilkins, Jim Farmer, Whitney Young, Rosa Parks, Ralph Abernathy, Fred Shuttlesworth, Jim Bevel, Bayard Rustin and I. And then, finally, Dr. King stepped up to deliver one of the most important speeches of his life. Again, as in Washington, he rose to the occasion:

> I know some of you are asking today, "How long will it take?" I come to say to you this afternoon however difficult the moment, however frustrating the hour, it will not be long, because truth pressed to the earth will rise again.
>
> How long? Not long, because no lie can live forever.
>
> How long? Not long, because you will reap what you sow.
>
> How long? Not long, because the arm of the moral universe is long but it bends toward justice.
>
> How long? Not long, because mine eyes have seen the glory of the coming of the Lord, trampling out the vintage where the grapes of wrath are stored. He has loosed the faithful lightning of his terrible swift sword. His truth is marching on.
>
> Glory hallelujah! *Glory hallelujah!*

Four and a half months after that day, on August 6, after a long, weaving journey through both houses of Congress, the 1965 Voting Rights Act was signed into law by Lyndon Johnson during a nationally televised midday ceremony at the U.S. Capitol. Earlier that morning I was invited to meet privately with the President in the Oval Office. Jim Farmer was there, along with a military officer—a black Army major named Hugh Robinson. This was my first visit to the

White House since the March on Washington, and my first one-on-one visit with a president.

Johnson dominated the conversation, his legs propped on a chair, his hands folded back behind his head. We talked for about twenty minutes, and near the end of the meeting the President leaned forward and said, "Now John, you've got to go back and get all those folks registered. You've got to go back and get those boys by the *balls.* Just like a bull gets on top of a cow. You've got to get 'em by the balls and you've got to *squeeze*, squeeze 'em till they *hurt.*"

I'd heard that Lyndon Johnson enjoyed talking in graphic, down-home terms, but I wasn't quite prepared for all those bulls and balls.

The signing that afternoon in the President's Room of the Capitol—the same room in which Abraham Lincoln signed the Emancipation Proclamation—was a powerfully moving moment for me. This law had teeth. Among its provisions were:

- the suspension of literacy tests in twenty-six states, including Alabama, Georgia and Mississippi, which had been the focal points of so much of our work
- the appointment of federal examiners to replace local officials as voter registrars
- authorization for the attorney general to take action against state and local authorities that use the poll tax as a prerequisite to voting

"The vote," President Johnson declared that day, "is the most powerful instrument ever devised by man for breaking down injustice and destroying the terrible walls which imprison men because they are different from other men."

After signing the bill, Johnson gave pens to Dr. King, Rosa Parks and several other civil rights "leaders," including me. I still have mine today, framed on the wall of my living room in Atlanta, along with a copy of the bill itself.

That day was a culmination, a climax, the end of a very long road. In a sense it represented a high point in modern America, probably the nation's finest hour in terms of civil rights. One writer called it the "nova of the civil rights movement, a brilliant climax which brought to a close the nonviolent struggle that had reshaped the South."

It was certainly the last act for the movement as I knew it. Something was born in Selma during the course of that year, but something died there, too. The road of nonviolence had essentially run out. Selma was the last act. Even that climactic day at Montgomery, at the end of the march from Selma, was darkened a few hours after Dr. King spoke by the murder of Viola Gregg Liuzzo, a thirty-nine-year-old white housewife from Detroit who had come down as a volunteer for the march. She was driving her Oldsmobile sedan back to Montgomery that night after transporting some marchers home to Selma after the march when she was shot to death on a lonely stretch of Highway 80 in Lowndes County—a stretch of road we had triumphantly walked over just days earlier. Four Klansmen were eventually arrested, tried and, not surprisingly, found "not guilty" of Mrs. Liuzzo's murder. The same four men were later tried on civil rights charges in Judge Johnson's courtroom and were convicted and sentenced to ten years in prison, but that was little consolation to Mrs. Liuzzo's family or to the many people in the movement—especially the younger ones—who saw her death as just one more reason to give up on this notion of nonviolence.

How could I blame them? As I later explained to a writer from *The New York Times* who asked me how I felt looking back on the campaign at Selma:

> We're only flesh. I could understand people not wanting to get beaten anymore. The body gets tired. You put out so much energy and you saw such little gain. Black capacity to believe white would really open his heart, open his life to nonviolent appeal, was running out.

It had been Selma that held us together as long as we did. After that, we just came apart.

Mississippi: The Fallen Paradise

Harper's Magazine, April 1965

◆

WALKER PERCY

A little more than one hundred years ago, a Mississippi regiment dressed its ranks and started across a meadow toward Cemetery Ridge, a minor elevation near Gettysburg. There, crouched behind a stone wall, the soldiers of the Army of the Potomac waited and watched with astonishment as the gray-clads advanced as casually as if they were on parade. The Mississippians did not reach the wall. One soldier managed to plant the regimental colors within an arm's length before he fell. The University Grays, a company made up of students from the state university, suffered a loss of precisely one hundred percent of its members killed or wounded in the charge.

These were good men. It was an honorable fight and there were honorable men on both sides of it. The issue was settled once and for all, perhaps by this very charge. The honorable men on the losing side, men like General Lee, accepted the verdict.

One hundred years later, Mississippians were making history of a different sort. If their record in Lee's army is unsurpassed for valor and devotion to duty, present-day Mississippi is mainly renowned for murder, church burning, dynamiting, assassination, night-riding, not to mention the lesser forms of terrorism. The students of the university celebrated the Centennial by a different sort of warfare and in the company of a different sort of general. It is not frivolous to compare the characters of General Edwin Walker and General Lee, for the contrast is symptomatic of a broader change in leadership in this part of the South. In any event, the major claim to fame of the present-day university is the Ole Miss football team and the assault of the student body upon the person of one man, an assault of bullying, spitting, and obscenities. The bravest Mississippians in recent years have not been Confederates or the sons of Confederates but rather two Negroes, James Meredith and Medgar Evers.

As for the Confederate flag, once the battle ensign of brave men, it has come to stand for raw racism and hoodlum defiance of the law. An art professor at Ole Miss was bitterly attacked for "desecrating" the Stars and Bars when he depicted the flag as it was used in the 1962 riot—with curses and obscenities. The truth was that it had been desecrated long before.

No ex-Mississippian is entitled to write with any sense of moral superiority of the tragedy which has overtaken his former state. For he cannot be certain in the first place that if he had stayed he would not have kept silent—or worse. And he strongly suspects that he would not have been counted among the handful, an editor here, a professor there, a clergyman yonder, who not only did not keep silent but fought hard.

What happened to this state? Assuredly it faced difficult times after the Supreme Court decision of 1954 and subsequent court injunctions which required painful changes in customs of long standing. Yet the change has been made peacefully in other states of the South. In Georgia before the 1965 voting bill was passed by Congress, over thirty-nine percent of Negroes of voting age were registered to vote. In Mississippi the figure was around six percent.

What happened is both obvious and obscure. What is obvious is that Mississippi is poor, largely rural, and has in proportion the largest Negro minority in the United States. But Georgia shares these traits. Nor is it enough to say that Mississippi is the state that refused to change, although this is what one hears both inside and outside the state. On the contrary, Mississippi has changed several times since the Civil War. There have been times, for example, when dissent was not only possible but welcome. In 1882 George Washington Cable, novelist and ex-Confederate cavalryman, addressed the graduating class at the University of Mississippi:

We became distended—mired and stuffed with conservatism to the point of absolute rigidity. Our life had little or nothing to do with the onward movement of the world's thought. We were in danger of becoming a civilization that was not a civilization, because there was not in it the element of advancement.

His address was warmly received by the newspapers of the region. It is interesting to speculate how these remarks would be received today at Ole Miss, if indeed Cable would be allowed to speak at all.

Two significant changes have occurred in the past generation. The most spectacular is the total defeat of the old-style white moderate and the consequent collapse of the alliance between the "good" white man and the Negro, which has figured more or less prominently in Mississippi politics since Reconstruction days. Except for an oasis or two like Greenville, the influential white moderate is gone. To use Faulkner's personae, the Gavin Stevenses have disappeared and the Snopeses have won. What is more, the Snopeses' victory has surpassed even the gloomiest expectations of their creator. What happened to men like Gavin Stevens? With a few exceptions, they have shut up or been exiled or they are running the local White Citizens' Council. Not even Faulkner foresaw the ironic denouement of the tragedy: that the Compsons and Sartorises not only should be defeated by the Snopeses but in the end should join them.

Faulkner lived to see the defeat of his Gavin Stevens—the old-style good man, the humanist from Harvard and Heidelberg—but he still did not despair, because he had placed his best hope in the youth of the state. Chick Mallison in *Intruder in the Dust*, a sort of latter-day Huck Finn, actually got the Negro Lucas Beauchamp out of jail while Gavin Stevens was talking about the old alliance. But this hope has been blasted, too. The melancholy fact is the Chick Mallisons today are apt to be the worst lot of all. Ten years of indoctrination by the Citizens' Councils, racist politicians, and the most one-sided press north of Cuba has produced a generation of good-looking and ferocious young bigots.

The other change has been the emigration of the Negro from Mississippi, reducing the Negro majority to a minority for the first time in a hundred years. At the same time, great numbers of Negroes from the entire South were settling in Northern ghettos. The chief consequence has been the failure of the great cities of the North to deal with the Negro when he landed on their doorstep, or rather next door. Mississippi has not got any better, but New York and Boston and Los Angeles have got worse.

Meanwhile, there occurred the Negro revolution, and the battle lines changed. For the first time in a hundred and fifty years, the old sectional division has been blurred. It is no longer "North" versus "South" in the argument over the Negro. Instead, there has occurred a diffusion of the Negro and a dilution of the problem, with large sections of the South at least tolerating a degree of social change at the very time Northern cities were beginning to grumble seriously. It seems fair to describe the present national mood as a grudging inclination to redress the Negro's grievances—with the exception of a few areas of outright defiance like northern Louisiana, parts of Alabama, and the state of Mississippi.

It is only within the context of these social changes, I believe, that the state can be understood and perhaps some light shed upon a possible way out. For, unfavorable as these events may be, they are nevertheless ambiguous in their implication. The passing of the moderate and the victory of the Snopeses may be bad things in themselves. Yet, history being the queer business that it is, such a turn of events may be the very condition of the state's emergence from its long nightmare.

During the past ten years Mississippi as a society reached a condition which can only be described, in an analogous but exact sense of the word, as insane. The rift in its character between a genuine kindliness and a highly developed individual moral consciousness on the one hand and on the other a purely political and amoral view of "states' rights" at the expense of human rights led at last to a sundering of its very soul. Kind fathers and loving husbands, when they did not themselves commit crimes against the helpless, looked upon such crimes with indifference. Political campaigns, once the noblest public activity in the South, came to be conducted by incantation. The candidate who hollers "nigger" loudest and longest usually wins.

The language itself has been corrupted. In the Mississippi standard version of what happened, noble old English words are used, words like "freedom," "sacredness of the individual," "death to tyranny," but they have subtly changed their referents. After the Oxford riot in 1962, the Junior Chamber of Commerce published a brochure entitled *A Warning for Americans,* which was widely distributed and is still to be found on restaurant counters in Jackson along with the usual racist tracts, mammy dolls, and Confederate flags. The pamphlet purports to prove that James Meredith was railroaded into Ole Miss by the Kennedys in defiance of "normal judicial processes"—a remarkable thesis in itself, considering that the Meredith case received one of the most exhaustive judicial reviews in recent history. The "warning" for Americans was the usual contention that states' rights were being trampled by federal tyranny. "Tyranny is tyranny," reads the pamphlet. "It is the duty of every American to be alert when his freedom is endangered."

Lest the reader be complacent about Mississippi as the only state of doublethink, the pamphlet was judged by the *national* Jay Cees to be the "second most worthy project of the year."

All statements become equally true and equally false, depending on one's rhetorical posture. In the end, even the rhetoric fails to arouse. When Senator Eastland declares, "There is no discrimination in Mississippi," and "All who are qualified to vote, black or white, exercise the right of suffrage," these utterances are received by friend and foe alike with a certain torpor of spirit. It does not matter that there is very little connection between Senator Eastland's utterances and the voting statistics of his home county: that of a population of 31,000 Negroes, 161 are registered to vote. Once the final break is made between language and reality, arguments generate their own force and lay out their own logical rules. The current syllogism goes something like this: 1. There is no ill-feeling in Mississippi between the races; the Negroes like things the way they are; if you don't believe it, I'll call my cook out of the kitchen and you can ask her. 2. The trouble is caused by outside agitators who are Communist-inspired. 3. Therefore, the real issue is between atheistic Communism and patriotic, God-fearing Mississippians.

Once such a system cuts the outside wires and begins to rely on its own feedback, anything becomes possible. The dimensions of the tragedy are hard to exaggerate. The sad and still incredible fact is that many otherwise decent people, perhaps even the majority of the white people in Mississippi, honestly believed that President John F. Kennedy was an enemy of the United States, if not a Communist fellow traveler.

How did it happen that a proud and decent people, a Protestant and Anglo-Saxon people with a noble tradition of freedom behind them, should have in the end become so deluded that it is difficult even to discuss the issues with them, because the common words of the language no longer carry the same meanings? How can responsible leadership have failed so completely when it did not fail in Georgia, a state with a similar social and ethnic structure?

The answer is far from clear, but several reasons suggest themselves. For one thing, as James Dabbs points out in his recent book *Who Speaks for the South?*, Mississippi was part of the Wild West of the Old South. Unlike the seaboard states, it missed the liberal eighteenth century altogether. Its tradition is closer to Dodge City than to Williamsburg. For another, the Populism of the eastern South never amounted to much here; it was corrupted from the beginning by the demagogic racism of Vardaman and Bilbo. Nor did Mississippi have its big city, which might have shared, for good and ill, in the currents of American urban life. Georgia had its Atlanta and Atlanta had the good luck or good sense to put men like Ralph McGill and Mayor Hartsfield in key positions. What was lacking in Mississippi was the new source of responsible leadership, the political realists of the matured city. The old moderate tradition of the planter-lawyer-statesman class had long since lost its influence. The young industrial interests have been remarkable chiefly for their discretion. When, for example, they did awake to the folly of former Governor Barnett's two-bit rebellion, it was too late. And so there was no one to head off the collision between the civil-rights movement and the racist coalition between redneck, demagogue, and small-town merchant. The result was insurrection.

The major source of racial moderation in Mississippi even until recent times has been, not Populism, but the white conservative tradition, with its peculiar strengths and, as it turned out, its fatal weakness. There came into being after

Reconstruction an extraordinary alliance, which persisted more or less fitfully until the last world war, between the Negro and the white conservative, an alliance originally directed against the poor whites and the Radical Republicans. The fruits of this "fusion principle," as it is called, are surprising. Contrary to the current mythology of the Citizens' Councils, which depicts white Mississippians throwing out the carpetbaggers and Negroes and establishing our present "way of life" at the end of Reconstruction, the fact is that Negroes enjoyed considerably more freedom in the 1880s than they do now. A traveler in Mississippi after Reconstruction reported seeing whites and Negroes served in the same restaurants and at the same bars in Jackson.

This is not to say that there ever existed a golden age of race relations. But there were bright spots. It is true that the toleration of the Old Captains, as W. J. Cash called them, was both politically motivated and paternalistic, but it is not necessarily a derogation to say so. A man is a creature of his time—after all, Lincoln was a segregationist—and the old way produced some extraordinary men. There were many felicities in their relation with the Negro—it was not all Uncle Tomism, though it is unfashionable to say so. In any case, they lost; segregation was firmly established around 1890 and lynch law became widespread. For the next fifty years the state was dominated, with a few notable exceptions, by a corrupt Populism.

What is important to notice here is the nature of the traditional alliance between the white moderate and the Negro, and especially the ideological basis of the former's moderation, because this spirit has informed the ideal of race relations for at least a hundred years. For, whatever its virtues, the old alliance did not begin to have the resources to cope with the revolutionary currents of this century. Indeed, the world view of the old-style "good" man is almost wholly irrelevant to the present gut issue between the Negro revolt and the Snopes counterrevolution.

For one thing, the old creed was never really social or political but purely and simply moral in the Stoic sense: if you are a good man, then you will be magnanimous toward other men and especially toward the helpless and therefore especially toward the Negro. The Stoic creed worked very well—if you were magnanimous. But if one planter was just, the next might charge eighty percent interest at the plantation store, the next take the wife of his tenant, the next lease convict labor, which was better than the sharecropper system because it did not matter how hard you worked your help or how many died.

Once again, in recent years, dissent became possible. During the depression of the 1930s and afterwards there were stirrings of liberal currents not only in the enthusiasm for the economic legislation of the Roosevelt Administration but also in a new awareness of the plight of the Negro. Mississippi desperately needed the New Deal and profited enormously from it. Indeed, the Roosevelt farm program succeeded too well. Planters who were going broke on ten-cent cotton voted for Roosevelt, took federal money, got rich, lived to hate

Kennedy and Johnson and vote for Goldwater—while still taking federal money. Yet there was something new in the wind after the war. Under the leadership of men like Hodding Carter in the Delta, a new form of racial moderation began to gather strength. Frank Smith, author of the book *Congressman from Mississippi,* was elected to Congress. Described by Edward Morgan as a "breath of fresh air out of a political swamp," Smith was one of the few politicians in recent years who tried to change the old racial refrain and face up to the real problems of the state. But he made the mistake of voting for such radical measures as the Peace Corps and the United Nations appropriation, and he did not conceal his friendship with President Kennedy. What was worse, he addressed mail to his constituents with a Mr. and Mrs., even when they were Negroes. Smith was euchred out of his district by the legislature and defeated in 1962 by the usual coalition of peckerwoods, super-patriots, and the Citizens' Councils.

But the most radical change has occurred in the past few years. As recently as fifteen years ago, the confrontation was still a three-cornered one, among the good white man, the bad white man, and the Negro. The issue was whether to treat the Negro well or badly. It went without saying that you could do either. Now one of the parties has been eliminated and the confrontation is face to face. "I assert my right to vote and to raise my family decently," the Negro is beginning to say. His enemies reply with equal simplicity: "We'll kill you first."

Yet the victory of the Snopeses is not altogether a bad thing. At least the choice is clarified. It would not help much now to have Gavin Stevens around with his talk about "man's struggle to the stars."

The old way is still seductive, however, and evokes responses from strange quarters. Ex-Governor Ross Barnett was recently revealed as a mellow emeritus statesman in the old style, even hearkening to the antique summons of noblesse oblige. A newspaper interview reported that the governor was a soft touch for any Negro who waylaid him in the corridor with a "Cap'n, I could sho use a dollar." The governor, it was also reported, liked to go hunting with a Negro friend. "We laugh and joke," the governor reminisced, "and he gets a big kick out of it when I call him Professor. There's a lot in our relationship I can't explain." No doubt, mused the interviewer, the governor would get up at all hours of the night to get Ol' Jim out of jail. It is hard to imagine what Gavin Stevens would make of this new version of the old alliance. Unquestionably, something new has been added. When Marse Ross dons the mantle of Marse Robert, Southern history has entered upon a new age. And perhaps it is just as well. Let Governor Barnett become the new squire. It simplifies matters further.

Though Faulkner liked to use such words as "cursed" and "doomed" in speaking of his region, it is questionable that Mississippians are very different from other Americans. It is increasingly less certain that Minnesotans would have performed better under the circumstances. There is, however, one peculiar social dimension wherein the state does truly differ. It has to do with the distribution, as Mississippians see it, of what is public and what is private. More precisely, it is the absence of a truly public zone, as the word is understood in most places. One has to live in Mississippi to appreciate it. No doubt, it is the mark of an almost homogeneous white population, a Protestant Anglo-Saxon minority (until recently), sharing a common tragic past and bound together by kinship bonds. This society was not only felicitous in many ways; it also commanded the allegiance of Southern intellectuals on other grounds. Faulkner saw it as the chief bulwark against the "coastal spew of Europe" and "the rootless ephemeral cities of the North." In any case, the almost familial ambit of this society came to coincide with the actual public space which it inhabited. The Negro was either excluded, shoved off into Happy Hollow, or admitted to the society on its own terms as good old Uncle Ned. No allowance was made—it would have been surprising if there had been—for a truly public sector, unlovely as you please and defused of emotional charges, where black and white might pass without troubling each other. The whole of the Delta, indeed of white Mississippi, is one big kinship lodge. You have only to walk into a restaurant or a bus station to catch a whiff of it. There is a sudden kindling of amiability, even between strangers. The salutations, "What you say now?" and "Y'all be good," are exchanged like fraternal signs. The presence of fraternity and sorority houses at Ole Miss always seemed oddly superfluous.

One consequence of this peculiar social structure has been a chronic misunderstanding between the state and the rest of the country. The state feels that unspeakable demands are being made upon it, while the nation is bewildered by the response of rage to what seem to be the ordinary and minimal requirements of the law. Recall, for example, President Kennedy's gentle appeal to the university the night of the riot when he invoked the tradition of L. Q. C. Lamar and asked the students to do their duty even as he was doing his. He had got his facts straight about the tradition of valor in Mississippi. But, unfortunately, the Kennedys had no notion of the social and semantic rules they were up against. When they entered into negotiations with the governor to get Meredith on the campus, they proceeded on the reasonable assumption that even in the arena of political give and take—i.e., deals—words bear some relation to their referents. Such was not the case. Governor Barnett did not double-cross the Kennedys in the usual sense. The double cross, like untruth, bears a certain relation to the truth. More serious, however, was the cultural confusion over the word "public." Ole Miss is not, or was not, a public school as the word is usually understood. In Mississippi as in England, a public school means a private school. When Meredith finally did walk the paths at Ole Miss, his fellow students cursed and reviled him. But they also wept with genuine grief. It was as if he had been quartered in their living room.

It is this hypertrophy of pleasant familial space at the expense of a truly public sector which accounts for the extraordinary apposition in Mississippi of kindliness and unspeakable violence. Recently, a tourist wrote the editor of the Philadelphia, Mississippi, newspaper that, although he expected the worst when he passed through the town, he found the folks in Philadelphia as nice as they could be. No doubt it is true. The Philadelphia the tourist saw is as pleasant as he said. It is like one big front porch.

How can peace be restored to Mississippi? One would like to be able to say that the hope lies in putting into practice the Judeo-Christian ethic. In the end, no doubt, it does. But the trouble is that Christendom of a sort has already won in Mississippi. There is more church news in the Jackson papers than news about the Ole Miss football team. Political cartoons defend God against the Supreme Court. On the outskirts of Meridian, a road sign announces: THE LARGEST PERCENTAGE OF CHURCHGOERS IN THE WORLD. It is a religion, however, which tends to canonize the existing social and political structure and to brand as atheistic any threat of change. "The trouble is, they took God out of everything," said W. Arsene Dick of Summit, Mississippi, founder of Americans for the Preservation of the White Race. A notable exception to the general irrelevance of religion to social issues is the recent action of Millsaps College, a Methodist institution in Jackson, which voluntarily opened its doors to Negroes.

It seems more likely that progress will come about—as indeed it is already coming about—not through the impact of the churches upon churchgoers but because after a while the ordinary citizen gets sick and tired of the climate of violence and of the odor of disgrace which hangs over his region. Money has a good deal to do with it, too; money, urbanization, and the growing concern of politicians and the business community with such things as public images. Governor Johnson occasionally talks sense. Last year the mayor and the business leaders of Jackson defied the Citizens' Councils and supported the token desegregation of the schools. It could even happen that Governor Johnson, the man who campaigned up and down the state with the joke about what NAACP means (niggers, alligators, apes, coons, possums), may turn out to be the first governor to enforce the law. For law enforcement, it is becoming increasingly obvious, is the condition of peace. It is also becoming more likely every day that federal intervention, perhaps in the form of local commissioners, may be required in places like Neshoba County where the Ku Klux Klan has been in control and law enforcement is a shambles. Faulkner at last changed his mind about the durability of the old alliance and came to prefer even enforced change to a state run by the Citizens' Councils and the Klan. Mississippians, he wrote, will not accept change until they have to. Then perhaps they will at last come to themselves: "Why didn't someone tell us this before? Tell us this in time?"

Much will depend on the residue of good will in the state. There are some slight signs of the long-overdue revolt of the ordinary prudent man. There must be a good many of this silent breed. Hazel Brannon Smith, who won a Pulitzer Prize as editor of the Lexington *Advertiser,* recently reported that in spite of all the abuse and the boycotts, the circulation of the paper continues to rise. The Mississippi Economic Council, the state's leading businessmen's group, issued a statement urging compliance with the 1964 Civil Rights Act and demanding that registration and voting laws be "fairly and impartially administered for all." In McComb, several hundred leading citizens, after a reign of terror which lasted for a good part of 1964, demanded not only law and order but "equal treatment under the law for all citizens."

It may be that the corner has been turned. Mississippi, in the spring of 1965, looks better than Alabama. But who can say what would have happened if Martin Luther King had chosen Greenwood instead of Selma? Mississippi may in fact *be* better just because of Selma—though at this very writing Ole Miss students are living up to form and throwing rocks at Negroes. Nor can one easily forget the 1964 national election. The bizarre seven-to-one margin in favor of Senator Goldwater attests to the undiminished obsession with race. It would not have mattered if Senator Goldwater had advocated the collectivization of the plantations and open saloons in Jackson; he voted against the 1964 Civil Rights Bill and that was that.

Yet there is little doubt that Mississippi is even now beginning to feel its way toward what might be called the American Settlement of the racial issue, a somewhat ambiguous state of affairs which is less a solution than a more or less tolerable impasse. There has come into being an entire literature devoted to an assault upon the urban life wherein this settlement is arrived at, and a complete glossary of terms, such as alienation, depersonalization, and mass man. But in the light of recent history in Mississippi, the depersonalized American neighborhood looks more and more tolerable. A giant supermarket or eighty thousand people watching a pro ball game may not be the most creative of institutions, but at least they offer a modus vivendi. People generally leave each other alone.

A Southerner may still hope that someday the Southern temper, black and white, might yet prove to be the sociable yeast to leaven the American lump. Indeed, he may suspect in his heart of hearts that the solution, if it comes, may have to come from him and from the South. And with good reason: the South, with all the monstrous mythologizing of its virtues, nevertheless has these virtues—a manner and a grace and a gift for human intercourse. And despite the humbuggery about the perfect love and understanding between us white folks and darkies down in Dixie, whites and blacks in the South do in fact know something about getting along with each other which the rest of the country does not know. Both black and white Southerner can help the country a great deal, though neither may choose to do so; the Negro for fear of being taken for Uncle Tom, the white from simple vengefulness: "All right, Yankee, you've been preaching at us for a hundred years and now you've got them and you're making a mess of it and it serves you right." It may well come to lie with the South in the near future, as it lay with the North in 1860, to save the Union in its own way. Given enough trouble in New York and Chicago, another ten years of life in the subways and urine in the streets, it might at last dawn on him, the Southerner, that it is not the South which is being put upon but the *country* which is in trouble. Then he will act as he acted in 1916 and 1941.

Someday a white Mississippian is going to go to New York, make the usual detour through Harlem, and see it for the foul cheerless warren that it is; and instead of making him happy as it does now, it is going to make him unhappy. Then the long paranoia, this damnable sectional insanity, will be one important step closer to being over.

This Quiet Dust

Harper's Magazine, April 1965

◆

WILLIAM STYRON

You mought be rich as cream
And drive you coach and four-horse team,
But you can't keep de world from moverin' round
Nor Nat Turner from gainin' ground.

And your name it mought be Caesar sure
And got you cannon can shoot a mile or more,
But you can't keep de world from moverin' round
Nor Nat Turner from gainin' ground.
                    —OLD-TIME NEGRO SONG

My native state of Virginia is, of course, more than ordinarily conscious of its past, even for the South. When I was learning my lessons in the mid-1930s at a grammar school on the banks of the James River, one of the required texts was a history of Virginia—a book I can recall far more vividly than any history of the United States or of Europe I studied at a later time. It was in this work that I first encountered the name Nat Turner. The reference to Nat was brief; as a matter of fact, I do not think it unlikely that it was the very brevity of the allusion—amounting almost to a quality of haste—which captured my attention and stung my curiosity. I can no longer quote the passage exactly, but I remember that it went something like this: "In 1831, a fanatical Negro slave named Nat Turner led a terrible insurrection in Southampton County, murdering many white people. The insurrection was immediately put down, and for their cruel deeds Nat Turner and most of the other Negroes involved in the rebellion were hanged." Give or take a few harsh adjectives, this was all the information on Nat Turner supplied by that forgotten historian, who hustled on to matters of greater consequence.

I must have first read this passage when I was ten or eleven years old. At that time my home was not far from Southampton County, where the rebellion took place, in a section of the Virginia Tidewater which is generally considered part of the Black Belt because of the predominance of Negroes in the population. (When I speak of the South and Southerners here, I speak of *this* South, where Deep South attitudes prevail; it would include parts of Maryland and East Texas.) My boyhood experience was the typically ambivalent one of most native Southerners, for whom the Negro is taken simultaneously for granted and as an object of unending concern. On the one hand, Negroes are simply a part of the landscape, an unexceptional feature of the local scenery, yet as central to its character as the pinewoods and sawmills and mule teams and sleepy river estuaries that give such color and tone to the Southern geography. Unnoticed by white people, the Negroes blend with the land and somehow melt and fade into it, so that only when one reflects upon their possible absence, some magical disappearance, does one realize how unimaginable this absence would be: it would be easier to visualize a South without trees, without *any* people, without life at all. Thus at the same time ignored by white people, Negroes impinge upon their collective subconscious to such a degree that it may be rightly said that they become the focus of an incessant preoccupation, somewhat like a monstrous, recurring dream populated by identical faces wearing expressions of inquietude and vague reproach. "Southern whites cannot walk, talk, sing, conceive of laws or justice, think of sex, love, the family, or freedom without responding to the presence of Negroes." The words are those of Ralph Ellison, and, of course, he is right.

Yet there are many Souths, and the experience of each Southerner is modified by the subtlest conditions of self and family and environment and God knows what else, and I have wondered if it has ever properly been taken into account how various this response to the presence of the Negroes can be. I cannot tell how typical my own awareness of Negroes was, for instance, as I grew up near my birthplace—a small seaside city about equally divided between black and white. My feelings seem to have been confused and blurred, tinged with sentimentality, colored by a great deal of folklore, and wobbling always between a patronizing affection, fostered by my elders, and downright hostility. Most importantly, my feelings were completely uninformed by that intimate knowledge of black people which Southerners claim as their special patent; indeed, they were based upon an almost total ignorance.

For one thing, from the standpoint of attitudes toward race, my upbringing was hardly unusual: it derived from the simple conviction that Negroes were in every respect inferior to white people and should be made to stay in their proper order in the scheme of things. At the same time, by certain Southern standards my family was enlightened: although my mother taught me firmly that the use of "lady" instead of "woman" in referring to a Negro female was quite improper, she writhed at the sight of the extremes of Negro poverty, and would certainly have thrashed me had she ever heard me use the word "nigger." Yet outside the confines of family, in the lower-middle-class school world I inhabited every day, this was a word I commonly used. School segregation, which was an ordinary fact of life for me, is devastatingly effective in accomplishing something that it was only peripherally designed to do: it prevents the awareness even of the existence of another race. Thus, whatever hostility I bore toward the Negroes was based almost entirely upon hearsay.

And so the word "nigger," which like all my schoolmates I uttered so freely and so often, had even then an idle and listless ring. How could that dull epithet carry meaning and conviction when it was applied to a people so diligently isolated from us that they barely existed except as shadows which came daily to labor in the kitchen, to haul away garbage, to rake up leaves? An unremarked paradox of Southern life is that its racial animosity is really grounded not upon friction and propinquity, but upon an almost complete lack of contact. Surrounded by a sea of Negroes, I cannot recall more than once—and then briefly, when I was five or six—ever having played with a Negro child, or ever having spoken to a Negro, except in trifling talk with the cook, or in some forlorn and crippled conversation with a dotty old grandfather angling for hardshell crabs on a lonesome Sunday afternoon many years ago. Nor was I by any means uniquely sheltered. Whatever knowledge I gained in my youth about Negroes, I gained from a distance, as if I had been watching actors in an all-black puppet show.

Such an experience has made me distrust any easy generalizations about the South, whether they are made by white sociologists or Negro playwrights, Southern politicians or Northern editors. I have come to understand at least as much about the Negro after having lived in the North. One of the most egregious of the Southern myths—one in this case propagated solely by Southerners—is that of the Southern white's boast that he "knows" the Negro.

Certainly in many rural areas of the South the cultural climate has been such as to allow a mutual understanding, and even a kind of intimacy, to spring up between the races, at least in some individual instances. But my own boyhood surroundings, which were semi-urban (I suppose suburban is the best description, though the green little village on the city's outskirts where I grew up was a far cry from Levittown), and which have become the youthful environment for vast numbers of Southerners, tended almost totally to preclude any contact between black and white, especially when that contact was so sedulously proscribed by law.

Yet if white Southerners cannot "know" the Negro, it is for this very reason that the entire sexual myth needs to be reexamined. Surely a certain amount of sexual tension between the races does continue to exist, and the Southern white man's fear of sexual aggression on the part of the Negro male is still too evident to be ignored. But the nature of the growth of the urban, modern South has been such as to impose ever more effective walls between the races. While it cannot be denied that slavery times produced an enormous amount of interbreeding (with all of its totalitarianism, this was a free-for-all atmosphere far less self-conscious about carnal mingling than the Jim Crow era which began in the 1890s) and while even now there must logically take place occasional sexual contacts between the races—especially in rural areas where a degree of casual familiarity has always obtained—the monolithic nature of segregation has raised such an effective barrier between whites and Negroes that it is impossible not to believe that theories involving a perpetual sexual "tension" have been badly inflated. Nor is it possible to feel that a desire to taste forbidden fruit has ever really caused this barrier to be breached. From the standpoint of the Negro, there is indifference or uncomplicated fear; from that of the white—segregation, the law, and, finally, indifference, too. When I was growing up, the older boys might crack wan jokes about visiting the Negro whorehouse street (patronized entirely, I later discovered, by Negroes plus a few Scandinavian sailors), but to my knowledge none of them ever really went there. Like Negroes in general, Negro girls were to white men phantoms, shadows. To assume that anything more than a rare and sporadic intimacy on any level has existed in the modern South between whites and Negroes is simply to deny, with a truly willful contempt for logic, the monstrous effectiveness of that apartheid which has been the Southern way of life for almost three-quarters of a century.

I have lingered on this matter only to try to underline a truth about Southern life which has been too often taken for granted, and which has therefore been overlooked or misinterpreted. Most Southern white people *cannot* know or touch black people and this is because of the deadly intimidation of a universal law. Certainly one feels the presence of this gulf even in the work of a writer as supremely knowledgeable about the South as William Faulkner, who confessed a hesitancy about attempting to "think Negro," and whose Negro characters, as marvelously portrayed as most of them are, seem nevertheless to be meticulously *observed* rather than *lived*. Thus in *The Sound and the Fury*, Faulkner's magnificent Dilsey comes richly alive, yet in retrospect one feels this is a result of countless mornings, hours, days Faulkner had spent watching and listening to old Negro servants, and not because Dilsey herself is a being created from a sense of withinness: at the last moment Faulkner draws back, and it is no mere happenstance that Dilsey, alone among the four central figures from whose points of view the story is told, is seen from the outside rather than from that intensely "inner" vantage point, the interior monologue.

Innumerable white Southerners have grown up as free of knowledge of the Negro character and soul as a person whose background is rural Wisconsin or Maine. Yet, of course, there is a difference, and it is a profound one, defining the white Southerner's attitudes and causing him to be, for better or for worse, whatever it is he is to be. For the Negro is *there*. And he is there in a way he never is in the North, no matter how great his numbers. In the South he is a perpetual and immutable part of history itself, a piece of the vast fabric so integral and necessary that without him the fabric dissolves; his voice, his black or brown face passing on a city street, the sound of his cry rising from a wagonload of flowers, his numberless procession down dusty country roads, the neat white church he has built in some pine grove with its air of grace and benison and tranquillity, his silhouette behind a mule team far off in some spring field, the wail of his blues blaring from some jukebox in a backwoods roadhouse, the sad wet faces of nursemaids and cooks waiting in the evening at city bus stops in pouring rain—the Negro is always *there*.

No wonder then, as Ellison says, the white Southerner can do virtually nothing without responding to the presence of Negroes. No wonder the white man so often grows cranky, fanciful, freakish, loony, violent: how else respond to a paradox which requires, with the full majesty of law behind it, that he deny the very reality of a people whose multitude approaches and often exceeds his own; that he disclaim the existence of those whose human presence has marked every acre of the land, every hamlet and crossroad and city and town, and whose humanity, however inflexibly denied, is daily evidenced to him like a heartbeat in loyalty and wickedness, madness and hilarity and mayhem and pride and love? The Negro may feel that it is too late to be known, and that the desire to know him reeks of outrageous condescension. But to break down the old law, to come to *know* the Negro, has become the moral imperative of every white Southerner.

I suspect that my search for Nat Turner, my own private attempt as a novelist to re-create and bring alive that dim and prodigious black man, has been at least a partial fulfillment of this mandate, although the problem has long since resolved itself into an artistic one—which is as it should be. In the late 1940s, having finished college in North Carolina and come to New York, I found myself haunted by that name I had first seen in the Virginia history textbook. I had learned something more of Southern history since then, and I had become fascinated by the subject of Negro slavery. One of the most striking aspects of the institution is the fact that in the 250 years of its existence in America, it was singularly free of organized uprisings, plots, and rebellions. (It is curious that as recently as the late 1940s, scholarly insights were lagging, and I could only have suspected then what has since been made convincing by such historians as Frank Tannenbaum and Stanley Elkins: that American Negro slavery, unique in its psychological oppressiveness—the worst the world has ever known—was simply so despotic and emasculating as to render organized revolt next to impossible.) There were three exceptions: a conspiracy by the slave Gabriel Prosser and his followers near Richmond in the year 1800, the plot betrayed, the conspirators hanged; a similar conspiracy in 1822, in Charleston, South Carolina, led by a free Negro named Denmark Vesey, who also was betrayed before he could carry out his plans, and who was executed along with other members of the plot.

The last exception, of course, was Nat Turner, and he alone in the entire annals of American slavery—alone among all those "many thousand gone"—achieved a kind of triumph.

Even today, many otherwise well-informed people have never heard the name Nat Turner, and there are several plausible reasons for such an ignorance. One of these, of course, is that the study of our history—and not alone in the South—has been tendentious in the extreme, and has often avoided even an allusion to a figure like Nat, who inconveniently disturbs our notion of a slave system which, though morally wrong, was conducted with such charity and restraint that any organized act of insurrectory and murderous violence would be unthinkable. But a general ignorance about Nat Turner is even more understandable in view of the fact that so little is left of the actual record. Southampton County, which even now is off the beaten track, was at that period the remotest backwater imaginable. The relativity of time allows us elastic definitions: 1831 was yesterday. Yet the year 1831, in the Presidency of Andrew Jackson, lay in the very dawn of our modern history, three years before a railroad ever touched the soil of Virginia, a full fifteen years before the use of the telegraph. The rebellion itself was of such a cataclysmic nature as practically to guarantee confusion of the news, distortion, wild rumors, lies, and, finally, great areas of darkness and suppression; all of these have contributed to Nat's obscurity.

As for the contemporary documents themselves, only one survives: the *Confessions of Nat Turner,* a brief pamphlet of some five thousand words, transcribed from Nat's lips as he awaited trial, by a somewhat enigmatic lawyer named Thomas Gray, who published the *Confessions* in Baltimore and then vanished from sight. There are several discrepancies in Gray's transcript but it was taken down in haste, and in all major respects it seems completely honest and reliable. Those few newspaper accounts of the time, from Richmond and Norfolk, are sketchy, remote, filled with conjecture, and are thus virtually worthless. The existing county court records of Southampton remain brief and unilluminating, dull lists, a dry catalogue of names in fading ink: the white people slain, the Negroes tried and transported south, or acquitted, or convicted and hanged.

Roughly seventy years after the rebellion (in 1900, which by coincidence was the year Virginia formally adopted its first Jim Crow laws), the single scholarly book ever to be written on the affair was published—*The Southampton Insurrection*, by a Johns Hopkins Ph.D. candidate named William S. Drewry, who was an unreconstructed Virginian of decidedly pro-slavery leanings and a man so quaintly committed to the *ancien régime* that, in the midst of a description of the ghastliest part of the uprising, he was able to reflect that "slavery in Virginia was not such to arouse rebellion, but was an institution which nourished the strongest affection and piety in slave and owner, as well as moral qualities worthy of any age of civilization." For Drewry, Nat Turner was some sort of inexplicable aberration, like a man from Mars. Drewry was close enough to the event in time, however, to be able to interview quite a few of the survivors, and since he also possessed a bloodthirsty relish for detail, it was possible for him to reconstruct the chronology of the insurrection with what appears to be considerable accuracy. Drewry's book (it is of course long out of print) and Nat's *Confessions* remain the only significant sources about the insurrection. Of Nat himself, his background and early years, very little can be known. This is not disadvantageous to a novelist, since it allows him to speculate—with a freedom not accorded the historian—upon all the intermingled miseries, ambitions, frustrations, hopes, rages, and desires which caused this extraordinary black man to rise up out of those early mists of our history and strike down his oppressors with a fury of retribution unequaled before or since.

He was born in 1800, which would have made him at the time of the insurrection thirty-one years old—exactly the age of so many great revolutionaries at the decisive moment of their insurgency: Martin Luther,* Robespierre, Danton,

---

*See Erik Erikson's *Young Man Luther* for a brilliant study of the development of the revolutionary impulse in a young man, and the relationship of this impulse to the father-figure. Although it is best to be wary of any heavy psychoanalytical emphasis, one cannot help believing that Nat Turner's relationship with his father, like Luther's, was tormented and complicated, especially since this person could not have been his real father, who ran away when Nat was an infant, but the white man who owned and raised him.

Fidel Castro. Thomas Gray, in a footnote to the *Confessions*, describes him as having the "true Negro face" (an offhand way of forestalling an assumption that he might have possessed any white blood), and he adds that "for natural intelligence and quickness of apprehension he is surpassed by few men I have ever seen"—a lofty tribute indeed at that inflammatory instant, with antebellum racism at its most hysteric pitch. Although little is known for certain of Nat's childhood and youth, there can be no doubt that he was very precocious and that he learned not only to read and write with ease—an illustrious achievement in itself, when learning to read and write was forbidden to Negroes by law—but at an early age acquired a knowledge of astronomy, and later on experimented in making paper and gunpowder. (The resemblance here to the knowledge of the ancient Chinese is almost too odd to be true, but I can find no reason to doubt it.)

The early decades of the nineteenth century were years of declining prosperity for the Virginia Tidewater, largely because of the ruination of the land through greedy cultivation of tobacco—a crop which had gradually disappeared from the region, causing the breakup of many of the big old plantations and the development of subsistence farming on small holdings. It was in these surroundings—a flat pastoral land of modest farms and even more modest homesteads, where it was rare to find a white man prosperous enough to own more than half a dozen Negroes, and where two or three slaves to a family was the general rule—that Nat was born and brought up, and in these surroundings he prepared himself for the apocalyptic role he was to play in history. Because of the failing economic conditions, it was not remarkable that Nat was purchased and sold several times by various owners (in a sense, he was fortunate in not having been sold off to the deadly cotton and rice plantations of South Carolina and Georgia, which was the lot of many Virginia Negroes of the period); and although we do not know much about any of these masters, the evidence does not appear to be that Nat was ill-treated, and in fact one of these owners (Samuel Turner, brother of the man on whose property Nat was born) developed so strong a paternal feeling for the boy and such regard for Nat's abilities that he took the fateful step of encouraging him in the beginnings of an education.

The atmosphere of the time and place was fundamentalist and devout to a passionate degree, and at some time during his twenties Nat, who had always been a godly person—"never owing a dollar, never uttering an oath, never drinking intoxicating liquors, and never committing a theft"—became a Baptist preacher. Compared to the Deep South, Virginia slave life was not so rigorous; Nat must have been given considerable latitude, and found many opportunities to preach and exhort the Negroes. His gifts for preaching, for prophecy, and his own magnetism seem to have been so extraordinary that he

grew into a rather celebrated figure among the Negroes of the county, his influence even extending to the whites, one of whom—a poor, half-cracked, but
respectable overseer named Brantley—he converted to the faith and baptized
in a mill pond in the sight of a multitude of the curious, both black and white.
(After this no one would have anything to do with Brantley, and he left the
county in disgrace.)

At about this time Nat began to withdraw into himself, fasting and praying, spending long hours in the woods or in the swamp, where he communed
with the Spirit and where there came over him, urgently now, intimations that
he was being prepared for some great purpose. His fanaticism grew in intensity,
and during these lonely vigils in the forest he began to see apparitions:

> I saw white spirits and black spirits engaged in battle, and the sun was darkened;
> the thunder rolled in the heavens and blood flowed in streams . . . I wondered
> greatly at these miracles, and prayed to be informed of a certainty of the meaning
> thereof; and shortly afterwards, while laboring in the fields, I discovered drops of
> blood on the corn as though it were dew from heaven. For as the blood of Christ
> had been shed on this earth, and had ascended to heaven for the salvation of sin-
> ners, it was now returning to earth again in the form of dew . . . On the twelfth day
> of May, 1828, I heard a loud noise in the heavens, and the Spirit instantly appeared
> to me and said the Serpent was loosened, and Christ had laid down the yoke he had
> borne for the sins of men, and that I should take it on and fight against the Serpent,
> for the time was fast approaching when the first should be last and the last should
> be first . . .

Like all revolutions, that of Nat Turner underwent many worrisome hesita-
tions, false starts, procrastinations, delays (with appropriate irony, Independence Day, 1830, had been one of the original dates selected, but Nat fell sick
and the moment was put off again); finally, however, on the night of Sunday,
August 21, 1831, Nat, together with five other Negroes in whom he had placed
his confidence and trust, assembled in the woods near the home of his owner of
the time, a carriage maker named Joseph Travis, and commenced to carry out
a plan of total annihilation. The penultimate goal was the capture of the
county seat, then called Jerusalem (a connotation certainly not lost on Nat,
who, with the words of the prophets roaring in his ears, must have felt like
Gideon himself before the extermination of the Midianites); there were guns
and ammunition in Jerusalem, and with these captured it was then Nat's purpose to sweep thirty miles eastward, gathering black recruits on the way until
the Great Dismal Swamp was reached—a snake-filled and gloomy fastness in
which Nat believed, with probable justification, only Negroes could survive,
and no white man's army could penetrate. The immediate objective, however,
was the destruction of every white man, woman, and child on the ten-mile
route to Jerusalem; no one was to be spared; tender infancy and feeble old age

alike were to perish by the axe and the sword. The command, of course, was that of God Almighty, through the voice of his prophet Ezekiel: "*Son of Man, prophesy and say, Thus saith the Lord; Say, a sword, a sword is sharpened, and also furbished; it is sharpened to make a sore slaughter . . . Slay utterly old and young, both maids and little children, and women . . .*" It was a scheme so wild and daring that it could only have been the product of the most wretched desperation and frustrate misery of soul; and of course it was doomed to catastrophe not only for whites but for Negroes—and for black men in ways which from the vantage point of history now seem almost unthinkable.

They did their job rapidly and with merciless and methodical determination. Beginning at the home of Travis—where five people, including a six-month-old infant, were slain in their beds—they marched from house to house on an eastward route, pillaging, murdering, sparing no one. Lacking guns—at least to begin with—they employed axes, hatchets, and swords as their tools of destruction, and swift decapitation was their usual method of dispatch. (It is interesting that the Negroes did not resort to torture, nor were they ever accused of rape. Nat's attitude toward sex was Christian and high-minded, and he had said: "We will not do to their women what they have done to ours.")

On through the first day they marched, across the hot August fields, gaining guns and ammunition, horses, and a number of willing recruits. That the insurrection was not purely racial, but perhaps obscurely pre-Marxist, may be seen in the fact that a number of dwellings belonging to poor white people were pointedly passed by. At midday on Monday their force had more than tripled, to the amount of nineteen, and nearly thirty white people lay dead. By this time, the alarm had been sounded throughout the county, and while the momentum of the insurgent band was considerable, many of the whites had fled in panic to the woods, and some of the farmers had begun to resist, setting up barricades from which they could fire back at Nat's forces. Furthermore, quite a few of the rebels had broken into the brandy cellars of the houses they had attacked and had gotten roaring drunk—an eventuality Nat had feared and had warned against. Nevertheless, the Negroes—augmented now by forty more volunteers—pressed on toward Jerusalem, continuing the attack into the next night and all through the following day, when at last obstinate resistance by the aroused whites and the appearance of a mounted force of militia troops (also, it must be suspected, continued attrition by the apple brandy) caused the rebels to be dispersed, only a mile or so from Jerusalem.

Almost every one of the Negroes was rounded up and brought to trial—a legalistic nicety characteristic of a time in which it was necessary for one to determine whether *his* slave, property, after all, worth eight or nine hundred dollars, was really guilty and deserving of the gallows. Nat disappeared immediately after the insurrection, and hid in the woods for over two months, when near-starvation and the onset of autumnal cold drove him from his cave and forced him to surrender to a lone farmer with a shotgun. Then he too was brought to trial in Jerusalem—early in November 1831—for fomenting a rebellion in which sixty white people had perished.

The immediate consequences of the insurrection were exceedingly grim. The killing of so many white people was in itself an act of futility. It has never been determined with any accuracy how many black people, not connected with the rebellion, were slain at the hands of rampaging bands of white men who swarmed all over Southampton in the week following the uprising, seeking reprisal and vengeance. A contemporary estimate by a Richmond newspaper, which deplored this retaliation, put the number at close to two hundred Negroes, many of them free, and many of them tortured in ways unimaginably horrible. But even more important was the effect that Nat Turner's insurrection had upon the institution of slavery at large. News of the revolt spread among Southern whites with great speed: the impossible, the unspeakable had at last taken place after two hundred years of the ministrations of sweet old mammies and softly murmured Yassuhs and docile compliance—and a shock wave of anguish and terror ran through the entire South. If such a nightmarish calamity happened there, would it not happen *here?*—here in Tennessee, in Augusta, in Vicksburg, in these bayous of Louisiana? Had Nat lived to see the consequences of his rebellion, surely it would have been for him the cruelest irony that his bold and desperate bid for liberty had caused only the most tyrannical new controls to be imposed upon Negroes everywhere—the establishment of patrols, further restrictions upon movement, education, assembly, and the beginning of other severe and crippling restraints which persisted throughout the slaveholding states until the Civil War. Virginia had been edging close to emancipation, and it seems reasonable to believe that the example of Nat's rebellion, stampeding many moderates in the legislature into a conviction that the Negroes could not be safely freed, was a decisive factor in the ultimate victory of the proslavery forces. Had Virginia, with its enormous prestige among the states, emancipated its slaves, the effect upon our history would be awesome to contemplate.

Nat brought cold, paralyzing fear to the South, a fear that never departed. If white men had sown the wind with chattel slavery, in Nat Turner they had reaped the whirlwind for white and black alike.

Nat was executed, along with sixteen other Negroes who had figured large in the insurrection. Most of the others were transported south, to the steaming fields of rice and cotton. On November 11, 1831, Nat was hanged from a live oak tree in the town square of Jerusalem. He went to his death with great dignity and courage. "The bodies of those executed," wrote Drewry, "with one exception, were buried in a decent and becoming manner. That of Nat Turner was delivered to the doctors, who skinned it and made grease of the flesh."

◆◆◆

Not long ago, in the spring of the year, when I was visiting my family in Virginia, I decided to go down for the day to Southampton County, which is a drive of an hour and a half by car from the town where I was born and raised. Nat Turner was of course the reason for this trip, although I had nothing particular or urgent in mind. What research it was possible to do on the event I had long since done. The Southampton court records, I had already been reliably informed, would prove unrewarding. It was not a question, then, of digging out more facts, but simply a matter of wanting to savor the mood and atmosphere of a landscape I had not seen for quite a few years, since the times when as a boy I used to pass through Southampton on the way to my father's family home in North Carolina. I thought also that there might be a chance of visiting some of the historic sites connected with the insurrection, and perhaps even of retracing part of the route of the uprising through the help of one of those handsomely produced guidebooks for which the Historical Commission of Virginia is famous—guides indispensable for a trip to such Old Dominion shrines as Jamestown and Appomattox and Monticello. I became even more eager to go when one of my in-laws put me in touch by telephone with a cousin of his. This man, whom I shall call Dan Seward, lived near Franklin, the main town of Southampton, and he assured me in those broad cheery Southern tones which are like a warm embrace—and which, after long years in the chill North, are to me always so familiar, reminiscent, and therefore so unsettling, sweet, and curiously painful—that he would like nothing better than to aid me in my exploration in whatever way he could.

Dan Seward is a farmer, a prosperous grower of peanuts in a prosperous agricultural region where the peanut is the unquestioned monarch. A combination of sandy loam soil and a long growing season has made Southampton ideal for the cultivation of peanuts; over 30,000 acres are planted annually, and the crop is processed and marketed in Franklin—a thriving little town of 7,000 people—or in Suffolk and Portsmouth, where it is rendered into Planters cooking oil and stock feed and Skippy peanut butter. There are other money-making crops—corn and soybeans and cotton. The county is at the northern-most edge of the cotton belt, and thirty years ago cotton was a major source of income. Cotton has declined in importance but the average yield per acre is still among the highest in the South, and the single gin left in the county in the little village of Drewryville processes each year several thousand bales which are trucked to market down in North Carolina. Lumbering is also very profitable, owing mainly to an abundance of the loblolly pines valuable in the production of kraft wood pulp; and the Union Bag–Camp Paper Company's plant on the Blackwater River in Franklin is a huge enterprise employing over 1,600 people. But it is peanuts—the harvested vines in autumn piled up mile after mile in dumpy brown stacks like hay—which have brought money to Southampton, and a sheen of prosperity that can be seen in the freshly painted farmhouses along the monotonously flat state highway which leads into Franklin, and the new-model Dodges and Buicks parked slantwise against the curb of some crossroads hamlet, and the gaudy, eye-catching signs that advise the wisdom of a bank savings account for all those surplus funds.

The county has very much the look of the New South about it, with its airport and its shiny new motels, its insistent billboards advertising space for industrial sites, the sprinkling of housing developments with television antennas gleaming from every rooftop, its supermarkets and shopping centers and its flavor of go-getting commercialism. This is the New South, where agriculture still prevails but has joined in a vigorous union with industry, so that even the peanut when it goes to market is ground up in some rumbling engine of commerce and becomes metamorphosed into wood stain or soap or cattle feed. The Negroes, too, have partaken of this abundance—some of it, at least—for they own television sets also, and if not new-model Buicks (the Southern white man's strictures against Negro ostentation remain intimidating), then decent late-model used Fords; while in the streets of Franklin the Negro women shopping seemed on the day of my visit very proud and well-dressed compared to the shabby stooped figures I recalled from the Depression years when I was a boy. It would certainly appear that Negroes deserve some of this abundance, if only because they make up so large a part of the work force. Since Nat Turner's day the balance of population in Southampton—almost 60 percent Negro— has hardly altered by a hair.

"I don't know anywhere that a Negro is treated better than around here," Mr. Seward was saying to the three of us, on the spring morning I visited him with my wife and my father. "You take your average person from up North, he just doesn't *know* the Negro like we do. Now for instance I have a Negro who's worked for me for years, name of Ernest. He knows if he breaks his arm—like he did a while ago, fell off a tractor—he knows he can come to me and I'll see that he's taken care of, hospital expenses and all, and I'll take care of him and his family while he's unable to work, right on down the line. I don't ask him to pay back a cent, either, that's for sure. We have a wonderful relationship, that Negro and myself. By God, I'd die for that Negro and he knows it, and he'd do the same for me. But Ernest doesn't want to sit down at my table, here in this house, and have supper with me—and he wouldn't want me in *his* house. And Ernest's got kids like I do, and he doesn't want them to go to school with my Bobby, any more than Bobby wants to go to school with *his* kids. It works both ways. People up North don't seem to be able to understand a simple fact like that."

Mr. Seward was a solidly fleshed, somewhat rangy, big-shouldered man in his early forties with an open, cheerful manner which surely did nothing to betray the friendliness with which he had spoken on the telephone. He had greeted us—total strangers, really—with an animation and uncomplicated good will that would have shamed an Eskimo; and for a moment I realized that, after years amid the granite outcroppings of New England, I had forgotten that this *was* the passionate, generous, outgoing nature of the South, no artificial display but a social gesture as natural as breathing.

Mr. Seward had just finished rebuilding his farmhouse on the outskirts of town, and he had shown us around with a pride I found understandable: there was a sparkling electric kitchen worthy of an advertisement in *Life* magazine, some handsome modern furniture, and several downstairs rooms paneled beautifully in the prodigal and lustrous hardwood of the region. It was altogether a fine, tasteful house, resembling more one of the prettier medium-priced homes in the Long Island suburbs than the house one might contemplate for a Tidewater farmer. Upstairs, we had inspected his son Bobby's room, a kid's room with books like *Pinocchio* and *The Black Arrow* and *The Swiss Family Robinson*, and here there was a huge paper banner spread across one entire wall with the crayon inscription: *"Two . . . four . . . six . . . eight! We don't want to integrate!"* It was a sign which so overwhelmingly dominated the room that it could not help provoking comment, and it was this that eventually had led to Mr. Seward's reflections about *knowing* Negroes.

There might have been something vaguely defensive in his remarks but not a trace of hostility. His tone was matter-of-fact and good-natured, and he pronounced the word Negro as *nigra*, which most Southerners do with utter naturalness while intending no disrespect whatsoever, in fact quite the opposite—the mean epithet, of course, is *nigger*. I had the feeling that Mr. Seward had begun amiably to regard us as sympathetic but ill-informed outsiders, non-Southern, despite his knowledge of my Tidewater background and my father's own accent, which is thick as grits. Moreover, the fact that I had admitted to having lived in the North for fifteen years caused me, I fear, to appear alien in his eyes, *déraciné*, especially when my acculturation to Northern ways has made me adopt the long "e" and say Negro. The racial misery, at any rate, is within inches of driving us mad: how can I explain that, with all my silent disagreement with Mr. Seward's paternalism, I knew that when he said, "By God, I'd die for that Negro," he meant it?

Perhaps I should not have been surprised that Mr. Seward seemed to know very little about Nat Turner. When we got around to the subject, it developed that he had always thought that the insurrection occurred way back in the eighteenth century. Affably, he described seeing in his boyhood the "Hanging Tree," the live oak from which Nat had been executed in Courtland (Jerusalem had undergone this change of name after the Civil War), and which had died and been cut down some thirty years ago; as for any other landmarks, he regretted that he did not know of a single one. No, so far as he knew, there just wasn't anything.

For me, it was the beginning of disappointments which grew with every hour. Had I really been so ingenuous as to believe that I would unearth some shrine, some home preserved after the manner of Colonial Williamsburg, a relic of the insurrection at whose portal I would discover a lady in billowing satin and crinoline, who for fifty cents would shepherd me about the rooms with a gentle drawl indicating the spot where a good mistress fell at the hands of the murderous darky? The native Virginian, despite himself, is cursed with a suffocating sense of history, and I do not think it impossible that I actually suspected some such monument. Nevertheless, confident that there would be something to look at, I took heart when Mr. Seward suggested that after lunch we all drive over to Courtland, ten miles to the west. He had already spoken to a friend of his, the Sheriff of the county, who knew all the obscure byways and odd corners of Southampton, mainly because of his endless search for illegal stills; if there was a solitary person alive who might be able to locate some landmark, or could help retrace part of Nat Turner's march, it was the Sheriff. This gave me hope. For I had brought along Drewry's book and its map which showed the general route of the uprising, marking the houses by name. In the sixty years since Drewry, there would have been many changes in the landscape. But with this map oriented against the Sheriff's detailed county map, I should easily be able to pick up the trail and thus experience, however briefly, a sense of the light and shadow that played over that scene of slaughter and retribution 134 years ago.

Yet it was as if Nat Turner had never existed, and as the day lengthened and afternoon wore on, and as we searched Nat's part of the county—five of us now, riding in the Sheriff's car with its huge star emblazoned on the doors, and its radio blatting out hoarse intermittent messages, and its riot gun protectively nuzzling the backs of our necks over the edge of the rear seat—I had the sensation from time to time that this Negro, who had so long occupied my thoughts, who indeed had so obsessed my imagination that he had acquired larger spirit and flesh than most of the living people I encountered day in and day out, had been merely a crazy figment of my mind, a phantom no more real than some half-recollected image from a fairy tale. For here in the back country, this horizontal land of woods and meadows where he had roamed, only a few people had heard of Nat Turner, and of those who had—among the people we stopped to make inquiries of, both white and black, along dusty country roads, at farms, at filling stations, at crossroad stores—most of them confused him, I think, with something spectral, mythic, a black Paul Bunyan who had perpetrated mysterious and nameless deeds in millennia past. They were neither facetious nor evasive, simply unaware. Others confounded him with the Civil War—a Negro general. One young Negro field hand, lounging at an Esso station, figured he was a white man. A white man, heavy-lidded and paunchy, slow-witted, an idler at a rickety store, thought him an illustrious racehorse of bygone days.

The Sheriff, a smallish, soft-speaking ruminative man, with the whisper of a smile frozen on his face as if he were perpetually enjoying a good joke, knew full well who Nat Turner was, and I could tell he relished our frustrating charade. He was a shrewd person, quick and sharp with countrified wisdom, and he soon became quite as fascinated as I with the idea of tracking down some relic of the uprising (although he said that Drewry's map was hopelessly out of date, the roads of that time now abandoned to the fields and woods, the homes burnt down or gone to ruin); the country people's ignorance he found irresistible and I think it tickled him to perplex their foolish heads, white or black, with the same old leading question: "You heard about old Nat Turner, ain't you?" But few of them had heard, even though I was sure that many had plowed the same fields that Nat had crossed, lived on land that he had passed by; and as for dwellings still standing which might have been connected with the rebellion, not one of these back-country people could offer the faintest hint or clue. As effectively as a monstrous and unbearable dream, Nat had been erased from memory.

It was late afternoon when, with a sense of deep fatigue and frustration, I suggested to Mr. Seward and the Sheriff that maybe we had better go back to Courtland and call it a day. They were agreeable—relieved, I felt, to be freed of this tedious and fruitless search—and as we headed east down a straight unpaved road, the conversation became desultory, general. We spoke of the North. The Sheriff was interested to learn that I often traveled to New York. He went there occasionally himself, he said; indeed, he had been there only the month before—"to pick up a nigger," a fugitive from custody who had been awaiting trial for killing his wife. New York was a fine place to spend the night, said the Sheriff, but he wouldn't want to live there.

As he spoke, I had been gazing out of the window, and now suddenly something caught my eye—something familiar, a brief flickering passage of a distant outline, a silhouette against the sun-splashed woods—and I asked the Sheriff to stop the car. He did, and as we backed up slowly through a cloud of dust, I recognized a house standing perhaps a quarter of a mile off the road, from this distance only a lopsided oblong sheltered by an enormous oak, but the whole tableau—the house and the glorious hovering tree and the stretch of woods beyond—so familiar to me that it might have been some home I passed every day. And of course now as recognition came flooding back, I knew whose house it was. For in *The Southampton Insurrection*, the indefatigable Drewry had included many photographs—amateurish, doubtless taken by himself, and suffering from the fuzzy offset reproduction of 1900. But they were clear enough to provide an unmistakable guide to the dwellings in question, and now as I again consulted the book I could see that this house—the monumental oak above it grown scant inches it seemed in sixty years—was the one referred to by Drewry as having belonged to Mrs. Catherine Whitehead. From this distance, in the soft clear light of a spring afternoon, it seemed most tranquil, but few houses have come to know such a multitude of violent deaths. There in the late afternoon of Monday, August 22, Nat Turner and his band had appeared, and they set upon and killed "Mrs. Catherine Whitehead, son Richard, and four daughters, and grandchild."

The approach to the house was by a rutted lane long ago abandoned and overgrown with lush weeds which made a soft, crushed, rasping sound as we rolled over them. Dogwood, white and pink, grew on either side of the lane, quite wild and wanton in lovely pastel splashes. Not far from the house a pole fence interrupted our way; the Sheriff stopped the car and we got out and stood there for a moment, looking at the place. It was quiet and still—so quiet that the sudden chant of a mockingbird in the woods was almost frightening—and we realized then that no one lived in the house. Scoured by weather, paintless, worn down to the wintry gray of bone and with all the old mortar gone from between the timbers, it stood alone and desolate above its blasted, sagging front porch, the ancient door ajar like an open wound. Although never a manor house, it had once been a spacious and comfortable country home; now in near-ruin it sagged, finished, a shell, possessing only the most fragile profile of itself. As we drew closer still we could see that the entire house, from its upper story to the cellar, was filled with thousands of shucked ears of corn—feed for the malevolent-looking little razorback pigs which suddenly appeared in a tribe at the edge of the house, eyeing us, grunting. Mr. Seward sent them scampering with a shied stick and a farmer's sharp "Whoo!" I looked up at the house, trying to recollect its particular role in Nat's destiny, and then I remembered.

There was something baffling, secret, irrational about Nat's own participation in the uprising. He was unable to kill. Time and time again in his confession one discovers him saying (in an offhand tone; one must dig for the implications): "I could not give the death blow, the hatchet glanced from his head," or, "I struck her several blows over the head, but I was unable to kill her, as the sword was dull . . ." It is too much to believe, over and over again: the glancing hatchet, the dull sword. It smacks rather, as in *Hamlet*, of rationalization, ghastly fear, an access of guilt, a shrinking from violence, and fatal irresolution. Alone here at this house, turned now into a huge corncrib around which pigs rooted and snorted in the silence of a spring afternoon, here alone was Nat finally able— or was he forced?—to commit a murder, and this upon a girl of eighteen named Margaret Whitehead, described by Drewry in terms perhaps not so romantic or farfetched after all, as "the belle of the county." The scene is apocalyptic—afternoon bedlam in wild harsh sunlight and August heat.

"I returned to commence the work of death, but those whom I left had not been idle; all the family were already murdered but Mrs. Whitehead and her daughter Margaret. As I came round the door I saw Will pulling Mrs. Whitehead out of the house and at the step he nearly severed her head from her body with his axe. Miss Margaret, when I discovered her, had concealed herself in the corner formed by the projection of the cellar cap from the house; on my approach she fled into the field but was soon overtaken and after repeated blows with a sword, I killed her by a blow on the head with a fence rail."

It is Nat's only murder. Why, from this point on, does the momentum of the uprising diminish, the drive and tension sag? Why, from this moment in the *Confessions*, does one sense in Nat something dispirited, listless, as if all life and juice had been drained from him, so that never again through the course of the rebellion is he even on the scene when a murder is committed? What happened to Nat in this place? Did he discover his humanity here, or did he lose it?

I lifted myself up into the house, clambering through a doorway without steps, pushing myself over the crumbling sill. The house had a faint yeasty fragrance, like flat beer. Dust from the mountains of corn lay everywhere in the deserted rooms, years and decades of dust, dust an inch thick in some places, lying in a fine gray powder like sooty fallen snow. Off in some room amid the piles of corn I could hear a delicate scrabbling and a plaintive squeaking of mice. Again it was very still, the shadow of the prodigious old oak casting a dark pattern of leaves, checkered with bright sunlight, aslant through the gaping door. As in those chilling lines of Emily Dickinson, even this lustrous and golden day seemed to find its only resonance in the memory, and perhaps a premonition, of death.

> *This quiet Dust was Gentlemen and Ladies,*
>   *And Lads and Girls;*
> *Was laughter and ability and sighing,*
>   *And frocks and curls.*

Outside, the Sheriff was calling in on his car radio, his voice blurred and indistinct; then the return call from the county seat, loud, a dozen incomprehensible words in an uproar of static. Suddenly it was quiet again, the only sound my father's soft voice as he chatted with Mr. Seward.

I leaned past the rotting frame of the door, gazing out past the great tree and into that far meadow where Nat had brought down and slain Miss Margaret Whitehead. For an instant, in the silence, I thought I could hear a mad rustle of taffeta, and rushing feet, and a shrill girlish piping of terror; then that day and this day seemed to meet and melt together, becoming almost one, and for a long moment indistinguishable.

When Watts Burned

Rolling Stone's The Sixties, 1977

◆

STANLEY CROUCH

It burst like a Mexican piñata stuffed full of statistics about economics, racism and frustration. Some said that it was a set-up, that the men who exhorted crowds on the streets in those first days and nights were not from Watts, but were strangers working for some violent cause—Marxists, or the ubiquitous CIA. I think it had more to do with younger blacks who were exchanging the Southern patience and diligence of Martin Luther King for the braggadocio of Malcolm X, made attractive by the Muslims' self-reliance program.

It also said something about the concepts of manhood, self-defense and "justifiable revenge" that dominated much more television time than did the real suffering of the civil rights workers. Every tactic of King's was contradicted by weekly war films, swashbucklers, Westerns, and detective shows. *Men* did not allow women and children to be beaten, hosed, cattle-prodded or blown up in Sunday school. Nonviolence, both as tactic and philosophy, was outvoted.

For all that, even though I was a member of the community and had seen many a confrontation between community people and police, I was not prepared for what I saw in these days. Sure, I had seen my street filled before with gang members beating each other over the head with tire irons, chains, bottles. But it was almost always possible for two police cars to break the thing up. And a year before the *big* riot, I had seen a smaller one take place at Jefferson High School when a pillhead had been arrested, and his sister, who had been trying to intervene, was pushed away. Bricks and bottles knocked down many police officers that day—but three drawn guns brought an end to it.

I had also read LeRoi Jones and James Baldwin, had felt enraged, but considered most of their threats no more than romantic literature, or at best, impotent fist-waving. Then, too, barbershops were always full of "would've, could've and should've" conversations about violent reactions to the racial tensions of the period.

I was hearing all of this, at nineteen, while writing speeches for an important person in Los Angeles's very nearly worthless poverty program. Since this person was an *expert* on the community, I was sent out there to find out what the disturbance was about in case the official ever had to speak authoritatively from a wellspring of hired information. Another street disturbance, I thought. Of course, I was wrong.

I never saw the very important woman who finally sparked it all. She was actually seen by very few, but for a moment she was every black woman victim of white racism. She was part of a crowd that gathered to watch the arrest of a black man. As the scene got heated, the story goes, she was singled out by the police and physically abused. But momentum swept away symbols, and she was soon forgotten as windows shattered under the weight of hurled bricks, tire irons and feet.

People were in the street that night, Wednesday, August 11, talking rebellious talk, throwing bottles, milling around the projects on Imperial Highway, a six-lane artery that ran east toward the white suburbs and west toward the Harbor Freeway, passing the borders of Watts.

They were still there the next day, and by that night they had started tearing things up. The next day, Friday the 13th, the crowds were bigger, covering the sidewalks of 103rd Street, a strip of stores that sold overpriced second-rate merchandise.

The police were obviously frightened—these black people did not avert their eyes, did not tremble and stutter, but stared into their white faces with a confident cynicism, a stoic rebelliousness, even a dangerous mischief. This was unusual for Los Angeles blacks, who long before had literally been whipped into shape by Chief Parker's thin blue line, a police force known in the community for shooting or clubbing first and asking questions later. No one was afraid of them now, and no one would follow the bullhorn orders to disperse. The police did not understand.

The store owners did. They left for home. Windows were smashed and goods snatched. A few arrests were made and bottles bounced off the windows of police cars. The police made a show of force, a slow-moving line of fifteen or twenty police cars, provoking more bottles and more bricks. The police pulled out and the surge began in full force, taking 103rd Street before leaping like the proverbial wildfire over the whole black community.

I had never seen anything like it before. It was a bloody carnival, a great celebration. Warring street gangs that had been shooting each other for the past two years were drunk in the park, laughing at overturned cars, stoning or stabbing random whites who mistakenly drove through the area, jubilantly shouting how "all the brothers are *together.*" Men stood in front of stores with their arms full of dreams—new suits, appliances, hats. The sky was full of smoke and there was occasional gunfire. Well-known local winos reached for Johnnie Walker Black and Harvey's Bristol Cream, leaving the cheaper stuff to feed the flames. The atmosphere at first was festive. Then on Saturday the National Guard went into action. With their arrival, the blood really began to flow. Within two days they had cordoned off the whole community.

Rumors sparked like random lightning about women and children being shot, and about subsequent cover-ups. Most of all, there was a feeling of occupation as the Jeeps rolled down the streets and the machine guns glinted in the sun, bayonets offering ugly invitations. Romantics thought the riot would take the state. But through the smoke I saw an older black woman emerge from a display window from which she had just stolen a new domestic worker's uniform. To me, she seemed to say what it was really all about.

After Watts

Violence in the City—An End or a Beginning?

A Report by the Governor's Commission on the Los Angeles Riots

The New York Review of Books, March 31, 1966

◆

Elizabeth Hardwick

The Disaster and then, after a period of mourning or shock, the Report. Thus we try to exorcise our fears, to put into some sort of neutrality everything that menaces our peace. The Reports look out upon the inexplicable in private action and the unmanageable in community explosion; they investigate, they study, they interview, and at last, they recommend. Society is calmed, and not so much by what is found in the study as by the display of official energy, the activity underwritten. For we well know that little will be done, nothing new uncovered—at least not in this manner; instead a recitation of common assumptions will prevail, as it must, for these works are rituals, communal rites. To expect more, to anticipate anguish or social imagination, leads to disappointment and anger. The Reports now begin to have their formal structure. Always on the sacred agenda is the search for "outside influence," for it appears that our dreams are never free of conspiracies. "We find," one of the Report goes, "no evidence that the Free Speech Movement was organized by the Communist Party, or the Progressive Labor Movement, or any other outside group." Good, we say, safe once more, protected from the ultimate.

It is also part of the structure of a Report that it should scold us, but scold in an encouraging, constructive way, as a mother is advised to reprimand her child. For, after all, are we to blame? To blame for riots, assassinations, disorderly students? The Reports say, yes, we are to blame, and then again we aren't. Oswald, friendless, and Watts, ignored. Well, we should indeed have done better—and they should have done better, too.

Watts—a strip of plastic and clapboard, decorated by skimpy palms. It has about it that depressed feeling of a shimmering, timeless afternoon in the Caribbean: there, just standing about, the melancholy bodies of young black boys—and way off, in the distance, the looming towers of a Hilton. Pale stucco, shacky stores, housing projects, laid out nicely, not tall, like rows of tomato vines. Equable climate, ennui, nothingness. Here? Why here? we demand to know. Are they perhaps, although so recently from little towns and rural counties of the South, somehow longing for the sweet squalor of the Hotel Theresa, the battered seats of the Apollo Theatre? This long, sunny nothingness, born yesterday. It turns out to be an exile, a stop-over from which there is no escape. In January there was a strange quiet. You tour the streets as if they were a battlefield, our absolutely contemporary Gettysburg. Here, the hallowed rubble of the Lucky Store, there once stood a clothing shop, and yonder, the ruins of a super market. The standing survivors told the eye what the fallen monuments had looked like, the frame, modest structures of small, small business, itself more or less fallen away from all but the most reduced hopes. In the evening the owners lock and bolt and gate and bar and then drive away to their own neighborhoods, a good many of those also infested with disappointments unmitigated by the year-round cook-out. Everything is small, but with no hint of neighborliness.

The promise of Los Angeles, this beckoning openness, newness, freedom. But what is it? It is neither a great city nor a small town. Sheer impossibility of definition, of knowing what you are experiencing exhausts the mind. The intensity and diversity of small-town Main Streets have been stretched and pulled and thinned out so that not even a Kresge, a redecorated Walgreen's, or the old gray stone of the public library, the spitoons and insolence of the Court House stand to keep the memory intact. The past resides in old cars, five years old, if anywhere. The Watts riots were a way to enter history, to create a past, to give form by destruction. Being shown the debris by serious, intelligent men of the district was like being on one of those cultural tours in an underdeveloped region. Their pride, their memories were of the first importance. It is hard to find another act in American history of such peculiarity—elation in the destruction of the lowly symbols of capitalism.

And now, how long ago it all seems. How odd it is to go back over the old newspapers, the astonishing photographs in *Life* magazine, the flaming buildings, the girls in hair curlers and shorts, the loaded shopping carts, "Get Whitey," and "Burn, baby, burn," and the National Guard, the crisis, the curfew, and Police Chief Parker's curtain line, "We're on top and they are on the bottom." In the summer of 1965 "as many as 10,000 Negroes took to the streets in marauding bands." Property damage was forty million; nearly four thousand persons were arrested; thirty-four were killed. A commission headed by John A. McCone produced a report called, "Violence in the City—An End or a Beginning?" (Imagine the conferences about the title!) It is somewhat dramatic, but not unnerving since its cadence whispers immediately in our ear of the second-rate, the Sunday Supplement, the *Reader's Digest*.

The Watts Report is a distressing effort. It is one of those bureaucratic documents, written in an ambivalent bureaucratic prose, and it yields little of interest on the surface and a great deal of hostility below the surface. (Bayard Rustin in *Commentary* shows brilliantly how the defects of Negro life are made to carry the blame for Negro behavior in a way that exonerates the conditions that produced the defects.) In our time, moral torpor and evangelical rhetoric have numbed our senses. The humble meters of the McCone Report are an extreme example of the distance a debased rhetoric puts between word and deed. A certain squeamishness calls the poor Negroes of Watts the "disadvantaged" and designates the police as "Caucasians." "A dull, devastating spiral of failure" is their way of calling to mind the days and nights of the Watts community.

The drama of the disadvantaged and the Caucasians opens on a warm night and a drunken driver. Anyone who has been in Watts will know the beauty and power of the automobile. It is the lifeline, and during the burning and looting, car lots and gasoline stations were exempt from revenge. Watts indeed is an island; even though by car it is not far from downtown Los Angeles, it has been estimated that it costs about $1.50 and one-and-a-half to two hours to get out of Watts to possible employment. One might wonder, as he reads the opening scene, why the police were going to tow the drunken driver's car away, rather than release it to his mother and brother who were trying to claim it? For this is a deprivation and frustration not to be borne in the freeway inferno. Without a car you are not truly alive; every sort of crippling, disabling imprisonment of body and mind attends this lack. The sight of the "Caucasians" and the hot night and the hatred and deprivation burst into a revolutionary ecstasy and before it was over it extended far beyond Watts, which is only the name for a small part of the community, into a much larger area of Negro residence.

And what is to be done, what does it mean? Was it gray, tired meat and shoes with composition soles at prices a little starlet might gasp at? Of course we know what the report will say, what we all say; all that is true and has nevertheless become words, rhetoric. It's jobs and headstarts and housing and the mother at the head of the family and reading levels and drop-outs. The Report mentions some particular aggravations: the incredible bungling of the poverty program in Los Angeles; the insult of the repeal of the Rumford Fair Housing

Act; the Civil Rights program of protest. The last cause is a deduction from the Byzantine prose of the report which reads: "Throughout the nation, unpunished violence and disobedience to law were widely reported, and almost daily there were exhortations, here and elsewhere, to take extreme and even illegal remedies to right a wide variety of wrongs, real and supposed." *Real* and *supposed;* in another passage the locution "many Negroes felt and *were encouraged to feel,*" occurs. These niceties fascinate the student of language. They tell of unseen enemies, real and supposed, and strange encouragements, of what nature we are not told.

Still, the Watts Report is a mirror: the distance its bureaucratic language puts between us and the Negro is the reflection of reality. The demands of those days and nights on the streets, the smoke and the flames, are simply not to be taken in. The most radical re-organization of our lives could hardly satisfy them, and there seems to be neither the wish nor the will to make the effort. The words swell as purpose shrinks. Alabama and California are separated by more than miles of painted desert. The Civil Rights movement is fellowship and Watts is alienation, separation.

"What can violence bring you when the white people have the police and the power? What can it bring you except death?"
"Well, we are dying a little bit every day."

The final words of the Report seem to struggle for some faint upbeat and resolution but they are bewildered and fatigued. "As we have said earlier in this report, there is no immediate remedy for the problems of the Negro and other disadvantaged in our community. The problems are deep and the remedies are costly and will take time. However, through the implementation of the programs we propose, with the dedication we discuss, and with the leadership we call for from all, our Commission states without dissent, that the tragic violence that occurred during the six days of August will not be repeated."

How hard it is to keep the attention of the American people. Perhaps that is what "communications" are for: to excite and divert with one thing after another. And we are a nation preeminent in communications. The Negro has been pushed out of our thoughts by the Vietnam war. Helicopters in Southeast Asia turned out to be far easier to provide than the respect the Negro asked for.

"The army? What about the army?"
"It's the last chance for a Negro to be a man . . . and yet it's another prison, too."

The months have gone by. And did the explosion in Watts really do what they thought afterward? Did it give dignity and definition? Did it mean anything in the long run? We know that only the severest concentration will keep the

claims of the Negro alive in America, because he represents all the imponder-
ables of life itself. Anxiety and uncertainty push us on to something else—to
words which seem to soothe, and to more words. As for Watts itself: the oddity
of its simplicity can scarcely be grasped. Its defiant lack of outline haunts the
imagination. Lying low under the sun, shadowed by overpasses, it would seem
to offer every possibility, every hope. In the newness of the residents, of the
buildings, of the TV sets, there is a strange stillness, as of something formless,
unaccountable. The gaps in the streets are hardly missed, where there is so
much missing. Of course it is jobs and schools and segregation, yes, yes. But beyond that something that has nothing to do with Negroes was trying to be destroyed that summer. Some part of new America itself—that "dull, devastating
spiral of failure" the McCone Commission imagines to belong only to the "disadvantaged" standing friendless in their capsule on the outskirts of downtown
Los Angeles.

The Brilliancy of Black

Esquire, January 1967

◆

Bernard Weinraub

Jesus Christ, His arms outstretched and pleading, is painted in lush blues and
pinks in the lobby. Inside the church, the aisles are filling with teen-agers, curiously quiet and solemn, who grip programs ("Harlem Youth Unlimited presents . . . 'The Role of Negro Youth in Shaping Their Destinies' "). Stepping
through the crowd a slight woman with a lost, desperate smile hands out a
"Come Ye Disconsolate" leaflet and cries out that Brothers and Sisters you are
all invited to view the Southern Baptist Stars on their twenty-second anniversary at Mount Moriah Baptist Church.

Outside, bare-chested little boys in sneakers watch the white television
men set up their cameras. A white cop, a pudgy man with roly-poly fingers and
a hard, blue-eyed Irish face, removes a handkerchief from his rear pocket,
scrubs off his forehead sweat and gazes up, up, up at the church—a De Mille
Corinthian setting that was once a movie theatre, the Alhambra. The Black
Muslims are distributing *Muhammad Speaks,* and the television men are ner-

vous and the teen-agers keep surging into the sweltering lobby past the mural of Jesus. It is dusk on Seventh Avenue and 116th Street in Harlem and it is warm and they are waiting for Stokely Carmichael.

Three months earlier, Stokely had taken over the Student Nonviolent Co-ordinating Committee and had coined those two words "Black Power" that aroused all the white folks and dismayed some of the powerful black folks. He had been on *Meet the Press* television and on the front page of *The New York Times* and had visited Mississippi and Washington, D.C. and Boston and now, finally, he was in Harlem.

The kids waited. They were fifteen, sixteen and seventeen, the boys in pressed olive-drab suits and seersucker jackets, the girls in sandals, dangling earrings, A-line skirts, and kerchiefs, quite chic, on their African cropped hair. They carried paperbacks and chatted quietly. For the past few months they had been in the Haryou-Act anti-poverty program where they worked with the community, and baby-sat for working mothers, and were taught what to wear when they took the A train downtown to apply for a job on Fifth Avenue. And they had read—and discussed—James Baldwin and Chester Himes and ex-plored in heated talks The Role of Negro Youth and The Problems of Negro Youth and What's Ahead for Negro Youth. And now Stokely, who used to play stickball on 137th Street, comes onstage with a half-dozen other speakers and the curious tenseness among the teen-agers bursts. They break into wild ap-plause.

Stokely is surrounded by friends. "Hey, baby, how ya' doin'?" he cries. . . . "Hey Thomas, why the hell aren't you back in Alabama doin' some work. . . . Hey, boy, you lookin' *good*." Stokely looks good too. He wears black Italian boots, a tight blue suit, white shirt, striped tie, a name chain on his wrist. He is six-feet-one and has the build of a basketball guard: a solid chest, slender waist, powerful legs. His smile dazzles—an open, unguarded, innocent smile.

. The first speaker is seventeen-year-old Clarissa Williams, a striking girl in a loose green dress. She has a gentle voice: "*Newsweek* and *Life* have conducted their own surveys of black people. Well, baby, no one has to tell us what the black community is like because we know it, we live it. We intend to be the gen-eration which will make black youth to be unlimited. We intend to be the gen-eration that says, Friends, we do not have a dream, we do *not* have a dream, we have a plan. So, TV men, do not be prepared to record our actions indoors, but be prepared to record our actions *on the streets*. . . ." The audience, and Stokely, applaud and cry, "Hit 'em hard, Sister."

Clarissa hits them harder and by the time she winds up her tough little speech the audience is electric. And then Stokely rises. His style dazzles. He shakes his head as he begins speaking and his body appears to tremble. His voice, at least in the North, is lilting and Jamaican. His hands move effortlessly. His tone—and the audience loves it—is cool and very hip. No Martin Luther

King We Shall Overcome oratory. No preacher harangue. No screaming. He speaks one tone above a whisper, but a very taut, suppressed whisper. His speech—he has made it dozens of times before—varies with the audience, the area, the news that day, his mood. Stokely's words flow musically and build and Stokely pounds into the microphone and stops and the music starts again. The audience is rapt.

"Brothers and Sisters, we have been living with The Man too long. Brothers and Sisters, we have been *in a bag* too long. *We have got to move to a position where we will be proud, be proud of our blackness.* From here on in we've got to stick together, Brothers and Sisters, we've got to join together and move to a new spirit and make of our community a community of love . . . LOVE. There's no time for shuckin' and jivin'. We've got to move fast and we've got to come together and we've got . . . we've got to realize . . . that this country was conceived in racism and dedicated to racism. And understand that we've got to move . . . WE HAVE GOT TO MOVE. . . . We've got to build to a position so that when L.B.J. says, 'Come heah, boy, I'm gonna send you to Veetnam,' we will say, 'Hell, no.' " ("Preach, boy, preach. . . . Tell 'em, Stokely. . . .")

"Brothers and Sisters, a hell of a lot of us are gonna be shot and it ain't just gonna be in South Vietnam. We've got to move to a position *in this country* where we're not afraid to say that any man who has been selling us rotten meat for high prices should have had his store bombed fifteen years ago. We have got to move to a position where we will control our *own* destiny. We have got to move to a position where we will have black people represent *us* to achieve *our* needs. This country don't run on love, Brothers, it's run on power and we ain't got none. Brothers and Sisters, don't let them separate you from other black people. Don't ever in your life apologize for your black brothers. Don't be ashamed of your culture because if you don't have culture, that means you don't exist and, Brothers and Sisters, we do exist. Don't ever, don't ever, don't *ever* be ashamed of being black because you . . . you are black, little girl with your nappy hair and your broad lips, and *you are beautiful.* Brothers and Sisters, I know this theatre we're in—it used to be the Alhambra. Well I used to come here on Saturday afternoon when I was a little boy and we used to see Tarzan here and all of us would yell like crazy when Tarzan beat up our black brothers. Well, you know Tarzan is on television now and from here on in I'm rooting for that black man to beat the hell out of Tarzan. . . ."

The audience roars and is on its feet and Stokely grins and waves. The audience keeps applauding. . . .

Stokely is in the East to build up support, to meet with S.N.C.C. workers in New York, Newark, Boston and Philadelphia. He will make speeches and hold private meetings and endure just a few interviews (he turns down many of them now because of "distortions"). At twenty-five, the most charismatic figure in the Negro movement, Stokely Carmichael rushes from ghetto to ghetto with the drive of a political candidate one week before Election Day. He sleeps just a few hours a night. He eats on the run and drinks milk to keep up his energy. In Mississippi and Alabama, during those five summers of unbearable heat, of prison, of beatings, of death threats, of rifle shots fired at him through car windows, Stokely smoked three packs of cigarettes a day. He doesn't smoke now and doesn't drink.

His base now—and S.N.C.C.'s headquarters—is in Atlanta and his itinerary in other cities is set up by the local S.N.C.C. office, mostly by twenty- and twenty-one-year-old Negroes whom Stokely led in the South. There are, inevitably, the fund-raising parties—S.N.C.C.'s funds have dropped—but mostly just meetings and speeches.

He spends the next day in Newark, a dismal, grey city which has more Negroes than whites. The highlight of the visit is a speech that evening at the anti-poverty board on Springfield Avenue, in the heart of the ghetto, and then a cocktail party at ten-fifteen across town. The anti-poverty board is packed with an older audience than in Harlem. There are mothers with children on their laps and grandmothers with grandchildren on their bosoms; old men in overalls, janitors, civil-service workers, LeRoi Jones, high-school students, tough-looking nineteen-year-olds leaning against the green stucco walls, and several white poverty workers.

Stokely instinctively knows the audience. He stares quickly across the room and then scribbles down notes on the back of an envelope. He rises to warm applause. He smiles.

"Is it okay if ah take off mah jacket?" he says in a too-Southern drawl.

The speech goes well. Stokely begins by warming up the elderly women in the audience and ends with a cry to the students. The themes are the same. "You gotta understand about white power. It's white power that brought us here in chains, it's white power that kept us here in chains and it's white power that wants to keep us here in chains. . . . What they've been able to do is make us ashamed of being black . . . ashamed. I used to come home from school and say, 'Hey, Momma.' And she used to say, 'Sssshh, you know how loud we are.' I wouldn't go outside eating watermelon, no sir. They say we're lazy, so we work from sunup to sundown to prove that we're not lazy. We are tired of working for them, of being the maids of the liberal white folks who consider us part of their families. . . . My mother was a maid for a lady in Long Island and this lady wanted me to go to college and she told my mother, 'Your boy is a bright colored boy and we want to help send him to college.' Well, I hated that woman. She gave my mother $30 a week and all the old clothes her kids didn't want. Well, I didn't want her old clothes. I didn't want her to help send me to college. I wanted my Momma." ("Tell it, Stokely. . . .")

"There is a system in this country that locks black people in, but lets one or two get out every year. And they all say, 'Well, look at that one or two. He's helping his race.' Well, Ralph Bunche hasn't done a damn thing for me. If he's helping his race, then he should come *home*. Brothers and Sisters, there's nothing wrong about being all white or all black. It's only when you use one to exploit the other—and we have been exploited. You gotta understand what they do. They say, 'Let's integrate.' Well integration means going to a white school because that school is good and the black school is bad. It means moving from a black neighborhood to a white neighborhood because one neighborhood, they tell you, is bad and the other is good. Well, if integration means moving to something white, moving to something good, then integration is just a cover for white supremacy. . . .

"Brothers and Sisters, we have to view ourselves as a community and not a ghetto and that's the only way to make it. The political control of every ghetto is outside the ghetto. We want political control to be *inside* the ghetto. Like the workers in the Thirties, like the Irish in Boston, we demand the right to organize the way we want to organize. Black power is the demand to organize around the question of blackness. We are oppressed for only one reason: because we are black. We must organize. Brothers and Sisters, the only way they'll stop me from organizing is if they kill me or put me in jail. And once they put me in jail I'll organize my brothers in prison. *Organize!*"

The back of Stokely's white shirt is drenched with sweat. As soon as he finishes the speech, the crowd rises and surrounds him and shakes his hand and Stokely seeks out the old ladies who cry, "My, my, *my*, you are somethin'" and gives the younger kids that special handshake reserved only for a black brother or sister—a handshake in which he clasps a hand with his right hand and places his left hand over the linked hands. (When a white man shakes his hand, the smile is guarded, the handclasp unsure, the left hand remains limp.)

Thirty minutes later the cocktail party on Porter Avenue awaits Stokely, who has stopped off in several Negro bars—not to drink, but to meet and talk with some of the customers. The party is given by a short, burly chemist and his wife in the yard in back of their twelve-room stucco house. At least forty people have paid $5 to see Stokely, with about a half-dozen S.N.C.C. workers admitted free. Weak Martinis and Whiskey Sours are ladled out and, curiously, the middle-aged white and Negro couples stand and drink together near the small swimming pool in the center of the yard. The younger white kids stand alone. The young Negroes stand beneath the Rose of Sharon, uncomfortable, hostile, waiting for Stokely.

He arrives late and in a bitter mood. In the car coming to the party Stokely has been told that David Frost, a candidate running in the upcoming Democratic Senatorial primary on an anti-Vietnam ticket, will also speak at the party. Stokely immediately feels that his name is being used to attract people for a political candidate, a *white* political candidate. The money isn't even going to S.N.C.C., as he had been told in New York, but to a local liberal group. Stokely is furious. He walks to the edge of the backyard and has a five-minute talk with Bob Fullilove, the local S.N.C.C. leader. Across the lawn, the young Negroes glower. . . . This is a real put-down, says one girl who is attending Rutgers Law School. Why the hell are they holding this in the backyard? Can't they hold it inside as if it were a regular, *formal* cocktail party? These people are not my kind of people . . . I don't like this scene, man. . . . This is bad news. . . .

Stokely and Fullilove end their talk and Stokely walks beneath the Rose of Sharon with the woman who accompanied him to the party, a six-foot-tall, very cool, very black-skinned woman with piled-high Nefertiti hair. She wears a tight white dress and is, she knows and Stokely knows and the entire party knows, the most stunning woman there. Stokely sips a Coke and the girl glowers at the crowd, which tries very hard to be casual, and not stare at her. A white man walks over, smiling, gripping his Martini.

"I just want to tell you, Mr. Carmichael, I saw you on TV and I really agreed with you on, uh, Vietnam and—"

Stokely cuts him off. "Thank you." Stokely gives him the white man's handshake.

"Attention, attention," cries the hostess, a short chubby woman in a knit dress. "Our guests are all here and our program is beginning."

The young Negroes appear startled. "What program?" Stokely frowns.

"I just want to say a few words," the woman goes on. "We have always been an integrated community. . . ." The Negroes begin shifting uncomfortably. "And we've never cared at all here about money or status, whatever that means."

"Shit," says Stokely in a loud whisper. "She don't know about status? Look at that swimming pool."

As soon as Frost begins speaking, Stokely leaves the backyard and walks toward the front of the house with his date. He leans against an elm, his left hand gentle on the young woman's shoulder. They chat in a whisper. A Negro girl, slightly drunk, and a white man come out of the house and Stokely glares at the girl. She walks over. "I like what you said about being proud of our blackness," she says.

"That means everyone," says Stokely in an angry whisper.

"Let's get out of here," says Stokely's date.

The girl looks at the white man and says, "Be proud of my blackness, my black womanness." She starts laughing and they walk away to a car.

Stokely watches them drive off.

"Let's leave," says Stokely's date.

They return to the backyard and within minutes Stokely—who had been scheduled to speak—and most of the young Negroes are gone; the whites and middle-aged Negroes are left alone.

Stokely is scheduled to take an eight o'clock flight the next morning to

Glens Falls, New York, and then be driven to Benson, Vermont, for a speech at a camp—he's not quite sure what type of camp or who will be there. At two minutes after eight Stokely's cab pulls up to the Mohawk Airlines terminal at LaGuardia Airport and Stokely leaps out and runs toward the ticket desk.

"I'm sorry," the ticket agent behind the desk says with a smile. "The flight just left."

"Oh no, oh no, oh *no*." Stokely pounds his fist on the desk.

"There *is* a flight leaving from Kennedy at eight-forty-five with a stop-off at Albany. And there's another at ten-thirty." The ticket agent smiles again.

Stokely walks away and shakes his head. "I took a cab from the Bronx [his mother's house]. It should have taken twenty minutes to get here. I kept saying, 'Use the bridge, use the bridge, man.' But that son of a bitch kept saying that Bruckner Boulevard was faster. Faster! It took an hour. Oh . . . oh that son of a bitch."

Stokely wears dark glasses, a black shirt with small-flowered print, dungarees and black shoes. He hails a cab for Kennedy Airport and once the cab starts Stokely lifts up the glasses and rubs his eyes—he had gone to bed at five that morning.

"They always do that in Atlanta," he says. "They always give us a hard time with flights down there."

He shakes his head again. The cab glides out of LaGuardia toward the Van Wyck Expressway. The traffic toward Manhattan is heavy; toward Kennedy Airport there are few cars. When Stokely is in New York, he generally spends the night in his mother's South Bronx home (the only Negro family on the block). He had not seen her on this trip, though, since she is working as a maid on a maritime line.

"She's a hard worker and a sharp gal," says Stokely, staring at the cars crawling toward New York. He turns. "She knew, she knows, that if you want to make it you got to hustle, and she hustled from the word go. She took no shit from no one. I got that from my mother. She used to tell me, 'You take nothing from no one, no matter who they are.' She knows the realities of life and she demanded, made sure, that I knew them too."

He smiles. "My old man was just the opposite." Stokely shakes his head and sighs. "He believed genuinely in the great American dream. And because he believed in it he was just squashed. Squashed! He worked himself to death in this country and he died the same way he started: poor and black."

"We came here in '52 from Port-of-Spain. That was a place that was mostly black. It was run by black people and everyone—the cops, the teachers, the civil servants—was black. We came here thinking that this was the promised land. Ha. We went up to the Bronx—I was eleven years old—and I saw this big apartment house we were going to and I said, 'Wow, Daddy, you own that whole thing?' And then eight of us climbed up to a three-room apartment.

"My old man . . ." Stokely takes off his glasses . . . "my old man would Tom. He was such a good old Joe, but he would Tom. And he was a very religious cat too—he was head deacon of the church and he was so honest, so very, very honest. He never realized people lied or cheated or were bad. He couldn't conceive of it. He just prayed and worked. Man, did he work. He worked as a cabdriver at night and went to school to study electricity and during the day he worked as a carpenter. He just thought that if you worked hard and prayed hard this country would take care of you. Well, I remember he tried to get into the carpenter's union—and this is a very racist thing. And the only way for him to get into the union was to bribe the business representative. Well, he would have none of that. So one day when my father is out, my mother calls up the business representative and tells him to come to the house and she gives him $50 and a bottle of perfume and my father gets into the union. And when my father comes home and finds out that he's in the union he says, 'You see. You work hard and pray hard and this country takes care.' And my mother and I . . . laughed. Wow. My old man was like the Man with the Hoe. He just felt that there were millions to be made in this country and he died at forty-two—just a poor black man."

The cab pulls up at the Eastern Airlines terminal in Kennedy Airport. Stokely walks in and within seconds a porter walks up and smiles broadly. "I usually hang out with the porters at the airports," he says, walking quickly through the terminal. "A lot of times I don't have money and they just pass the hat. They're good people. In Memphis last week they bought me a steak dinner."

He walks to Gate 2 where a Mohawk flight is taking off at eight-forty-five. He waits ten minutes on standby but the flight is filled. He trudges back to the ticket desk and makes a reservation for the ten-thirty flight and then phones S.N.C.C. to tell them to notify the camp. By now Stokely is hungry and he walks into the cocktail lounge and restaurant in the heart of the terminal. The alcoholics, the hangers-on, the bored travelers, the women catching the nine o'-clock flight to Mexico City line the bar, sipping Bloody Marys and beer and Scotch, straight. A waiter hustles over and says, no, the restaurant is not open at this hour, but there's another restaurant at the end of the corridor. A woman at the bar, blonde, tall, tanned, in her late forties, carrying a large white pillbox, turns and stares through dark glasses at Stokely—this hulking, dungareed figure in dark glasses too. Their eyes meet. The woman smiles, just slightly, and Stokely stares at her for a moment and then turns away and walks out.

"Man, this place says something. You can get a drink at nine o'clock, but you can't get food."

At a table in the restaurant Stokely calls the waitress "M'am" and orders orange juice, bacon and eggs, English muffins and two glasses of milk.

"I used to drink," he says with a smile. "I used to like wine. I used to know a hell of a lot of guys who drank wine all day."

The waitress brings his orange juice and he sips it. "In Harlem I used to know a lot of guys like that. I used to know a lot of guys who were addicts and they were some beautiful cats. I'm not kidding. They had this ability, this profound ability to understand life."

While Stokely's father struggled and his mother worked as a maid to help support the family—Stokely has four sisters—he often spent days and weeks with his aunts on Lenox Avenue and 142nd Street in Harlem. "I like Harlem," says Stokely. "It's a very exciting place. It represents life, real life. On one block you have a church and right next door is a bar and they're both packed. On Saturday night people are always in constant motion. You get all of life's contradictions right there in one community: all the wild violence and all the love can be found in Harlem. You get the smells of human sweat and all sorts of bright colors and bright clothes and people in motion. You get preachers on one side of a street and nationalists on the other."

The waitress brings the rest of the order.

Stokely Carmichael grew up in the Bronx and Harlem, a bright, wild, aggressive boy. He attended P.S. 39, P.S. 34, and P.S. 83 and was involved, almost as soon as the family moved to New York, in fistfights and gang intrigues. In the Bronx, he was the only Negro member of the Morris Park Avenue Dukes and was, he admits, a specialist in stealing hubcaps and car radios.

In 1956 quite suddenly Stokely broke with the past. He was admitted to the Bronx High School of Science, a school for some of the brightest children in New York. "My freshman year I wanted to leave," Stokely recalls. "I couldn't intellectually compete with those cats. They were doctors' sons and lawyers' sons and read everything from Einstein to *The Grapes of Wrath*. The only book I knew was *Huckleberry Finn*. It was clear to me I couldn't compete. My mother wouldn't accept it though. She wanted me to go to Science and she would have it no other way. No questions asked. 'Remember one thing,' she would say, 'they're white, they'll make it. You won't unless you're on the top.' "

Stokely began reading—Marx, Darwin, Camus, anything he was given. "I began to read as quickly as I could; anything that anybody mentioned. It was naïve at the time, but it was sincere." For the first time, his friends were upper middle-class whites, wealthy kids who would go on to Harvard, Columbia, Brandeis. He began going out with white girls and making the Greenwich Village scene. He was invited to parties on Park Avenue.

Even as he persisted in friendships with white men and women, however, Stokely realized that the white and black worlds he knew were not linking; in fact they were splitting, irrevocably, apart. "I learned at Science that white people, liberal white people, could be intellectually committed but emotionally racist. They couldn't see *through*. I was everybody's best friend. They would say to me, 'Oh, you're so different.' And they didn't know any other black people. What they meant was I didn't meet their image of black people. And their image, their responses, are governed by the thought that Negroes *are* inferior. I was an exception. I was the accepted Negro. But other Negroes weren't like me. They were bums, lazy, unambitious, inhuman, and that attitude was extended to me. They would say to me, 'Oh, you dance so well,' when I couldn't dance so well. Or they would say to me, 'Oh, you're so sensitive.' Well the only thing I was sensitive to was the fact that they all had maids and they saw no inconsistency between being my friend and exploiting a black maid—paying her $30 a week while they went off and made a damned good living. I went to parties on Park Avenue and they called their maids by their first name and the maids were smiling and serving and I knew full well what was going on in their minds and I knew they didn't want to take all that shit. All these kids—these filthy rich kids—they all had maids and my mother was a maid."

When Stokely was a high-school senior, he began reading about the first sit-ins in the South. His first reaction was negative. "What I said was, 'Niggers always looking to get themselves in the paper, no matter how they did it.' My opinion was that they didn't know what they were doing."

Within months, though, he met several students involved in the sit-ins. As the civil-rights movement spread quickly across the South, Stokely's commitment—and fascination—grew. First, he picketed Woolworth's in New York and then sat-in in Virginia and North Carolina. He turned down scholarships to several white schools and enrolled at Howard University, mostly because he could keep working in the movement while at a Negro school. At Howard, he met other civil-rights activists and immediately engaged in sit-ins and the early freedom rides through Mississippi, Georgia and Alabama. The first ride and the first arrest was in Jackson, Mississippi in 1961. . . .

By now Stokely had finished breakfast at the airport and walked to Gate 2 to board the plane. Almost as soon as he took his seat he began shivering—he is always cold—and he grabbed a blanket off the rack. The plane started and Stokely peered through the window at the rows of A-frame houses below, the cars, the Manhattan skyline. "I went down South when I was nineteen. I was a kid who took nothing from no one. And, man, I took it." He smiled. "In Mississippi, the beatings are by the cops, not by mobs. The mobs, they throw wild punches and if you're cool you can miss them. But the cops are out to get your ass and you get three cops in a back room who are out to get your ass and. . . ." He shook his head. "In Jackson, before they put me in jail, the cops rode me up and down in an elevator; they kept kicking and using billy clubs and pressing the buttons using their fist. I wanted . . . I just wanted to get my hands on one of them. But like you had to cover your head and . . . and . . . you keep thinking why don't you leave me alone. Why don't you beat your wives instead and just leave me alone?"

Stokely then spent time in jail. "Fifty-three days. Oh, lord, fifty-three days in a six-by-nine cell. Twice a week to shower. No books, nothing to do. They would isolate us. Maximum security. And those guards were out of sight. They did not play, *they did not play*. The sheriff acted like he was scared of black folks and he came up with some beautiful things. One night he opened up all the windows, put on ten big fans and an air conditioner and dropped the temperature to 38 degrees. All we had on was T-shirts and shorts. And it was so cold, so *cold*, all you could do was walk around for two nights and three days, your teeth chattering, going out of your mind, and it getting so cold that when you touch the bedspring you feel your skin is gonna come right off.

"I don't go along with this garbage that you can't hate, you gotta love. I don't go along with that at all. Man you *can*, you *do* hate. You don't forget that Mississippi experience. You don't get arrested twenty-seven times. You don't smile at that and say love thy white brother. You don't forget those beatings and, man, they were rough. Those mothers were out to get revenge. You don't forget. You don't forget those funerals. I knew Medgar Evers, I knew Willie Moore, I knew Mickey Schwerner, I knew Jonathan Daniels, I met Mrs. Liuzzo just before she was killed. You don't forget those funerals."

The worst experience was what Stokely calls a two-day nervous breakdown just before the Selma-to-Montgomery march. "I was in the Ben Moore Hotel in Montgomery, getting ready to go downstairs, when they locked the doors. I couldn't get out. And downstairs were the marchers, and the cops began beating and using hoses. I couldn't stand it. I was by my window and I looked down and saw the cops beating and I couldn't get out. I was completely helpless. There was no release. I kept watching and then I began screaming and I didn't stop screaming. Some guys took me to the airport later and I kept screaming and I tried to kick in a couple of windows at the airport. Oh, man."

He shakes his head slowly. "There have been people in the movement who have cracked. Like you can't help it. You always work on the assumption that the worst things will happen, you always work on the assumption that you're going to die. I used to say that the only way they'll stop me is if they kill me. I still think that's true. What bothers me now is if I live through all this I just hope I don't get tired or give up or sell out. That's what bothers me. We all have weaknesses. I don't know what mine are. But if they find out they'll try to destroy me. It's a question of them finding out what my weaknesses are—money, power, publicity, I don't know. And sometimes . . . sometimes . . . you just get so tired too."

Stokely peers out the window at the clean, azure sky and shivers beneath the blanket. Within seconds, he is asleep.

Twenty minutes later the plane is landing at Albany Airport where Stokely will catch a plane for Glens Falls. He steps down the ramp and begins singing: "The empty-handed painter on your street is drawing crazy patterns on your sheet."

He grins and walks into the terminal. "Man, that Dylan is a wild guy."

With thirty minutes free before the next plane leaves, Stokely steps into the airport luncheonette and orders a vanilla ice cream soda. The waitress leaves and Stokely turns toward several persons at the counter reading newspapers. "Look at that, look at *that*," he says, laughing, pointing to the sports page headline of The New York *Daily News:* "Operate on Whitey's Arm."

"If they flipped that over and put it on the front page they'd sell a million copies," he laughs.

Within the hour Stokely arrives in the small Glens Falls airport—three hours late. As soon as he climbs off the plane, a smiling, crew-cut youth waves and walks over and introduces himself. He is Frank Levy, a Ph. D. candidate in economics at Yale and a member of the camp's staff.

Stokely struggles into Levy's red MG and they drive off to the camp, about fifty miles away. Stokely asks Levy about the camp and is told that it's called the Shawnee Leadership Institute, an annual two-week summer camp for teenagers who hold discussions on "issues" and listen to invited guest speakers. (The next day, Lord Caradon, the British Ambassador to the United Nations, was coming up.) There are about seventy campers and a staff of thirty, mostly college and graduate students.

Stokely likes Levy and they begin kidding about Vermont: "I wonder if everyone up here smokes pot." The car crosses New York into Vermont on Route 4 and passes Deak's grocery and Frank's Taxidermist. "I've never been to Vermont before," says Stokely.

The elms and pines are just starting to blaze with autumn colors and Stokely settles back and gazes silently at the countryside. He waves at farm boys—who wave back—and laughs as they ride past Crumley's grocery in Fort Ann. "A town like this and you go out of your mind," he exclaims. "I read someplace that suicide rates are very high in Vermont—they must be sick of cutting all that grass."

Just outside of Fort Ann, the car breaks down. Stokely moans and shakes his head and begins laughing. "This is my day," he says. The fan belt is broken and Stokely and Levy struggle with the new belt. After twenty minutes they are off again.

As soon as Stokely arrives at the camp he appears startled, then amused. "Wow," he says, as a half-dozen teen-age interracial couples, their arms around each other, surround the car, "Hey, like I had visions when I heard the name of the camp of old Protestant ladies sitting around campfires talking about love." They shake his hand and escort him to the dining room.

Once inside, Stokely is greeted by an old friend, Julian Houston, who is president of the Student Government at Boston University. Stokely grins and gives Julian the "black" handshake and embraces him. "Man, you should be workin' down in Alabama," cries Stokely.

With Houston and several other camp leaders, Stokely sits down at a wooden table while the campers, awestruck, watch him. Plates of ham and cheese and rolls are brought out and Stokely eats hungrily while a long-haired girl strums a guitar and sings "Ain't Gonna Study War No More."

After the plates are cleared away, all the campers are called into the wooden dining room. Stokely removes his shoes and begins speaking quietly.

"Black people have not only been told that they are inferior, but the system maintains it. We are faced in this country with whether or not we want to be equal and let white people define equality for us on their terms as they've always done and thus lose our blackness or whether we should maintain our identity and still be equal. This is Black Power. The fight is whether black people should use their slogans without having white people say, 'That's okay.' You have to deal with what white means in this country. When you say Black Power you mean the opposite of white and it forces this country to deal with its own racism. The 1954 school desegregation decision was handed down for several reasons. It was a political decision—and it was *not* based on humanitarianism, but was based on the fact that this country was going further into nonwhite countries and you could not espouse freedom and have second-class citizens in your own country. The area in which we move now is politics and within a political context. People kept saying that segregation and racism was wrong because it was immoral. But they still didn't come to grips with the two essential things: we are poor and we are black. You can pass 10,000 bills but you still haven't talked about economic security. When someone is poor, it's not because of cultural deprivation, it's not because they need to be uplifted and head-started. When someone is poor, it's because they have no money, that's all. That's all. They say it's our fault, *our fault* that we're poor when in fact it's the system that calculates and perpetuates poverty. They say black people don't know money, that they'll drink it away, they won't work. But we never had money, and it's presumptuous to tell us we won't be thrifty, brave, clean and reverent. You know who the biggest welfare group is in this country? You know who they are? You think it's the black people? Well, it's not. It's the farmers. They are the biggest welfare group in this country. But the difference between them and us is that they run their own programs, they control their own resources and they get something out of it. We must, *we must* take over and control our resources and our programs. And if we don't, the black people will wake up again tomorrow morning, still poor, still black, and still singing *We Shall Overcome.*"

The audience responds warmly and as soon as Stokely finishes, the questions begin. Stokely calls on a burly Negro youth who speaks in a thick drawl.

"Stokely, do you believe in God?"

Stokely stares at the youth. "That's a personal question."

The youth smiles. "Oh."

"Where you from?" Stokely asks.

"St. Augustine, Florida, Stokely."

"What you do down there?"

"I worked in the field. Cotton, tobacco, you name it. I worked for $2 a day since I was so high. I worked for $2 a day until I heard Dr. King down there and then I knew I had to join the movement."

"Right." Stokely turns from the boy to the audience. "The reason I joined the movement was not out of love. It was out of hate. I hate white supremacy and I'm out to smash it."

A pause. An older woman rises, a white woman. "Stokely," she asks, a tremor in her voice, "What can we do? What can the whites do?"

"You must seek to tear down racism. You must seek to organize poor whites. You must stop crying 'Black supremacy' or 'Black nationalist' or 'racism in reverse' and face certain facts: that this country is racist from top to bottom and one group is exploiting the other. You must face the fact that racism in this country is a white, not a black problem. And because of this, you, *you* must move into white communities to deal with the problem. We don't need kids from Berkeley to come down to Mississippi. We don't need white kids to come to black communities just because they want to be where the action is.

"Look," says Stokely, leaning forward, speaking in a loud whisper. "Every white man in this country can announce that he is our friend. Every white man can make us his token, symbol, object, what have you. Every white man can say, 'I am your friend.' Well from here on in we're going to decide who is our friend. We don't want to hear any words, we want to see what you're going to do. The price of being the black man's friend has gone up.

"And you must understand," he says, his voice rising, "that as a person oppressed because of my blackness, I have common cause with other blacks who are oppressed because of *their* blackness. It must be to the oppressed that I address myself, not to members—even friends—of the oppressing group."

The audience stirs. Stokely suggests they walk outside so he can get some good country air. Within minutes, the teen-agers sit in a semicircle beneath an evergreen, chatting quietly with Stokely who is lying on his side, his elbow dug into the grass, his chin in his hand. . . .

By dusk, with the apricot-colored sky streaked with violet, the campers implore Stokely to stay the night. He'd love to, he says, he needs the rest and this marvelous clean air, but there are meetings and speeches and appointments the next day.

With Julian Houston, Stokely climbs into a car driven by a Roman Catholic priest from Boston who is on the camp's staff.

"Stokely," says the priest, driving quickly down the darkening road, "what should church people do?"

Stokely pauses. "They should start working on destroying the church and building more Christ-like communities. It's obvious, Reverend, that the church doesn't want Christ-like communities. Christ—he taught some revolutionary stuff, right? And the church is a counterrevolutionary force."

The priest drives a moment in silence. "What should the priest's job be?"

"To administer, through his actions, the teachings of Jesus Christ," says Stokely. "I would also make every church a plain building that could be used for other things, a building that will not be embellished."

"What's next for you, Stokely?" asks the priest.

"Next?" Stokely smiles. "How does the victim move to equality with the executioner? That's what's next. We are the victims and we've got to move to equality with our executioners." He pauses. "Camus never answers that question, does he? We are the victims, they are the executioners. Every real relationship is that—victim and executioner. Every relationship. Love, marriage, school, everything. This is the way this society sees love. You become a slave to somebody you love. You love me, you don't mess around with anyone else. One is the victim, the other the executioner. . . ."

It is dark now and chilly and Stokely begins shivering. He begins gossiping with Houston about old friends who have been lost to the poverty program, the Peace Corps, graduate schools.

At the airport in Burlington, Stokely is told that the plane to New York has been delayed an hour. He shakes his head—"It's my day"—and walks around with Houston. He then has two sandwiches and two glasses of milk and averts the stares of several men at the bar who recognize him.

The plane finally arrives. Stokely shakes hands with the priest and Houston and walks wearily up the ramp. He is cold and tired and sleeps listlessly on the trip to New York.

Shortly before eleven the plane lands at Kennedy Airport. Stokely has a date downtown in Manhattan but decides, instead, just to return to the Bronx and go to sleep. By now he is exhausted. The lack of sleep, the missed and delayed flights, the car trips, the questions, sandwiches on the run, the pressures have taken their toll. He walks through the terminal, breathing heavily, peering blankly through his dark glasses. Once outside, he decides to take a taxi and starts walking to the first cab in line. The driver, who is white, stares at Stokely—dungarees, dark glasses, carrying a paper bag of ham sandwiches, looking vaguely ominous—and drives past him to pick up a laughing white couple who carry cardboard cases of tax-free liquor. Stokely tenses, clenches his fist and takes a deep breath and turns toward the second cabdriver in line. This driver, who is a young Negro, has watched Stokely and is now smiling faintly. Stokely walks over, looks at the cabdriver and begins smiling too. He then opens the door and climbs into the cab and returns home for just a brief rest.

Representative

The New Yorker, April 1, 1967

◆

Charlayne Hunter-Gault

Julian Bond, the twenty-seven-year-old Negro whom the Georgia legislature twice refused to seat last year, because he supported draft-card burners ("I would not burn my own draft card, but I admire the courage of those who do"), was seated in January by the United States Supreme Court and has just completed the first half of a two-year term of office. When we learned that he was to give a speech at a banquet on behalf of the Southern Conference Educational Fund (S.C.E.F.) at the Roosevelt Hotel the other night, we walked over there to hear what he had to say. We paused in the lobby long enough to pull out our program and read that S.C.E.F. is "the oldest interracial organization at work in the South to end all forms of segregation, discrimination, and injustice," and that it now feels itself challenged by events "to undertake anew the task of changing the mind-set of the white community and organizing at the grassroots level that coalition of black and white which will have the strength to bring about a truly democratic society." Then we took the stairs to the ballroom, on the mezzanine, where the banquet was being held, and as soon as we entered we spotted the tall young legislator standing in a pool of light and looking handsome and a trifle bored as several men adjusted floodlights for a television news interview. We introduced ourself, and Mr. Bond stepped from behind the lights and told us that this would be his third talk of the day. He said that he had spoken at Cheyney State College, near Philadelphia, and then had appeared on a Philadelphia television program, and that after the S.C.E.F. speech he was going straight to bed, because he had to make a speech in Rhode Island the next day.

"Every weekend has been like this," Mr. Bond said, in a quiet, even voice that had traces of a Southern accent. "My wife, Alice, and our three kids—a girl of four and two boys, one three and the other ten months—haven't been very happy about the trips I've had to take, but I've spoken in cities and towns from Georgia to California."

We asked Mr. Bond if his speeches fell into different categories.

"Two," he answered, with a smile. "That is, I have only two speeches that I give. The one that I give less frequently is about the two movements in this country—civil rights and peace—and how they ought to learn from each other. The other speech is a history of the Movement, which I usually call 'What Next for the Negro?' or 'Civil Rights—1960 to the Present Day,' or something that conveys that general idea."

"What next for the Movement?" we asked.

"The 1965 Civil Rights Bill changed the Movement," Mr. Bond said, without hesitation. "Many people who had previously supported the Movement thought that the passage of that bill meant the job was done. Others did not like the involvement of S.N.C.C., C.O.R.E., S.C.E.F., and S.C.L.C. in the anti-war protests. Then Black Power led to the final falling away. And for the Movement lack of interest is more killing than lack of money."

Mr. Bond paused long enough to light a cigarette, and continued, "On the other hand, the Movement people are more interested now in local programs, which don't necessarily make front-page splashes, the way the sit-ins did— things like backing candidates for the Board of Supervisors of Sunflower County, in Mississippi, and getting federal registrars to go there. That's Eastland's county, you know, and there is not one single federal registrar anywhere in it. The Movement used to spend most of its time trying to get federal legislation on housing, voting, and public accommodations. It has come to realize now that laws by themselves are never going to change the face of the country, since even the laws that exist today are not being enforced. That is why the emphasis now is on more local thrust—more contained thrust, if you will."

We asked Mr. Bond about his first session in the Georgia House of Representatives.

"Well, fortunately for me, several of my friends from Fulton County had been seated the year before, and since we are seated according to counties, we were all together," he said. "They kept me filled in. I had campaigned on a promise to introduce a minimum-wage bill for domestic workers, and when I was prevented from taking my seat, Ben Brown, an old friend from the sit-in days, and John Hood, another colleague, introduced it, but it didn't get out of committee. In fact, it barely got into committee. I myself introduced three privileged resolutions, the most radical of which was for official recognition of Negro History Week in Georgia. The others were for recognition of Dr. Benjamin E. Mays on his retirement after twenty-seven years as president of Morehouse College, and for recognition of Morehouse on its hundredth anniversary. My three, along with the hundreds of others for recognition of all kinds of things, passed. One of my biggest problems in the legislature was getting used to the flowery language."

When it was time for Mr. Bond to give his speech at the Roosevelt, we noted an absence of flowery language and a tendency to come straight to the point. He spoke briefly of the National Conference for New Politics and of the need for race consciousness. ("Negroes must not forget race consciousness as long as they are victims of racism," he said.) Then he spoke of the early Negro activists and the heritage of dissent they helped to create in this country. Finally, he made his main point by means of four quotations. The first was from a Negro newspaper of 1842:

> If war be declared, shall we fight with the chains upon our limbs? Will we fight in defense of a government which denies us the most precious right of citizenship? . . . We ask these questions. . . . The states in which we dwell have twice availed themselves of our *voluntary services*, and have repaid us with chains and slavery. Shall we a third time kiss the foot that crushes us? . . . No!

Mr. Bond's voice rose, then fell at an even pitch as he introduced his next quotation—from Henry McNeal Turner, one of twenty-seven Negroes who were expelled from the Georgia legislature in 1868:

> The black man cannot protect a country if the country doesn't protect him; and if, tomorrow, a war should arise, I would not raise a musket to defend a country where my manhood is denied. . . . I will say this much to the colored men of Georgia. . . . Never lift a finger nor raise a hand in defense of Georgia, unless Georgia acknowledges that you are men, and invests you with the rights pertaining to manhood.

Mr. Bond paused for a moment, then continued with a quotation from a newspaper article by Lewis Douglass, son of Frederick Douglass, written in 1899:

> It is a sorry, though true, fact that wherever this government controls, injustice to dark races prevails. The people of Cuba, Porto Rico, Hawaii and Manila know it well, as do the wronged Indian and outraged black man in the United States. . . . The question will be asked: How is it that such promises are made to Filipinos thousands of miles away while the action of the administration in protecting dark citizens at home does not even extend to a promise of any attempt to rebuke the outlawry which kills American citizens of African descent for the purpose of gratifying bloodthirstiness and race hatred? . . . It is hypocrisy of the most sickening kind to try to make us believe that the killing of Filipinos is for the purpose of good government and to give protection to life and liberty, and the pursuit of happiness.

Mr. Bond's last quotation was from W. E. B. DuBois, who wrote in 1904:

> I believe in the Prince of Peace. I believe that War is Murder. I believe that armies and navies are at bottom the tinsel and braggadocio of oppression and wrong; and I believe that the wicked conquest of weaker and darker nations by nations white and stronger but foreshadows the death of that strength.

Mr. Bond was quiet for a few seconds, then asked the audience to consider those statements in the light of events today, and sat down.

The Second Coming
of Martin Luther King

Harper's Magazine, August 1967

◆

DAVID HALBERSTAM

He is perhaps the best speaker in America of this generation, but his speech before the huge crowd in the UN Plaza on that afternoon in mid-April was bad; his words were flat, the drama and that special cadence, rooted in his Georgia past and handed down generation by generation in his family, were missing. It was as if he were reading someone else's speech. There was no extemporizing; and he is at his best extemporaneously, and at his worst when he reads. There were no verbal mistakes, no surprise passions. (An organizer of the peace march said afterwards, "He wrote it with a slide rule.") When he finished his speech, and was embraced by a black brother, it seemed an unwanted embrace, and he looked uncomfortable. He left the UN Plaza as soon as he could.

On that cold day of a cold spring Martin Luther King, Jr. made a sharp departure from his own past. He did it reluctantly; if he was not embittered over the loss of some old allies, he was clearly uneasy about some of his new ones. Yet join the peace movement he did. One part of his life was behind him, and a different and obviously more difficult one lay ahead. He had walked, marched, picketed, protested against legal segregation in America—in jails and out of jails, always in the spotlight. Where he went, the action went too. He had won a striking place of honor in the American society: if he was attacked as a radical, it was by men whose days were past. If his name was on men's room walls throughout the South, he was celebrated also as a Nobel Prize–winner, the youngest one in history; he was our beloved, *Time* Magazine's man of the year; his view of Christianity was accepted by many Americans who could never have accepted the Christianity of Billy Graham. In the decade of 1956 to 1966 he was a radical America felt comfortable to have spawned.

But all that seemed long ago. In the year 1967, the vital issue of the time was not civil rights, but Vietnam. And in civil rights we were slowly learning some of the terrible truths about the ghettos of the North. Standing on the platform at the UN Plaza, he was not taking on George Wallace, or Bull Connor, or Jim Clark; he was taking on the President of the United States, challenging what is deemed national security, linking by his very presence much of the civil-rights movement with the peace movement. Before the war would be ended, before the President and King spoke as one on the American ghettos— if they ever would—his new radicalism might take him very far.

On both these issues there had been considerable controversy and debate within the King organization, especially among those people who care most deeply for King, and see him as the possessor of a certain amount of moral power. On the peace issue none of King's associates really questioned how he felt; rather they questioned the wisdom of taking a stand. Would it hurt the civil-rights movement? Would it deprive the Negroes of King's desperately needed time and resources? And some of these peace people, were they really the kind of people King wanted to play with? On the ghettos there were similar problems.

No one is really going to accomplish anything in the ghettos, goes the argument, until the federal government comes in with massive programs. In the meantime King can only hurt and smear his own reputation; he will get dirt on his hands like the other ward heelers if he starts playing with practical day-by-day politics in the North. In the North, in addition to the white opponents, there are all the small-time Negro operators who will be out to make a reputation by bucking Martin King. Yet the ghettos exist, and to shun them is to lose moral status.

II

After the New York peace rally I traveled with King for ten days on the new paths he had chosen. It was a time when the Negro seemed more than ever rebellious and disenchanted with the white; and when the white middle class— decent, upright—seemed near to saturation with the Negro's new rebellion. The Negro in the cities seemed nearer to riots than ever; the white, seeing the riots on TV, wanted to move further away from the Negro than ever before. A terrible cycle was developing. At press conference after press conference he said no, he didn't think his stand on Vietnam was hurting the civil-rights movement or damaging the Negro cause with the President; no, he didn't think Stokely Carmichael's cry of black power had hurt the Negroes; no, he didn't plan to run for the Presidency. It was a week which began in New York with an announcement that King would go to the Holy Land in the fall on a pilgrimage.

Then came the first question: "And do you relate this to Vietnam?" No, King said, there were no political implications.

A Negro reporter who had been out to St. Alban's Hospital in Queens and had talked to the soldiers there said, "The war doesn't bother them. The soldiers are for it."

Later, on the way to the airport (most of King's life is spent going to airports, and it is the only time to talk to him), King's top assistant, Andy Young, commented on the fact that the Vietnam question had come from a Negro reporter. "It always does," he said. "Every time we get the dumb question, the patriot question, it's a Negro reporter." A New York minister said it was the Negro middle class wanting respectability and playing it close on Vietnam. "They're very nervous on Vietnam, afraid they're going to lose everything else." King added, "Yes, they're hoping the war will win them their spurs. That's not the way you win spurs." The ghettos, he said, were better on the war issue than the middle class.

III

The most important stop on King's trip would be Cleveland, where he was thinking of making a major summer effort to break down some of the ghetto barriers. It is a strange thing the way a city can rise to national and international fame over racial problems. Sometimes it is predictable. The word was always out in the South, for instance, that Birmingham was a tough city with a tough police force and Bull Connor; Negroes in Georgia and Mississippi knew about Bull Connor fifteen years before. Little Rock, which we once heard so much about, was an accident, its crisis deriving from its own succession laws and Orval Faubus' ambition.

Now there are cities imprinted on our memories that we barely know about, cities which we have forgotten, but in the Negro world, and in that part of the white world which is trying to cope with the coming fire, the word is out: Cleveland, where four people died in riots last summer, is likely to be a very tough place with all the worst aspects of the ghetto, and almost none of the safety valves. Unlike New York, where Mayor John Lindsay at least visits the slums, Mayor Ralph Locher seems to have written off the Negro vote, and to depend on the Italians, the Poles, and other white minorities. The Negro ministers there are interested in King's coming in for the summer action program, and though this is early May, a chilly day, and King is asking someone to find him a topcoat, there is a feeling that we will hear a good deal more about Cleveland before the summer is over, probably more than we want to.

King is edgy because the Negro community is divided. He does not want to get caught in a cross fire, and he is sensitive to what happened with his ill-fated organizing effort in Chicago last year.

Yet there are advantages in Cleveland. It is smaller than Chicago, better laid out geographically, and the Mayor is not so smart as Daley. His Chicago machine has enough Negro support to keep the Negro community divided; Locher's indifference to the Negroes in Cleveland may eventually force them to unite. But they must be brought together by someone from the outside. Here, then, is one of the ironies: for years the crisis was in the South, and Northern Negroes sent money and support there. In the process the most skilled leadership rose up in the South, fashioned out of the crises faced there, while in general the Northern leadership, so far lacking such direct and dramatic crises, lacks prestige; it must summon help from the South.

King is met at the airport by one of the older Negro ministers who is representing the Negro Ministers' Association. The preacher is about sixty, very pleased to be meeting King. As soon as we are in the car he starts talking about an earlier King speech and how much he liked it. Everyone else smiles politely, and there is a murmur of approval from King, which dies as the preacher continues, "I mean the way you got up there, Doctor King, and you told those Negroes they got to improve themselves, they got to help themselves more, isn't anyone else going to help them, and they got to clean up themselves, clean up their houses, clean up the filth in the streets, stop livin' like pigs, they've got to wash up. They can't just wait for someone to come to their doors with a welfare check, they got to help themselves."

There is silence in the car as he continues, his voice gaining in enthusiasm as he carries on, for he is preaching now, and driving a little faster too.

King says nothing, but from the back of the car, quite softly, the Reverend Bernard Lee, a King assistant, says, "You got to have something worth cleaning up, Reverend," almost as an apology.

The tension rises a little in the car; King is silent, and Bernard Lee speaks again. "It's easier said than done, Reverend. You've got six generations just trying to make do, and they've given up fighting."

But the Cleveland Reverend keeps on; the Negroes have got to clean it up; they've lost these homes.

This time it is Andy Young: "You ain't lost it, Reverend. They lost it for you. You never had it."

In all this King has said nothing, letting Lee and Young do the stalking. (Later I am to find that this is his standard technique, holding back, letting others talk themselves out, allowing his men to guide the conversation to the point where it can be finally summed up by him.) "Well, Reverend," King finally says, "these communities have become slums not just because the Negroes don't keep clean and don't care, but because the whole system makes it that way. I call it slummism—a bad house is not just a bad house, it's a bad school and a bad job, and it's been that way for three generations, a bad house for three generations, and a bad school for three generations."

Then Andy Young starts telling of a home-owning community in Atlanta. Recently somewhat lower-class white, it was now turning quickly black, and somewhat middle-class black: "And so, of course, as soon as they've moved they all get together and have a big meeting about how to keep the neighborhood clean . . . and they want that garbage picked up, you know all that, and in the middle of the meeting, a man stands up at the back of the room and he tells them they're kidding themselves. 'Forget it,' he says, 'just forget it, because you're not going to get these services. I work for the sanitation department and I want you to know that they've just transferred twenty men out of this area, so you can just forget it all.' "

"Same old story," Bernard Lee says. "Negroes buy houses and immediately the services stop, and these aren't Negroes on relief, Reverend."

King, to ease the tension, asks about the Negro community of Cleveland, and the preacher becomes so eloquent on the subject of the division within the Negro church community that Andy Young finally says, "Reverend, go back all the way to the New Testament. Even Peter and Paul couldn't get together."

"But *they* got it. They already got theirs, and we're trying to get our share," the preacher says.

King then asks, Is the Mayor a racist? No, says the preacher, it's not racism, "it's just ignorance. He doesn't know the pulse of the new Negro. The wrong kind of people are advising him, telling him handle the Negro this way, give him just a very little bit of this and a very little bit of that; give him a pacifier, not a cure, a sugar tit, that's what we used to call it in the South, a sugar tit, just enough to take away the appetite but doesn't fill you up . . . feed one man, give one man a job, and you've taken care of the Negroes." As he finishes, one can sense the relaxation in the car. The preacher has rehabilitated himself, he's not as much of a Tom as you think.

Then King starts talking about the cities. So very few of the mayors have the imagination to deal with the complexity of the problems, and the handful who do can't really handle it because they lack the resources. The problems are so great that they must go to the federal government, but most of them don't even know the problems in their own cities. It is almost as if they are afraid to try to understand, afraid where that trip would lead them. "Why, this Mayor Locher here in Cleveland," he says, "he's damning me now and calling me an extremist, and three years ago he gave me the key to the city and said I was the greatest man of the century. That was as long as I was safe from him down in the South. It's about the same with Daley and Yorty too; they used to tell me what a great man I was."

IV

That was a simpler time. He had exuded love and Christian understanding during the nation's dramatic assault on legal segregation. In retrospect it was not so much Martin Luther King who made the movement go, it was Bull Connor; each time a bomb went off, a head smashed open, the contributions would mount at King's headquarters. They bombed King's own house, an angry black mob gathered ready to do violence, and King came out and said, "We want to love our enemies. I want you to love our enemies. Be good to them and let them know you love them. What we are doing is right and God is with us." And, of course, it was a time of television, we could tune in for a few minutes and see the cream of Negro youth, the slack-jawed whites answering their love with illiterate threats and violence, shouting what they were going to do to the niggers, and reveling in this, spelling their own doom.

King was well prepared for his part in that war; the weapon would be the white man's Christianity. He knew his people, and he could bring to the old cadences of the Southern Negro preacher the new vision of the social gospel which demanded change in America. He was using these rhythms to articulate the new contemporary subjects they were ready to hear ("America, you've strayed away. You've trampled over nineteen million of your brethren. All men are created equal. Not some men. Not white men. All men. America, rise up and come home"). Before Birmingham, the Montgomery bus strike was a success, and other victories followed. Grouped around King were able young ministers, the new breed, better educated; in a changing South he became the single most important symbol of the fight against segregation, culminating in his great speech before the crowd which had marched to Washington in 1963. Those were heady years, and if not all the battles were won, the final impression was of a great televised morality play, white hats and black hats; lift up the black hat and there would be the white face of Bull Connor; lift up the white hat and there would be the solemn black face of Martin King, shouting love.

V

But in Cleveland in 1967 the Negro ministers are in trouble. They are poorly educated products of another time when a call to preach, a sense of passion, was judged more important than what was being said. Their great strength is organization; they try to hold their own separate congregations together. They get their people out of jail and they get them on welfare, and if that is not very much, there is nothing else.

But now they are divided—by age, by denomination, by style, by petty jealousies. They have not yet found the unifying enemy which bound their contemporaries together in the South, and they are unable to deal with the new young alienated Negroes, for whom their talk about damnation and salvation is at best camp; in the ghettos they cannot help those who need aid most. They are frightened by the Nationalists and Muslims, the anger spawned in the streets, the harshness and bitterness of these new voices, the disrespect to elders, the riots. In the South in the 'fifties all the preachers were on the outside looking in, but here in the North there is sometimes the illusion that they have made it and opened the door to the Establishment. So there is double alienation, not just black from white but black from black middle class.

When King arrives in Cleveland, he is immediately hustled off to a meeting of the ministers. The meeting lasts more than three hours, and there is a general agreement that King should come into Cleveland to organize; there is some doubt expressed because of what happened to his Chicago program, doubts which some of the ministers counter by listing otherwise unknown accomplishments and blaming the white press.*

Afterwards, King has dinner in a Negro restaurant with eight key preachers, some of them old friends. At least one went to Stockholm with him to get the Nobel Prize, and he is letting people know about that. There is something here of a self-consciously jovial atmosphere, curiously reminiscent of white Rotary clubs in the South. King takes the menu and tells one preacher he sees something just right for him. "What's that?" the preacher asks. "*Cat*fish!" King says. There is a considerable ritual of joke telling, most of the jokes dealing with very old wealthy men interested in marriage with young and pretty women. One very wealthy old man is finally permitted to marry, and the Lord says after some deliberation that he can marry a forty-year-old woman. The old man thinks about this some, and then asks, "Lord, would two twenties be all right?"

King laughs enthusiastically, and then tells the story of the young, well-educated minister who visits a church as a guest pastor; he is introduced to the congregation by the pastor as "Dr. So and So." The preacher is embarrassed, and he says, "Sorry, Reverend, I'm not a doctor."

"You're an ordained minister, aren't you?" asks the older man, quite surprised. The younger man nods, and the older preacher says, "Well, then, you're an *automatical* doctor."

Everyone tells King how glad they are to learn what a success the Chicago program was, and that they should have known that the distortions were the fault of the white press. The white press is soundly castigated. "Even here in Cleveland," one of the ministers says, "why, some white reporter asks Martin a question about the Mayor and Martin makes the answer that he thinks the Mayor is apathetic, and the next day the headline says, 'King Attacks Mayor.' They got to sell newspapers that way."[†]

---

*But many white reporters sympathetic to King, who thought the most important thing that could happen in America last year was for King to succeed in Chicago, consider his Chicago program a failure and a great tragedy. The problems had just been too great, the divisions within the Negro community too sharp, and the Daley machine too clever for him. The Daley machine was like nothing he had ever been up against before, with its roots in the Negro community. To this day there is no love by King for Daley, but there is considerable respect for Daley as a political operator. King sees Daley as a man for whom the machine is an end in itself, a man with little social vision, but with a sense of how social uses can be tailored to the perpetuation of the machine.

†Yet there is an increasing difficulty in covering racial news. Two years ago if a white reporter even hinted that there was division in the movement, he was accused of trying to create that very division. As the divisions became more obvious, each time you were with an established leader like Roy Wilkins, he would complain how the press *invented* radical leaders, created by the white press because of its guilt feelings. The next day you might be in Harlem talking with one of the more radical Negroes, and he would give a bitter discourse on how the white press played up only Whitney Young and Roy Wilkins; the white press was out to make the Negroes think that this mild leadership was all they had.

The dinner is pleasant, a discussion of the problems of Cleveland ("the middle-class Negroes are our problem, they've all gone to Shaker Heights and don't give a damn about being Negro anymore"); King says yes, it's the same all over. Finally there is some mild joking and one of the preachers, very dark in skin, points to another and says how much darker the other is. There is almost a reproach in King's remark: "It's a new age," he says, "a new time. Black is beautiful."

Just as they are about to break up one old friend, the one who went to Stockholm, starts talking about what a great man Martin Luther King is, how he is sent to them from Above. Then the preacher tells about the Nobel Prize ceremonies in Stockholm and Martin King, Senior. "There was to be a huge party afterwards," he explains, "and the champagne was all ready to be popped, and Daddy King stopped them. He's a complete teetotaler, and he said, 'Wait a minute before you start all your toasts to each other. We better not forget to toast the man who brought us here, and here's a toast to God.' And then he said, 'I always wanted to make a contribution, and all you got to do if you want to contribute, you got to ask the Lord, and let Him know, and the Lord heard me and in some kind of way I don't even know He came down through Georgia and He laid His hand on me and my wife and He gave us Martin Luther King and our prayers were answered and when my head is cold and my bones are bleached the King family will go down not only in American history but in world history as well because Martin King is a Nobel Prize–winner.' When he finished everyone was so moved, why the champagne just stayed there, and they made the toast to God and the champagne just stayed there afterwards. No one drank any, not even Bayard Rustin."

There was a moment of silence, and then one of the other ministers said, "Yes, sir, the Negro preacher is something. He sure is. God has use for him even when the Negro preacher didn't know what he was saying himself."

VI

The Kings of Atlanta are aristocrats of power and influence in the Negro world in the way that the Lodges have been among the Yankees and the Kennedys are among the Irish. The Negro church, particularly in the South, has always been the Negroes' great cultural base. The Baptist church was the church with the largest mass base, untouched by the white man. He did not appoint its preachers, he did not control them. One of the big churches of Atlanta, the greatest city of the South, is the Ebenezer Baptist Church. To have been pastor of it was to have a real base in the Negro community, not just of Atlanta, but in Negro America. Its pastor fifty years ago was a man named A. D. Williams, considered one of the finest preachers of his time; his sweet and gentle daughter married an ambitious young rural Negro from Georgia named Martin Luther King.

Martin King Senior, M. L. Senior, or Daddy King in Atlanta is probably not so outstanding as his son, but he is in many ways more interesting. He is a man of great intensity and willpower, not entirely committed to nonviolence; he goes along with it for his son's sake, but some of those who have physically pushed or hit Martin Junior would regret it if they tried it on his father.

Martin King Junior's reminiscences of his childhood are largely gentle stories; the inevitable hurts are bathed in the love of his parents. But Martin King Senior's stories of his boyhood are stories of violent racial confrontations with the whites of that day. Every angry face is still sketched in full detail, every taunt, every humiliation, every cheating recalled.

As a boy King Senior was the best Bible student around; he went to Atlanta, worked hard, studied at night, married Reverend Williams' daughter, and became assistant pastor of Ebenezer, where today he is pastor and his son Martin Junior is assistant pastor. By this time his father-in-law was treasurer of the National Baptist Convention, a powerful position which took him all over the country. The Williams family and the Kings came to know the important Negroes in other cities. To this day whenever there is a city in racial trouble King Senior knows the names of all the important people and preachers in town.

Martin King Senior instilled in his family a sense of pride and confidence; every time there was an incident involving the children King Senior repeated to them: Don't be ashamed, you're as good as anyone else. The family grew up well-to-do. "Not wealthy really," says young Martin King, "but Negro-wealthy. We never lived in a rented house and we never rode too long in a car on which payment was due, and I never had to leave school to work."

Six years ago in a loving and prophetic piece about him, James Baldwin quoted a friend's saying of King, quoted and requoted it because Baldwin felt it told so much about King: "He never went around fighting with himself like we all did." (The Baldwin essay was prophetic in that it saw the darkening clouds for any Negro leader; it was also poignant. Baldwin saw King as "a younger much-loved and menaced brother; he seemed slight and vulnerable to be taking on such odds," and one senses, reading it, that King with his happy home as a young man, and with the warmth of his present home, is somebody Baldwin would like to have been.)

As a young man he grew up in the world of preachers; by the time he went off to college, to Morehouse (father, grandfather, and great-grandfather had gone there; it was where you went) he had decided to become a doctor; he was an agnostic. Part of the reason was a contempt for the Southern Negro preacher, the low level of intellectual training, the intense emotionalism.

He had simply turned on the church: "If God was as all-powerful and as good as everyone said, why was there so much evil on the face of the earth?" Later at Morehouse several teachers, including Dr. Benjamin Mays, the president, and Dr. George Kelsey, a philosophy professor, convinced him that religion could be intellectually respectable; he returned, and then went on to

Crozier Theological Seminary in Pennsylvania. There for the first time he entered the white world. He was terribly aware of their whiteness and his blackness, and the stereotypes they had of Negroes. Negroes were always late for things, Martin King was always first in a classroom. Negroes were lazy and indifferent, Martin King worked hard and studied endlessly. Negroes were dirty, Martin King was always clean, always properly, perhaps too properly, dressed. Negroes were always laughing, Martin King was deadly serious. If there was a school picnic, Martin King did not eat watermelon.

He had gone in 1951 from Crozier to Boston University to study for his Ph.D., and entered there the social and intellectual world of the Northern Negro. King felt Morehouse had committed him to work in the South, and besides it was 1955 when he took his degree, the year after the Supreme Court decision outlawing school segregation. King had three offers to stay in the North, including one teaching position, but he chose a small church in Montgomery. He arrived just in time to be there when Rosa Parks' feet hurt, and he was catapulted to national prominence with the bus strike. He was the new boy in a divided city, and he became the leader of the Montgomery Improvement Association precisely because he was both new and yet known and respected through his family.

VII

In Cleveland King was to meet with both the preachers and the Black Nationalists, who have the support of the alienated young people.

The leader of the Nationalists is a tall mystic young man named Ahmed, who has a particular cult of his own combining racism and astrology—the darkness of the white man and the darkness of the skies. Earlier in the year he predicted that May 9 would be the *terrible day* when the black ghetto erupted. He made this prediction partly because there was to be an eclipse of the sun that day. Everyone laughed, old Ahmed, that crazy astrologer, but the police picked up him and a group of his followers that day just in case. Ahmed is mocked not only by the whites, but by the preachers as well. To them he represents nothing, has no job, all he does is talk.

King's people, however, believe Ahmed has a considerable, if somewhat fluid, influence. At first Ahmed and his men put out the word they were not interested in meeting with King; they were down on preachers, and he was a sort of Superpreacher. "He's really a Tom, you know," one of them told a King aide, "and one thing we don't need, that's more lectures from more Toms."

King went out to meet with them, however; he talked with them, but more important he listened to them, and it went surprisingly well. While he spoke nonviolence to them he did tell them to be proud of their black color, that no emancipation proclamation, no act of Lyndon Johnson, could set them free unless they were sure in their own minds they liked being black. And of course he talked with them on Vietnam, and they liked that also. The most important thing, however, was the simple act of paying attention to them. In Cleveland, King's people believe, the Nationalists are extremely important. Cleveland has particularly restless youths, up from Mississippi, either born there, or the first-generation children of parents born there. They are ill prepared for the cities. They come to these compact places like Hough, so that finally the inner ghetto is filled with the completely hopeless, floating, and rootless. It is estimated that one-third of the people in the inner ghetto change residence every year.

"There's a little power in these street gangs," one Negro says, "but power that doesn't go beyond a few blocks. Within those few blocks a man can be pretty big, you know he can shout, 'This is wrong, this is wrong, this is wrong.' But it doesn't go much beyond that. Past Fifty-fifth Street (the ghetto line), they're nothing, so they speak for the poor, but only to the poor."

That night the meeting was stormy. There had been some talk that Ahmed and his people might walk out, but they remained inside and, indeed, dominated the meeting. "The preachers were afraid of them, but they weren't afraid of the preachers," said one of King's aides. Outside one of Ahmed's followers had decided to lecture to other younger Negroes: "Do you think ol' whitey, he's going to come by and say, 'Why there's Chuck Hill. He's a good black man. I'm going to spare that good black Chuck Hill.' No, whitey's not going to do that. He's going to shoot you down like all the others. Whitey doesn't care about any black man."

Inside the meeting, one of the more conservative ones said something about good things coming and the need for only a little more patience, and Ahmed jumped up angrily and said, "How can you trust a man that would kidnap a little child, bring him to a country he raped, put him down on stolen property, and then say, 'Just you wait a few days, I'm going to give you your freedom and lots of other good things'?"

A few minutes later there was a heated debate between Ahmed and a middle-class Negro. Ahmed had been talking, giving his program, when the man rose and shouted:

"Have you got a job? Have you got a job? Have you got a job?"

Ahmed answered, "My job is to free the minds of my people."

"No no no!" the man shouted. "Do you have an eight-hour job? Do you have an eight-hour job?"

"My job is a twenty-four-hour job," Ahmed replied, "and as a matter of fact, it's got just as much risk and danger as your job. Anytime you want to switch I'd be delighted."

The next day King's people were delighted with Ahmed. "He was so warm, so beautiful last night," one of them said, and in the middle of the press conference the next day announcing that King planned to come to Cleveland to organize for better housing and jobs, a King aide suggested to a Negro reporter that he ask Ahmed, sitting next to King, what he thought of King. Ahmed answered that King was a black brother; there was a happy sigh of relief from King's people.

VIII

One wonders whether King's alliance with the Nationalists can last. King is hot and they are cool; he overstates and they understate; he is a preacher and their God is dead. They are of the ghetto the way Malcolm X was, and like Malcolm they are flawed by it; that was his great strength. King is not of the ghetto, he is not flawed (*he never went around fighting with himself like we all did*), he is of the South. The people he touches most deeply are the people they left behind.

When one raises this question with Andy Young, he talks about the church being a force with young people, but one senses that he shares some of the doubts. He tells of when they went to Rochester, during the riots there. The Negro youths refused to talk with them until they beat them at basketball, beat them at shooting craps, proved they weren't squares. He tells of how the tough kids in Chicago didn't want to meet King. They finally did, and they were impressed with him, with the sheer power of his moral presence, but when he left they slipped right back into the gangs.

"We see the ghettos now as a form of domestic colonialism," Andy Young says. "The preachers are like the civil servants in Ghana, doing the white man's work for them." King has decided to represent the ghettos; he will work in them and speak for them. But their voice is harsh and alienated. If King is to speak for them truly, then his voice must reflect theirs, it too must be alienated, and it is likely to be increasingly at odds with the rest of American society.

His great strength in the old fight was his ability to dramatize the immorality he opposed. The new immorality of the ghettos will not be so easy to dramatize, for it is often an immorality with invisible sources. The slum lords are evil enough, but they will not be there by their homes waiting for King and the TV crews to show up, ready to split black heads open. The schools are terrible, but there is no one man making them bad by his own ill will, likely to wait there in the school yard with a cattle prod. The jobs are bad, but the reasons Negroes aren't ready for decent jobs are complicated; there won't be one sinister hillbilly waiting outside the employment agency grinding cigarettes into the necks of King and his followers.

IX

King admits he is becoming a more radical critic of the society, and that the idea of "domestic colonialism" represents his view of the North. I suggest that he sounded like a nonviolent Malcolm; he says no, he could never go along with black separatism. For better or worse we are all on this particular land together at the same time, and we have to work it out together.

Nevertheless, he and his people are closer to Malcolm than anyone would have predicted five years ago—and much farther from their more traditional allies like Whitney Young and Roy Wilkins. King's people are privately very critical of both men; they realize that both work through the white Establishment to get things for Negroes, that they often have to tolerate things they privately consider intolerable because they feel in the long run this has to be done. The white man is there, he owns 90 per cent of it, and the only course is to work through his Establishment. King's people privately feel that this is fine, but that the trouble is the white Establishment has become corrupt, and in modeling yourself after it and working with it and through it, you pick up the same corruptions.

There are some very basic differences at issue here, much deeper than the war in Vietnam (though King's people see Vietnam as an example of the difference, for they believe that some high-level Negro acceptance of Vietnam is effected not because of agreement with the Johnson Administration's position, but as a price to pay in order to get other things from the Administration). In the split it is King who is changing, not Young or Wilkins. "For years," King says, "I labored with the idea of reforming the existing institutions of the society, a little change here, a little change there. Now I feel quite differently. I think you've got to have a reconstruction of the entire society, a revolution of values."

This means, he says, the possible nationalization of certain industries, a guaranteed annual income, a vast review of foreign investments, an attempt to bring new life into the cities. His view of whites has also changed deeply in the last year; previously he believed that most of America was committed to the cause of racial justice, "that we were touching the conscience of white America," that only parts of the white South and a few Northern bigots were blocking it. But after Chicago he decided that only a small part of white America was truly committed to the Negro cause, mostly kids on the campuses. "Most Americans," he would say, "are unconscious racists."

X

King is a frustrating man. Ten years ago *Time* found him humble, but few would find him that way today, though the average reporter coming into contact with him is not exactly sure why; he suspects King's vanity. One senses that he is a shy and sensitive man thrown into a prominence which he did not seek but which he has come to accept, rather likes, and intends to perpetuate. Colleagues find him occasionally pretentious; and the student leaders have often called him De Lawd, a title both mocking, and at the same time a sign of respect.

Being with him is a little like being with a Presidential candidate after a long campaign; he has been through it all, there has been too much exposure, the questions have all been asked before; the reporters all look alike, as do the endless succession of airport press conferences. King on the inside seems the same as King on the outside—always solemn, always confident, convinced that there is a right way and that he is following it; always those dark, interchangeable suits; the serious shirt and responsible tie.

He has finally come to believe his myth, just as the people in the Pentagon believe theirs and the man in the White House believes his; he sticks to the morality of his life and of his decisions, until there becomes something of a mystic quality to him. His friend, Reverend Wyatt Tee Walker, who is not a mystic, and indeed something of a swinger and finds King almost too serious says, "I am not a mystic but I am absolutely convinced that God is doing something with Martin King that He is not doing with anyone else in this country." And Martin Luther King Senior believes his son is "a prophet. That's what he is, a prophet. A lot of people don't understand what he's doing and don't like it, and I tell them he *has* to do these things, things that aren't popular. Prophets are like that, they have special roles. Martin is just a twentieth-century prophet."

Friends believe King has become decreasingly concerned with worldly things, and has no interest in money. There are many fine Negro homes in Atlanta, but King's is not one of them; he lives in a small house right near one of the ghettos. He takes little money from his church and tends to return a good deal to it; despite this attitude his children are protected because Harry Belafonte, a friend of King's, has set up an educational trust fund for each one.

XI

From Cleveland we flew to Berkeley for a major speech. Berkeley is now the center for the new radicalism in America, and King was likely to get a very warm response there; Berkeley would make him forget about the ghettos. Thousands of cheering young people would be there, applauding him. They would be there not because he led the March on Washington, for those days are easily forgotten (to some of them the March smacks of Tomism now), but because he is saying what they want to hear on Vietnam.

It was Vietnam, of course, which linked him with the new radicalism. His dissent was coming; that had been obvious for some time. Last winter when the peace groups and the New Left planned a major peace demonstration for the spring, the head of it was the Reverend James Bevel, a top King deputy who had organized for King in both Birmingham and Chicago. Bevel is the radical wing of the Southern Christian Leadership Conference, deeply Biblical and mystic, weaving in the new politics with the Old Testament. He is also something of a link between King and SNCC.

Bevel is an intense, fiery man, and these days the words genocide and race war come quickly to his lips, and he is obsessed with Vietnam: *"The war in Vietnam,"* he has said, *"will not end until Jesus Christ rises up in the Mekong Delta; the*

Lord can't hear our prayers here in America, because of all the cries and moans of His Children in the Mekong Delta, and that is all He can hear as long as the war continues, so forget your prayers until the war is over, America."

King's Southern Christian Leadership Conference is a rather loosely knit organization, and at Atlanta headquarters, there is a certain fear of what are now called Bevelisms. Recently there was a sharp kickback when Bevel spoke at a Catholic college and apparently made some remarks slurring the Virgin Mary. A young Jesuit questioned him sharply, and Bevel said, yes, he was interested in Mary, "but which Mary, all the thousands of Marys walking the streets of the ghettos, the thousands of peasant Marys being killed in the Mekong Delta, or some chick who lived thousands of years ago?"

The far-left groups who organized the peace march went for Bevel because they wanted King. King had seemed interested himself, but very slightly so. They contacted Bevel and they found he was interested, and ended up coming to their meetings. "Then the question was," one of them said, "could he deliver King? He said he could and he promised, but weeks went by and no King. We began to wonder. Then finally he came through."

They wanted King because they wanted a mass basis; they already had the automatics, the pacifists, their very own, but they wanted a broader constituency. As one peace organizer said, "There were a lot of people we felt wanted to come in on this, you know, good-hearted Americans for whom someone like King would make it easier, be a good umbrella. We could then call some of these unions and church groups and just middle-aged people who were nervous about coming in, who wanted to come in a little bit, but didn't like the whole looks of it, and we could say, Look here, we've got King, and it makes them all breathe easier. They think, Why it's King, it's all right, it's safe."

King repeats over and over again that he does not take stands because of what Stokely Carmichael says. Nonetheless, someone like Carmichael creates pressures to which King must inevitably react in order to retain his position. King would have reacted to the pressures of the ghettos and of Vietnam anyway, but without pressure and the alternative voices of a Stokely or a Floyd McKissick, he might have done it more at his choosing in his own good time. Stokely's outspoken stand on Vietnam made King's silence all the more noticeable. For King is a moralist, a fairly pragmatic one, and he does not intend to lose his position with young, militant, educated Negroes.

What was decisive in Bevel's role was that a trusted lieutenant in the most important of King's projects wanted out so he could join the peace movement. *That* moved King. Here was one more sign that a bright and passionate friend judged Vietnam more important than civil rights. It was symbolic of what King saw the war doing; taking all the time, money, energy, and resources of America away from its ghetto problems and focusing them thousands of miles away on a war the wisdom of which he doubted in the first place.

There are friends who feel that other factors affected him profoundly too, one of these being the right of a *Negro* to speak out. This had come to a point in early March at a fund-raising evening in Great Neck. King, Whitney Young, and John Morsell of the NAACP had appeared for an evening of speeches, questions, and answers. The subject of Vietnam came up, and King was asked how he felt. He answered with a relatively mild criticism of the war, the morality of it, and what it was doing to America.

Young was asked the same question and he dissented. There was the other war here in the ghettos, and that was the war the Urban League was fighting; he as an individual couldn't speak for the Urban League, but then he made his personal stand clear: communism had to be stopped just as Hitler should have been stopped in World War II. As the evening was breaking up, Young and King got into a brief but very heated argument. Young told King that his position was unwise since it would alienate the President, and they wouldn't get anything from him. King angrily told him, "Whitney, what you're saying may get you a foundation grant, but it won't get you into the kingdom of truth." Young quite angrily told King that he was interested in the ghettos, and King was not. "You're eating well," Young said.

King told Young that was precisely why he opposed the war, because of what it was doing to the ghettos. The argument, with a number of people still standing around, was so heated that King's lawyer quickly broke it up. Afterwards King felt badly about having spoken so angrily in public, and telephoned Young to apologize. They talked for more than an hour, failing of course to resolve their very basic differences.

This had happened to him once before. In 1965, when he was fresh from the Nobel Prize, King had briefly opposed the war and called for negotiations. There was a violent reaction. President Johnson got in touch with him and persuaded him to talk with that wooer-of-the-strayed, Arthur Goldberg. Goldberg assured him that peace was in the air. Similarly, King admits he was stunned by the extent of the pressure and reaction to him. "They told me I wasn't an expert in foreign affairs, and they were all experts," he said. "I knew only civil rights and I should stick to that." So he backed down, feeling a little guilty and suspecting he had been told that it wasn't a Negro's place to speak on Vietnam. This continued to rankle him, and after the Great Neck meeting he felt that if he had *backed* the war he would have been welcomed aboard, but that if he didn't back the war it was his place to remain silent.

XII

Though King says he could never live under communism, he does not see the chief division in the world as between the communist and capitalist. His is a more U Thantian view, with the division being between the rich and the poor, and thus to a large degree the white and nonwhite (the East European nations would become Have nations, to the surprise of many of their citizens). His view of violence in Vietnam and violence in Angola are quite different. Yet he is also terribly American, more American than he knows; his church is Western, his education is Western, and he thinks as a Westerner, though an increasingly alienated one.

He does not particularly think of the war in Vietnam as a racial one (although the phrase "killing little brown children in Vietnam" slips in); rather he sees the American dilemma there as one of face-saving, of an inability to end a miscalculation and a tendency to enhance it with newer and bigger miscalculations. Because there is a good deal of conservatism in King, there was a lively debate among his advisers as to whether he could go into the Spring Mobilization. The Call to the march had the whole works, genocide and race war; and a number of King allies, traditional liberals, advised him against it. The old ladies in Iowa wouldn't buy it.

But after much negotiating, which King's people clearly enjoyed, it was finally decided he should go in without signing the Call. "I went in because I thought I could serve as a bridge between the old liberals and the New Left," he says. He is still somewhat wary of much of the peace movement, however; he does not know all the people as he does in civil rights, and he lacks a sure touch for the vocabulary of peace. He is also angry about having been ambushed by the New Politics people who leaked to the press in Boston recently that King was considering running for President; he was not yet considering it, and he felt they were trying to push him faster than he wanted to go; he remains wary of some of the peace people, and he realizes they are all out to exploit his name for their own purposes.

His stand on Vietnam is not necessarily the most popular one he has ever taken. It is popular on the campuses, of course, but it has hurt him with the editorial writers (Vietnam and civil rights don't mix), gladdened George Wallace, hurt him in the suburbs, and it has made the ghettos a little uneasy.

Peace is not a sure issue in the ghettos. There have been wars in which the Midwest provided many of the boys, and the small towns rallied around them. There are no picket fences in the ghettos and the American Legion posts are weaker there, but right now *our boys* are coming from the ghettos, and so it is a very delicate issue. One radical Negro leader thought Vietnam would be an easy whipping boy until he began to hang around Harlem bars, where he found you don't knock the war (black faces under green berets) and so he toned down his attacks. But some of King's best friends fear that Roy Wilkins may be wiser than King about how Negroes in the ghetto feel about Vietnam.

XIII

But Berkeley is another country. We went there one sunny day, and they were ready for him. They came to pick him up early in the afternoon, a young Negro dean and some bright young students, and they predicted a great reception for him—a demonstration for a King-Spock ticket.

We rode out together and I relaxed while a young student editor interviewed King; she had her questions all written down (Declining U.S. moral status in the world? Answer, yes. Doing this because of Stokely? Answer, no). The ride was pleasant, and the students were talking about the dove feeling on the campus, and King said, "I guess it's not too popular to be a hawk at Berkeley," and someone asked if he's for their right of dissent. "I'm too deeply committed to the First Amendment to deny the right of dissent, even to hawks," he said.

On the campus there are a lot of young men wearing pins which say simply, "October 16." That is their day, they explain, when all over the country they plan to go down to recruiting centers and turn in their draft cards. On the campus there are numerous signs saying "King-Spock."

His speech there is an attack on American values; it cites Berkeley as the conscience of the academic community and the center for new values ("we have flown the air like birds, and swum the sea like fishes but we have not learned the simple act of walking the earth like brothers"). It is looser and more natural than the peace-march one, and the biggest ovation of the day comes when King denies that he and Berkeley are against our boys in Vietnam:

"We're for our boys. We're their best friends back home, because we want them to come home. It's time to come home. They've been away too long."

A few minutes later, after answering questions (no, he will not run for President, though he is touched by their support; indeed he says they must be careful who runs against Johnson, perhaps it will be "Mr. Nixon, or your good Governor") he heads for a meeting of the Afro-American students.

Suddenly a white graduate student steps out and blocks his way. "Dr. King," the student says, "I understand your reservations about running for President, but you're a world figure, you're the most important man we've got, you're the only one who can head a third-party ticket. And so when you make your decision, remember that there are many of us who are going to have to go to jail for many years, give up our citizenship, perhaps. This is a very serious thing."

King is stunned; this requires more than a half minute, and the student presses on: "This is the most serious thing in our lives. Politically you're the only meaningful person. Spock isn't enough. So please weigh our jail sentences in the balance when you make your decision."

I have watched King with dozens of people as he nods and half-listens, and this is the first time I have ever seen anyone get to him. He waits for a moment, for the student to say more, and then realizes there is nothing more to say, and he finally says, "Well, you make a very moving and persuasive statement."

That meeting had shaken King a little, and on the way back to San Francisco we talked about the sense of alienation of the students. At the meeting one of the students claimed that the white man was planning to exterminate all American Negroes, every last one, that the war in Vietnam was being used solely for that purpose as a testing ground for weapons. "He really believed that," King said, "really believed that." Another student was deeply committed to separatism—move away from the white community completely, forget all the whites. "What's your program?" King had asked, "What are you offering?" But all he had was more radical rhetoric. Another student had advocated more violence, but King had answered, "We don't need to talk mean, we need to act mean."

In the car King mused that the trouble with the people who talk mean is that they're always gone when the trouble finally strikes. "They lead you there and then they leave." Then he mentioned a confrontation with Charles Evers, the very able head of the NAACP in Mississippi. He said Charles had really whipped a crowd up one night, putting it to them on violence and the need for it, and King had finally said, "Look here, Charles, I don't appreciate your talking like that. If you're that violent, why you just go up the highway to Greenwood and kill the man who killed your own brother." And they applauded.

The students, King said, were disenchanted with white society, there had been too few victories, and they were losing faith in nonviolence—this and a sense of guilt over their own privileged status. Some of this is good, the fact that they identify with the ghettos much more than they did ten years ago, but there is also the danger of paranoia. One of the white students had mentioned how influential the autobiography of Malcolm X is with the students, both black and white, and added, "You won't believe this, but my conservative old Republican grandmother has just read it and she thinks it's marvelous, a book of love."

"That is what we call the power to become," King said, "the ability to go on in spite of. It was tragic that Malcolm was killed, he was really coming around, moving away from racism. He had such a sweet spirit. You know, right before he was killed he came down to Selma and said some pretty passionate things against me, and that surprised me because after all it was my own territory down there. But afterwards he took my wife aside, and said he thought he could help me more by attacking me than praising me. He thought it would make it easier for me in the long run."

The car finally reached the hotel. He had covered 3,000 miles in the last few days, and now he was ready to recross the country, five stops on the way. The people, the faces, the audiences, the speeches were already blending into each other; even the cities were becoming interchangeable. Only the terrible constancy of the pressures remained. One sensed him struggling to speak to and for the alienated while still speaking to the mass of America, of trying to remain true to his own, while not becoming a known, identified, predictable, push-button radical, forgotten because he was no longer in the mainstream. The tug on him was already great, and there is no reason to believe that in the days ahead it would become any less excruciating.

Martin Luther King Is *Still* on the Case

Esquire, August 1968

◆

GARRY WILLS

Of course, Mailer had an instinct for missing good speeches—at the Civil
Rights March in Washington in 1963 he had gone for a stroll just a little
while before Martin Luther King began, "I have a dream," so Mailer—trust-
ing no one else in these matters, certainly not the columnists and the commentators—would never know whether the Reverend King had given a
great speech that day, or revealed an inch of his hambone.

—NORMAN MAILER
The Armies of the Night

"Nigger territory, eh?" He was a cabdriver, speculative; eyed the pistol incongruous beside him on the seat, this quiet spring night; studied me, my two small
bags, my raincoat. The downtown streets were empty, but spectrally alive.
Every light in every store was on (the better to silhouette looters). Even the
Muzak in an arcade between stores reassured itself, at the top of its voice, with
jaunty rhythms played to no audience. Jittery neon arrows, meant to beckon
people in, now tried to scare them off. The curfew had swept pedestrians off the
street, though some cars with white men in them still cruised unchallenged.

"Well, get in." He snapped down every lock with four quick slaps of his
palm; then rolled up his window; we had begun our safari into darkest Memphis. It *was* intimidating. Nothing stirred in the crumbling blocks; until, almost
noiseless—one's windows are always up on safari—an armored personnel car-
rier went nibbling by on its rubber treads, ten long guns bristling from it
(longer because not measured against human forms, the men who bore them
were crouched behind the armored walls); only mushroom helmets showed,
leaning out from each other as from a single stalk, and, under each, bits of elfin
face disembodied.

At last we came to lights again: not the hot insistence of downtown; a
lukewarm dinginess of light between two buildings. One was modern and well-
lit; a custodian sat behind the locked glass door. This is the headquarters of a
new activism in Memphis, the Minimum Salary Building (designed as national

headquarters for raising the pay of ministers in the African Methodist Episcopal Church and now encompassing other groups). Its director, Reverend H. Ralph Jackson, was a moderate's moderate until, in a march for the striking sanitation workers, he was Maced by police. Since then his building has been a hive of union officials, Southern Christian Leadership Conference staff, and members of various human-rights organizations.

Next to it is the Clayborn Temple, a church from which marchers have issued almost daily for the past two months. Marchers fell back to this point in their retreat from the scuffle that marred Dr. King's first attempt to help the strikers. Some say tear gas was deliberately fired into the church; others that it drifted in. But the place *was* wreathed with gas, and a feeling of violated sanctuary remains. Churches have been the Negro's one bit of undisputed terrain in the South, so long as they were socially irrelevant; but this church rang, in recent weeks, with thunderous sermons on the godliness of union dues.

I pay the cabdriver, who resolutely ignores a well-dressed young couple signaling him from the corner, and make my way, with bags and coat, into the shadow of the church porch. In the vestibule, soft bass voices warn me. I stop to let my eyes, initiated into darkness, find the speakers and steer me through their scattered chairs. They are not really conversing; their meditative scraps of speech do not meet each other, but drift off, centripetally, over each one's separate horizon of darkness. This uncommunicative, almost musical, slow rain of words goes on while I navigate my way into the lighted dim interior of the church.

About a hundred people are there, disposed in every combination: family groups; clots of men, or of women; the lean of old people toward each other, the jostle outward of teen-agers from some center (the church piano, a pretty dress on a hanger); or individuals rigid in their pews as if asleep or dead. The whole gathering is muted—some young people try to pick out a hymn on the piano, but halfheartedly. There are boxes of food, and Sunday clothes draped over the backs of pews. The place has the air of a rather lugubrious picnic—broken up by rain, perhaps, with these few survivors waiting their chance to dash out through the showers to their homes. Yet there is a quiet sense of purpose, dimly focused but, finally, undiscourageable. These are garbage collectors, and they are going to King's funeral in Atlanta. It is ten P.M.; in twelve hours the funeral will begin, 398 miles away.

They have been told different things, yesterday and today, by different leaders (some from the union, some from S.C.L.C.). They have served as marshals in the memorial march that very afternoon, and preparations for that overshadowed any planning for this trip. Some have been told to gather at ten o'clock; some at eleven. They believe there will be two buses, or three; that they will leave at eleven, or at twelve; that only the workers can go, or only they and their wives, or they and their immediate families. Yesterday, when they gathered for

marshals' school, a brusque young Negro shouted at them to arrive sharply at
ten: "We're not going by C. P. Time—Colored People's Time. And if you don't
listen now, you won't find out how to get to Atlanta at all, 'cause *we'll* be on the
plane tomorrow night." The speaker seemed to agree with much of white Memphis that "you have to know how to talk to these people."

And so they wait. Some came before dark, afraid to risk even a short walk
or drive after curfew. Some do not realize the wait will be so long; they simply
know the time they were asked to arrive. Most will have waited three hours before we start; some, four or five. I try to imagine the mutters and restlessness of
a white group stranded so long. These people are the world's least likely revolutionaries. They are, in fact, the precisely *wrong* people—as the Russian field-
worker was the wrong man to accomplish Marx's revolt of the industrial
proletariat.

People such as these were the first "Memphians" I had met in any number. That
was four days ago. And my first impression was the same as that which nagged
at me all night in the church: these Tennessee Negroes are not unlikely, they
are impossible. They are anachronisms. Their leaders had objected for some
time to J. P. Alley's "Hambone" cartoon in the local paper; they say, rightly, that
it offers an outdated depiction of the Negro. Nonetheless, these men *are* Hambones. History has passed them by.

I saw them by the hundred, that first morning, streaming past the open
casket in a hugger-mugger wake conducted between the completion of the em-
balmer's task and the body's journey out to the Memphis airport. I had arrived
in Memphis several hours after King's death; touched base at the hotel, at the
police station, at the site of the murder—dawn was just disturbing the sky;
flashbulbs around and under the balcony still blinked repeatedly against the
room number—306—like summer lightning. As the light strengthened, I
sought out the funeral home police had mentioned—R. S. Lewis and Sons.

Clarence Lewis is one of the sons, he has been up all night answering the
phone, but he is still polite; professionally sepulchral, calm under stress. "They
brought Dr. King here because we have been connected with the Movement for
a long time. We drove him in our limousines when he was here last week [for
the ill-fated march]. They brought the body to us from the morgue at ten-thirty
last night, and my brother has been working on it ever since. There's so much
to do: this side [he pulls spread fingers down over his right cheek and neck] was
all shot away, and the jawbone was just dangling. They have to reset it and then
build all that up with plaster." I went through the fine old home (abandoned to
trade when the white people moved from this area) into a new addition—the
chapel, all cheap religious sentiment, an orange cross in fake stained glass.
There are two people already there, both journalists, listening to the sounds
from the next room (Clarence calls it, with a mortician's customary eu-

phemism, "the Operating Room"), where a radio crackles excerpts from Dr. King's oratory, and men mutter their appreciation of the live voice while they work on the dead body. We comment on the ghoulishness of their task—knowing ours is no less ghoulish. We would be in there, if we could, with lights and cameras; but we must wait—wait through an extra hour of desperate cosmetic work. We do it far less patiently than Memphis garbage men wait in their church. "Hell of a place for Dr. King to end up, isn't it?" the photographer says. "And one hell of a cause—a little garbage strike."

When, at eight o'clock, the body is brought out, bright TV lights appear and pick out a glint of plaster under the cheek's powder. Several hundred people file past; they have sought the body out, in their sorrow, and will not let it leave town without some tribute. But not one white person from the town goes through that line.

Those who do come are a microcosm of the old Southern Negro community. Young boys doff their hats and their nylon hair caps—their "do rags"—as they go by. A Negro principal threatened to expel any child from a local high school who came to class with an "Afro" hairdo. Possessive matrons take up seats in the back, adjust their furs, cluck sympathetically to other women of their station, and keep the neighborhood record straight with bouts of teary gossip. They each make several passes at the coffin; sob uncontrollably, whip out their Polaroid cameras, and try an angle different from that shot on their last pass. One woman kisses the right cheek. Clarence Lewis was afraid of that: "It will spoil the makeup job. We normally put a veil over the coffin opening in cases of this sort; but we knew people would just tear that off with Dr. King. They want to see him. Why, we had one case where the people lifted a body up in the coffin to see where the bullet had gone into a man's back."

Outside, people mill around, making conversation, mixing with stunned friendliness, readjusting constantly their air of sad respect. Again, the scene looked like a disconsolate picnic. Some activists had called him "De Lawd." He always had to be given either his title ("*Doctor* King," even the *Reverend Doctor* King") or his full historic name ("Luther Martin King" one prim lady mourner called him in the funeral home, understandably stumbling over the big mouthful). Even that title "Doctor"—never omitted, punctiliously stressed when whites referred to him, included even in King's third-person references to himself—had become almost comical. He was not only "De Lawd," but "De Lawd High God Almighty," and his Movement was stiff with the preacher-dignities of the South; full of Reverends This and Bishops That and Doctors The-Other. No wonder the militants laughed at it all. And now, damned if he hadn't ended up at a Marc Connelly *fish fry* of a wake—right out of *The Green Pastures.*

Connelly learned to read by poring over the pages of the Memphis *Commercial Appeal* and he learned his lesson well: he was able to create a hambone God: "Dey's gonter to be a deluge, Noah, an' dey's goin' to be a flood. De Levees is gonter bust an' everything dat's fastened down is comin' loose." These are unlikely people, I thought at that sad fish fry, to ride out the deluge whose signs had already thundered from several directions on the night King died. But then, so was Noah an unlikely candidate. Or Isaac, who asked: "Does you want de brainiest or the holiest, Lawd?" "I want the holiest. I'll make him brainy." And there was one note, at King's makeshift wake, not heard anywhere in Connelly's play. As one of the mammy types waddled out the front door, she said with matter-of-fact bitterness to everyone standing nearby: "I wish it was Henry Loeb lying there"—handsome lovable Henry Loeb, the city's Mayor, who would later tell me, in his office, how well he liked his Negroes; unaware, even now, that they are not his. Connelly's "darkies" do not hate white people: "the white folk" simply do not exist in his play, which was meant to fortify the Southern conviction that "they have their lives and we have ours," an arrangement convenient to the white and (so whites tell themselves) pleasant for all. The whites get servants, and the blacks get fish fries. That whole elaborate fiction was shattered by the simple words, "I wish it was Henry Loeb." Massah's not in the cold, cold ground. She wishes he were. These people may be Hambones, but not J. P. Alley's kind. They are a paradox, a portent white Memphis still must come to grips with—hambone militants, "good darkies" on the march. When even the stones rise up and cry out, the end has come for Henry Loeb's South.

The signs of it are everywhere—at the Lorraine Motel, where King died; it is an extension of the old Lorraine Hotel, once a white whorehouse. Then, when the neighborhood began to go black, it was thrown to a Negro buyer as, in the South, old clothes are given to "the help." A man named William Bailey bought it, and laboriously restored it to respectability. King stayed there often on his visits to Memphis. It is now a headquarters for the S.C.L.C.'s Project Memphis, a program designed—as its assistant director says—"to make Memphis pay for the death of Dr. King." Yet the Lorraine is run by a man who could pose for "Uncle Ben" rice ads—an ex–Pullman porter who is still the captain of porters at a Holiday Inn. He works for the white man, and does it happily, while he owns and runs a black motel where activists plot their campaigns. "I'm very proud to be part of the Holiday Inn family," he told me. "Why, the owners of the whole chain call me Bill Bailey." That's the Negro Henry Loeb has always known. It is the other side of him—the owner of the Lorraine, the friend of Dr. King—that is the mystery.

King made the mistake of staying, on his penultimate visit to Memphis, at one of the posher new Holiday Inns—in the kind of place where Bill Bailey works, not in the motel he owns. The Memphis paper gleefully pointed out that King *could* stay in the Inn because it had been integrated—"without demonstrations." But the Lorraine is not integrated (except in theory). Neither was the white flophouse in which the sniper lurked. It is good that King came back to the real world, the de-facto segregated world, to die. He was in the right place, after all. Memphis indeed, had taught him to "stay in his place"—a thing it will come to regret. For "his place" is now a command post, a point where marches are planned, and boycotts, and Negro-history classes.

These garbage men are that new thing, Hambones in rebellion—and they have strange new fish to fry. The people who filed past King's body had said no to the whole city of Memphis; said it courteously, almost deferentially (which only made it more resounding); they had marched every day under their employers' eyes; boycotted the downtown; took on, just for good measure, firms like Coca-Cola and Wonder Bread and Sealtest Milk; and were ready, when the time came, to join with King in taking on Washington. Patience radiates from them like a reproach. Perhaps that is why the white community does not like to see them in a mass—only in the single dimension, the structured encounter that brings them singly into the home or the store for eight hours of work. These Negroes seem almost too patient—wrong people for rebels. Yet their like has already made a rebellion. A tired woman in Montgomery was the wrong sort to begin all the modern civil-rights activism; but Rosa Parks did it. King was drawn into that first set of marches and boycotts almost by accident—as he was involved, finally, in the garbage men's strike: "Dat's always de trouble wid miracles. When you pass one you always gotta r'ar back an' pass another."

The buses were late. They were supposed to arrive at eleven-thirty for loading baggage (each man had been told to bring toothbrush, change of underwear, change of outer clothes if he wanted it, and most wanted it.) Besides, there had been talk of a bus for teen-agers, who were now giggling and flirting in the dark vestibule (surrendered to them by their elders). Jerry Fanion, an officer of the Southern Regional Conference, scurried around town looking for an extra bus; like all Negroes, he was stopped everywhere he went. Police recognized him, and they had been alerted about the men who would be leaving their homes for the funeral; but they made him get out of the car anyway, and laboriously explain himself. He never did get the bus. Later in the week, the teen-agers made a pilgrimage to King's grave.

Meanwhile, the wives in the Clayborn Temple still did not know whether they could go with their husbands. About eleven-thirty, T. O. Jones showed up, with P. J. Ciampa. Jones is the spheroid president of the sanitation local—a man too large in some ways and too small in others for any standard size of shirt, coat, pants. He is content with floppy big pants and a windbreaker that manages to get around him, but only by being too long in the sleeves and too wide in the shoulders. He is a quiet man in his early forties, determined but vague, who began the strike by going to the office of the Director of Public Works and—when the Director told him there was an injunction against any strike by city employees—changing into his "prison clothes" on the spot.

Ciampa is the fiery Italian organizer who came into town for the union and amused people with televised arguments against Mayor Loeb (who insisted that all negotiations be carried on in public). Jones and Ciampa have lost the list of men signed up for the buses; they don't know how many buses are coming, how many can ride on each. They try to take two counts—of workers alone, and workers with their wives; but it's difficult to keep track of those who wander in and out of shadows, doors, anterooms.

After an hour of disorder, it becomes clear that everyone can fit into the three buses if folding chairs are put down the aisles. T. O. had told me to save a seat for him, but the chairs in the aisle barricade us from each other. I sit, instead, with a sleepy young man who describes the route we *have* to take, and then finds confirmation of his theory, with a kind of surprised triumph, all along the way. The route one travels through Mississippi and Alabama is a thing carefully studied by Southern Negroes. After giving T. O. a check for the bus drivers, Ciampa went back to the hotel, T. O. swung onto the lead bus, and we pulled out.

In the seat behind me, a woman is worried over the teen-agers still standing by the church, hoping they will get a bus. "How they gonna get home?" she asks. "Walk, woman," her husband growls. "But what of the curfew?" "What of it?" "I don't trust those police. If I hadn't got on the bus with you, I'd have stayed all night in the church." As the bus rolls through downtown Memphis, on its way South, the woman sees cars moving. "What are they doing out during the curfew? Why aren't *they* stopped?" She knows, of course. Her husband does not bother to answer her.

In our bus, all the animation comes from one voice in the back. A tall laughing man I had watched, in the church, as he moved from one cluster to another, mixing easily, asked to sit beside me while I was still saving a seat for T. O. I was sorry later I had not said yes. As the riders shouldered sleepily into their chair backs, he joked more softly, but showed no signs of fatigue himself—though he had been a marshal all the long afternoon of marching. And as fewer and fewer responded to him, he moved naturally from banter and affectionate insults to serious things: "That Dr. King was for us." The response is a sigh of yesses. "He didn't have to come here." A chorusing of nos. As he mused on, the crowd breathed with him in easy agreement, as if he were thinking for them. This "audience participation" is what makes the Southern preacher's sermon such an art form. I had been given a dazzling sample of it three days before in the garbage men's meeting at the United Rubber Workers Union Hall. That was the day after King's death, and a formidable lineup of preachers was there to lament it. They all shared a common language, soaked in Biblical symbol: Pharaoh was Mayor Loeb, and Moses was Dr. King, and Jesus was the Vindicator who would get them their dues checkoff. But styles were different, and response had to be earned. The whole hall was made up of accompanists for the improvising soloist up front. When he had a theme that moved them, they cheered him on: "Stay there!" "Fix it." "Fix it up." "Call the roll." "*Talk* to me!" "Talk *and a half.*" The better the preacher, the surer his sense of the right time to tarry, the exact moment to move on; when to let the crowd determine his pace,

when to push against them; the lingering, as at the very edge of orgasm, prolonging, prolonging; then the final emotional breakthrough when the whole
audience "comes" together.

Memphis is not really the birthplace of the blues, any more than Handy
was the father of them; but these are the same people who created the form—
the triple repeated sighing lines, with a deep breathing space between each,
space filled in with the accompanists' "break" or "jazz." That is the basic pattern for the climactic repetitions, subtle variations, and refrains of the
preacher's art. That kind of sermon is essentially a musical form; and the
garbage men are connoisseurs. When a white pastor from Boston got up, he
gave them slogans and emotion; but without a response from the audience—
he didn't know the melody.

Nor did all the black preachers succeed, or win equal acceptance. The surprise of the afternoon, at least for me, came when an S.C.L.C. delegation
reached the hall, and the Reverend James Bevel got up to preach. He and his associates looked almost out of place there amid the "do rags" and scarred ebony
skulls; they were immaculately dressed, with educated diction, wearing just
the proper kind of "natural" and a beard.

Bevel was the fourteenth, and last, speaker of the afternoon. It seemed that
earlier emotional talks would have drained these men of all response left them
after the shock of the preceding night. But Jim Bevel slowly built them up, from
quiet beginnings, to an understanding of what it means to be "on the case."
(This is a phrase he invented a year ago to describe musicians who are perfectly
interacting; it is now an S.C.L.C. phrase of wide applicability.) "Dr. King died on
the case. Anyone who does not help forward the sanitation workers' strike is
not on the case. You getting me?" (They're getting him.) "There's a false rumor
around that our leader is dead. *Our* leader is not dead." ("No!" They know
King's *spirit* lives on—half the speeches have said that already.) "That's a *false*
rumor!" ("Yes!" "False." "Sho' nuff." "*Tell* it!") "Martin Luther King is not—"
(yes, they know, not dead; this is a form in which expectations are usually satisfied, the crowd arrives at each point *with* the speaker; he outruns them at peril
of losing the intimate ties that slacken and go taut between each person in the
room; but the real artist takes chances, creates suspense, breaks the rhythm deliberately; a snag that makes the resumed onward flow more satisfying)—
"Martin Luther King is not our *leader!*" ("No!" The form makes them say it, but
with hesitancy. They will trust him some distance; but what does he mean? The
"Sho' nuff" is not declamatory now; not fully interrogatory, either; circum-
flexed.) "*Our* leader—("Yes?")—is the *man*—("*What* man?" "Who?" "Who?"
Reverend Abernathy? Is he already trying to supplant King? The trust is almost
fading)—who led *Moses* out of *Israel.*" ("*Thass* the man!" Resolution; all doubt
dispelled; the bridge has been negotiated, left them stunned with Bevel's virtuosity.) "*Our* leader is the man who went with Daniel into the lions' den."
("Same man!" "Talk some.") "*Our* leader is the man who walked out of the

grave on Easter morning." ("Thass the leader!" They have not heard, here in hamboneland, that God is dead.) "Our leader never sleeps nor slumbers. He cannot be put in jail. He has never lost a war yet. *Our* leader is *still on the case.*" (*"That's it!"* *"On* the case!") "Our leader is not dead. One of his prophets died. We will not stop because of that. Our staff is not a funeral staff. We have friends who are undertakers. We *do business.* We *stay on the case,* where our leader is."

It is the most eloquent speech I have ever heard. I was looking forward, a day later, to hearing Bevel again, before a huge audience in the Mason Temple. He was good—and gave an entirely different speech. But the magic of his talk to the sanitation workers was gone. It was not merely the size of the crowd (though that is important—the difference between an intimate combo and some big jazz band only partially rehearsed). The makeup of the crowd was also different. Those in the Union Hall were predominantly male. Men accompany; women compete—they talk over the preacher's rhythms. Their own form is not the jazz combo, but the small group of gospel singers, where each sister fights for possession of the song by claiming a larger share of the Spirit. In a large place like the Mason Temple, women set up nuclei around the hall and sang their own variations on the sermon coming out of the loudspeakers.

But that night in the bus, there was no fighting the jolly voice that mused on "Dr. King's death." Responses came, mingled but regular, like sleepy respirations, as if the bus's sides were breathing regularly in and out. This is the subsoil of King's great oratory, of the subtly varied refrains: "I have a *dream . . . I* have a dream today." He must have been a great preacher in his own church; he could use the style out in the open, before immense crowds. He made the transition more skillfully than Bevel had—and far better than Abernathy does. That very day, the Monday before King's funeral, Abernathy had paused long on the wrong phrases: "I do not *know . . .* I do not *know."* He had let the crowd fool him by their sympathy; he took indulgence for a *demand* to linger. He did not have King's sure sense of when to move.

I suppose I heard thirty or forty preachers on that long weekend of religious eloquence; but not one of them reached King's own level of skill in handling a crowd. That was the mystery of King. He was the Nobel Prize–winner and a Southern Baptist preacher; and, at places like the Washington Mall in 1963, the two did not conflict but worked together. As the man in the bus kept saying, "He was for *us."* ("Unh-*hmmn!"*) "He was *one* with us." ("That he was." "That he was.")

But King's rapport with his people was not the natural thing it seems now. He had to learn it, or relearn it. The man's voice rose behind us in the bus: "You know what Dr. King said?" ("What?") "He said not to mention his Nobel Prize when he died." ("Thass what he *said."*) "He said, 'That don't mean nothing.' " ("Sho' nuff.") "What matters is that *he* helped *us."* ("Thass the truth." "That *is* the truth." *"That* is.")

In several ways. King was very bright, a quick study. He skipped two grades to finish high school at the age of fifteen. He was ordained at eighteen; graduated from college at nineteen. It was a fast start, for a career that is one long quick record of youthful accomplishment. He got his theology degree at the age of twenty-two. While a pastor (from the age of twenty-five), he got his Ph.D. from Boston University at twenty-six. And he went direct from graduate school to a position of national leadership. His major achievements were already behind him when he became the youngest man (thirty-five) to receive the Nobel Prize. He was dead before he reached the age of forty; and there are constant little surprises in remembering how young he was—as when Harry Belafonte, speaking in Memphis, referred to King as his junior by a year. Was "De Lawd" really younger than that baby-faced singer? And why did we never think of him as young?

He had the strained gravity of the boy who has moved up fast among his elders. That unnatural dignity is in his writing, too, which labors so for gravity that it stretches grammar: "President Kennedy was a strongly contrasted personality . . . trying to sense the direction his leadership could travel." His acceptance speech will not rank with the great Nobel speeches: "transform this *pending* cosmic elegy into a creative psalm . . . unfolding events which surround . . . spiral down a militaristic stairway . . . blood-flowing streets. . . ."

The young King wanted to study medicine. He majored in sociology at Morehouse College. He thought preachers not quite intellectually respectable, though his father and grandfather and great-grandfather had all been preachers. Even when he accepted ordination, he thought he should become a theologian-minister, perhaps a professor, rather than a mere preacher. He took his first parish—in Montgomery—to get "pastoring background" before accepting a teaching post. To the end of his life he talked of turning to an academic career.

But he was never convincing as a scholar. An account of his own intellectual development reads as if it were lifted from a college catalog: "My intellectual journey carried me through new and sometimes complex doctrinal lands, but the pilgrimage was always stimulating, gave me a new appreciation for objective appraisal and critical analysis, and knocked me out of my dogmatic slumber." He was not even a very perceptive commentator on the men who created his doctrine of civil disobedience—Thoreau and Gandhi. When he began the Montgomery boycott, he liked to refer vaguely to Hegel as the prophet of "creative tensions." It was not till someone suggested more likely patrons of nonviolent rebellion that he began referring to Gandhi and Gandhi's American forerunner—*referring* to them—as saints. He never really discusses their philosophy. And his most ambitious defense of civil disobedience—the Letter from a Birmingham Jail, written eight years after the Montgomery boycott—does not even *refer* to Gandhi or Thoreau. Instead, King uses tags from Augustine and Aquinas (hardly anti-authoritarians). Nor does the Letter deserve high marks for logic. It offers as the model of civil disobedience, not Gandhi, but Socrates, the stock Platonic figure suborned for all noble causes, but something of an embarrassment in this context, since Plato makes him preach history's most rigorous sermon against civil disobedience in the *Crito.* The Letter gives three qualifications for a valid act of civil disobedience: 1) that it be open, 2) that it be loving (nonviolent), and 3) that those engaged in it accept their punishment willingly. Then he gives as a historical example of this the Boston Tea Party, whose perpetrators: 1) were clandestine (they disguised themselves as Indians), 2) were armed for violence (they forced wharf guards away and were ready to repel any interruption), and 3) evaded all punishment (Sam Adams and his Committee of Correspondence *dared* England to attempt punishment). Indeed, none of the historical examples of civil disobedience given in King's Letter meets the three requirements he had just set up.

Like Moses, he was not "de brainiest." He only knew one book well—the Bible. It was enough. All the other tags and quotes are meant to give respectability to those citations that count—the phrases sludged up in his head from earliest days like a rich alluvial soil. He could not use these with the kind of dignity he aspired to unless he were more than "just a preacher." Yet the effect of that *more* was to give him authority *as* a preacher. By trying to run away from his destiny, he equipped himself for it. He became a preacher better educated than any white sheriff; more traveled, experienced, poised. He was a Hambone who could say "no" and make it sound like a cannon shot.

It is interesting to contrast him with another preacher's son—James Baldwin. Baldwin became a boy preacher himself as a way of getting out into the secular world. King became a student as a way of getting into a larger world of *religion,* where the term "preacher" would not be a reproach. He needed a weightiness in his work which only that "Doctor" could give him. He needed it for personal reasons—yes, he had all along aspired to be "De Lawd"—and in order to make Southern religion relevant. That is why King was at the center of it all: he was after *dignity,* which is the whole point of the Negro rebellion. His talent, his abilities as a "quick study," his versatility, his years studying philosophy and theology (for which he had no real natural bent) were means of achieving power. His books and degrees were all tools, all weapons. He had to put that "Doctor" before his name in order to win a "Mister" for every Southern Negro. They understood that. They rejoiced in his dignities as theirs. The Nobel Prize *didn't* matter except as it helped them. As T. O. Jones put it, "There can never be another leader we'll have the feeling for that we had for him."

Our three buses had a long ride ahead of them—ten hours, an all-night run, through parts of Mississippi, Alabama, and Georgia. They were not luxury buses, with plenty of room; the Greyhound company had run out of vehicles and leased these from a local firm. One could not even stretch one's legs in the aisle; the folding chairs prevented that. Ten hours there. Ten hours back.

Minutes after our departure, the man behind me said, "We're in Mississippi now." "Oh no!" his wife groaned. It is well to be reminded that our citizens are afraid to enter certain states. The man most frightened was T. O. Jones. He knows what risks an "uppity" Negro takes in the South. He does not give out his address or phone number. The phone is changed automatically every six months to avoid harassment. He has lived in a hotel room ever since the beginning of his union's strike, so his wife and two girls will not be endangered by his presence in the house. "This is risky country," he told me. "And it gets more dangerous as you go down the road. That Mississippi!" We were going down the road.

The lead bus had no toilet, and the chairs in the aisle effectively barricaded it from anyone's use in the other buses. The technique for "rest stops" was for all three buses to pull off into a darkened parking lot; the chairs were folded; then people lined up at the two toilets (one bus for men, one for women). At our first stop, some men began to wander off into the trees, but T. O., sweating in the cool night, churning all around the buses to keep his flock together, warned them back. "Better not leave the bus." I asked him if he expected trouble. "Well, we're in Mississippi, and folk tend to get flustered at—" He let it hang. He meant at the sight of a hundred and forty Negroes pouring out of buses in the middle of the night. "You didn't see that man over there, did you—in the house by the gas station? There was a man at the door." Some had tried to go near the dark station, to get Cokes from an outdoor vending machine. T. O. pulled them back to the buses. He carries his responsibility very self-consciously.

Back in the bus, there was a spasm of talk and wakefulness after our stop. The deep rumbling voice from the rear got chuckles and approval as he mused on the chances of a strike settlement. "We got Henry Loeb on the run now." ("Yeah!" "Sure do!") "He don't know what hit him." Fear is not surprising in the South. This new confidence is the surprising thing. I had talked to a watery little man, back in the church, who seemed to swim in his loose secondhand clothes—a part-time preacher who had been collecting Memphis' garbage for many years. What did he think of the Mayor? "Mr. Loeb doesn't seem to do much thinking. He just doesn't *understand*. Maybe he can't. The poor man is just, y'know—kinda—*sick*." It is King's word for our society, a word one hears everywhere among the garbage men; a word of great power in the Negro community—perhaps the key word of our decade. It is no longer a question of courage or fear, men tell each other; of facing superior white power or brains or resources. It is just a matter of understanding, of pity. One must be patient with the sick.

Henry Loeb does not look sick. He is vigorous, athletic, bushy-browed, handsome in the scowling-cowboy mold of William S. Hart and Randolph

Scott. And he has a cowboy way of framing everything as part of his personal code: "*I* don't make deals. . . . *I* don't believe in reprisals. . . . *I* like to conduct business in the open." There is an implicit contrast, in that repeatedly emphasized pronoun, with all the other shifty characters in this here saloon. He even has a cowboy's fondness for his mount"—the P.T. boat he rode during the war, a loving if unskilled portrait of which hangs behind his desk. (His office biography makes the inevitable reference to John F. Kennedy.)

Loeb is an odd mixture of the local and the cosmopolitan. He comes from a family of Memphis millionaires; he married the Cotton Carnival Queen. Yet as a Jew he could not belong to the Memphis Country Club (he has become an Episcopalian since his election as Mayor); and he went East for his education. A newsman who knows him made a bet with me: "When he hears you are from a national magazine he will not let five minutes go by without a reference to Andover or Brown." When I went into his office, he asked for my credentials before talking to me (he would later boast that he talks to anyone who wants to come see him). Then he asked where I live. Baltimore. "Oh, do you know so-and-so?" No. Why? "He was in my class at Andover, and came from Baltimore." That newsman could clean up if he made his bets for money.

Loeb did not mention Brown. But he did not need to. As I waited for him in his office, his secretary took the Dictaphone plug out of her ear and began flipping through her dictionary, and confided to me, as she did so, "The Mayor was an English major at Brown University, and he uses words so big I can't even find them." Later, his executive assistant found occasion to let me know that his boss was "an English major at Brown University."

But the Mayor also plays the role of local boy protecting his citizens from carpetbaggers out of the North. He has the disconcerting habit of leaving his telephone amplifier on, so that visitors can hear both ends of a conversation; and when a newspaperman with a pronounced Eastern accent called him for some information, he amused local journalists, who happened to be in his office, by mimicking the foreigner in his responses. When a group of white suburban wives went to his office to protest his treatment of the garbage strikers, he listened to them, then slyly asked the five who had done most of the talking where they were from; and his ear had not betrayed him—not one was a native "Memphian." He has a good ear for classes, accent, background. He wanted to know where I had gone to college. The South is very big on "society."

But Loeb has no ear at all for one accent—the thick, slow drawl of men like T. O. Jones. He knows they haven't been to college. I asked him whether he thought he could restore good relations with the Negro community after the sanitation workers settlement. "There is good understanding now. I have Negroes come to me to firm up communications—I won't say to reestablish them, because they had not lapsed." I told him I attended a mass rally at Mason Temple, where more than five thousand Negroes cheered as preacher after preacher attacked him. "Well, you just heard from a segment of the community whose personal interests were involved. Why, I have open house every Thursday, and just yesterday I had many Negroes come in to see me about different things." Imagine! And Massah even talked to them! And they came right in the front door, too! It is the conviction of all Henry Loebs that the great secret of the South, carefully hidden but bound to surface in the long run, is the Negro's profound devotion to Henry Loeb. After all, look at everything he has done for them. "*I* took the responsibility of spending fifteen thousand dollars of city money—multiplied many times over by federal food stamps—to feed the strikers." *Noblesse oblige.*

The odd thing is that white Memphis really *does* think that—as citizen after citizen tells you—"race relations are good." Its spokesman cannot stop saying, "How much we have done for the Negro" (the Southern bigot is nothing but the Northern liberal caricatured—we have *all* done so much for the Negro). A journalist on the *Press-Scimitar*, the supposedly "liberal" paper in town, says, "We have been giving Negroes the courtesy title" (that is, calling Mr. and Mrs. Jones *Mr.* and *Mrs.* Jones) "ever since the Korean War." (It embarrassed even the South to call the parents of a boy killed in action *John* and *Jane* Jones.) But the executive secretary of the local N.A.A.C.P. was considered a troublemaker when, arrested in a demonstration supporting the strikers, she held up the booking process time after time by refusing to answer the officer's call for "Maxine" instead of Mrs. Smith. ("Why, *isn't* your name Maxine?" one honestly befuddled cop asked her.)

Mrs. Smith is one of the many Negroes who protested the morning paper's use of the "Hambone" cartoon. But she ran up against the typical, infuriating response: "Hambone" was actually the white man's way of saying how much he *loves* the Negro. It was begun in 1916 by J. P. Alley, who—this is meant to settle the question once for all—won a Pulitzer Prize for attacking the Klan. It was kept up by the Alley family (one of whom is married to the morning paper's editor), and Memphis felt it would lose a precious "tradition" if their favorite darkie disappeared from their favorite newspaper—as, at last, a month after King's death, he did; with this final salute from the paper: "Hambone's nobility conferred a nobility upon all who knew him."

Nowhere is the South's sad talk of "tradition" more pitiful than in Memphis. The city was founded as part of a land deal that brought Andrew Jackson a fortune for getting Indians to give up their claims to the site. The city's great Civil War hero—to whom Forrest Park is dedicated—could not belong to the antebellum equivalent of the Memphis Country Club because he was not a "gentleman"—that is, he was not a slave *owner* but a slave *trader.* After the war, however, he took command of the Ku Klux Klan, which made him "society." The Memphis Klan no doubt boasted of all the things it did for the Negro, since it *was* more selective and restrained than the Irish police force, which slaughtered forty-six Negroes in as many hours during 1866. Later in the century, yellow fever drove the cotton traders out of town; and Irish riffraff took over; the municipality went broke, surrendered its charter, and ceased to exist as a city for a dozen years. Then, just as Memphis regained its right of self-government, a small-town boy from Mississippi, Ed Crump, came up the pike and founded the longest-lasting city "machine" of this century. The main social event for the town's "aristocracy"—the Cotton Carnival—goes back only as far as 1931, when it was begun as a gesture of defiance to the Depression: the city is built on a bluff, and run on the same principle.

When Dr. King's planned second march took place, four days after his death, men built the speaker's platform inconveniently high up, so Mrs. King would be standing before the city emblem, above the doors of City Hall, when she spoke. It was meant, of course, as a rebuke to the city. But her standing there, with that background, is henceforth the only tradition Memphis has worth saving.

Yet the city keeps telling itself that "relations are good." If that is so, why was Henry Loeb guarded by special detectives during and after the strike? (One sat in during my session with him; they stash their shotguns under his desk.) Why did some white ministers who supported the strike lose their jobs? Why are black preachers called Communists in anonymous circulars? But the daily papers will continue to blink innocently and boast on the editorial page: "Negro football and basketball players figure prominently in all-star high-school teams selected by our Sports Department." What *more* do they want?

When dawn came, our buses had reached Georgia, the red clay, the sparse vegetation. By the time we entered Atlanta, it was hot; the funeral service had already begun at Ebenezer Church. The bus emptied its cramped, sleepy load of passengers onto a sidewalk opposite the courthouse (Lester Maddox is hiding in there behind *his* bodyguard, conducting the affairs of office on a desk propped up, symbolically, with shotguns). The garbage men who brought their good clothes have no opportunity to change. The women are especially disappointed; the trip has left everyone rumpled. Men begin to wander off. T. O. does not know what to do. He ends up staying where the bus stopped, to keep track of his flock. Some men get the union's wreath over to the church. Others walk to Morehouse College. But for most, the long ride simply puts them in the crowd that watches, at the Capitol, while celebrities march by.

It was a long ride for this; and the ride back will seem longer. The buses leave Atlanta at eight-thirty on the night of King's burial, and do not reach Memphis until six the next morning. But no one regretted the arduous trip. T. O. told me he *had* to go: "We were very concerned about Dr. King's coming to help us. I talked with the men, and we knew he would be in danger in Memphis. It was such a saddening thing. He was in Memphis for only one reason—the

Public Works Department's work stoppage. This is something I lay down with, something I wake up with. I know it will never wear away."

A week after the funeral, Mayor Loeb finally caved in to massive pressures from the White House. The strike was settled, victoriously. At the announcement, T. O. blubbered without shame before the cameras. It was the culmination of long years—almost ten of them—he had poured into an apparently hopeless task, beginning back in 1959 when he was fired by the city for trying to organize the Public Works Department. After the victory I went with him to an N.A.A.C.P. meeting where he was introduced, to wild applause, by Jesse Turner, head of the local chapter: "Our city fathers tell us the union has been foisted on us by moneygrubbing outsiders. Well, here's the outsider who did it all, Carpetbagger Jones." The applause almost brought him to tears again: "I was born in Memphis, and went to school here. I haven't been out of the state more than three days in the last ten years. Is that what they mean by an outsider?" A man got up in the audience and said, "When my wife saw you on television, she said 'I feel sorry for that fat little man crying in public.' But I told her, 'Don't feel sorry for him. I've seen him for years trying to get something going here, and getting nowhere. *He* just *won.*' "

When the strike was still on, Henry Loeb, if asked anything about it, liked to whip out his wallet and produce the first telegram he got from the union's national office, listing nine demands. He would tick off what he could and couldn't do under each heading, giving them all equal weight, trying to bury in technicalities the two real issues—union recognition and dues checkoff. When I went to see him after the settlement, he brought out the tired old telegram, now spider-webbed with his arguments and distinctions. Then he searched the grievance-process agreement for one clause that says the final court of appeal is the Mayor (still built on a bluff). He assured me that, no matter how things look, *he* does not make deals. They really settled on *his* terms. But isn't there a dues checkoff? No. The *city* does not subtract union dues before pay reaches the men; their credit union does (a device the union had suggested from the outset). What about recognition of the union; wasn't that guaranteed? No, it was not. There is no contract, only a memorandum signed by the City Council. Well, is that not a binding agreement—i.e., a contract? "No, it is a *memorandum*" (see how useful it is to be an English major?)—"but we have a way of honoring our commitments." The code. Well, then, didn't the union get a larger raise than the Mayor said it would? Not from the *city*. Until July 1, when all city employees were scheduled for a raise, the extra demands of the union will be met by a contribution of local businessmen. *Noblesse oblige*—see what we have done for our Negroes. Will the Mayor handle promised union agitation by the hospital and school employees in a new way, after the experience of the garbage strike? "No. Nothing has changed."

Wrong again, Henry. Everything has changed. The union is here to stay, it will spread: Jesse Epps and P. J. Ciampa and T. O. Jones will see to that. The S.C.L.C. is here to stay: Jim Bevel is in charge of Project Memphis. The city is his case now, and he is on it. A coalition of local preachers that backed the strikers has made itself a permanent organization, Community on the Move for Equality; preachers like James Lawson, better educated than some Brown graduates, are convinced that the God of Justice is not dead, not even in Memphis. Most important, Memphis is now the place where Dr. King delivered one of his great speeches—those speeches that will outlive his labored essays.

The excerpt most often published from that last speech told how King had been to the mountaintop. But those who were there at the Mason Temple to hear him, the night before he died, remember another line most vividly.

He almost did not come to that meeting. He was tired; the weather was bad, he hoped not many would show up (his first march had been delayed by late spring *snows* in Tennessee); he sent Ralph Abernathy in his stead. But the same remarkable people who rode twenty hours in a bus to stand on the curb at his funeral came through storm to hear him speak on April 4. Abernathy called the Lorraine and told King he could not disappoint such a crowd. King agreed. He was on his way.

Abernathy filled in the time till he arrived with a long introduction on King's life and career. He spoke for half an hour—and set the mood for King's own reflection on the dangers he had faced. It was a long speech—almost an hour—and his followers had never heard him dwell so long on the previous assassination attempt, when a woman stabbed him near the heart. The papers quoted a doctor as saying that King would have died if he had sneezed. "If I had sneezed," he said, he would not have been in Birmingham for the marches. "If I had sneezed—" ("Tell it!" He was calling the roll now, talking "and a half," tolling the old cadences.) He could never, had he sneezed, have gone to Selma; to Washington for the great March of 1963; to Oslo. Or to Memphis.

For the trip to Memphis was an important one. He did not so much climb to the mountaintop there as go back down into the valley of his birth. Some instinct made him return to the South, breathing in strength for his assault on Washington, which he called the very last hope for nonviolence. He was learning, relearning, what had made him great—learning what motels to stay at; what style to use; what were his roots. He was learning, from that first disastrous march, that he could not come in and touch a place with one day's fervor; that he had to *work with* a community to make it respond nonviolently as Montgomery had, and Birmingham, and Selma.

It is ironic that the trouble on that first march broke out on Beale Street, where another man learned what his roots were. W. C. Handy did not come from Memphis, like Bessie Smith; he did not grow up singing the blues. He learned to play the trumpet in Alabama from a traveling bandmaster, a real

Professor Harold Hill. Then he went North, to tootle transcribed Beethoven on "classical cornet" afternoons in Chicago. It was only when he came back South, and saw that the native songs *worked* better with audiences, that he began to write down some of those songs and get them published.

King, after largely ineffectual days in Chicago, returned to Memphis, the deracinated Negro coming home. Home to die. His very oratory regained majesty as he moved South. He had to find out all over what his own movement was about—as Marc Connelly's "Lawd" learns from his own creation: "Dey cain't lick you, kin dey Hezdrel?" Bevel said the leader was not Martin King. That was true, too, in several ways. In one sense, Rosa Parks was the true leader. And T. O. Jones. All the unlickable Hezdrels. King did not sing the civil-rights blues from his youth. Like Handy, he got them published. He knew what *worked*—and despite all the charges of the militants, no other leader had his record of success. He was a leader who, when he looked around, had armies behind him.

This does not mean he was not authentic as a leader. On the contrary. His genius lay in his ability to articulate what Rosa Parks and T. O. feel. Mailer asks whether he was great or was hamboning; but King's unique note was precisely his *ham* greatness. That is why men ask, now, whether *his* kind of greatness is obsolete. Even in his short life, King seemed to have outlived his era. He went North again—not to school this time, but to carry his movement out of Baptist-preacher territory—and he failed. The civil-rights movement, when it left the South, turned to militancy and urban riots. Men don't sing the old songs in a new land.

Yet it may be too soon to say that the South's contribution has been made. After all, the first two riots in 1968 were in South Carolina and Tennessee. The garbage strike opens a whole new possibility of labor-racial coalition in those jobs consigned exclusively to Negroes throughout the South. And, more important, the Northern Negro, who has always had a love-hate memory for the South, begins to yearn for his old identity. The name for it is "soul."

The militant activists insist on tradition (Africa) and religion (Muslimism, black Messianism, etc.) and community (the brothers). Like the young King, many Negroes feel the old Baptist preachers were not dignified. Better exotic headdress and long gowns from Africa than the frock coat of "De Lawd." But the gowns and headgear *are* exotic—foreign things that men wear stiffly, a public facade. There are more familiar Negro traditions and religion and community. Black graduate students have earned the right to go back to hominy and chitlins and mock anyone who laughs. The growth of "soul" is a spiritual return to the South—but a return with new weapons of dignity and resistance. Religion, the family, the past can be reclaimed now without their demeaning overtones. In this respect, the modern Negro is simply repeating, two decades later, King's brilliant maneuver of escape and reentry. He got the best of both worlds—the dignity that could only be won "outside," and the more familiar things which that dignity can transform. King was there before them all.

He remained, always, the one convincing preacher. Other civil-rights pioneers were mostly lawyers, teachers, authors. They learned the white man's language almost too well. King learned it, too; but it was always stiff. He belonged in the pulpit, not at the lectern. Bayard Rustin, with his high dry professional voice and trilled r's, cannot wear the S.C.L.C.'s marching coveralls with any credibility. The same is true, in varying measure, of most first-generation "respectable" leaders. Some of them would clearly get indigestion from the thinnest possible slice of watermelon, Adam Powell, of course, can ham it with the best; but his is a raffish rogue-charm, distinguished by its whiff of mischief. King, by contrast, was an Uncle Ben with a degree, a Bill Bailey who came home—and turned the home upside down. That is why he infuriated Southerners more than all the Stokelys and Raps put together. In him, they saw *their* niggers turning a calm new face of power on them.

King had the self-contained dignity of the South without its passivity. His day is not past. It is just coming. He was on his way, when he died, to a feast of "soul food"—a current fad in Negro circles. But King was there before them. He had always loved what his biographer calls, rather nervously, "ethnic delicacies." He never lost his "soul." He was never ashamed. His career said many things. That the South cannot be counted out of the struggle yet. That the Negro does not have to go elsewhere to find an identity—he can make his stand on American soil. That even the Baptist preacher's God need not yield, yet, to Allah. God is not dead—though "De Lawd" has died. One of His prophets died.

IV

Twilight

◆◆◆

By 1968, the "White Only" signs were down, blacks were winning elections, and the battle shifted from fighting segregation to trickier terrain. "Affirmative action" entered the language; the country began to realize that the problem of poverty was more intractable than Jim Crow. King's next great crusade was to have been the Poor People's Campaign, in Washington: a massive demonstration on behalf of economic justice. Pat Watters (1927–1999) journeyed to the Mall after King's assassination. Watters had been a newspaper reporter in the South, but the force of the movement drove him from the ranks of the objective to the staff of the Southern Regional Council, a progressive organization based in Atlanta. His clear-eyed assessment of what he found in Resurrection City (the Poor People's Campaign's main camp in the center of the capital) evokes the profound disappointment of life after King.

As the seventies began, Peter Goldman (1933–), a *Newsweek* senior editor, summed up a decade of the magazine's groundbreaking coverage of race with a book entitled *Report from Black America*. Beginning in 1963, *Newsweek* launched the first extensive survey of African-American opinion and had, in 1967, published a landmark editorial, "The Negro in America: What Must Be Done." Goldman's book drew on *Newsweek*'s research and reporting; the chapter excerpted here is " 'We in a War—Or Haven't Anybody Told You That?' "

One day in 1970, Tom Wolfe (1931–), then writing for *New York* magazine, happened to be visiting *Harper's*. Wandering into David Halberstam's office, Wolfe saw an invitation to an event at the conductor Leonard Bernstein's Manhattan apartment in honor of the Black Panthers. Wolfe, who was then thinking of writing a novel about New York society on the scale of Thackeray's *Vanity Fair,* thought the spectacle at the Bernsteins' might make a good chapter. He copied down the reply number on the card and called it. "I'm Tom Wolfe with *New York* magazine and I accept," he said—and the ploy worked. When Wolfe arrived at the appointed hour, there was a cardboard table outside the apartment and his name was on the list. By the time the evening ended, Wolfe knew he couldn't hold back what he had seen for a novel. The result: "Radical Chic: That Party at Lenny's," a brilliant portrait of the liberal elite's fascination with the Black Panthers.

Alice Walker (1944–) describes her reasons, a decade after the March on Washington, for building a life in the South. In his book *The Rage of a Privileged Class,* Ellis Cose (1951–) put his finger on an important new phenomenon: that many of the outward trappings of progress and success merely masked inward fury and frustration for professional blacks in the 1980s and 1990s. In the summer of 1985, Cose was running the Institute on Journalism Education, and one of the programs was a training session for middle managers. Fifty percent were people of color, so Cose decided to host an evening seminar on whether management was different for them than for whites. "It was a fascinating night," Cose recalls, "and soon the participants, particularly the blacks, were finishing each other's sentences. That's where the seed was planted."

Calvin Trillin (1935–) had covered the South in the Atlanta bureau of *Time* from 1960 to 1961, but soon left the newsmagazine for *The New Yorker*. There, his first piece was "An Education in Georgia," an epic 1963 account of the struggle of Charlayne Hunter and Hamilton Holmes to integrate the University of Georgia. In the 1995 article collected here, Trillin takes readers inside the files of Mississippi's Sovereignty Commission, an arm of the state government that spied on its own citizens at the height of the movement.

Finally, in a Pulitzer Prize–winning essay, Howell Raines (1943–) remembers his family's complex relationship with its housekeeper. "I had wanted to find Grady for years but had lost track of her," Raines says. "Then I was visiting Birmingham one day and my sister had run into a relative of Grady's and had gotten her telephone number. So I called her, and we got back together." The reunion shed light on the ambiguities that long characterized relations between the races in the South.

"Keep On A-Walking, Children"

New American Review, January 1969

◆

PAT WATTERS

I had decided during the week after they killed Dr. King that I would go to Washington for the Poor People's Campaign—whenever it would be they wanted white people there. What prompted me to go was not my respect for Dr. King's life, the special feeling that Southerners in the civil rights movement had for his style and spirit. It was not even the sense of our loss, or the knowledge (never to be shaken) of all the hope—Southern and, in the way of Southern hopes and lost causes, naïve—which had been destroyed. In those nightmare days of the spring of 1968, I felt too despondent or too angry for these motives to have much force. Acting out of numbness, I went to find out what would happen now, what there was left to hold onto, what the future of the civil rights movement could possibly be.

There was a time of strong hope that what Dr. King preached—his grandly universalist faith in mankind, couched in a Southern Negro Baptist idiom— might, if not prevail, at least enter and renew the core of American culture. At the very least, the greatest of the Southern nonviolent demonstrations (and most of these were organized not by his SCLC, but by SNCC and CORE) had dramatized for the nation, like a man teetering on a high wire, the precarious course that American democracy had now taken, the fateful tension between the spirit that Dr. King preached and the spirit of obscene violence attracted to these demonstrations. The bullet through John Kennedy's brain signaled the breaking point of the teetering balance. From then on, violence—obscene violence—became more and more dominant, and the spirit that Dr. King embodied progressively declined until the bullet that destroyed him made us recognize that it was defeated. (I make a distinction about violence, calling "obscene" the kind which has come to prevail in the American psyche: a hysterical objectiveless, morbid, unrealistic, *neurotic* violence, in quality much the same as the Southern racist violence I happen to know well.)

Our poets know about the killing of the spirit of nonviolence, the capture of America by the spirit of obscene violence—especially those whose medium is journalism, whose muse is paranoia. They have told it, like the Old Testament prophets, over and over in the course of filing their suspicions, their distrust, their theories of national and international conspiracy. Whether the intricate webs of facts and surmises by which they weave their poetry are in themselves true or not is irrelevant: it is the metaphor these poets of paranoia make that holds the truth, and the nation, in its avid reading of all this stuff about Oswald, Garrison, etc., in its enthusiasm for the play *MacBird*, knows the truth of that metaphor. The CIA, it is often said in their poetry, engineered the assassinations, as it has engineered violent events around the world, for its own ugly purpose. This purpose, in sum, is to make prevalent and permanent in this land the spirit of violence whose medium is the Cold War, whose rationale is that there is a strategy, an ideology, more important than all and any human life, and whose ultimate obscenity is nuclear holocaust. True, not true—in the factual sense? Who is to say? True, metaphorically? Look about you. When they killed Robert Kennedy, when that obscene spirit killed him, if it said anything at all, it said: do not even allow yourself to hope, against all evidence, just to hope there might be chance for something else, for the spirit embodied in the words, the efforts, the life of Dr. King.

And when the time came to attend the sad finale to his efforts, the Poor People's Campaign, there was no longer even any of the rage I had intermittently felt; nor the idea of going there not as a journalist but as a participant—white, Southern, middle-aged, middle class, without ideology, really, not radical only radically angry—to show them, by God, they just couldn't get away with it, couldn't kill what Dr. King stood for. That was gone. For the knowledge was there, underscored by the assassination of Robert Kennedy, that they had indeed killed it, that it was gone in this nation, and that violence, obscene violence, unclear violence controlled.

So when I arrived in Washington on June 18, it was with much the same feeling that has hung over the liberal establishment for some time now, and has spread to those varieties of left-of-center people who had thought they were better than the liberals: numbness, let us call it, weariness, the sense of going through the motions because there is not even energy enough, will enough, to call a halt to say no more of this, it is hopeless. I had not understood this malaise in the liberals before, seeing diabolical motives in their willingness these past several years to keep on trying all those obsolete methods—study groups, pilot studies, conferences, papers—in situations that demanded drastic action, certainly not more words. But now I was in Washington, a notebook in my inside coat pocket, though stuck there indecisively. I had always gone to these events as a reporter—first as a newspaperman, later as a representative of the Southern Regional Council and its small magazine, *New South*. The Southern Regional Council is a civil rights organization whose role has been mainly fact-gathering, setting the record straight rather than direct action. Normally, I had worked with the conviction that trying to tell the truth had importance, could make a difference. But this time I didn't know that I would act even as a reporter, knowing that I wouldn't participate as a marcher—would perhaps just stand around, observe, absorb the full meaning of the thing.

"This will be the whimper," a friend who had observed a good bit of the Poor People's Campaign heretofore in Washington during the spring and the summer had said, "with which the Movement will die." I had once before just stood there and taken in the full impact of an event. That had been John Kennedy's assassination. Until a month before I had been a newspaperman for eleven years, and when the flash came from Dallas, my every instinct was to get up from my new job, rush out, and begin putting together a story. Instead I had to sit there and just feel what had happened. Journalism is a cold and callous calling; out of the necessity to get the news while it is breaking, the best workers have a conditioning and an ability to divert all the energy of their emotion into the skills of gathering information and writing it coherently. Sometimes this can be a blessing.

My notes on the three days in Washington reflect my inner ambivalence; they are fragmentary, disinterested, without passion. (On the first view of Resurrection City: "A-frame huts. Mud. Handball mud-encrusted in the middle of mudhole. Sewage pipes in mud alongside ditch. Mess tent: dried mud on plywood floor. Sign: 'Please Brother, Clean Up.'") I was neither participant, fully feeling observer, nor reporter. On the eve of the Solidarity Day march, I stepped out of the Dupont Plaza (not the best of hotels but luxurious enough to make ludicrous the notion that I was there in solidarity with the starving children of Mississippi). Over in Dupont Circle a demonstration was being formed, a line of maybe two hundred ready to go, an even mixture of white and black, mostly young, excited, even ebullient. They were a contingent of the National Welfare Rights Organization, a group recently formed to organize welfare recipients. A young Negro had given fliers to a good-looking girl, and he was trying to get the older guy beside her on the bench—in a business suit, frowning, shaking his head—to take one of them. "At least read it, get both sides of things," he was saying to the man. Conditioned by what I had read and heard of the Poor People's Campaign, the Black Power attempts at bullying the Indians and Mexicans, conditioned by encounters with Southern varieties of Negroes emancipated into an ability to express racial animosity, bad manners, or strong-arm predilections, I had been walking warily amid this crowd of demonstrators, as among Southern whites at a Citizens Council meeting or a straight political rally. I was waiting for one of those ugly, defeating episodes of inane nastiness which has become the coin of all social intercourse in our cities and has spread finally into the nonviolent movement that Dr. King founded. But here this young Negro, proffering his flier about welfare rights, was smiling, was sincere, was simply trying to get the guy to read the thing—truth in open encounter. The guy kept refusing it, the Negro looked at the girl, who was dutifully glancing over hers. "He with you?" he asked, as though she could do something about the other's intransigence, but she only nodded, sloe-eyed, smiling up. No intimidation here, nor white guilty fear. Just people. (In the next two days I would keep coming back to Dupont Circle—a circle of sanity, a place of the future where people might just be people.)

The line had started moving out, cops all over the place directing it, with gaps every twenty people or so. I asked the young Negro where they were going. "We are going to have dinner with Wilbur Mills," he said, his accent Northern. The Welfare Rights people had just gotten to town for the march the next day, and were taking the opportunity to embarrass the member of the House of Representatives they held most to blame for their many, I am certain, just grievances. Mills lived, he said, about a mile away. I was to meet some friends who might be able to fill me in on Resurrection City; since I was going in the same direction, I fell in behind a segment of the march, my notebook hidden.

It was a good-natured crowd moving along the sidewalk, and the residents of the area (a lot of them, I was to learn, Washington's hippies and students) seemed to welcome the diversion of the demonstration and to support the marchers. But after we got about a block, the cops intervened and began to hold things up. I stood around awhile, and got to thinking it would be this way at every intersection, and felt impatient, then felt how futile it was to try to embarrass a man like Mills who would measure any such effort down to the most minute calibers of power, and conclude quickly that here was no threat, no power, that could affect him. ("Congress Wake Up To What's Going On," said a big sign.) So I left the march, not having really joined it, and went over to the next block and watched it from each parallel intersection. An old crazy-hair lady stood alongside it at one intersection, hands on hips, not liking it at all. One of the friends I was to meet was watching it outside the restaurant, and we stood together as it went by, a segment singing weakly, "Ain't goin' let nobody turn me 'round," one young man throwing his whole soul into the song, his thin shoulders squared, head thrown back, his pinched face suggesting the fanatical college student drawn inevitably to the Movement, but his close-clipped, home-style haircut belying this, suggesting that he was a bona-fide welfare recipient. "Ain't goin' let nobody turn me 'round," and it occurred to me that nobody much but the crazy-hair old lady seemed to want to, she now moving on by us, muttering, stopping to pick up a bit of paper littered there by some bad citizen, then dropping it angrily, as she would like to drop the demonstration, in a garbage can. Later, I read in the paper that some of these demonstrators were arrested, in some technical contretemps with the cops over where it was improper for them to be.

There had been a familiar feeling about that walking out of the hotel into a demonstration. It was like arriving in Selma or Albany during Dr. King's direct-action campaigns, the plunging from the gray world of everyday into a world where everyday wrongs had been disinterred, brought forth for confrontation, the demonstrations a focus for seeing what is ordinarily not seen, for making tension and conflict the norm of every day (often every hour), as in a battle. Washington has known some of this, I thought, with the Poor People's Campaign. But then I learned that the march I had stumbled on was a rarity, not the minor skirmish I had supposed.

Much of the malaise afflicting Resurrection City, I was also to learn, stemmed from the lack of action for people who had come for a crusade of direct action. It was not the much-publicized mud, which was no different from niggertown alley mud, fragranced with garbage and excretion whenever rain comes in the South; no worse than ghetto filth. Nor was it the social pathology said to be stalking the encampment at night—sped by wine, drugs, and other torments. Nor was it even the cruel and heartbreaking irony of the discovery in the muddy misery of the place that their own "brothers" named to the role of security police, given clubs and power over them, became suddenly the beasts that all white cops were known to be. No, none of these. We know even from the pale empathy of print that the culture of poverty contains all of this and worse, and has its mechanisms—not only brutalization, the blunting of sensibility—whereby people deal with it, even as the culture of affluence contains its own versions of viciousness and has its martini mechanisms for coping. It was the lack of action that had sent so many away, back to familiar mud, and hunger and crime and *idleness*. The capacity of Resurrection City was three thousand. At the peak of occupancy around May 20, about a month after Dr. King's murder, there were 2,650 residents, and many more had been turned away. By the time of the Solidarity Day march, there were no more than eight hundred people left. Some had gone home; others had drifted off to the Washington ghetto; nearly all remaining were Negro, with maybe twenty or twenty-five whites, mostly from West Virginia, some from Chicago, still dwelling among them. Indians and Mexican-Americans, out of bureaucratic ineffectiveness, out of dismay at conditions, and out of hostility from the Negroes, never had lived in any number in Resurrection City, but had encamped in nearby schools and churches. Of 125 Indians who came, no more than fifteen or twenty were still there for Solidarity Day; of four hundred Mexican-Americans, two hundred were left.

Idleness, maybe we will come to know from the Poor People's Campaign, is, along with hunger, the bane of the poor. Robert Coles has written of an organizing instinct in the human mind which tries to impose a routine on the days of idleness, of nothing to do, of purposelessness among the starving people of the rural South. Murray Kempton, standing about with reporters (in our isolation) at Resurrection City, spoke of that sense of disorder that comes upon the ghetto, upon individual souls in the ghetto as afternoon starts, as the hope of the morning dies and the realization sinks in that here is another day wasted, another day that will come to nothing; this is the time that the wine-drinking starts, the pathology begins to stir. How much of what had moved the poor to far-off, unfriendly Washington, to Resurrection City, I now asked myself, was merely the hope of something to do, a surcease from futility? (They go, said my good friend who had helped recruit them in rural Alabama, because they know that things at the campaign can't be any worse than back home. We both had thought it was only food that they hungered for.)

Occasionally during those long weeks a demonstration would be announced on the rarely idle loudspeaker system of the "City," and people would bestir themselves, begin to build a life of a day on the announcement, getting ready, girding themselves. Then there would be delays and falterings, and usually the thing would be called off. But more often, there would not even be the announcement of a demonstration. The people were getting enough to eat (although the fine plans for three hot meals a day never were realized; not always, even, was supper hot). From an adequate diet there was unaccustomed energy. But the energy was not used, was frustrated.

The few "good" demonstrations that had occurred stood out in the memory of those involved; they hinted at what might have been. There had been the time, about two weeks before Solidarity Day, when everyone was together. The march was on the Justice Department to protest the unconstitutional arrest of Mexican-American youngsters in a Los Angeles school walkout. Mexican-Americans were at the head of the march, behind them, whites, and then blacks. There was a driving rain. The singing, the solidarity defied the rain, and for the moment defied Washington—shook a mighty fist at all its alien grandeur and haughtiness.

So the little march that I saw on the eve of Solidarity Day was a big thing, and I suppose I should have known this merely from having seen the physical setting of Resurrection City, the reification of all the South's niggertowns, the Northern city ghettos. I had earlier in the day walked down one side of it, up the other. They had finally laid a trail of planks and plywood through the mud, leading by the huts of habitation, the larger huts of headquarters and officialdom, and the gathering places, like Martin Luther King Plaza—a wooden platform from which Dr. Ralph Abernathy made his pronouncements. I notice that I headed my notes "Tent City," a nostalgic slip, harking back to the desperate little enterprise of 1966, in Lowndes County, Alabama, where Negroes evicted from the land for attempting to register to vote took refuge in tents and sought in vain to call attention to their plight. There were other unsuccessful Southern antecedents. Strike City, in Tribbett, Mississippi, was a tent encampment for the farm laborers who in 1965, in a grandly hopeless gesture against the law of supply and demand, attempted to bargain collectively with the planters. And then there was the Tent City, also in 1966, set up in Washington itself, a little band of the dispossessed and hungry people who had tried to take over an abandoned air force base in Greenville, Mississippi, and had been efficiently carried out of it, old folks and little children, by the United States military.

Our time is expanded, broadened out, filled almost to the bursting point with event; that was all two and three years ago as time has been measured since antiquity—linearly—but how many years of antiquity's slim pacing of event? It seems like a decade, even a century ago. When that Washington Tent City was encamped on Lafayette Square, the newly formed Citizens Crusade Against Poverty was holding a poor people's convention—incongruously, indeed surrealistically—within the luxurious confines of the International Inn. In one of the first public displays of the unruliness and just plain undeservingness of the poor (there was considerable comment in the liberal press), the delegates there, led by some of the toughest of Mississippi's grass-roots Negro leaders—which is to say some of the most misused and lied-to people in the world—set upon such speakers as Walter Reuther with boos and catcalls and an alarming disregard for parliamentary procedure. How long ago, how far back in our innocence; we were sorry the President and the nation and its Congress didn't respond to those various tent cities. But we had other things going; the Poverty Program seemed so hopeful, founded in the notion that the poor, with proper direction and encouragement, could democratically rid themselves of the taints and defects that prevented them from sharing in the affluent society. There was little thought then that it was the society itself that was tainted and defective.

Tents are honest temporary shelters. Somehow, plywood built into the shape and size of tents has no honesty, no integrity. A man is not demeaned by having to bend over to get into a tent; he does so for the sake of being able to strike the thing in the morning and go on his way. But permanent plywood tents press down on the soul, bend heads and shoulders toward indignity. Middle-class mindlessness designed and built those abominations and set them down on lawn grass with the same insensitivity that housed a crusade against poverty in a plastic and glass-bubble modern motel, and with the same deadly unrealism that expected democratic procedures, used against the poor a million times, to sustain them, to hold up under them.

Resurrection City itself felt like an African village seen in the movies—that sense of imperfect planning conveyed by the huts, of an unknown communal culture, perhaps more sociable than ours, with black babies waddling barefoot in the mud. There also was a feel of the South, the porch somebody had incongruously stuck out in front of one of the huts, three men seated on it, chairs tilted back to the plywood wall. And there was a sense of the circus—controlled chaos, the big top soon to rise—the same as there was on the Selma-to-Montgomery march produced by the essential Americanism of Dr. King and the metaphors of protest he had projected.

Little groups were gathered in discussion, one felt endless discussion: tableaux of black young men, a white in their group; or two whites sitting on their haunches; or an old garrulous Southern Negro woman talking at once to everyone and no one. There was hostility toward the stranger—the white, the besuited, unbearded with press tag affixed, notebook out in the open—but mostly I was struck by the aloofness of these people, the demand that their privacy in this place be respected. There had been the time when, as a reporter, I would have, without second thought, moved among such people, talked with them. In part I would have done so simply because I was interested in them, glad of the chance to meet them, to hear what they had to say, to share a common view. That part had been genuine and good; but there had also been another, not very pretty part: the unspoken, maybe even, for some of them, unrecognized enactment of a mutually demeaning ritual: of my eliciting, their showing, the pathos, the tragedy, the ugliness of their situation, and the humor and braveness and beauty of their response: this to be put down in my notebook, to be filled out, built up, bodied forth in quotes, the alive words of suffering people for the American consumers of words, of authenticity, of real human material. No more. Or at least not here. The people had apparently been exposed too much in Washington to the truth of how little America cares about their humanity. So they do not speak to the straight stranger, nor look at him, even in the intimacy of the one waiting while the other negotiates a single plank through a mud puddle. Or they show contempt by demanding a cigarette or money.

I remember my shock, the first upsetting of my conditioned expectations of the Movement Negroes of the South, and most of all, of SNCC, when in the summer of 1964, Freedom Summer, I went into the SNCC-run office of COFO in Jackson, Mississippi, and had a Negro youth ask me for money. That was not the way the Movement had been run heretofore; there was too much mutual respect for that sort of thing, despite my expense account and good living made out of writing about the Movement, despite their poverty and their beyond-belief braveness. I had not learned then to be aware of the implications of our relative positions, their incongruity in the real meanings of that movement to which we were both devoted; and he had not learned that begging might have utility beyond the momentary need for money, that begging by such as him from such as me could be an exquisite insult. For a time the activists of the Movement accepted those white Southerners (and there were damn few of them) who were able to support direct action. In this context, some of us, reporters and others, developed a sort of proprietary feeling about the Movement; we liked to advise and criticize it, using as a standard those best and most beautiful moments of it that we had seen. Sometimes we could be relevant and constructive; but sometimes our attitude degenerated into that of the connoisseur—carping and superficial. In any case, the Movement's penetration to ever deeper and more painful truth about American society has ended this rule. We have come a ways since, that long-ago kid at COFO and myself.

Wordlessly, I handed out cigarettes to three young black men before one of the huts, and we all four lit up, and I tried to think of some way not to get just a quote. I could not. They read my press tag. (I had decided to wear it out of dread of some mean, stupid scene with the security police.) One of the young men said, "Tell the truth about us when you write." I had heard that so many times from the whites in the South; there was no longer any shock at hearing it, too, from Negroes, and with probably more justification, but again renouncing the old politeness, the old mutual respect that had been so pleasant. "He can write anything he wants to," another of them said, turning, disgusted, cynical, bending his head down to go into his hut. "It's a free country."

An old Negro man, from the South, from the country, unlearned in or maybe too wise for blanket hostility, the gratuitous, meaningless insult, asked politely for a cigarette, and then went on to say that he was praying for rain on Solidarity Day "so all them visitors can get baptized in our mud." He laughed, and I laughed. Maybe he was paying for his cigarette in the old unconscious ways with a quote. Maybe he wasn't. But it was like old times.

There was a faint sense in Resurrection City of a struggle of wills, of the constructive and, let us say, softer side of humanity against the harsh and destructive. A dribble painting executed with skill on a hut's outer wall was carefully signed. The God's Eye Bakery was dispensing hot brown bread and apple butter to all comers, straight strangers even, with a joy in the goodness of it. At the Child Care Center, a large, three-room plywood construction with a blessedly squared-off roof, not cramping down on the children, there was a sense of purpose, of busy people. Crayon and fingerpaint art was all over the walls; children were moving about in the random way of preschoolers; a sign on the wall said to take a free toothbrush. A boy of about five in a corner cried all the woe of his time in life, and one of a number of pretty, mud-stained white girls went quickly to him, knelt to him, comforted him, ended sitting on the floor and engaging him in some game. Two middle-aged, middle-class local Negro women were in charge, both with experience in professional day-care work. They talked of their thirty-five charges, including some infants, in that gentle way— not condescending, nor pitying, but more nearly awed—that their middle-aged, middle-class counterparts in the Child Development Group of Mississippi speak of theirs: these selfsame bright-eyed little kids flowering forth their potential, their beauty, freed for a time from torpor and listless quarrelsomeness by the advent in their lives of one hot meal a day.

Back outside, an old white man with dancing eyes began to talk of the greatness of America, that it could produce such a thing as Resurrection City. Another of his kind interrupted a conversation of a beautiful young woman with straight black hair, high cheekbones, and tan skin, a Negro professional civil rights worker who had been assigned to work with the Indians. She had been telling how every time an Indian got singled out for any role of leadership he was immediately discredited with the others, and she was saying, as the old man hove up, "I'm just a token Indian." "No, no," he reassured her. "You're an Indian—" as though nothing could be worse than what she really was. He went on his way, had an afterthought, returned to tell it. "If it weren't for the Indians, we wouldn't have this country, would we? We stole it from them."

Shortly before they killed Dr. King, I heard that he had been made hopeful once more by the success in recruiting the other races for the Poor People's Campaign; he regarded it as evidence that his dream of welding all the poor together could be achieved. There had been little enough during the past few years to encourage him. His organization (if the scattering of outposts and individual preachers across the South could be called an organization) and funds had shrunk. His Chicago adventures had been near disasters (the old tactic of exposing at its most vicious the normally hidden brutality of segregation had worked as dramatically in Chicago as it had in the South, but there was little willingness in the nation even to acknowledge the brutality it was shown, let alone act upon the Northern ghetto problems). His influence in the White House was long since gone, the condemnation of the Vietnam war having ended all contact. He had been badly used by Stokely Carmichael *et al.* during the Meredith March of 1966, his presence having drawn the press and thus given the leaders of the Black Power schism a national platform as well as a stalking horse for their new doctrine. Finally, Dr. King and his movement undoubtedly had been hurt by the riots in the Northern ghettos. Almost nowhere in the South had there been anything like them.

We know in the South (from the beginning of our lives) that it is insanity we fight when we oppose racism, when we exercise our civil liberties. You handle insanity as delicately, cautiously as you can, not out of political moderation or humane feeling, but out of self-preservation. This was at the essence of the strategy (as distinct from the philosophy) of Dr. King's nonviolent movement. To have that self-preserving caution, that pitting of the sane against the insane, suddenly blown up by outbursts of an answering insanity from the ghettos must have been to know anguish and despair of an exquisite kind. Back in 1965, Bayard Rustin had stated with Southern clarity the case against black violence when he remarked of the new breed of black militants: "They think [Malcolm X] can frighten white people into doing the right thing. To believe this, of course, you must be convinced, even if unconsciously, that at the core of the white man's heart lies a buried affection for Negroes—a proposition one may be permitted to doubt." Not the least of the reasons Dr. King found himself in Memphis in the fateful spring of 1968 was the pressure on him to show, as in a staging ground for the Washington campaign, that nonviolent demonstrations could still be achieved, could resist the agents and impulses of the riot insanity. And of course the insanity did arise, preparing the ground for that more effective lethal white variant of it that ended his life.

Naturally enough, in the process of all the vicissitudes of recent years, Dr. King's headquarters staff had shown signs of demoralization. Unlike the old SNCC and CORE, Dr. King's organization had always had a tendency toward soft middle-class living. I remember my innocent shock (the same connoisseur's shock of being panhandled by a SNCC kid) at overhearing a big SCLC leader in 1963 in Albany, Georgia, where the demands on the people for sacrifice and suffering were great, speak of dreading to go into the heat, the noise of the nightly mass meetings which the people loved so much, this being his form of sacrifice and suffering. There were other men of power on the SCLC staff of whom there was universal agreement among us bystanders that SCLC, Dr. King, and the Movement would long have been better off without. There was never any hint that Dr. King would get rid of such men. Ralph Abernathy was to show a similar disinclination: some said it was because Mr. Abernathy felt more comfortable around such men, lesser men than himself, than around the lean, aggressive younger activists who came back to SCLC for the Poor People's Campaign. I don't think this motive was ever part of Dr. King's tolerance for them. I think that in a way so genuine it was innate with him, he believed in the good, the positive in all men to a degree that made of little significance to him those gradations in demonstrated goodness—or more to the point here, ability—by which the rest of us judge individuals. His leadership was to draw the best from each man, not seek better and better men. This is the *ne plus ultra*, of course, of radical leadership, a concept ancient enough, but in our time of *surplus* human beings, an entirely alien one.

After his death, reports came from the spontaneous drawing together in grief of his staff, from their staff meetings, a retreat they held, that there was to be a renaissance of the old movement spirit, a renewed unity and dedication. Everything one now heard in Washington about the staff seemed to deny this, or to indicate a deterioration of the new spirit. The most public criticism was that of the unwillingness of the staff to live in the squalor of Resurrection City. There were gleeful reports of a bill of at least fifteen thousand dollars run up by the staff at the motel where most of them stayed. More devastating to the effect of the campaign was the confusion of command, the absence of leadership and authority which developed in Washington, manifest in the failures to get demonstrations going, to satisfy the hunger for purposefulness in the poor people. The style of the Southern movement had always included a fine little bit of chauvinism, a deliberate baiting of the Northern fetish for efficiency. In all its major campaigns, SCLC had indulged this indifference to routines and planning to dangerous degrees. Apparently in Washington it got out of hand. Previously it had been the defect of a greater virtue—a spontaneity that provided energy, morale. Now it seemed the expression of collapsed morale from whatever wide variety of causes among the individuals on the staff.

Thus, the connoisseur of the Movement might make his pronouncements and judgments, like a literary critic or sportswriter. The press is expert at this; the Poor People's Campaign has been subjected to it everywhere, from *The Village Voice* to *Business Week*. What do any of us know of the real forces at work on any group, any organization, any collection of people, even on that most intimate grouping of all, our own families? What happens to the men who make such a movement? I speak of hopelessness. What do we know of the dimensions of hopelessness (or hope) in a man at the head of a demonstration line in the Black Belt South marching into the face of his worst childhood fears? I remember Dr. King's inarticulateness in Albany during one of the first arrests there: the words, the inspiration, the incredible bravery coming that time not from him but from one of those he led, seeking the best in them—an unlettered country preacher falling on his knees in the street, praying in the breath-gasping, ungrammatical idiom of his religious tradition, inchoate, wild-sounding prayer, pulling the demonstrators to his own exalted state.

I do not presume to judge, then, or even to insist that these surface things I have told even begin to explain what happened to the Poor People's Campaign. It is fair and accurate to report, though, that on the eve of the Solidarity Day march, no one was hopeful, no one was predicting, from the performance of SCLC in the simple mechanics of organizing for such an event, much of a crowd. It will be the whimper, my friend had said. It happened, though, that I had had occasion the previous week to be reading a random assortment of out-of-town papers, and I had been struck with how nearly all of them—in the South, New England, Pittsburgh, such places—had their little stories saying a thousand from here, a busload from there, were getting themselves ready to go to the march. Apparently much of this was spontaneous, with no great organizational effort behind it—a minister here, a Negro leader there, getting it up. So I had a hunch that the crowd would be better than anyone had a right to hope; and through the hot morning, watching the people gathering around the Washington Monument, seeing them steadily coming, like so many picnickers, I felt some little sense of satisfaction, and, seeing such a quietly ordered and decent-looking crowd, I found myself, in an old reflex of the Movement's magic, beginning to hope. We had counted crowds so many times, the numbers in a church, the size of the demonstration, as though to find some mystical magical number, as though to quantify the miracle occurring before our eyes was somehow to solidify it, certainly Americanize it. The essence of Dr. King's movement—perhaps like that of his people, the Negro South—derived more from the East than the West: spiritual, indeed mystical, involving the absorbing of the individual in the will and consciousness of the many, just as his demonstrations made use of methods and mechanisms not much drawn on anymore in the West—singing, chanting, religious exaltation. I can still see Claude Sitton of *The New York Times* running up and down the line of the demonstrations in St. Augustine, Florida, sweating in the balmy, tropical night heat, counting the number that was willing, incredibly, night after night, to march to the town square and get beaten with clubs and steel pipe and bicycle chains, and then be arrested for their pains. It was important to get the exact number. During the morning in Washington people kept saying, "How would you estimate the crowd?" "Would you say fifty thousand?" We had sat up late the night before, talking, dolefully talking, as we had so many nights since the assassinations, and the hangover I had was like so many since then, indeed one big one since then, a hangover of impotent grief and anger that would not sweat away in that godawful morning of Washington humidity. So I tended to be short with my stock answer, that I don't think it's possible to estimate a crowd, that if you can't count them (count their legs and divide by two, we used to say), then you just don't know, and it becomes a guessing game, an issue of contention between those who are for the crowd and those against it. Sure enough, the next day, Ralph Abernathy called a press conference to quarrel with *The Washington Post*'s estimate of fifty thousand.

Less was said about the quality of the crowd. There was, as always at these things, the most recent one having been Dr. King's funeral, the sense of being at a reunion, or convention, the seeing and greeting and talking with members of a community who came from all over, mostly up and down the Eastern seaboard—people with ties to the Movement, with mutual memories. Occasionally, one of them would say of the day's crowd that—yes, it was different, different from that great, joyous throng in 1963 in Washington, for example. Some would say that it was better—younger, more serious. Others would say it seemed lifeless, hopeless, going through the motions. I couldn't tell. My notes at one point say flatly, "not young predominantly, not poor—the same kind of middle-class, well-intentioned, naïve crowd that has always turned out for these things—maybe even more whites than there used to be."

The crowd flowed slowly around the Washington Monument. At the base, one of those inevitable "entertainment" sessions went on, with maybe half the crowd gathered around it. Pete Seeger sang, the good Southern idiom of "The Crawdad Song" ("You git a line, I'll git a pole . . . We'll go down to that crawdad hole . . .") ringing out over the more than ordinarily inhuman loudspeaker system. There is a verse to "The Crawdad Song" that Seeger understandably refrained from using: "Yonder comes a nigger with a sack on his back; yonder comes a nigger with a sack on his back . . . Got more crawdads than he can pack . . ." There is a spirit in which that verse can be sung which would not be offensive to Negroes, Southern Negroes, a spirit of white and black sharing subtleties of humor, the anomaly of a nigger ever having more of anything than he can pack, the humbleness of that creature, the crawdad diminutive cousin of the lobster, capable in the tradition of turnip greens, pigs' snouts, of being cooked into exquisite fare, as in crayfish bisque. We have not seen the time, even that joyous time of the March on Washington in 1963, when such an explanation could be broached to such a crowd. We shall not likely see it, ever. To try it even in print is to risk offending good people and court the contumely of various kinds of fools, including Black Power ones. And yet—who wants to live in a land where you can't try to say the unsayable?

In the headquarters tent, around noon, I watched Ralph Abernathy being greeted, hugged, posed for pictures, being treated like a potentate by various old friends of his, and new ones. He looked tired, as Dr. King used to look during these climaxes of his adventures in innovative political action. Ralph Abernathy is a likable man, more so on the level of how-de-do, haven't seen you in a long time, than Dr. King ever was. I always admired his preaching. He gets a tone of the sardonic and at the same time of Elizabethan, Gargantuan outrage into his voice that is eloquent; it sang for a while in his speech later in the day. His children and Dr. King's have been among the tiny token of desegregation at the grammar school where my children go; he and I sat together one PTA meeting and listened to his daughter and my son and two of Dr. King's youngsters in a choral group on the stage singing "Dixie." We looked at each other, shook our heads, laughed. I watched him and Dr. King once in Albany, going to all the Negro dives and poolrooms to plead that there be no repetition of the previous night's disruption of a demonstration by throwing bricks at police. That was in 1962, and in those innocent, pre-Northern riots, pre–Black Power times, the plea prevailed; in these encounters, we reporters, connoisseurs, agreed, Abernathy, of the two men of God down among the sinners, had the surest common touch, was the most effective. It was said that much of the ineffectiveness and the doldrums in Resurrection City stemmed from a flaw in the command system which demanded that he make every decision, however minor, although he was nearly always unavailable, caught as now in talk by handwringers and hangers-on. Be that as it may, the march was, true to form, to cliché, going to be late.

When, finally, the Reverend Jesse Jackson got the march officially under way, fully half the marchers had already ambled the short distance of its course across the green and alongside the reflecting pool to the Lincoln Memorial. With marvelous ability to ignore this plain reality, Jackson was officiously instructing who should be where in the march—the Resurrection City residents first, the Mule Team people (their mule team in some bureaucratic snag left across the river in a Washington suburb) second, etc.

I noticed, ambling along the march route, that many of the Resurrection City residents were sitting it out in the familiarity of the shade of their huts, some of them standing along the fence, looking at, even talking to the marchers. There was a clear division: the march was in one tradition (that of the old, lately lamented coalition of white liberals, labor and religious figures, and Negro sacrifices, the former unable to deliver such crucial items as votes but ever able to bargain, the latter depended upon to deliver whatever was demanded—votes, lives); Resurrection City was in another tradition, one that was done with coalition. "We Marched at Selma, 1965, Washington, 1968," said what may have been the saddest of all the hand-lettered signs on the plywood of the A-frame huts. A button to complement it was worn by a middle-aged, middle-class lady, innocent of innocents: "Think Poor."

The dust, the crowding, the heat were worse than even in the morning's hangover dread I had imagined. Finally I sat down in some shade, apart from all of it; there were maybe a hundred of us along there. They played "The Star-Spangled Banner." I stood up. I always have, though never since the age of twelve, I reckon, with any meaning in it. Maybe six others in our shade did too.

About this time two buses marked "Congressional Delegation" pulled up, and I watched the occupants descend from their air-conditioning right into the worst of the heat and crowdedness. To a man, they stood a moment, staring down at what they (and there were precious few of them) had come here to be part of. I watched their faces—these politicians' faces, whore-trained to simulate any desired emotion—one after the other falter and fall for an instant into honest expressions, mostly of dismay, a few of panic, fear. And then I watched Senator McCarthy arrive. He had given us the first faint, fitful start of real hope since the assassinations with the news that morning of the New York primary returns. The Secret Service men and the soldiers were scurrying before and after him, their heads swinging unnaturally fast in sweeps of observation, scanning like electronic instruments for killers. McCarthy's face as he scurried along was all twisted, maybe squinting in the glare—but maybe showing his distaste for this ritual of his arrival, along with all the rest of ritual which he has so eloquently disdained.

When Humphrey arrived a little later, they booed him. It was one of the few good moments. Another was when a large group, more than a hundred, did their marching through the length of the reflecting pool, waving their signs, clapping, singing the old Movement songs, "Sing A-men . . . Amen . . . Amen. Amen. Amen." They were refreshed, alive—having fun. The filthy water sparkled in their hair.

I ran into John Lewis, who was the old SNCC's brave, gentle leader. Of all the young activists who were inspired by Dr. King (SNCC sprang full-grown from the belly of an SCLC conference), Lewis was probably the closest to him in spirit and in a still unfaltering ability to accept each person as he is, on his own terms. More than one automatically ironic reporter was to note that the famous words that were stricken from John Lewis' speech at the 1963 march would have been pale beside the inflammatory idiom of this day's speeches. One reporter somehow got into print in a paper that should have known better the comment that John Lewis had become in the years since that 1963 speech entirely respectable, a man who now wore an Ivy League suit. He always had. I remember seeing him, still dazed, still in pain, wearing such a suit a few days after the most spectacular of his countless brave acts: he and Hosea Williams leading the march that tried to cross the Edmund Pettus bridge in Selma, and was beaten back and trampled by Alabama troopers and other savages on horseback. John Lewis had been with Robert Kennedy, had talked with him just before they killed him. His grief, as it had been over Dr. King, was terrible to see. I had somewhere in one of those long days of all our grief snarled out, "Why in the hell doesn't somebody put a bullet through the brain of one of theirs, the worst of theirs," and John turned on me, as harsh as I ever heard him speak, and said, "Hush that kind of talk. We're sick—sick with violence." This most hopeful of all the men I have known in the Southern movement spoke of going to this march but not expecting much. I had seen him during the morning. He confided that he had noticed a lot of bureaucrat types in the crowd, the kind who come to anything only as a command performance. "It wouldn't surprise me," John Lewis said wistfully, "to see the President show up."

A sign, "Jobs Or Income For All," had been abandoned, stuck on its flimsy stick in the middle of a mud puddle. I made notes: a big Negro man with a hand that dwarfs his sign stick: "America Why Not Now?" A stooped middle-class white woman, kerchief on her gray head, a bearded kid behind her, a grayhaired priest, a solemn Negro man, hand on hip, head bent, listening to Roy Wilkins, four girls sitting in grass, the day's dust coating their mini-skirts, an elderly nun, a middle-class Negro woman with glasses on a chain around her neck, a white mother and son eating sandwiches, a news cameraman asleep. A banner proclaiming that Ripon Republicans Join Poor People's Struggle is held by three young men, somehow looking fresh in their business suits, like a television commercial. A Negro man from out of the Washington wilderness paces slowly with his sandwich board: "I am the true prophet. This land is going to be bombed with nuclear. This is the end for the nations of Christianity. This is the meaning of doom's day."

It was the alienated young, in all their modes of hairstyle and dress, who got to me most: a tall young Negro in a robe, his happy discovery of a style really expressive of himself, a princeliness, ferociousness formerly denied him; or the young in Resurrection City in all their brooding privacy and silence. They stirred buried sources of anxiety I didn't know I had. I began to feel that this nation was going off the track. I had been reared in the surly listlessness of the Southern Depression, had come of age in the hysteria of World War II, had matured in the Southern civil rights struggle, had witnessed the insurrection of the white South, after the 1954 Supreme Court decision and Dr. King's counterrevolution. But here in Washington I felt for the first time that the orderly path, those parallel lines between which our struggles had been confined, seemed certain always to be confined, twisting and turning, moving forward and backward, those lines that seemed so certainly, so permanently drawn— really could be ripped apart, torn away, and new ones drawn. Perhaps they would be more stirring lines, but they would lead through the air there in Resurrection City, all of that nameless hostility. Knowing the Southern darkness, the murderous insanity that had created this hostility in its image and now awaited it, lips pursed; considering the sad inevitabilities of revolution; considering some of the psychological specimens I had known of the nucleus of the New Left in the South; considering that being *under* thirty no more assures a sense of consequences than being Negro or white does, or being poor, I felt a fear of the future like none I had ever known.

The speeches were as dull, as remote from the reality of Resurrection City as the routine program designed them to be. There was the usual gossip among the connoisseurs about the mighty power struggle going on within SCLC, exemplified by Mrs. Coretta King's taking so much time for her part of the program (her speech was acutely intelligent, her courage and beauty that had shown through all the obscene spectacle of the assassination's aftermath on display once more). Such talk of power struggles trailed Dr. King through his career, struggles that seem integral to any organized effort of Southerners, white and black, their zest for exaggerating the ordinary maneuverings of clique and faction in any human endeavor being one of their more debilitating traits. By far the best of the speeches was the fiery tirade of Reies Lopes Tijerina, by all accounts a monomaniac, centering on lands swindled from his ancestors: "I stand before the eyes of the world to accuse the United States of America of organized criminal conspiracy against my people. I accuse the United States of cultural genocide against the Spanish-American people. . . . I accuse the U.S.A. of violating all the human rights of the people of the Southwest." The ellipsis marks one of those lapses into the ludicrous, the noting of which proved irresistible to some of the best of reporters covering the Poor People's Campaign, stimulated as they were by all the incongruities of American society's disparate body of castoffs, misfits, not-neededs: Indians whose ancestors practiced slavery denouncing it, Negroes cheering Mexicans in denunciations of the Supreme Court. In the counts of his indictment Lopes Tijerina accused America of slaughtering sixty million buffaloes to divide the Indians into poverty and genocide.

But the dominant presences, haunting the event, hovering over it, were not the suffering poor but the martyred dead. *Their* theme was played in endless variations by the crowd, the man in a business suit festooned with buttons as big as saucers in memory of John F. Kennedy and Martin Luther King, Jr., a family grouping, grandparents to babies, sitting under a tree with their home-made sign propped up that said "This Family Believes in That Dream," and that displayed magazine photographs of both Kennedys and Dr. King. Ralph Abernathy in his oration at the end of the day evoked the memory of a few of the many lesser-known martyrs: "four little girls in the Sunday School of the Six-teenth Street Baptist Church in Birmingham, Alabama, died at the hands of a mad bomber. . . . We met with some success in Selma. But it cost us the lives of Reverend James Reeb, Mrs. Viola Liuzzo, and Jimmy Lee Jackson. . . . Medgar Evers was murdered, and hundreds of unknown black men sleep in the bloody soil and waters of the Southland." Over it all, looking down on it with his mournful, gravedigger's face, was the first martyr of them all, the seated Lincoln.

Dr. Abernathy's speech was probably the best he has ever made. But by the time the program wound its weary way to him, it was evening and at least half the crowd had wandered away: many, no doubt, back to their air-conditioned hotels and motels to sanely watch the program wind down on television; the people from Resurrection City were nearly all back in the heat and stench and mud of their turf. Those who had remained were mostly unheeding, sunk in the heat torpor. The program, I realized, had been built on the old model that accommodated Dr. King—building up slowly, lengthily, to his appearance, last on the program, longest to speak. But Dr. King was a celebrity they would wait to see; Dr. King was an orator capable of pulling back the long-since-wandered attention, reviving energy, bringing to climax and fruition all the day's walking, talking, weary waiting, all the day's emotion. Dr. Abernathy could not evoke this excitement; he remains a preacher, one of the best in the Negro Southern Baptist tradition of virtuosity, but he is no celebrity. Who even heard what he had to say out there in the weary afternoon heat, his preacher rhythm ringing all kinds of nuances out of his words, like early jazz: "We have been taught by two hundred and five years of bitter experience that we cannot trust the leadership of this nation. We cannot trust the elected representatives of Congress. We cannot trust the administration—whether Democratic or Republican—to fulfill the promise to the disinherited. . . ."

And who in the restless crowd there was listening, even when the moments of thunder came: "I see nothing in my Bible about the riches of the world or this nation belonging to Wilbur Mills or Russell Long; nor do they belong to General Motors, the grape growers in California, the cotton kings in Mississippi, and the oil barons in Texas. But I read in my Bible that the earth is the Lord's and the fullness thereof, and there is no need of God's children going hungry in 1968."

Who listened to Dr. Abernathy say: "I will not sink so low as to imitate the very worst of white Western civilization violence. The United States Government is the leader of the violent movement in the world. They believe in fire power. . . ."

Maybe the poets of paranoia were listening. Maybe the seated Lincoln, who had his own powerful prophetic style. A nation cannot survive half slave, half free. Nor can an individual. Yet that was precisely our predicament, we out there in the innocent, unaware middle-class crowd, just as much as the most beset citizen of Resurrection City. We talk about economic intimidation of Negroes in the Black Belt. But consider as well the poor young devil, white and privileged, graduated by the skin of his teeth a few years before from a second-rate college, with two babies and a third on the way, a mortgage on the house, and a superfluity of installment-credit appliances and vehicles. Then think of his political position vis-à-vis that of the manager of his office (no need to go up the chain of intimidation to the president of the company). Then speak of economic intimidation, half slave, half free. A middle-aged friend had said, look to the kids, not the Negroes. (C. Wright Mills said it, too.) The main question of our time, my friend had said, is whether the kids are going to decide to free us or enslave us. Either way, the nation could stand—but not as now, full of people divided against themselves.

The Solidarity Day march ended in anticlimax, the familiar mournful music of "We Shall Overcome" floating lifeless over the reflecting pool where a Washington Negro slum kid, fully clothed, swam slowly in the muck. "We are not afraid" floated into Resurrection City, arousing what memories there? What derision? Or perhaps no reaction at all, the most chilling characteristic of its somber mood, the blank stare of depression's rage. They swayed, hand in middle-class hand, black and white innocents together, singing the swan song of the Movement as I had known it, loved it, Dr. King's movement that came cutting through the edge of all my conditioned resistance to emotion, to belief, to such a thing as hope, and consumed my life for a long time, shaped it, put me down at one specified reference point on the map of the world of my times, and held me there, South-caught. No one had heard Ralph Abernathy. They never really heard Dr. King either, most of the middle class, half slave and half free, even the most sensitive and human of them who had comprised the Movement's crowds over the years, like the one dwindling away now from the Lincoln Memorial. And those who had heard him, his people, the basis of all he said and the way he said it—they were over there in Resurrection City.

I had watched a group of six or so young blacks standing in the street in front of the Lincoln Memorial during Dr. Abernathy's sermon. They were typical of their generation—slim, full of nervous energy, a sense of freedom of motion that was well beyond the American norm, with all the eccentricity of adornment that is their conformity. They were having a great time of it, cheering the speech, intoning with perfect timing the amen's, the "Yes, tell it, brother" responses which weld the crowd in a Negro church into one personality, one being—greater than the sum of the individuals, perhaps; certainly different from it. These kids were not listening to the honest, harsh, just words of the speech, its tedious linear development of meaning, but were responding to the familiar rhythms of the preacher's style, and their responses were mocking, jeering—as much of themselves and the best of their vaunted black heritage as of poor old preacher Abernathy. A friend came along and pointed one of them out as the young gentleman known as Sweet Willie, who was leader of that gang which in Memphis disrupted the last attempt of Dr. King to work his miracle of nonviolence. My friend called him over and presented me to him (in the way of these things, a recommendation of me for future reference, wherever our paths might cross). I shook his hand, looked into his unfriendly, glancing-away eyes. To a segregationist white Southerner, shaking hands with a nigger has been the most anathematic gesture of all, and I sensed in the listless hand I shook there as Abernathy spoke, as Lincoln looked down, the same loathfulness of contact. The Urban Coalition, the latest of the Establishment's teams to wrestle with race relations, has taken unto its breast such fellow power politicians as Sweet Willie; so have the centers of American innocence like the liberal church and sincere liberal politics; somehow I found myself not charmed with him.

The sensed violence (which was only the more volatile and less evil aspect of the mood of Resurrection City) broke loose that night, after a storm had rung down the curtain on the Solidarity Day march. I read about it in *The Washington Post:* six "youths" with tent poles confronting six cops, the youths talking about getting whiteys, honkies; the cops pushing them back; a crowd coming from Resurrection City, throwing bottles; fifty more cops rushing in; a tense confrontation, as we say, finally ending without, as we say, serious mishap. The story also noted "seventeen reported assaults" within Resurrection City that night, but contained no details because the Resurrection City residents acting as "security police" would not let reporters in, or tell them anything. The story also noted that some security police were drunk during the previous day's march, and pushed around tourists as well as Resurrection City residents. Subsequently, the *Post* carried a story quoting a security policeman who alleged that violence, theft, and rape had been commonplace throughout the existence of Resurrection City and who was now quitting because of the lack of law enforcement there. The story would be subsequently cited the following week by the authorities bent on getting Resurrection City gone forever. The SCLC people would point out that whatever pathology was on display in

Resurrection City was typical of all the hidden environments of poverty they were protesting. The speaker who, early in the campaign, had said that Resurrection City was better than the ghettos if there were no murders nor death from overdose of drugs there was much quoted.

But this would seem a trifle disingenuous; after all, Resurrection City had not been planned by Dr. King as a showcase of the criminality of the poor. There had been talk of a "model city." Haunting the failure of responsibility in regard to the security police situation and general welfare (the showers that never materialized, the less adequate than promised diet, for example) was the memory of the old faith, held most militantly by SNCC, that all the evils of this world could be cured if the poor people could only be put in charge. If you know the wisdom, the resources of strength, courage, and doggedness in the poor people of the rural South with whom the old SNCC worked (it being more clear in the South than elsewhere that poverty is not the fault of the poor, not a signal of failure, but the result of systematic repression, and the inability of the economic system to provide adequate jobs and wages), you can understand that old SNCC romanticism of the poor. I remember defending it to a friend in New York and having him, as we drove the intricate complexity of the expressways there, wave his hands about at all the arranged system of signals and signs, and say in exasperation, "Do you think Mrs. Hamer could run all this?" And of course I could wave my hands and holler, "Who needs all this?" But the point is, the main point perhaps of Resurrection City, is that we do need all of the social organization, social responsibility, humane planning, intelligent administration we can get. The one point on which the Right and the Left agree is that the social system is breaking down, like an old locomotive being driven at faster and faster speeds. We most likely will see it run off the tracks. But we won't likely see the system abolished. From what I have seen of the thinking that would make the revolution, we would end up with the same old malfunctioning society in new hands. Give Sweet Willie his choice of blowing up the Pentagon or becoming the head general in charge of it. His swagger stick and systems analysis would be the envy of the military world.

I went back to Resurrection City the next day, in the hope that seeing it on the morning after might reveal more of its truth, make it somehow seem less unhealthy. But the violence of the early morning hours, while I slept, was apparently the only thing that was left to happen there. In the morning's muggy sun and mud, that same silent torpor was upon it. Once more, I walked its length and back again: the same few unfriendly encounters, and the same unwillingness, inability, on my part to invade the privacy of the people. At the front gate, a number of the families, looking like Southerners, were gathered with their paperbag baggage: the stout Negro women, thinly strong Negro men, solemn-eyed Negro children of the rural South, apparently going home. Had they come only for the march? Or had they been there all along, and finally had had enough of Resurrection City last night? Or had they decided, like me, that the march proclaimed the end of what had once been the one bright hope in their lives? I looked into the fatigued, introspective eyes of one of those women, wanting to ask—but not able to.

A young guy demanded a cigarette, and then started in on his need for money. I heard my name shouted and then apparently his, and a laughing Southern voice saying, "What a pair to find here together." It was Lawrence Guyot from Mississippi, the head of the Mississippi Freedom Democratic Party. He had also been part of the Mississippi challenge at Atlantic City in 1964, which had been an earlier ending, the killing of the hope in SNCC, the final convincing evidence to them that you couldn't work within the system, between those lines of orderly progress, reform, and that you couldn't trust white people—from the most powerful man of them all on down. The other man, it seemed, was from Greenwood, Mississippi, where the bravest of all the voter registration campaigns had been double-crossed by the Kennedy Justice Department, where Jimmy Travis had been shot in the neck with an automatic rifle, where for the first time national attention had been paid to the desperate, child-starving poverty of the rural South—followed by a brief, fitful spurt of free food and clothing. That was in 1963. Some of the toughest SNCC workers had wept at seeing the people coming with rags tied on their feet in lieu of shoes, grateful for whatever had been given; the workers were also grieved to see the entirely to be expected results of privation that showed in some of the poor, the trickery, the taking any way they could some of them, more than their share of the Thanksgiving basket, missionary largesse sent down from rich America. Conditions were no less desperate in 1963 than in 1968 or the years between in the rural South. Now the nation's attention was attracted again. But the old SNCC was gone; they had killed all that good in it, that young, hard-boiled, tough good which, nurtured on the unexpected, stupendous success of the sit-ins, had for a time behind it the belief that anything— no limits, no caution—could be achieved, or at least tried. The good in the poor people could prevail. What organization now, what leader, could be said to elicit and speak for that good? Now, the violence that is built into the victim of injustice and neglect, the greediness that had so grieved SNCC, seems more likely to be the poor people's contribution to the new order. Guyot soon went his way, a good guy, full of talk about plans for the delegate challenge—this time in Chicago.

All morning the loudspeakers had been heralding a demonstration. It was to have started around lunchtime; I had resigned myself to another no-lunch day when it still had not started a good two hours later. People had formed their line; they were waiting for the word to go. In charge was Hosea Williams, a brave SCLC activist from Savannah, Georgia, as well as a self-promoter of prodigious energy, a man with a knack for antagonizing people needlessly, the kind of man you want in a revolution to lead troops but somehow not get back in time to help form the new government. Finally he gave the order for the line of about fifty people to start marching through Resurrection City, from the front gate toward the back one, and off we set, the old familiar formation: we reporters, notebooks in hand, off to the side; they marching, singing the good old songs—"Ain't goin' let nobody turn me 'round," "If you miss me in the back of the bus and you can't find me nowhere, Come on up to the front of the bus, and I'll be driving up there," "Come by here, my Lord, Come by here, oh, Lord, Come by here. . . ." It was to these very songs, in coincidental fact, that I had responded most in that personal religious experience which had been my introduction to Dr. King's movement, a long time ago. It seemed a mockery to hear those songs now, dodging along through the mud, seeing the blank looks that the vast majority of Resurrection City's residents gave the demonstrators and their song, summing up so many betrayals of good words, good people, so many disappointments, disillusionments.

The march through the mud of Resurrection City added no more than fifteen people to the little line. Hosea called them into a huddle in the grass just outside the rear gate. Then he strode over ostentatiously to the press contingent (consisting of me, a lanky young man from *The Washington Post*, and a very black young man from some African publication) and yelled, "Y'all go on over away from us so we can discuss things." I stuck my hand out to him, said howdy. "Yeah," he said in a tone suggesting he wished I hadn't stuck my hand out to him. "Y'all go on over yonder."

I thought this would be where they called the march off, but no, it started off again, Hosea heading back into Resurrection City, and a tall young man who looked remarkably like Stokely Carmichael (but no kin—somebody finally asked him) in charge. We went through the field that had been yesterday's staging area for the march, up the hill toward the Washington Monument. They kept singing those good old songs, cops bumping alongside on motorcycles, motors roaring. We passed three Negro teen-agers with Afro haircuts, sitting under a tree; one had a saxophone, and blew riffs at the demonstration. "Get a gun, brother," yelled one of the demonstrators, last of the legions of Dr. King's nonviolent army.

"Michael, row the boat ashore," they sang, approaching the Washington Monument. I got my first inkling, then, of something else that might be considered a prime cause of what ailed Resurrection City. There were rows of tourists sitting on little benches all around the base of the monument, and the brave song of the little marching band wavered as they approached those tourists, sitting in their slick-magazine informal wear—melting-pot American families, American primitives, all kinds—and before the marchers had got past

all those cold eyes, the song had died completely. The only sound was the flapping of all those American flags ringing the monument, so gallantly streaming. It was not like marching down to the courthouse, through the familiarity
of the town square in the South, every inch of the way known, every nuance of
the angry, hostile, sneering response of those ol' crackers just as familiar. In the
South, we have shared the physical world, every town and city being two
towns, black Atlanta, white Atlanta, the business section common property,
and the rivers and the woods used separately but jointly, with all that intricacy
of rules of separation over which so much of the energy of the Southern civil
rights movement was consumed. Up here, godamighty, in the ghetto cities of
the North, they don't even do that, don't share the land: this pile of monument
concrete, these big, rich-as-a-bank-looking buildings.

The Department of Agriculture proved to be the target of this demonstration,
the lair of that most evildoing of all the middle-class innocents, Orville W.
Freeman, standing accused on national television of starving little newborn
babies to death in the interest of showing his boss one of those two-million-
dollar bookkeeping gains so dear to the boss's not at all innocent heart. The entrance at which the march stopped had marble columns (the big house of the
plantation), and behind these, taller than a man, gates of close iron rods; then
the building itself, tall, marble, intimidating. The cops were in clusters (I
counted twenty-two at one point) across the street in the park (orderly and for-
bidding-looking, these parks, not like the woods, not like parks back home),
and there were about a dozen men in business suits standing and watching the
demonstrators in front of the building, no more than four of these newsmen,
the others looking like cops, like FBI, like authority. One uniformed cop kept
walking up close to the demonstrators, standing in a long line thinly stretched
across the front of that wide building; he poked a Polaroid camera at one or another of them, and then stepped back quickly to peel off his print, as you might
take a picture of an alligator as close-up as you could. A young Negro man who
had made the march on crutches broke out in a sudden tirade, perhaps in defiance of the bigness, the business suits, the strangeness surrounding him. He
hollered, something about America being the richest nation in the world, veins
standing out on his forehead, and then his voice died out, like the song back at
the monument, and, self-consciously, he hollered out: "I'm tryin' to tell it like it
is, Brother."
    There was a little flurry of surprise, and style, when a gleaming truck
rolled up, and, within a few minutes, a beautiful buffet lunch was laid out on a
long table. The demonstrators quietly formed a line, and with no show of exuberance over this fine little fillip, with that same subdued mood of their singing,
they filled their plates and sat down to eat around the entranceway of the
place. Workers within looked down from high windows on the scene, blank,

white faces. No one would say who had provided the food, paid for it. The truck was from a Negro-owned catering service; its three attendants were Negro, one of them a squat, big-shouldered man wearing a sweat shirt with "Black Liberation" lettered on it, and an inked-on design of stars and a crescent. While they ate, he stared with hating eyes, like white Southerners when they can catch your eye, at all the whites bustling around in their business suits. I long ago had learned how to avoid such eyes. My stomach was gnawing in its own faint, middle-class knowledge of hunger. In the old days, the press would have been offered food, would have had to make one of those delicate little decisions of whether partaking would impair the image, the myth of their objectivity (getting both sides of questions about which there can be no debate, like the right of Negroes to register to vote). Now none was offered.

The demonstrators were about half white, half Negro, all ages, the whites including a mother with her baby, and a stringy, tough-looking lady who looked like she was from the hill country. Their differences were eclipsed by the familiar larger separation of the two realities, the two worlds of such a situation: the demonstrators in theirs, a crisis scene of long-built emotion, one that was soon to culminate in a high, fearful, brave moment of life, maybe the highest of a lifetime; and the rest of us in ours, just a little out of the ordinary routine, doing the job, getting along, making a day, one in ten thousand of them. While we were waiting for the demonstrators to finish their lunch, a photographer spoke to one of the cops about how, thank God, in just two hours he would be out on a boat fishing, then about getting his daughter married the coming weekend. In the South during the Movement's past, these moments before the confrontation would have tremendous dramatic tension, for there was always a real sense of the drum-stir, the chain-rattle, the death-touch of totalitarianism, the shivering awareness that in this world, the limitlessness of human cruelty can be unleashed in licensed, uniformed, drilled numbers on the helpless, the hapless, the normal, decent run of no-better-and-no-worse-than-they-should-be humanity. Violence would victimize them all, the demonstrators but also the bureaucrats, the cops, the tourist come up with his green cap on to take a picture of this whole thing, his wife harping at him to get on up closer, ask that man to move out of the way. And this destruction of decency would be done at the will not of a monster, a De Sade, but at the behest of merely the type of life-hating, twisted, mean little son-of-a-bitch that we have all known, some stingy little storekeeper, some smirking little clerk. You can almost taste that meanness in your mouth, horrible and human, in the South, the George Wallaces squeezing their abominable ways up out of it every generation, the real horror of our heritage down there. But here in official, marble Washington, the potential horror had a further dimension, something purely mechanical and alien, a monstrosity of machines and mathematics that had moved on beyond any humanly evil origins, beyond human control—the efficient, functional *technique* that was starving Southern children, burning Vietnamese ones, and moving inevitably on to its own final and total solution.

After lunch, one of the bustling little business-suit men came forward and took charge. He was a baldheaded gent who had stared with some puzzlement previously at my press badge, which said I represented *New South,* a publication not likely known in his circles. I had put him down at the time as a bureaucrat (a cop would have asked about the badge, or not been so obviously staring). He turned out to be Joseph M. Robertson, assistant secretary for administration. The leaders of the march told him they wanted an audience with Secretary Freeman. He said to give him fifteen minutes, and with ten of them still to go, he bustled back and said to the leaders that he was sorry but he had to report that the secretary would not see the demonstrators. Mr. Freeman would be happy to confer with Mr. Abernathy at any time but not . . . he didn't say "rabble" but the inference was plain.

The leaders, some of the demonstrators, the press, the cops, we were all gathered around him for the announcement. "But these are the people," the young man who resembled Stokely said. "The people . . ." Robertson shook his head, the gesture signifying how entirely futile it was to argue with him; it was out of his hands. So the leader ended with: "I'll tell the people there's nothing you can do. This is just a small minority of the people in this country who are starving." He threw the words at the bald, bland-faced Robertson, and I harkened to that, to the insult and accusation in his voice. Maybe it would move the man.

The confrontation was reminding me of a time when I had helped two men try to get a boat for Daufuskie Island, South Carolina. It was in a spring of the long ago in Washington, the very same time that the poor were first showing some of the less benign side of what hunger and hurt does to people, that time of the convention of the poor staged by the Citizens Crusade Against Poverty. Could it have been only two years ago, way back there in 1966? Two citizens of Daufuskie Island had come to the convention to try out a scheme they had. Their island lies just above Hilton Head, which is a notable new resort whose development in the 1950's resulted forthwith in that action of state and federal authority in mutual accord and purposefulness necessary to the construction of a causeway to connect it to the mainland and all its tourist money. I cherish the memory of Hilton Head and its splendid, entirely untouched beach, and the assemblage of tourists every day around the luxury motel swimming pool, their finely, fashionably tanned backs to the beach.

Well, Daufuskie had not yet been bought up for development and exploitation. Most of its inhabitants are Negro; some of the few whites there, like most of the Negroes, trace their ancestry on the island back to the days of slavery.

The two citizens who came to Washington shared this distinction: the ancestors of the white one of them (a rough-hewn gentleman with a game leg, beyond middle-age, articulate in his coastal brogue) had owned the ancestors of the black one of them (a grave, elderly black farmer, articulate with his eyes and the wrinkling of his brows but seldom-spoken). Their island had no causeway, inhabited as it was just by poor people, and no other means beyond motor boats of getting to and back from the mainland. Daufuskie's two citizens in Washington wanted no part of a causeway; what they wanted was a boat, a big boat, big enough to haul crops and cars and the other heavy cargo necessary to develop farming on Daufuskie. The United States Government, they understood, had a lot of boats, just the kind they needed, sitting around unused in harbors. So, since they were up here in Washington anyhow for the convention, they thought they would just ask their government if they couldn't have one of those boats. They thought they would ask the President.

I got drawn into the boat thing by a friend of mine who had a penchant for this kind of situation, a feeling for the people we call poor, like the two Daufuskie Islanders, who fit none of the imagery of the word. In an ebullient mood, we bundled into a taxi and set off to see the President. All four of us were in the way of Southerners richly delighted with the scheme, capable of laughing at it and at the same time of believing in the possibility of confounding mighty Washington and all its ambiguous marble bigness and complexity by this specific, simple-minded need of a boat. Someday the rest of the nation will realize that it has been by this keen sense of the specific—the refusal ever to get embroiled in generalities, in dangerous abstraction, principle, ideals—that the Southerner has ever out-tricked them, out-traded them: losing the war but winning the peace; spreading the taint of systematized racism through the nation; corrupting, capturing, ruining the Congress; making fools of all adversaries.

The taxi driver was not amused, hearing us. They will put you'uns in jail, he warned. Better not try to go in his office. Find a phone booth and call him up. He deposited us at one, shaking his head. We spent the morning around the phone booth, the white man of the Daufuskie team doing all the calling, telling his story with its insulting threat over and over to startled receptionists on down a line (the President, it seemed, was gone to South America, darn the luck, he reported early on), not getting angry but being plenty forceful, emphasizing his words occasionally by banging on the metal tray of the phone booth with his stubby fist, saying loudly enough for us to hear once, "Well, don't you see, we want to be part of the United States, we're drifting off, we may wind up in Cuba." The other member of the team stood straight as a pole, patient and solemn through it all, glancing occasionally at the sun, measuring all the time this was taking. I stood alongside him, thinking of a couple of former newspaper colleagues of mine who were now fancy Presidential correspondents, wondering what they would think to find me here, standing, waiting with the Daufuskie fellows, after a boat. Finally, the talker emerged, grinning. "The Vice President's gonna see us." He had an appointment; there was just time for a gleeful, hopeful lunch.

Humphrey's outer office told much of what the world was later to learn from his actions about the essential gimcrackery of his soul. I recollect a replica of a wagon train; a lot of pharmaceutical paraphernalia; a number of those certificates and diplomas by which Americans convince themselves that they know more than they know they know, that they have achieved more than they know they have; and an Indian motto, appropriately engraved, something to the effect that you shouldn't criticize a fellow until you've walked in his moccasins. (How many times, one wonders, did Hubert Humphrey in those four years console himself with this wisdom?)

We presented the spectacle that we were, and our little story, to a receptionist who recovered her aplomb quickly, and said she was sorry to inform us that the Vice President actually couldn't see us but that an aide of his would— a very important one, she implied. We went on into his office, some of our impertinency having been chipped away by that same combination of big-building, big-people, big-nation awesomeness whose effect on the demonstrators I was later in my life to note. The Negro farmer of the Daufuskie team showed the effect most openly, the fingers of his big, strong farmer's hands clinched together, the knuckles taut knots, and his forehead wrinkled into an eloquent tight knot of concentration and, yes, awe.

The aide looked at us and listened to us with something of the air of a man suffering from the phobia that haunts a friend of mine, that his daily hangover has come at last to be of such severe proportions that it has snapped his mind, unhinged him at last from reality. At one point he said, "A *boat?*" with exquisite expressiveness, and at another, "Now let me get this straight, you say you need a boat?" The white Daufuskie Islander did most of the talking, telling the story straight through, about how the young people were leaving, a paradise for them lost, how the people who stayed were suffering, all for the lack of a boat, of how it didn't used to matter about not having a boat because most of the livings on the island were made by oyster fishing, but now there was only farming to do, and hence the need of the boat to haul the crops ashore, because the United States Government—and here was our punch line, our threat, our insult, and the old islander pushed it hard at the aide—had forbidden oyster fishing anymore because the water around the island is so polluted that the oysters will kill you if you eat them. It was a time when the administration of which Mr. Humphrey's office was so elevatedly a part was still claiming vehemently that it wished to do things about such domestic problems as pollution, and the story about the oysters had its effect on the aide, his eyes walling even more than when we walked in. He plunged into the kind of crisp summing-up questions and ordering of the facts of the case that is a ritual with his kind. At one point, all engrossed in the thing, he asked, "How many now are there of you on the island?" And being told, he asked, "And how many of these have incomes below the poverty level?" And being told, "Ever' one of 'em, ever' last one of us," he exclaimed, "Good. Good."

He sent us finally to a man in the Office of Economic Opportunity, a man he called with a great display of how important it was, how much it meant for him to call the man, not just send us over there. Seeing us out the door with his eyes still walling, he made a little joke about "have to be careful how you pronounce the name of that island of yours, heh heh," which did not sit well with the two Daufuskie Islanders at all, impressed as they were, jubilant as they were. Letting out some of their steam, they pegged along, the game-legged one setting the pace, through seemingly endless tunnels that whistled with unearthly subterranean winds. "This is where they send everybody who dares to come up here asking for a boat," said my friend who had got me into all this.

We ended up, the four of us and the high-ranking bureaucrat to whom we had been sent, on our knees on the floor of his office, studying an elaborate mariner's map of the island that the white islander had brought. When the bureaucrat tried to unsettle him with highly specific questions about the kind of boat he wanted, he was easily able to unsettle the bureaucrat with a knowledgeable, well-prepared list of specifications for exactly the kind of boat needed. We left with the man's words ringing in our ears. "Now I'm not sure, you understand, I can't say for certain, but I think it can be done, I think we can swing it—but don't get your hopes up, don't be too hopeful."

Hopeful. Actually, he did swing it; Daufuskie did get its boat. I was in Charleston a short while before Solidarity Day, and heard how a fine brandnew boat and other improvements for the island had resulted from our venture. I was to read a short while later another bit of news about Daufuskie Island: in the Democratic primary, a qualified and peace-campaigning Negro candidate for Congress had run against the incumbent from their district; and all the islanders, "ever' last one of 'em," had voted for the warmonger, racist L. Mendel Rivers. Maybe it was out of gratitude at getting the boat. I also read, not a long while after our call on the Humphrey aide, that he had been forced to resign, because of some indiscretion in the politics of his, and Mr. Humphrey's, home state. I like to think he was indiscreet on the side of decency, and that our confronting him with the reality of the need for a boat in the unreality of that office, that world he dwelt in, might have had something to do with it.

But all of that might have occurred in another age, even another country. Nobody at the Department of Agriculture (already implicated in just about every racist practice against Negroes in the rural South through every administration of every liberal President over the years) was about to be pushed around by any Southern specifics of starvation, any mere insults, any reality. The demonstrators huddled and very briefly decided what they would do: "We're going to go on to the next order of business," they warned Robertson, and formed a line of march, singing "Do What the Spirit Say Do." They were in a column of twos, and in the same bookkeeper's voice that would say it outside of a gas chamber, a minor bureaucrat said to the major bureaucrat, Robertson, "Now we've got a chance at last for a reasonably accurate count of them."

I thought they were folding up—another demonstration, another day come to naught—and I asked a middle-aged Negro man if they were going back to Resurrection City. "Ask the man at the front of the line," he snapped, in that almost shamefaced nastiness of any minor functionary under orders not to talk to outsiders. I trailed along as they turned the corner, not back toward that wretched place I guess they called home. I watched with admiration as they turned another corner and gravely began peeling off to sit in all the many doorways of the Agriculture Department buildings on both sides of the street. Somewhere along the way they had become supplied with the personal belongings that demonstrators take to jail, toothbrushes, combs, the like. It was well-organized, clean, efficient, as were the arrests that began quickly to follow. With the dignity and style of the old movement, the demonstrators passively resisted the police, some going limp, some walking slowly, one Negro man standing as he was frisked. Then, as he was led to a police bus, he began to sing: "Oh Freedom, oh Freedom, oh Freedom over me, Before I'll be a slave, I'll be buried in my grave, and go home to my Lord and be free," singing over and over the old brave words, alive for a hopeful little moment there again.

I watched Robertson's face as he ordered the beginning of the arrests; he had the look of a man trying to clean rats out of his cellar. The white cops' faces had that look of grim, morbid excitement worn by their Southern counterparts in similar circumstances. One Negro cop was holding back people on the sidewalk while demonstrators were being removed from the door. A nondescript Negro man was among these he held back; he growled something about Black Power to the cop. This cop's face was flinty; he had the flat nose, the flesh tones of an Indian. He was angry—surely in part at being where he was, doing what he was doing (not what the spirit say do).

They sang as they waited, in twos and threes blocking each of the doorways, to be arrested. A blonde girl, college-age, was among those going limp. A cop said, "I'd grab that broad by the hank of the hair." Two Negro cops did the removal job at one of the doorways; talking to the kids, preparing to lift them, their faces seemed friendly. One of the kids did the little jerking motions that make such a task more difficult. "Don't act like a child," one of the Negro cops grunted.

Faces were peering down from all the windows. You would expect them to be full of concern, or anger, or sympathy—or something. For the most part, they were not. As four cops lifted a young Negro, a pretty black girl looked down and smiled. While these arrests were taking place, other demonstrators had lain down in the driveways to the parking lots of some of the buildings. A car was unable to get out and the driver, a middle-aged guy with his gray-faced wife beside him, was sitting on his horn. I moved with the cops and the press toward this development, and in the middle of the street, I heard from above a voice of anger—at last—coming from one of the windows. A pretty blonde was yelling down, "No. No. You're not going to arrest them." She was angry not because of the suppression of decency, of reality going on down there, but because the cops were getting the man out of his car. But it wasn't to arrest him. He had to sign something, a complaint, I suppose, so they could begin removing the driveway blockers.

A fat Negro man, spectator of all this, yelled up at the blonde: "Shut yo' mouth. Mind yo' business."

She yelled back at him: "I work."

It seemed to sum it all up, both sides of the shibboleth. I watched the orderly, systematic clearing of one driveway after another. In one, there were three girls and two boys of college age, black and white together, and a country-looking, older white woman. All their faces, so disparate—the white girls' full of that innocent bloom of assured middle-class security—had a shared calmness, coolness. Here is the best hope, I thought. Here is the other side of the prophecy made by my friend: the basis for believing that the young might free us, or help us find courage to fight for our freedom. The quiet calm of their absolute conviction was what struck this muddled and fearful middle-aged observer; this was the way it had been in SNCC, this was the way it must have been through history, for those who were able, really able, to resist tyranny and stupidity. They could laugh at what made me cringe; they could march through tear gas and get their heads beat with the same sort of apparent inner certainty that it doesn't matter that what they believe in will prevail. And what they believe in—here, around the world, South African whites among them even—has been so uniformly right: against war, against racism, against poverty; against the monstrosity of *technique;* and being for, in every conceivable context, the liberation and enhancement of the human spirit, I noticed that the elderly country-looking lady was right there with them. It was not really a matter of chronological age. It was a matter of the best in people coming out, quietly fighting, serenely sure. They won't kill this, I thought.

It was getting toward my plane time. I didn't regret having to leave, as once I would have—indeed would not have left, back when these dramas demanded the reporter's loyalty to see them through, to be there as witness to whatever might be the worst atrocity, to be there as witness so the worst atrocity might not occur. The press by this time was on the scene in great numbers. I chatted a few moments with Charlayne Hunter, who, after making news by integrating the University of Georgia, had covered a lot of these demonstrations in the South. "I'm leaving," I said. "I've seen all this before." As the arrests got started, as the bureaucrat Robertson jerked his stiff face around, as the cops pushed their pistol-strength into the demonstrators, as the inevitable white loudmouth heckled unhindered behind police lines, I had felt a good and healthy rise in me of Southern chauvinism, a desire to yell at the cops, the bureaucrats, "You're no better, no better than the worst of ours." It was the first time I had seen this Northern ability to duplicate, down to the last self-righteous gesture, Southern racism, Southern dehumanization. In a few short minutes there, I had lost something, a part of my provinciality, the Southerner's collective inferiority complex; and I had lost something else, too—a little more of the respect for and confidence in men and institutions that is the glue which holds a society together. Long weak and watery in the South, the glue was becoming the same, evidently, in Washington and in the rest of the nation. Once the Southerner opposed to racism could console himself with the thought: I am virtually alone down here, but I am of the majority in the nation. No more.

I had left my bags at a friend's office near my hotel. I decided to take one last walk through Resurrection City, hoping maybe to get a better feel of it, or to get a better feeling about it, before catching a cab. But when I got to the back gate, a cop was there who refused to let me enter. I started to begin one of those contests of authority with him, using my press card, but realized it wasn't worth it, no more than trying to talk with those silent, bitter people.

I went away and sat in the cool green of Dupont Circle, watching all its diversity of types, like colorful and busy birds: the hippies; a boy on his knees patiently following a pigeon across the grass; the old people of both races; one Negro with an empty golf bag, not new, enigmatically on the bench beside him; the straight people, mostly walking through—a beautiful blonde baby-girl type, so young, so slim, carrying a big bag of groceries; a tall young man in his Haspel cord carrying a courier case under one arm, a shopping sack in the other hand, walking long strides, head back, a farmer, a pioneer. And there were even a few of those I sensed to be a new breed, a blend of what the hippies seek, what old people come to after finally getting their values settled, what the young straights have in the way of confidence and control: a plump young mother in an indifferent dress that sagged and rippled all around the hem, her black hair unfashionably long, watching her two fat babies playing in the sandpile; a young Negro with three Negro girls beside him, sketching the park scene. Someone began a loud, melodious, free whistling. This, I thought, is what a Resurrection City should be like: this tolerance in all these people in all their diversity, each for the others.

I went on to get my bag, and at the next corner, a drab little drama ensued.

A slovenly young white woman was yelling at a group of six or seven people waiting at the bus stop. I saw that she was yelling at the one Negro among them, a stout, dignified matriarchal woman. "Communists," the fat girl screamed drunkenly. "Communists. Why don't you go back to Africa?" All the worst of the racist insults poured out of the girl, anachronistic, almost refreshing in their direct ugliness. The Negro woman stood there, swollen with outrage. "We never come from Africa," she said finally in that voice Southern Negroes use with drunks of theirs, with idiots and the insane, with unruly white children. When I came out of my friend's office with my bag, the fat drunk white girl was out in the middle of the street, the light against her. A young white guy at the bus stop yelled at her, "Hey you—you're the one breaking the law." The girl wheeled back around: "Faggot. Faggot. You burned your draft card. You faggot." She passed me at the next corner where I was trying to catch my cab, crossed with the light, and then stood, face blank with all her meaningless rage, as the light changed three times. She was still standing there, hulking, murderous, pitiful, when I got my cab.

The episode had the feel of the worst I had experienced at Resurrection City, standing by the main gate, listening to Murray Kempton, who was extemporizing his bedazzling sort of intricate instant analysis of everything I had been seeing. An old Negro man—thin, city-looking, defeated in his face—came up to us. Drunk, wine-drunk by the look of his eyes, he said to get out. We both had been through these minor moments of nastiness many times before; I from whites, mostly, but blacks in recent times, Kempton I guess, plenty of both, and we knew that the only thing to do was avoid any personal touch with this drunk, like avoiding the hate stare of the racist when you walk into a Southern restaurant in the company of a Negro. We moved away slowly, the old guy behind us, cursing us, his voice low, as though if he properly yelled, it would end the magic of our obeying him. We wouldn't look back at him, kept walking slowly, continuing our conversation. He came closer and put his hand on my shoulder, still saying to get out, cursing us, and walking in a pantomime of pushing me out, no force in his hand, no ability really to heave me the hell out of there.

The feebleness of his anger reminded me of the time I sat listening to a racist harangue from the state superintendent of schools in Georgia, shortly after the 1954 school decision. He was an old man, a good, gentle product of white Southern Methodism, a good educator by Southern standards, which meant that he really cared about the children rather than merely for the prerogatives and power of his job. His tirade was of that same weak and feeble quality as the drunk Negro's heave-ho; somewhere in the midst of it, he got Jesus into it, as was natural for his generation and his religious tradition, and I burst out, surprised at myself: "Leave Jesus out of this." His old eyes were startled for a minute, and then hurt, and for a long time afterward I felt bad about hurting him needlessly, for he was old, and unregenerate on the race thing, and, I thought, harmless. Later I came to know how harmful such innocent old men in positions of power were to be to the South, to humanity, how ruinous the workings of the innocent were in America. And now I finally knew, too, that to burst out at him, on the most elemental of human terms, was better than not to—better than not to fight him, not even to look at him.

The radio in the taxicab described what happened to the demonstration after I left it, how it attracted other columns of marchers, more police, how it spread into the street, how the police had to use "necessary restraint with their billy clubs." Some who were there later told me the cops started it; others said it was one group of Negroes bent on violence. Either way, it is the same: the violence is the thing, neither side anymore has any real control of it.

I read a few days later of Abernathy's final march and arrest, and of the expeditious way that they ran the few remaining people out of Resurrection City, and then destroyed it, and got grass to growing there again almost overnight. Out of that sorry episode, Jack Nelson of the *Los Angeles Times* wrote the best single newspaper story on the civil rights movement I have ever read— about how efficient the government was in enforcing the penny-ante law it used to clear Resurrection City out of the landscape and consciousness of Washington, D.C., but how inefficient that same government had been over many long years in enforcing the vital, basic laws (voter registration, protection of civil rights, not to mention human life; farm programs and job opportunities; the feeding of hungry children) that would make life livable for the poor. How sorry a record of incredible failure.

It was like reading about the old regime leading up to the French or Russian revolution: the Greek-tragedy sense of disaster drawing on, of forces and events out of control. I passed the White House on one of the nights there in Washington, and a Washington friend in the car exclaimed that he never had seen it so lit up before, spotlights like they use in prison yards illuminating every inch of the grounds, this bastion of the greatest of all the nickel-nursing switchers-off of unused forty-watt bulbs in America. We all surmised that he was afraid, that man in there, of the poor people down in Resurrection City, and afraid of all the gatherings of the innocents who had come spontaneously, out of the last saving remnants of decency and goodness within America. One of the main reasons he did not run again, I was told by a Washington friend privy to such secrets, was that he was afraid he would be killed during the campaign and not just embarrassed to death by those demonstrations that followed him everywhere the police and military didn't keep them out.

As my plane climbed above Washington, I pondered the valedictory feeling about the Movement that had been dogging me for the past two days and nights, the sense of an ending. It was not dead in its organizational forms or its plans and campaigns (John Lewis would come back from Washington two weeks after I did, quietly optimistic, telling of the fine new scheme for the poor people's embassy up there). It was just dead within me. It had acquainted me with a kind of hope, a universal kind of hope for humanity, that my generation had been conditioned not to know. My life, my work had fed on that hope through crucial years of my lifetime. Now that hope was gone. I had never, like the innocents, been a niggerlover. It seems to me that the premise underlying all that Dr. King knew and taught was that to love everybody without ever loving anybody is as meaningless as hating everybody. Black Power is deep in that meaninglessness, which the riots so graphically express. So do the assassinations. Black violence has not killed a single real enemy of black people, of humanity; it has killed its own. And the vehemence of the verbal violence of Black Power has been much less a threat than an advantage to these enemies, while only the true friends of the Black Powerists, black and white masochistically together, expect it to overcome.

It would be cathartic to draw lines and say I am the enemy of all these, Black Powerists and white niggerlovers, just as I have been the enemy of all the white racists in the South. But the Southern sun bores itself into your bones, sweats such dogmatism out of you. Like all liberals down there, Negro and white, Dr. King included, I know that humanity is too complex, too mysterious to draw rigid lines and expect to contain much reality in them. The lines have to be drawn on principles, not on people.

There was a time when just about every black person I saw agreed with me on principles, which involved essentially the Bill of Rights and the failure to exercise and enforce it where Negro citizens of the South were concerned. Thus I felt we were united in a struggle, the Movement, to achieve those principles, that enforcement, which denied to some were meaningless to all. This unity no longer exists. So now it is necessary to judge each Negro I meet on the criteria by which we judge all other people—a natural and, indeed, better way: some are with you, some are enemies of your most important principles and values. And so one looks among them, as one looks among whites, for those who believe in what is summed up in the Bill of Rights, and who are aware of all the ways the Bill of Rights is raped in America, not just as regards Negroes, but whites as well. This, then, has been Black Power's most constructive effect: that it has removed from whites the last shred of romantic, paternalistic, indiscriminate idealization of Negroes, and that it has removed Negroes from the obligations, the expectations unrealistically put upon them by whites, to do, in sum, the impossible.

There was some justification for the expectation. In the South, Negro leaders and Negro people fought for their civil liberties with the kind of courage, the kind of selflessness that white liberals were incapable of when the Cold War insanity, and its first agent, Joe McCarthy, clenched a fist around *their* civil liberties. Whites, the likes of me, looked at the Negro movement, Dr. King's movement, once it had stirred hope within them, to do more than oppose the racial injustices of the South. What we came to expect was that Negroes, with their demonstrations, their new-found ability to force action by the offering of their bodies to the clubs of the cops and the murderousness of the unlicensed terrorists, would change American society, would right its wrongs, would correct the fatal malfunctions of its systems. Despite all that hopelessness I carried up there to Washington, I must have had some small hope left that the Movement, spread now to the poor of all races, still might just do it, might reactivate the conscience of society. This had been the ultimate delusion: that the least powerful, and then, even, the least able could do a job that may well not be accomplished even should it be tackled by the most powerful, the most able. At last, the delusion was dead.

I got my two drinks fetched as fast as tourist accommodations allow, and ignored my seat-mate, a young soldier, through most of the first one. But the soldier asked me for a cigarette (damn it, I seemed to be counting out my last hopes for the Movement in bummed cigarettes) and seemed as anxious as I was for the stewardess to bring the drinks. We got to talking. His voice was Southern, which sounded good to me. He had drunk, he said, the day before, a full quart of grain alcohol, and still hadn't quite got over it. He said that the first drink just about burned out his whole mouth and throat and head.

"I took it straight," he said.

"Should have cut it with grapefruit juice," I said out of the vastness of my own military experience.

"Yeah, I did after that first one."

He mentioned that he was a cook. Oh-oh, I thought, remembering that all the army cooks of my time had been certifiably insane.

A colored man, he said, had given him the grain alcohol as a going-away present for his leave. "He comes around every night and I give him all the food we have left over. His family needs it, other families. I don't see any harm in that. We waste so damn much food." I said I didn't see any harm in it, either.

The soldier was from East Point, a suburb of Atlanta, a stronghold of the kind of people who believe in Lester Maddox. His daddy was a policeman. "Makes it rough," he said. "I like to go to these bars, my favorite ones, and the cops come in and see me and first thing go tell my dad I was there." I asked him what he planned to do when he got out. He said he would be a computer operator, an ambition entirely out of my generation's experience, but sounding like a likely one.

"I still have to go back and finish high school; I got kicked out my senior year for dumping a whole big load of fireworks into a toilet in the boys' restroom. It blew out all the plumbing."

I laughed, but shouldn't have. He didn't, and I knew from my own son's recent experience with authority, with the close-knittedness nowadays of school and police authority (the educators are cops; the cops educate), that this wasn't a laughing matter anymore, that Huck Finn and Penrod are not tolerated in a society that is deadly serious, that he had felt the shiver of the threat of jail, of authoritarian power.

The army, he said, had matured him; he wouldn't ever do a fool stunt like that again. He had been to Vietnam. I fought off the juxtaposition of images, the guilty criminal putting fireworks in the boys' john and society's hero wreaking unspeakable havoc with the explosives and other chemicals they use in Vietnam: I'd had enough ironic juxtapositions for one trip. He said he had been wounded—showing me a scar on his wrist—by a grenade. "I know," he said (the plane was circling to land), "what we are fighting for over there."

"Oh yeah," I said, half-believing from the conviction in his voice that he did, that he would reveal a meaning in all this world of meaninglessness to me.

"They got my buddy," he said, "the same attack. A mortar. He didn't have a chance. And I said to myself right then, I'll kill every goddamn gook I can get my hands on. That's what this war is all about."

It was hot in Atlanta when we got down. The cab driver complained of the unrelenting quality of the goddamned heat in that ageless, always surprised, equinox after equinox, complaint of the Southerner. The Movement is dead, I said to myself. And there is no hope that lasts. They have known that for some time in other places: in France they have embodied it now into a philosophy; in India, they have nurtured their religion on it. Negroes in the South have known it, through slavery and since then—existing, making do. How did the SNCC kids, with all their reading of Camus, miss that? Keeping on, those of them still at it, coining their rhetoric from the metal of hope, showing in all their hate-talk now only the other side of the love-talk, anything to avoid accepting hopelessness. Dr. King knew about that. Making do, as Southern Negroes always have done, with an irrelevant and irrational religion, he forged a world-view of staggering insight. Making do with the worst of his followers by drawing the best out of them, he built a movement that shook America, almost converted some of it, at the very least put an end to Southern institutionalization of racism. And then he had seen his philosophy and strategy of nonviolent change lose influence, had seen America steadily moving in the opposite direction from the one he sought. You get down to hopelessness, finally, his kind of hopelessness, and then you see that it is still possible to keep on, to find meaning in meaninglessness, like the Negroes with no food and no purpose, like the demonstrators in that driveway. "Keep on a-walking, children," Dr. King used to say in the hot, fervent, sacred little churches of the Movement's great days, "don't you get weary. We are headed toward the promised land."

"We in a War—Or Haven't Anybody Told You That?"

Report from Black America, 1969

◆

PETER GOLDMAN

They roared on two wheels into Burma Road—Harlem's unaffectionate nickname for its stretch of Lenox Avenue—and burned to a stop outside the Royal Flush Bar. The car belonged to Joe-Joe, a chunky ebony 20-year-old who earned it by sticking through high school and graduating into a job at the post office. But the dude who led everybody into the artificial midnight of the Royal Flush and popped for beers all around was just naturally J.B., a young man of obtrusive flash and dash in hip-hugging black gabardines, a crisp yellow shirt and a new stingy-brim straw hat. J.B. was 20, too, but he had quit high school early and got himself a hustle. He was a numbers runner, with a bankroll built out of Harlem's dimes and quarters, and he had it made.

Outside, the streets cooked in the August sun; the bloods were idling on the corners and the stoops, slugging wine from bottles wrapped in brown paper bags; the talk, as it did every summer now, fastened mostly on the latest news of riot and retaliation in the ghettos of urban America. "The Man, he worried now," J.B. was saying, "cause he know we ain't takin' no more his shit. Anybody come rollin' into a city with tanks *got* to be afraid of somethin'. Anyplace you see a tank, you *know* there got to be a war goin' on, right? And that's what this is, baby—war!"

"That's right, that's right," said Skeeter, a spindly kid who quite clearly neither expected nor demanded anything of life except a place at J.B.'s heels. Skeeter was 19 and nowhere, a jobless dropout living with an aunt and a sister. A fierce stammer helped shame him out of high school when he was 14, and he still wasn't talking much. Except when J.B. said something; then Skeeter would say, "That's right."

Someone wondered what Rap Brown was into those days. "That's my man!" J.B. exclaimed. "Ain't nobody in the world gonna get nothin' if he don't fight for it. The black man's been takin' low too long."

"That's right," Skeeter blurted. But Joe-Joe half disagreed—not on the necessity of making a fight but on what the fighting was really about. "I used to watch ole Stokely up there on TV tellin' off the white people," he said. "I thought he was crazy, cause I thought he was gonna get hisself killed—like

Malcolm. But you know, when a man says what all the time you been thinkin', you wonder if maybe *you* ain't crazy. I mean like if you feel inside knotted all the time, maybe it's better if you make some noise." He sipped at his beer. "Like the time I broke my big toe cuttin' the fool [roughhousing] out at Coney Island. I went on limpin' around grinnin', not lettin' on to nobody I was hurt. But I finally had to tell 'em cause I couldn't stand it no more. And like, you know, these two cats crossed their arms and made like a seat and carried me to the beach clinic. Now supposin' I hadn't said nothin'?"

So Joe-Joe guessed that if Harlem ever rioted again he would join in. "Man," he said, grinning broadly, "you know my sister wouldn't let me in the street that last time. But I bet I'm goin' to get somethin' next time. I just might break me some windows, grab me some rags and throw me some bottles."

J.B. didn't know. "I wouldn't mind knockin' me some cracker heads together," he said—but, like any budding entrepreneur, he worried that rioting might be bad for business. Still, in the end, he guessed he would join in, too. "I mean," he said, "that's where it's at."

"That's right," Skeeter said. "That's right."

White America had, by the end of the 1960s, accumulated a vast literature on rioting in the ghetto, some of it intelligent, some banal, some provocative, some pedantic—and hardly any of it quite so educational as an hour in any black slum in the nation. Joe-Joe had it right—the riots were the black man's desperate cry to whites that he was hurting and that he couldn't stand any more. But rioting is the most primitive form of communication; it evoked shock, fear, guilt, anger and finally a sort of numb acceptance of periodic violent insurrections in the casbah as an ordinary part of urban life. "What shocked me most," said a Detroit matron in the midst of the devastating riot there, "was how *normal* it seemed to have those soldiers standing outside Hudson's department store when I went shopping." To be so inured to rioting was finally and tragically to miss the message of the rioters. For what Joe-Joe and J.B. and the kids on a thousand corners were trying to tell America was that, for them, life as their elders had lived it simply was no longer supportable. When a young man growing up in the suffocating emptiness of the ghetto reaches that unhappy pass, the issue is no longer whether or not riots are moral. The question becomes whether or not they will be useful—or at least be fun while they last.

It was a judgment on America that so many of the ghetto young came to that pass and acted on it in the middle and late 1960s. A "white racist" when the decade began was somebody who put a bedsheet over his head and said "nigguh" in public in a Southern accent. When the '60s ended, America *as a society* had been pronounced racist by President Johnson's impeccably responsible riot commission—a verdict which may or may not have accurately stated the nation's collective intent but which most certainly described the results. That some white Americans finally asked themselves the question was no doubt a hopeful sign. That black Americans were able to raise it only at the most terrible cost—by resort to violence at a pitch and a frequency without precedent in the history of this violent land—may have been the sorriest fact of all.

The cost was devastating indeed. The fire this time flared first in Harlem in 1964, burned high in Watts in 1965 and roared to a crescendo in the ten months between July 1967 (when Newark and Detroit exploded) and April 1968 (when Martin Luther King's assassination set off what amounted to a single coast-to-coast rebellion). The statistics of those five years were unreliable and in the last analysis nearly meaningless. It was enough to record that more than 200 people, most of them blacks, died in the streets; that at least 10,000 were injured and 60,000 arrested; that whole streets were plundered, whole blocks laid waste by fire; that the occupation of American cities by soldiers armed for war became an everyday spectacle of summer; that, by the end of the decade, hardly a city or a town with a black enclave big enough to be called a ghetto had escaped at least a brush with catastrophe. The epidemic touched not only such acknowledged urban disaster areas as Newark but such progressively run "model" cities as Detroit and New Haven—a spread that suggested how little such distinctions mean to black people as against the everyday desperation of ghetto life.

Desperation was precisely the point of the riots; they were important not so much for the physical damage they wreaked as for the social and the psychic damage they revealed. Harlem began it all but Watts was the watershed—the revolt of the colonials in a sun-washed, palm-shaded paradise a continent's distance from the stifling tenements of black Manhattan. The ashes there were still warm when Martin Luther King ventured in to try to make peace, and his first speaking stop in the ghetto told everything about the way the currents were running. "We must join hands—" he began. "And *burn!*" a black kid whooped, and everybody laughed. King struggled through his speech, but he canceled the rest of his schedule in Watts and soon left town. Neither he nor The Movement was ever quite the same again. A whole ideology of rioting flowered in the ghetto after Watts; Rap Brown and SNCC proposed celebrating August 18, the anniversary of the uprising, as Independence Day—the day when the blacks "stopped moaning 'We Shall Overcome' and started swinging to 'Burn, Baby, Burn.' "* And where the ideology didn't take, the fever did. Whites were recurringly shocked not only by the fury of the riots but by the unbridled joy of the rioters. "It's like laughing at a funeral," said New Jersey's Governor Richard Hughes, haggard and hollow-eyed after a pre-dawn riot tour

*The battle cry actually was the signature phrase of a locally popular black disc jockey, and, before Watts, it had nothing to do with Molotov cocktails. To "burn," in the black argot of the day, actually meant something like to "groove" or to "wail"—to improvise brilliantly in singing, soloing or just living.

of Newark's Central Ward. Not quite. "The chronic riot of their day-to-day lives is, as far as they're concerned, no better than the acute riots," Kenneth Clark, the black psychologist, observed. "They don't have anything to lose, *including* their lives. It's not just desperation—it's what-the-hell."

The riots were all the more ominous for the very fact that they flared in a community so heavily inclined to nonviolence as a strategy of protest—and so stubbornly hopeful that nonviolence would carry the day. Nearly two-thirds of the Negroes in the *Newsweek* Poll believed that the blacks had more to lose than to gain by resorting to violence and that, in any event, they could win their rights without it. This faith, for all the devastation of the latter '60s, was as strong at the end of the decade as it had been at the beginning. "You can catch more flies with honey than with vinegar," a 42-year-old Pittsburgh housewife told a Gallup interviewer. "We have nothing to fight *with*," said a Denver printer, 41 years old. "Violence," a 29-year-old steel-mill worker in Kansas City offered, "will only get a lot of people killed without winning anything. We *are* winning without violence."

Yet there was peril in taking too much comfort in the great sentiment for nonviolence. It ought to surprise no one that black people, like everybody else, preferred war to peace; the far more stunning figure was that fully a fifth of all Negroes—and more than a third of the Northern ghetto young—simply did not believe that their struggle could be won by peaceful means. They remained a minority within a minority—but there are quite enough of them, in James Baldwin's phrase, to ring down the curtain on the American dream. "We aren't going to get anything unless we take it," said a 21-year-old student in Baltimore. "The white man has no reason to give us anything when he can keep us where we are." A college freshman in Pittsburgh: "It's gonna be *three* eyes for an eye." A machine operator in Philadelphia, 42 years old: "There's a time for everything. Sometimes a brick must be thrown." A Pittsburgh house-wife: "We got to get to *all* white people, and some of them, honey, only listen to violence." A waitress of 39 in Kansas City: "I used to feel that nonviolence was the way. But I'm changing and I don't know why. I think violence may be the only thing they understand."

There was, moreover, a painful ambivalence in black America's view of the rioting of the summers just past. Negroes on balance shared the white man's abhorrence of the burning, the thieving and the killing. But they parted company on what those acts meant. Lyndon Johnson probably spoke for the white American consensus when, in a stricken TV report to the nation on the Detroit riot, he said, "First—let there be no mistake about it—the looting, arson, plunder and pillage which have occurred are not part of a civil-rights protest. That is crime—and crime must be dealt with forcefully, swiftly, cer-tainly . . ." Black people were by no means so certain. They agreed that the *ac-tions* of the rioters were criminal, but they tended to see the rioting very much

as a political act—an outcry at the just and widely shared grievances of the
Negro community. So, for them, the riots in fact were continuous with the civil-
rights protest of the 1950s and '60s. And so the fire and the blood were not
simple criminality run rampant; they were, for many blacks, the more or less
regrettable excesses of a righteous struggle toward freedom.

A poll can only begin to suggest what so traumatic a train of events meant
to Negro America. But the *Newsweek* survey figures were nevertheless revealing as a post mortem on five riot summers:

> ■ Negroes on balance did not believe that the riots were justified, but very
> nearly a third did—a reservoir of black anger deeper and more desper-
> ate than most whites dreamed possible.

Americans—for all their revolutionary beginnings as a nation—grew up
believing that no level of grievance, however broadly based or acutely felt,
could justify resorting to violence. Negroes share that article of democratic
faith with whites; it was accordingly less startling that 48 per cent of them said
the rioting was not justified than that 31 per cent felt it was—a riot constituency equivalent to nearly 4 million of America's 12.5 million adult blacks.
For a comparable fraction of the nation's whites to feel pressed to the point of
rebellion would surely be recognized as a disaster demanding the most drastic
relief measures; the New Deal did not wait for the cities to start burning. No
such effort has yet been mounted in the ghettos, however, and the ideology of
rioting as a legitimate expression of discontent could only be strengthened as a
result. That notion by 1969 had already become the prevailing view among
Northern middle-income blacks—the leadership class in the ghetto. And there
was evidence in other surveys that many Negroes who did not consider rioting
justified were in fact deploring the acts of war—not its underlying motives. A
30 per cent minority of the Watts Negroes spoke favorably of the riot there in a
UCLA poll, but majorities of two and three to one thought that it had been a
purposeful act of protest and that its targets—police, merchants and whites
in general—deserved whatever they got. "People want *recognition*," a Watts
filling-station worker told *Newsweek* long afterward, "and the only way they
were gone get it was riot. The *only* way. See, we don't want to overthrow the
country—we just want what we ain't got."

> ■ Negroes do not think of the rioters as hoodlums—the common judg-
> ment of white Americans—but as a representative slice of the black
> community; as people, in short, much like themselves.

White people, as one of UCLA's riot-study papers accurately observed, have
squandered a good deal of time and energy constructing a mythology of "bad

Negroes" (a tiny minority who make riots) and "good Negroes" (the vast long-suffering majority who are said to cower before them). This comfortable fantasy ought to have been punctured by warfare on the scale of Watts, Newark and Detroit, in which at least 10 to 20 per cent of the ghetto actually tasted combat and many more were approving or at least acquiescent spectators. The rioters, as psychiatrist Alvin Poussaint once put it, "range from the plain damn angry to those with fantasies of taking over, to those who want a TV set, to those angry at their father and mother, to those caught up in hysteria, to those who will act only when they see the cops shoot someone . . . Rage is common to all of them." That is a far cry from dismissing them as the dregs of black society—a view indulged by many whites and few blacks. Who riots? A fourth of the Negroes blamed mostly hoodlums. But fully as many thought that the rioters were mainly "good people"—and 41 per cent guessed that both sorts were involved. What this collective verdict announces to white America is that conditions of life in the ghetto are so oppressive that the law-abiding as well as the lawless—the "good Negro" as well as the "bad"—may feel driven to rebel. Ernest D., a foundry worker at decent wages and with no criminal record, was driving home in Milwaukee's ghetto when a pride of rioters swirled by. "I got out of my car," he recounted later, still plainly surprised at the fact, "and asked 'em what was goin' on. They said they wanted their freedom. I asked what kind of freedom and they said black power. So I just started fightin' too."

■ The widely held view of the ghetto—against the weight of the evidence—is that rioting works.

"This nation," Bayard Rustin once remarked sadly, "is teaching the poor that they *ought* to riot lest they get nothing. Tell them in the spring that you are going to riot in the summer and they will vote money. Or after a riot. In Watts they wanted a hospital. They didn't get it. They rioted. Now they have one; it's not up yet and it's not very good, but after the riot they came in with plans. In Chicago, the children wanted sprinklers on the fireplugs. Riots. Then Mayor Daley came along personally with eight-dollar sprinklers." The victories, as Rustin went on to note, are usually cheap and often meaningless, and every riot increased the risks of bringing down repression on the heads of the blacks. But the balance of sentiment in Negro America in 1969 was that, like them or not, the riots had not hurt and probably had helped the cause. The feeling was by no means unanimous. The poorest blacks, contrary to much of the folklore of the day, felt rather strongly that the rioting had done more harm than good. But the relatively affluent were even more firmly convinced that it had advanced the struggle, and their view prevailed, 40 to 29 (with an additional 16 per cent doubtful that rioting made much difference one way or the other). That their optimism bore so little tangible relation to reality did not shake those who shared it; some notice from white people, and some attention to the problems of the blacks, was for them clearly better than nothing—even if it had to be bought at the great pain and the greater peril of insurrection. "Black people," Watts community worker Ferman Moore said cheerlessly, "now know that if you burn down a city or two, the power structure is going to dump a bushel basket of money on top of you to try to quiet you down. And they realize that the white boy who *built* the power structure did it by violence and force—by kicking the shit out of the British, then the Indians and now the black and brown people. Yes, sir, we have a fine example to follow, and who can fault us? It's in the finest American tradition."

■ The restraints on rioting are crumbling among the young in the Northern ghettos—the children of the city of destruction.

The under-30 generation in the ghetto came of age during a decade of black revolt. They were witness to the televised affluence of white people and the real-life defeat of their own fathers; they were exposed daily to the bright promise and the bitter disappointments of the Negro revolution; they were schooled in the work ethic and then graduated into a job market frozen at depression unemployment levels; they lived in a milieu where racial hatreds and revanchist passions that had been suppressed for decades were suddenly out in the open. They were precisely the blacks who had, in Clark's phrase, passed beyond desperation to what-the-hell. "I can't lose by rioting," said one of them, an Oakland gang kid. "Done lost. Been lost. Gonna be lost some more. I'm sayin' to The Man, 'You includin' me in this game or not?' An' I know his answer, so I'm gettin' ready to get basic." He might have been speaking for a generation. The under-30 Northern blacks believed by 47 to 32 that the riots were justified; by 74 to 18 that the rioters were partly or principally "good people"; by 50 to 20 that rioting helped the cause. And one in six said he would join a riot if it happened—an extraordinarily large pool of combatants waiting for a war and utterly reckless of the odds against winning it. "I don't mind gettin' killed," a street-corner kid in Chicago told *Newsweek*'s Marvin Kupfer. "When I'm dead, they'll tell my kid, 'He died for a good cause.' "

So, in sum, the poll reveals sizable numbers in every sector of the black community—and most of all in the volatile age group that makes riots—who see the street mutinies of the late '60s in something quite like revolutionary terms: a series of explosions that were broadly based, purposeful, rooted in real grievances and helpful in the common cause of Negroes everywhere. What polls cannot tell about riots is their emotional content for the individuals and the communities who actually experience them—a psychic dimension even more disturbing than the statistics in what it told about the state of mind of black men in white America. "At the level of individuals," Frantz Fanon once wrote, discussing the Algerian rebels, "violence is a cleansing force. It frees the native from his inferiority complex, and from his despair and inaction; it makes him fearless and restores self-respect." The vices and virtues of comparing the situation of Negroes in America with the lot of colonials in Africa can, of course, be debated inconclusively forever. Yet there is eye-witness evidence aplenty that rioting, for many American blacks, may in fact have been an exhilarating and even a liberating experience—an expression of power by the powerless, an act of revenge by the vanquished, an assertion by the Invisible Man that he really exists.

New Jersey's Governor Hughes glimpsed that inner reality in the carnival gaiety of the Newark looters; what he saw as laughing at a funeral may have been more like rejoicing at a birth. Ernest D., the Milwaukee foundry worker, experienced it when he poked his fist through a shattered store window in search of an intangible piece of goods called freedom. And Dr. Frederick J. Hacker, a white psychiatrist from the University of Southern California, recorded it in a remarkable report on the Watts riots in the West Coast magazine *Frontier.* "For the Negroes," said Hacker, who interviewed some of them before and after the riot, "what happened . . . *was* justified legally and morally. Where the police saw black criminals tearing apart law and order with a cascade of Molotov cocktails, the Negroes of Watts watched freedom fighters liberating themselves with blood and fire." Hacker found widespread acknowledgment that burning, looting and lawbreaking are bad things to do—and surprising little shame, guilt or regret about having done them. Quite to the contrary, the riot in important ways was "psychologically analogous to the Hungarian Revolution and the Boston Tea Party." It was plain damned fun ("Violence makes you feel good—at least for a while") and far more: "It was the metamorphosis of the Negroes of southeastern Los Angeles from victims—historical objects—to masters . . . The people of Watts felt that for those four days they represented all Negroes; the historical plight of the Negroes; all the rebellions against all injustice." Most of them, Hacker wrote, knew that they couldn't win; all that mattered to them was the exercise of their will and their stunted pride. "What must be understood by the rest of America," he said, "is that, for the lower-class Negro, riots are not criminal but a legitimate weapon in a morally justified civil war."

The exhilaration, as Hacker noted, is a function of action and does not long survive the war. But the pride does. Watts Negroes began throwing an annual summer festival on the anniversary of their rebellion well before Rap Brown suggested it, and independence was precisely what they were celebrating. And in postwar Detroit, with the acrid scent of smoke still souring the air, *Newsweek*'s John Dotson found a few of the children of the city of destruction sitting on a rail and staring idly across Dexter Avenue into a solid block of charred ruins.

"Those buildings goin' up was a pretty sight," said one of them, a lanky spidery-legged kid whose hand-me-down pants ended a shin's length short of his shoes. "I sat right here and watched 'em go. And there wasn't nothin' them honkies could do but sweat and strain to put it out."

"Yeah, man," a pal chimed in, "it's about time those honkies started earnin' their money in this neighborhood."

"You know," the long-legged kid said, "we made big news. They called this the worst race riot in history."

"Yeah," another boy, mountainously beefy, echoed, "we got the record, man. They can forget all about Watts and Newark and Harlem. This where the riot to end all riots was held."

They were silent for a moment.

"That little girl that got shot, man," the long-legged boy said. "She shouldn't of got shot."

"That's the breaks, brother," the beefy youth replied, absently patting at the deep waves in his processed hair. "We in a war—or haven't anybody told you that?"

Everyone laughed.

The language of war, by the end of the 1960s, was common currency in the ghetto—and so was a deep, fatalistic assumption that acts of war would keep recurring in the years to come. Would there be more riots? Two-thirds of the nation's blacks thought so—a level of expectation verging on that point where possibility can become probability. And there was talk everywhere of a turn from the spontaneous violence of the riots to the strategic violence of revolution. Malcolm X, Stokely Carmichael, Rap Brown and the Black Panthers successively urged Negroes to take up arms; by 1969, no fewer than a fourth of all Negroes—and a third of the ghetto young—agreed that they ought at least to have guns, whether or not they used them. Police periodically aborted what they said were terrorist plots—one to blow the head off the Statue of Liberty, another to dynamite Macy's, still another to assassinate Negro moderates like Whitney Young and Roy Wilkins. Street battles broke out with all the surface appearances of guerrilla warfare—the worst and most notorious of them a summer 1968 shoot-out between police and a little troop of armed nationalists led by a half-hinged street astrologer named Fred (Ahmed) Evans. Three cops and seven blacks died; Evans was sentenced to the electric chair for murder; tales flew, in and out of print, that the blacks had gulled police into a carefully plotted ambush.

It mattered little that the evidence for this theory was flimsy, or that most of the proliferating reports of sniping by supposed ghetto *guerrilleros* in the late 1960s proved on close examination to have been minor or plain fictitious. What mattered was what people believed was happening, and the combination of incendiary black rhetoric and inflamed white imaginations was quite enough to lead them to believe the worst. "May the deaths of '68 signal the beginning of the end of this country," Rap Brown wrote his followers from jail early that year. "Resistance is not enough. Aggression is the order of the day." Blacks as well as whites took such prophecies at face value. Were newer, more exotic forms of violence on the way? "There *couldn't* be any more, could there?" an elderly Houston man replied. "Lord have mercy on all of us if something else happen." But the widespread expectation was that something else would. "Racial war," said a Philadelphia electronics plant foreman, 34 years old. "Suicide squads," said a 28-year-old Harlem housewife. "Real revolution," a Denver schoolteacher ventured. "Sabotage," a middle-aged Pittsburgh woman predicted, "and whites intimidating Negroes, and child, all hell will break loose when that happens—bombings, shooting, fires . . ."

Tactical violence remained a possibility for the 1970s; whites tended greatly to overestimate the number of practicing revolutionaries in the ghetto, but a very few *plastiqueurs* could wreak very considerable havoc. Neither was the nation safely past the riot era. The rebellions percolated down in the latter 1960s from the big cities into small-to-middling towns and suburbs; they spread from the streets into the schools; they started earlier and died out later until the "long hot summer" stretched from winter to winter. And tensions tightened dangerously between militants and the police. The militants, said Terry Ann Knopf, research associate at Brandeis University's Lemberg Center for the Study of Violence, "really believe the police are out to kill them all. They stockpile arms. The police infiltrators learn of the stockpiles and law enforcement gets nervous. They begin surveillance. The spying makes militants more nervous and more sure of extermination. The stage is set for battle." And battles flared in the late 1960s: the Evans shoot-out in Cleveland, a duel between the cops and a group of black separatists meeting at a ghetto church in Detroit, the running and generally lopsided combat between police and the Panthers.

Yet there were signs by the decade's end that rioting on the cataclysmic scale of Watts, Newark or Detroit might at last be passing into history. The riots over King's assassination were like some last furious Walpurgisnacht in the ghetto—a transcontinental firestorm on a scale with the trauma that set it going. Street disorders in the days and months thereafter were at least as numerous and as widespread as in the summers before. But their intensity was considerably banked; it was almost as if the worst of the fury had spent itself in those terrible April days and nights after King died. The *Newsweek* Poll a year later asked blacks whether or not they would join a riot. Eleven per cent said they would. That is, of course, a startlingly large number to confess so violently angry a cast of mind to strangers. But the more telling fact may be that the number was down significantly from the 15 per cent who said yes in the days three years earlier when insurrection in the ghetto was still relatively new.

There were a number of theories as to why this should be so, each with some claim to credibility. Among them were these:

- *The Inoculation Theory.* This view holds that a riot is an act of cathar-sis—a spontaneous rising that may be satisfying once but is too har-rowing and too exhausting to go through a second time. "Cities which have had the bath of full-scale rioting are likely to have been washed out," said a black Federal intelligence source with well-laid wires into the ghetto. The record of a half-dozen years of rioting was indeed sug-gestive: lightning rarely struck twice with deadly force in the same place, and by the end of the decade, most places had been struck once. The riots, in short, were running out of cities to happen in; the ghetto, having tasted war, began to reassert its deeply grained will for peace.

- *The Hangover Theory.* A related hypothesis is that the ghetto wakes up the morning after a riot to discover that it has sustained most of the death and all of the destruction—and that it has achieved little if any-thing for its pain. The riots were a kamikaze assault on white America's conscience; the results—a faltering white liberalism on one hand and a quickening white backlash on the other—set many blacks wondering whether white America really had enough conscience to justify the cost. "The stupid thing about riots," said Earl Raines, a tough-minded young lawyer who headed the Los Angeles NAACP, "is why should you burn down your own home? The man in the ghetto lived in despair for so long—he just couldn't communicate with The Man downtown. To him, picking up a Molotov cocktail was his way of grabbing The Man's attention. The Watts riot was a time of glee for black people. But later they tallied up the damage and found out they'd lost the game. It wasn't even close."

- *The Police-Are-Getting-Better Theory.* The riot commission was appalled by the "indiscriminate and excessive force" often used to put down riots—a rather delicate phrase for a form of collective madness in which panicky cops and militiamen fired on anything that moved or made noise, including one another; in which densely populated tenements were powdered with .50-caliber machine-gun fire; in which the dead included not only looters and fire-bombers but old men, women and children. The police-are-getting-better theory presumed that lawmen had learned from disastrous experience. Their response to the King as-sassination riots was, relatively speaking, a model of sophistication—a show of maximum force at maximum speed and with a minimum of random gunplay. (The national death toll was 43 scattered among a dozen cities—still high, perhaps, but that many were killed in Detroit alone in 1967.) And department after department got religion about riot-prevention as well as riot-control measures: sharpened intelligence operations, serious community-relations programs and increased use of mobile commando units trained to nip riots surgically before they start.

■ *The Police-Are-Getting-Worse Theory.* This view insisted that, for all the appearance of reform, the police were in fact arming for Armageddon—an overt war of repression against the ghetto. The notion, of course, was most inflamed among the militants: the withering police pressure that destroyed some of them and drove others into exile persuaded them that Armageddon was already on. But the view was surprisingly current among ordinary blacks as well. At the height of the Newark rioting in 1967, a ghetto kid stood on a street corner watching the white firepower parade by and screamed in helpless rage, "The Man have *everything!*" Not yet; there were, in the wake of that angry summer, tales of the police stockpiling still more: high-powered rifles, machine guns, tanks, gas, helicopter gunships and miscellaneous other exotica of war unheard of this side of Vietnam. And none of it eased the paranoia which is one of the afflictions of life in the ghetto. "These people aren't stupid," said Los Angeles's Raines. "They know The Man is just waiting for them to do something wrong so he can come in and mow them down."

■ *The Lull-Between-Storms Theory.* Some black spectators read the winding down of the street war less as a turning point than as a pause—a time for the Negro community, in its own argot, to get it together and consider which way to move next. Militants and moderates alike in this period preached against the spontaneous insurrections of the past— the moderates because they had never believed in insurrection and the militants because they no longer believed in spontaneity. Various groups channeled the energies of the young into conventional politics, or community organization, or militant protest; even the Panthers stacked their guns out of sight and laid on their breakfast-for-children program. Yet a vein of pessimism underlay the lull-between-storms theory—a presumption that all these moral equivalents to war would fail and that violence in some form, probably but not necessarily more organized and more selective than the riots, almost certainly would follow. "All blacks are angry, very angry," said William Grier, a black psychiatrist and co-author (with Price Cobbs) of the book *Black Rage.* "Every black person in this country is a smoldering keg of dynamite. I would say the big riots are over. But the riots were not an end point by any means."

All of these elements no doubt were at play in the ghetto by the end of the 1960s, operating at least temporarily as a check on mass violence where the normal restraints had been overrun by events. None of them, naturally, guaranteed that the danger had run its course, or would so long as grievance remained the norm of the ghetto. J.T., a wasted young man of 23, came home from Vietnam to Chicago's West Side with no skills, no job, no future and so no vista beyond the street corner where he spends his days and nights jiving with his friends. "All you guys want to give is a dollar an hour," he said bitterly. "Man, I can *beg* more than that right on this corner. They didn't tell me I was going to be just another nigger when I got back home." So J.T. was indeed a keg of dynamite waiting for a match. "I want to burn down every building in this town," he said. "Let me do that and I'll be grateful to The Man for the rest of my life."

There are thousand of J.T.'s in the ghetto; they are bitter, alienated and potentially destructive, and, as Rap Brown once noted, matches only cost a penny. Yet the evidence is that their numbers are diminishing—at least partly because the riots turned out, in one important sense, to have worked after all. They scarred black America, to be sure, and they carried the very real risk of white backlash and white reprisal. But they created even as they destroyed, wakening a sense of community among the blacks—and giving many of them, often for the first time, a sense that they actually did have something to lose by rioting. Whites have always had a tendency somewhat to overstate the disorganization of the ghetto; blacks over the centuries have been forced by the fact of exclusion and the hard necessities of survival to develop their own parallel structure of churches, colleges, fraternal orders, burial societies and black betterment organizations. But their history in white America has always encouraged a sort of atomization of the Negro community—an ethos of Making It in which the object has been the escape of the talented few from the ghetto and from the shame of blackness.

The riots changed black America. They were, however, ugly and terrifying, a rare communal experience, a series of explicitly racial rebellions that cut across the wide class divisions of the Negro community, and their net effect tended more toward fusion than fission. The fleeting exhilaration of action, as USC's Dr. Hacker noted, was succeeded in Watts "by a strange sense of pride and accomplishment which is actually the finding of a national and racial identity. . . . The riots welded them together, and now they feel capable of carving a new fate, not just passively enduring their present existence." Detroit's Mayor Jerome Cavanagh, an urban politician of rare sensitivity, thought he detected a movement from "the militancy of despair" before the insurrections to "a militancy of hope" afterward. That rising militancy heightened the new introspective mood called black awareness; it brought many of the Negro middle class to the pained rediscovery of their kinship with the ghetto poor; it flowered in the explosion of community organizing efforts in the slums. Despair fragments; war unites. Before the riots, said psychiatrist Grier, "it was rare for a black man to use the term 'brother' to another black man and have each share a conception of its meaning. The secular meaning of brotherhood rose out of the riots."

Men who discover the fragile beginnings of community will not lightly risk them in war. Yet, to America's shame, it took war for those beginnings to be discovered, and the decision as to whether war would recur did not rest exclusively with the blacks. "In the ghettos of America," Hubert Locke, a black former police official, wrote in an unpublished epilogue to his book *The Detroit Riot of 1967*, "the fear of violence itself is tempered by a deep-seated desire, conscious or unconscious, to see white America pay dearly for 300 years of white injustice. . . . Unless the nation wages a vigorous and massive campaign to eradicate its injustices, the ability of or the basis for black people to decide clearly against violence and for a stable and just social order is virtually nil."

And the clock was running. In Watts one summer, while much of the community was celebrating its rebirth by riot, an authentic American ruin named Henry J. lay flat on his back on a lot in the burnt-out block called Charcoal Alley No. 1, sipped at a 50-cent bottle of Applejack wine and delivered a soliloquy to a sunny and utterly indifferent sky. He had, he announced, spent 12 of his 28 years in jail; as a consequence, he could not find work; there was a carwash job in Torrance, but Torrance was 20 miles away and he had no car. So he lay in the grass and drank Applejack and told the sky, "Fuck whitey. I don't believe in nothin'. I feel like they ought to burn down the whole world. Just let it burn down, baby."

Radical Chic: That Party at Lenny's

New York, June 8, 1970

◆

Tom Wolfe

At 2 or 3 or 4 A.M., somewhere along in there, on August 25, 1966, his forty-eighth birthday, in fact, Leonard Bernstein woke up in the dark in a state of wild alarm. That had happened before. It was one of the forms his insomnia took. So he did the usual. He got up and walked around a bit. He felt groggy. Suddenly he had a vision, an inspiration. He could see himself, Leonard Bernstein, the *egregio maestro*, walking out on stage in white tie and tails in front of a full orchestra. On one side of the conductor's podium is a piano. On the other is a chair with a guitar leaning against it. He sits in the chair and picks up the guitar. A guitar! One of those halfwitted instruments, like the accordion, that are made for the Learn-to-Play-in-Eight-Days E-Z-Diagram 110-IQ fourteen-year-olds of Levittown! But there's a reason. He has an anti-war message to deliver to this great starched white-throated audience in the symphony hall. He announces to them: "I love." Just that. The effect is mortifying. All at once a Negro rises up from out of the curve of the grand piano and starts saying things like, "The audience is curiously embarrassed." Lenny tries to start again, plays some quick numbers on the piano, says, "I love. *Amo ergo sum.*" The Negro rises again and says, "The audience thinks he ought to get up and walk out. The audience thinks, 'I am ashamed even to nudge my neighbor.'" Finally, Lenny gets off a heartfelt anti-war speech and exits.

For a moment, sitting there alone in his home in the small hours of the morning, Lenny thought it might just work and he jotted the idea down. Think of the headlines: BERNSTEIN ELECTRIFIES CONCERT AUDIENCE WITH ANTI-WAR APPEAL. But then his enthusiasm collapsed. He lost heart. Who the hell was this Negro rising up from the piano and informing the world what an ass Leonard Bernstein was making of himself? It didn't make sense, this superego Negro by the concert grand.

Mmmmmmmmmmmmmmmmmm. These are nice. Little Roquefort cheese morsels rolled in crushed nuts. Very tasty. Very subtle. It's the way the dry sackiness of the nuts tiptoes up against the dour savor of the cheese that is so nice, so subtle. Wonder what the Black Panthers eat here on the hors d'oeuvre trail? Do the Panthers like little Roquefort cheese morsels rolled in crushed nuts this way, and asparagus tips in mayonnaise dabs, and *meatballs petites au Coq Hardi,* all of which are at this very moment being offered to them on gadrooned silver platters by maids in black uniforms with hand-ironed white aprons . . . The butler will bring them their drinks . . . Deny it if you wish to, but such are the *pensées métaphysiques* that rush through one's head on these Radical Chic evenings just now in New York. For example, does that huge Black Panther there in the hallway, the one shaking hands with Felicia Bernstein herself, the one with the black leather coat and the dark glasses and the absolutely unbelievable Afro, Fuzzy-Wuzzy-scale, in fact—is he, a Black Panther, going on to pick up a Roquefort cheese morsel rolled in crushed nuts from off the tray, from a maid in uniform, and just pop it down the gullet without so much as missing a beat of Felicia's perfect Mary Astor voice . . .

Felicia is remarkable. She is beautiful, with that rare burnished beauty that lasts through the years. Her hair is pale blond and set just so. She has a voice that is "theatrical," to use a term from her youth. She greets the Black Panthers with the same bend of the wrist, the same tilt of the head, the same perfect Mary Astor voice with which she greets people like Jason, John and

D.D., Adolph, Betty, Gian-Carlo, Schuyler, and Goddard, during those *après-*concert suppers she and Lenny are so famous for. What evenings! She lights the candles over the dining-room table, and in the Gotham gloaming the little tremulous tips of flame are reflected in the mirrored surface of the table, a bottomless blackness with a thousand stars, and it is that moment that Lenny loves. There seem to be a thousand stars above and a thousand stars below, a room full of stars, a penthouse duplex full of stars, a Manhattan tower full of stars, with marvelous people drifting through the heavens, Jason Robards, John and D. D. Ryan, Gian-Carlo Menotti, Schuyler Chapin, Goddard Lieberson, Mike Nichols, Lillian Hellman, Larry Rivers, Aaron Copland, Richard Avedon, Milton and Amy Greene, Lukas Foss, Jennie Tourel, Samuel Barber, Jerome Robbins, Steve Sondheim, Adolph and Phyllis Green, Betty Comden, and the Patrick O'Neals . . .

. . . and now, in the season of Radical Chic, the Black Panthers. That huge Panther there, the one Felicia is smiling her tango smile at, is Robert Bay, who just forty-one hours ago was arrested in an altercation with the police, supposedly over a .38-caliber revolver that someone had, in a parked car in Queens at Northern Boulevard and 104th Street or some such unbelievable place, and taken to jail on a most unusual charge called "criminal facilitation." And now he is out on bail and walking into Leonard and Felicia Bernstein's thirteen-room penthouse duplex on Park Avenue. Harassment & Hassles, Guns & Pigs, Jail & Bail—they're *real,* these Black Panthers. The very idea of them, these real revolutionaries, who actually put their lives on the line, runs through Lenny's duplex like a rogue hormone. Everyone casts a glance, or stares, or tries a smile, and then sizes up the house for the somehow delicious counterpoint . . . Deny it if you want to! but one *does* end up making such sweet furtive comparisons in this season of Radical Chic . . . There's Otto Preminger in the library and Jean vanden Heuvel in the hall, and Peter and Cheray Duchin in the living room, and Frank and Domna Stanton, Gail Lumet, Sheldon Harnick, Cynthia Phipps, Burton Lane, Mrs. August Heckscher, Roger Wilkins, Barbara Walters, Bob Silvers, Mrs. Richard Avedon, Mrs. Arthur Penn, Julie Belafonte, Harold Taylor, and scores more, including Charlotte Curtis, women's news editor of *The New York Times,* America's foremost chronicler of Society, a lean woman in black, with her notebook out, standing near Felicia and big Robert Bay, and talking to Cheray Duchin.

Cheray tells her: "I've never met a Panther—this is a first for me!" . . . never dreaming that within forty-eight hours her words will be on the desk of the President of the United States . . .

This is a first for me. But she is not alone in her thrill as the Black Panthers come trucking on in, into Lenny's house, Robert Bay, Don Cox the Panthers' Field Marshal from Oakland, Henry Miller the Harlem Panther defense captain, the Panther women—Christ, if the Panthers don't know how to get it all together, as they say, the tight pants, the tight black turtlenecks, the leather coats, Cuban shades, Afros. But real Afros, not the ones that have been shaped and trimmed like a topiary hedge and sprayed until they have a sheen like acrylic wall-to-wall—but like funky, natural, scraggly . . . wild . . .

These are no civil-rights Negroes *wearing gray suits three sizes too big—*

—no more interminable Urban League banquets in hotel ballrooms where they try to alternate the blacks and whites around the tables as if they were stringing Arapaho beads—

—*these are* real men!

Shoot-outs, revolutions, pictures in *Life* magazine of policemen grabbing Black Panthers like they were Vietcong—somehow it all runs together in the head with the whole thing of how *beautiful* they are. *Sharp as a blade.* The Panther women—there are three or four of them on hand, wives of the Panther 21 defendants, and they are so lean, so *lithe,* as they say, with tight pants and Yoruba-style headdresses, almost like turbans, as if they'd stepped out of the pages of *Vogue,* although no doubt *Vogue* got it from them. All at once every woman in the room knows exactly what Amanda Burden meant when she said she was now anti-fashion because "the sophistication of the baby blacks made me rethink my attitudes." God knows the Panther women don't spend thirty minutes in front of the mirror in the morning shoring up their eye holes with contact lenses, eyeliner, eye shadow, eyebrow pencil, occipital rim brush, false eyelashes, mascara, Shadow-Ban for undereye and Eterna Creme for the corners . . . And here they are, right in front of you, trucking on into the Bernsteins' Chinese yellow duplex, amid the sconces, silver bowls full of white and lavender anemones, and uniformed servants serving drinks and Roquefort cheese morsels rolled in crushed nuts—

But it's all right. They're *white* servants, not Claude and Maude, but white South Americans. Lenny and Felicia are geniuses. After a while, it all comes down to servants. They are the cutting edge in Radical Chic. Obviously, if you are giving a party for the Black Panthers, as Lenny and Felicia are this evening, or as Sidney and Gail Lumet did last week, or as John Simon of Random House and Richard Baron, the publisher, did before that; or for the Chicago Eight, such as the party Jean vanden Heuvel gave; or for the grape workers or Bernadette Devlin, such as the parties Andrew Stein gave; or for the Young Lords, such as the party Ellie Guggenheimer is giving next week in *her* Park Avenue duplex; or for the Indians or the SDS or the G.I. coffee shops or even for the Friends of the Earth—well, then, obviously you can't have a Negro butler and maid, Claude and Maude, in uniform, circulating through the living room, the library, and the main hall serving drinks and canapés. Plenty of people have tried to think it out. They try to picture the Panthers or whoever walking in bristling with electric hair and Cuban shades and leather pieces and the rest of it, and they try to picture Claude and Maude with the black uniforms coming up and saying, "Would you care for a drink, sir?" They close their eyes and try to picture it *some way,* but there *is* no way. One simply cannot see that moment. So the current wave of Radical Chic has touched off the most desperate search for white servants. Carter and Amanda Burden have white servants. Sidney Lumet and his wife Gail, who is Lena Horne's daughter, have three white servants, including a Scottish nurse. Everybody has white servants. And Lenny and Felicia—they had it worked out before Radical Chic even started. Felicia grew up in Chile. Her father, Roy Elwood Cohn, an engineer from San Francisco, worked for the American Smelting and Refining Co. in Santiago. As Felicia Montealegre (her mother's maiden name), she became an actress in New York and won the *Motion Picture Daily* critics' award as the best new television actress of 1949. Anyway, they have a house staff of three white South American servants, including a Chilean cook, plus Lenny's English chauffeur and dresser, who is also white, of course. Can one comprehend how perfect that is, given . . . the times? Well, many of their friends can, and they ring up the Bernsteins and ask them to get South American servants for them, and the Bernsteins are so generous about it, so obliging, that people refer to them, goodnaturedly and gratefully, as "the Spic and Span Employment Agency," with an easygoing ethnic humor, of course.

The only other thing to do is what Ellie Guggenheimer is doing next week with her party for the Young Lords in her duplex on Park Avenue at 89th Street, just ten blocks up from Lenny and Felicia. She is giving her party on a Sunday, which is the day off for the maid and the cleaning woman. "Two friends of mine"—she confides on the telephone—"two friends of mine who happen to be . . . not white—that's what I hate about the times we live in, the *terms*—well, they've agreed to be butler and maid . . . and I'm going to be a maid myself!"

Just at this point some well-meaning soul is going to say, Why not do without servants altogether if the matter creates such unbearable tension and one truly believes in equality? Well, even to raise the question is to reveal the most fundamental ignorance of life in the great co-ops and townhouses of the East Side in the age of Radical Chic. Why, my God! servants are not a mere convenience, they're an absolute psychological necessity. Once one is into that life, truly into it, with the morning workout on the velvet swings at Kounovsky's and the late mornings on the telephone, and lunch at the Running Footman, which is now regarded as really better than La Grenouille, Lutèce, Lafayette, La Caravelle, and the rest of the general Frog Pond, less ostentatious, more of the David Hicks feeling, less of the Parish-Hadley look, and then—well, then, the idea of not having servants is unthinkable. But even that does not say it all. It makes it sound like a matter of convenience, when actually it is a sheer and fundamental matter of—*having servants.* Does one comprehend?

God, what a flood of taboo thoughts runs through one's head at these Radical Chic events . . . But it's delicious. It is as if one's nerve endings were on red alert to the most intimate nuances of status. Deny it if you want to! Nevertheless, it runs through every soul here. It is the matter of the marvelous contradictions on all sides. It is like the delicious shudder you get when you try to force the prongs of two horseshoe magnets together . . . *them* and *us* . . .

For example, one's own servants, although white, are generally no problem. A discreet, euphemistic word about what sort of party it is going to be, and they will generally be models of correctness. The euphemisms are not always an easy matter, however. When talking to one's white servants, one doesn't really know whether to refer to blacks as *blacks, Negroes,* or *colored people.* When talking to other . . . well, *cultivated* persons, one says *blacks,* of course. It is the only word, currently, that implicitly shows one's awareness of the dignity of the black race. But somehow when you start to say the word to your own white servants, you hesitate. You can't get it out of your throat. Why? *Counter-guilt!* You realize that you are about to utter one of those touchstone words that divide the cultivated from the uncultivated, the attuned from the unattuned, the *hip* from the dreary. As soon as the word comes out of your mouth—you know it before the first vocable pops on your lips—your own servant is going to size you up as one of those *limousine liberals,* or whatever epithet they use, who are busy pouring white soul all over the black movement, and would you do as much for the white lower class, for the domestics of the East Side, for example, fat chance, sahib. Deny it if you want to! but such are the delicious little agonies of Radical Chic. So one settles for *Negro,* with the hope that the great god Culturatus has laid the ledger aside for the moment . . . In any case, if one is able to make that small compromise, one's own servants are no real problem. But the elevator man and the doorman—the death rays they begin projecting, the curt responses, as soon as they see it is going to be one of *those* parties! Of course, they're all from Queens, and so forth, and one has to allow for that. For some reason the elevator men tend to be worse about it than the doormen, even; less sense of *politesse,* perhaps.

Or—what does one wear to these parties for the Panthers or the Young Lords or the grape workers? What does a woman wear? Obviously one does not want to wear something frivolously and pompously expensive, such as a Gerard Pipart party dress. On the other hand one does not want to arrive "poormouthing it" in some outrageous turtleneck and West Eighth Street bell-jean combination, as if one is "funky" and of "the people." Frankly, Jean vanden Heuvel—that's Jean there in the hallway giving everyone her famous smile, in which her eyes narrow down to f/16—frankly, Jean tends too much toward the funky fallacy. Jean, who is the daughter of Jules Stein, one of the wealthiest men in the country, is wearing some sort of rust-red snap-around suede skirt, the sort that English working girls pick up on Saturday afternoons in those absolutely *berserk* London boutiques like Bus Stop or Biba, where everything looks chic and yet skimpy and raw and vital. Felicia Bernstein seems to understand the whole thing better. Look at Felicia. She is wearing the simplest little black frock imaginable, with absolutely no ornamentation save for a plain gold necklace. It is perfect. It has dignity without any overt class symbolism.

Lenny? Lenny himself has been in the living room all this time, talking to old friends like the Duchins and the Stantons and the Lanes. Lenny is wearing a black turtleneck, navy blazer, Black Watch plaid trousers and a necklace with a pendant hanging down to his sternum. His tailor comes here to the apartment to take the measurements and do the fittings. Lenny is a short, trim man, and yet he always seems tall. It is his head. He has a noble head, with a face that is at once sensitive and rugged, and a full stand of iron-gray hair, with sideburns, all set off nicely by the Chinese yellow of the room. His success radiates from his eyes and his smile with a charm that illustrates Lord Jersey's adage that "contrary to what the Methodists tell us, money and success are good for the soul." Lenny may be fifty-one, but he is still the *Wunderkind* of American music. Everyone says so. He is not only one of the world's outstanding conductors, but a more than competent composer and pianist as well. He is the man who more than any other has broken down the wall between elite music and popular tastes, with *West Side Story* and his children's concerts on television. How natural that he should stand here in his own home radiating the charm and grace that make him an easy host for leaders of the oppressed. How ironic that the next hour should prove so shattering for this *egregio maestro!* How curious that the Negro by the piano should emerge tonight!

A bell rang, a dinner-table bell, by the sound of it, the sort one summons the maid out of the kitchen with, and the party shifted from out of the hall and into the living room. Felicia led the way, Felicia and a small gray man, with gray hair, a gray face, a gray suit, and a pair of Groovy but gray sideburns. A little gray man, in short, who would be popping up at key moments . . . to keep the freight train of history on the track, as it were . . .

Felicia was down at the far end of the living room trying to coax everybody in.

"Lenny!" she said. "Tell the fringes to come on in!" Lenny was still in the back of the living room, near the hall. "Fringes!" said Lenny. "Come on in!"

In the living room most of the furniture, the couches, easy chairs, side tables, side chairs, and so on, had been pushed toward the walls, and thirty or forty folding chairs were set up in the middle of the floor. It was a big, wide room with Chinese yellow walls and white moldings, sconces, pier-glass mirrors, a portrait of Felicia reclining on a summer chaise, and at the far end, where Felicia was standing, a pair of grand pianos. A pair of them; the two pianos were standing back to back, with the tops down and their bellies swooping out. On top of both pianos was a regular flotilla of family photographs in silver frames, the kind of pictures that stand straight up thanks to little velvet- or moiré-covered buttresses in the back, the kind that decorators in New York recommend to give a living room a homelike lived-in touch. "The million-dollar *chatchka* look," they call it. In a way it was perfect for Radical Chic. The nice part was that with Lenny it was instinctive; with Felicia, too. The whole place looked as if the inspiration had been to spend a couple of hundred thousand on the interior without looking pretentious, although that is no great sum for a thirteen-room co-op, of course . . . Imagine explaining all that to the Black Panthers. It was another delicious thought . . . The sofas, for example, were covered in the fashionable splashy prints on a white background covering deep downy cushions, in the Bill Baldwin or Margaret Owen tradition—without it looking like Billy or Margaret had been in there fussing about with teapoys and japanned chairs. *Gemütlich* . . . Old Vienna when Grandpa was alive . . . That was the ticket . . .

Once Lenny got "the fringes" moving in, the room filled up rapidly. It was jammed, in fact. People were sitting on sofas and easy chairs along the sides, as well as on the folding chairs, and were standing in the back, where Lenny was. Otto Preminger was sitting on a sofa down by the pianos, where the speakers were going to stand. The Panther wives were sitting in the first two rows with their Yoruba headdresses on, along with Henry Mitchell and Julie Belafonte, Harry Belafonte's wife. Julie is white, but they all greeted her warmly as "Sister." Behind her was sitting Barbara Walters, hostess of the *Today Show* on television, wearing a checked pants suit with a great fluffy fur collar on the coat. Harold Taylor, the former "Boy President" of Sarah Lawrence, now fifty-five and silver-haired, but still youthful-looking, came walking down toward the front and gave a hug and a big social kiss to Gail Lumet. Robert Bay settled down in the middle of the folding chairs. Jean vanden Heuvel stood in the back and sought to focus . . . f/16 . . . on the pianos . . . Charlotte Curtis stood beside the door, taking notes.

And then Felicia stood up beside the pianos and said: "I want to thank you all very, very much for coming. I'm very, very glad to see so many of you here." Everything was fine. Her voice was rich as a woodwind. She introduced a man named Leon Quat, a lawyer involved in raising funds for the Panther 21, twenty-one Black Panthers who had been arrested on a charge of conspiring to blow up five New York department stores, New Haven Railroad facilities, a police station, and the Bronx Botanical Gardens.

Leon Quat, oddly enough, had the general look of those fifty-two-year-old men who run a combination law office, real estate, and insurance operation on the second floor of a two-story taxpayer out on Queens Boulevard. And yet that wasn't the kind of man Leon Quat really was. He had the sideburns. Quite a pair. They didn't come down just to the intertragic notch, which is that little notch in the lower rim of the ear, and which so many tentative Swingers aim their sideburns toward. No, on top of this complete Queens Boulevard insurance-agent look, he had real sideburns, to the bottom of the lobe, virtual muttonchops, which somehow have become the mark of the Movement.

Leon Quat rose up smiling: "We are very grateful to Mrs. Bernstein"—only he pronounced it "steen."

"STEIN!"—a great smoke-cured voice booming out from the rear of the room! It's Lenny! Leon Quat and the Black Panthers will have a chance to hear from Lenny. That much is sure. He is on the case. Leon Quat must be the only man in the room who does not know about Lenny and the Mental Jotto at 3 A.M. . . . For years, twenty at the least, Lenny has insisted on -stein not -steen, as if to say, I am not one of those 1921 Jews who try to tone down their Jewishness by watering their names down with a bad soft English pronunciation. Lenny has made such a point of -stein not -steen, in fact, that some people in this room think at once of the story of how someone approached Larry Rivers, the artist, and said, "What's this I hear about you and Leonard Bernstein"—steen, he pronounced it—"not speaking to each other any more?"—to which Rivers said, "STEIN!"

"We are very grateful . . . for her marvelous hospitality," says Quat, apparently not wanting to try the name again right away.

Then he beams toward the crowd: "I assume we are all just an effete clique of snobs and intellectuals in this room . . . I am referring to the words of Vice-President Agnew, of course, who can't be with us today because he is in the South Pacific explaining the Nixon doctrine to the Australians. All vice-presidents suffer from the Avis complex—they're second best, so they try harder, like General Ky or Hubert Humphrey . . ." He keeps waiting for the grins and chuckles after each of these mots, but all the celebrities and culturati are nonplussed. They give him a kind of dumb attention. They came here for the Panthers and Radical Chic, and here is Old Queens Boulevard Real Estate Man with sideburns on telling them Agnew jokes. But Quat is too deep into his weird hole to get out. "Whatever respect I have had for Lester Maddox, I lost it when I saw Humphrey put his arm around his shoulder . . ." and somehow Quat begins disappearing down a hole bunging Hubert Humphrey with lumps of old Shelley Berman material. Slowly he climbs back out. He starts telling about the oppression of the Panther 21. They have been in jail since February 2, 1969, awaiting trial on ludicrous charges such as conspiring to blow up the Bronx Botanical Gardens. Their bail has been a preposterous $100,000 per person, which has in effect denied them the right to bail. They have been kept split up and moved from jail to jail. For all intents and purposes they have been denied the right to confer with their lawyers to prepare a defense. They have been subjected to inhuman treatment in jail—such as the case of Lee Berry, an epileptic, who was snatched out of a hospital bed and thrown in jail and kept in solitary confinement with a light bulb burning over his head night and day.

The Panthers who have not been thrown in jail or killed, like Fred Hampton, are being stalked and harassed everywhere they go. "One of the few higher officials who is still . . . in the clear"—Quat smiles—"is here today. Don Cox, Field Marshal of the Black Panther Party."

"Right on," a voice says to Leon Quat, rather softly. And a tall black man rises from behind one of Lenny's grand pianos . . . *The Negro by the piano* . . .

The Field Marshal of the Black Panther Party has been sitting in a chair between the piano and the wall. He rises up; he has the hard-rock look, all right; he is a big tall man with brown skin and an Afro and a goatee and a black turtleneck much like Lenny's, and he stands up beside the piano, next to Lenny's million-dollar *chatchka* flotilla of family photographs. In fact, there is a certain perfection as the first Black Panther rises within a Park Avenue living room to lay the Panthers' ten-point program on New York Society in the age of Radical Chic. Cox is silhouetted—well, about nineteen feet behind him is a white silk shade with an Empire scallop over one of the windows overlooking Park Avenue. Or maybe it isn't silk, but a Jack Lenor Larsen mercerized cotton, something like that, lustrous but more subtle than silk. The whole image, the white shade and the Negro by the piano silhouetted against it, is framed by a pair of bottle-green velvet curtains, pulled back.

And does it begin now?—but this Cox is a cool number. He doesn't come on with the street epithets and interjections and the rest of the rhetoric and red eyes used for mau-mauing the white liberals, as it is called.

"The Black Panther Party," he starts off, "stands for a ten-point program that was handed down in October 1966 by our Minister of Defense, Huey P. Newton . . ." and he starts going through the ten points . . . "We want an educational system that expresses the true nature of this decadent society" . . . "We want all black men exempt from military service" . . . "We want all black men who are in jail to be set free. We want them to be set free because they have not had fair trials. We've been tried by predominantly middle-class, all-white juries" . . . "And most important of all, we want peace . . . see . . . We want peace, but there can be no peace as long as a society is racist and one part of society engages in systematic oppression of another" . . . "We want a plebiscite by the United Nations to be held in black communities, so that we can control our own destiny" . . .

Everyone in the room, of course, is drinking in his performance like tiger's milk, for the . . . Soul, as it were. All love the tone of his voice, which is Confidential Hip. And yet his delivery falls into strangely formal patterns. What are these block phrases, such as "our Minister of Defense, Huey P. Newton"—

"Some people think that we are racist, because the news media find it useful to create that impression in order to support the power structure, which we have nothing to do with . . . see . . . They like for the Black Panther Party to be made to look like a racist organization, because that camouflages the true class nature of the struggle. But they find it harder and harder to keep up that camouflage and are driven to campaigns of harassment and violence to try to eliminate the Black Panther Party. Here in New York twenty-one members of the Black Panther Party were indicted last April on ridiculous charges of conspiring to blow up department stores and flower gardens. They've had twenty-seven bail hearings since last April . . . see . . ."

—But everyone in here loves the *sees* and the *you knows.* They are so, somehow . . . *black* . . . *so funky* . . . so metrical . . . Without ever bringing it fully into consciousness everyone responds—communes over—the fact that he uses them not for emphasis but for punctuation, metrically, much like the *uhs* favored by High Church Episcopal ministers, as in, "And bless, uh, these gifts, uh, to Thy use and us to, uh, Thy service"—

". . . they've had twenty-seven bail hearings since last April . . . see . . . and every time the judge has refused to lower the bail from $100,000 . . . Yet a group of whites accused of actually bombing buildings—they were able to get bail. So that clearly demonstrates the racist nature of the campaign against the Black Panther Party. We don't say 'bail' any more, we say 'ransom,' for such repressive bail can only be called ransom.

"The situation here in New York is very explosive, as you can see, with people stacked up on top of each other. They can hardly deal with them when they're *un*organized, so that when a group comes along like the Black Panthers, they want to eliminate that group by any means . . . see . . . and so that stand has been embraced by J. Edgar Hoover, who feels that we are the greatest threat to the power structure. They try to create the impression that we are engaged in criminal activities. What are these 'criminal activities'? We have instituted a breakfast program, to address ourselves to the needs of the community. We feed hungry children every morning before they go to school. So far this program is on a small scale. We're only feeding fifty thousand children nationwide, but the only money we have for this program is donations from the merchants in the neighborhoods. We have a program to establish clinics in the black communities and in other ways also we are addressing ourselves to the needs of the community . . . see . . . So the people know the power structure is lying when they say we are engaged in criminal activities. So the pigs are driven to desperate acts, like the murder of our deputy chairman, Fred Hampton, in his bed . . . see . . . in his sleep . . . But when they got desperate and took off their camouflage and murdered Fred Hampton, in his bed, in his sleep, see, that kind of shook people up, because they saw the tactics of the power structure for what they were . . .

"We relate to a phrase coined by Malcolm X: 'By any means necessary' . . . you see . . . 'By any means necessary' . . . and by that we mean that we recognize that if you're attacked, you have the right to defend yourself. The pigs, they

say the Black Panthers are armed, the Black Panthers have weapons . . .
see . . . and therefore they have the right to break in and murder us in our beds.
I don't think there's anybody in here who wouldn't defend themselves if somebody came in and attacked them or their families . . . see . . . I don't think
there's anybody in here who wouldn't defend themselves . . ."

—and every woman in the room thinks of her husband . . . with his
cocoa-butter jowls and Dior Men's Boutique pajamas . . . ducking into the
bathroom and locking the door and turning the shower on, so he can say later
that he didn't hear a thing—

"We call them pigs, and rightly so," says Don Cox, "because they have the
way of making the victim look like the criminal, and the criminal look like the
victim. So every Panther must be ready to defend himself. That was handed
down by our Minister of Defense, Huey P. Newton: Everybody who does not
have the means to defend himself in his home, or if he does have the means and
he does not defend himself—we expel *that man* . . . see . . . As our Minister of
Defense, Huey P. Newton, says, 'Any unarmed people are slaves, or are slaves in
the real meaning of the word' . . . We recognize that this country is the most
oppressive country in the world, maybe in the history of the world. The pigs
have the weapons and they are ready to use them on the people, and we recognize this as being very bad. They are ready to commit genocide against those
who stand up against them, and we recognize this as being very bad.

"All we want is the good life, the same as you. To live in peace and lead the
good life, that's all we want . . . see . . . But right now there's no way we can do
that. I want to read something to you:

" 'When in the course of human events, it becomes necessary for one people to dissolve the political bands which have connected them with another,
and . . .' " He reads straight through it, every word. " '. . . and, accordingly, all
experience hath shown, that mankind are more disposed to suffer, while evils
are sufferable, than to right themselves by abolishing the forms to which they
are accustomed. But when a long train of abuses and usurpations, pursuing
invariably the same object, evinces a design to reduce them under absolute
despotism, it is their right, it is their duty, to throw off such government, and to
provide new guards for their future security.'

"You know what that's from?"—and he looks out at everyone and hesitates before laying this gasper on them—"That's from the Declaration of Independence, the American Declaration of Independence. And we will defend
ourselves and do like it says . . . you know? . . . and that's about it."

The "that's about it" part seems so casual, so funky, so right, after the
rhetoric of what he has been saying. And then he sits down and sinks out of
sight behind one of the grand pianos.

The thing is beginning to move. And—hell, yes, the *Reichstag fire!* Another
man gets up, a white named Gerald Lefcourt, who is chief counsel for the Pan-

ther 21, a young man with thick black hair and the muttonchops of the Movement and that great motor inside of him that young courtroom lawyers ought to have. He lays the Reichstag fire on them. He reviews the Panther case and then he says:

"I believe that this odious situation could be compared to the Reichstag fire attempt"—he's talking about the way the Nazis used the burning of the Reichstag as the pretext for first turning loose the Gestapo and exterminating all political opposition in Germany—"and I believe that this trial could also be compared to the Reichstag trial . . . in many ways . . . and that opened an era that this country could be heading for. That could be the outcome of this case, an era of the Right, and the only thing that can stop it is for people like ourselves to make a noise and make a noise now."

. . . and not be Krupps, Junkers, or Good Germans . . .

". . . We had an opportunity to question the Grand Jury, and we found out some interesting things. They all have net worths averaging $300,000, and they all come from this neighborhood," says Lefcourt, nodding as if to take in the whole Upper East Side. And suddenly everyone feels, really *feels*, that there are two breeds of mankind in the great co-ops of Park Avenue, the blue-jowled rep-tied Brook Club Junker reactionaries in the surrounding buildings . . . and the few *attuned* souls here in Lenny's penthouse. ". . . They all have annual incomes in the area of $35,000 . . . And you're supposed to have a 'jury of your peers' . . . They were shocked at the questions we were asking them. They shouldn't have to answer such questions, that was the idea. They all belong to the Grand Jury Association. They're somewhat like a club. They have lunch together once in a while. A lot of them went to school together. They have no more understanding of the Black Panthers than President Nixon."

The Junkers! Leon Quat says: "Fascism always begins by persecuting the least powerful and least popular movement. It will be the Panthers today, the students tomorrow—and then . . . the Jews and other troublesome minorities! . . . What price civil liberties! . . . Now let's start this off with the gifts in four figures. Who is ready to make a contribution of a thousand dollars or more?"

All at once—nothing. But the little gray man sitting next to Felicia, the gray man with the sideburns, pops up and hands a piece of paper to Quat and says: "Mr. Clarence Jones asked me to say—he couldn't be here, but he's contributing $7,500 to the defense fund!"

"Oh! That's marvelous!" says Felicia.

Then the voice of Lenny from the back of the room: "As a guest of my wife"—he smiles—"I'll give my fee for the next performance of *Cavalleria Rusticana.*" Comradely laughter. Applause. "I *hope* that will be four figures!"

Things are moving again. Otto Preminger speaks up from the sofa down front: "I geeve a t'ousand dollars!"

Right on. Quat says: "I can't assure you that it's tax deductible." He smiles. "I wish I could, but I can't." Well, the man looks brighter and brighter every minute. He knows a Radical Chic audience when he sees one. Those words are magic in the age of Radical Chic: it's *not* tax deductible.

The contributions start coming faster, only $250 or $300 at a clip, but faster . . . Sheldon Harnick . . . Bernie and Hilda Fishman . . . Judith Bernstein . . . Mr. and Mrs. Burton Lane . . .

"I know some of you are caught with your Dow-Jones averages down," says Quat, "but come on—"

Quat says: "We have a $300 contribution from Harry Belafonte!"

"No, no," says Julie Belafonte.

"I'm sorry," says Quat, "it's Julie's private money! I apologize. After all, there's a women's liberation movement sweeping the country, and I want this marked down as a gift from *Mrs.* Belafonte!" Then he says: "I know you want to get to the question period, but I know there's more gold in this mine. I think we've reached the point where we can pass out the blank checks."

More contributions . . . $100 from Mrs. August Heckscher . . .

"We'll take *anything*!" says Quat. "We'll take it all!" . . . He's high on the momentum of his fund-raiser voice . . . "You'll leave here with nothing!"

But finally he wraps it up. A beautiful ash-blond girl with the most perfect Miss Porter's face speaks up. She's wearing a leather and tweed dress. She looks like a Junior Leaguer graduating to the Ungaro Boutique.

"I'd like to ask Mr. Cox a question," she says. Cox is standing up again, by the grand piano. "Besides the breakfast program," she says, "do you have any other community programs, and what are they like?"

Cox starts to tell about a Black Panther program to set up medical clinics in the ghettos, and so on, but soon he is talking about a Panther demand that police be required to live in the community they patrol. "If you police the community, you must live there . . . see . . . Because if he lives in the community, he's going to think twice before he brutalizes us, because we can deal with him when he comes home at night . . . see . . . We are also working to start liberation schools for black children, and these liberation schools will actually teach them about their environment, because the way they are now taught, they are taught not to see their real environment . . . see . . . They get Donald Duck and Mother Goose and all that lame happy jive . . . you know . . . We'd like to take kids on tours of the white suburbs, like Scarsdale, and like that, and let them see how their oppressors live . . . you know . . . but so far we don't have the money to carry out these programs to meet the real needs of the community. The only money we have is what we get from the merchants in the black community when we ask them for donations, which they *should give*, because they are the exploiters of the black community"—

—and *shee-ut*. What the hell is Cox getting into that for? Quat and the little gray man are ready to spring in at any lonesome split second. For God's sake, Cox, don't open that can of worms. Even in this bunch of upholstered skulls there are people who can figure out just *who* those merchants are, what group, and just how they are *asked* for donations, and we've been free of that little issue all evening, man—don't bring out *that* ball-breaker—

But the moment is saved. Suddenly there is a much more urgent question from the rear: "Who do you call to give a party? Who do you call to give a party?"

Every head spins around . . . Quite a sight . . . It's a slender blond man who has pushed his way up to the front ranks of the standees. He's wearing a tuxedo. He's wearing black-frame glasses and his blond hair is combed back straight in the Eaton Square manner. He looks like the intense Yale man from out of one of those 1927 Frigidaire ads in *The Saturday Evening Post,* when the way to sell anything was to show Harry Yale in the background, in a tuxedo, with his pageboy-bobbed young lovely, heading off to dinner at the New Haven Lawn Club. The man still has his hand up in the air like the star student of the junior class.

"I won't be able to stay for everything you have to say," he says, "but who do you call to give a party?"

In fact, it is Richard Feigen, owner of the Feigen Gallery, 79th near Madison. He arrived on the art scene and the social scene from Chicago three years ago . . . He's been moving up hand over hand ever since . . . like a champion . . . Tonight—the tuxedo—tonight there is a reception at the Museum of Modern Art . . . right on . . . a "contributing members'" reception, a private viewing not open to mere "members" . . . But before the museum reception itself, which is at 8:30, there are private dinners . . . right? . . . which are the *real* openings . . . in the homes of great collectors or great climbers or the old Protestant elite, marvelous dinner parties, the real thing, black tie, and these dinners are the only true certification of where one stands in this whole realm of Art & Society . . . The whole game depends on whose home one is invited to before the opening . . . And the game ends as the host gathers everyone up about 8:45 for the trek to the museum itself, and the guests say, almost ritually, "God! I wish we could see the show from here! It's too delightful! I simply don't want to *move!*" . . . And of course, they mean it! Absolutely! For them, the opening is already over, the hand is played . . . And Richard Feigen, man of the hour, replica 1927 Yale man, black tie and Eaton Square hair, has dropped in, on the way, *en passant,* to the Bernsteins', to take in the other end of the Culture tandem, Radical Chic . . . and the rightness of it, the exhilaration, seems to sweep through him, and he thrusts his hand into the air, and somehow Radical Chic reaches its highest, purest state in that moment . . . as Richard Feigen, in his tuxedo, breaks in to ask, from the bottom of his heart, "Who do you call to give a party?"

Choosing to Stay at Home: Ten Years After the March on Washington

The New York Times Magazine, August 26, 1973

◆

ALICE WALKER

Our bus left Boston before dawn on the day of the March. We were a jolly, boisterous crowd who managed to shout the words to "We Shall Overcome" without a trace of sadness or doubt. At least on the surface. Underneath our bravado there was anxiety: Would Washington be ready for us? Would there be violence? Would we *be* Overcome? Could *we* Overcome? At any rate, we felt confident enough to try.

It was the summer of my sophomore year in college in Atlanta and I had come to Boston as I usually did to find a job that would allow me to support myself through another year of school. No one else among my Boston relatives went to the March, but all of them watched it eagerly on TV. When I returned that night they claimed to have seen someone exactly like me among those milling about just to the left of Martin Luther King, Jr. But of course I was not anywhere near him. The crowds would not allow it. I was, instead, perched on the limb of a tree far from the Lincoln Memorial, and although I managed to see very little of the speakers, I could hear everything.

For a speech and drama term paper the previous year my teacher had sent his class to Atlanta University to hear Martin Luther King lecture. "I am not interested in his politics," he warned, "only in his speech." And so I had written a paper that contained these lines: "Martin Luther King, Jr. is a surprisingly effective orator, although *terribly* under the influence of the Baptist church so that his utterances sound overdramatic and too weighty to be taken seriously." I also commented on his lack of humor, his expressionless "oriental" eyes, and the fascinating fact that his gray sharkskin suit was completely without wrinkles—causing me to wonder how he had gotten into it. It was a surprise, therefore, to find at the March on Washington that the same voice that had seemed ponderous and uninspired in a small lecture hall was now as electrifying in its tone as it was in its message.

Martin King was a man who truly had his tongue wrapped around the roots of Southern black religious consciousness, and when his resounding voice swelled and broke over the heads of the thousands of people assembled at the Lincoln Memorial I felt what a Southern person brought up in the church *always* feels when those cadences—not the words themselves, necessarily, but the rhythmic spirals of passionate emotion, followed by even more passionate pauses—roll off the tongue of a really first-rate preacher. I felt my soul rising from the sheer force of Martin King's eloquent goodness.

> There are those who are asking the devotees of civil rights, "When will you be satisfied?" We can never be satisfied as long as the Negro is the victim of the unspeakable horrors of police brutality. We can never be satisfied as long as our bodies, heavy with the fatigue of travel, cannot gain lodging in the motels of the highways and the hotels of the cities. We cannot be satisfied as long as the Negro's basic mobility is from a smaller ghetto to a larger one. We can never be satisfied as long as our children are stripped of their selfhood and robbed of their dignity by signs stating "For white only." We cannot be satisfied as long as a Negro in Mississippi cannot vote and a Negro in New York believes he has nothing for which to vote. No, we are not satisfied and we will not be satisfied until justice rolls down like waters and righteousness like a mighty stream.

And when he spoke of "letting freedom ring" across "the green hills of Alabama and the red hills of Georgia" I saw again what he was always uniquely able to make me see: that I, in fact, had claim to the land of my birth. Those red hills of Georgia were mine, and nobody was going to force me away from them until I myself was good and ready to go.

> . . . Some of you have come here out of great trials and tribulations. Some of you have come fresh from narrow jail cells. Some of you have come from areas where your quest for freedom left you battered by storms of persecution and staggered by the winds of police brutality. . . . Go back to Mississippi, go back to Alabama, go back . . . to Georgia . . . knowing that somehow this situation can and will be changed. . . . This is our hope. This is the faith that I go back to the South with. With this faith we will be able to hew out of the mountain of despair a stone of hope.

Later I was to read that the March on Washington was a dupe of black people, that the leaders had sold out to the Kennedy administration, and that all of us should have felt silly for having participated. But whatever the Kennedy administration may have done had nothing to do with the closeness I felt that day to my own people, to King and John Lewis and thousands of others. And it is impossible to regret hearing that speech, because no black person I knew had ever encouraged anybody to "Go back to Mississippi . . . ," and I knew if this challenge were taken up by the millions of blacks who normally left the South for better fortunes in the North, a change couldn't help but come.

This may not seem like much to other Americans, who constantly move about the country with nothing but restlessness and greed to prod them, but to the Southern black person brought up expecting to be run away from home—because of lack of jobs, money, power, and respect—it was a notion that took root in willing soil. We would fight to stay where we were born and raised and destroy the forces that sought to disinherit us. We would proceed with the revolution from our own homes.

I thought of my seven brothers and sisters who had already left the South and I wanted to know: Why did they have to leave home to find a better life?

I was born and raised in Eatonton, Georgia, which is in the center of the state. It is also the birthplace of Joel Chandler Harris, and visitors are sometimes astonished to see a large iron rabbit on the courthouse lawn. It is a town of two streets, and according to my parents its social climate had changed hardly at all since they were children. That being so, on hot Saturday afternoons of my childhood I gazed longingly through the window of the corner drugstore where white youngsters sat on stools in air-conditioned comfort and drank Cokes and nibbled ice-cream cones. Black people could come in and buy, but what they bought they couldn't eat inside. When the first motel was built in Eatonton in the late fifties the general understanding of *place* was so clear the owners didn't even bother to put up a "Whites Only" sign.

I was an exile in my own town, and grew to despise its white citizens almost as much as I loved the Georgia countryside where I fished and swam and walked through fields of black-eyed Susans, or sat in contemplation beside the giant pine tree my father "owned," because when he was a boy and walking five miles to school during the winter he and his schoolmates had built a fire each morning in the base of the tree, and the tree still lived—although there was a blackened triangular hole in it large enough for me to fit inside. This was my father's tree, and from it I had a view of fields his people had worked (and briefly owned) for generations, and could walk—in an afternoon—to the house where my mother was born; a leaning, weather-beaten ruin, it was true, but as essential to her sense of existence as one assumes Nixon's birthplace in California is to him. Probably more so, since my mother has always been careful to stay on good terms with the earth she occupies. But I would have to leave all this. Take my memories and run north. For I would not be a maid, and could not be a "girl," or a frightened half-citizen, or any of the things my brothers and sisters had already refused to be.

In those days few blacks spent much time discussing hatred of white people. It was understood that they were—generally—vicious and unfair, like floods, earthquakes, or other natural catastrophes. Your job, if you were black, was to live with that knowledge like people in San Francisco live with the San Andreas Fault. You had as good a time (and life) as you could, under the circumstances.

Not having been taught black history—except for the once-a-year hanging up of the pictures of Booker Washington, George Washington Carver, and Mary McLeod Bethune that marked Negro History Week—we did not know how much of the riches of America we had missed. Somehow it was hard to comprehend just how white folks—lazy as all agreed they were—always managed to get ahead. When Hamilton Holmes and Charlayne Hunter were first seen trying to enter the University of Georgia, people were stunned: Why did they want to go to that whitefolks' school? If they wanted to go somewhere let 'em go to a school black money had built! It was a while before they could connect their centuries of unpaid labor with white "progress," but as soon as they did they saw Hamp and Charlayne as the heroes they were.

I had watched Charlayne and Hamp every afternoon on the news when I came home from school. Their daring was infectious. When I left home for college in Atlanta in 1961 I ventured to sit near the front of the bus. A white woman (may her fingernails now be dust!) complained to the driver and he ordered me to move. But even as I moved, in confusion and anger and tears, I knew he had not seen the last of me.

My only regret when I left Atlanta for New York two and a half years later was that I would miss the Saturday-morning demonstrations downtown that had become indispensable to education in the Atlanta University Center. But in 1965 I went back to Georgia to work part of the summer in Liberty County, helping to canvass voters and in general looking at the South to see if it was worth claiming. I suppose I decided it *was* worth something, because later, in 1966, I received my first writing fellowship and made eager plans to leave the country for Senegal, West Africa—but I never went. Instead I caught a plane to Mississippi, where I knew no one personally and only one woman by reputation. That summer marked the beginning of a realization that I could never live happily in Africa—or anywhere else—until I could live freely in Mississippi.

I was also intrigued by the thought of what continuity of place could mean to the consciousness of the emerging writer. The Russian writers I admired had one thing in common: a sense of the Russian soul that was directly rooted in the soil that nourished it. In the Russian novel, land itself is a personality. In the South, Faulkner, Welty, and O'Connor could stay in their paternal homes and write because although their neighbors might think them weird—and in Faulkner's case, trashy—they were spared the added burden of not being able to use a public toilet and did not have to go through intense emotional struggle over where to purchase a hamburger. What if Wright had been able to stay in Mississippi? I asked this not because I assumed an alternative direction to his life (since I readily admit that Jackson, Mississippi, with the stilling of gunfire, bombings, and the surge and pound of black street resistance, is about the most boring spot on earth), but because it indicates Wright's lack of choice. And that a man of his talent should lack a choice is offensive. Horribly so.

Black writers had generally left the South as soon as possible. The strain of creation and constant exposure to petty insults and legally encouraged humiliations proved too great. But their departure impoverished those they left behind. I realized this more fully when I arrived in Jackson to live and discovered Margaret Walker, the author of *For My People*, already there, a natural force, creating work under unimaginable pressures and by doing so keeping alive, in the thousands of students who studied under her, not only a sense of art but also the necessity of claiming one's birthright at the very source. I do not know if, in her case, settling in the South was purely a matter of choice or preference, but in the future—for other black artists—it might and *must* be.

And so, ten years after the March on Washington, the question is: How much has the mountain of despair dwindled? What shape and size is the stone of hope?

I know it is annoying this late in the day to hear of more "symbols" of change, but since it is never as late in the day in Mississippi as it is in the rest of the country I will indulge in a few:

One afternoon each week I drive to downtown Jackson to have lunch with my husband at one of Jackson's finest motels. It has a large cool restaurant that overlooks a balalaika-shaped swimming pool, and very good food. My husband, Mel Leventhal, a human-rights lawyer who sues a large number of racist institutions a year (and wins) (and who is now thinking of suing the Jackson Public Library, because a. they refused to issue me a library card in my own name, and b. the librarian snorted like a mule when I asked for a recording of Dr. King's speeches—which the library didn't have), has his own reasons for coming here, and the least of them is that the cooks provide excellent charbroiled cheeseburgers. He remembers "testing" the motel's swimming pool in 1965 (before I knew him)—the angry insults of the whites as blacks waded in, and the tension that hung over everyone as the whites vacated the pool and stood about menacingly. I remember the cold rudeness of the waitresses in the restaurant a year later and recall wondering if "testing" would ever end. (We were by no means alone in this: one of the new black school-board members still lunches at a different downtown restaurant each day—because she has been thrown out of all of them.) It is sometimes hard to eat here because of those memories, but in Mississippi (as in the rest of America) racism is like that local creeping kudzu vine that swallows whole forests and abandoned houses; if you don't keep pulling up the roots it will grow back faster than you can destroy it.

One day we sat relaxing in the restaurant and as we ate watched a young black boy of about fifteen swimming in the pool. Unlike the whites of the past, the ones in the pool did not get out. And the boy, when he was good and tired, crawled up alongside the pool, turned on his back, drew up his knees—in his tight trunks—and just lay there, oblivious to the white faces staring down at him from the restaurant windows above.

"I could *swear* that boy doesn't know what a castration complex is," I said, thinking how the bravest black "testers" in the past had seemed to crouch over themselves when they came out of the water.

We started to laugh, thinking of what a small, insignificant thing this sight should have been. It reminded us of the day we saw a young black man casually strolling down a street near the center of town arm in arm with his high-school sweetheart, a tiny brunette. We had been with a friend of ours who was in no mood to witness such "incorrect" behavior, and who moaned, without a trace of humor: "Oh, why is it that as soon as you do start seeing signs of freedom they're the wrong ones!"

But would one really prefer to turn back the clock? I thought of the time, when I was a child, when black people were not allowed to use the town pool, and the town leaders were too evil to permit the principal of my school to build a pool for blacks *on his own property.* And when my good friend a teenager from the North (visiting his grandmother, naturally) was beaten and thrown into prison because he stooped down on Main Street in broad daylight to fix a white girl's bicycle chain. And now, thinking about these two different boys, I was simply glad that they are still alive, just as I am glad we no longer have to "test" public places to eat, or worry that a hostile waitress will spit in our soup. They will inherit Emmett Till soon enough. For the moment, at least, their childhood is not being destroyed, nor do they feel hemmed in by the memories that plague us.

It is memory, more than anything else, that sours the sweetness of what has been accomplished in the South. What we cannot forget and will never forgive. My husband has said that for her sixth birthday he intends to give our daughter a completely *safe* (racially) Mississippi, and perhaps that is possible. For her. For us, safety is not enough any more.

I thought of this one day when we were debating whether to go for a swim and boat ride in the Ross Barnett Reservoir, this area's largest recreational body of water. But I remembered state troopers descending on us the first time we went swimming there, in 1966 (at night), and the horror they inspired in me; and I also recall too well the man whose name the reservoir bears. Not present fear but memory makes our visits there infrequent. For us, every day of our lives here has been a "test." Only for coming generations will enjoyment of life in Mississippi seem a natural right. But for just this possibility people have given their lives, freely. And continue to give them in the day-by-day, year-by-year hard work that is the expression of their will and of their love.

Blacks are coming home from the North. My brothers and sisters have bought the acres of pines that surround my mother's birthplace. Blacks who thought automatically of leaving the South ten years ago are now staying. There are more and better jobs, caused by more, and more persistent, lawsuits: we have learned for all time that nothing of value is ever given up voluntarily. The racial climate is as good as it is in most areas of the North (one would certainly hesitate before migrating to parts of Michigan or Illinois), and there is still an abundance of fresh air and open spaces—although the frenetic rate of economic growth is likely to ugly up the landscape here as elsewhere. It is no longer a harrowing adventure to drive from Atlanta to Texas; as long as one has money one is not likely to be refused service in "the motels of the highways and the hotels of the cities." The last holdouts are the truck stops, whose owners are being dragged into court at a regular rate. Police brutality—the newest form of lynching—is no longer accepted as a matter of course; black people react violently against it and the city administrations worry about attracting business and their cities' "progressive" image. Black people can and do vote (poll watchers still occasionally being needed), and each election year brings its small harvest of black elected officials. The public schools are among the most integrated in the nation, and of course those signs "White Only" and "Colored" will not hurt my daughter's heart as they bruised mine—because they are gone.

Charles Evers, the famous mayor of Fayette, is thinking—again—of running for the Mississippi governorship. James Meredith is—again—thinking of running for the same position. They make their intentions known widely on local TV. Charles Evers said in June, at the tenth commemoration of his brother Medgar's assassination, "I don't think any more that I will be shot." Considering the baldness of his political aspirations and his tenacity in achieving his goals, this is a telling statement. The fear that shrouded Mississippi in the sixties is largely gone. "If Medgar could see what has happened in Mississippi in the last few years," said his widow, Myrlie Evers, "I think he'd be surprised and pleased."

The mountain of despair *has* dwindled, and the stone of hope has size and shape, and can be fondled by the eyes and by the hand. But freedom has always been an elusive tease, and in the very act of grabbing for it one can become shackled. I think Medgar Evers and Martin Luther King, Jr., would be dismayed by the lack of radicalism in the new black middle class, and discouraged to know that a majority of the black people helped most by the Movement of the sixties has abandoned itself to the pursuit of cars, expensive furniture, large houses, and the finest Scotch. That in fact the very class that owes its new affluence to the Movement now refuses to support the organizations that made its success possible, and has retreated from its concern for black people who are poor. Ralph Abernathy recently resigned as head of the Southern Christian Leadership Conference because of lack of funds and an $80,000.00 debt. This is more than a shame; it is a crime.

A friend of mine from New York who was in SNCC in the sixties came to Mississippi last week to find "spiritual nourishment." "But I found no nourishment," he later wrote, "because Mississippi has changed. It is becoming truly American. What is worse, it is becoming the North."

Unfortunately, this is entirely possible, and causes one to search frantically for an alternative direction. One senses instinctively that the beauty of the Southern landscape will not be saved from the scars of greed, because Southerners are as greedy as anyone else. And news from black movements in the North is far from encouraging. In fact, a movement *backward* from the equalitarian goals of the sixties seems a facet of nationalist groups. In a recent article in *The Black Scholar*, Barbara Sizemore writes:

> The nationalist woman cannot create or initiate. Her main life's goal is to inspire and encourage man and his children. Sisters in this movement must beg for permission to speak and function as servants to men, their masters and leaders, as teachers and nurses. Their position is similar to that of the sisters in the Nation of Islam. When Baraka is the guiding spirit at national conferences only widows and wives of black martyrs such as Malcolm X and Martin Luther King, Jr. and Queen Mother Moore can participate. Other women are excluded.

This is heartbreaking. Not just for black women who have struggled so *equally* against the forces of oppression, but for all those who believe subservience of any kind is death to the spirit. But we are lucky in our precedents; for I know that Sojourner Truth, Harriet Tubman—or Fannie Lou Hamer or Mrs. Winson Hudson—would simply ignore the assumption that "permission to speak" *could be given them*, and would fight on for freedom of all people, tossing "white only" signs and "men only" signs on the same trash heap. For in the end, freedom is a personal and lonely battle, and one faces down fears of today so that those of tomorrow might be engaged. And that is also my experience with the South.

And if I leave Mississippi—as I will one of these days—it will not be for the reasons of the other sons and daughters of my parents. Fear will have no part in my decision, nor will lack of freedom to express my womanly thoughts. It will be because the pervasive football culture bores me, and the proliferating Kentucky Fried Chicken stands appall me, and neon lights have begun to replace the trees. It will be because the sea is too far away and there is not a single mountain here. But most of all, it will be because I have freed myself to go; and it will be My Choice.

A Hostile and Welcoming Workplace

The Rage of a Privileged Class, 1993

◆

ELLIS COSE

The evening had been long and the dinner pleasant, with hosts who were a portrait of success. Their suburban home was spacious and tastefully furnished. Their children—three away in college and two in elementary school—were academically accomplished, popular, and athletic. Both parents held advanced degrees from Harvard and were well respected in their fields. For two whose beginnings had been fairly modest, they had more than ample grounds for contentment, even conceit.

As the husband and I sat nursing after-dinner drinks, his cheery mood progressively turned more pensive, and he began to ruminate on his achievements since earning his MBA. By any normal standard, he had done exceedingly well. Within years after graduation, he had risen to a senior position in a national supermarket chain. Shortly thereafter he had taken a job as manager of a huge independent supermarket and had used that as a base from which to launch his own business. He had thought the business would make him wealthy. Instead, he had gone bankrupt, but in the end had landed on his feet with yet another corporate job.

Still, he was not at all pleased with the way his career was turning out. At Harvard, he had always assumed that he would end up somewhere near the top of the corporate pyramid, as had most of his white peers. Yet shortly after graduation he had begun to sense that they were passing him by, so he had opted for the entrepreneurial route. Now that his business had failed and he was again mired in the upper layers of middle-management, he found it galling that so many of his white classmates had prospered with such seeming ease. A considerable number had become corporate royalty, with seven-figure compensation packages, access to private planes, and other accouterments of status and power about which he could only dream. Despite the good life he had, he felt he deserved—and had been denied—so much more.

In the course of conducting interviews for this book, I heard that complaint again and again—not always with the same degree of bitterness or the same doleful sense that opportunity had permanently slipped away, but always with a sadness born of the conviction that for black superachievers success not only came harder but almost invariably later and at a lower level than for comparably credentialed whites.

Wallace Ford, a graduate of Dartmouth College and Harvard Law School, is characteristic. Comparing himself to whites with similar skills, experience, and education, Ford concluded, "I should probably be doing more than I'm doing now." At the time he was New York City's commissioner for business services and, though only in his early forties, had already held a series of impressive-sounding positions: president of the Harlem Lawyers Association, first vice president at Drexel Burnham Lambert Inc., president of the State of New York Mortgage Agency, and others. Still, by his lights, he had under-achieved, whether because of "bad luck, bad decisions, race," or "a combina-tion of all three," he wasn't sure. But wherever the primary fault lay, he was certain that race had played a role.

"It's always a factor somewhere," said Ford. "It may not always be up front. It may be in the bushes, or lurking in someone's mind, but it's always there." Not that in the circles he frequented people were likely to vent racial animosities freely. "But you look at a situation and say, *I know.* By having gone to places like Dartmouth and Harvard . . . working with the governor, working with the mayor, [working with] people who are moving up . . . you realize that there's no magic." Yes, some of the stars who had briefly flickered near him before shoot-ing high into the sky were brilliant and extremely well educated, but never so bright that he was "blinded from across the table." So he found himself asking: *Why can they do fifty-million-dollar deals with little more than projections on the back of an envelope?* And why were others, blacks who were "offering to give up mom, dad, and all their kids," able to get only crumbs? "You realize that a lot of it has to do with a lot of factors—race, who you know. Certain people are accorded the opportunity to do X. As you go up the ladder, much is made available to a few."

Even the few blacks who get near the top, who become senior executives in Fortune 500 companies, must ask themselves why they are "not next in line to be chairman [or] CEO of the whole thing," Ford surmised. Just as those brainy blacks who went to top law schools and then found themselves woefully un-deremployed must ask themselves: *Why?* "My mind cannot accept the fact that of all the [black] people I went to law school with, only half a dozen of them have achieved partnerships in any of the New York law firms."

In his alumni publications, Ford reads of so many whites succeeding so spectacularly, and he wonders why does it not seem to happen for blacks: "With degrees up and down the line, you get jobs, you get opportunities, but you can't achieve any pinnacle that you might think you'd like to compete for." The re-sult is frustration and confusion. "You usually end up suspecting that race is a factor," but the truth is difficult to know. "People aren't saying, 'You black son of a bitch.' " The only real solution, Ford muses, may be for blacks to start more businesses themselves.

Such pessimism from one blessed with so many advantages may strike many readers as strange. But among those of Ford's race and class, his per-spective is widely shared.

Darwin Davis, senior vice president with the Equitable Life Assurance Society, came along at a time when opportunities such as those enjoyed by Wallace Ford were all but unimaginable for blacks. After getting his bachelor's degree in business administration from the University of Arkansas in 1954, he returned to his hometown of Flint, Michigan, marched into General Motors headquarters, and inquired about a job. He was told politely but firmly that applications for the management training program were not accepted from "colored people." Devastated, Davis went into the army, then got a master's degree in education and went on to teach mathematics in the Detroit school system. Ten years later, when America's cities erupted in riots, corporations began to open their doors to blacks; Davis got a job at Equitable and did well there. Still, for all the barriers thrown in his way, he believes that those now making their way through the corporate labyrinth may be having an even rougher time. "They have even worse problems because they've got MBAs from Harvard. They went to Princeton. They went to all these places and did all these things that you're supposed to do. . . . And *things* are supposed to happen."

Instead of "things" happening, instead of careers taking off, blacks are being stymied. They are not running into a glass ceiling, says Davis, but into one made of cement and steel. So many young people of his son's generation have about them an "air of frustration" and are surrounded by a wall of gloom "that's just as high now as it was thirty years ago."

Davis's observations are similar to those of management consultant Edward Jones, whose surveys tapped into the frustration raging among black graduates of the nation's top business schools—apparently not a phenomenon that the schools themselves have chosen to explore. Calls to the public relations departments of several of them, including the business schools at Harvard, Stanford, the University of Chicago, and Northwestern, elicited a curious sense of incuriosity about how their minority graduates were faring in the outside world. No one had any idea, I was told again and again, of how well black business graduates were doing relative to whites. But the research being done in the area, carried out largely by black scholars, tends to confirm the perceptions of Ford, Davis, and Jones.

Several years ago, Edward Irons and Gilbert Moore, professors of finance and economics, respectively, conducted a pioneering study of black professionals in banking. The scholars interviewed 125 black bankers in ten different states, distributed one thousand questionnaires (of which nearly one-third were completed and returned) to black bankers in twenty-two states, and reviewed sixteen years' worth of relevant Equal Employment Opportunity Commission statistics. The result was *Black Managers: The Case of the Banking Industry*, published in 1985. Despite the authors' dry prose, their findings were compelling, painting a poignant and depressing picture of the plight of blacks in banking.

Like every other researcher I know of who has asked any large number of black professionals how they are faring, Irons and Moore found a cornucopia of discontent. Interviewees repeatedly complained of being left out of the informal communications network, of "not being in on things." Few reported having "mentors" or anyone high within their organizations who took a supportive interest in their careers. By and large, they judged themselves less likely to be promoted than their white peers and felt they had to expend an inordinate amount of effort trying to make whites "comfortable" with them. They admitted to being under great stress, and many (particularly among the black men in the sample) seemed to be fleeing the field—which led the authors to observe that "black males who have the same high self-image . . . and aggressive personality as white males must either 'walk softly' or face the prospect of being driven out of the industry, out of frustration." Irons and Moore, who had been prepared to find some measure of unhappiness, expressed shock at the magnitude and pervasiveness of the problems they uncovered.

Phyllis Wallace, professor emeritus at Sloan School of Management at the Massachusetts Institute of Technology, reported equally dismal results after systematically examining the experiences of her former students. For five years (from 1980 through 1984), she tracked recent Sloan graduates, trying to compare the progress of blacks and whites who were "similar . . . in every way." She found that virtually from the outset the blacks began to fall behind the whites in terms of income and status in their companies. In part that had to do with the professions they entered. Numerous whites, for instance, went into financial services and management consulting—fields that tended to pay young people extremely well and to promote rapidly during the years of her study. Yet "not a single one of our black students went into the management consulting industry," perhaps, she speculates, because those companies sought employees they thought had potential to attract big-spending clients. Blacks, who "were not seen as able to bring in million-dollar contracts," generally gravitated to Fortune 500 firms.

Once there, said Wallace, they tended to get "stuck in a staff job," and they progressed significantly more slowly than whites. "It was just more difficult for them to be promoted," she observed. "They had to demonstrate over and over again that they were worthy of promotion." Wallace was so concerned by the discrepancies in mobility that she kept in touch with many of the black graduates beyond the period of her research. Eventually, after six or seven years, she found that some received a "double promotion." After initially being held back, they were "finally given the stamp of approval." The result, said Wallace, if not exactly parity with their white classmates, was at least a partial closing of the gap.

Ella Bell, a visiting associate professor at Sloan who has also taught at Yale's school of organization and management, agrees with many of Wallace's findings, but she believes that more recent graduates (unlike those studied by Wallace) have learned to avoid the sinkhole of corporate staff jobs. "The ones that I know of are in bottom-line positions. They are not going into staff positions. . . . They are savvy enough to know you do not do that." What they have not learned, however, is how to stay on the same track as similarly credentialed whites.

"Once they get into these companies, they're astounded," said Bell, "because they feel, 'I went to Yale. I went to Harvard, Sloan, or Stanford. Somehow that's supposed to polish the floor for me so I can just slide on through.' And that does not happen, for a lot of different reasons—race being a factor in that. What usually happens is that blacks will get in with these credentials. They'll make it one or two years, and then all of a sudden they start getting this real fuzzy kind of feedback—what I call static feedback—from their supervisors. Somehow they're 'not good team players.' They're 'too outspoken, too aggressive.' Another favorite one is that they 'just don't know how to develop people.' All of this is subjective, nothing that you can fix. . . . And when you ask for examples it gets even flimsier."

As a result, blacks find that "they're not where they want to be. . . . They knew—some of them knew—it was going to be tough." But they also assumed that they would be okay. "Then reality sets in, that they're not going to be okay. They're not getting the positions. They're not getting what was promised . . . a chance to really do some cutting-edge work. So there's a lot of disappointment, and a lot of turnover. . . . A lot of my students, particularly from Yale, [change jobs] within the first two years. One was a brilliant guy from Ghana. He's now gone back to Ghana. . . . I know two others who are looking for jobs right now. It has not turned out the way they thought it would be."

Bell acknowledges that some do "cross over and make it," but they seem to be exceptions to the general rule. And though she believes that white uneasiness with blacks may play some role in black disappointments, the reality is "more complicated." Once upon a time, she recalls, many whites seemed painfully uncomfortable with blacks, "and there are still signs of that. But I've spoken to managers, white males, who are very high up . . . and they talk about having their black colleagues to their homes, to Christmas parties. . . . It's not comfort that's the issue." The issue, as she sees it, is whether those managers are able to see blacks as capable of carrying the company forward, of representing to the company's myriad constituencies the same things white senior executives would represent.

Black women, she believes, face especially daunting challenges, for even as white men are wondering, "Can I really mentor a black female?" black female managers are trying to deflect any suggestion that they may be sleeping with the white boss. For the most part, the women's efforts—at least in that area— seem to be successful. "When I go into companies," said Bell, "I will often hear that white women worked their way up sexually. . . . Very rarely do I hear that about black women." Not that she presumes it to be true when said of white women, but with black women it's rarely even suggested as a possibility: "That's not one of the mythologies you hear."

Sharon Collins, a sociologist with the University of Illinois in Chicago, is no more upbeat than Bell and the others. Collins's professional interest in black managers began in 1980, following Ronald Reagan's election as president, when she noticed a new anxiety among many black professionals she knew. Blacks who had been doing nicely, "who were driving Mercedes and going to Oak Street and buying suits, . . . were scared—simply because of this change in political administrations." The reason, she concluded after reflection and research, was that for blacks, middle-class status was largely a "politically dependent condition." A disproportionate number of blacks worked for the government, often in "black-related" agencies. Others owed their jobs to "legislation that forced employers to hire blacks." Still others were in positions that "depended on money being funneled from the government into the private sector in all sorts of ways," from job-training programs to minority set asides. If the government had not been looming in the background, "these people would not have been hired for the most part." And with Reagan coming into power, many understandably worried that they would soon lose their tenuous grip on middle-class status.

A few years later (in 1986 and 1987), Collins interviewed seventy-six black senior executives with Fortune 500 companies. She intentionally picked those near the top of the corporate pyramid to see whether blacks at that rarefied level also feared losing their status, and whether they had managed to gain recognition for reasons unrelated to race. "So, essentially, I went to people who actually looked like their white counterparts from all external criteria," said Collins. They had good educations, impressive titles, and huge salaries. But they were also largely pigeonholed by race she discovered. Two-thirds of them had progressed through what she defined as race-related jobs (meaning positions in such areas as affirmative action, community relations, and minority affairs), and half of that number were still in those jobs—even though their titles, in many instances, gave little indication of that.

"There was a constant issue in their careers," said Collins. They were either trying to avoid "black" jobs or trying to get out of them or being penalized for being in them—"because those jobs are going nowhere," and many of those seemingly successful people "won't go one step further than they are now." Indeed, when she returned to interview the executives in 1992, she found that a number had left their companies, a circumstance she attributed largely to the fact that with corporate restructuring proceeding apace, many in minority-related fields were seen as expendable and were let go.

Even among those who were not trapped in race work, Collins found a large measure of discontent. "Very few of them felt really satisfied," she said. "These are ambitious guys, very ambitious, and their eyes are on the prize," yet many were concluding that they were simply not regarded in the same way as their white peers.

Collins recalled one manager who made an especially strong impression on her. "If ever there was a company man, this man is it," she said. He "can hardly say anything without putting it in terms of what's good for the company." Through a long and distinguished career, he had endeavored to earn that company's unconditional respect, clearing every hurdle placed in his path and making every sacrifice required. And he had positioned himself, finally, to reap the rewards of his exertions. But now, despite all his labors, people were passing him by as they moved into jobs he thought he should have. Like many blacks in the same situation, he was having a hard time sorting out whether and to what extent his race was holding him back, but he had reluctantly admitted that racial discrimination was the only explanation that made sense to him.

What did he really want? wondered Collins. "Is it to be seen as if he is white? Or for race not to matter?" If so, "think of how much a black person has to sell of himself to try to get race not to matter. . . . You have to ignore the insults. You have to ignore the natural loyalties. You have to ignore your past. In a sense, you have to just about deny yourself." Collins kept thinking about his pain, she added, and about the price of his denial. "He knows the final threshold is there, and he's losing hope that he can cross it."

Results of a 1991 survey by the Executive Leadership Council were somewhat more upbeat than the bleak portrait painted by Collins and her fellow academics. The council, a Washington-based organization of black executives (most vice presidents or higher at Fortune 500 companies), polled fifty of its fifty-five members and found a bare majority—52 percent—agreeing that their companies created a "comfortable and supportive work environment for African Americans." But even members of this relatively contented group were far from sanguine. Asked to identify the "major restraining force" on their careers, most responded "racism."

"Most executives agreed that the racism they face is covert, elusive, and heavily masked," wrote Jeffalyn Johnson, who analyzed the data for ELC. The survey also found that the executives felt at particular risk of having their careers derailed or of being labeled "troublemakers" if they aggressively promoted the hiring of women and minorities. Johnson concluded that in order to rise, "African-American executives might have to make difficult value decisions between their 'black identity' and orientation and corporate acculturation."

Francine Soliunas, legal counsel for Illinois Bell, has seen black executives cut themselves off from other blacks in their quest to be more acceptable to management. Yet "even those among us who have achieved the ultimate power . . . [are] at some point . . . let know, in some way, shape, or form, that they are [considered] 'nigger[s].' " The message, she says, is transmitted in any number of ways. People quietly make you aware at meetings that they doubt you know what you're talking about. Executives totally outside your area of expertise endeavor to prove that they are more expert than you. The message, as she sees it, is unmistakable, and translates as: "You think you have power? You don't really have power, because I can take away that power anytime I want." As a consequence, even those blacks who are not initially inclined to align themselves with other blacks often end up doing so: "They get religion, if you will. They become part of the networking effort. They speak out more. They are less concerned about the impact in terms of it affecting their positions because their positions have already been affected."

Despite the harshness of her observations, Soliunas is not dissatisfied with her own life. As counsel, her rank is equal to assistant vice president. "I'm comfortable with my level of achievement and my rate of achievement in corporate America," she says. "I've had three promotions in the twelve years I've been here. That's two more than the average lawyer." Nonetheless, she believes that corporate America has violated a morally binding contract, "the contract being if you work, study hard, and excel in your education, and if you work hard and excel on your job, you will have the opportunities—even if you're only that very small fraction that they allow to slip through the gates. I think even those of us who are that small fraction . . . have to recognize that we still confront major, major barriers, even after we've slipped through."

For Soliunas to complain of racism in corporate America even as she expresses satisfaction with her personal achievements is not as contradictory as it may seem. Like other black executives I interviewed, she does not judge her progress in relation to an ideal (and color-blind) standard but in relation to other opportunities in the corporate world. And by that measure she feels she is doing well, particularly in a profession dominated by white males to a greater extent than much of the corporate world.

"Typically corporate lawyers . . . are the white-haired, three-piece black-pin-striped-suit gentlemen," says Soliunas. "They are not little chubby black women who have white-haired, three-piece-suit-wearing gentlemen as their clients. And so, on any number of occasions in working for Illinois Bell, I've walked into court with my clients and the judge immediately starts directing his questions to my clients on the assumption that they're the lawyer and I'm the client."

Gender, race, and raiment incongruities notwithstanding, Soliunas is confident that many of her white colleagues recognize her talents and give her credit for her accomplishments. But she also senses from some of them an attitude of " 'How dare you to put yourself on the same plane with me! How dare you to challenge me! How dare you to think that you have the option to question my power and my authority!' And I think it's very subtle . . . It's communicated . . . when there's a meeting and there are discussions going on and you express a dissenting opinion. Or you challenge someone who is deemed to be the authority on the issue. . . . I see a very different reaction from my challenging them than I've seen with white females. . . . I don't see it with a lot of white men. It's not a pervasive attitude. But it is an attitude and it is present in white males of power who can influence your career."

Soliunas, who came to Illinois Bell after working as a litigator in county, state, and federal government, acknowledges that her career in the private sector did not get off to the most auspicious start. Before her first promotion, two white males were moved up. A white female and two other white males advanced along with her. All the males were promoted to higher positions, all had been at the company for less time than she, and all had less experience as lawyers. She is not certain that race accounts for her slower start. A number of plausible reasons could be offered, including the fact that at the time her area of specialization was not sufficiently broad. But "no one took me by the hand and said, 'You know, you've got to move out of labor now if you want to move into a [higher] position.' "

Soliunas finds fulfillment not only in having risen in the company, but in helping others. "My satisfaction comes from knowing that I have positioned myself in a way that allows me to have a tremendous amount of power in terms of being able to impact policy in a number of ways, but specifically with respect to minorities in the corporation. . . . If there is a decision to terminate, a decision that may negatively impact a minority or a female, a decision that has to do with money, particularly compensation that may have some negative impacts, I'm the one that they talk to." But getting there wasn't easy, and "when it happened for me, it happened very late in the game."

Basil Paterson, the former deputy mayor of New York, makes a similar point more poignantly. "Every day I realize that I'm further ahead than I ever thought I would be in my life," yet "by any standard that is uniquely American, I'm not successful. It's too late for me to get rich because I spent too much time preparing for what I've got. . . . Most of us are ten years behind what we should have been. We couldn't get credentials until we were older than other folks." And he is not at all sure that the next generation will have it much better. He recently received a résumé from a black graduate of a prestigious law school who claimed she wanted experience in international commerce. "She can't get international commerce working for me," Paterson pointed out, speculating that she had come to him because she saw few opportunities elsewhere.

Certainly, in law—as in other professions—when blacks are asked how they are doing, they consistently say they are not doing nearly as well as whites tend to assume. In 1992, when the Association of the Bar of the City of New York surveyed minority associates at the city's major law firms, the pollsters found that blacks in particular felt isolated and neglected.

Largely as a result of the efforts of Conrad Harper, president of the association, 169 law firms and corporate law departments had signed a "Statement of Goals" the previous year pledging to improve retention and promotion rates for nonwhites and calling for a 10 percent minority hiring rate between 1992 and 1997. The 1992 survey, conducted by a subcommittee of the Committee to Enhance Professional Opportunities for Minorities charged with implementing that agreement, was far too small to yield firm generalizations, including only twenty-three blacks, twenty-one Asian-Americans and Pacific Islanders, nine Hispanics, three "others," and three who did not give their race. Nevertheless, its findings were consistent with the stories I heard in my own research, and with virtually every survey I have seen that has tried to assess the feelings of black professionals. And the picture it painted was sobering.

Sixty-one percent of blacks felt their work experiences were "clearly different from [those of] nonminority lawyers" at their firms. Only 9.5 percent of Asians/Pacific Islanders and none of the Hispanics felt that way. Thirty percent of the blacks said they were "judged differently from nonminority lawyers," with another 30 percent unsure. Only 20 percent unequivocally said they were judged in the same way compared to 89 percent of the Hispanics and 76 percent of the Asians/Pacific Islanders. Sixty-one percent of blacks thought their firms had a poor "commitment to the retention of minority lawyers," as did 67 percent of Hispanics and 29 percent of Asians/Pacific Islanders.

In a statement released with the survey, Harper said: "The implication of this modest, not scientific yet persuasive survey, augmented by the undeniable lack of advancement of African-American lawyers to the partnership level, is that such lawyers perceive far more race-related barriers to their professional development than do other minority lawyers. . . . To communicate openly across cultures requires a comfort level that does not presently seem to exist in law firms."

That observation was driven home by an accompanying bar association report, which stated, "Most law firms, no doubt, believe that they have created an environment in which the perceptions described in the survey would be unwarranted. However, the fact that these perceptions may come as a surprise is explained by some of the comments made in follow-up interviews. . . . A third generation African-American lawyer described himself as not feeling 'entitled to complain' because he was 'lucky to be there.' "

Harper, the first African American elected to head the association, was made a partner in Simpson Thacher & Barlett in 1974. At the time, there were only two other black partners in major New York law firms. Over the years, the number has climbed to more than thirty. And through that entire period, Harper said, he had often heard black associates complain of being treated "differently." He and the handful of other black partners saw the bar association's foray into survey research as part of a process of making the profession "more hospitable to blacks and other minorities," and of underlining the point that simply hiring black associates was not the same as putting them on an equal footing with whites.

That Harper, Francine Soliunas, Sharon Collins, and the others quoted above should find so much evidence of corporate inhospitality to blacks may be a matter of skewed perceptions, or of what Senator Moynihan insists is a tendency of middle-class blacks to wallow in a "legacy of grievance . . . inappropriate to their condition." Another possibility is that the grievances are real: that corporate America, in ways more persistent and pervasive than most whites realize, is playing a cruel trick on those who thought they could escape the curse of discrimination simply by adhering to the rules; that what the would-be trailblazers discover is that following the rules carries few guarantees—for those of any race; that while a good education, hard work, and high performance can increase the odds of success, a host of other factors, having nothing to do with ability or merit, ultimately dictates how high one can rise; and that those other factors often differ as a function of race.

Part of the problem, as management consultant Edward Jones pointed out, is that though Americans constantly "talk about merit . . . we can't even define what it is." Outside of sports and certain technical specialties, merit tends to be defined subjectively, primarily by attaching complimentary labels to those who are thought to be meritorious: people who are "fast starters," who "have potential," who show style or demonstrate leadership or otherwise have the mystical "right stuff" that will take them to the top. Once they have risen, as predicted, it is assumed they did so on merit—a reassuring if circular assumption. But what it fails to take into account is the real possibility that merit, objectively defined, has relatively little to do with who gets ahead.

A 1984 study by sociologist James Rosenbaum (published as *Career Mobility in a Corporate Hierarchy*) took a hard look at career advancement in one large company. Rosenbaum, who had full access to personnel records, tracked one cohort's progress through the corporation over a thirteen-year period. In the end, he had processed some 20 million discrete pieces of data and had concluded that careers developed very differently—and along much narrower tracks—than generations of management had assumed.

Whereas management (and employees) believed that good work could be rewarded at any stage of a career, Rosenbaum found that early job assignments and early promotions had an enduring influence "independent of the most salient individual attributes." In other words, those who were designated as "fast starters" did significantly better throughout their careers than others—irrespective of actual ability or performance. He also discovered that people tended to be categorized very quickly, often before they were aware of it. "Even employees who were on the fast track learned about it gradually. . . . They reported noticing the extra attention they were receiving, they began to infer that they were getting special treatment, and later they realized that they were advancing more quickly than their peers."

This process, noted Rosenbaum, was in important respects just the opposite of the meritocracy many assumed to be operating. For if there is to be true equality of opportunity within a corporation, "employees must know the rules of the game, they must start at similar positions, and they must be allowed to begin the tournament when they are ready to compete." His findings, he said, "raise doubts about each of these points." He added that a system that tracked employees so early in the process was "particularly weak at discovering errors of exclusion. It does not have any way to bring former losers back into the competition for top positions." The likelihood of worthy employees being excluded was compounded, he observed, in "sponsored" programs, in which management selects workers presumed to have high potential and moves their careers along. Yet many large corporations, and certainly most major law firms, operate in precisely this way.

Conrad Harper, for instance, recalls that early in his career he did not realize that he was being groomed for success until one of his firm's eminences pulled him aside and told him he would be working very closely with a certain senior partner. "There is no such thing as a self-made partner in a major law firm," Harper says. "One cannot advance in places like this without a godfather." But as Rosenbaum found, a system based on mentorship, or on early tracking of future corporate stars, "carries the risk that the term 'high-potential people' does not so much describe a type of person as it describes a predefined role to which some individuals will be assigned regardless of their personal qualities."

Some of Rosenbaum's research was foreshadowed by sociologist Robert Merton, who explained the concept of the "self-fulfilling prophecy" in a famous article in *The Antioch Review* in 1948. His inspiration came from W. I. Thomas's observation that "if men define situations as real, they are real in their consequence." A series of studies in the 1960s and 1970s explored the concept in the classroom and found, at least in some instances, that student performance seemed to be largely shaped by teacher expectations. According to Ray Rist, who investigated a predominantly black school in St. Louis, "If the teacher expects high performance, she receives it, and vice versa." He found that once students were tracked into ability groups—largely on the basis of appearance and dress—there was virtually no movement either up or down.

Rosenbaum's study, an analysis of general career mobility, was radically different from Rist's, but he too found that once people were put into tracks, they tended to stay in them. And while his research was not designed to look specifically at race, his findings have clear racial implications. If in fact blacks tend to be tracked into certain areas, and if in fact blacks are therefore destined to progress more slowly than whites, and if in fact the real reasons for advancement have less to do with ability than with attributes one is *a priori* assumed to possess, then it is only to be expected, given certain widespread racial assumption in America, that very few blacks, however accomplished, manage to get near the top of the corporate hierarchy.

Furthermore, if in fact many whites get ahead in large part because they are beneficiaries of a congenial stereotype (which presupposes that executives and corporate lawyers are white), of early high-profile job assignments (which whites are more likely to get), of mentors (whom whites have an easier time acquiring), and of wide latitude to fail (but also to triumph), then it should not be much of a mystery why even those blacks who do get into corporate management sometimes feel so bitter.

In career development, as Rosenbaum notes, the loss of even a few years can be critical. And yet, if the testimony of those I interviewed is to be believed, blacks almost automatically lose the years it typically takes to make a corporation comfortable with them. By the time the corporation finally does become comfortable and acknowledges abilities, the fast trackers (who are almost always white) have already moved on—so that even the most talented blacks often end up in slower lanes. When someone like Basil Paterson says, "It's too late for me," he is not speaking for himself alone, but for thousands upon thousands of other blacks who wonder how much better they would be doing in a fairer world.

If the phenomenon of the false meritocracy were a thing of the past, Moynihan's dismissal of black middle-class discontent would make a great deal of sense. But the little evidence that exists on blacks with fast-track credentials indicates that for whatever reason, they generally are not getting on the track, certainly in nothing approaching the proportions of their white peers. And given all the stories of disappointed young achievers who walk away from corporations in disgust, like Professor Bell's black MBAs, it seems premature, at the very least, to pronounce their problems little more than figments of their collective imagination.

This is not to say that blacks are altogether faultless. As Illinois Bell's Francine Soliunas put it, "I don't think it is all corporate America's making. I think we have had opportunities to perhaps build stepping stones to that [glass] ceiling to break through and we've choked . . . by not learning what it is that we have to do in order to break though, and not being willing to do it because of some fear, real or imagined, that we will compromise our blackness or our femininity, or whatever else it is." Nor am I arguing that corporations or major law firms are openly hostile to blacks. Naked hatred and open hostility are— thank God—largely relics of a wretched past. Still, many institutions and the individuals within them have trouble seeing blacks in the same light in which they customarily see whites.

Ross Perot demonstrated that in 1992 when he addressed the national convention of the NAACP and persisted in referring to blacks as "you people," dwelling on anecdotes of his parents' personal kindnesses to black hobos and blue-collar employees. No one accused Perot of being a racist—if a racist is defined as one who hates another racial group. What he was charged with was unwitting condescension, with assuming that simply because his audience was black, it would relate to stories about black bums—which implied that in Perot's mind the most important bond between members of the audience was an interest in the benevolence of whites towards blacks. It is hardly conceivable, for instance, that he would have addressed middle-class whites as "you people" or regaled them with stories of his father's generous treatment of tramps, whatever their color.

Corporate America is full of people like Perot, people who, without intending to create racial hurdles or hostility, manage to create a fair amount of both. That they cannot see what they have done is due partly to the fact that they meant no harm and partly to a disinclination to examine whether the assumptions they hold dear are in accord with reality.

In December of 1992, in an elegy for the demise of the marriage of the Prince and Princess of Wales, the *New York Times* editorialized, "On July 29, 1981, millions of Americans rose at dawn to watch a young woman who actually looked like a princess (golden hair, blue eyes, and a whopper of a tiara) marry a prince who didn't exactly look like one (he's no Tom Cruise). But what the heck. The music was swell, St. Paul's Cathedral never looked better and, all in all, it was the kind of wedding that even money can't buy." No one with any sense would argue that running a major American corporation is equivalent to being the Prince of Wales, but senior corporate executives and senior partners in law firms are also expected to conform to a certain image. And though their positions may not require golden hair and blue eyes, they do require the ability to look like—and be accepted as—the ultimate authority. To many Americans that image still seems fundamentally incongruous with kinky hair and black skin.

State Secrets

The New Yorker, May 29, 1995

◆

CALVIN TRILLIN

When it comes to the operations of the Mississippi State Sovereignty Commission, I have always been partial to the smaller stories. Consider, for example, the Grenada, Mississippi, baby inspection. In the early sixties, a white woman in Grenada, a county seat in the north-central part of the state, gave birth to an out-of-wedlock baby, and there were rumors around town that the baby had been fathered by a black man. The State Sovereignty Commission had been established by the legislature in 1956, in the days when the white South was erecting its defenses against the decision of the United States Supreme Court, in *Brown v. Board of Education*, that segregation in public education is unconstitutional. The Commission was charged to "do and perform any and all acts and things deemed necessary and proper to protect the sovereignty of the State of Mississippi, and her sister states, from encroachment thereon by the federal government." Being an agency that always interpreted that mission broadly, it dispatched one of its investigators, Tom Scarbrough, to see if Grenada had truly been the scene of what Southern politicians of that era tended to call the mongrelization of the races.

After interviewing a number of Grenada residents, Scarbrough accompanied the local sheriff for an inspection of the baby under suspicion. It's easy to envision those two officials of the State of Mississippi trying to edge in close to the crib—large men, as I imagine them, with the sheriff wearing a pistol and further burdened, perhaps, by what people in regular contact with the Southern law-enforcement community come to think of as a sheriff's belly. In Scarbrough's report, which ran four or five thousand words, he wrote, "I was looking at the child's fingernails and the end of its fingers very closely." From this I assume that he believed African ancestry could be detected by the presence of distinctive half-moons at the cuticles—a theory that was an article of faith in my grade school in Missouri, during a period when I was also persuaded for a while that Japanese people had yellow blood. The baby's fingernails might have been too small for a conclusive half-moon search. Scarbrough said in his report, "We both agreed we were not qualified to say it was a part Negro child, but we could say it was not 100 percent Caucasian." Perhaps sensing this indecision, the mother parried shrewdly: the baby's father, she said, was Italian.

Even as a connoisseur of the smaller stories, I acknowledge that the big stories do carry a certain impact. Officially, the files of the State Sovereignty Commission remain sealed until a lawsuit to open them, which began in federal district court in 1977, is finally resolved. But the activity surrounding the suit has already dislodged formerly secret information that has resulted in front-page headlines about stories that made front-page headlines the first time around. It is now known, for instance, that an early black applicant to the University of Southern Mississippi who was convicted of several crimes and thrown into prison was framed; an alternative plan was to murder him. It is known that during the 1964 trial of Byron De La Beckwith for the murder of Medgar Evers the Sovereignty Commission investigated potential jurors for the defense and furnished such capsule biographies as "He is a contractor and believed to be Jewish." It is known that the Sovereignty Commission got weekly reports from paid spies within the Council of Federated Organizations (COFO), the umbrella organization of the 1964 voter-registration effort known as the Mississippi Summer Project, and that it distributed license-plate numbers of COFO cars, including the one that Michael Schwerner and James Chaney and Andrew Goodman had been riding in before they were murdered, in Neshoba County, that summer.

In 1990, such stories, based on State Sovereignty Commission documents, ran for eight pages one day in the Jackson *Clarion-Ledger,* which reported not only that a black newspaper editor had been on the Commission's payroll—one of his duties was to run a story, furnished by the Sovereignty Commission, that linked Martin Luther King, Jr., to the Communist Party—but that the *Clarion-Ledger* itself had routinely killed stories that the Sovereignty Commission wanted killed and run stories that the Sovereignty Commission wanted run. According to a memo quoted in the *Clarion-Ledger* in 1990 by Jerry Mitchell, the reporter who revealed many of the Sovereignty Commission documents, the Commission had even prevailed on the Jackson newspapers to drop the honorific "Rev." from the names of ministers who were civil-rights activists: "Our friends of the press could drop their titles from news articles and if queried they could say they do not consider them as ministers 'as how can a man profess to serve God when he is actually serving atheistic Communism?' "

For me, practically any document in the secret files of the State Sovereignty Commission has a certain resonance: at the beginning of the sixties, I was in and out of Mississippi, originally as a reporter for the Southern bureau of *Time.* I can now place the source, say, of a front-page Jackson *Daily News* item that I've kept all these years—an item that begins, under a four-column headline, "Mississippi authorities have learned that the apparently endless 'freedom' rides into Mississippi and the south were planned in Havana, Cuba, last winter by officials of the Soviet Union." Reading about Tom Scarbrough's fingernail inspection brings back into focus what I came to think of during my time in the South as a regional obsession with yard-sale anthropology. Any number of white people explained to me, for instance, that the brains of black people were capable of processing specific statements but not general or abstract statements. (My response was always "Give me an example.")

But, as I go through the State Sovereignty Commission material now available, what I still find most interesting is how small a deviation from the Mississippi way of life was required to attract the attention of Scarbrough or one of his colleagues—a pastor's attendance at an interracial meeting or a professor's choice of a suspect textbook or a student's attendance at the wrong concert. That was the aspect of the Commission that had most fascinated me from the start—from the time, in 1961, when I spent a few days in the state to look into revelations that the Sovereignty Commission had tried to smear a senior at the

University of Mississippi named Billy Barton, who was running for the editor-
ship of the Ole Miss newspaper. The rumors that had been spread about Billy
Barton accused him of, among other things, being a protégé of Ralph McGill—
an accusation that Barton, of course, vehemently denied. He said he had never
met Ralph McGill, the Atlanta newspaperman who was then widely considered
by people outside the South to be the region's most distinguished journalist;
and he voluntarily took a lie-detector test to confirm that statement.

Because Barton's file became public and could easily be shown to be nonsense, the case provoked some weekly newspaper editors in Mississippi into crit-
icizing the Commission as a sort of cornpone Gestapo that had got out of hand.
But in 1961 the Mississippi State Sovereignty Commission had no reason to
fear grumbling from a few county weeklies. It acknowledged, in a speech given
around the state, that it kept a file on "persons whose utterances or actions indicate they should be watched with suspicion on future racial attitudes." It
openly contributed five thousand dollars of taxpayers' money every month to
the Citizens Council—sometimes referred to as the uptown Klan—which
claimed a membership of ninety thousand and was considered the most influential political force in the state. Several members of the Citizens Council's executive committee also sat on the Sovereignty Commission, and some
observers considered the Commission to be basically a device for providing the
Citizens Council with the resources and legitimacy of the state. Except for the
smattering of editorials provoked by the Billy Barton case, there was little significant opposition to any of this. Partly through the economic intimidation
that was the specialty of the Citizens Council, most of Mississippi's small store
of moderate and liberal whites had been silenced or driven from the state.

One of those who remained, an Ole Miss history professor named James W.
Silver, wrote in the early sixties that "Mississippi is the way it is not because of
its views on the Negro—here it is simply 'the South exaggerated'—but because
of its closed society, its refusal to allow freedom of inquiry or to tolerate 'error
of opinion.' " (Even before those words were printed in an influential book by
Silver called *Mississippi: The Closed Society,* the director of the State Sovereignty
Commission had written to the chairman of the university's board of trustees
outlining what a Commission report described as "various reasons why Dr.
James Silver could be terminated from his position at the University of Mississippi without any risk of losing the University's accreditation.") Being guilty of
an error of opinion did not require a drastic deviation from the Mississippi
mainstream: at the time, the Citizens Council's definition of subversive organizations was broad enough to include both the Methodist Church and the
United States Air Force. In other Southern states, agencies similar to the State
Sovereignty Commission tended to be modest operations that left it to law-
enforcement agencies to keep extensive files on people suspected of being potential "race mixers." The Mississippi State Sovereignty Commission, which

had no law-enforcement duties, estimated that its files included information on ten thousand people. Mississippi was the only place where a state agency saw its duty as coördinating all aspects of the effort to maintain white supremacy, including propaganda films, thought control, and baby inspection. A completely closed society in one out of fifty states was not possible, of course, but any effort in that direction had to include the attention to minutiae which I found so fascinating.

After I began going to Mississippi, there were times when I had to remind myself that I was in one of the fifty states. In those days, a reporter from a magazine published in New York could feel like a visitor to a foreign land almost anywhere in the Deep South. White people who weren't simply hostile would often explain certain fundamental truths in the tone that a citizen of some exotic but long-established country might use to enlighten a slightly dim American tourist on rudimentary history: Northerners didn't understand Negroes the way Southerners did; local Negroes were perfectly content; race trouble was caused by outside agitators, who were mostly Communists. In almost any Southern state, there were leaders who made daily pronouncements that seemed foreign to what American children were supposedly taught in school (even the schools I went to in Missouri, which were segregated by law at the time) about equality and opportunity in the Land of the Free. But only Mississippi seemed to have come close to shutting out the rest of the country.

In Mississippi in 1961, there didn't seem to be any other side; it was as if a secret agreement had been made to insist that day be called night, and the entire white population of the state had been in on it. Everything appeared to be under control. The segregation of the races was complete. Voting was essentially a privilege limited to white people. Until a sit-in at the Jackson public library by students from Tougaloo, a black college on the outskirts of town, the demonstrations then sweeping other Southern cities were not seen in Jackson. Those who ran the state operated as if the Mississippi way of life were invulnerable. The State Sovereignty Commission was actually sending various prominent Mississippians to Northern service-club luncheons to talk about the tranquillity of Mississippi's race relations. The premise was not that the movement had not yet arrived in Mississippi but that it would never arrive.

In Alabama, the Freedom Riders, who came through a couple of months after the Billy Barton controversy, were attacked in Anniston and Birmingham and Montgomery; in Mississippi, residents lined the road as the bus passed, like an army under orders to stand down, and the Freedom Riders were politely arrested in the Jackson bus station for breach of peace. The next day, the governor, Ross Barnett, welcomed the reporters who were covering the Freedom Ride, and the mayor of Jackson gave each one an honorary Jackson police badge. I still have mine. (There were three black reporters on the bus, and they had not been arrested. "Professional courtesy," the police chief explained.) Among reporters in the South, Alabama was considered more dangerous then, but Mississippi, where strangers might say hello on the street and ask you how you were enjoying your visit, was somehow more ominous. Sometimes after working in Mississippi for a few days I'd drive to Memphis to write my copy and send it out. When I called my office, in Atlanta, I'd say, "I've slipped over the border."

By 1964, when Paul B. Johnson, Jr., became governor, the Mississippi monolith was beginning to show cracks. It had taken some serious hits, like the desegregation of Ole Miss, and there was enough activity by the race mixers to make Johnson's term among the busiest four years in the State Sovereignty Commission's history. Documents and reports and correspondence that the Commission routinely sent to Governor Johnson's office constitute the largest collection of Commission papers now accessible to the public. They were among the papers that the Johnson family donated to the University of Southern Mississippi, in Hattiesburg, and they were made accessible in 1989 through a state court order obtained by the *Clarion-Ledger.* The picture that emerges from the Paul Johnson papers is of a Sovereignty Commission staff, which was never very large, dashing around the state in an effort to spy on a voter-registration drive here and put an end to a boycott there. Still, as I went through the files in the W. D. McCain Library and Archives of U.S.M. one day not long ago, I found that the Commission always seemed to have time for missions of the baby-inspection variety. In 1965, for instance, Governor Johnson received a letter, written in longhand, from a couple in Biloxi. "Dear Governor Johnson," it began. "We regret to say that for the first time in our lives we need your help very badly. We are native Mississippians and are presently living in Biloxi. Our only daughter is a freshman at the University of Southern Miss. She has never before caused us any worry. However, she is in love with a Biloxi boy who looks and is said to be part Negro. . . ."

"Your recent letter and your situation fills me with great apprehension," the Governor wrote back at once. "I am having this matter investigated to the fullest." Tom Scarbrough had already been dispatched to the Gulf Coast to investigate the lineage of the suitor—presumably under orders to exercise a level of discretion that would have made a close inspection of fingernails out of the question. In a three-thousand-word report Scarbrough concluded that the young man was from a group of people in Vancleave, Mississippi, who were sometimes called "red-bones" or "Vancleave Indians"—people who had always gone to white schools and churches but had always been suspected by their neighbors of being part black. (I once did a piece about a similar group, called the Turks, in South Carolina, and the standard opinion of longtime neighbors was reflected by a woman who told me, "Oh, they got some of it in 'em, all right.") The possibility of arranging to have the suitor drafted—a solution hinted at in the letter from his girlfriend's distraught parents—was looked into and dropped when it became apparent that he was too young for the draft. I couldn't find any indication in the McCain Library files that the Sovereignty Commission was able to break up the romance, but in what other state in what other period of American history could parents of no great influence write to the governor about a suitor they considered inappropriate and have the governor get right on the case?

At the McCain Library, the people who brought me a library cart full of files and collected documents to be photocopied could not have been more helpful—a fact that I would have found unremarkable except that, not having been in Mississippi on matters concerning race since the summer of 1964, when I reported on the Mississippi Summer Project for *The New Yorker,* I still remembered the narrowed eyes and suspicious looks that had in those days made me long for the moment when I could slip over the border. The University of Southern Mississippi is now integrated, of course. There are a thousand black students at Ole Miss, where the admission of one, James Meredith, once caused something close to an insurrection—unless you accept the argument of the film the Sovereignty Commission distributed about those events, which was that the federal marshals were responsible for the violence. If the librarians helping me had heard on the radio news that morning about a court ruling against a man who said he had been passed over for the job of Jackson chief of police because of racial bias, they probably hadn't been startled even for a moment by hearing later in the account that the man in question is white and the new police chief and the former police chief are both black.

Some of the people helping me with my copying weren't yet born in 1960, when W. D. McCain, the Southern Mississippi president after whom the library is named, went to Chicago to deliver a State Sovereignty Commission speech that said, among other things, "We maintain that Negroes receive better treatment and more consideration of their welfare in Mississippi than in any state in the nation" and "The Negroes prefer that control of the government remain in the white man's hands." Unless members of the library staff had reason to go through the files themselves, they would have no way of knowing that it was President McCain who received a memorandum from the director of the Sovereignty Commission dated March 2, 1964, with instructions on how to handle a black man who had announced that he was applying to the university. Confirming a conversation, the director wrote that McCain or his registrar should say to the applicant, "We have information that you are a homosexual. We also have sufficient information to prove it if necessary. If you change your mind about enrolling at an all-white university we will say no more about it. If you persist in your application, we will give this information to the press."

What I had missed in Mississippi was the transition. That took a while, the pace set partly by the gradual increase in registered black voters. In 1973, a Mississippi governor vetoed the appropriations bill for the State Sovereignty Commission, although his public explanation was not that its activities were wrong or silly but that they overlapped with the activities of other agencies. In 1977, the Commission, by then moribund, was finally abolished. That left the question of what would become of its files. This was only fifteen years after Mississippi university presidents were delivering Sovereignty Commission speeches in the North and bar-association leaders were presiding over Citizens Council chapters in the Delta and virtually all Mississippi politicians were behaving in ways that black voters would have found distinctly unappealing. By an overwhelming majority, the Mississippi House of Representatives passed a bill that read, in part, "The Secretary of State is hereby directed to destroy the said files in their entirety."

A court injunction prevented that, and the legislature instead voted to seal the files for fifty years. The injunction was part of a suit to open the files, brought by the American Civil Liberties Union of Mississippi, among others, on behalf of all those who had been spied on or smeared or harassed by the Mississippi State Sovereignty Commission. The plaintiffs eventually included a collection of old comrades from the civil-rights movement. There was the Delta Ministry, a National Council of Churches project, and two of its staff members. There was Ken Lawrence, the Mississippi director for an American Friends Service Committee project on government surveillance that had been one of the inspirations for the suit. There was the A.C.L.U. itself. There were two non-blacks who had been faculty members at Tougaloo—Edwin King, the college chaplain, and John R. Salter, Jr., sometimes known in Jackson as "the mustard man" because of a noted newspaper picture in which he is shown covered with condiments poured on him during a lunch-counter sit-in. It's a picture that brings into focus one of the strongest images I have of those days in the South: black college students, dressed in what they might wear to church on Sunday, are sitting at a lunch counter, staring straight ahead, their backs to the white hoodlums who are tormenting them. Recalled thirty years later, the image seems to have an improbable clarity—as if the production designer of a morality play had gone overboard in distinguishing the good guys from the bad guys.

The suit to open the files of the State Sovereignty Commission has now been going on for eighteen years. The bare outline of its history has something in common, I think, with the history of the civil-rights movement itself—challenging what seems to be a powerful, and even monolithic, institution, persevering despite delay after delay, and breaking up into internal discord by the time the prize seems to be at hand. In this instance, the powerful and monolithic institution presented itself in the form of Federal District Court Judge W. Harold Cox, the most openly racist jurist on the federal bench. Judge Cox's response to the suit strikes me as more or less the equivalent of the policy put together by Southern white politicians in the years just after the *Brown v. Board*

of Education decision of 1954—a policy that went by the name of massive resistance.

Harold Cox was one of the first judges appointed by two politicians whose
pictures still occupy a place of honor in the homes of some Mississippi black
people—John and Robert Kennedy. His selection was supposed to clear the way
for action on other judicial nominees in the Senate Judiciary Committee, then
run by Senator James O. Eastland, of Mississippi, a friend of Cox's from the time
they were students. As it turned out, many of the Southern judges who were
then nominated by the Kennedys and passed on expeditiously by the committee were considered by the civil-rights community to be nearly as hostile as Cox
was; Cox, though, was the only one who referred to black people from the
bench with words like "niggers" and "chimpanzees." In those days, the federal
judges who were the most resolute about dismantling the South's system of
legal white supremacy tended to be Republicans appointed by Dwight D. Eisenhower—the old sort of Southern Republicans, whose party affiliation might
have signified nothing more ideological than having been born in a hill county
that had been unenthusiastic about Secession in the first place. I once wrote
that a foreign traveller who knew nothing about the Republican Party except
what he gathered from observing federal judges in the South in those days
could have easily mistaken it for the party of Lincoln.

Judge Cox's response to the suit asking for access to the State Sovereignty
Commission files was to dismiss it on his own motion. There was a successful
appeal to the Fifth Circuit, of course, but in the six years until Cox's retirement
little progress was made. In 1984, the judge who inherited the case, William H.
Barbour, Jr., granted the plaintiffs the right to discovery, meaning that Ken
Lawrence could read every bit of what had survived as the files of the Mississippi State Sovereignty Commission—eight filing cabinets full of documents,
locked in a vault at the state archives. Lawrence, a white radical from Chicago
who had spent many years in Mississippi, was peculiarly suited to the task. He
had always had an interest in government attempts to spy on and harass the
left, and, even before the A.F.S.C. project began, he had accumulated a number
of Sovereignty Commission documents. He is, by nature, a collector. He now
lives in State College, Pennsylvania, because it is home to the American Philat-
elic Society; he serves on the society's board and writes a column on United
States stamps for its magazine. He owns what he believes to be one of the country's finest collections of Holocaust mail. When he was given access to the Sovereignty Commission files, he assembled photocopies in a twelve-volume
plaintiff's exhibit, organized into nearly a hundred categories. Some of the categories were general, such as Spying on Organized Labor and Spying on Elementary School Curricula and Invasion of Personal Privacy and Interference
with and Denial of Voting Rights. Some were specific, such as Developing an
Informer on Freedom Riders in Prison and Investigating B'nai B'rith and Tar-

geting Michael Schwerner and Targeting Rust College and Spying on an Italian Filmmaker in Natchez.

Judge Barbour decided in favor of the plaintiffs. In 1989, he ruled that the evidence—"generally unrebutted by the defendants"—proved that "the State of Mississippi acted directly through its State Sovereignty Commission and through conspiracy with private individuals to deprive the Plaintiffs of rights protected by the Constitution to free speech and association, to personal privacy, and to lawful search and seizure." He said that opening the files "would further the general principle of informed discussion of the actions of government, while to leave the files closed would perpetuate the attempt of the State to escape accountability." Those referred to in the files would have the opportunity to add corrective information, Judge Barbour ruled, and then the public would have the same access to the documents that it had to other papers in the state archives. At the time of Barbour's decision, the governor and the attorney general were young, reform-minded men who carried no baggage from the sixties; the attorney general announced that the State of Mississippi would not appeal.

That would have been that, except that by the time Judge Barbour handed down his decision a split among the plaintiffs had divided them into two subclasses, which the Judge called the access class and the privacy class. The access class, which represented those who wanted the public to have virtually unrestricted access to the files, included the A.C.L.U. itself and almost everyone else on the plaintiff side. The privacy class consisted of John Salter and Ed King, the two former Tougaloo faculty members. Their view was that unlimited access would be a way of recirculating the Commission's dirt—compounding the damage that the spying and smearing had done to innocent people in the first place. The privacy class appealed Barbour's ruling, and the Fifth Circuit directed Barbour to construct a plan that would protect privacy. The plan that Judge Barbour came up with included mechanisms by which victims of the State Sovereignty Commission—but not informers or people who had been acting for the state—would be given an opportunity to ask that their names be blocked out. Salter, who is now retired in North Dakota, dropped out of the case, but King, maintaining that the plan would not go far enough in protecting the privacy of innocent parties, appealed to the Fifth Circuit again. Because of that appeal, the case continues, and so does the disagreement between Ed King and the rest of the plaintiffs about just how much of the secret past needs to be uncovered.

"I don't think I'm either insane or a traitor," Ed King said within a few seconds of our meeting. He is aware that people say that he must have something to fear from public access to the files, or that he can't bear to see the case end because he is still living in the sixties, or that he has simply gone over the edge.

Ken Lawrence, who believes that opening the files is "a weapon of the struggle," makes no bones about considering King the enemy. "People assume that I couldn't be carrying on this fight on principle," King told me. "I must be covering something up." But among those who disagree with him there are some people who do believe that he is carrying on the fight on principle—that he is, in the words of one of them, "pure of heart." Even those people, though, are tired of looking at documents about the case that King has annotated. Even those people tend to respond to the mention of Ed King's name with a sigh and a rolling of the eyes. King is aware of that, too.

King's bitterest critics would not deny that he was an authentic hero of the civil-rights struggle. At a time when few white Mississippians would have publicly supported even the theoretical right of black people to demonstrate, he was active in the sit-in movement. He was the only white candidate on the slate of a statewide mock election carried on in November of 1963—an election that turned out to be the precursor of the Mississippi Summer Project. In those days, I was always curious about what might cause a white person in a place like Mississippi to abandon the views on race he had grown up with and openly join the movement that his family and friends and neighbors so despised. King tends to credit his apostasy to the Methodists—an indication that the subversion hunters of the Citizens Council might have been, in their own special way, on the right track. Growing up in a conventionally segregationist family in Vicksburg, King went to Millsaps, a liberal-arts college in Jackson connected to the Methodist Church. The very fact that the Methodists had healed their Civil War split—unlike, say, the American Baptists and the Southern Baptists— meant that, even in Mississippi, Methodists were exposed to a national-church point of view on race. King, who was heading toward divinity school, says he found that view persuasive. On the other hand, among the Paul Johnson papers at U.S.M. I came across the report of a surprise visit to King's mother made by the State Sovereignty Commission director, who concluded from the conversation that one of two Millsaps sociology professors named in the report must have been the prime influence in transforming Ed King into a race mixer.

In "Local People," a study of the civil-rights struggle in Mississippi, which recently won the Bancroft Prize, the historian John Dittmer wrote that King became "the most visible white activist in the Mississippi movement, and he paid a heavy price for honoring his convictions. King was ostracized by his family, scorned by his colleagues in the clergy, and later shunned by the 'New South' white moderates who entered the political arena only after it was safe to do so." He still bears the scars of a dreadful car wreck that occurred at the height of the Jackson demonstrations. At one point, he went through an acrimonious divorce. He now works for the University of Mississippi Medical Center, in Jackson, teaching sociology to people who are studying to be physical therapists and medical technicians. Those who feel kindly toward him tend to say, even if they are about to say that he is insane or is living in the past, that he is one of the many people who might have been damaged in the movement.

To me, Ed King didn't sound insane—just highly focussed. He says that, far from having changed his mind about access as it became clear what was in the files, he had simply assumed from the start that the names of innocent parties would be blocked out, as they are in F.B.I. files obtained through the Freedom of Information Act. He has any number of specific problems with the privacy protections proposed by Judge Barbour. He thinks, for instance, that insufficient distinction is made between "the dirty spies who each week turned in their neighbors" and someone who might have made a remark at a party which found its way into a report after some phrase like "Information was received from . . ." He says that notification in newspaper advertisements about how to arrange to have your name blocked out would mean nothing to people who have no reason to think that their names would be in such files in the first place. What if, he says, a report on a black minister who allowed COFO to use his church for mass meetings in 1964 includes the allegation that he dipped into church funds and had affairs with certain women in the congregation? Why would those women, who may have had nothing at all to do with the civil-rights movement, think that their names might be in the files of the State Sovereignty Commission? How would a veteran of the movement who might think it amusing to have been called a Communist by the Sovereignty Commission know that he was also called a drug addict or an adulterer? What about those whose request to have their names blocked out is denied on the ground that they were informers or state agents? Should they have to hire a lawyer just to protect their privacy? King and his former allies have talked about these points for hours—for instance, they have discussed one formula or another for defining an informer by, say, number of contacts or whether payment was received—but he says he will not be satisfied unless it is agreed to block out the name of everyone who could be in any way considered a victim or a bystander rather than an oppressor. He often repeats the simplest formulation of his viewpoint: "We need to know what the government did, but not to whom."

Whatever dangers unrestricted access would bring are, of course, already present in the several years' worth of Sovereignty Commission documents accessible to anyone willing to go to the McCain Library at the University of Southern Mississippi and ask for the Paul Johnson papers. If the ready availability of the Johnson collection since 1989 has caused any instances of divorce or mortification or blackmail, they have not become public knowledge. What I saw in the Johnson documents seemed to confirm what I'd heard from people familiar with the files as a whole: there is relatively little material that people would find personally embarrassing or damaging, particularly thirty years after the fact. One report from someone who spied for the Commission during the summer of 1964 says that the students occupying what the civil-rights volunteers called Freedom Houses were especially careful not to engage in any behavior that would give the police an excuse to arrest them. In King's view, though, "if only a dozen people are affected, they have their rights."

I did feel uneasy about reading a few of the documents I saw in the McCain Library—a report that mentioned the treatment of one jailed demonstrator for a social disease, for instance, and a medical report that seemed to be a psychiatric workup of a young man admitted to the state mental hospital. On the other hand, I felt exhilarated by another document. It was the report of a spy in the COFO office which mentioned someone I knew—a woman who had come to the South even before 1964 to work with the Student Nonviolent Coördinating Committee. The spy, who was identified on his reports as "Operator #79," wrote, "The 'strong' females on the permanent office staff have told me earlier of a revolution among females, 'the women's fight for equality with men.' To the students, this is a deeply serious matter. I have watched it gain momentum over the past months. There are many male supporters of this new 'thing.' " My acquaintance was named as one of the new thing's ringleaders. I sent her a copy of the report. I figure that if she ever gets into a dispute with other feminists about who does and who doesn't have bona fides in the movement, the report that Operator #79 filed in July of 1964 will trump anything in the room.

The largest chunk of Commission documents to have surfaced during the litigation over access to the files was put into circulation by Erle Johnston, who happens to be the only surviving director of the Mississippi State Sovereignty Commission. In 1989, Johnston borrowed part of Ken Lawrence's plaintiff's exhibit from an unsuspecting legal secretary and headed straight for the copying store. Liberator of the files is an unusual role for a former director of the Sovereignty Commission to play—it might be assumed that the people who actually worked for the Commission would have a strong interest in keeping everything locked tightly in the basement of the state archives—but Johnston was an unusual Sovereignty Commission director. Although he succeeded a former sheriff and preceded a former F.B.I. man, he himself was a former editor and publisher of the Scott County *Times*, in Forest, Mississippi. I had last run into him in the office of Governor Ross Barnett in 1961, the day I got my Jackson police badge; he was then the Sovereignty Commission's public-relations director. I've always had vivid memories of that occasion because Governor Barnett, who was known for grandiloquent speech, said to me—in as gracious a way as he could manage, since all Mississippi officials were trying hard to be polite—that something *Time* had said about him a few years before was "a malicious, pusillanimous, herbivorous lie." Johnston was amiable then, and he remains amiable. He has always been a man who tries to get along. A book he wrote on the period, *Mississippi's Defiant Years: 1953–1973*, includes testimonials from both William F. Winter, a relatively liberal governor in the early eighties, and William J. Simmons, the longtime administrator of the Citizens Council. It also contains a tribute to Aaron Henry and Charles Evers, "the two most visible and aggressive black civil-rights leaders in Mississippi during the 'defiant years' "—sort of in the spirit of a trial lawyer lifting a glass to his adversary after a particularly rancorous day in court.

Johnston maintains that he has nothing to fear from public access to the files, since they would portray him as a "practical segregationist" rather than an authentic hater. More or less retired at seventy-seven, he likes to talk about having hired black people when he was mayor of Forest and making speeches as Sovereignty Commission director that enraged the Citizens Council, but he seems half resigned to being considered a villain. "I'm the only one left," he told me when I stopped by Forest to see him. "I'm the one they can point the finger at and say, 'There goes that monster.' " Anyone who wanted to defend or condemn Johnston's behavior at the Sovereignty Commission could find plenty of supporting material for either in the papers of Paul Johnson. This was in a period when thugs were beginning to crawl out of the cracks that had been made in Mississippi's confident defense, and there are reports in the U.S.M. papers showing that the Sovereignty Commission under Johnston's leadership quietly settled some confrontations before the dynamite-and-shotgun crowd could take over. There are papers reflecting the attempt of the Citizens Council and its even kookier cousin, Americans for the Preservation of the White Race, to get Johnston fired for suspicion of moderation. On the other hand, the U.S.M. files also show that it was Erle Johnston who wrote the University of Mississippi trustees trying to get James Silver fired and Erle Johnston, on a similar errand at Rust College, who sent the trustees a report smearing their president as "a known liar and ladies' man." The memo instructing McCain on how to blackmail an applicant to the University of Southern Mississippi into withdrawing his application was also signed by Erle Johnston.

It isn't likely that the files under court seal hold documents that would drastically affect the reputation of Erle Johnston, and what is true of him is thought to be true of most people who were well known in what he calls the defiant years. Nobody I talked to in Mississippi believes that what remains secret includes many more front-page stories. Judge Barbour has estimated that three-quarters of the papers locked away at the state archives have already been seen in one way or another. Also, it is taken for granted that some of the more explosive material gathered by the State Sovereignty Commission was long ago weeded out. Most of the segregationist politicians of that era are out of politics by now, or dead. The paucity of dramatic stories about prominent black people who were discovered to have been spies is such that one man who seems to have been an operative known as Agent X, a congressional aide named R. L. Bolden, has been exposed in the media again and again—most recently last January by *Dateline NBC*, in the tone of voice that might have been used if a reporter for a TV news-magazine show had beat Stanley to Living-stone.

Among those familiar with the material, there is general agreement that a lot of what's in the files amounts to newspaper clippings and turgid essays ("Comments on 'Yesterday's Constitution Today,' a Textbook Taught at the University of Mississippi") and spying reports so mundane that they have the sound of the "Social Notes" column in a country weekly. ("Bill Kopic, mentioned in previous reports, returned to Jackson the week of December 13," wrote a spy placed as a secretary in the offices of some civil-rights lawyers. "You will recall that he went to New York to take his bar examination again. He does not know whether or not he passed this time. Henry Aronson was out of town during the Holidays. He was in New York and Seattle during this time.")

Also, the Mississippi State Sovereignty Commission, like any other government agency, generated a lot of paper that had more to do with justifying next year's appropriation than with completing the job at hand. There are pages in the files, for instance, concerning Erle Johnston's efforts to bring about the firing of A. D. Beittel, a Tougaloo president who had been openly supportive of civil-rights demonstrations; a week after Johnston flew to New York to put his case before Tougaloo trustees, it was announced that Beittel's contract would not be renewed. But John Dittmer, who has studied the incident in some detail, is convinced that Johnston, finding out from a spy at Tougaloo that Beittel was going to be forced out, staged the campaign so that the State Sovereignty Commission could take credit—a theory that Erle Johnston has been only too happy to embrace. ("I was always looking for something I could do to satisfy the white power structure without doing something terrible.")

At times, the State Sovereignty Commission was indeed capable of forcing people from their jobs, but its predilection for sending large men to examine tiny fingernails can make it seem more ludicrous than ominous. A phrase that keeps popping up in current descriptions of its activities is "Keystone Cops." A passage in a 1964 report reflects the level of sophistication the Commission sometimes demonstrated in the area of Cold War skulduggery: "In order to receive regularly publications of communist front organizations and preferring that the Sovereignty Commission not be on their mailing lists, we made arrangement with John Kochtitzky, Jr., to be the subscriber and deliver the publications to our office each week. We wanted a name which sounded 'Russian-ish.' " In 1964, when the Commission began dealing with the Mississippi Summer Project volunteers, many of them students from first-rank Northern universities, reports from investigators and spies began to include sentences like "The Kirschenbaum boy said that he did not believe in Jesus Christ."

Of course, what sound like Keystone Cops antics now were probably not funny at all thirty years ago—certainly not to the Kirschenbaum boy if he was being questioned at the side of a lonely country road around dusk by armed officials of the State of Mississippi who wanted to know exactly what he had against the Saviour. In those days, being called a Communist was also considerably less amusing than it might be now. It's difficult for anyone sitting in the McCain Library in 1995, several years after the end of the Cold War, to take seriously references to the role of the Red Menace in the events of 1964, when black Americans in Mississippi were routinely denied even the elementary American right to vote and a number of people went to the state with the goal of helping to remedy that situation. But Communism was serious business at the time. A Mississippi politician who was asked why black people were not allowed to vote in his state might answer that certain people involved in the voter-registration campaign had once been to a meeting of an organization cited by the House Un-American Activities Committee as a Communist front. Case closed.

The civil-rights movement itself was seriously split over the question of whether accepting the assistance of organizations that could easily be attacked as subversive was counterproductive, or perhaps even immoral. Association with such organizations could mean the loss of funding in the North, because the concern—some would say obsession—with Communism was national. It was the federal government, in the form of the attorney general's office and congressional committees, that gathered lists of subversive organizations. In one of the clippings I ran across in Mississippi, Erle Johnston is quoted as saying that the State Sovereignty Commission "operated like a state-level F.B.I." That characterization seemed grandiose, given the Sovereignty Commission's penchant for bloodline inspections, but then I started thinking about what the F.B.I. was up to at that time—bugging motel rooms in order to embarrass or blackmail Martin Luther King, Jr., gathering information on law-abiding citizens right down to the names of people they had spoken to at the high-school reunion or the Hadassah dinner dance. Mississippi was not the only state government to keep secret files on its residents. "The Police Threat to Political Liberty," the report that came out of the American Friends Service Committee project on surveillance, has chapters not just on Jackson but also on Seattle and Baltimore and Los Angeles and Philadelphia.

In a way, the code phrases Mississippi used—"state sovereignty" for its system of white supremacy, "federal encroachment" for the national pressure to change—offered an accurate reflection of the situation. The Mississippi way of life was always vulnerable to contact with national institutions—the Methodist Church or the United States Air Force or the United States Court of Appeals for the Fifth Circuit. For many years, though, the pressure from Washington was not much more than nominal. Federal civil-rights legislation was bottled up by a powerful bloc of Southern senators. The Presidents in office in the decade after the Brown decision, when Mississippi was doing its best to run what James Silver called the Closed Society, did not treat the restoration of civil rights to black people in the South as a national priority. Dwight D. Eisenhower was identified with the view that you can't legislate morality. John F. Kennedy seemed to consider segregation a deplorable but essentially unalterable regional situation that was inconvenient mainly because it caused embarrassment overseas. Even Northern politicians who were particularly critical of Mississippi's single-race elections would not challenge their legitimacy, as Ed King and other delegates of the Freedom Democratic Party found out at the Democratic National Convention of 1964 when they tried to get seated in place of the all-white delegation from Mississippi. Reading through State Sovereignty Commission documents did not change my view that Mississippi had been sui generis, but it did remind me that the Closed Society had existed quite comfortably for years within the society of the United States of America. When I was in Mississippi in those days, I may have had thoughts of slipping over the border, but I was in my own country the entire time.

Of the hundreds of white people who went to Mississippi in the summer of 1964, committed to working for the benefit of black people, one is still at it. His name is Rims Barber, and he is one of the named plaintiffs in the suit to open the files of the State Sovereignty Commission. A Presbyterian minister from Chicago, Barber worked for the Delta Ministry for a dozen years and the Children's Defense Fund for another dozen. For the past four or five years, he has been lobbying the Mississippi Legislature as a one-man organization called the Mississippi Human Services Agenda. He works out of a ramshackle house a couple of blocks from the capitol, sharing quarters with other lingering troublemakers, like the Environmental Justice Project and Congregations for Children—the Methodists, again. One room of the old house is supposed to be the office of the Mississippi Human Services Agenda, but Barber seems to have migrated to one corner of a large conference table in what was once a living room—a room whose walls have posters like one showing a smiling little girl above the legend "The Arms Race May Kill Her. So Might Poverty. Help Fight Both." When I walked in, he waved an arm at the disorder around him and said, "Welcome to the Freedom House of the nineties." It did look like a Freedom House during what civil-rights workers sometimes called Freedom Summer and Erle Johnston, out of an old habit, still refers to as the Invasion. Sitting there in a rickety folding chair next to the messy conference table, I felt for a moment that we were back in 1964, when Jackson seemed full of the eager students referred to by one white woman I met as "those COFO things."

"Why are you still here?" I asked.

"Ignorance and stubbornness," Barber said.

Rims Barber believes that the State Sovereignty Commission files should be opened under the privacy guidelines constructed by Judge Barbour. He thinks that most of the dirt in the files was spread when it was acquired, and that the rest wouldn't make much difference at this point anyway. "I know there are lies in there," he said. "So what? You can tell that they're lies. And they're thirty years old. I have seen some of the lies in there—one that says we paid people to register to vote. If you smudged that over, you wouldn't know what kind of lies they were telling, and if you smudged my name out there'd be no way the lie could be checked. Also, it reflects the thinking of these people. They *believed* that. It's important to know what they thought. And without names it isn't real."

Barber first worked in the capitol in 1968, as an administrative assistant to the state's first black legislator since Reconstruction, and even then he was irritated by hints that legislators he dealt with every day might have seen Sovereignty Commission documents about him that he had never seen himself. There are now forty-two black legislators, and they form the core around which Barber tries to build coalitions on issues having to do with poverty and welfare and crime and education. Republicans dominate Mississippi politics now, and they are not the sort of Republicans that Dwight D. Eisenhower might have appointed to the federal bench. They are modern right-wing Republicans who talk about smaller government and personal responsibility and how idyllic everything was in the fifties—a period, Barber is quick to point out, in which women were in the kitchen and black people were in the back of the bus. These days, of course, there are a lot of people in Washington as well as in Mississippi talking about the evils of federal encroachment on areas of life that should be the province of the states. People around the country who refer to federal agents as "jackbooted thugs" speak of the Tenth Amendment with as much fervor as Ross Barnett and the Citizens Council once did. If all of them were united in a national umbrella organization, State Sovereignty Commission wouldn't be a bad name.

In that sense, I suppose you could say that Mississippi is now more like the rest of the country—or that the rest of the country is more like Mississippi—but not in ways that please Rims Barber. While I was in Jackson, the legislature was dealing with a measure to introduce caning into prisons and a measure to privatize certain areas of welfare. "Nobody says 'nigger' anymore," Barber says. "It's usually in code words." But he sees the issues he deals with now as simply extensions of what was being fought over in 1964. In fact, he sometimes says, "The gains we made are hanging by a thread, and they want to cut the thread." If you're talking to Rims Barber in what he calls the Freedom House of the nineties, the documents in the State Sovereignty Commission files don't seem to be about a peculiar and encapsulated era in American history.

Before I left the house, I asked Barber if he had expected the lawsuit to open the files to take this long.

"No," he said. "But then I didn't expect the civil-rights movement to take this long, either."

Grady's Gift

The New York Times Magazine, December 1, 1991

◆

HOWELL RAINES

Grady showed up one day at our house at 1409 Fifth Avenue West in Birmingham, and by and by she changed the way I saw the world. I was 7 when she came to iron and clean and cook for $18 a week, and she stayed for 7 years. During that time everyone in our family came to accept what my father called "those great long talks" that occupied Grady and me through many a sleepy Alabama afternoon. What happened between us can be expressed in many ways, but its essence was captured by Graham Greene when he wrote that in every childhood there is a moment when a door opens and lets the future in. So this is a story about one person who opened a door and another who walked through it.

It is difficult to describe—or even to keep alive in our memories—worlds that cease to exist. Usually we think of vanished worlds as having to do with far-off places or with ways of life, like that of the Western frontier, that are remote from us in time. But I grew up in a place that disappeared, and it was here in this country and not so long ago. I speak of Birmingham, where once there flourished the most complete form of racial segregation to exist on the American continent in this century.

Gradystein Williams Hutchinson (or Grady, as she was called in my family and hers) and I are two people who grew up in the '50s in that vanished world, two people who lived mundane, inconsequential lives while Martin Luther King Jr. and Police Commissioner T. Eugene (Bull) Connor prepared for their epic struggle. For years, Grady and I lived in my memory as child and adult. But now I realize that we were both children—one white and very young, one black and adolescent; one privileged, one poor. The connection between these two children and their city was this: Grady saw to it that although I was to live in Birmingham for the first 28 years of my life, Birmingham would not live in me.

Only by keeping in mind the place that Birmingham was can you understand the life we had, the people we became and the reunion that occurred one day not too long ago at my sister's big house in the verdant Birmingham suburb of Mountain Brook. Grady, now a 57-year-old hospital cook in Atlanta, had driven out with me in the car I had rented. As we pulled up, my parents, a retired couple living in Florida, arrived in their gray Cadillac. My father, a large, vigorous man of 84, parked his car and, without a word, walked straight to Grady and took her in his arms.

"I never thought I'd ever see y'all again," Grady said a little while later. "I just think this is the true will of God. It's His divine wish that we saw each other."

This was the first time in 34 years that we had all been together. As the years slipped by, it had become more and more important to me to find Grady, because I am a strong believer in thanking our teachers and mentors while they are still alive to hear our thanks. She had been "our maid," but she taught me the most valuable lesson a writer can learn, which is to try to see—honestly and down to its very center—the world in which we live. Grady was long gone before I realized what a brave and generous person she was, or how much I owed her.

Then last spring, my sister ran into a relative of Grady's and got her telephone number. I went to see Grady in Atlanta, and several months later we gathered in Birmingham to remember our shared past and to learn anew how love abides and how it can bloom not only in the fertile places, but in the stony ones as well.

I know that outsiders tend to think segregation existed in a uniform way throughout the Solid South. But it didn't. Segregation was rigid in some places, relaxed in others; leavened with humanity in some places, enforced with unremitting brutality in others. And segregation found its most violent and regimented expression in Birmingham—segregation maintained through the nighttime maraudings of white thugs, segregation sanctioned by absentee landlords from the United States Steel Corporation, segregation enforced by a pervasively corrupt police department.

Martin Luther King once said Birmingham was to the rest of the South what Johannesburg was to the rest of Africa. He believed that if segregation could be broken there, in a city that harbored an American version of apartheid, it could be broken everywhere. That is why the great civil rights demonstrations of 1963 took place in Birmingham. And that is why, just as King envisioned, once its jugular was cut in Kelly Ingram Park in Birmingham in 1963, the dragon of legalized segregation collapsed and died everywhere—died, it seems in retrospect, almost on the instant. It was the end of "Bad Birmingham," where the indigenous racism of rural Alabama had taken a new and more virulent form when transplanted into a raw industrial setting.

In the heyday of Birmingham, one vast belt of steel mills stretched for 10 miles, from the satellite town of Bessemer to the coal-mining suburb of Pratt City. Black and white men—men like Grady's father and mine—came from all over the South to do the work of these mills or to dig the coal and iron ore to feed them. By the time Grady Williams was born in 1933, the huge light of their labor washed the evening sky with an undying red glow. The division of tasks within these plants ran along simple lines: white men made the steel; black men washed the coal.

Henry Williams was a tiny man from Oklahoma—part African, part Cherokee, only 5 feet 3 inches, but handsome. He worked as the No. 2 Coal Washer at Pratt Mines, and he understood his world imperfectly. When the white foreman died, Henry thought he would move up. But the dead man's nephew was brought in, and in the natural order of things, Henry was required to teach his new boss all there was to know about washing coal.

"Oh, come on, Henry," his wife, Elizabeth, said when he complained about being passed over for a novice. But he would not be consoled.

One Saturday, Henry Williams sent Grady on an errand. "Go up the hill," he said, "and tell Mr. Humphrey Davis I said send me three bullets for my .38 pistol because I got to kill a dog."

In his bedroom later that same afternoon, he shot himself. Grady found the body. She was 7 years old.

Over the years, Elizabeth Williams held the family together. She worked as a practical nurse and would have become a registered nurse except for the fact that by the early '40s, the hospitals in Birmingham, which had run segregated nursing programs, closed those for blacks.

Grady attended Parker High, an all-black school where the children of teachers and postal workers made fun of girls like Grady, who at 14 was already working part-time in white homes. One day a boy started ragging Grady for being an "Aunt Jemima." One of the poorer boys approached him after class and said: "Hey, everybody's not lucky enough to have a father working. If I ever hear you say that again to her, I'm going to break your neck."

Grady finished high school in early 1950, four weeks after her 16th birthday. Her grades were high, even though she had held back on some tests in an effort to blend in with her older classmates. She planned to go to the nursing school at Dillard University, a black institution in New Orleans, but first she needed a full-time job to earn money for tuition. That was when my mother hired her. There was a state-financed nursing school in Birmingham, about 10 miles from her house, but it was the wrong one.

Between the Depression and World War II, my father and two of his brothers came into Birmingham from the Alabama hills. They were strong, sober country boys who knew how to swing a hammer. By the time Truman was elected in 1948, they had got a little bit rich selling lumber and building shelves for the A.&P.

They drove Packards and Oldsmobiles. They bought cottages at the beach and hired housemaids for their wives and resolved that their children would go to college. Among them, they had eight children, and I was the last to be born, and my world was sunny.

Indeed, it seemed to be a matter of family pride that this tribe of hard-handed hill people had become prosperous enough to spoil its babies. I was doted upon, particularly, it occurs to me now, by women: my mother; my sister, Mary Jo, who was 12 years older and carried me around like a mascot; my leathery old grandmother, a widow who didn't like many people but liked me because I was named for her husband.

There was also my Aunt Ada, a red-haired spinster who made me rice pudding and hand-whipped biscuits and milkshakes with cracked ice, and when my parents were out of town, I slept on a pallet in her room.

Then there were the black women, first Daisy, then Ella. And finally Grady.

I wish you could have seen her in 1950. Most of the women in my family ran from slender to bony. Grady was buxom. She wore a blue uniform and walked around our house on stout brown calves. Her skin was smooth. She had a gap between her front teeth, and so did I. One of the first things I remember Grady telling me was that as soon as she had enough money she was going to get a diamond set in her gap and it would drive the men wild.

There is no trickier subject for a writer from the South than that of affection between a black person and a white one in the unequal world of segregation. For the dishonesty upon which such a society is founded makes every emotion suspect, makes it impossible to know whether what flowed between two people was honest feeling or pity or pragmatism. Indeed, for the black person, the feigning of an expected emotion could be the very coinage of survival.

So I can only tell you how it seemed to me at the time. I was 7 and Grady was 16 and I adored her and I believed she was crazy about me. She became the weather in which my childhood was lived.

I was 14 when she went away. It would be many years before I realized that somehow, whether by accident or by plan, in a way so subtle, so gentle, so loving that it was like the budding and falling of the leaves on the pecan trees in the yard of that happy house in that cruel city in that violent time, Grady had given me the most precious gift that could be received by a pampered white boy growing up in that time and place. It was the gift of a free and unhateful heart.

Grady, it soon became clear, was a talker, and I was already known in my family as an incessant asker of questions. My brother, Jerry, who is 10 years older than I, says one of his clearest memories is of my following Grady around the house, pursuing her with a constant buzz of chatter.

That is funny, because what I remember is Grady talking and me listening—Grady talking as she did her chores, marking me with her vision of the way things were. All of my life, I have carried this mental image of the two of us:

I am 9 or 10 by this time. We are in the room where Grady did her ironing. Strong light is streaming through the window. High summer lies heavily across all of Birmingham like a blanket. We are alone, Grady and I, in the midst of what the Alabama novelist Babs Deal called "the acres of afternoon," those legendary hours of buzzing heat and torpidity that either bind you to the South or make you crazy to leave it.

I am slouched on a chair, with nothing left to do now that baseball practice is over. Grady is moving a huge dreadnought of an iron, a G.E. with stainless steel base and fat black handle, back and forth across my father's white shirts. From time to time, she shakes water on the fabric from a bottle with a sprinkler cap.

Then she speaks of a hidden world about which no one has ever told me, a world as dangerous and foreign, to a white child in a segregated society, as Africa itself—the world of "nigger town." "You don't know what it's like to be poor and black," Grady says.

She speaks of the curbside justice administered with rubber hoses by Bull Connor's policemen, of the deputy sheriff famous in the black community for shooting a floor sweeper who had moved too slowly, of "Dog Day," the one time a year when blacks are allowed to attend the state fair. She speaks offhandedly of the N.A.A.C.P.

"Are you a member?" I ask.

"At my school," she says, "we take our dimes and nickels and join the N.A.A.C.P. every year just like you join the Red Cross in your school."

It seems silly now to describe the impact of this revelation, but that is because I cannot fully re-create the intellectual isolation of those days in Alabama. Remember that this was a time when television news, with its searing pictures of racial conflict, was not yet a force in our society. The editorial pages of the Birmingham papers were dominated by the goofy massive-resistance cant of columnists like James J. Kilpatrick. Local politicians liked to describe the N.A.A.C.P. as an organization of satanic purpose and potency that had been rejected by "our colored people," and would shortly be outlawed in Alabama as an agency of Communism.

But Grady said black students were joining in droves, people my age and hers. It was one of the most powerfully subversive pieces of information I had ever encountered, leaving me with an unwavering conviction about Bull Connor, George Wallace and the other segregationist blowhards who would dominate the politics of my home state for a generation.

From that day, I knew they were wrong when they said that "our Negroes" were happy with their lot and had no desire to change "our Southern way of life." And when a local minister named Fred L. Shuttlesworth joined with Dr. King in 1957 to start the civil rights movement in Birmingham, I knew in some deeply intuitive way that they would succeed, because I believed that the rage that was in Grady was a living reality in the entire black community, and I knew that this rage was so powerful that it would have its way.

I learned, too, from watching Grady fail at something that meant a great deal to her. In January 1951, with the savings from her work in our home, she enrolled at Dillard. She made good grades. She loved the school and the city of New Orleans. But the money lasted only one semester, and when summer rolled around Grady was cleaning our house again.

That would be the last of her dream of becoming a registered nurse. A few years later, Grady married Marvin Hutchinson, a dashing fellow, more worldly than she, who took her to all-black nightclubs to hear singers like Bobby (Blue) Bland. In 1957, she moved to New York City to work as a maid and passed from my life. But I never forgot how she had yearned for education.

Did this mean that between the ages of 7 and 14, I acquired a sophisticated understanding of the insanity of a system of government that sent this impoverished girl to Louisiana rather than letting her attend the tax-supported nursing school that was a 15-cent bus ride from her home?

I can't say that I did. But I do know that in 1963, I recognized instantly that George Wallace was lying when he said that his Stand in the School House Door at the University of Alabama was intended to preserve the Constitutional principle of states' rights. What he really wanted to preserve was the right of the state of Alabama to promiscuously damage lives like Grady's.

It is April 23, 1991. I approach the locked security gate of a rough-looking apartment courtyard in Atlanta. There behind it, waiting in the shadows, is a tiny woman with a halo of gray hair and that distinctive gap in the front teeth. Still no diamond. Grady opens the gate and says, "I've got to hug you."

Grady's apartment is modest. The most striking feature is the stacks of books on each side of her easy chair. The conversation that was interrupted so long ago is resumed without a beat.

Within minutes we are both laughing wildly over an incident we remembered in exactly the same way. Grady had known that I was insecure about my appearance as I approached adolescence, and she always looked for chances to reassure me, preferably in the most exuberant way possible. One day when I appeared in a starched shirt and with my hair slicked back for a birthday party, Grady shouted, "You look positively raping."

"Grady," my mother called from the next room, "do you know what you're saying?"

"I told her yeah. I was trying to say 'ravishing.' I used to read all those True Confession magazines."

Reading, it turned out, had become a passion of Grady's life, even though she never got any more formal education. For the first time in years, I recall that it was Grady who introduced me to Ernest Hemingway. In the fall of 1952, when I had the mumps and *The Old Man and the Sea* was being published in *Life*, Grady sat by my bed and read me the entire book. We both giggled at the sentence: "Once he stood up and urinated over the side of the skiff. . . ."

Partly for money and partly to escape a troubled marriage, Grady explains, she had left Birmingham to work in New York as a maid for $125 a month. Her husband had followed.

"So we got an apartment, and the man I worked for got him a job," Grady recalls. "And we got together and we stayed for 31 years, which is too long to stay dead."

Dead, I asked? What did that mean?

For Grady it meant a loveless marriage and a series of grinding jobs as a maid or cook. And yet she relished the life of New York, developing a reputation in her neighborhood as an ace gambler and numbers player. Through an employer who worked in show business, she also became a regular and knowledgeable attender of Broadway theater.

There were three children: Eric Lance, 37, works for the New York subway system; Marva, 33, is a graduate of Wilberforce University and works in the finance department at Coler Memorial Hospital in New York; Reed, 29, works for a bank in Atlanta, where Grady is a dietetic cook at Shepherd Spinal Center. It has not been a bad life and is certainly richer in experiences and perhaps in opportunities for her children than Grady would have had in Birmingham.

At one point Grady speaks of being chided by one of her New York–raised sons for "taking it" back in the old days in Birmingham.

"He said, 'I just can't believe y'all let that go on,' " she says. "I said: 'What do you mean y'all? What could you have done about it?' What were you going to do? If you stuck out, you got in trouble. I always got in trouble. I was headstrong. I couldn't stand the conditions and I hated it. I wanted more than I could have.

"I always wanted to be more than I was," she adds. "I thought if I was given the chance I could be more than I was ever allowed to be."

I felt a pang of sympathy for Grady that she should be accused of tolerating what she had opposed with every fiber of her being. But how can a young man who grew up in New York know that the benign city he saw on visits to his grandmother each summer was not the Birmingham that had shaped his mother's life?

Among black people in the South, Grady is part of a generation who saw their best chances burned away by the last fiery breaths of segregation. It is difficult for young people of either race today to understand the openness and simplicity of the injustice that was done to this dwindling generation. When you stripped away the Constitutional falderal from Wallace's message, it was this: He was telling Grady's mother, a working parent who paid property, sales and income taxes in Alabama for more than 40 years, that her child could not attend the institutions supported by those taxes.

Even to those of us who lived there, it seems surreal that such a systematic denial of opportunity could have existed for so long. I have encountered the same disbelief in the grown-up children of white sharecroppers when they looked at pictures of the plantations on which they and their families had lived in economic bondage.

For people with such experiences, some things are beyond explanation or jest, something I learn when I jokingly ask Grady if she'd like her ashes brought back to Pratt City when she dies.

"No," she answers quite firmly, "I'd like them thrown in the East River in New York. I never liked Alabama. Isn't that terrible for you to say that? You know how I hate it."

Word that I had found Grady shot through my family. When the reunion luncheon was planned for my sister's house, my first impulse was to stage-manage the event. I had learned in conversations with Grady that she remembered my mother as someone who had nagged her about the housework. None of the rest of us recollected theirs as a tense relationship, but then again, none of us had been in Grady's shoes. In the end I decided to let it flow, and as it turned out, no one enjoyed the reunion more than Grady and my mother.

"You're so tiny," Grady exclaimed at one point. "I thought you were a great big woman. How'd you make so much noise?"

My mother was disarmed. In the midst of a round of stories about the bold things Grady had said and done, I heard her turn to a visitor and explain quietly, in an admiring voice, "You see, now, that Grady is a strong person."

Grady is also a very funny person, a born raconteur with a reputation in her own family for being outrageous. It is possible, therefore, to make her sound like some '50s version of Whoopi Goldberg and her life with my family like a sitcom spiced with her "sassy" asides about race and sex. But what I sensed at our gathering, among my brother, sister and parents, was something much deeper than fondness or nostalgia. It was a shared pride that in the Birmingham of the '50s this astonishing person had inhabited our home and had been allowed to be fully herself.

"She spoke out more than any person I knew of, no matter what their age," my sister observed. "She was the first person I'd ever heard do that, you see, and here I was 18 years old, and you were just a little fellow. This was the first person I'd ever heard say, 'Boy, it's terrible being black in Birmingham.' "

As Grady and my family got reacquainted, it became clear that my memory of her as "mine" was the narrow and selfish memory of a child. I had been blind to the bonds Grady also had with my brother and sister. Grady remembered my brother, in particular, as her confidant and protector. And although they never spoke of it at the time, she looked to him as her guardian against the neighborhood workmen of both races who were always eager to offer young black girls "a ride home from work."

"Even if Jerry was going in the opposite direction," Grady recalled, "he would always say: 'I'm going that way. I'll drop Grady off.' "

In my brother's view, Grady's outspokenness, whether about her chores or the shortcomings of Birmingham, was made possible through a kind of adolescent cabal. "The reason it worked was Grady was just another teen-ager in the house," he said. "There were already two teen-agers in the house, and she was just a teen-ager, too."

But it is also hard to imagine Grady falling into another family led by parents like mine. They were both from the Alabama hills, descended from Lincoln Republicans who did not buy into the Confederate mythology. There were no plantation paintings or portraits of Robert E. Lee on our walls. The mentality of the hill country is that of the underdog.

They were instinctive humanitarians. As Grady tells it, my father was well known among her relatives as "an open man" when it came to the treatment of his employees. I once saw him take the side of a black employee who had fought back against the bullying of a white worker on a loading dock—not a common occurrence in Birmingham in the '50s.

The most powerful rule of etiquette in my parents' home, I realize now, was that the word "nigger" was not to be used. There was no grand explanation attached to this, as I recall. We were simply people who did not say "nigger."

The prohibition of this one word may seem a small point, but I think it had a large meaning. Hill people, by nature, are talkers, and some, like my father, are great storytellers. They themselves have often been called hillbillies, which is to say that they understand the power of language and that the power to name is the power to maim.

Everyone in my family seems to have known that my great long afternoon talks with Grady were about race. Their only concern was not whether I should be hearing such talk, but whether I was old enough for the brutality of the facts.

"I would tell Howell about all the things that happened in the black neighborhoods, what police did to black people," Grady recalled to us. "I would come and tell him, and he would cry, and Mrs. Raines would say: 'Don't tell him that anymore. Don't tell him that. He's too young. Don't make him sad.' He would get sad about it."

Grady told me in private that she recalled something else about those afternoons, something precise and specific. I had wept, she said, on learning about the murder of Emmett Till, a young black boy lynched in Mississippi in 1955.

To me, this was the heart of the onion. For while some of the benefits of psychotherapy may be dubious, it does give us one shining truth. We are shaped by those moments when the sadness of life first wounds us. Yet often we are too young to remember that wounding experience, that decisive point after which all is changed for better or worse.

Every white Southerner must choose between two psychic roads—the road of racism or the road of brotherhood. Friends, families, even lovers have parted at that forking, sometimes forever, for it presents a choice that is clouded by confused emotions, inner conflicts and powerful social forces.

It is no simple matter to know all the factors that shape this individual decision. As a college student in Alabama, I shared the choking shame that many young people there felt about Wallace's antics and about the deaths of the four black children in the bombing of the Sixteenth Street Baptist Church in September 1963. A year later, as a cub reporter, I listened to the sermons and soaring hymns of the voting rights crusade. All this had its effect.

But the fact is that by the time the civil rights revolution rolled across the South, my heart had already chosen its road. I have always known that my talks with Grady helped me make that decision in an intellectual sense. But I had long felt there must have been some deeper force at work, some emotional nexus linked for me, it seemed now on hearing Grady's words, to the conjuring power of one name—Emmett Till—and to disconnected images that had lingered for decades in the eye of my memory.

Now I can almost recall the moment or imagine I can: Grady and I together, in the ironing room. We are islanded again, the two of us, in the acres of afternoon. We are looking at *Life* magazine or *Look*, at pictures of a boy barely older than myself, the remote and homely site of his death, several white men in a courtroom, the immemorial Mississippi scenes.

Thus did Grady, who had already given me so much, come back into my life with one last gift. She brought me a lost reel from the movie of my childhood, and on its dusty frames, I saw something few people are lucky enough to witness. It was a glimpse of the revelatory experience described by Graham Greene, the soul-shaking time after which all that is confusing detail falls away and all that is thematic shines forth with burning clarity.

Our reunion turned out to be a day of discovery, rich emotion and great humor. Near the end of a long lunch, my sister and my brother's wife began pouring coffee. In classic Southern overkill, there were multiple desserts. Grady spoke fondly of my late Aunt Ada's artistry with coconut cakes. Then she spoke of leaving Birmingham with "my dreams of chasing the rainbow."

"I used to say when I was young, 'One day I'm going to have a big house, and I'm going to have the white people bring me my coffee,' " Grady said, leaning back in her chair. "I ain't got the big house yet, but I got the coffee. I chased the rainbow and I caught it."

Of course, Grady did not catch the rainbow, and she never will. Among the victims of segregation, Grady was like a soldier shot on the last day of the war. Only a few years after she relinquished her dream of education, local colleges were opened to blacks, and educators from around the country came to Birmingham looking for the sort of poor black student who could race through high school two years ahead of schedule.

Grady's baby sister, Liz Spraggins, was spotted in a Pratt City high-school choir in 1964 and offered a music scholarship that started her on a successful career in Atlanta as a gospel and jazz singer. Grady's cousin Earl Hilliard, who is 10 years younger than she, wound up at Howard University Law School. Today he is a member of the Alabama Legislature. When Grady and I had lunch with the Hilliards, the family was debating whether Earl Jr. should join his sister, Lisa, at Emory or choose law-school acceptances at Stanford, Texas or Alabama.

If Grady had been a few years younger, she would have gone down the road taken by her sister and cousin. If she had been white, the public-education system of Alabama would have bailed her out despite her poverty. Even in 1950, fatherless white kids who zipped through high school were not allowed to fall through the cracks in Alabama. But Grady had bad timing and black skin, a deadly combination.

At some point during our reunion lunch, it occurred to everyone in the room that of all the people who knew Grady Williams as a girl, there was one group that could have sent her to college. That was my family. The next morning, my sister told me of a regretful conversation that took place later that same day.

"Mother said at dinner last night, 'If we had just known, if we had just known, we could have done something,' " Mary Jo said. "Well, how could we have not known?"

Yes, precisely, how could we not have known—and how can we not know of the carnage of lives and minds and souls that is going on among young black people in this country today?

In Washington, where I live, there is a facile answer to such questions. Fashionable philosophers in the think tanks that influence this Administration's policies will tell you that guilt, historical fairness and compassion are outdated concepts, that if the playing field is level today, we are free to forget that it was tilted for generations. Some of these philosophers will even tell you that Grady could have made it if she had really wanted to.

But I know where Grady came from and I know the deck was stacked against her and I know who stacked it. George Wallace is old, sick and pitiful now, and he'd like to be forgiven for what he, Bull Connor and the other segs did back then, and perhaps he should be. Those who know him say that above all else he regrets using the racial issue for political gain.

I often think of Governor Wallace when I hear about the dangers of "reverse discrimination" and "racial quotas" from President Bush or his counsel, C. Boyden Gray, the chief architect of the Administration's civil rights policies. Unlike some of the old Southern demagogues, these are not ignorant men. Indeed, they are the polite, well-educated sons of privilege. But when they argue that this country needs no remedies for past injustices, I believe I hear the grown-up voices of pampered white boys who never saw a wound.

And I think of Grady and the unrepayable gift she gave with such wit, such generosity, to such a boy, so many years ago.

Grady told me that she was moved when she went to a library and saw my book, an oral history of the civil rights movement entitled *My Soul Is Rested.* It is widely used on college campuses as basic reading about the South, and of everything I have done in journalism, I am proudest of that book.

I was surprised that Grady had not instantly understood when the book came out in 1977 that she was its inspiration. That is my fault. I waited much too long to find her and tell her. It is her book really. She wrote it on my heart in the acres of afternoon.

Acknowledgments

This is a highly personal anthology. No attempt has been made to be exhaustive or encyclopedic. I have tried to avoid straightforward political manifestos in favor of narratives or journalism. The movement is a vast subject, and readers will no doubt argue with the book, wondering how such a collection could fail to include a favorite author, or a memorable piece. So be it: I welcome the debate. My goal was to give a flavor of what life was like as the movement unfolded, to capture its ambiguities and lingering tensions, and to give readers a chance to see, in one place, what a handful of the nation's best writers had to say about our most important twentieth-century domestic drama. The choices are not driven by ideology, but by the editorial instinct to lay out as many of the key perspectives as possible; in other words, the fact that a piece is republished here should not be interpreted as an endorsement of that particular voice or view.

The most important thanks, naturally, go to the writers, living and dead, whose work is included here. I am grateful to Russell Baker, Ellis Cose, Stanley Crouch, Marshall Frady, Charlayne Hunter-Gault, Peter Goldman, David Halberstam, Howell Raines, William Styron, Calvin Trillin, Bernard Weinraub, Garry Wills, and Tom Wolfe for sharing stories with me about the writing of their pieces.

John Egerton and David J. Garrow answered many questions; I am one of countless readers in their debt, and I am fortunate they are my friends. Egerton's *Speak Now Against the Day: The Generation Before the Civil Rights Movement in the South* (1994) and Garrow's *Bearing the Cross: Martin Luther King, Jr., and the Southern Christian Leadership Conference* (1986) are essential reading on America in the twentieth century. I also owe thanks to Barbara Epstein, Lewis Lapham, Harry Evans, Jack Bass, Julia Reed, Malcolm Jones, David Remnick, George Plimpton, Manie Barron, James H. Cone, the late C. Eric Lincoln, Holly George-Warren, Richard Somerset-Ward, Peter Osnos, Vern Smith, Kathy Deveny, Kenneth Auchincloss, Nancy Cooper, Chris Shay, Mike Hill, Janelle Duryea, Sofia and Herbert Wentz, and the terrific Research Center staff of *Newsweek*.

I drew on numerous secondary sources for the essay that opens the book and the subsequent section introductions. The following volumes were especially useful: David Bradley's introduction to the 1988 Thunder's Mouth Press edition of Richard Wright's *Twelve Million Black Voices;* Victoria Glendinning's *Rebecca West: A Life;* Alex Haley's *The Autobiography of Malcolm X;* James H. Cone's *Martin & Malcolm & America;* and Joseph Blotner's *Robert Penn Warren: A Biography.*

At *Newsweek,* I am grateful to Rick Smith, Mark Whitaker, Ann McDaniel, and Evan Thomas for their innumerable kindnesses. Thanks, too, to Amanda Urban, friend and counselor; and without ICM's Richard Abate's tireless efforts to obtain permissions, there would be no book at all. Richard was a thoughtful colleague whose good cheer and wise insights were invaluable. At Random House, I was the lucky beneficiary of Jonathan Karp's formidable editorial gifts. And to Keith, of course, I owe the most.

Permissions Acknowledgments

"The Negro Revolt Against 'The Negro Leaders'" by Louis E. Lomax was originally published in *Harper's Magazine.* Copyright © 1960 by Louis Lomax.

Grateful acknowledgment is made to the following for permission to reprint previously published material:

AMERICAN PLAY COMPANY: "American Segregation and the World Crisis" by William Faulkner from *The Segregation Decisions.* Copyright © 1955 by William Faulkner. Reprinted by permission of American Play Company.

JAMES BALDWIN ESTATE: "The Dangerous Road Before Martin Luther King" was originally published in *Harper's Magazine,* 1955, by James Baldwin. Collected in *The Price of the Ticket* (New York, N.Y.: St. Martin's Press, 1985). Copyright © 1985 by James Baldwin. Reprinted by arrangement with the James Baldwin Estate.

DON CONGDON ASSOCIATES, INC.: "This Quiet Dust" from "Voices in Black & White: Writings on Race" from *Harper's Magazine* by William Styron. Copyright © 1965 by Harper's, renewed in 1993 by William Styron. Reprinted by permission of Don Congdon Associates, Inc.

STANLEY CROUCH: "When Watts Burned" from *The Sixties* by Stanley Crouch. Originally appeared in *Rolling Stone.* Copyright © 1977 by Stanley Crouch. Reprinted by permission of the author.

DOUBLEDAY, A DIVISION OF RANDOM HOUSE, INC.: "Liar by Legislation" from *First Person Rural* by Hodding Carter. Copyright © 1963 by Hodding Carter. Originally appeared in *Look.* Reprinted by permission of Doubleday, a division of Random House, Inc.

BARBARA EPSTEIN, LITERARY EXECUTOR OF THE MURRAY KEMPTON ESTATE: "He Went All the Way"; "Next Day"; "The Soul's Cry"; "Upon Such a Day" from *America Comes of Middle Age, Columns 1950–1962* by Murray Kempton. Copyright © 1963. Reprinted by permission of Barbara Epstein, Literary Executor of the Murray Kempton Estate.

FARRAR, STRAUS & GIROUX, LLC: Excerpt from "Appendix" from *Mystery and Manners* by Flannery O'Connor. Copyright © 1969 by the Estate of Mary Flannery O'Connor. "Mississippi: The Fallen Paradise" from "Life in the South" from *Signposts in a Strange Land* by Walker Percy. Originally appeared in *Harper's Magazine.* Copyright © 1991 by Mary Bernice Percy. Excerpt from "Radical Chic" from *Radical Chic & Mau-Mauing the Flak Catchers* by Tom Wolfe. Originally appeared in *New York.* Copyright © 1970 by Tom Wolfe. Reprinted by permission of Farrar, Straus & Giroux, LLC.

DAVID HALBERSTAM AND INTERNATIONAL CREATIVE MANAGEMENT, INC.: "The Second Coming of Martin Luther King" from *Harper's Magazine* by David Halberstam. Copyright © 1967 by David Halberstam. Reprinted by permission of David Halberstam and International Creative Management, Inc.

HARCOURT, INC.: "Choosing to Stay at Home: Ten Years After the March on Washington" from *In Search of Our Mothers' Gardens* by Alice Walker. Copyright © 1973 by Alice Walker. Reprinted by permission of Harcourt, Inc.

HARPERCOLLINS PUBLISHERS, INC.: "A Hostile and Welcoming Workplace" from *The Rage of the Privileged Class* by Ellis Cose. Copyright © 1993 by Ellis Cose. Reprinted by permission of HarperCollins Publishers, Inc.

JOHN HAWKINS & ASSOCIATES, INC.: "Inheritors of Slavery" by Richard Wright from *Twelve Million Black Voices: A Folk History of the Negro in the United States.* Copyright © 1941 by Richard Wright. Reprinted by permission of John Hawkins & Associates, Inc.

HOWARD UNIVERSITY: "The Moral Aspects of Segregation" by Benjamin E. Mays from *The Segregation Decisions.* Copyright © 1995 by Benjamin Mays. Reprinted by permission of Howard University.

CHARLAYNE HUNTER: "Representative" by Charlayne Hunter from *The New Yorker.* Copyright © 1967 by Charlayne Hunter. Reprinted by permission of the author.

Index

ABC, 7, 301, 302
Abernathy, Juanita, 313
Abernathy, Ralph D.
  in Memphis, 405
  and Montgomery bus boycott, 138, 140, 153
  as orator, 397
  and Poor People's Campaign, 418, 423, 425, 426, 430–31, 432, 438, 446
  resignation from SCLC of, 484
  and Selma, 302, 310, 313, 316
  as trying to supplant King, 396
Abyssinia Baptist Church (Harlem), 53
Adair, Mrs. R. T., 140
Adams, Sam, 285, 399
Adams, Sherman, 150
affirmative action, 409, 491
Africa/Africans, 127–28, 231, 445, 457. See also South Africa
African Americans. See blacks
African Methodist Episcopal Church, 390
Agent X, 512–13
Agnew, Spiro, 471
agriculture, and inheritors of slavery, 13–31
Agriculture, U.S. Department of, and Poor People's Campaign, 436–38, 441–43, 444, 446
Ahmed (Black Nationalist). See Evans, Fred
Akins, G. H., 115
Alabama
  Carmichael in, 355, 361
  communism in, 521
  Freedom Riders in, 503
  legislature/Senate of, 527
  NAACP in, 521
  National Guard in, 312, 314
  poll-tax law in, 307
  and Senate refusal to let Wallace succeed himself, 248–49
  state troopers in, 296–99, 300, 304, 314, 428
  voter rights/registration in, 317, 416
  Wallace's impact on, 238, 248
  Wallace's popularity in, 247
  See also Selma-to-Montgomery march; Wallace, George C.; specific city or town
Alabama Christian Movement for Human Rights, 291
Alabama Council on Human Relations, 138
Alabama State University/College, 139–40, 270, 305, 309
Albany, Georgia, 289, 416–17, 423, 424, 426
Albert Pick Motel (Montgomery, Alabama), 308–9
Algeria, 457
All the King's Men (Warren), 108–9
Allen, Ivan, 240
Alley, J. P., 391, 393, 402
A.M.E. Zion Church (Montgomery, Alabama), 140
American Civil Liberties Union (A.C.L.U.), 506, 508
American Friends Service Committee (AFSC), 506, 507, 514
Americans for the Preservation of the White Race, 326, 512
Americus, Georgia, 289
Amoroso, Pat, 155
Amos n' Andy (TV/radio program), 155, 157–58
Amsterdam News, 276
Angelou, Maya, 4, 6, 10, 61–74
Angola, 386
Anniston, Alabama, 503
apartheid, 231, 518

Arkansas
  NAACP in, 275–76
  "Uncle Toms" in, 188
Armstrong, Louis, 42
Army, U.S., 31, 312, 314, 351, 448–49
Aronson, Henry, 513
Ashmore, Robert T., 87, 88, 89, 102
Asia, views about American segregation
  in, 127–28
Asian-Americans, 495
Associated Press, 141
Association of the Bar of the City of New
  York, 494–95
Atlanta, Georgia
  black homeowners in, 373–74
  bus segregation in, 481
  bus trip from Memphis to, 389–91,
    394–97, 399–400, 403–4, 405
  and character of Georgia, 322
  churches in, 377–78
  demonstrations in, 481
  desegregation in, 149
  as divided city, 436
  as headquarters of civil rights organi-
    zations, 355, 384, 409
  Hutchinson in, 517, 518, 522
  and King, 277, 377, 383, 390, 403–4
  lynchings in, 31
  and black leaders' appeal to Eisen-
    hower, 149–50
Atlanta University, 478, 481
Atlantic City, New Jersey, 434
Autobiographical Notes (Baldwin), 4
The Autobiography of Malcolm X (Malcolm
  X and Haley), 108
Avedon, Mrs. Richard, 465
Avedon, Richard, 465
Azbell, Joe, 139

baby inspections, 499–500, 503,
  504–5
"Back to Africa" movement, 229
Baez, Joan, 289, 291, 315
Bailey, William, 393
Baker, Russell, 281, 288–92
Baker, Wilson, 299
Baldwin, James, 4, 7–8, 10, 41–57, 287,
  346, 353, 378, 399, 453

"The Ballot or the Bullet" (Malcolm X
  speech), 109
Baltimore Afro-American, 30, 277
Baptist Church, 377, 378, 406, 478,
  509
Barber, Rims, 515–16
Barber, Samuel, 465
Barbour, William H., Jr., 507, 508, 510,
  512, 515
Barbour County, Alabama, 241, 259,
  260–61, 263–65, 307
Barnett, Ross, 231, 322, 324, 325, 503,
  511, 516
Baron, Richard, 466
Barton, Billy, 502, 503
Bates, Daisy, 275–76
Battles, Charles, 114, 115
Bay, Robert, 465, 470
Beittel, A. D., 513
Belafonte, Harry, 290, 291, 315, 383,
  398, 476
Belafonte, Julie, 465, 470, 476
Bell, Ella, 489–91, 498
Bellamy, Fay, 303
Ben Moore Hotel (Montgomery, Ala-
  bama), 362
Bennett, Tony, 315
Benny, Jack, 156, 159
Berkeley, California, King in, 383,
  386–88
Bernstein, Felicia, 464–65, 467, 469,
  470, 471, 475
Bernstein, Judith, 476
Bernstein, Leonard, 315, 410, 463–77
Berry, Lee, 471
Bess, Doc, 154
Bethune, Mary McLeod, 481
Bevel, James, 293, 294, 313, 316,
  383–84, 396–97, 405, 406
Bible
  Abernathy's references to, 430–31
  and black leadership, 269
  and Black Muslims, 221–22
  and Earle murder trial, 90, 91
  King's knowledge of/references to,
    153, 285, 399
  as source of justification for segrega-
    tion, 118, 127, 143, 178, 179–80,
    196

as source of sermons, 395
and Turner insurrection, 337
Bilbo, Theodore G., 275, 322
Bill of Rights, 285, 447
Billingsley, Orzell, 307
Birmingham, Alabama
demonstrations/violence in, 4, 149,
291, 301, 430, 518
Freedom Riders in, 503
and Grady-Raines relationship, 411,
517–22, 524–25
King in, 375, 383, 405, 518, 521
media in, 521
police in, 372, 518, 521
segregation in, 149
Wallace campaign in, 258–60
Wallace rally in, 109
The Birmingham News, 244
Birmingham University Hospital, 306
Black Boy (Wright), 3
*Black Managers: The Case of the Banking
Industry* (Irons and Moore), 488–89
"Black Moses," myth of, 271–72
Black Muslims, 108, 218–34, 277, 346,
352, 375, 406, 485
Black Nationalists, 375, 379–81
Black Panthers (civil rights organization),
249, 283, 410, 458, 459, 461,
464, 465–77. *See also specific person*
Black Panthers (high school football
team), 35–36
Black Power
and black leadership, 272, 278
Bond's views about, 368
and Carmichael, 7, 353, 356, 364, 371
constructive effects of, 447
and future of civil rights movement,
447
and King, 422
and Poor People's Campaign, 415,
426, 442
and riots/violence, 447, 455
rise of, 7, 283
black supremacy, 219
Blacks
anger of, 461–62
Arabs compared with, 200
as community, 462–63
dignity of, 275, 277–78, 399, 407

divisiveness among, 7, 21, 130,
220–21, 223–24, 228, 372, 374,
376n, 443, 462
hoaxes played against, 36–38
images of, 33–34, 379, 391, 499
as individuals, 275–80
Newsweek's survey of opinions of, 410
as superachievers, 486–99
white ignorance about, 174, 221,
330–32, 341, 360–61
Bloody Sunday, in Selma, Alabama,
292–318
Blough, Roger, 239
B'Nai B'Rith, 224, 507
Bolden, R. L., 512–13
Bolt, Ben, 89, 91
Bond, Alice, 367
Bond, Julian, 283, 303, 367–69
Bosses of the Buildings, 15, 22, 23, 30, 31
Boston Tea Party, 399, 457
Boston University, King at, 379, 398
Bowen, Charles M., 289
Boynton, Amelia, 295, 298
Bradley, Mamie, 274
Branch, Taylor, 106–7, 150–53
Brando, Marlon, 290, 291
Braves (baseball team), 5, 165
Breasted, James Henry, 227
"The Brilliancy of Black" (Weinraub),
283, 352–66
Brommer, Pauline, 114
Bronx Botanical Gardens, threats
against, 470, 471
Bronx High School of Science, 360
Brooklyn Dodgers, 156, 275
Brooks, John, 269
Brooks, Sadie, 146
Brooks, Stella, 146
Brotherhood of Sleeping Car Porters, 7,
272
Brown, Ben, 368
Brown, Rap, 407, 450, 452, 457, 458,
459, 462
Brown v. Board of Education (1954)
as beginning of civil rights movement,
429
and black leadership, 271
Carmichael's comments about, 364
impact of, 122

Brown v. Board of Education (1954)
    (*cont'd*)
  and Mississippi as Closed Society, 319,
    500, 506–7, 514
  and Montgomery bus boycott, 136,
    137
  and moral aspects of segregation, 124,
    125–26, 127
  and South Carolina, 129–30
  and unconstitutionality of separate
    but equal, 105
  and Warren's article, 107
  and what blacks want, 184, 186, 187
  and White's letter from Florida, 166
Brown's Chapel (Selma, Alabama), 292,
    293, 299, 302, 304, 306, 313
Bruce, James, 288–89
Bryant, Roy, 111, 113
Building Services International Union,
    Local 144 (New York City), 289
Bunche, Ralph, 122, 223, 291, 313,
    316, 356
Burden, Amanda, 466, 467
Burden, Carter, 467
"Burn, Baby, Burn," 452, 452*n*
Burris, C. E., 114
Burwell Infirmary (Selma, Alabama),
    300
buses
  in Atlanta, 481
  and Memphis-Atlanta trip for King's
    funeral, 389–91, 394–97,
    399–400, 403–4, 405
  Supreme Court decisions about, 147
  White's views about segregation on,
    166
  See also specific city or state
Bush, George C., 527
Butler, Mac Sim, 143
Byrnes, James E., 131, 132

Cable, George Washington, 319–20
Calloway, Cab, 158
Cambridge, Maryland, 289–90
Cannon, Poppy, 273–74
Capitol Building (Washington, D.C.), Vot-
    ing Rights Act signed at, 316
Carlton, Sidney, 111, 112

Carmichael, Stokely
  and Black Power, 7, 371
  influence on black youth of, 450–51
  and King, 384, 387, 407, 422
  look-alike of, 435, 438
  and shattering of American society,
    238
  and violence, 458
  Weinraub piece about, 283, 352–66
Carter, Eugene, 146
Carter, Hodding, 107, 324
Carver, George Washington, 122, 314,
    481
Carver project (Selma, Alabama), 293,
    299, 306
Cash, W. J., 323
Catledge, Turner, 6
Cavanagh, Jerome, 462
CBS, 307
celebrities
  at March on Washington, 290, 291
  and Selma-to-Montgomery
    march/Bloody Sunday, 295, 313,
    315–16
  See also specific person
Celler, Emanuel, 252
Central High School (Little Rock,
    Arkansas), 159, 160, 275–76
Central Intelligence Agency (CIA), 346,
    414
Chad Mitchell Trio, 315
Chamber of Commerce, 321
Chandler, Len, 315
Chaney, James, 501
Chapin, Schuyler, 465
Charleston, South Carolina, 333, 441
Charlotte, North Carolina, 149
Charlottesville, Virginia, 149
Chatham, Gerald, 111
Cheerleaders, 203, 204, 205, 206–8
Chestnut, J. L., 307
Cheyney State College, 367
Chicago *Defender*, 30
Chicago Eight, 466
Chicago, Illinois
  King in, 372, 375–76, 376*n*, 381,
    382, 383, 406, 422
  McCain speech in, 505
  in 1968, 434

riots in, 455, 456
wash-pot incident in, 274
children
    and inheritors of slavery, 24–25,
        28–29, 30
    and Little Rock integration, 159, 160
    and Nashville integration crisis,
        113–15
    and New Orleans school integration,
        207–8
    and Poor People's Campaign, 421
Children's Defense Fund, 515
Christianity
    and Angelou, 70
    and Baldwin's family, 45, 52
    and character of Mississippi, 326
    King's views about, 152, 370, 374,
        375
    as legend, 55
    and lunch-counter demonstrations,
        269
    Malcolm X's views about, 219, 221,
        222, 224, 231, 232
    and Montgomery bus boycott, 135,
        143, 144, 151, 152, 153
    and moral aspects of segregation, 124,
        127
    and reasons for segregation, 183
churches
    and Baldwin's youth, 43
    in Cleveland, 374
    and inheritors of slavery, 26–27
    King's views about, 381
    in Memphis, 390
    in Mississippi, 326
    role in black life of, 377
    See also ministers; religion; specific
        church
Ciampa, P. J., 394–95, 405
C.I.O. (Congress of Industrial Organiza-
    tions), 92, 93, 94, 102
circus, White's views about, 161–64,
    165
cities, 374. See also slums/ghettos; specific
    city
Citizens Council
    in Mississippi, 107, 129, 320, 323,
        324, 326, 502, 506, 509, 512,
        516

    and Montgomery bus boycott, 135,
        137, 138, 139, 141, 147, 148, 152
    and violence, 193
    and Warren's interviews about the
        future, 190, 193, 194
    white views about, 182
Citizens Crusade Against Poverty, 419,
    438–39
City of St. Jude (Montgomery, Alabama),
    315, 316
civil disobedience, 298–99
civil liberties, 447
Civil Rights Act (1964), 282, 327
Civil Rights Commission, U.S., 307
civil rights movement
    as civic fairy tale, 4
    future of, 413, 429, 446–49
    history of, 367–68
    King's role in, 374–75, 406–7, 413,
        425, 449
    martyrs of, 430
    Montgomery bus boycott as beginning
        of, 394
    Nelson's story about, 446
    in North, 406
    oral history of, 528
    and peace movement, 367–68,
        370–71, 383, 384, 386
    roots of, 4–8
    sources and images about, 3–4
    as spectator sport, 160–61
    and subversive organizations, 514
    as surprise to blacks, 159
    Voting Rights Act as "nova" of, 317
    Watters's expectations for, 420–21
Civil War
    battles of, 168
    centennial of end of, 282, 319
    civil rights movement's roots in, 5
    impact on Constitution of, 191
    impact on twentieth century events of,
        95
    Malcolm X's views about, 220, 232,
        233
    Mississippi's role in, 318–19
    and poor white trash, 181
    Southern inability to forget, 247
    and Southern romanticism, 177
    in Yazoo, 33

Clarendon County (South Carolina), 129

Clark, Edward, 98, 102, 103

Clark, Jim, and Bloody Sunday, 7, 294, 296, 299, 300, 301, 304, 309, 311, 370

Clark, Kenneth, 453

Clark, Ramsey, 313

Clark, Tom C., 81

Clarksdale, Mississippi, 172, 195

Clayborn Temple (Memphis, Tennessee), 390, 394–95

Clayton, Alabama, 261, 263–66

Clement, Frank, 115

Cleveland, Ohio, 109, 372–74, 375–77, 379–81, 459

Cloud, John, 296, 297

"The Club" (Vestavia, Alabama), 259

Cobbs, Price, 461

COFO. See Council of Federated Organizations

Cohn, Roy Elwood, 467

Cold War, 414, 447, 513, 514

Cole, Nat King, 156

Coles, Robert, 417

Collins, LeRoy, 149, 304

Collins, Sharon, 491–92, 496

colonialism, 121, 222, 381, 457

color, skin, shades of, 34, 227

Colored People (Gates), 154–61

Columbia, South Carolina, 130

Colvin, Claudette, 140

Comden, Betty, 465

communism
in Alabama, 521
and black leadership, 273
and emergence of civil rights movement, 6
King accused of being involved in, 501
King's views about, 385–86
and lack of respect for law, 191
Malcolm X's views about, 224
and ministers as communists, 403
Mississippians' blame on, 322, 501, 503, 510, 513, 514
and outside agitators as communists, 503
and Poor People's Campaign, 445
and segregation, 149

Wallace's views about, 252
and Watts, 348
Young's (Whitney) views about, 385

Community on the Move for Equality, 405

Confederacy, Wallace's views about, 252

Confederate flags, 321

Confessions of Nat Turner, 333–34, 335, 345

Congregations for Children, 515

Congress of Racial Equality (CORE), 225, 271n, 279, 303, 368, 413, 423

Congress, U.S., 277, 286–87, 306, 427

Connelly, Marc, 392, 393, 406

Connor, T. Eugene (Bull), 291, 370, 372, 374, 375, 517, 521, 527

Constitution, U.S., 136, 147, 152, 182–83, 191, 285, 308, 311, 508, 523

Copland, Aaron, 465

CORE. See Congress of Racial Equality

Cose, Ellis, 410, 486–99

cotton, 17–19, 22–24, 25, 27, 29, 65, 339

Council of Federated Organizations (COFO), 420, 421, 501, 510, 511, 515

Courtland, Virginia, 341–42, 343. See also Jerusalem, Virginia

Cox, Don, 465, 472–74, 476–77

Cox, W. Harold, 506–7

"The Crawdad Song," 425–26

"The Creation" (James Weldon Johnson), 68

Cross, Bonham, 130–31

Crouch, Stanley, 282–83, 346–48

Crozier Theological Seminary, 379

Crump, Ed, 403

Cuba, 232, 501

Culbertson, Henry, 82

Culbertson, John Bolt, 91, 92–94, 95, 98, 99, 102, 103

Curtin, Andrew G., 285

Curtis, Charlotte, 465, 470

Dabbs, James, 322

Dadisman, Carl, 154–55

Daley, Richard, 372, 374, 376*n*, 455
dancing, 28
Daniels, Jonathan, 362
Danville, Virginia, 288–89
Darin, Bobby, 290
Dartmouth College
   minority graduates of, 487
   Wallace speech at, 237–38
Dateline NBC (TV program), 512
Daufuskie Island, South Carolina,
   438–41
Davis, Darwin, 488
Davis, Humphrey, 519
Davis, Ossie, 291, 315
Davis, Sammy, Jr., 315
De La Beckwith, Byron, 500–501
Deal, Babs, 520
death
   Baldwin's views about, 54
   Dickinson's poem about, 345
   as theme in Poor People's Campaign
      speeches, 430
Debs, Eugene V., 285
Declaration of Independence, 127, 474
Delta Democrat-Times (Greenville, Missis-
   sippi), 107
Delta Ministry, 506, 515
democracy
   and jazz music, 217
   and riots/violence, 413, 454
   and segregation, 120–23, 127, 130,
      135, 137, 147, 152, 193
   and Selma-to-Montgomery
      march/Bloody Sunday, 308,
      309–11
   Southern blacks' hope for a future of,
      216–17
   Wallace as representative of dark side
      of, 240
   Wallace's views about, 242–43
Democratic National Convention (1964),
   515
demonstrations
   as aftermath of Bloody Sunday, 306,
      308
   and black leadership, 271
   spirituality as basis of, 278–79
   *See also type of demonstration or specific
      demonstration*

Depression (1930s), 323, 340, 403,
   429
Detroit Free Press, 284
Detroit, Michigan
   Black superachievers in, 488
   criticisms of NAACP in, 273
   riots/violence in, 41, 192, 283, 451,
      452, 453, 455, 457, 459, 460,
      462, 463
Devine, Father, 275
Devlin, Bernadette, 466
Dexter Avenue Baptist Church (Mont-
   gomery, Alabama), 7, 134, 153,
   316, 398
Dick, W. Arsene, 326
Dickinson, Emily, 345
Dillard University, 519, 522
diner, Baldwin's experiences at New Jer-
   sey, 45–48
discrimination
   and March on Washington, 286
   in Mississippi, 321
   and black leadership, 268, 277
   "reverse," 527
   in workplace, 486–99
District of Columbia. *See* March on Wash-
   ington; Poor People's Campaign;
   Washington, D.C.
Dittmer, John, 509, 513
Doar, John, 249, 302, 304, 313
Donaldson, Ivanhoe, 306
Dotson, John, 457
Douglass, Frederick, 272, 369
Douglass, Lewis, 369
Doyle, Andrew, 115–17
Drewry, William S., 334, 338, 342,
   343–44
Drewryville, Virginia, 339
Du Bois, W.E.B., 67, 369
Duchin, Peter and Cheray, 465, 469
Dunbar, Paul Lawrence, 67
Durham, North Carolina, 149
Dylan, Bob, 291

Earle, Willie, murder of, 75–104
Easterly, J. B., 131–32
Eastland, James O., 227, 231, 321–22,
   368, 507

Eatonton, Georgia, 480
Ebenezer Baptist Church (Atlanta, Georgia), 377–78, 403
Ebony magazine, 157
Eckstine, Billy, 315
economic issues, 220, 232, 233–34, 323–24, 340, 431. *See also* Depression (1930s); Poverty
education
  black attitudes about, 44–45
  Malcolm X's views about, 232
  in Mississippi, 507
  separate but equal, 35–36
  and white supremacy, 232
  See also *Brown v. Board of Education; schools*
"An Education in Georgia" (Trillin), 411
Egypt, and Black Muslims, 226–27
Eisenhower, Dwight D., 149–50, 178, 233, 277, 507, 514, 516
elections
  of 1964, 327, 515
  of 1968, 387, 427
  Mississippi mock (1963), 509
Elkins, Stanley, 333
Ellington, Duke, 158
Ellison, Ralph, 4, 10, 107–8, 214–18, 329, 332
Emancipation Proclamation, 15–16, 233, 317, 379
Emerson, William, 119
Engelhardt, Sam, 148
Environmental Justice Project, 515
Epps, Jesse, 405
Equal Employment Opportunity Commission (EEOC), 488
equal opportunity, 122, 126, 127, 486–99
equality
  Malcolm X's views about, 232, 233
  and March on Washington, 286, 287
Esquire magazine
  Weinraub article for, 283, 352–66
  Wills's article in, 284, 389–407
ethnology, 178
Europe, views about American segregation in, 127–28
Evans, Fred (Ahmed), 379–81, 458, 459
Evers, Charles, 388, 484, 512

Evers, Medgar, 291, 319, 362, 430, 484, 500–501
Evers, Myrlie, 484
Executive Leadership Council (ELC), 492

families, and inheritors of slavery, 24–25, 28–29
Fanion, Jerry, 394
Fanon, Frantz, 456–57
Farm Credit Administration, 9
farm factories, 23, 29
Farmer, Jim, 303, 316
farming/farmers, 13–31, 187. *See also* Agriculture, U.S. Department of; sharecroppers
Fat Joy, 77, 86, 97, 101, 102–3
Faubus, Orval, 231, 372
Faulkner, William, 4, 5, 105–6, 120–23, 172, 216, 320, 324, 325, 326, 331–32, 481
Fayette, Mississippi, 484
Federal Bureau of Investigation (FBI)
  and Earle-Brown murders, 81–82, 87, 91, 93, 95
  files of, 510
  and King, 514
  and Poor People's Campaign, 436
  and Selma-to-Montgomery march, 298, 300, 307, 312
  Southern attitudes about, 173
federal government
  and inheritors of slavery, 21–22
  Mississippi's views about, 514, 516
  southern views about, 95
  See also Congress, U.S.; Supreme Court, U.S.; *specific person or department*
Feigen, Richard, 477
films, Mississippi criticized in, 172
First Amendment, 387
First Baptist Church (Greenville, South Carolina), 76
First Baptist Church (Montgomery, Alabama), 138
First Baptist Church (Nashville, Tennessee), 268
First Baptist Church (Selma, Alabama), 299
"fish and loaves committee," 312

Fishman, Bernie, 476
Fishman, Hilda, 476
Fisk University, 268
Florida, 5, 161–66
"folk," and Wallace, 240–41, 244, 248–49
folk tradition, 24
Folsom, James E., 149, 256, 259
Ford, Wallace, 487, 488, 490
Forest, Mississippi, 511, 512
Forman, Jim, 302, 303, 304–5, 308, 309, 310–11, 313
Fort Nashborough, 171–72
Fort Smith, Arkansas, 149
Fortune 500 corporations, Collins's interviews of black executives with, 491–92
Foss, Lukas, 465
Foster, Marie, 295
Fowler, U. G., 88, 89, 91, 99
Frady, Marshall, 5, 108–9, 235–66
Franklin, Virginia, 339, 340
Fredenthal, David, 98
Fredericksburg, Virginia, 149
Free Speech Movement, 348
freedom
    Malcolm X's views about, 220, 234
    and segregation, 121–23
Freedom Houses, 511, 515, 516
Freedom of Information Act, 510
Freedom Riders, 106, 218, 302, 305, 501, 503, 507
Freedom Singers (Mississippi), 291
Freeman, Orville W., 436, 438
Frontier magazine, 457
Frost, David (Democratic candidate), 356, 357
Fruit of Islam, 219
Fullilove, Bob, 357
Fulton County, Georgia, 368
fund raising, 303, 312, 355, 374, 385, 475–76

Galbraith, John Kenneth, 238
Gallup poll, 453
Gandhi, Mahatma, 132, 136, 269, 278, 285, 295, 398, 399
gangs, street, 380, 381, 456

garbage strike (Memphis), 390, 392, 394, 395, 396, 400, 401, 403, 404–5, 406
Garrison, William Lloyd, 285
Garvey, Marcus, 229
Gates, Henry Louis, Jr., 6, 107, 154–61
Gates, Rocky, 157, 159
Gayle, W. A., 135, 136, 141, 142, 145
General Motors Corporation, management program at, 488
Georgia
    Bond case in, 367–69
    Carmichael in, 361
    legislature of, 367–69
    lynchings in, 31
    Mississippi compared with, 319, 322
    Negro History Week in, 368
    racist harangue from state superintendent in, 445–46
    voting rights/registration in, 317, 319, 481
    Walker's childhood/youth in, 480
    See also specific city or town
Gettysburg, Pennsylvania, Civil War battle at, 318–19
Gilmore, Georgia, 146
Gilstrap, Ed, 83–84
Ginsberg, Allen, 239
Glendora, Mississippi, Melton murder in, 194–95
Goldman, Peter, 410, 450–63
Goldwater, Barry, 239, 324, 327
Good Samaritan Hospital (Selma, Alabama), 299, 300, 301–2, 303
Goodman, Andrew, 501
Governor's Commission on the Los Angeles Riots, 283, 348–52
Graetz, Robert S., 134, 137, 142–44, 149
Graham, Billy, 226, 239, 370
Graham, Philip, 5
Grand Ole Opry, 259
Granger, Lester, 270–71
Gray, C. Boyden, 527
Gray, Fred D., 138–39, 140, 141, 142, 307
Gray, Thomas, 333–34, 335
Great Dismal Swamp, 336–37
Great Migration, 9–10, 30–31, 320

Great Neck, Long Island, Young (Whit-
   ney)-King disagreement in, 385
Green, Adolph, 465
The Green Pastures (film), 158, 159, 392
Green, Phyllis, 465
Greenberg, Jack, 308–9
Greene, Amy, 465
Greene, Graham, 517, 526
Greene, Milton, 465
Greensboro, North Carolina, 149
Greenville, Mississippi, 107, 320, 419
Greenville, South Carolina, 10–11,
   75–104
Greenwood, Mississippi, 112, 327, 388,
   434
Gregory, Dick, 291, 313, 315
Grenada, Mississippi, 499–500
Grier, William, 461, 462
Griffin, Marvin, 149
Griffith, Jacqueline Faye, 113
Griffith, M. J., 113
Guggenheimer, Ellie, 466, 467
Gurwit, Monty, 164
Guyot, Lawrence, 434

Hacker, Frederick J., 457, 462
Halberstam, David, 283–84, 370–88,
   410
Haley, Alex, 108, 218–34
Hall, David, 314
Hall, Grover C., Jr., 139, 145
"Hambone" cartoon (Alley), 391, 393,
   394, 402, 406
Hamer, Fannie Lou, 433, 485
Hamilton, Roy, 179
Hampton, Fred, 472, 473
Handy, W. C., 396, 405–6
The Hangover Theory, 460
Hardwick, Elizabeth, 283, 348–52
Hardy, B. E., 130
Harlem (New York City)
   Baldwin in, 10, 48–57
   black youth in, 450–51
   Carmichael in, 352–54, 355, 360
   Ellison's article about, 214–18
   King in, 452
   Malcolm X in, 219, 229
   psychological character of, 215–18

riots/marches in, 7, 41, 48–50,
   54–56, 308, 452, 458
as symbol of black alienation, 215,
   216
Harnick, Sheldon, 465, 476
Harper, Conrad, 494–95, 496, 497
Harper, Oscar, 262, 263
Harper's Magazine
   Angelou's article in, 61–74
   Ellison's article in, 214–18
   Halberstam as writer for, 283
   Halberstam's article in, 370–88
   Lomax's article in, 7, 108, 268–80
   Morris as editor of, 10
   Percy's article in, 318–28
   Styron's work in, 282, 328–45
   See also Morris, Willie
Harris, Joel Chandler, 480
Hartsfield, Mayor, 322
Harvard Law School Forum, Malcolm X
   speaks before, 230
Harvard University, minority graduates
   of, 486, 487, 488, 490
Haryou Act anti-poverty program,
   353
The Hate That Hate Produced (Mike Wal-
   lace documentary), 108, 109
hatred
   Baldwin's views about, 48, 56
   black self-, 220
   Carmichael's comments about, 362,
      365
   and Earle murder trial, 91
   King's views about, 145
   and Malcolm X-Haley interview, 220,
      222, 228
   and Montgomery bus boycott, 145
   and Nashville integration crisis, 115
   and Wallace, 243
   Warren's interviews about, 171, 181,
      199–200
Hayes, Harold, 284
Heckscher, Mrs. August, 465, 476
Hellman, Lillian, 465
Helms, James, 156
Hemingway, Ernest, 172, 216, 522
Henderson, Annie, 63–74
Henry, Aaron, 512
Herodotus, 227

heroes
  for New South, 196
  in 1950s, 275
Heschel, Abraham, 313
Heston, Charlton, 290, 291
Hicks, James, 276
Hill, Chuck, 380
Hilliard, Earl, 527
Hilton Head, 438
Himes, Chester, 353
Hispanics, 415, 417, 418, 429, 495
Historical Commission of Virginia, 339
Hitler, Adolf, and Malcolm X-Haley inter-
  view, 219, 224
Hoffa, James, 275
Holiday Inn (Memphis, Tennessee),
  393
Holmes, Hamilton, 411, 481
Holocaust, American segregation com-
  pared with, 128
Holt Street Baptist Church (Montgomery,
  Alabama), 107, 134, 137, 140
homosexuality, 506
Hood, John, 368
Hoover, Herbert, 240–41
Hoover, J. Edgar, 473
Horne, Lena, 289, 290, 467
"A Hostile and Welcoming Workplace"
  (Cose), 410, 486–99
Hot Springs, Arkansas, 149
Hotel Albert, attack on King at, 298
Hotel Braddock (Harlem), start of race
  riot at, 54–55
House Un-American Activities Commit-
  tee (HUAC), 275, 514
Houston, Julian, 363, 365–66
Howard University, 361
Hudson, Mrs. Winson, 485
Hudson's Department Store (Detroit,
  Michigan), 451
Hughes, Langston, 67, 108
Hughes, Richard, 452–53, 457
human rights, 321
Humphrey, Hubert, 247, 427, 440, 441,
  471
Humphries, Earl, 82
Hungary, Soviet rape of, 149
Hunter-Gault, Charlayne, 160, 283,
  367–69, 411, 444, 481

Hurd, Roosevelt Carlos, Sr., 77, 78, 81,
  82, 85, 86, 93, 97, 98, 100, 101,
  102
Hutchinson, Gradystein Williams, Raines
  relationship with, 411, 517–28
Hutchinson, Marvin, 522
hymns, 28, 289, 290

"I Have a Dream" speech (King), 281,
  285–86, 389, 397
"I Know Why the Caged Bird Sings"
  (Angelou), 61–74
idealism, 196–97, 279
Illinois Bell, 492–94, 498
Imitation of Life (film), 158–59
Indians, 313, 415, 417, 422, 429
individual, divisions within the, 195–201
Ingram, Rex, 159
The Inoculation Theory, 460
Institute of Journalism Education, 410
intellectuals, 243, 244, 255–56, 325
Invisible Man (Ellison), 107–8
Irons, Edward, 488–89

Jack & Jill (magazine), 159
Jackson, Dr. (Selma dentist), 309
Jackson, H. Ralph, 390
Jackson, Jesse, 426
Jackson, Jimmy Lee, 313, 430
Jackson, Mahalia, 292
Jackson, Sullivan, 304, 309
Jackson, William, 116, 117
Jackson Clarion-Ledger (Mississippi), 501,
  504
Jackson Daily News (Mississippi), 501
Jackson, Mississippi
  Carmichael arrest in, 361
  and character of Mississippi, 321,
    323, 326
  demonstrations/sit-ins in, 4, 503, 506,
    509
  SNCC in, 420
  Walker's views about, 481–82
  Welty's reporting about, 10, 57–61
jazz, 217, 396
Jefferson High School (Los Angeles, Cali-
  fornia), violence at, 346

Jefferson, Thomas, 127
Jennings, Robert, 116
Jerusalem, Virginia, 336–37, 338, 341.
    See also Courtland, Virginia
Jesus Christ, as black, 226
Jet magazine, 157
Jews/Jewish, 124, 127, 128, 206,
    224–25, 226, 401, 501
Jim Crow system
    Baldwin's experience with, 45–48
    and Earle murder trial, 100–101
    legalization of, 5
    in military, 31
    and Montgomery bus boycott, 132–33
    in New Jersey, 7
    in 1950s, 6
    poverty problem as replacement for,
        409
    in Virginia, 334
    White's (E. B.) views about, 107
Johnson, Bailey, 63, 65, 66, 68, 69–70, 71
Johnson, Frank M., Jr., 147, 302, 303,
    304, 305, 307–8, 309, 310, 311,
    314, 318
Johnson, Governor (Mississippi), 326
Johnson, James Weldon, 67, 68
Johnson, Jeffalyn, 492
Johnson, Lawrence, 289
Johnson, Luci, 308
Johnson, Lyndon
    Carmichael's comments about, 354
    and civil rights movement, 379
    civil rights/voting rights speech of,
        309–10
    and Daufuskie Islanders, 439–40
    and elections of 1968, 387
    Forman's speech about, 310
    and King, 370–71, 382, 385, 387,
        422
    Lewis (John) meets, 316–17
    and Mississippi, 324
    as myth, 383
    and racism of white society, 451
    on riots, 453
    and Selma-to-Montgomery march,
        300, 302, 306, 308, 310, 312,
        316, 317
    and shattering of American society,
        239

    and Vietnam, 382, 385, 422
    and voting rights legislation, 306,
        309–10, 316–17
    and Wallace, 246, 308
Johnson, Marguerite. *See* Angelou, Maya
Johnson, Paul B., Jr., 504–5, 509
    papers of, 512–25
Johnson, Roosevelt, 289
Johnson, Willie, 38, 66–67, 68, 69, 70,
    71, 73
Johnston, Erle, 511–12, 513, 514, 515
Jones, Clarence, 475
Jones, Edward, 488–89, 496
Jones, LeRoi, 346, 355
Jones, T. O., 394–95, 399, 400, 401,
    403, 404, 405
Jones, Walter B., 147
journalism
    role in civil rights movement of, 5
    Watters's views about, 415
    See also media
judges, Southern, 507
Judgment at Nuremberg (film), 7, 301
Judiciary Committee (U.S. Senate), 507
Justice, U.S. Department of, 300, 302,
    304, 308, 418, 434
justice/injustice
    Baldwin's views about, 57
    King's views about, 148, 153

Kasper, John, 106, 114–15, 116–18,
    119
Katzenbach, Nicholas, 304
"Keep on A-Walking, Children" (Wat-
    ters), 409, 413–49
Kelly, Robert, 119
Kelsey, George, 378
Kempton, Murray, 4, 6, 106, 111–19,
    417–18, 445
Kennedy, John F.
    assassination of, 413, 415, 430
    black appointments of, 232
    black leadership meets with, 286–87
    civil rights program of, 287
    inauguration of, 286
    judicial appointments of, 507
    and King's "I Have A Dream" speech, 4
    King's views about, 398

and Loeb, 401
and March on Washington, 286–87,
   479
and Mississippi, 160, 321, 322, 324,
   325
and segregation, 514–15
Kennedy, Robert F., 252, 321, 414, 428,
   507
Kilpatrick, James J., 521
Kimbell, Elmer, 194–95
King, Coretta Scott, 313, 403, 429, 485
King, Edwin, 506, 508–10, 511, 515
King, Martin Luther, Jr.
   in Albany, Georgia, 416–17, 424, 426
   assassination of, 7, 284, 413, 452,
      459, 460
   Atlanta University speech of, 478
   Baldwin (James) compared with, 399
   in Berkeley, 383, 386–88
   in Birmingham, 375, 383, 405, 518,
      521
   and black leadership, 269, 276–78,
      407, 423, 425
   and Black Panthers, 283
   and Black Power, 422
   and Brown (Rap), 407
   and Carmichael, 384, 387, 407, 422
   Carmichael compared with, 353–54
   in Chicago, 372, 375–76, 376n, 381,
      382, 383, 406, 422
   childhood/youth of, 378
   children of, 426
   in Cleveland, 372–74, 375–77,
      379–81
   as conservative, 386
   death threats against, 293, 316
   death/funeral of, 389–94, 397,
      403–4, 405, 413, 414, 425, 430
   dignity of, 407
   and divisiveness among blacks, 7
   "double-dealing" of, 304–5
   education of, 378–79, 398
   and FBI, 514
   first political speech of, 150–53
   and Forman's speech, 311
   Gates's views about, 159–60
   Halberstam's interview with, 283–84,
      370–88
   in Harlem, 452

   "I Have a Dream" speech of, 4, 281,
      285–86, 389, 397
   influence on others of, 159, 365
   on justice, 153
   and LBJ, 370–71, 382, 385, 387, 422
   and LBJ's speech on civil rights/voting
      rights, 309, 310
   Letter from a Birmingham Jail of,
      298–99
   and Lewis, 427, 428
   and Liuzzo murder, 317–18
   and Malcolm X, 224, 381–82, 388
   and March on Washington, 281,
      285–87, 375, 383, 389, 397, 405,
      478, 479
   and media, 374–75, 376, 376n, 386
   in Memphis, 391–94, 405, 423, 432
   and Meredith march of 1966, 422
   and middle class, 484
   and Montgomery bus boycott, 7, 106,
      134, 136, 137, 140, 141, 142,
      144, 145, 146, 147, 148, 149,
      150–53, 375, 379, 394, 398,
      405
   as myth, 383
   and NAACP, 276–77
   Nobel Prize for, 370, 376, 377, 385,
      397, 398, 399
   and nonviolence, 134, 148, 374, 378,
      379, 399, 405, 413, 415, 422,
      423, 449
   as orator, 397, 405, 406, 430,
      478–79
   physical attacks on, 149, 277, 298,
      405
   and Poor People's Campaign, 409,
      422, 430, 433
   and power struggles, 429
   as preacher, 399, 407
   and presidency, 371, 386, 387
   rapport with people of, 397–98
   recordings of speeches of, 482
   and religion, 378–79
   return to South of, 406–7
   role in civil rights movement of,
      374–75, 406–7, 413, 425, 449
   and Selma, Alabama, 292, 293–94,
      295, 302–5, 309–11, 313,
      315–17, 405, 416–17, 420

King, Martin Luther, Jr. *(cont'd)*
Selma monument of, 293
and SNCC, 383
"soul" of, 406–7
and spirituality of demonstrations, 278
and students, 382, 383, 386–88
and Vietnam, 7, 370–71, 372, 380,
382, 383, 384, 385–86, 387–88,
422
and Voting Rights Act, 316, 317
and Watts, 346
and Wilkins, 276–78
Wills's article about, 389–408
King, Martin (M. L.) "Daddy," Sr.,
377–78, 383
King family, 377
Kipling, Rudyard, 67
Kirby, George, 315
Kleeman (Rowan colleague), 139, 140
Knopf, Terry Ann, 459
Knoxville, Tennessee, 149
Kochtitzky, John, Jr., 513
Ku Klux Klan
and inheritors of slavery, 19
and Liuzzo murder, 318
in Memphis, 402–3
in Mississippi, 326
and Montgomery bus boycott, 145,
147, 152
and Nashville integration crisis, 113,
114, 115
whites warning blacks about, 6, 69
Kupfer, Marvin, 456

labor, 153, 272, 390–91, 404–5, 406,
507. *See also* garbage strike (Memphis)
Lamar, L.Q.C., 325
Lancaster, Burt, 290, 291
Lane, Mr. and Mrs. Burton, 465, 469,
476
language
in Mississippi, 321–22
of report about Watts, 351
Larsen, Jack Lenor, 472
Lautler, Louis, 277
law profession, minorities in, 494–95,
499
Lawrence, Ken, 506, 507, 509, 511

Lawson, James, Jr., 268, 405
leadership, black
and black leadership class, 271
and "Black Moses" myth, 271–72
and Black Muslims, 223–24, 277
and black newspapers, 273, 276,
277
congressional leaders meet with,
286–87
divisiveness among, 276–78, 303
and Eisenhower, 149–50, 277
and individual black, 270–80
and Kennedy, 286–87
and King, 407, 423
and "Leader of Leaders," 272
and liberals, 277
local, 270, 276
Lomax's criticisms of, 109
and March on Washington, 286–87
and masses, 269–80
and media, 376n
and migration of blacks, 31
and Montgomery bus boycott, 271,
276, 279
national, 270–71
and New Gospel, 269–71
in 1950s, 268–80
in 1960s, 283
and nonviolence, 279
and Poor People's Campaign, 423
and power, 272, 278
and prerequisites for becoming a
leader, 272
revolt against, 268–70
and riots, 454
and school integration, 270, 273, 275
and Selma-to-Montgomery march,
295
and separate but equal, 272, 273
and students, 268–71, 275–76, 278,
279, 280
summit meeting of, 276–77
and World War II, 274–75
See also specific person or organization
Leary, Timothy, 239
Leatherer, Jim, 313
Leave It to Beaver (TV program), 156
Lee, Bernard, 373–74
Lee, Cager, 313
Lee, Robert E., 252, 319

Lee, Sinclair, Jr., 113
Lefcourt, Gerald, 474–75
Legal Defense and Education Fund,
    NAACP, 274, 279–80, 308–9
Letter from a Birmingham Jail, King's,
    398–99
"Letter from the South" (E. B. White),
    107
Leventhal, Mel, 482, 483
Levy, Frank, 363
Lewis, Clarence, 391–92
Lewis, John, 7, 282, 283, 292–318,
    427–28, 447, 479
Lexington *Advertiser*, 327
libel laws, 194, 196
liberals
    and black leadership, 277
    Carmichael's comments about, 360
    and civil rights in 1958, 277
    and Earle murder trial, 92–94
    and future of civil rights movement,
        447–48
    limousine, 468
    and Montgomery bus boycott,
        135–36
    and Poor People's Campaign, 414,
        427, 432
    and Radical Chic, 468
    and riots, 460
    and Wallace, 239, 243, 244
    and white reasons for segregation,
        180
    Wolfe's portrait of, 410
    See also moderates
Liberty County, Georgia, 481
Lieberson, Goddard, 465
Liebling, A. J., 240–41
Life magazine
    Black Panther photographs in, 466
    and Earle murder trial, 98, 102–3
    and King assassination, 284
    Pius XII article in, 226
    surveys of blacks by, 353
    and Till murder trial, 174, 526
    and Wallace, 251
    Warren's article on desegregation for,
        107
    Watts' photographs in, 349
Lincoln, Abraham, 156, 177, 233, 272,
    285, 287, 317, 323, 507

Lincoln Memorial (Washington, D.C.)
    and March on Washington, 4, 281,
        290, 291, 478–79
    and Poor People's Campaign, 426,
        430, 431–32
Lindsay, John, 372
Lingo, Al (Alabama state trooper), 294,
    296, 304, 307–8
Lingo, Al (SNCC member), 294
Lions Club, 164, 195
"Litany at Atlanta" (Du Bois), 67
literacy tests, 317
Little Rock, Arkansas, 4, 149, 159, 160,
    275–76, 277
Little Rock Nine, 276
Liuzzo, Viola Gregg, murder of, 317–18,
    362, 430
Locher, Ralph, 372, 374
Locke, Hubert, 463
Loeb, Henry, 393, 394, 395, 400–402,
    403, 404–5
Lomax, Louis E., 7, 108, 109, 220–21,
    268–80
Long, Huey, 240–41, 243
Long, Russell, 430
Look magazine
    Carter's article in, 209–14
    Till murder photographs in, 526
Lopes Tijerina, Reies, 429
Lords of the Land, 15, 16, 17–27, 29,
    30, 31
Lorraine Motel (Memphis, Tennessee),
    284, 393–94, 405
Los Angeles, California, 282–83, 323,
    352, 418, 460. *See also* Watts
Los Angeles Times, 446
Louis, Joe, 156, 275
Lowndes County, Alabama, 418
Lucy, Autherine, 160, 169, 192
The Lull-Between-Storms Theory, 461
Lumet, Gail, 465, 466, 467, 470
Lumet, Sidney, 466, 467
lunch-counter demonstrations, 268–69,
    278, 279, 506
Lynchburg, Virginia, 149
lynchings, 31–32, 104, 193, 206, 223,
    270. *See also* Earle, Willie: trial
    about murder of; Till, Emmett: mur-
    der of
Lynne, Seybourn, 147

McCain Library and Archives (University of Southern Mississippi), 504–14
McCain, W. D., 505, 512
McCarthy, Eugene, 241, 427
McCarthy, Joseph, 239, 447
McClendon, Emanuel, 289
McComb, Mississippi, 327
McCone (John A.) Commission Report, 350–52
McGill, Ralph, 107, 322, 502
McKissick, Floyd, 384
McLuhan, Marshall, 267
McNair, Bob, 240
Macy's Department Store (New York City), threats against, 458
Maddox, Lester, 241, 403, 448, 471
Mailer, Norman, 239, 389, 406
Malcolm X
  assassination of, 388, 451
  "ballot or bullet" speech of, 109
  early life of, 228–29
  Haley's interview with, 108, 218–34
  impact on civil rights movement of, 282
  influence of, 388, 473
  and King, 381–82, 388
  Lomax as debater of, 109
  as Muhammad's disciple, 108
  in prison, 226, 230
  Rustin's views about, 422–23
  and violence, 458, 473
  and Watts, 346
manners, 109, 267, 327
Mants, Bob, 295
March on Washington (1963), 281, 285–92, 306, 312, 317, 375, 383, 389, 397, 405, 410, 425, 426, 428
  ten years after, 478–85
Marchant, John B., 89–90
Marshall, Thurgood, 232, 274, 279–80
marshalls, U.S., 206, 207, 208, 304, 312, 505
Martin, J. Robert, Jr., 86–87, 93, 96, 99, 101, 102
Martin, James, 256, 266
Martin Luther King Plaza (Washington, D.C.), 418
martyrs, of civil rights movement, 430
Mason Temple (Memphis, Tennessee), 397, 401, 405

Massachusetts Institute of Technology, 489, 490
Mathis, Johnny, 315
May, Elaine, 315, 316
Mays, Benjamin E., 105–6, 123–28, 368, 378
media
  in Birmingham, 521
  and black leadership, 376n
  and Black Muslims, 277
  and Carmichael, 353
  and Earle lynching trial, 79
  and emergence of civil rights movement, 6
  and Freedom Summer, 420
  and King, 374–75, 376, 376n, 386
  and March on Washington, 286
  in Memphis, 393, 402, 403
  in Mississippi, 320, 503–4
  and Montgomery bus boycott, 139, 147, 148
  and Poor People's Campaign, 424, 435, 436, 437, 438, 443, 444
  and riots, 453, 456
  and Selma-to-Montgomery march/Bloody Sunday, 296, 297–98, 300, 301, 302, 303, 306, 307, 308, 314
  Southern views about northern, 173, 200–201
  Southern violence against, 205
  and Voting Rights Act (1965), 316
  and Wallace, 251, 266
  See also television
Medical Committee for Human Rights, 294, 312
Meet the Press (TV program), 353
Melton, Clinton, 194–95
Memphis Commercial Appeal, 392
Memphis Press-Scimitar, 402
Memphis, Tennessee
  Belafonte speech in, 398
  bus trip to Atlanta from, 389–91, 394–97, 399–400, 403–4, 405
  churches/ministers in, 390, 403, 405
  Depression in, 403
  first "Memphians" of, 391
  garbage strike in, 390, 392, 394, 395, 396, 400, 401, 403, 404–5, 406

"good race relations" in, 402
King in, 7, 284, 405, 423, 432,
    489–94
KKK in, 402–3
march in, 403
media in, 393, 402, 403
NAACP in, 402, 404
police in, 390
Project Memphis, 393, 405
Trillin in, 504
violence in, 192
See also Loeb, Henry
Menotti, Gian-Carlo, 465
mentors, 497
Meredith, James, 160, 232, 319, 321,
    325, 422, 484, 505
Meridian, Mississippi, 326
Merton, Robert, 497
Methodist Church, 509, 514, 515
Methodist Episcopal Church (Stamps,
    Arkansas), 61–63
Mexican Americans. See Hispanics
middle class
    in Cleveland, 377
    and economic issues, 431
    lack of radicalism among, 484
    and Poor People's Campaign, 431
    and riots, 454, 462–63
    and SCLC, 423
    and Vietnam, 372
    in workplace, 486–99
migrant labor, 29
The Mike Wallace Show (TV program), 108
Milam, J. W., 111, 112, 113, 194
militancy, 406, 462. See also violence;
    specific person or organization
military, U.S., 419. See also Army, U.S.;
    National Guard
Miller, Henry, 465
Mills, C. Wright, 431
Mills, Wilbur, 416, 430
Millsaps College, 326, 509
Milwaukee, Wisconsin, riots in, 455, 457
ministers
    and Baldwin's father as minister, 43
    in Cleveland, 372, 373, 375–77, 379,
        380
    as communists, 403, 501
    divisiveness among, 374, 375

and Forman's speech, 311
and inheritors of slavery, 26–27
King's views about, 378–79, 398
in Memphis, 390, 403, 405
in Mississippi, 501
and Montgomery bus boycott, 133,
    134, 138, 140, 141, 144, 145,
    146, 148, 149
pay of, 190
and Selma-to-Montgomery march,
    306, 312, 313, 316
and sermons as art form, 395–96
title for, 501
Warren's interviews of, 179–80, 191,
    197, 198
See also specific person
Minneapolis, Minnesota, Rowan in,
    140–41
Minneapolis Tribune, 130, 140–41
minorities, Malcolm X's views about,
    227, 233
miscegenation, 179, 189
Mississippi
    black leadership in, 419
    black migration from, 320
    and black revolution, 320–21
    blacks as farmers in, 187
    and Brown decision, 319, 500, 506–7,
        514
    Carmichael in, 353, 355, 361–62
    character of, 318–28, 481–85
    Citizens Councils in, 107, 129, 320,
        323, 324, 326, 502, 506, 509,
        512, 516
    as Closed Society, 319, 500, 506–7,
        514, 515
    discrimination in, 321
    dissent in, 323
    in early and mid-1960s, 282
    economic issues in, 323–24
    education in, 26, 507
    elections in, 515
    and federal government, 516
    films as critical of, 172
    Freedom Riders in, 501
    Georgia compared with, 319, 322
    KKK in, 326
    language in, 321–22
    leadership in, 322

Mississippi *(cont'd)*
legislature in, 506, 515, 516
libel laws in, 194
media in, 320, 503–4
mock election (1963) in, 509
moderates in, 320–24, 509, 512
NAACP in, 388
Percy's views about, 318–28
police in, 503, 505, 511, 514
Populism in, 322, 323, 326
public and private in, 325–26
Republican Party in, 516
restoration of peace to, 326–28
schools in, 326
SNCC in, 302, 511
state troopers in, 483
Summer Project in, 501
transition in, 505–6
violence in, 319, 326, 505
voting rights/registration in, 317,
319, 321–22, 327, 501, 503, 504,
505–6, 507
Walker in, 481–85
Warren's interviews in, 181
white conservative tradition in,
322–23
See also Mississippi State Sovereignty
Commission; University of Southern
Mississippi; *specific city or town*
Mississippi Economic Council, 327
Mississippi Freedom Democratic Party,
434, 515
Mississippi Freedom Summer, 515
Mississippi Human Services Agenda, 515
Mississippi State Sovereignty Commission, 411, 499–516
Mississippi Summer Project, 306, 501,
505, 509, 513
Mitchell, Henry, 470
Mitchell, Jerry, 501
mobs
and inheritors of slavery, 19
See also Earle, Willie: trial about mur-
der of
moderates, 320–24, 338, 461, 509,
512
Money, Mississippi, Till murder in, 106,
111–13
Montgomery *Advertiser*, 135–36, 137,
138, 139, 143, 144, 145

Montgomery, Alabama
bus boycott in, 7, 106, 107, 132–53,
271, 276, 279, 375, 379, 394,
398, 405
Carmichael in, 362
Citizens Council in, 135, 137, 138,
139, 141, 147, 148, 152
demonstrations in, 305, 308, 309
Freedom Riders in, 503
King in, 375, 379, 394, 398, 405
KKK in, 145, 147
march to capitol in, 310
and nonviolence, 317–18, 405
police in, 305, 309, 362
violence in, 309, 310, 362
See also Selma-to-Montgomery march
(March 1965)
Montgomery Improvement Association,
134, 146, 275, 276, 277, 379
Moon, Henry, 271
Moore, Edna Jean, 114
Moore, Ferman, 456
Moore, Gilbert, 488
Moore, Queen Mother, 485
Moore, Willie, 362
Morehouse College, 368, 378, 398, 403
Morgan, Edward, 324
Morgan, Juliette, 136–37
Morrah, Bradley, Jr., 89, 90–91
Morris, Willie, 3, 6, 10, 32–41, 282
Morsell, John, 385
Mount Moriah Baptist Church (Harlem),
352–53
Moynihan, Patrick, 496, 498
Muhammad, Elijah, 108, 219–22, 224,
227, 228, 230–34
Murray v. University of Maryland,
126–27
Murrow, Edward R., 159
music, 28–29. *See also* jazz
My Soul Is Rested (Raines), 528

NAACP. *See* National Association for the
Advancement of Colored People
Nashville, Tennessee
integration crisis in, 106, 113–19
KKK in, 113, 114, 115
lunch-counter demonstrations in,
268, 269

march on Capitol at, 179
police in, 268, 269
violence in, 4
Nation of Islam. *See* Black Muslims
National Association for the Advancement of Colored People (NAACP)
in Alabama, 521
in Arkansas, 275–76
and Black Muslims, 224, 225
black newspapers/journals, 30, 79, 273, 276, 277, 369
and *Brown* decision, 271
early criticisms by blacks of, 273
internal problems of, 273–75
joke about, 326
Legal Defense and Education Fund of, 274, 279–80, 308–9
and Little Rock, 277
in Los Angeles, 460
and March on Washington, 287, 290
in Memphis, 402, 404
in Mississippi, 388
and Montgomery bus boycott, 141, 146, 147, 271, 276
Perot speech before, 498–99
rise to power of, 272
and school integration, 271, 273
and SCLC, 382
and Selma-to-Montgomery march, 312
and University of Alabama integration, 192
and Vietnam, 385
and violence, 193
and Warren's interviews about the future, 190
National Baptist Convention, 378
National Conference for New Politics, 368
National Council of Churches, 506
National Guard, 149, 160, 282–83, 312, 314, 347, 349
National Limited (Parkersburg), 155
National Lutheran Council, 137
National Welfare Rights Organization, 415, 416
Native Americans. *See* Indians
nazism/fascism, 224, 273, 301, 475. *See also* Rockwell, George Lincoln
"Negro," as psychological island, 13
"The Negro in America: What Must Be Done" (*Newsweek* editorial), 410

Negro History Week, 368, 481
Negro Ministers' Association, 373
"The Negro Revolt Against 'The Negro Leaders'" (Lomax), 108, 109, 268–80
Nelson, Jack, 446
Neshoba County, Mississippi, 501
New American Review, Watters's piece in, 408, 413–49
New Deal, 323, 454
New Gospel, 269–71
New Hampshire, Wallace's campaign in, 235–38
New Haven, Connecticut, 452
New Haven Railroad, threats against, 470
New Hope, Alabama, 254
New Jersey
Baldwin in, 10, 45–48
Jim Crow system in, 7, 45–48
New Left, 383, 386, 429
New Orleans, Louisiana, 5, 42, 43, 107, 192, 203–8
New Politics, 386
The New Republic, Welty's article in, 10, 57–61
New South, 196–201, 340, 509
New South magazine, 414, 438
New York City
and black migration, 320
Hutchinson in, 522, 523, 524
Lindsay as mayor of, 372
Radical Chic in, 463–77
slums in, 372
standard of living of blacks in, 132
See also Harlem
New York Post, 106
The New York Review of Books, Hardwick article for, 348–52
The New York Times
Baker's article in, 281, 288–92
Carmichael interview in, 353
Catledge as full-time reporter for South for, 6
Lewis interview in, 318
Prince and Princess of Wales editorial in, 499
Reston's article in, 281, 285–87
and Selma-to-Montgomery march, 297–98, 300, 303, 318

The New York Times Magazine
  Raines piece in, 517–28
  Walker's piece in, 478–85
The New Yorker
  Hunter-Gault article in, 283, 367–69
  Trillin article in, 411, 499–516
  West report for, 10–11, 75–104
  White's "Letter from the South" in,
    107, 161–66
Newark, New Jersey
  Carmichael in, 354, 355–56
  riots in, 283, 452–53, 455, 457, 458,
    459, 461
Newman, Paul, 290
Newport News, Virginia, 149
Newsweek
  coverage of race in America by, 410
  survey of black opinion in, 353, 410,
    453, 454, 456, 459
  and Wallace, 108, 251
Newton, Huey P., 472, 474
Nichols, Mike, 465
Nixon, E. D., 7, 144
Nixon, Richard M., 247, 251–52, 387,
    446, 465, 475
Nobel Prize, for King, 370, 376, 377,
    385, 397, 398, 399
nonviolence
  and black leadership, 279
  black opinions about, 453
  and CORE, 413
  and death of King, 413
  end of era of, 317–18, 346
  and Forman's language, 311
  and future of civil rights movement,
    449
  and King, 134, 148, 374, 378, 379,
    399, 405, 413, 415, 422, 423, 449
  and King Sr., 378
  and Montgomery bus boycott, 134
  and riots, 453
  and SCLC, 413
  and SNCC, 413
Norfolk, Virginia, 149
North
  civil rights movement in, 406
  as promised land, 30–31, 216–17
  riots in, 422
  See also specific city or state

North Carolina
  Carmichael in, 361
  lynchings in, 104
Northwestern University, minority grad-
    uates of, 488
"Notes of a Native Son" (Baldwin), 7–8,
    10, 41–57

O'Connor, Flannery, 109, 267, 481
Odetta, 315
Office of Economic Opportunity, U.S., 441
Ole Miss. *See* University of Southern Mis-
    sissippi
"on the case," 396
O'Neal, Patrick, 465
"Operator #79," 511
Ottley, Peter, 289
ownership, and inheritors of slavery, 16,
    21, 24
Oxford, Mississippi, 4, 321

"A Pageant of Birds" (Welty), 10, 57–61
Panther 21, 466, 470, 471, 473,
    474–75
Parker, Police Chief (Los Angeles, Califor-
    nia), 347, 349
Parks, Rosa, 6–7, 107, 132–33, 140,
    151, 152, 316, 317, 379, 394, 406
"Parting the Waters: America in the King
    Years" (Branch), 106–7, 150–53
Paterson, Basil, 494, 498
Patterson, John, 248, 307
Peace Corps, 324, 366
peace movement
  Bond's views about, 367–68
  and civil rights movement, 367–68,
    370–71, 383, 384, 386
  and King, 370–71, 384
  See also Vietnam
peanuts, 339–40
Peek, Floyd, 116
Penn, Mrs. Arthur, 465
Percy, Walker, 282, 318–28
Perkins, Anthony, 315
Perkins, Della, 146
Perot, Ross, 498–99
Peter, Paul and Mary, 291, 315, 316

Petersburg, Virginia, 149
Pettus Bridge (Selma, Alabama), 7, 282, 295–97, 307, 313–14, 428
Philadelphia, Mississippi, 326
Phipps, Cynthia, 465
photographs, role in civil rights movement of, 4–5, 7
Pierce, Larry, 307
Pine Bluff, Arkansas, 149
Pittsburgh *Courier*, 30
Pius XII (pope), 226
plantations/planters, 15, 16, 17–19, 21, 22, 23, 26, 29, 30, 323–24, 335
Plato, 399
Playboy magazine, Malcolm X interview in, 108, 218–34
Plessy v. Ferguson (1896), 5, 126–27
Poe, Edgar Allan, 67
police
    in Albany, Georgia, 289, 426
    in Birmingham, 372, 518, 521
    and Black Panthers, 459, 465, 473–74, 476–77
    and Carmichael, 352, 362
    in Cleveland, 379
    coercion by, 87
    in Detroit, 459
    and Earle-Brown murders, 80, 87, 88
    and future of civil rights movement, 448
    in Jackson, Mississippi, 505
    at Little Rock, 160
    Malcolm X's views about, 229
    and March on Washington, 289
    and martyrs of civil rights movement, 437
    in Memphis, 390
    in Mississippi, 503, 511, 514
    and Montgomery bus boycott, 133, 135, 136, 138, 141, 142, 305, 309, 362
    and Nashville integration crisis, 113, 114, 115, 116, 117, 268, 269
    in New Orleans, 206, 207
    and Poor People's Campaign, 416, 432, 435, 436, 437, 438, 442–43, 444, 446
    and riots, 458
    and violence in 1970s, 459

Wallace's views about, 255
    in Washington, D.C., 416, 432, 435, 436, 437, 438, 442–43, 444, 446
    and Watts, 347, 350, 454
    in Yazoo, Mississippi, 38–39
The Police-Are-Getting-Better Theory, 460–61
The Police-Are-Getting-Worse Theory, 461
politicians, and March on Washington, 286–87
poll taxes, 307, 317
Poole, Elijah. *See* Muhammad, Elijah
Poor People's Campaign, 409, 413, 414–20, 422, 423–38, 441–45, 446
poor whites, 15, 19, 20, 21, 71–72, 99, 181, 306, 323, 337
Popham, John, 6
Populism, 322, 323, 326
Portsmouth, Virginia, 149
Poussaint, Alvin, 455
poverty, 350–51, 419, 433, 434. *See also* Poor People's Campaign; slums/ghettos
Powell, Adam Clayton, 274–75, 407
Powell, W. J., 140
power, 19, 180, 242, 272, 278. *See also* Black Power
preachers. *See* ministers; *specific person*
Preminger, Otto, 465, 470, 475
presidency
    and King, 371, 386, 387
    Malcolm X's views about, 233
Princeton University, minority graduates of, 488
Progressive Labor Movement, 348
Project Memphis (SCLC), 393, 405
Prosser, Gabriel, 333
public and private, in Mississippi, 325–26

Quat, Leon, 470–72, 475, 476–77

R. S. Lewis and Sons Funeral Home, 391–92
"Radical Chic: That Party at Lenny's" (Wolfe), 410, 463–77

Radical Republicans, 323
radio, late-night, 157
The Rage of the Privileged Class (Cose),
    410, 486
Raines, Earl, 460, 461
Raines, Howell, 411, 517–28
Raines, Jerry, 520, 524
Raines, Mary Jo, 520, 527
Randolph, A. Philip, 7, 272, 276, 277,
    313
Random House, 466
Ray, Cecil, 117
Ray, James Earl, 284
Reader's Digest, 108, 174
Reagan, Ronald, 239
Reconstruction, 270, 320, 323
rednecks, 179, 201
Reeb, James J., 306–7, 308, 309, 430
Reed, Roy, 297–98
religion
    as basis of mass involvement in civil
        rights movement, 270, 279–80
    Carmichael's comments about,
        365–66
    and King, 370, 374, 375
    in Mississippi, 326
    and moral aspects of segregation, 124
    and "soul," 406
    and Turner insurrection, 335–36, 337
    and Warren's interviews about the
        future, 197–98
    See also Bible; churches; ministers
Report from Black America (Goldman),
    410, 450–63
Republican Party, 156, 181, 287, 507,
    516, 525
Reston, James, 281, 285–87
Resurrection City, 409, 415–20,
    421–22, 423, 426–36, 442, 444,
    445, 446
Reuther, Walter, 419
Reynolds, Frank, 301
Ribicoff, Adam, 232
Richmond, Virginia, 149, 269, 333,
    334, 338
Ricks, Willie, 303
riots
    black opinions about, 453–57
    and democracy, 454

desperation as point of, 451, 452
and King's assassination, 459, 460
legacy of, 462–63
and media, 453, 456
and nonviolence, 453
and police, 458
in slums/ghettos, 451–63
spread of, 459
theories about, 460–62
and violence, 452–53, 458, 461
Ripon Republicans, 428
Rist, Ray, 497
Rivers, L. Mendel, 441
Rivers, Larry, 465, 471
Rives, Richard T., 147
Roanoke, Virginia, 149
Robards, Jason, 465
Robbins, Jerome, 465
Robertson, Joseph M., 438, 442, 444
Robeson, Paul, 122, 275
Robinson, Hugh, 316
Robinson, Jackie, 156, 275
Robinson, Jimmie George, 298
Robinson, JoAnn, 139–40
Rockwell, George Lincoln, 231, 286
Roebuck, Alabama, 260
Rolling Stone, Crouch article for, 283,
    346–48
Romantics, and Watts riot, 348
Romney, George, 252
Roosevelt, Franklin D., 233, 323
Roosevelt, Mrs. Franklin D., 274
Roosevelt Hotel (New York City), 367–69
Rosenbaum, James, 496–97, 498
Ross, Harold, 10, 11
Rowan, Carl T., 6, 106, 129–49
Rumford Fair Housing Act, 350–51
Russell, Nipsey, 315
Russia. *See* Soviet Union
Rust College, 508, 512
Rustin, Bayard, 316, 350, 377, 407,
    422–23, 455
Ryan, D. D., 465
Ryan, John, 465

St. Augustine, Florida, 425
St. Martin, Doctor, 204
Salter, John R., Jr., 506, 508

Sanders, Carl, 240
Saturday Evening Post, 108
Savannah, Georgia, 435
Scarbrough, Tom, 500, 501, 504
Schlesinger, James, 238
schools
    and black leadership, 270, 273, 275
    and inheritors of slavery, 25, 26, 30
    integration of Nashville, 113–19
    in Mississippi, 326
    in New Orleans, 203–8
    in Stamps, Arkansas, 66
    in Yazoo, Mississippi, 35–36
    See also *Brown v. Board of Education;*
        education
Schwerner, Michael "Mickey," 362, 501,
    507–8
SCLC. *See* Southern Christian Leadership
    Conference
Seeger, Pete, 425–26
segregation
    Bible as justification for, 118, 127,
        143, 178, 179–80, 196
    and communism, 120–23, 149
    death of legalized, 4
    and democracy, 120–23, 127, 135,
        137, 147, 149, 152, 193
    and discrimination, 187
    and freedom, 121–23
    Holocaust compared with, 128
    King's first political speech about,
        150–53
    main reasons for legal, 124–25
    as moral issue, 123–28, 198, 201–2
    and psychological character of blacks,
        217
    and "states' rights," 179
    and stigma of inferiority, 124–26, 130
    and violence, 123, 137, 144, 179,
        185, 191, 192–93
    and Warren's interviews about the
        future, 190–94
    what blacks feel at exclusions of,
        189–90
    white reasons for, 175–83
    See also *specific person, organization, city,
        state, or demonstration*
Segregation: The Inner Conflict in the South
    (Warren), 8, 107, 167–202

self-fulfilling prophecy, 497
Sellers, Clyde, 138, 139, 141, 142
Selma, Alabama
    and end of nonviolence, 317
    King in, 292, 293–94, 295, 302–5,
        309–11, 313, 315–17, 405,
        416–17, 420
    Malcolm X in, 388
    unrest in, 137
    violence in, 4, 430
    See also Selma-to-Montgomery march
        (March 1965)
Selma Times-Journal, 295, 299
Selma-to-Montgomery march (March
    1965), 7, 282, 292–318, 362, 420,
    427. *See also* Bloody Sunday
senators, Southern, 514
separate but equal, 5, 25, 35–36, 105,
    126–27, 166, 185, 193–94, 272,
    273. See also *Brown v. Board of Edu-
    cation*
separatism
    King's views about, 381, 388
    Malcolm X's views about, 220, 222,
        232, 234
sermons, as art form, 395–96
servants, and Radical Chic, 466–67,
    468, 469
Seward, Bobby, 341
Seward, Dan, 339, 340–44, 345
Shabazz, Betty, 485
Shabazz, Malik. *See* Malcolm X
Shakespeare, William, 67–68
sharecroppers, 15–17, 21, 23, 190, 323,
    523–24
Shawnee Leadership Institute (Vermont),
    363–65
sheriffs
    baby inspection by, 500
    and Carmichael in jail, 362
    and Earle-Brown murders, 81, 90
    and Montgomery bus boycott, 143
    and Selma-to-Montgomery march,
        308
    and Styron's Southampton County,
        Virginia, trip, 342–44, 345
    and Till murder, 112–13
    Wallace's views about, 255
Shores, Arthur, 307

Shuttlesworth, Fred L., 149, 291, 316, 521

Silver, James W., 502, 512, 514

Silver Moon bar (Selma, Alabama), 306

Silvers, Bob, 465

Simkins, George, 271n

Simmons, William J., 512

Simon, John, 466

Simone, Nina, 315

Sims, Albert, 82

sit-ins, 308, 361, 368, 434, 503, 509

Sitton, Claude, 425

Sixteenth Street Baptist Church (Birmingham, Alabama), 430, 526

Sizemore, Barbara, 485

slavery, 5, 233, 338
    inheritors of, 13–32
    in Virginia, 332–38

Sloan School of Management (MIT), 489, 490

slums/ghettos, 372–74, 379–81, 384, 385, 386, 388, 417–18, 422, 451–63. *See also* Resurrection City

Smith, Alberta, 140

Smith, Frank, 324

Smith, George, 112–13

Smith, Gerald L. K., 177

Smith, Hazel Brannon, 327

Smith, Kelly Miller, 268, 269

SNCC. *See* Student Nonviolent Coordinating Committee

social gospel, 375

sociology/sociologists, 183, 233

Solidarity Day, 415, 416, 417, 418, 421, 424, 431, 432, 441

Soliunas, Francine, 492–94, 496, 498

Sommerton, South Carolina, 130

Sondheim, Steve, 465

"soul," 406–7

South
    black return to, 483–84
    Civil War defeat as central fact about, 247
    inferiority complex of, 44, 97
    King's return to, 406–7
    myths of the, 330–31
    survival of, 267
    Wallace as political and cultural articulation of, 241–42

South Africa, 97, 128, 231, 252, 443, 518

South Carolina, 129–32, 147, 406, 504. *See also specific city or town*

Southampton County, Virginia, 329, 332–45

The Southampton Insurrection (Drewry), 334, 338, 342, 343–44

Southern Baptist, 174, 196, 413, 430

Southern Christian Leadership Conference (SCLC)
    Abernathy resigns from, 484
    Atlanta as headquarters of, 384
    Bevel as head of left-wing of, 383
    and black leadership, 276, 277
    and CORE, 423
    debt of, 484
    demoralization in, 423–24
    fund raising by, 303, 312
    and history of civil rights movement, 368
    in Memphis, 390, 393, 405
    and middle class, 423
    and NAACP, 276, 382
    and nonviolence, 413
    and Poor People's Campaign, 423–24, 432–33
    power struggle within, 429
    and Rustin, 407
    and Selma-Montgomery march/Bloody Sunday, 292, 293, 294, 295, 299, 303–10, 312
    and SNCC, 303, 304–5, 306, 427–28
    and Urban League, 382
    and Vietnam, 368

Southern Conference Education Fund (SCEF), 367, 368

Southern Historical Association, 105–6

Southern Presbyterian Church, 118

Southern Regional Conference, 394

Southern Regional Council, 149, 278, 409, 414–15

Soviet Union, 149, 179, 224, 232, 275, 446, 481, 501

Spingarn Medal (NAACP), 276

Spock, Benjamin, 387

sports, integration of professional, 155–56, 165

Spraggins, Liz, 527
Spring Mobilization, 386
Stamps, Arkansas, Angelou's youth in, 61–74
Stanford University, minority graduates of, 488, 490
Stansell, Roy, 88
Stanton, Frank and Donna, 465, 469
Stark, Willie (fictional character), 109
"State Secrets" (Trillin), 411, 499–516
state troopers
  in Alabama, 296–99, 300, 304, 314, 428
  in Mississippi, 483
"states' rights," 179, 321, 522
Statue of Liberty, threats against, 458
Steele, Rosa, 314
Stein, Andrew, 466
Stein, Jules, 468
Steinbeck, John, 5, 107, 203–8
Stokes, Ernest, 82
storytelling, 25–26
Strider, H. C., 6
Strike City (Tribbett, Mississippi), 418–19
Stroud, Fred, 118–19
Student Nonviolent Coordinating Committee (SNCC)
  Atlanta as headquarters of, 355
  and Carmichael's trips, 354–57, 359
  changes in, 434
  control of, 283, 353
  conviction of, 443
  and Freedom Summer, 420
  fund raising by, 355
  and history of civil rights movement, 368
  killing of hope in, 434
  and King, 383
  in Mississippi, 511
  and nonviolence, 413
  and poverty, 434
  romanticism of poor by, 433
  and SCLC, 303, 304–5, 306, 427–28
  and Selma-to-Montgomery march/Bloody Sunday, 293, 299, 302–6, 308, 311, 312
  and Vietnam, 368
  and Watts, 452
  See also specific person

students
  and black leadership, 268–71, 275–76, 278, 279, 280
  in Civil War, 319
  and King, 382, 383, 386–88
  and Watts, 349
Students for a Democratic Society (SDS), 466
Styron, William, 5–6, 10, 282, 328–45
Sullins, Marvin, 116
Summit Meeting of Negro Leadership, 276
Sumner, Mississippi, and Till murder, 111–13
Sunflower County, Mississippi, 368
Supreme Court, U.S.
  and Bible as part of common law in South Carolina, 91
  and Bond decision, 367
  and character of Mississippi, 319, 326
  lack of respect for, 191
  Malcolm X's views about, 220, 225
  Mexican-Americans' denunciation of, 429
  and Montgomery bus boycott, 152
  and Plessy v. Ferguson (1896), 5, 126–27
  and segregation on intrastate buses, 147, 148
  Southern Baptist Convention support for, 174
  and Warren's interviews about the future, 197
  and white reasons for segregation, 183
  See also Brown v. Board of Education
Surrney, Lafayette, 303
Sweet Willie, 432, 433

Tallahassee, Florida, 149
Talmadge, Herman, 149
Tannenbaum, Frank, 333
tattoos, LOVE and HATE, 98–99
taxi drivers, and Earle murder, 76–104
Taylor, Harold, 465, 470
Taylor, Lowell, 155

teachers
  blacks as, 131–32, 174, 176–77, 199,
    260, 270, 273
  and inheritors of slavery, 26
  and Nashville integration crisis, 114
  in South Carolina, 131–32
  visit to Stamps, Arkansas, of, 66–67
  Warren's interviews of, 174, 176–77,
    190, 199
television
  blacks on, 155–61
  and Carmichael, 352–53
  and King, 374–75
  and March on Washington, 287
  in 1950s, 155–61
  and Poor People's Campaign, 436
  riots on, 453, 456
  role in civil rights movement of, 4–5,
    107, 155–61, 207, 371
  signing of Voting Rights Act on, 316
  and Wallace, 243, 248
Tennessee, 402, 406. See also Memphis,
    Tennessee
Tennessee Agricultural and Industrial
    University, 268
Tent City (Washington, D.C., 1966), 419
Tenth Amendment, 516
Texas, lynchings in, 31
Thalhimers department store (Rich-
    mond, Virginia), demonstration at,
    269
"This Quiet Dust" (Styron), 282,
    328–45
Thomas, W. I., 497
Thompson, Maude, 58–61
Thoreau, Henry David, 136, 269, 278,
    285, 398
Thurmond, Strom, 256
Till, Emmett Louis
  and Chicago wash-pot incident, 274
  murder of, 6, 106, 111–13, 159, 172,
    189, 193, 194, 195, 274, 483,
    525, 526
Time magazine
  King article in, 370, 382
  and Wallace, 251
tobacco, 335
Tocqueville, Alexis de, 270
Today Show (NBC-TV), 159

Tougaloo College, 503, 506, 508, 513
Tourel, Jennie, 465
trains, segregation on, 155
Travels with Charley (Steinbeck), 5, 107,
    203–8
Travis, Jimmy, 434
Travis, Joseph, 336, 337
Trenholm, H. C., 270
Tribbett, Mississippi, 418–19
Trillin, Calvin, 411, 499–516
Trinity Lutheran Church (Montgomery,
    Alabama), 134, 142
Truman, Harry S, 233, 519
Truth, Sojurner, 485
Tubman, Harriet, 485
Turks, in South Carolina, 504
Turner, Albert, 295
Turner, Henry McNeal, 369
Turner, Jesse, 404
Turner, Nat, 282, 329, 332–45, 334n
Turner, Samuel, 335
Tuscaloosa, Alabama, 4, 191
Tuskegee Institute, 305, 309
"Twenty West Fortieth Street" (NAACP
    headquarters, New York), 276

"Uncle Toms," 186–88, 323, 327, 359,
    374, 379
United Nations (UN), 223, 324, 370,
    472
United Press International (UPI), 299,
    302
United Rubber Workers Union Hall
    (Memphis, Tennessee), 395, 397
University of Alabama, 108, 160,
    169–70, 180, 192, 307, 522
University of Arkansas, 488
University of California at Los Angeles
    (UCLA), poll at, 454
University of Chicago, 488
University of Georgia, 160, 283, 411,
    444, 481
University of Maryland, 126–27
University of Southern Mississippi
  and character of Mississippi, 318–19,
    320, 321, 325, 326, 327
  integration of, 160, 232, 319, 325,
    504, 505, 512

and Mississippi State Sovereignty Commission, 500, 501–2, 504–15
and students in Civil War, 318
Urban Coalition, 432
Urban League, 225, 270–71, 272, 312, 382, 385, 466

Valkar, Kyle, 289
Vancleave, Mississippi, 504
Vanden Heuvel, Jean, 465, 466, 468, 470
Vanderbilt University, 268
Vatican, 224
Vermont, Carmichael's trip to, 358, 363–66
Vesey, Denmark, 333
Vestavia, Alabama, 259–60
Vietnam
    and Bernstein, 463–64
    and Bevel, 383–84
    and black middle class, 372
    Carmichael's comments about, 354
    and Johnson, 422
    and King, 7, 370–71, 372, 380, 382, 383, 384, 385–86, 387–88, 422
    and LBJ, 382, 385, 422
    and NAACP, 385
    Selma's Blood Sunday compared with, 300
    Wallace's views about, 237
    and Watts, 351
    See also peace movement
vigilantes, 240
violence
    Abernathy's views about, 431
    and Black Power, 447
    checks on mass, 461–62
    and civil rights movement in North, 406
    and colonialism, 121
    and death of King, 413
    and future of civil rights movement, 447
    King's views about, 386, 388
    and martyrs of civil rights movement, 430
    against media, 205
    in 1960s, 452
    in 1970s, 459

and police-black relations, 38–39
    rednecks as cause of, 201
    and riots, 452–53, 458, 461
    Rustin's views about, 422–23
    and segregation, 123, 137, 144, 146, 149, 179, 185, 191, 192–93
    spread of, 149
    and Wallace, 239, 240
    and Warren's interviews about the future, 191, 192–93
    See also lynchings; Turner, Nat; specific demonstration/riot or city
"Violence in the City—An End or a Beginning?" (Watts report), 350–52
Virginia
    Carmichael in, 361
    Depression in, 340
    Jim Crow system in, 334
    moderates in, 338
    nineteenth century, 332–38
    plantations in, 335
    pre–World War II years in, 5–6
    slavery in, 331–32
    Styron's youth in, 328–29, 330
    Turner insurrection in, 332–45
voting rights
    and black leadership, 270, 277
    and LBJ, 306, 309–10
    SCLC sponsors drive for, 277
    and Selma-to-Montgomery march/Bloody Sunday, 308
    See also specific state
Voting Rights Act (1965), 7, 281, 282, 306, 316–17, 319, 368

Wagner, Robert (New York mayor), 291
Walker, Alice, 4, 410, 478–85
Walker, Edwin, 319
Walker, Margaret, 482
Walker, Martha, 146
Walker, Wyatt Tee, 383
Walker's Cafe (Selma, Alabama), 306
Wall Street, Wallace's views about, 248
Wallace, George C.
    and Alabama Senate's refusal to let Wallace succeed himself, 248–49
    as classic demagogue, 243

Wallace, George C. (cont'd)
  and "folk," 240–41, 244, 247,
    248–49
  Frady article about, 5, 235–66
  Johnson's (Frank) relationship with,
    307
  and King, 370, 386
  and LBJ, 246, 308
  1964 candidacy of, 242–43, 246,
    255–56
  and 1966 Alabama gubernatorial
    campaign, 244, 247–48, 249–66
  1968 presidential campaign of,
    108–9, 235–39, 240–41, 242–43,
    247–48
  Raines's views about, 521, 522, 523,
    526, 527
  and Selma-to-Montgomery march,
    299, 304, 306–8, 310, 313, 316
  and states' rights, 522
  and University of Alabama, 108, 160
  and violence, 239, 240
  as Warren's Willie Stark, 108–9
  Watson as important in life of, 263,
    266
Wallace, Lurleen, 109, 242, 247,
    249–50, 252, 257, 261, 263, 264,
    265, 266
Wallace, Mike, 108, 109
Wallace, Momma Mae, 263–64, 266
Wallace, Phyllis, 489
Walters, Barbara, 465, 470
A Warning for Americans (Chamber of
    Commerce brochure), 321
Warren, Earl, 105, 179, 247
Warren, Robert Penn, 4, 8, 107, 108–9,
    167–201
wash-pot incident, 274
Washington, Booker T., 122, 481
Washington, D.C.
  police in, 416, 432, 435, 436, 437,
    438, 442–43, 444, 446
  See also March on Washington; Poor
    People's Campaign; Resurrection City
Washington Monument
  and March on Washington, 288–89,
    290
  and Poor People's Campaign, 424,
    425, 435
The Washington Post, 425, 432, 435

Washington Prayer Pilgrimage (1957),
    276
Watson, Billy, 263, 266
Watt, Sam, 86, 87, 88, 89, 90, 94, 95
Watters, Pat, 409, 413–49
Watts (Los Angeles)
  blame for, 348–52
  burning of, 4, 282–83, 346–48, 452,
    454, 455, 457, 458, 459, 460,
    462, 463
  Crouch article about, 282–83,
    346–48
  National Guard in, 282–83
  report about, 348–52
"We Shall Overcome" (song), 304, 310,
    364, 431, 452, 478
Weaver, Robert, 232
Weinraub, Bernard, 283, 352–66
welfare, 364, 375, 415, 416, 516
Welty, Eudora, 10, 57–61, 481
West, Ben, 118, 119
West, Rebecca, 4, 10–11, 75–104
West family, 306
West Virginia, Gates's youth in, 107,
    154–61
White, E. B., 4, 5, 107, 161–66
White, Josh, 291
White, Viola, 140
White, Walter, 273–74
White Citizens Council. See Citizens
    Council
white conservative tradition, in Missis-
    sippi, 322–23
White House
  and Poor People's Campaign, 446
  protests outside of, 308
"White Only" signs, 4, 25, 409, 480, 484
white power, 272, 278, 355
white supremacy, 19, 218, 232, 365, 514
Whitehead, Catherine, 344, 345
Whitehead, Margaret, 344–45
Whitehead, Richard, 344
whites
  help for blacks in Montgomery bus
    boycott from, 142
  King's views about, 382
  lack of knowledge about blacks of,
    330–32, 341, 360–61
Who Speaks for the South? (Dabbs), 322
Wilkerson, Milton, 289

Wilkins, Roger, 465
Wilkins, Roy, 274, 276–78, 287, 290, 316, 376n, 382, 386, 428, 458
Williams, A. D., 377, 378
Williams, Bert, 154, 155
Williams, Clarissa, 353
Williams, Elizabeth, 519
Williams, Grady. *See* Grady
Williams, Henry, 519
Williams, Hosea, 7, 293, 294, 295, 296, 297, 300, 303, 308–9, 313, 428, 434–35
Williams, James, 289
Williams, Roger, 285
Williamsburg, Virginia, 322
Wills, Garry, 284, 389–407
Wilson, A. W., 140
Winston-Salem, North Carolina, 149
Winter, William F., 512
Winters, Shelley, 315
Wofford, Thomas, 84–85, 91, 94–96, 99, 101, 103
Wolfe, Tom, 410, 463–77
women
    at bereavement times, 51
    of Black Panthers, 466
    in corporate America, 490–94
    fight for equality of, 511
    as inheritors of slavery, 16
    in 1970s, 485
Woolworth's (New York City), demonstrations at, 361
workplace, minorities in, 410, 486–99
World War I, 29–30, 31
World War II, 6, 32–41, 45–50, 274–75, 429. *See also* Detroit, Michigan: race riots in; Harlem (New York City): race riots in
Wright, Herbert, 270
Wright, Mose, 111–13
Wright, Richard, 3, 9, 13–32, 108

Yale University, minority graduates of, 490
Yazoo, Mississippi, 3, 9–10, 32–41
Yorty, Sam, 374
Young, Andrew, 294, 302, 303, 308–9, 313, 371–72, 373–74, 381
Young, Whitney, 316, 376n, 382, 385, 458
Young Lords, 466, 467, 468

About the Type

This book was set in Fairfield, the first typeface from the hand of the distinguished American artist and engraver Rudolph Ruzicka (1883–1978). In its structure, Fairfield displays the sober and sane qualities of the master craftsman whose talent has long been dedicated to clarity. It is this trait that accounts for the trim grace and vigor, the spirited design and sensitive balance, of this original typeface.

Chicago; BPP, Attica

Boston; Atlanta Bakke, Miami
Chicago